UNDOCUMENTED WINDOWS 2000 SECRETS

UNDOCUMENTED WINDOWS 2000 SECRETS

A PROGRAMMERS COOKBOOK

SVEN B. SCHREIBER

ADDISON–WESLEY

Boston San Francisco New York Toronto Montreal
London Munich Paris Madrid Capetown
Sydney Tokyo Singapore Mexico City

The publisher offers discounts on this book when ordered in quantity for special sales. For more information, please contact:

Pearson Education Corporate Sales Division
One Lake Street
Upper Saddle River, NJ 07458
(800) 382-3419
corpsales@pearsontechgroup.com

Visit AW on the Web: www.awl.com/cseng/

Library of Congress Cataloging-in-Publication Data

Schreiber, Sven B., 1958–
Undocumented Windows 2000 secrets: a programmer's cookbook / Sven B.Schreiber
p. cm.
Includes bibliographical references and index.
ISBN 0-201-72187-2
1. Microsoft Windows (Computer file) 2. Operating systems (Computers)
I. Title.
QA76.73.O63S389 2001
005.4'4769—dc21

00–054836

ISBN 0-201-72187-2
Text printed on recycled paper
1 2 3 4 5 6 7 8 9 10—CRS—0403020100
First printing, April 2001

To all the people in the world who never stopped asking "why" . . .

Contents

Preface

After finishing the manuscript of my first book, *Developing LDAP and ADSI Clients for Microsoft Exchange* (Schreiber 2000) in October 1999, I was honestly convinced for some time that I would never write a book again. Well, this phase didn't last long, as the pages you are reading right now prove. Actually, I was already starting to think about writing another book as early as November 1999 while I was playing around with the latest release candidate of Microsoft Windows 2000. Examining the kernel and its interfaces and data structures, I was very pleased to find that this operating system—despite its ugly name that reminded me too much of Windows 95 and 98—was still a good old Windows NT.

Poking around in the binary code of operating systems has always been one of my favorite pastimes. Just a couple of weeks before I had the idea to write this book, my article "Inside Windows NT System Data" (Schreiber 1999), showing how to retrieve internal system data by means of the undocumented kernel API function *NtQuerySystemInformation()*, had been published in *Dr. Dobb's Journal*. The preparatory research to this article left me with a huge amount of unpublished material that longed for being printed somewhere, and so I yelled: "Hey, how about a book about Windows 2000 Internals?" Because of the obvious similarities between Windows NT 4.0 and Windows 2000, plus my pile of interesting undocumented information too valuable to be buried, this seemed to be a great idea, and I am proud that this idea took the physical form of the book you are holding in your hands. While transforming the stuff I had collected into something that was readable by other people, I discovered lots of other interesting things, so this book also features a great deal of brand-new material that I hadn't planned to include beforehand.

Addison-Wesley has a long and glorious tradition of publishing books of this kind. The list of milestones is long, containing the two-volume printed version of Brown and Jim Kyle's classic "Interrupt List," *PC Interrupts* and *Network Interrupts* (Brown and Kyle 1991, 1993, 1994, available online at *http://www.cs.cmu.edu/afs/cs.cmu.edu/user/ralf/pub/WWW/files.html*); two editions of *Undocumented DOS* (Schulman et al., 1990, 1993); the Windows 3.1 update thereof, titled *Undocumented Windows* (Schulman et al., 1992); Matt Pietrek's *Windows Internals* (Pietrek 1993); as well as `DOS Internals` by Geoff Chappell (Chappell 1994) and *Dissecting DOS* by Michael Podanoffsky (Podanoffsky 1994). Other authors have contributed invaluable material in other areas such as PC hardware programming (Sargent III and Shoemaker 1994, van Gilluwe 1994). Andrew Schulman and Matt Pietrek both have written two more books of this "undocumented" kind about Windows 95, this time for IDG Books Worldwide (Schulman 1994, Pietrek 1995). However, what has been painfully missing in the past few years was a similar book for Windows NT system programmers. Fortunately, some information has been made available in article form. For example, Matt Pietrek has filled some parts of this huge gap in his "Under the Hood" column (e.g., Pietrek 1996a-d) in *Microsoft Systems Journal* (*MSJ*, meanwhile transformed into *MSDN Magazine*), and `The NT Insider` journal, published bimonthly by Open Systems Resources (OSR), is an indispensable source of know-how (check out *http://www.osr.com/publications_ntinsider.htm* for a free subscription). We should also not forget about the incredible SysInternals Web site operated by Mark Russinovich and Bryce Cogswell at *http://www.sysinternals.com*, who have brought us numerous powerful utilities—some even including full source code—that really should have been part of the Microsoft Windows NT Resource Kit.

For a long time, the Microsoft Windows NT Device Driver Kit (DDK) has been the only comprehensive source of information about Windows NT system internals. However, the DDK documentation is tough to read—some people even say it's anything but didactic. Moreover, the DDK is documenting just a small part of the available system interfaces and data structures. The largest part belongs to the category of the so-called internal features. This has made it next to impossible to write nontrivial kernel-mode software for Windows NT without searching for additional information somewhere else. In the past, however, reliable documentation and sample code was hard. This situation improved somewhat in 1997 when *The Windows NT Device Driver Book* by Art Baker and Rajeev Nagar's *Windows NT File System Internals* appeared. The year 1998 was marked by the heavily revised update of Helen Custer's two-volume set *Inside Windows NT* and *Inside the Windows NT File System* (Custer 1993, 1994) by David Solomon (Solomon 1998), who added a lot of new, previously unpublished material. In early 1999, *Windows NT Device Driver Development*, written by NT kernel-mode experts Peter G. Viscarola and W. Anthony Mason, was published (Viscarola and Mason 1999). Both are consulting partners of Open Systems Resources (OSR), and the OSR people are well known for their excellent kernel-mode driver and file system programming courses, so having their first-hand knowledge in printed form was a real benefit. In the same year, Edward N. Dekker and Joseph M. Newcomer's *Developing Windows NT Device Drivers* (Dekker and Newcomer 1999) appeared. Both books were probably the first comprehensive and *practically useful* NT kernel-mode programming tutorials. If you want to read thoughtful and accurate reviews about several Windows NT driver programming books, including some of those mentioned above, just peek into the November/December 1999 issue of *The NT Insider* (Open Systems Resources 1999c).

In late 1999, more authors delved into the depths of the Windows NT kernel. A trio of system programmers and consultants from Puna, India, Prasad Dabak, Sandeep Phadke, and Milind Borate, brought us the first *Undocumented Windows NT* book (Dabak, Phadke, and Borate 1999). Because it was published before the release of the final version of Windows 2000, it covers Windows NT 3.51 and 4.0 and the latest 2000 beta then available. After this overdue release, another must-have book for anyone in Windows 2000 system programming appeared in January 2000: Gary Nebbett's *Windows NT/2000 Native API Reference* (Nebbett 2000). His work provides a thorough, comprehensive, and extraordinarily detailed documentation of `all` API functions and the structures they involve, providing the first opportunity to double-check my findings about `NtQuerySystemInformation()` in *Dr. Dobb's Journal* (Schreiber 1999). I was pleased to see that not only did our technical details match perfectly but so did most of the symbolic names we had chosen independently. This book should have been published by Microsoft years earlier!

You may think that everything has already been said about the internals of Windows 2000. Not so! The internal functions and data structures inside the kernel involve such a vast area of knowledge that they can hardly be covered by just two books. The book you're reading now is just one of the building blocks required for a better understanding of the architecture of Windows 2000. Hopefully, the coming years will bring many more publications of this kind. One recent publication is the third edition of *Inside Windows NT*. Because it covers many of the new features introduced with Windows 2000, it is consequently now called *Inside Windows 2000* (Solomon and Russinovich 2000). This third edition is a genuine member of the former *Inside Windows NT* series. In this edition, Mark Russinovich is co-author with David Solomon, which is a reliable indicator that this book can be bought blindly. There is no significant overlap between the contents of *Inside Windows 2000* and *Undocumented Windows 2000 Secrets: A Programmer's Cookbook,* so it is probably a good idea to have both on the shelf.

THE TOPICS DISCUSSED IN THIS BOOK

If I had to compare this book with its predecessors, I'd say it's written in the tradition of the old *Undocumented DOS* volumes (Schulman et al., 1990, 1993). I treasured these books back in the days of DOS programming, because they involved an ideal trade-off between comprehensiveness and an in-depth treatment of an essential subset of topics. In my opinion, it is nearly impossible to write a comprehensive documentation of the internals of a complex operating system in a single volume without losing detail. If you don't opt for a multitome encyclopedia, you can either write a reference handbook, such as Nebbett's (Nebbett 2000), or focus on specific topics, as Andrew Schulman and friends did. Nebbett didn't leave much for other reference authors, but the in-depth documentation of special Windows NT/2000 topics is still a wide-open field.

Like *Undocumented DOS*, this book of introduces Windows 2000 programming topics that I have found both interesting and useful. In the "undocumented" business, there is always a danger of doing "art for art's sake." Unveiling undocumented features of an operating system is usually very exciting and fulfilling for the person doing the work, but might be quite irrelevant for others. Not everything that is undocumented is automatically useful as well. Some operating system internals are just internals in their strictest sense, that is, implementation details. However, many internals of Microsoft systems are much more than that. Microsoft has a notorious reputation for intentionally preventing the developer community from knowing too much about their target operating system. My favorite example is the ingenious and extremely useful MS-DOS Network Redirector Interface described in Chapter 8 of the second edition of *Undocumented DOS* (Schulman et al., 1993). Much time would have been saved and much trouble avoided if Microsoft had documented this wonderful interface when they introduced it. Unfortunately, Microsoft has pursued this information policy with the follow-up systems Windows 3.x, Windows 9x, Windows NT, and Windows 2000. However, books such as this are being written to provide further information.

After introducing you to the basic architecture of Windows 2000 and helping you to set up your workstation for Windows 2000 kernel spelunking, this book leads you through some very exciting corners inside the world of kernel programming. Typically, each chapter first discusses the essential theory you need to know about the topic, and then immediately presents sample code to illustrate the respective features. The language chosen for the samples is plain C. The probability is high that the readers of this book are comfortable with C, and this language is well supported by Microsoft's Windows 2000 development tools.

This book deliberately does `not` attempt to give a broad overview of the architecture of the Windows 2000 kernel, although it discusses parts of it in some chapters. If you are looking for such information, see *Inside Windows 2000* (Solomon and Russinovich 2000) instead, which takes a very general and theoretical approach to the Windows 2000 internals. Neither *Inside Windows 2000* nor the *Undocumented Windows 2000 Secrets: A Programmers Cookbook Windows NT/2000 Native API Reference* (Nebbett 2000) provide practical code examples and full-featured sample applications that interact live with the system contains reprinted code samples in abundance, accompanying the Windows 2000 concepts and features under discussion. The companion CD contains all of this code in ready-to-run applications that you can extend, tear to shreds for use in other applications, or simply use as is. Basically, you will be led through the following topics:

- Using the Windows 2000 debugging interfaces
- Loading, parsing, and using the Windows 2000 symbol files
- Dissecting the Microsoft PDB file format
- Interfacing to the kernel's Native API
- Writing simple kernel-mode drivers
- Exploring Windows 2000 system memory
- Hooking and monitoring calls to the Native API
- Calling kernel functions from user-mode applications
- Calling nonexported kernel functions
- Exploring the world of Windows 2000 kernel objects

You also will learn many more details about the system both in the text and samples. My foremost intention while writing the manuscript was to share with you anything I knew about the topics covered.

THE ORGANIZATION OF THIS BOOK

After considering which sequence of chapters would be optimal for all potential readers of this book, I have arranged the seven chapters in the order that I thought would be best for a novice Windows 2000 system programmer. Therefore, any new concepts or techniques introduced in a chapter are explained at their first appearance. Consequently, newbies should read the chapters sequentially as they appear in the book. This approach may bore expert readers who look for more "off-road" information. However, it is easier for an expert to skip over familiar details than for a novice to keep up if the material is presented in a nondidactic sequence.

Here is what awaits you in each chapter:

- **Chapter 1** begins with a guided tour through setup and use of the Windows 2000 Kernel Debugger, because this is one of the most helpful tools for system exploration. Other highlights are the official Windows 2000 debugging interfaces in the form of the `psapi.dll`, `imagehlp.dll`, and `dbghelp.dll` components. The chapter closes with detailed descriptions of the layouts of Microsoft CodeView and Program Database (PDB) files, complemented by a sample symbol file parser DLL and an accompanying client application.

- **Chapter 2** introduces the Windows 2000 Native API, discussing the main system service dispatcher, the various API function groups exported by ntdll.dll and ntoskrnl.exe, and the data types most frequently used by these components.
- **Chapter 3** is a short and easy introduction to basic kernel-mode driver development. It is by no means intended as a tutorial for heavy-duty hardware driver developers. It simply points out essential information required to understand the sample code in subsequent chapters, including loading and unloading driver modules at runtime via the Service Control Manger interface. Probably the most interesting highlight is the description of the customizable driver wizard included with full source code on the companion CD.
- **Chapter 4** is certainly the most challenging chapter for readers suffering from hardware phobia, because it starts with a detailed description of the Intel Pentium CPU features used by the Windows 2000 memory manager. Anyone who survives this section is rewarded by extensive sample code of a memory spy device that supports the visualization of prohibited memory regions and internal memory manager data structures. Also included is a Windows 2000 memory map that outlines how the system makes use of the vast 4-GB address space offered by the Pentium CPU family.
- **Chapter 5** explains in detail how you can hook Native API functions, mainly focusing on call parameter monitoring and file/registry tracking. This chapter makes heavy use of inline assembler code and CPU stack twirling.
- **Chapter 6** proposes a general-purpose solution for something that is commonly considered impossible in the Windows 2000 programming paradigm: calling kernel-mode code from user-mode applications. The sample code in this chapter builds a bridge from the Win32 subsystem to the main kernel interfaces inside ntoskrnl.exe, hal.dll, and other core components. The chapter also describes how to call nearly any kernel function as long as its entry point is provided in the Windows 2000 symbol files.
- **Chapter 7** delves deeply into the mysterious Windows 2000 object manager. The internal structure of kernel objects is one of the best-kept secrets, because Microsoft doesn't give you more information about an object than an opaque void* pointer. This chapter unveils what this pointer really points to, and how object structures and handles are maintained and managed by the system. As a special feature, the layout of process and thread

objects is discussed in detail. The last section of the chapter is a sample application that displays the hierarchical arrangement of kernel objects by tracing the relations of various undocumented object structures.

- **Appendix A** is related to Chapter 1 and contains all commands and command options of the Windows 2000 Kernel Debugger.
- **Appendix B** is related to Chapter 2 and summarizes several API functions exported by the Windows 2000 kernel modules.
- **Appendix C** provides an extensive collection of Windows 2000 constants and data types in alphabetical order. This reference list documents several undocumented kernel structures introduced and used throughout the book.

As you see, this book discusses much information that merits the attribute "undocumented," and some of the material has never been published before.

THE AUDIENCE OF THIS BOOK

Undocumented Windows 2000 Secrets: A Programmer's Cookbook is intended for system programmers who want to maximize the features of their target operating system. First disclaimer: If the target platform of your software is Windows 95, 98, or Me (Millennium Edition), don't read any further. Because of the architectural differences of the Windows 9x/Me and NT/2000 platforms, you won't benefit from reading this book. Second disclaimer: This book does not contain information on the Alpha processor or multiprocessor systems—I will target the 32-bit Intel i386 single-processor platform exclusively. Third disclaimer: Be aware that this text is not written for the faint-hearted. You will be faced with programming techniques the average Win32 programmer has never seen. The Windows 2000 kernel is an entirely different world, bearing little resemblance to the Win32 subsystem built upon it. Some of the interfacing techniques introduced toward the end of the book might be new to even experienced kernel-mode programmers. Let me put it this way: This is the book your high-school teachers and Microsoft representatives have always warned you about!

If you are still reading on, you are obviously an open-minded, courageous person who wants to know everything about the things lurking beneath the surface of the Windows 2000 operating system. That's great! Even if you won't use the know-how you gain from this book on a daily basis, you will certainly benefit from it. Knowing what is going on under the surface of an application interface is always advantageous. It facilitates debugging and optimization, and helps avoid unwanted side effects caused by misconceptions about the hidden mechanics of the system.

The only expertise I'm expecting from my readers is "talking C" fluently and basic knowledge of Win32 programming. If you have already written kernel-mode drivers, you're in an even better position, but that's not a requirement. You will find an introduction to kernel-mode driver programming in this book, telling you everything you need to know within its scope. However, please note that this is not a comprehensive kernel-mode tutorial. If you are specifically interested in kernel-mode driver development, please get one of the good books that deal with this topic exclusively (e.g., Viscarola and Mason 1999, or Dekker and Newcomer 1999).

Some chapters of this book include heavy use of inline assembly language (ASM). I don't expect you to have thorough ASM programming experience, but a basic knowledge of ASM will be certainly helpful. If you have never written a line of ASM code, you may find these chapters difficult or you may choose to skip them entirely. However, I encourage you to read at least parts of them, only skipping the subsections that explain the details of the ASM code. Because the ASM code snippets used in the samples are always well encapsulated in C function wrappers, you can usually ignore their internals and still benefit from the remaining material that surrounds them.

THE CONVENTIONS USED IN THIS BOOK

The target operating system of this book is Windows 2000. However, you will find that most of the information also applies to Windows NT 4.0, and most of the sample applications run on this platform as well. Note that I am not covering Windows NT 3.x. Although it is probably outdated now, NT 3.51 has been my favorite NT so far because it was relatively small and fast and did not burn up too many CPU MIPS in its user interface. With respect to Windows NT 4.0, I have done everything to keep the software compatible with this version, because it is still in use. Many companies have designed their corporate networks for the classic Windows NT domain concept, and they will need time to adopt the new Active Directory paradigm introduced with Windows 2000. In some cases, it is not possible to provide common code for both operating system versions because of differences in the layout of some internal data structures. Therefore, some portions of the sample code contain version checking and separate execution paths for different versions.

Concerning terminology, when I use the term Windows 2000, it usually includes Windows NT 4.0 as well. Remember that this funny name is just a marketing gimmick to propel the sales of a system that should have been named Windows NT 5.0. In the same way, the term Windows NT without a version specification refers to the NT platform in general, including Windows 2000 and Windows NT 4.0. Note again that Windows NT 3.x is not on the list. In discussing version-specific features, I will use the terms Windows 2000 and Windows NT 4.0 in a contrasting fashion, pointing out the respective differences.

THE SAMPLE CODE ON THE CD

The sample code included on the companion CD and partially reprinted in this book has been written for Microsoft Visual C/C++ 6.0 with Service Pack 3. If you want to rebuild or change the samples, you should also install the latest releases of the Win32 Platform Software Development Kit (SDK) and the Windows 2000 Device Driver Kit (DDK). These development kits contain the latest header file and import library updates. Be sure to set the compiler's and linker's search paths appropriately to guarantee that the SDK and DDK files are found before the header and library files installed with Visual C/C++. Both kits are distributed on CD or DVD as part of the Microsoft Developer Network (MSDN) Professional and Universal Subscriptions. If you aren't a subscriber yet, go for it! You will receive all updates of Microsoft's operating systems and development kits, plus more than 1 gigabyte of first-hand technical documentation. The subscription is somewhat expensive, but I think it is worthwhile. More information is available from Microsoft's MSDN Web site at *http://msdn.microsoft.com/subscriptions/prodinfo/overview.asp*.

The CD included with this book contains both the C source code of all samples and compiled and linked binary builds thereof for immediate use. All directories are set up as Microsoft Visual Studio 6.0 expects them: There is a base directory for each module containing the source files (C code and header files, resource scripts, definition files, project and workspace information, etc.) and a subdirectory called `release` holding the binaries (executables, object code, import libraries, etc.). *Figure P-1* outlines the overall directory structure of the CD. All source and project files are found in the `\src` tree. It contains a subtree for each sample project, plus a `common` directory for header and library files shared by them. The `\bin` directory contains all `.exe`, `.dll`, and `.sys` files of the samples, allowing you to start all applications directly from the CD. The `\tools` tree is a collection of third-party tools that I thought would be helpful for readers of this kind of book.

To rebuild a sample, simply copy the module's base directory including the `release` subdirectory to the folder where you are keeping your own projects. The base directory contains `.dsw` and `.dsp` workspace and project definition files providing build information for Visual Studio. Rebuilding is easy: Open the `.dsw` file in Visual Studio, choose the active configuration (e.g., Release) and select **Build \ Build** or **Build \ Rebuild All** from the main menu. Please note that some header files contain additional linker directives in the form of `#pragma` statements. This neat trick allows you to rebuild all samples with default Visual Studio settings—no need to enter anything into the project setting dialogs.

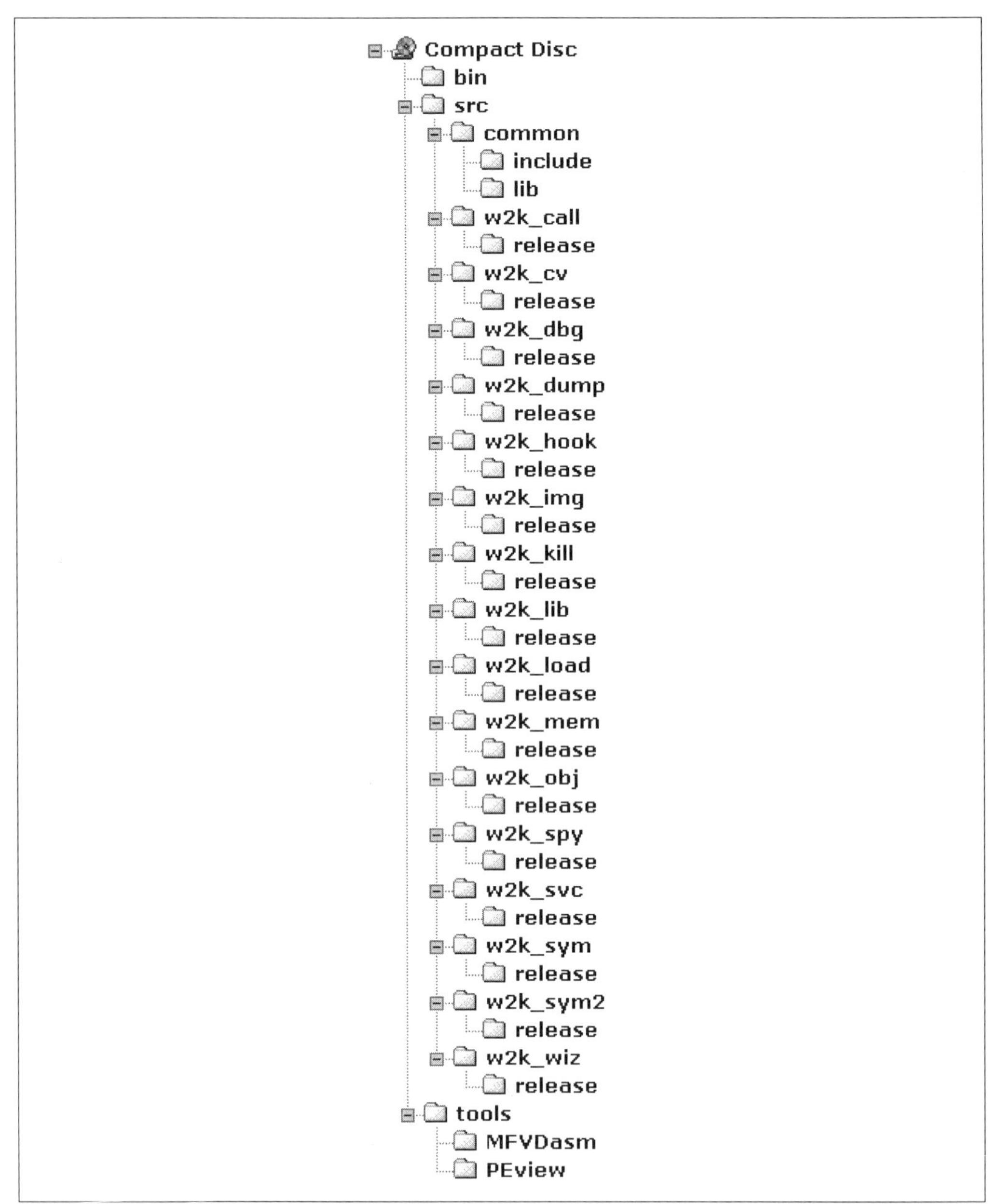

FIGURE P-1. *Directory Structure of the Sample CD*

Because most of the code is guaranteed to be `not` Windows 9x compatible, I did not provide support for ANSI characters. The native character set of Windows 2000 is Unicode, featuring 16-bit characters. Therefore, strings are defined as `WORD` arrays or pointers, except for the rare occasions that the system actually expects ANSI strings. This makes it a lot easier, doesn't it? Good Win32 programmers always try to support both ANSI and Unicode side by side to give legacy operating systems such as Windows 95 and 98 a fair chance to execute their code. This problem does not arise here—the code presented in this book usually goes well below the Win32 layer, so we can make full use of all native features of Windows 2000. The only notable exception is the `w2k_img.dll` library project and its companion application `w2k_sym2.exe`, both discussed toward the end of Chapter 1. The DLL supports both ANSI and Unicode, and the application is compiled for ANSI. This is the only sample application on the CD that runs even on Windows 95.

There are manifold dependencies between the sample projects on the CD. For example, the kernel-mode driver `w2k_spy.sys` and the utility library `w2k_lib.dll` are referenced by several applications, introduced in different chapters. *Figure P-2* outlines these dependencies. The diagram should always be read from left to right. For example, the `w2k_obj.exe` application imports API functions from `w2k_call.dll` and `w2k_lib.dll`, and `w2k_call.dll` in turn relies on `w2k_lib.dll` and `w2k_img.dll`, additionally performing Device I/O Control calls into `w2k_spy.sys`. This means that you should always place the dependent files into the same directory with `w2k_obj.exe` to be able to run this application reliably. Note that I have added `imagehlp.dll` and `psapi.dll` to the diagram, although they are Microsoft components. This is just to emphasize that the `w2k_dbg.dll` library relies on these additional DLLs, whereas the other sample programs do not.

One of the sample modules should be mentioned explicitly here: It is the "Windows 2000 Utility Library" found in the `w2k_lib` directory branch. As well as hosting large portions of the sample code reprinted in the following chapters, it also contains lots of Win32 boilerplate code not specifically related to the focus of this book that you might want to reuse in other projects. It features memory, registry, object pool, and linked-list management, CRC32 computation, pseudo–random number generation, operating system and file version checking, and much more. The huge `w2k_lib.c` file is a repository of general-purpose code I have written for myself in the past few years, and it is intended to make the life of Win32 programmers somewhat easier. Enjoy!

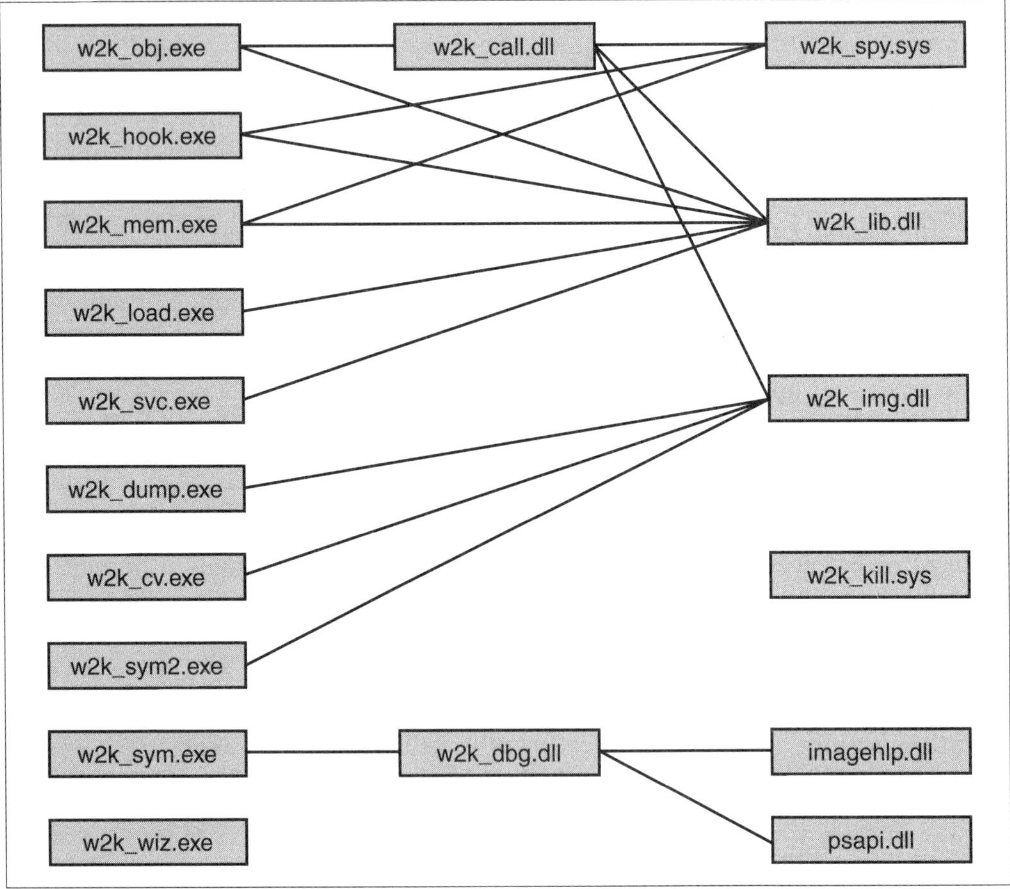

FIGURE P-2. *Dependencies of the Sample Programs*

THE THIRD-PARTY TOOLS ON THE CD

Along with the sample code I wrote exclusively for this book, the companion CD contains valuable tools contributed by others. I am indebted to Jean-Louis Seigné and Wayne J. Radburn for allowing me to distribute their finest tools on this CD. In the `\tools` directory, you will find the following goodies:

- *The Multi-Format Visual Disassembler* (MFVDasm) is written by Jean-Louis Seigné, who has been in the Windows software development business since 1990. Actually, MFVDasm is much more than just a disassembler—it is a Portable Executable (PE) file cruncher, disassembler, hex dump utility, and ASM code browser in one. The `\tools\MFVDasm` directory on the CD contains a fully functional timed demo version, protected with the Softlocx software produced by BitArts. You can get an unlimited version by paying US$100.00 to Jean-Louis Seigné via credit card. The latest version of MFVDasm is available at *http://redirect.to/MFVDasm*; inquiries about the software should be emailed to *MFVDasm@redirect.to*.

- The *PE and COFF File Viewer* (PEview) is contributed by Wayne J. Radburn and is given royalty-free as a special bonus for the readers of this book. Wayne is a die-hard Win32 assembly language programmer like me, except that he is still doing the job while I have moved to C. Application programming in ASM is tough, so you can be sure that Wayne is a true expert. PEview is certainly the most versatile PE file browser I'm aware of, and it is an essential tool for operating system spelunkers. It provides a quick and easy way to view the structure and content of 32-bit Portable Executable (PE) and Component Object File Format (COFF) files, and it supports the viewing of `.exe`, `.dll`, `.obj`, `.lib`, `.dbg`, and other file types. Meet Wayne on the Web at *http://www.magma.ca/~wjr/*, or send email to *wjr@magma.ca*.

Because this is third-party software, included here by special license agreement with the respective authors, neither Addison-Wesley nor I take any responsibility for its usage. Please read the licensing information displayed by these programs for more details.

THE "WITHOUT WHOM" SECTION

Before writing my first book, I wasn't aware that so many people participate in a book's production process. Writing the manuscript is just one of many steps to be taken until the first printed copy appears on the shelves of the bookstores. This section is dedicated to the numerous people who have contributed substantially to the making of this book.

First, I want to thank Gary Clarke, formerly of Addison-Wesley, for putting this book project onto the track. Unfortunately, Gary left Addison-Wesley just before the first manuscript line was written, but fate brought me together again with Karen Gettman and Mary Hart, who coordinated the manuscript creation phase of my first book. This was good luck; I can't think of a better team for the birth of a new book. However, my joy halted abruptly just as I was writing the last paragraphs of Chapter 7, when I got notice that Mary left Addison-Wesley. Fortunately, Emily Frey jumped in and saved the day. I'm also indebted to Mamata Reddy, who coordinated the book's production, Curt Johnson, Jennifer Lawinski, and Chanda D. Leary-Coutu of the marketing team, Katie Noyes for doing the cover artwork, and Beth Hayes for faithfully copyediting my raw manuscript. Several other people at Addison-Wesley whose names are unknown to me were involved in the production and marketing of this book, and I thank them all from my heart. Additionally, special thanks go to my queen of hearts Gerda B. Gradl, my parents Alla and Olaf Schreiber, and my colleague Rita Spranger for continuous encouragement and support throughout the entire project—writing a book is sometimes a lonesome job, and it is good to have someone with whom to talk about it sometimes.

And finally, a big, big "thank you" to Roine Stolt, leader of the Swedish Progressive-Rock band *The Flower Kings* (*http://www.users.wineasy.se/flowerkings/*), for his unbelievable, indescribable music, which has been an endless source of inspiration to me during manuscript writing. He always keeps on reminding me that "Stardust we are."

We believe in the light,
We believe in love,
Every precious little thing.
We believe you can still surrender,
You can serve the Flower King.

NOTE: *Excerpt from "The Flower King" by Roine Stolt, 1994. Used by kind permission.*

CHAPTER 1

Windows 2000 Debugging Support

Because much of the information found in this book is of the so-called undocumented kind, some of it is available only by peeking inside the operating system code. The Windows 2000 Device Driver Kit (DDK) provides a powerful debugger that does a great job in this respect. This chapter begins with detailed step-by-step instructions to set up a full-fledged debugging environment on your machine. While reading the following chapters, you will frequently go back to the Kernel Debugger to extract operating system internals of various kinds. If you are becoming bored with the Kernel Debugger, you might want to tailor your own debugging tools. Therefore, this chapter also includes information about the documented and undocumented Windows 2000 debugging interfaces, including detailed inside information about Microsoft symbol files. It features two sample libraries with companion applications that list processes, process and system modules, and various kinds of symbol information buried inside the Windows 2000 symbol files. As a special bonus, you will find the first public documentation of the Microsoft Program Database (PDB) file format at the end of this chapter.

SETTING UP A DEBUGGING ENVIRONMENT

"Hey, I don't want to debug a Windows 2000 program. First of all, I want to *write* one!" you might shout out after reading this headline. "Right!" I say, "That's what you are going to do!" But why should you start the voyage by setting up a debugging environment? The answer is simple: The debugger is sort of a backdoor into the operating system. Of course, this has not been the primary intention of the persons who wrote this tool. However, every good debugger must be able to tell you something useful about the system while you are stepping through the execution of your own code or after your application has died unexpectedly. It is not quite acceptable to report an eight-digit crash address that points somewhere into the 4GB address space, leaving you figuring out alone what really happened. The debugger should at least tell you which module's code the offending code was executing last, and, ideally, it should also tell you the name of the function where the application passed away. Therefore, the debugger usually must know much more about the system than is printed in the programming manuals, and you can use this knowledge to explore the internals of the system.

Windows 2000 comes with two native debuggers: `WinDbg.exe` (pronounced like "WindBag") is a Win32 GUI application, and `i386kd.exe` is its console-mode equivalent. I have worked with both versions for some time and finally decided that `i386kd.exe` is the better one because it has a more powerful set of options. Recently, however, it seems that `WinDbg.exe` has improved, causing the people at Open Systems Resources (OSR) to include an article titled "There's a New WinDBG in Town—And It Doesn't Suck Anymore" in the May/June 2000 edition of *The NT Insider* (Open Systems Resources 2000). Nevertheless, all examples in this book that somehow involve a Windows 2000 debugger relate to `i386kd.exe`. As you might have guessed, the `i386` portion of the name refers to the target processor platform (Intel 386 family in this case, including all Pentium versions), and `kd` is short for Kernel Debugger. The Windows 2000 Kernel Debugger is a very powerful tool. For example, it knows how to make use of the symbol files distributed on the Windows 2000 setup CDs, and therefore can give you invaluable symbolic information about almost any address in system memory. Moreover, it will disassemble binary code, list hex dumps of memory contents in various formats, and even show you the layout of some key structures of the kernel. And it gives away this information for free—the debugger's command interface is fully documented in its online help.

Preparing for a Crash Dump

This is the good news. The bad news is that you have to do some preparatory work before the Kernel Debugger will obey you. The first obstacle is that debugging usually involves two separate machines connected by a cable—one running the debugger, the other one hosting the debuggee. However, there is a much easier way, eliminating the necessity of a second machine, if live debugging is not a requirement. For example, if a buggy application throws an unhandled exception causing the infamous NT "Blue Screen Of Death" (BSOD) to pop up, you can choose to save the memory image that was in effect right before the crash to a file and examine this *crash dump* after rebooting. This technique is usually called *post mortem* debugging (*post mortem* is Latin and means "after death"), and it is one of the preferred methods used throughout this book. Our primary task here is to explore system memory, and for most situations, it doesn't matter whether the memory under examination is alive or a snapshot of the last breath of a dead system. However, some interesting insights can be gained by peeking into the innards of a live system using a kernel-mode driver, but this is a topic to be saved for later chapters.

A crash dump is simply a copy of the current memory contents flushed to a disk file. Therefore, the size of a complete crash dump file is (almost) the same as the amount of physical RAM installed on the machine—in fact, it is a bit less than that. The crash dump is written by a special routine inside the kernel in the course of handling the fatal exception. However, this handler doesn't write the memory contents immediately to the target file. This is a good idea, because the disk file system might not be in good health after the crash. Instead, the image is copied to the page file storage, which is part of the system's memory manager. Therefore, you should increase the total size of your page files to at least twice the size of physical memory. Twice? Wouldn't the same size be enough? Of course—just enough for the crash dump. However, the system will attempt to copy the crash dump image to a real disk file during bootstrap, and this means that the system might run out of virtual memory if it can't free the page file memory occupied by the image in time. Usually, the system will cope with this situation, just throwing some annoying "low on virtual memory" warnings at you while thrashing the disk, but you can save a lot of time by making the page file large enough whenever you are expecting an increased probability of a Blue Screen.

That said, you should proceed now by starting the Windows 2000 Control Panel utility and changing the following settings:

- Increase the overall size of your page files to at least twice the amount of installed RAM. To this end, open the **System** applet, select the **Advanced** tab of the **System Properties** dialog, and click the **Performance Options...** button. In the **Virtual memory** frame, click the **Change...** button, and change the value in the **Maximum size (MB)** field if it doesn't match your physical memory configuration. Figure 1-1 is a sample snapshot taken on the system on which I am currently writing these lines. I have 256 MB of RAM inside my tower, so 512 MB is just enough. Click **Set** after changing the settings, and confirm all open dialogs except the **System Properties** by pressing their **OK** buttons.
- Next, configure the system to write a crash dump file on every Blue Screen. In the **System Properties** dialog, click the **Startup and Recovery...** button, and examine the **Write Debugging Information** options. You should select the **Complete Memory Dump** option from the drop-down list to get a faithful copy of the entire memory contents. In the **Dump File** box, enter the path and name of the file where the dump will be copied to from the page file. `%SystemRoot%\MEMORY.DMP` is a commonly used setting (Figure 1-2). Check or uncheck the **Overwrite any existing file** option according to your own preference, and confirm all open dialogs.

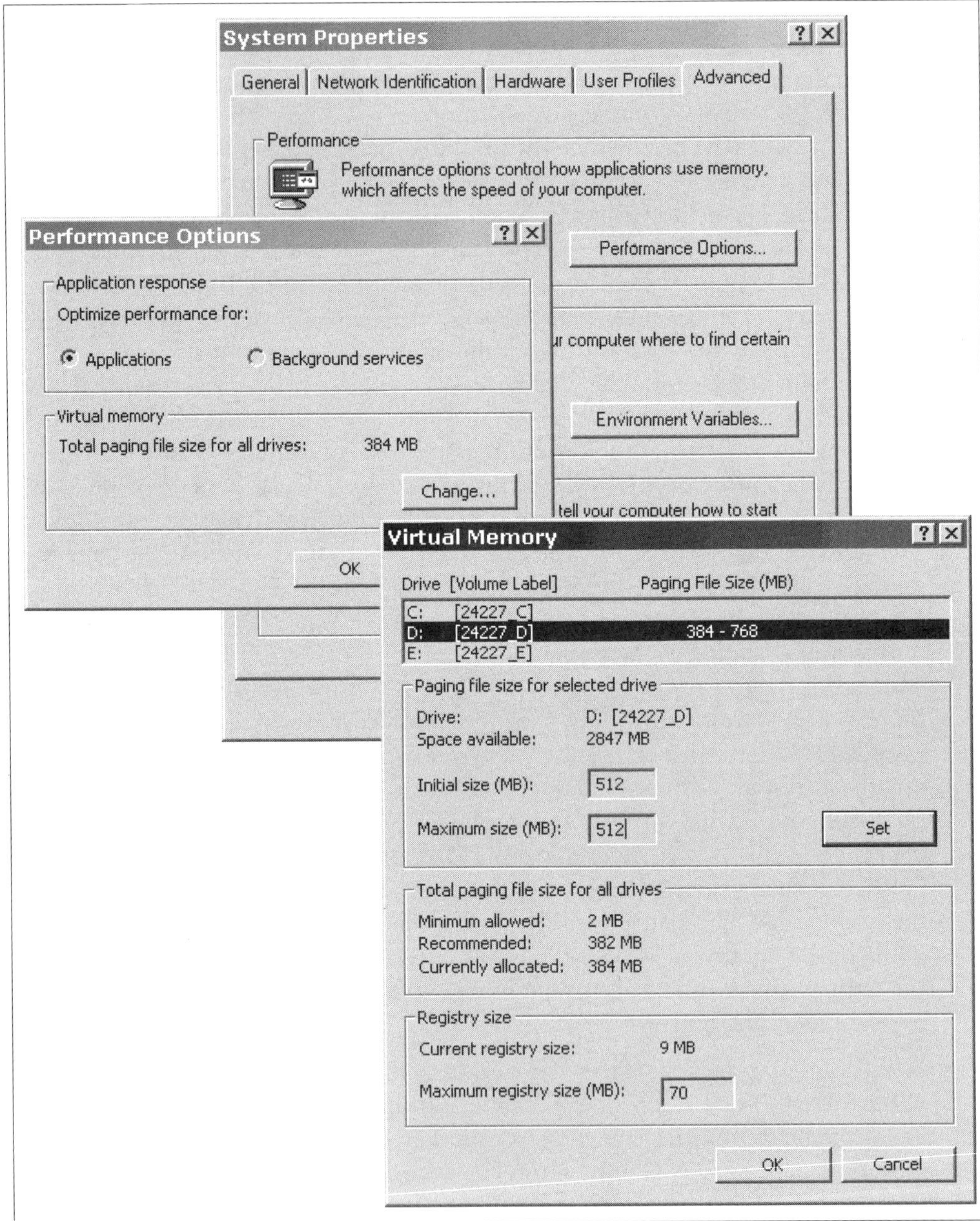

FIGURE 1-1. *Setting the Size of the Page File Storage*

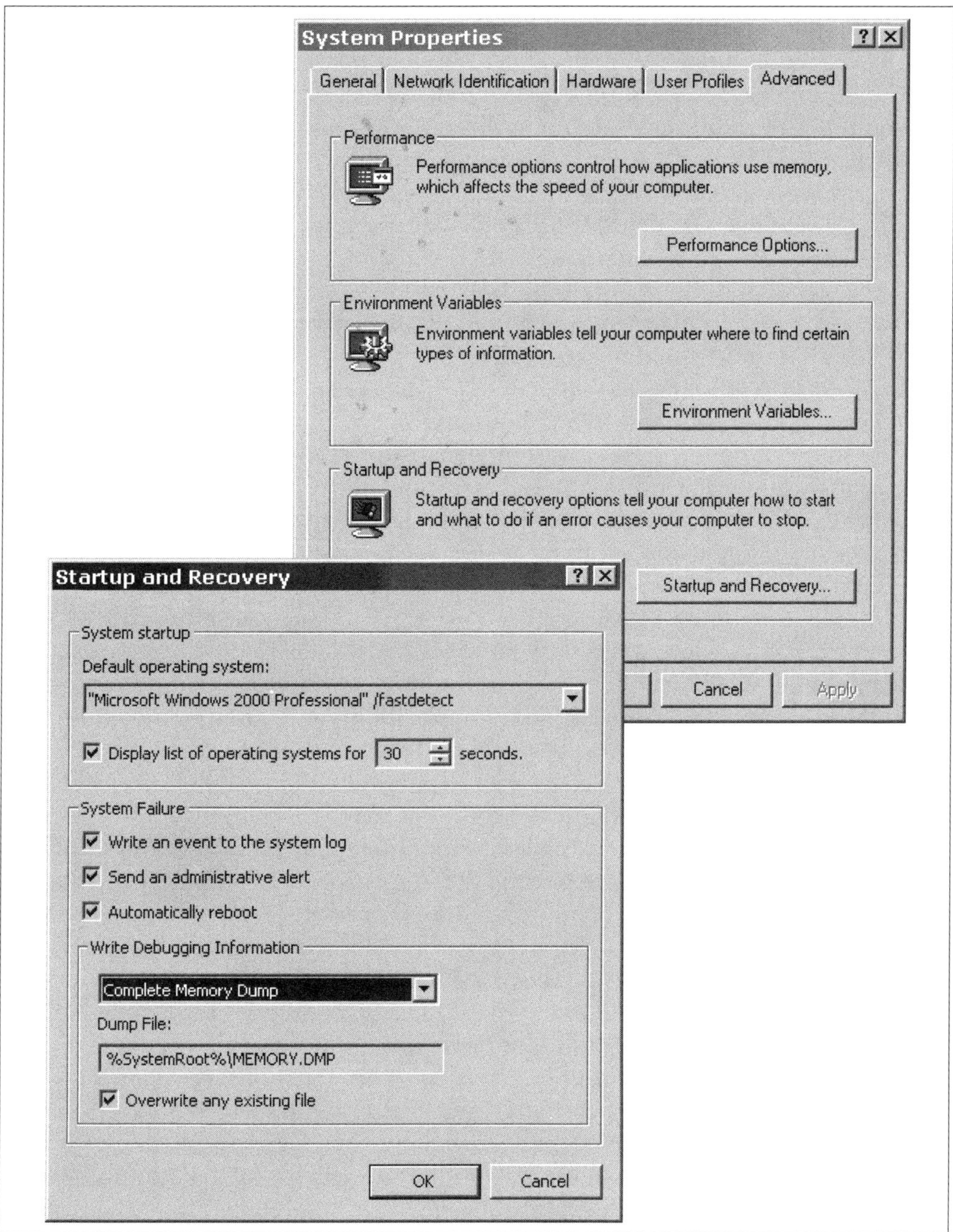

FIGURE 1-2. *Choosing Crash Dump Options*

CRASHING THE SYSTEM

After having set up the system for a crash dump, it is time to do the most horrible thing in the life of a Windows 2000 system programmer: Let's crash the system! Usually, you will get the dreaded Blue Screen whenever Damocles' sword is hanging above your head—typically when a production deadline is due in a few hours. Now that you are willing to crash the system, you are probably unable to find any unstable piece of software that will do the job. Try David Solomon's neat trick described in the second edition of *Inside Windows NT*. This is his proposal:

> *"How can you reliably generate a crash dump? Just kill the Win32 subsystem process (csrss.exe) or the Windows NT logon process (winlogon.exe) with the Windows NT Resource Kit tool kill.exe. (You must have administrator privileges to do this.)" (Solomon [1998], p. 23.)*

Surprise, surprise! This trick doesn't work anymore on Windows 2000! On first sight, that's bad luck, but on the other hand, it is good news. What do you think about an operating system that can be trashed so easily by a tiny and simple tool officially distributed by Microsoft? In fact, it is good that Microsoft has closed this security gap. However, we are now in need of an alternative way to tear down the system. At this point, it is time for an old and simple NT rule: "If anything seems to be impossible in the Win32 world, just write a kernel-mode driver, and it will work out all right!" Windows 2000 manages Win32 applications very carefully. It constructs a wall between the application and the kernel, and anyone trying to cross this border will be shot without mercy. This is good for the overall stability of the system, but bad for programmers who need to write code that has to touch hardware. Contrary to DOS, where any application was allowed to do anything to the hardware, Windows 2000 is very picky in this respect. This doesn't mean that accessing hardware on Windows 2000 is impossible. Instead, this kind of access is restricted to a special kind of module called kernel-mode driver.

I can tell you now that I will present a short introduction to kernel-mode driver programming in Chapter 3. For now, it should suffice to say that crashing the system is one of the easiest things a kernel-mode driver can do. Windows 2000 doesn't provide an error recovery mechanism for drivers going berserk—even the faintest attempt to perform an illegal operation is immediately answered with a Blue Screen. Of course, the simplest and least dangerous violation of the rules is reading from an invalid memory address. Because the system explicitly catches all memory accesses through a NULL pointer, which is probably one of the most common errors in C programming, a NULL pointer read is the ideal operation to force a benign system crash. This is exactly what the `w2k_kill.sys` driver on the sample CD does. This very simple piece of software will also be one of the first kernel-mode driver projects presented in this book.

Listing 1-1 is a tiny excerpt from `w2k_kill.c`, containing nothing but the bad code that triggers the Blue Screen. When writing senseless code such as this, be aware that the brilliant optimizer built into Visual C/C++ might counteract your efforts. It tracks all code and tends to eliminate any instructions that don't have permanent side effects. In the example below, the optimizer's hands are tied because the `DriverEntry()` function insists on returning the value found at address zero as its return value. This means that this value has to be moved to CPU register `EAX`, and the easiest way to do this is by means of the `MOV EAX, [0]` instruction, which will throw the exception we have been waiting for.

The `w2k_load.exe` application presented in Chapter 3 can be used to load and start the `w2k_kill.sys` driver. If you are mentally ready to kill your Windows 2000 system, proceed as follows:

- Close all applications.
- Insert the accompanying sample CD.
- Choose **Run...** from the **Start** menu.
- Enter `d:\bin\w2k_load w2k_kill.sys` into the edit box, replacing `d:` with the drive letter of your CD-ROM drive, and click **OK.**

After this click, `w2k_load.exe` will attempt to load the `w2k_kill.sys` file located in the CD's `\bin` directory. As soon as the `DriverEntry()` routine is executed, the Blue Screen will appear, with a message similar to the one shown in Figure 1-3, and you will see a counter on the screen being incremented from 0 to 100 (or so) while the memory contents are dumped to the page file storage. If you have checked the **Automatically reboot** option in the **Startup and Recovery** dialog (see Figure 1-2), the system will reboot immediately after the crash dump is finished. When the system is ready for logon, wait for some time until the disk LED is no longer flashing. It takes some time to copy the crash dump image from the page file storage to the target disk file defined in the **Startup and Recovery** options (see Figure 1-2), especially if you have plenty of physical memory. Disturbing the system in this phase, for example, by shutting it down too early, might yield an invalid crash dump file that will be refused by the Kernel Debugger.

```
NTSTATUS DriverEntry (PDRIVER_OBJECT pDriverObject,
                      PUNICODE_STRING puRegistryPath)
    {
    return *((NTSTATUS *) 0); // read through NULL pointer
    }
```

LISTING 1-1. *A NULL Pointer Read Operation in Kernel-Mode Crashes the System*

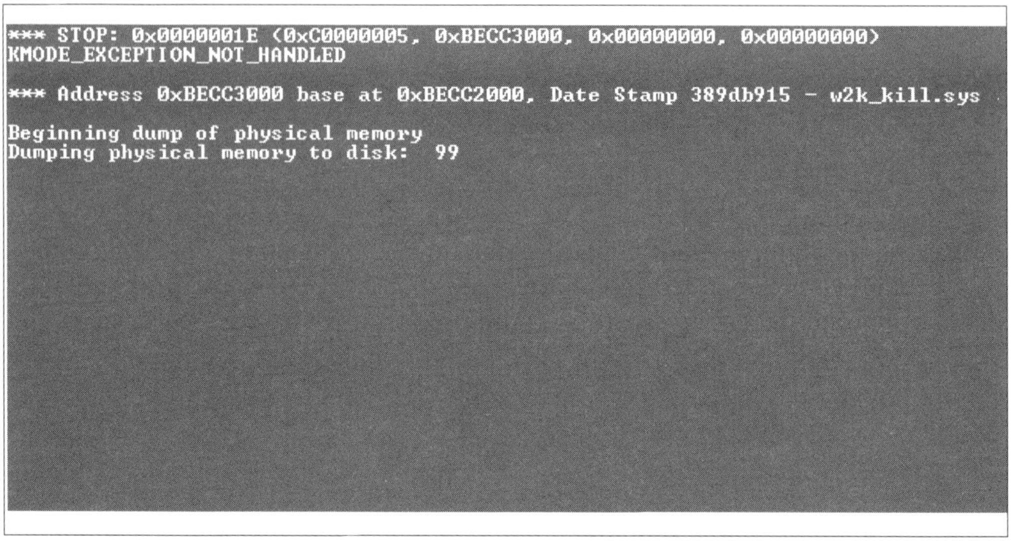

```
*** STOP: 0x0000001E (0xC0000005, 0xBECC3000, 0x00000000, 0x00000000)
KMODE_EXCEPTION_NOT_HANDLED

*** Address 0xBECC3000 base at 0xBECC2000, Date Stamp 389db915 - w2k_kill.sys

Beginning dump of physical memory
Dumping physical memory to disk:  99
```

FIGURE 1-3. *Execution of* `w2k_kill.sys` *Yields a Nice Blue Screen*

In Figure 1-3, the system displays the name of the module that contains the offending code (`w2k_kill.sys`), as well as the address of the instruction that caused the exception (`0xBECC3000`). This address will probably be different on your system, because it varies with the hardware configuration. Driver load addresses generally are not deterministic, similar to DLL load addresses. Please write down the indicated address—you will need it later after installing and configuring the Kernel Debugger.

A short note of caution is appropriate here: Crashing the system intentionally is not something you should do every day. Although the offending `w2k_kill.sys` code itself is benign, the time of its execution might be unfortunate. If the NULL pointer read occurs while another thread is in the course of doing something important, the system might shut down before this thread has a chance to clean up. For example, the active desktop tends to complain after the reboot that something horrible has happened and that it needs to be restored. Therefore, carefully check that the machine isn't working on precious data and that all cached data has been flushed to disk before you crash the system. The best time is when the disk has calmed down after a bootstrap. Note that neither the author nor the publisher of this book shall be liable for any damages resulting from system crashes forced by the `w2k_kill.sys` driver.

INSTALLING THE SYMBOL FILES

After rebooting, you have a snapshot of a Windows 2000 system, including a bad kernel-mode driver, caught in the course of a NULL pointer read. Peeking into this file is as good as examining the memory of a live system. Of course, this snapshot is like a dead animal body—it can't react anymore to external stimuli, but that shouldn't worry you now. What comes next is the setup of the symbol files that shall be used by the Kernel Debugger while you are dissecting the crash dump.

MSDN subscribers have to look for the symbol files on the CD named *Windows 2000 Customer Support—Diagnostic Tools*, which is part of the dark green *Development Platform (English)* CD set. Inserting the CD into the drive will start the Windows 2000 Internet Explorer with a file named `\DBG.HTM`. Here you can click on various setup options. If you are running the free build of Windows 2000, **Install retail symbols** is the correct choice. For the checked build, choose **Install debug symbols** instead. You can also use the classic symbol file setup by opening the Explorer and double-clicking the files `\SYMBOLS\I386\RETAIL\SYMBOLSX.EXE` (Figure 1-4) or `\SYMBOLS\I386\DEBUG\SYMBOLSX.EXE`, which are exactly the actions attached to the setup hyperlinks embedded in the `\DBG.HTM` file. The setup utility will copy several `.dbg` and `.pdb` files from the `SYMBOLS.CAB` archive to various subdirectories of the system's symbol root, which is named `%systemroot%\Symbols` by default. The `%systemroot%` token symbolizes the value of the environment variable `systemroot`, indicating the installation directory of the Windows 2000 system. In the example below, it is the `D:\WINNT` directory.

On startup, the Windows 2000 Kernel Debugger will try to locate the symbol files by evaluating the environment variable `_NT_SYMBOL_PATH` (note the leading underscore), so it is a good idea to define this variable right now. Again, you have to start the **System** applet from the Control Panel and select the **Advanced** tab, this time clicking the **Environment Variables...** button. Next, click the **New...** button in the **System variables** frame, and enter the **Variable Name:** and **Variable Value:** as shown in Figure 1-5, replacing `D:\WINNT` by the `%systemroot%` path of your system. After confirming all dialogs, symbol setup is complete.

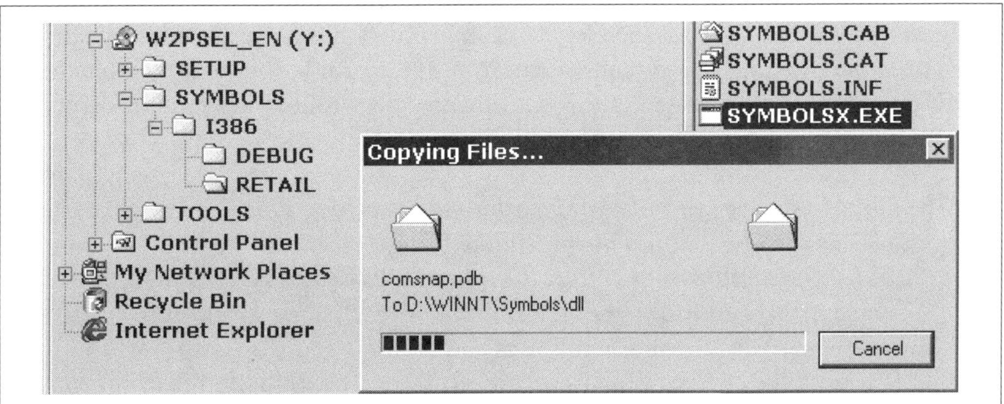

FIGURE 1-4. *Installing the Windows 2000 Retail Symbols*

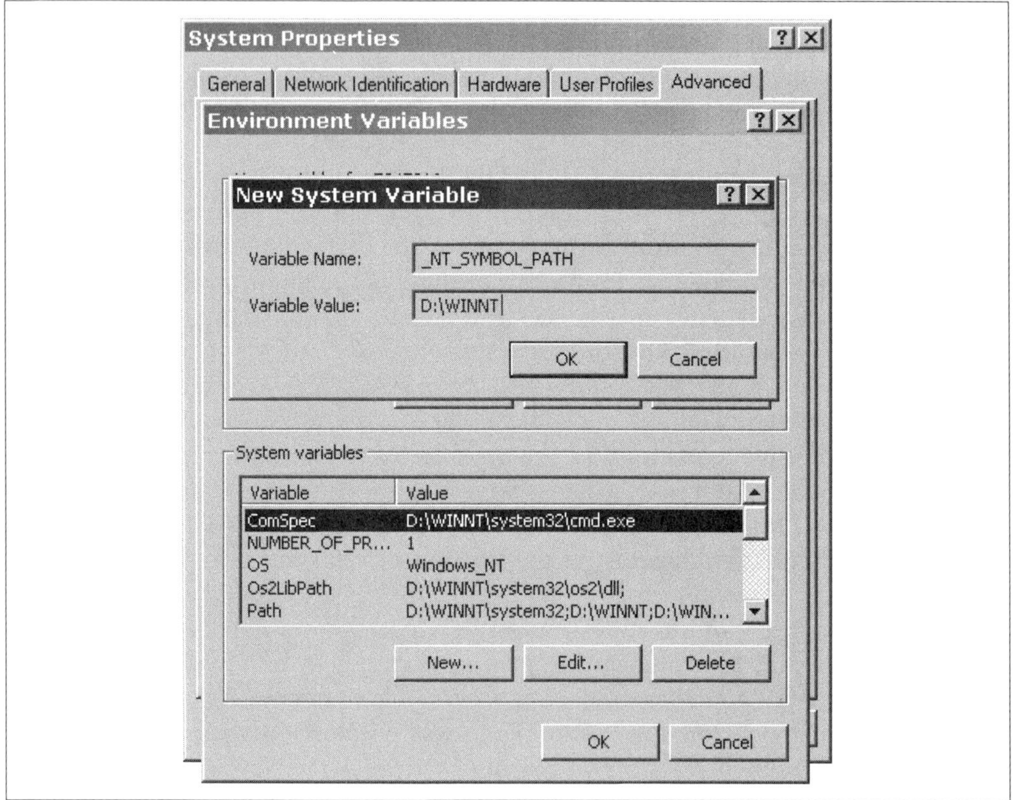

FIGURE 1-5. *Defining the Environment Variable* `_NT_SYMBOL_PATH`

The Microsoft documentation is somewhat unclear about which directory path must be assigned to the `_NT_SYMBOL_PATH` variable. The kernel-mode debugging chapters of the DDK say that the `Symbols` subdirectory has to be included, yielding a value of `d:\winnt\symbols` or equivalent. In the Platform Software Development Kit (SDK) documentation of the `dbghelp.dll` library, the symbol path setup is described a bit differently:

> *"The library uses the symbol search path to locate debug symbols* `(.dbg file)` *for* `.dll`, `.exe`, *and* `.sys` *files by appending "*`\symbols`*" and "*`\dll`*" or "*`\exe`*" or "*`\sys`*" to the path. For example, the typical location of symbol files for* `.dll` *files is* `c:\mysymbols\symbols\dll`. *For* `.exe` *files, the location is* `c:\mysymbols\symbols\exe`.*"*
> *[...] "If you set the* `_NT_SYMBOL_PATH` *or* `_NT_ALT_SYMBOL_PATH` *environment variable, the symbol handler searches for symbol files in the following order:*

1. *The current working directory of the application.*
2. *The* _NT_SYMBOL_PATH *environment variable.*
3. *The* _NT_ALT_SYMBOL_PATH *environment variable.*
4. *The* SYSTEMROOT *environment variable."*

(MSDN Library - April 2000 \ Platform SDK \ Base Services \ Debugging and Error Handling \ Debug Help Library \ About DbgHelp \ Symbol Handling \ Symbol Paths)

This sounds more like setting _NT_SYMBOL_PATH to d:\winnt rather than d:\winnt \symbols. To find out which point of view is correct, I tried both variants and was glad to see that it doesn't matter which one you choose. The Kernel Debugger finds the symbol files one way or another. If you suspect now that the _NT_SYMBOL_PATH value doesn't matter at all, try to set it to an invalid path—the debugger will refuse to run.

SETTING UP THE KERNEL DEBUGGER

The last step in the debugging environment setup is the installation and configuration of the Kernel Debugger. If you have already installed the Windows 2000 DDK, you can use the debuggers found in the \NTDDK\bin directory. The Kernel Debugger executable is named i386kd.exe. An alternative way is to install the debugging tools from the MSDN CD *Windows 2000 Customer Support—Diagnostic Tools,* from which you have already taken the symbol files. Just click on the **Install Debugging Tools** link on the setup page \DBG.HTM, or start the setup in the classic way by double-clicking \TOOLS\I386\DBGPLUS.EXE in the Explorer panel. This setup utility will copy the tools to a directory named \Program Files\Debuggers\bin.

After installing the Kernel Debugger, it is a good idea to create a shortcut that invokes i386kd.exe with the parameters you need. If you want to examine the crash dump file generated after the w2k_kill.sys Blue Screen, you can use the -z command line switch to specify the path of this file, directing the debugger to load this memory image at startup. Figure 1-6 illustrates typical shortcut properties.

Now everything is set up for the first debugging session. If you double-click the debugger's shortcut, you should see a console window like the one shown in Figure 1-7. The kd> prompt in front of the flashing cursor indicates that the Kernel Debugger is ready to accept commands. Before doing anything else, please check that the symbol search path displayed below the copyright banner is set to the correct location. If not, there is probably a typo in the environment variable specifying this path (see Figure 1-5). The start message also shows that the debugger has loaded three extension DLLs. i386kd.exe features a powerful extension mechanism that allows the basic command set to be augmented by custom commands implemented in a separate DLL. Because these additional commands have to be preceded by the "bang" character "!" to distinguish them from the built-in set, they usually are called *bang commands.* Some of them are extremely useful, as you will see later.

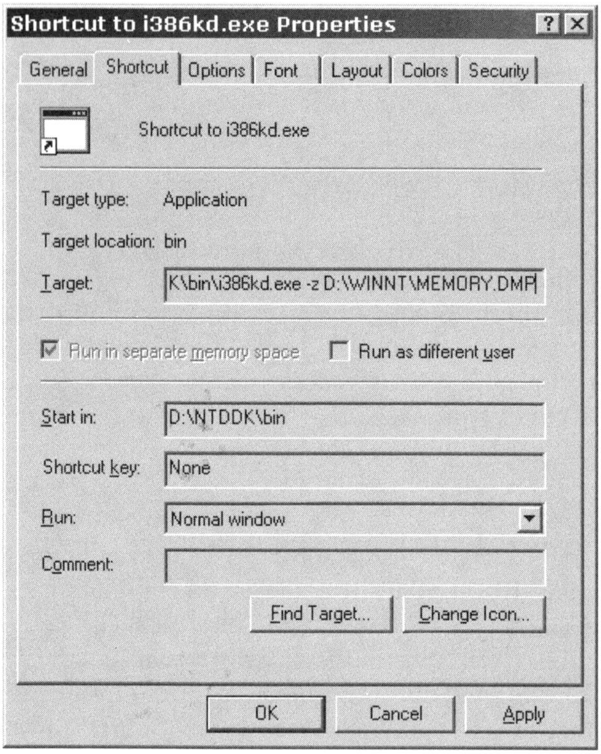

FIGURE 1-6. *Creating a Kernel Debugger Shortcut*

In Figure 1-7, I have entered one of the built-in commands: `u becc3000`. The `u` mnemonic means, of course, "unassemble," and `becc3000` is the hexadecimal start address where disassembly begins. By default, the number radix is 16, but you can change this setting with the `n` command, for example, `n 10` if you prefer decimal notation. You can always force a number to be interpreted as a hexadecimal by using the `0x` prefix borrowed from the C language. The address `becc3000` is the memory location where the `w2k_kill.sys` crash dump occurred (see Figure 1-3). Please try the `u` command with the address reported by your system after crashing. You should get a `mov eax,[00000000]` instruction, too, as shown in Figure 1-7, although the address is probably different. Otherwise, you are probably peeking into the wrong crash dump file—please check your Kernel Debugger shortcut in this case (see Figure 1-6). The `mov eax,[00000000]` instruction, loads a 32-bit value from the virtual address `0x00000000` to CPU register `EAX`, so it is obviously the implementation of the C expression `return *((NTSTATUS *) 0)` in Listing 1-1, and constitutes a NULL-pointer read operation. There is no special exception handler installed for this type of error, therefore, the system reports a `KMODE_EXCEPTION_NOT_HANDLED` error on the Blue Screen, as demonstrated by Figure 1-3. If you want, you can learn more about this common error code in *The NT Insider* (Open Systems Resources 1999b).

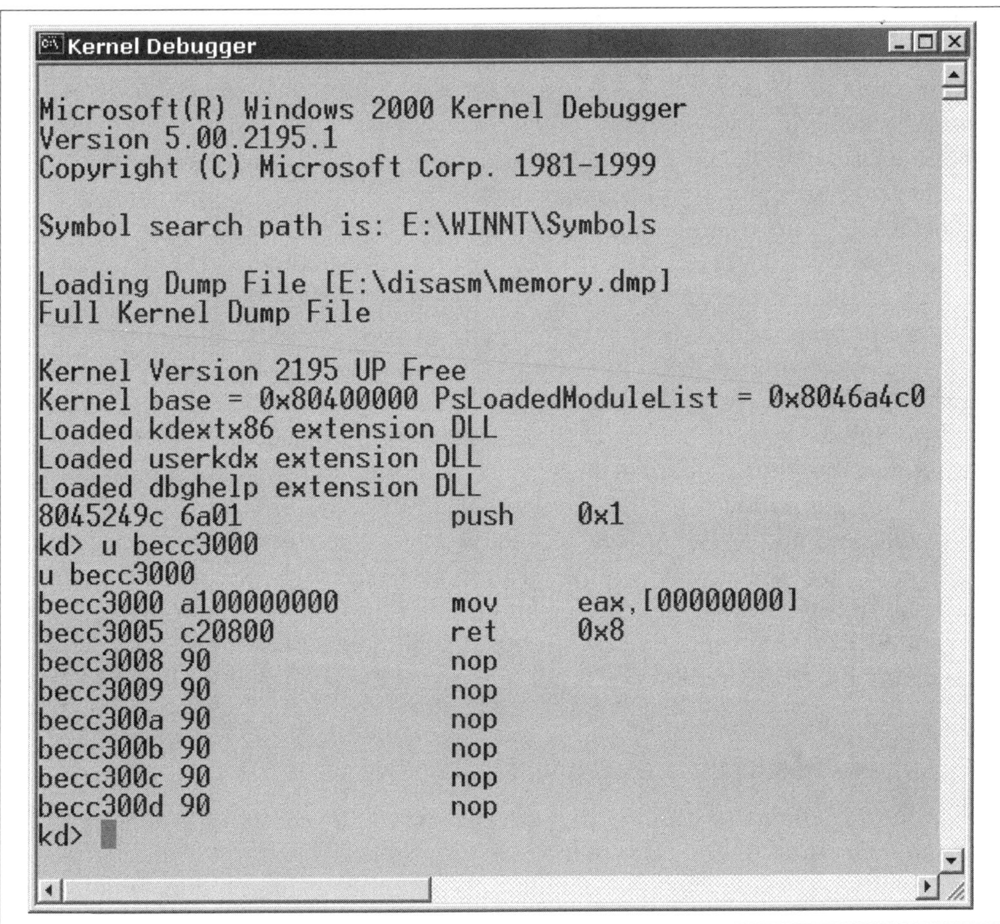
```
Microsoft(R) Windows 2000 Kernel Debugger
Version 5.00.2195.1
Copyright (C) Microsoft Corp. 1981-1999

Symbol search path is: E:\WINNT\Symbols

Loading Dump File [E:\disasm\memory.dmp]
Full Kernel Dump File

Kernel Version 2195 UP Free
Kernel base = 0x80400000 PsLoadedModuleList = 0x8046a4c0
Loaded kdextx86 extension DLL
Loaded userkdx extension DLL
Loaded dbghelp extension DLL
8045249c 6a01             push    0x1
kd> u becc3000
u becc3000
becc3000 a100000000       mov     eax,[00000000]
becc3005 c20800           ret     0x8
becc3008 90               nop
becc3009 90               nop
becc300a 90               nop
becc300b 90               nop
becc300c 90               nop
becc300d 90               nop
kd>
```

FIGURE 1-7. *Initiating a Kernel Debugger Session*

KERNEL DEBUGGER COMMANDS

Although the debugger commands are intended to be mnemonic, it is sometimes hard to recall them at the right time. Therefore, I have collected them in Appendix A, Table A-1, as a quick reference. This table is an edited version of the debugger's help output generated by the `?` command. The various types of arguments required for the commands are compiled in Table A-2.

As already mentioned, the Kernel Debugger can execute external commands known as *bang commands* that are implemented in one or more associated extension DLLs. Whenever a command name is prefixed by an exclamation mark (the so-called *bang* character), this name is looked up in the export lists of the loaded extension DLLs. If a match is found, the command is handed over to the DLL. Figure 1-7 shows that the Kernel Debugger loads the extensions `kdextx86.dll`, `userkdx.dll`, and dbghelp.dll, in this order. The latter is located in the same directory as the i386kd.exe application; the former pair is available in four versions: free versus checked build for Windows NT 4.0 (subdirectories nt4fre and nt4chk), and free versus checked build for Windows 2000 (subdirectories w2kfre and w2kchk), respectively. Normally, the debugger will use a default search order when locating the handler of a bang command. However, you can override the default by specifying a module name before the command name, separated by a dot. For example, both the kdextx86.dll and userkdx.dll extensions export a help command. Typing !help will yield the help screen of the kdextx86.dll module by default. To execute the help command of userkdx.dll, you have to type !userkdx.help (or !userkdx.help -v if you need more verbose help). By the way, you can write your own debugger extensions if you know the rules. An excellent how-to article can be found in *The NT Insider* (Open Systems Resources 1999a). It is targeting WinDbg.exe rather than i386kd.exe, but because both debuggers use the same extension DLLs, most of the information is applicable to i386kd.exe as well.

Tables A-3 and A-4 in Appendix A show the output generated by the help commands of kdextx86.dll and userkdx.dll, respectively, slightly corrected and heavily edited for better readability. You will notice that these tables list far more commands than documented in the Microsoft DDK, and some commands obviously have additional optional parameters not mentioned in the DDK documentation.

The Top Ten Debugging Commands

Tables A-1 to A-4 demonstrate in an impressive way that the Kernel Debugger and its standard extensions offer a large number of commands. Therefore, I will discuss in detail some of the commands that are most useful for the exploration of Windows 2000 internals.

u: *Unassemble Machine Code*

You have already used the u command after starting the Kernel Debugger to check whether the loaded crash dump file is OK. The u command has three forms:

1. u <from> disassembles eight machine instructions, starting at address <from>.
2. u <from> <to> starts disassembly at address <from>, and continues until reaching or transcending address <to>. The instruction at this address, if any, is not included in the listing.
3. u (without arguments) restarts disassembly from the address where a previous u command stopped (no matter whether it had arguments or not).

Of course, disassembling large code portions with this command is quite annoying, but it comes in handy if you just need to know what is occurring at a specific address. Perhaps the most interesting feature of the `u` command is its ability to resolve symbols referenced by the code—even internal symbols not exported by the target module. However, in disassembling complete Windows 2000 executables, using the `Multi-Format Visual Disassembler` on the companion CD is much more fun. More on this product will follow later in this chapter.

`db`, `dw`, and `dd`: Dump Memory `BYTEs`, `WORDs`, and `DWORDs`

If the memory contents you are currently interested in are binary data rather than machine code, the debugger's hex dump commands do a great job. Depending on the data types you are expecting at the source address, one of the variants `db` (for `BYTEs`), `dw` (for `WORDs`), or `dd` (for `DWORDs`) applies.

- `db` dumps a memory range in two panels. On the left-hand side, the contents are displayed as two-digit 8-bit hexadecimal quantities; the right-hand panel shows the same data in ASCII format.
- dw displays the contents of a memory range as four-digit 16-bit hexadecimal quantities. An ASCII panel is not included.
- `dd` displays the contents of a memory range as eight-digit 32-bit hexadecimal quantities. An ASCII panel is not included.

For this command set, the same arguments as for the `u` command can be used. Note, however, that the data located at the `<to>` address are always included in the hex dump listing. If no arguments are specified, the next 128-byte block is displayed.

`x`: Examine Symbols

The `x` command is very important. It can create lists of symbols compiled from the installed symbol files. It is typically used in one of the following three forms:

1. `x *!*` displays a list of all modules for which symbols can be browsed. After startup, only the `ntoskrnl.exe` symbols are available by default. The symbols of other modules can be added by issuing the `.reload` command.
2. `x <module>!<filter>` displays a list of symbols found in the symbol file of `<module>`, applying a `<filter>` that may contain the wildcards `?` and `*`. The `<module>` name must be one of the list yielded by the `x *!*` command. For example, `x nt!*` lists all symbols found in the kernel's symbol file `ntoskrnl.dbg`, and `x win32k!*` lists the symbols provided by `win32k.dbg`. If the debugger reports "Couldn't resolve 'x ...'", try the command again after reloading all symbols by means of the `.reload` command.

3. x <filter> displays a subset of all available symbols, matched against a <filter> expression. Essentially, this is a variant of the x <module>!<filter> command, in which the <module>! part has been omitted.

Along with the symbol names, the associated virtual addresses are shown. For function names, this is the function's entry point. For variables, it is a pointer to the base address of the variable. The most notable thing about this command is that its output includes many internal symbols, not just those found in the executable's export table.

ln: List Nearest Symbols

The ln command is certainly my favorite, because it gives quick and easy access to the installed symbol files. It is the ideal complement to the x command. Whereas the latter is great if you need an address listing of various operating system symbols, the ln command is used to look up individual symbols by address or name.

- ln <address> displays the name of the symbol found at or preceding the given <address>, as well as the next known symbol following this address.
- ln <symbol> resolves the given <symbol> name to its virtual address and then proceeds like the ln <address> command.

Like with the x command, the debugger is aware of all exported and several nonexported internal symbols. Therefore, it is an important aid for anyone who tries to make sense of unknown pointers occurring somewhere in a disassembly listing or hex dump. Note that the u, db, dw, and dd commands also accept symbols where addresses are expected.

!processfields: List EPROCESS Members

As the bang character preceding the name imples, this is a command from a debugger extension module—kdextx86.dll, in this case. This command displays the names and offsets of all members of the—formally undocumented—EPROCESS structure used by the kernel to represent processes, as shown in Example 1-1.

```
kd> !processfields
!processfields
 EPROCESS structure offsets:
    Pcb:                                      0x0
    ExitStatus:                               0x6c
    LockEvent:                                0x70    LockCount:       0x80
    CreateTime:                               0x88
    ExitTime:                                 0x90
```

```
LockOwner:                          0x98
UniqueProcessId:                    0x9c
ActiveProcessLinks:                 0xa0
QuotaPeakPoolUsage[0]:              0xa8
QuotaPoolUsage[0]:                  0xb0
PagefileUsage:                      0xb8
CommitCharge:                       0xbc
PeakPagefileUsage:                  0xc0
PeakVirtualSize:                    0xc4
VirtualSize:                        0xc8
Vm:                                 0xd0
DebugPort:                          0x120
ExceptionPort:                      0x124
ObjectTable:                        0x128
Token:                              0x12c
WorkingSetLock:                     0x130
WorkingSetPage:                     0x150
ProcessOutswapEnabled:              0x154
ProcessOutswapped:                  0x155
AddressSpaceInitialized:            0x156
AddressSpaceDeleted:                0x157
AddressCreationLock:                0x158
ForkInProgress:                     0x17c
VmOperation:                        0x180
VmOperationEvent:                   0x184
PageDirectoryPte:                   0x1f0
LastFaultCount:                     0x18c
VadRoot:                            0x194
VadHint:                            0x198
CloneRoot:                          0x19c
NumberOfPrivatePages:               0x1a0
NumberOfLockedPages:                0x1a4
ForkWasSuccessful:                  0x182
ExitProcessCalled:                  0x1aa
CreateProcessReported:              0x1ab
SectionHandle:                      0x1ac
Peb:                                0x1b0
SectionBaseAddress:                 0x1b4
QuotaBlock:                         0x1b8
LastThreadExitStatus:               0x1bc
WorkingSetWatch:                    0x1c0
InheritedFromUniqueProcessId:       0x1c8
GrantedAccess:                      0x1cc
DefaultHardErrorProcessing          0x1d0
LdtInformation:                     0x1d4
VadFreeHint:                        0x1d8
VdmObjects:                         0x1dc
DeviceMap:                          0x1e0
ImageFileName[0]:                   0x1fc
VmTrimFaultValue:                   0x20c
Win32Process:                       0x214
Win32WindowStation:                 0x1c4
```

EXAMPLE 1-1. *Cracking the* EPROCESS *Structure*

Although this command shows the members' offsets only, you can easily guess the corresponding types. For example, the `LockEvent` member is located at offset *0×70*, and the next member follows at offset *0×80*, so this member requires 16 bytes, which looks rather like a `KEVENT` structure. Don't worry if you don't know what a `KEVENT` is—I will discuss kernel object structures in Chapter 7.

`!threadfields:` List *ETHREAD* Members

This command is another great option offered by the `kdextx86.dll` debugger extension. Like the `!processfields` command, it displays the member names and offsets of yet another formally undocumented structure named `ETHREAD`, which represents threads. Example 1-2 shows a sample output.

`!drivers:` List Loaded Drivers

The `kdextx86.dll` goodie `!drivers` shows detailed information about all currently running kernel and file system modules. If a crash dump image is examined, this list reflects the system state at the time of the crash. Example 1-3 is an excerpt of a sample run on my machine. Note that the last line before the summary shows our bad Windows 2000 killer device at base address `0xBECC2000`, which is obviously one of the hexadecimal numbers reported on the Blue Screen after the `w2k_kill.sys` crash (see Figure 1-3).

```
kd> !threadfields
!threadfields
 ETHREAD structure offsets:
    Tcb:                                    0x0
    CreateTime:                             0x1b0
    ExitTime:                               0x1b8
    ExitStatus:                             0x1c0
    PostBlockList:                          0x1c4
    TerminationPortList:                    0x1cc
    ActiveTimerListLock:                    0x1d4
    ActiveTimerListHead:                    0x1d8
    Cid:                                    0x1e0
    LpcReplySemaphore:                      0x1e8
    LpcReplyMessage:                        0x1fc
    LpcReplyMessageId:                      0x200
    ImpersonationInfo:                      0x208
    IrpList:                                0x20c
    TopLevelIrp:                            0x214
    ReadClusterSize:                        0x21c
```

```
ForwardClusterOnly:                    0x220
DisablePageFaultClustering:            0x221
DeadThread:                            0x222
HasTerminated:                         0x224
GrantedAccess:                         0x228
ThreadsProcess:                        0x22c
StartAddress:                          0x230
Win32StartAddress:                     0x234
LpcExitThreadCalled:                   0x238
HardErrorsAreDisabled:                 0x239
```

EXAMPLE 1-2. *Cracking the* ETHREAD *Structure*

```
kd> !drivers
!drivers
Loaded System Driver Summary

Base       Code     Size        Data     Size       Driver Name    Creation Time
80400000   142dc0   (1291 kb)   4d680    (309 kb)   ntoskrnl.exe   Wed Dec 08 00:41:11 1999
80062000    13c40   (  79 kb)    34e0    ( 13 kb)        hal.dll   Sun Oct 31 00:48:14 1999
f0810000     1760   (   5 kb)    1000    (  4 kb)    BOOTVID.DLL   Thu Nov 04 02:24:33 1999
f0400000     bdc0   (  47 kb)    22a0    (  8 kb)        pci.sys   Thu Oct 28 01:11:08 1999
f0410000     99c0   (  38 kb)    18e0    (  6 kb)     isapnp.sys   Sat Oct 02 22:00:35 1999
f09c8000      760   (   1 kb)     520    (  1 kb)   intelide.sys   Fri Oct 29 01:20:03 1999
f0680000     42e0   (  16 kb)     e80    (  3 kb)    PCIIDEX.SYS   Thu Oct 28 01:02:19 1999
f0688000     64a0   (  25 kb)     a20    (  2 kb)   MountMgr.sys   Sat Oct 23 00:48:06 1999
bffe3000    192c0   ( 100 kb)    2b00    ( 10 kb)     ftdisk.sys   Mon Nov 22 20:36:23 1999
f0900000     12e0   (   4 kb)     640    (  1 kb)   Diskperf.sys   Fri Oct 01 02:30:40 1999
[...]
bf255000     fc40   (  63 kb)    2120    (  8 kb)     wdmaud.sys   Wed Oct 27 20:40:45 1999
f0670000     9520   (  37 kb)    1f40    (  7 kb)   sysaudio.sys   Mon Oct 25 21:28:14 1999
f094c000      d40   (   3 kb)     860    (  2 kb)     ParVdm.SYS   Tue Sep 28 05:28:16 1999
f0958000      a00   (   2 kb)     480    (  1 kb)   PfModNT.sys    Thu Dec 16 05:14:08 1999
bf0dd000    35520   ( 213 kb)    59e0    ( 22 kb)         rv.sys   Tue Nov 30 08:38:21 1999
bf191000     d820   (  54 kb)    1280    (  4 kb)       Cdfs.SYS   Mon Oct 25 21:23:52 1999
bed9a000    11f20   (  71 kb)    2ac0    ( 10 kb)      ipsec.sys   Tue Nov 30 08:08:54 1999
beaaf000        0   (   0 kb)       0    (  0 kb)      ATMFD.DLL   Header Paged Out
be9eb000    16f60   (  91 kb)    ccc0    ( 51 kb)     kmixer.sys   Wed Nov 10 07:52:30 1999
becc2000      200   (   0 kb)     a00    (  2 kb)   w2k_kill.sys   Sun Feb 06 19:10:29 2000
TOTAL:     79c660   (7793 kb)  15c160   (1392 kb)      (    0 kb     0 kb)
```

EXAMPLE 1-3. *Displaying Information about System Modules*

`!sel`: Examine Selector Values

If issued without arguments, the `!sel` command implemented by `kdextx86.dll` dumps the parameters of 16 consecutive memory selectors in ascending order. You can issue this command repeatedly until "Selector is invalid" is reported to get a list of all valid selectors (Example 1-4). Memory selector handling will be covered extensively in Chapter 4, and I will present sample code there that demonstrates how you can crack selectors in your own applications.

```
kd> !sel
!sel
0000  Bas=00000000 Lim=00000000 Bytes DPL=0 NP
0008  Bas=00000000 Lim=000fffff Pages DPL=0  P Code  RE A
0010  Bas=00000000 Lim=000fffff Pages DPL=0  P Data  RW A
0018  Bas=00000000 Lim=000fffff Pages DPL=3  P Code  RE A
0020  Bas=00000000 Lim=000fffff Pages DPL=3  P Data  RW A
0028  Bas=80244000 Lim=000020ab Bytes DPL=0  P TSS32    B
0030  Bas=ffdff000 Lim=00000001 Pages DPL=0  P Data  RW A
0038  Bas=00000000 Lim=00000fff Bytes DPL=3  P Data  RW A
0040  Bas=00000400 Lim=0000ffff Bytes DPL=3  P Data  RW
0048  Bas=00000000 Lim=00000000 Bytes DPL=0 NP
0050  Bas=80470040 Lim=00000068 Bytes DPL=0  P TSS32    A
0058  Bas=804700a8 Lim=00000068 Bytes DPL=0  P TSS32    A
0060  Bas=00022ab0 Lim=0000ffff Bytes DPL=0  P Data  RW A
0068  Bas=000b8000 Lim=00003fff Bytes DPL=0  P Data  RW
0070  Bas=ffff7000 Lim=000003ff Bytes DPL=0  P Data  RW
0078  Bas=80400000 Lim=0000ffff Bytes DPL=0  P Code  RE
kd> !sel
!sel
0080  Bas=80400000 Lim=0000ffff Bytes DPL=0  P Data  RW
0088  Bas=00000000 Lim=00000000 Bytes DPL=0  P Data  RW
0090  Bas=00000000 Lim=00000000 Bytes DPL=0 NP
0098  Bas=00000000 Lim=00000000 Bytes DPL=0 NP
00a0  Bas=814985a8 Lim=00000068 Bytes DPL=0  P TSS32    A
00a8  Bas=00000000 Lim=00000000 Bytes DPL=0 NP
00b0  Bas=00000000 Lim=00000000 Bytes DPL=0 NP
00b8  Bas=00000000 Lim=00000000 Bytes DPL=0 NP
00c0  Bas=00000000 Lim=00000000 Bytes DPL=0 NP
00c8  Bas=00000000 Lim=00000000 Bytes DPL=0 NP
00d0  Bas=00000000 Lim=00000000 Bytes DPL=0 NP
00d8  Bas=00000000 Lim=00000000 Bytes DPL=0 NP
00e0  Bas=f0430000 Lim=0000ffff Bytes DPL=0  P Code  RE A
00e8  Bas=00000000 Lim=0000ffff Bytes DPL=0  P Data  RW
00f0  Bas=8042dce8 Lim=000003b7 Bytes DPL=0  P Code  EO
00f8  Bas=00000000 Lim=0000ffff Bytes DPL=0  P Data  RW
```

EXAMPLE 1-4. *Displaying Selector Parameters*

Shutting Down the Debugger

You can kick the Kernel Debugger out of the system by simply closing the console window it is running in. However, the clean way to shut it down is using its `q` command, where "q" stands for—you guessed it—"quit."

MORE DEBUGGING TOOLS

On the book's companion CD, you will find another pair of valuable debugging tools contributed by two "e-friends" of mine. I am very glad that they allowed me to put fully functional versions of their great tools onto the CD. Wayne J. Radburn's *PE and COFF File Viewer* (PEview) is a special FreeWare edition for the readers of this book. Jean-Louis Seigné's *Multi-Format Visual Disassembler* (MFVDasm) comes in an uncrippled but timed demo version. This section is a short introduction to both tools.

MFVDasm: The Multi-Format Visual Disassembler

MFVDasm is not just a simple assembly listing generator. In fact, it is more an assembly code browser with several nice navigation features. Figure 1-8 shows a snapshot of an MFVDasm session in which I examined the Windows 2000 I/O Manager function `IoDetachDevice()`. Figure 1-8 does not show the color you would see on the screen. For example, all function labels, as well as jumps and calls to named destinations, are displayed red. Jumps and calls to anonymous addresses (i.e., addresses that are not associated with an exported symbol) are blue, and references to symbols dynamically imported from other modules are violet. All reachable destinations are underlined, indicating that you can click on them to scroll the code pane to the address. Using the **Back** and **Forward** buttons on the toolbar, you can navigate through the history of branches, much like flipping through the visited pages in an Internet browser.

In the right-hand pane, you can randomly select a symbol or target address to which you can jump. Of course, this list can be sorted by clicking on the column header buttons. On the lower edge of this pane, MFVDasm has tabs that allow switching between **Symbols, HexDump,** and **Relocations.** The hex dump view can be quite useful if you are disassembling a code section that contains embedded strings. MFVDasm doesn't choke on very large files such as `ntoskrnl.exe`, as some other popular disassemblers do, and, of course, the assembly code can be saved to a text file. Many more options are accessible via the main menu and the context menus that appear if you right-click on one of the window panes. If you need more information, visit Jean-Louis Seigné's MFVDasm home site at http://redirect.to/MFVDasm.

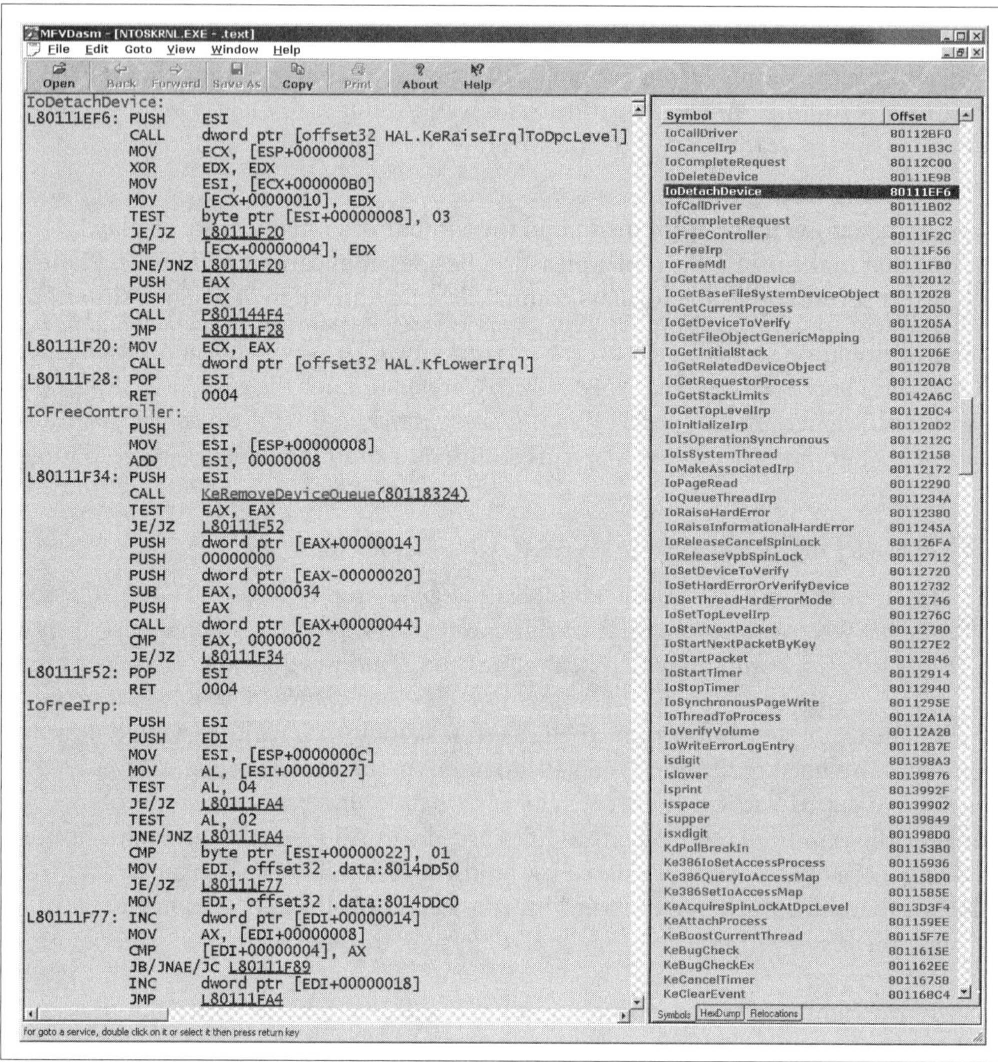

FIGURE 1-8. *MFVDasm Disassembling* `ntoskrnl.Io` DetachDevice()

PEVIEW—THE PE AND COFF FILE VIEWER

Although MFVDasm shows lots of details about the internal structure of a Portable Executable (PE) file, its strength is code browsing. On the other hand, PEview doesn't show you more than a hex dump of a code file section, but is considerably more detailed about the file structure. Figure 1-9 is a snapshot of PEview displaying the various parts of `ntoskrnl.exe` in tree form. If you click on a leaf node in the left-hand pane, the right-hand pane displays everything there is to know about the binary contents of this item. In Figure 1-9, I have selected the `IMAGE_OPTIONAL_HEADER` structure, which is a member of the `IMAGE_NT_HEADERS` structure located near the beginning of the executable.

If you take a closer look to the PEview toolbar, you see navigation arrows that allow scrolling through the file structure (vertical arrows) and the navigation history (horizontal arrows). The main menu and the toolbar offer many more display options that make using this tool a pleasure. Besides applications and DLLs, PEview can dissect several other file formats commonly encountered in debugging situations, such as object files, import libraries, and symbol files. More information is available at Wayne J. Radburn's Web site at http://www.magma.ca/~wjr/.

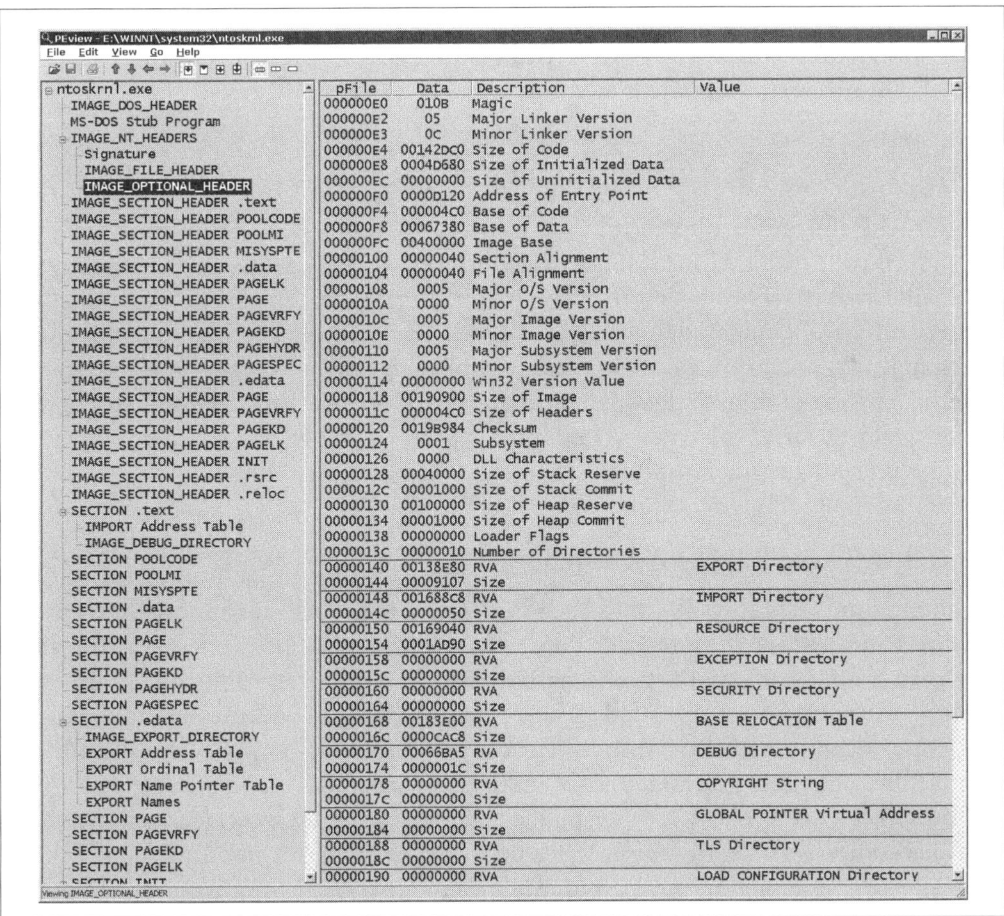

FIGURE 1-9. *PEview Dissecting the PE File Structure of* `ntoskrnl.exe`

As mentioned in the Preface, Wayne writes his Win32 software in assembly language (ASM). Yes, this is not only possible but also quite easy if you have the necessary tools. In fact, ASM programming is much easier on the Win32 platform than it was in the old DOS and Windows 3.x days, because you can take full advantage of the CPU's 32-bit instruction set. Wayne actively supports Win32 ASM by providing extensive sample code on his Web site. I have been a die-hard ASM programmer myself, but I retired from it after discovering that the Microsoft Visual C optimizer does a much better job than a human ASM coder, because it can use all sorts of tricks that an ASM programmer should never use—the code would be unreadable and almost impossible to maintain. The results of my ASM efforts are publicly available in the form of a FreeWare package for the Microsoft Macro Assembler (MASM). It is called *Win32 Assembly Language Kit (WALK32)* and can be downloaded from my Web site. Just go to http://www.orgon.com/pub/asm/ and get all files that contain the letters "walk" in the file name. However, be aware that I have abandoned WALK32, and will not support or update it anymore.

WINDOWS 2000 DEBUGGING INTERFACES

The Kernel Debugger is a powerful tool for everyone interested in exploring the internals of the system. However, its user interface is somewhat poor, and sometimes you might wish to have even more powerful commands. Fortunately, Windows 2000 offers two fully documented debugging interfaces that enable you to add debugging functionality to your applications. These interfaces are far from luxurious, but they have the blessing of official documentation by Microsoft. In this section, I will take you on a short tour of these debugging interfaces, showing what they can do for you and how you can get the most out of them.

psapi.dll, imagehlp.dll, and dbghelp.dll

For a long time, Windows NT had been criticized for its lack of support for the Windows 95 `ToolHelp32` interface. Some of the critics were possibly not aware that Windows NT 4.0 came with an alternative debugging interface of its own, buried inside a system component named `psapi.dll`, distributed with the Win32 SDK. This DLL, together with `imagehlp.dll` and `dbghelp.dll`, comprise the officially documented debugging interfaces of Windows NT and 2000. The five letters PSAPI are the acronym of Process Status Application Programming Interface, and this interface comprises a set of 14 functions providing system information about device drivers, processes, memory usage and modules of a process, working sets, and memory-mapped files. `psapi.dll` supports both ANSI and Unicode strings.

The other pair of debugging DLLs, `imagehlp.dll` and `dgbhelp.dll`, cover a different range of tasks. Both export a similar set of functions, with the major difference that imagehlp.dll offers more functions, whereas dbghelp.dll is a redistributable component. This means that Microsoft allows you to put dbghelp.dll into the setup package of your applications if it relies on that DLL. If you choose to use imagehlp.dll instead, you must take the one that is currently installed on the target system. Both DLLs provide a rich set of functions for parsing and manipulating PE files. However, their most outstanding feature probably is their ability to extract symbols from the symbol files you have installed for use with the Kernel Debugger. To guide your decision as to which DLL you should choose, I have compiled all functions exported by imagehlp.dll and dgbhelp.dll in Table 1-1, where the middle and right-hand columns show which functions are not supported by which component. An entry of N/A means "not available."

TABLE 1-1. *Comparison of* imagehlp.dll *and* dbghelp.dll

NAME	**imagehlp.dll**	**dbghelp.dll**
BindImage		N/A
BindImageEx		N/A
CheckSumMappedFile		N/A
EnumerateLoadedModules		
EnumerateLoadedModules64		
ExtensionApiVersion	N/A	
FindDebugInfoFile		
FindDebugInfoFileEx		
FindExecutableImage		
FindExecutableImageEx		
FindFileInSearchPath		
GetImageConfigInformation		N/A
GetImageUnusedHeaderBytes		N/A
GetTimestampForLoadedLibrary		
ImageAddCertificate		N/A
ImageDirectoryEntryToData		
ImageDirectoryEntryToDataEx		
ImageEnumerateCertificates		N/A
ImageGetCertificateData		N/A
ImageGetCertificateHeader		N/A
ImageGetDigestStream		N/A
ImagehlpApiVersion		
ImagehlpApiVersionEx		

(continued)

TABLE 1-1. *(continued)*

NAME	imagehlp.dll	dbghelp.dll
ImageLoad		N/A
ImageNtHeader		
ImageRemoveCertificate		N/A
ImageRvaToSection		
ImageRvaToVa		
ImageUnload		N/A
MakeSureDirectoryPathExists		
MapAndLoad		N/A
MapDebugInformation		
MapFileAndCheckSumA		N/A
MapFileAndCheckSumW		N/A
ReBaseImage		N/A
ReBaseImage64		N/A
RemovePrivateCvSymbolic		N/A
RemovePrivateCvSymbolicEx		N/A
RemoveRelocations		N/A
SearchTreeForFile		
SetImageConfigInformation		N/A
SplitSymbols		N/A
StackWalk		
StackWalk64		
sym	N/A	
SymCleanup		
SymEnumerateModules		
SymEnumerateModules64		
SymEnumerateSymbols		
SymEnumerateSymbols64		
SymEnumerateSymbolsW		
SymFunctionTableAccess		
SymFunctionTableAccess64		
SymGetLineFromAddr		
SymGetLineFromAddr64		
SymGetLineFromName		
SymGetLineFromName64		

TABLE 1-1. *(continued)*

NAME	imagehlp.dll	dbghelp.dll
SymGetLineNext		
SymGetLineNext64		
SymGetLinePrev		
SymGetLinePrev64		
SymGetModuleBase		
SymGetModuleBase64		
SymGetModuleInfo		
SymGetModuleInfo64		
SymGetModuleInfoEx		
SymGetModuleInfoEx64		
SymGetModuleInfoW		
SymGetModuleInfoW64		
SymGetOptions		
SymGetSearchPath		
SymGetSymbolInfo		
SymGetSymbolInfo64		
SymGetSymFromAddr		
SymGetSymFromAddr64		
SymGetSymFromName		
SymGetSymFromName64		
SymGetSymNext		
SymGetSymNext64		
SymGetSymPrev		
SymGetSymPrev64		
SymInitialize		
SymLoadModule		
SymLoadModule64		
SymMatchFileName		
SymEnumerateSymbolsW64		
SymRegisterCallback		
SymRegisterCallback64		
SymRegisterFunctionEntryCallback		
SymRegisterFunctionEntryCallback64		
SymSetOptions		

(continued)

TABLE 1-1. *(continued)*

NAME	`imagehlp.dll`	`dbghelp.dll`
SymSetSearchPath		
SymUnDName		
SymUnDName64		
SymUnloadModule		
SymUnloadModule64		
TouchFileTimes		N/A
UnDecorateSymbolName		
UnMapAndLoad		N/A
UnmapDebugInformation		
UpdateDebugInfoFile		N/A
UpdateDebugInfoFileEx		N/A
WinDbgExtensionDllInit	N/A	

In the sample source code following in this section, I will demonstrate how `psapi.dll` and `imagehlp.dll` are used for the following programming tasks:

- Enumeration of all kernel components and drivers
- Enumeration of all processes currently managed by the system
- Enumeration of all modules loaded inside a process' virtual address space
- Enumeration of all symbols of a given component, if available

The `psapi.dll` interface is not particularly well designed. It provides a minimum of functionality, although it would have been easy to add a bit more convenience. Also, this DLL queries quite a bit of information from the kernel and then throws away most of it, leaving only tiny bits and pieces.

Because the `psapi.dll` and `imagehlp.dll` functions are not part of the standard Win32 API, their header files and import libraries are not automatically included in your Visual C/C++ projects. Therefore, the four directives in Listing 1-2 should show up somewhere in your source files. The first pair pulls in the required header files, and the latter pair establishes the dynamic links to the API functions exported by both DLLs.

```
#include <imagehlp.h>
#include <psapi.h>

#pragma comment (linker, "/defaultlib:imagehlp.lib")
#pragma comment (linker, "/defaultlib:psapi.lib")
```

LISTING 1-2. *Adding* `psapi.dll` *and* `imagehlp.dll` *to a Visual C/C++ Project*

SAMPLE CODE ON THE CD

On the CD accompanying this book, two sample projects are included that are built on `psapi.dll` and `imagehlp.dll`. One of them is `w2k_sym.exe`—a Windows 2000 symbol browser that extracts symbol names from an arbitrary symbol file, provided you have installed it (see Setting Up a Debugging Environment). The symbol table can be sorted by name, address, and data size, and a wildcard filter can be applied as well. As an additional bonus, `w2k_sym.exe` also lists active system module/driver names, running processes, and modules loaded inside any process. The other sample project is the debugging support library `w2k_dbg.dll`, which contains several convenient wrappers around `psapi.dll` and `imagehlp.dll` functions. `w2k_sym.exe` relies entirely on this DLL. The source code of these projects is located in the CD directories `\src\w2k_dbg` and `\src\w2k_sym`, respectively.

Table 1-2 lists the functions that are used by `w2k_dbg.dll`. The column A/W indicates for all functions involving strings whether ANSI (A) or 16-bit wide Unicode characters (W) are supported. As noted earlier, `psapi.dll` supports both ANSI and Unicode. Unfortunately, `imagehlp.dll` and `dbghelp.dll` aren't that clever and require 8-bit ANSI strings for several functions. This is somewhat annoying because a Windows 2000 debugging application usually will not run on Windows 9x and therefore could use Unicode characters without reservation. With `imagehlp.dll` included in your project, you will either have to use ANSI or occasionally convert Unicode strings back and forth. Because I definitely hate to work with 8-bit strings on a system capable of handling 16-bit characters, I have opted for the latter approach. All functions exported by `w2k_dbg.dll` that involve strings expect Unicode characters, so you don't need to be concerned about character size issues if you are reusing this DLL in your own Windows 2000 projects.

On the other hand, `imagehlp.dll` and `dbghelp.dll` have an interesting feature that `psapi.dll` lacks: They are already fit for Win64—the 64-bit Windows every developer is frightened of, because nobody really knows how difficult it will be to port Win32 applications to Win64. These DLLs export Win64 API functions, and that's OK—maybe we will be able to use them someday.

TABLE 1-2. *Debugging Functions Used by* w2k_dbg.dll

NAME	A/W	LIBRARY
EnumDeviceDrivers		psapi.dll
EnumProcesses		psapi.dll
EnumProcessModules		psapi.dll
GetDeviceDriverFileName	A/W	psapi.dll
GetModuleFileNameEx	A/W	psapi.dll
GetModuleInformation		psapi.dll
ImageLoad	A	imagehlp.dll
ImageUnload		imagehlp.dll
SymCleanup		imagehlp.dll
SymEnumerateSymbols	A/W	imagehlp.dll
SymInitialize	A	imagehlp.dll
SymLoadModule	A	imagehlp.dll
SymUnloadModule		imagehlp.dll

I don't go into `psapi.dll` and `imagehlp.dll` in depth. This book focuses on undocumented interfaces, and the interfaces of both DLLs are satisfactorily documented in the Platform SDK. However, I don't want to bypass them completely because they are closely related to the Windows 2000 Native API, discussed in Chapter 2. Moreover, `psapi.dll` is a good example of why an undocumented interface might be preferable to a documented one. Its interface is not only spartan and clumsy—it might even return inconsistent data in certain situations. If I had to write and sell a professional debugging tool, I would not build it on this DLL. The Windows 2000 kernel offers powerful, versatile, and much better-suited debugging API functions. However, they are almost completely undocumented. Fortunately, many system utilities provided by Microsoft make extensive use of this API, so it has undergone only slight changes across Windows NT versions. Yes, you have to revise and carefully test your software on every new NT release if you are using this API, but its benefits more than outweigh this drawback.

Most of the following code samples are taken from the source code of `w2k_dbg.dll`, found in the CD accompanying this book in the file `\src\w2k_dbg\w2k_dbg.c`. This library encapsulates several steps that you would have to take separately in convenient opaque functions that return rich information sets. The data is returned in properly sized, linked lists, with optional indexes imposed on them for sorting and other such functions. Table 1-3 lists the API functions exported by this DLL. It is a long list, and discussing each function is beyond the scope of this chapter, so you are encouraged to consult the source code of the companion application `w2k_sym.exe` for details about the typical usage (see `\src\w2k_sym\w2k_sym.c` on the CD).

TABLE 1-3. `w2k_dbg.dll` *API Function Set*

FUNCTION NAME	DESCRIPTION
dbgBaseDriver	Return the base address and size of a driver, given its path
dbgBaseModule	Return the base address and size of a DLL module
dbgCrc32Block	Compute the CRC32 of a memory block
dbgCrc32Byte	Bytewise computation of a CRC32
dbgCrc32Start	CRC32 preconditioning
dbgCrc32Stop	CRC32 postconditioning
dbgDriverAdd	Add a driver entry to a list of drivers
dbgDriverAddresses	Return an array of driver addresses (`EnumDeviceDrivers()` wrapper)
dbgDriverIndex	Create an indexed (and optionally sorted) driver list
dbgDriverList	Create a flat driver list
dbgFileClose	Close a disk file
dbgFileLoad	Load the contents of a disk file to a memory block
dbgFileNew	Create a new disk file
dbgFileOpen	Open an existing disk file
dbgFileRoot	Get the offset of the root token in a file path
dbgFileSave	Save a memory block to a disk file
dbgFileUnload	Free a memory block created by `dbgFileLoad()`
dbgIndexCompare	Compare two entries referenced by an index (used by `dbgIndexSort()`)
dbgIndexCreate	Create a pointer index on an object list
dbgIndexCreateEx	Create a sorted pointer index on an object list
dbgIndexDestroy	Free the memory used by an index and its associated list
dbgIndexDestroyEx	Free the memory used by a two-dimensional index and its associated lists
dbgIndexList	Create a flat copy of a list from its index
dbgIndexListEx	Create a flat copy of a two-dimensional list from its index
dbgIndexReverse	Reverse the order of the list entries referenced by an index
dbgIndexSave	Save the memory image of an indexed list to a disk file
dbgIndexSaveEx	Save the memory image of a two-dimensional indexed list to a disk file
dbgIndexSort	Sort the list entries referenced by an index by address, size, ID, or name
dbgListCreate	Create an empty list
dbgListCreateEx	Create an empty list with reserved space
dbgListDestroy	Free the memory used by a list
dbgListFinish	Terminate a sequentially built list and trim any unused memory
dbgListIndex	Create a pointer index on an object list

(continued)

TABLE 1-3. *(continued)*

FUNCTION NAME	DESCRIPTION
dbgListLoad	Create a list from a disk file image
dbgListNext	Update the list header after adding an entry
dbgListResize	Reserve memory for additional list entries
dbgListSave	Save the memory image of a list to a disk file
dbgMemoryAlign	Round up a byte count to the next 64-bit boundary
dbgMemoryAlignEx	Round up a string character count to the next 64-bit boundary
dbgMemoryBase	Query the internal base address of a heap memory block
dbgMemoryBaseEx	Query the internal base address of an individually tagged heap memory block
dbgMemoryCreate	Allocate a memory block from the heap
dbgMemoryCreateEx	Allocate an individually tagged memory block from the heap
dbgMemoryDestroy	Return a memory block to the heap
dbgMemoryDestroyEx	Return an individually tagged memory block to the heap
dbgMemoryReset	Reset the memory usage statistics
dbgMemoryResize	Change the allocated size of a heap memory block
dbgMemoryResizeEx	Change the allocated size of an individually tagged heap memory block
dbgMemoryStatus	Query the memory usage statistics
dbgMemoryTrack	Update the memory usage statistics
dbgModuleIndex	Create an indexed (and optionally sorted) process module sub-list
dbgModuleList	Create a flat process module sub-list
dbgPathDriver	Build a default driver path specification
dbgPathFile	Get the offset of the file name token in a file path
dbgPrivilegeDebug	Request the debug privilege for the calling process
dbgPrivilegeSet	Request the specified privilege for the calling process
dbgProcessAdd	Add a process entry to a list of processes
dbgProcessGuess	Guess the default display name of an anonymous system process
dbgProcessIds	Return an array of process IDs (`EnumProcesses()` wrapper)
dbgProcessIndex	Create an indexed (and optionally sorted) process list
dbgProcessIndexEx	Create a two-dimensional indexed (and optionally sorted) process/module list
dbgProcessList	Create a flat process list
dbgProcessModules	Return a list of process module handles (`EnumProcessModules()` wrapper)
dbgSizeDivide	Divide a byte count by a power of two, optionally rounding up or down

TABLE 1-3. *(continued)*

FUNCTION NAME	DESCRIPTION
dbgSizeKB	Convert bytes to KB, optionally rounding up or down
dbgSizeMB	Convert bytes to MB, optionally rounding up or down
dbgStringAnsi	Convert a Unicode string to ANSI
dbgStringDay	Get the name of a day given a day-of-week number
dbgStringMatch	Apply a wildcard filter to a string
dbgSymbolCallback	Add a symbol entry to a list of symbols (called by `SymEnumerateSymbols()`)
dbgSymbolIndex	Create an indexed (and optionally sorted) symbol list
dbgSymbolList	Create a flat symbol list
dbgSymbolLoad	Load a module's symbol table
dbgSymbolLookup	Look up a symbol name and optional offset given a memory address
dbgSymbolUnload	Unload a module's symbol table

ENUMERATING SYSTEM MODULES AND DRIVERS

`psapi.dll` can be instructed to return a list of active kernel modules currently residing in memory. This is a fairly simple task. The `psapi.dll` function `EnumDeviceDrivers()` receives an array of `PVOID` slots, which it fills with the image base addresses of the active kernel-mode drivers, including the basic kernel modules `ntdll.dll`, `ntoskrnl.exe`, `win32k.sys`, `hal.dll`, and `bootvid.dll`. The reported values are the virtual memory addresses where the contents of the respective executable files have been mapped. If you examine the first few bytes at these addresses with the Kernel Debugger or some other debugging tool, you will clearly recognize the good old DOS stub program, starting with Mark Zbikowski's famous initials "MZ," and containing the message text, "This program cannot be run in DOS mode" or something similar. Listing 1-3 shows a sample invocation of `EnumDeviceDrivers()`, including this function's prototype at the top for your convenience.

`EnumDeviceDrivers()` expects three arguments: an array pointer, an input size value, and a pointer to an output size variable of type `DWORD`. The second argument specifies the size of the supplied image address array in bytes (!), and the third argument receives the number of bytes copied to the array. Therefore, you have to divide the resulting size by `sizeof (PVOID)` to obtain the number of addresses copied to the array. Unfortunately, this function doesn't help you to find out how large the output array should be, although it actually knows how many drivers are running. It just tells you how many bytes were returned, and, if the buffer is too small, it conceals the number of bytes that didn't fit in. Therefore, you have to employ a dull trial-and-error loop to determine the correct size, as demonstrated in Listing 1-3, assuming that the

```
BOOL WINAPI EnumDeviceDrivers (PVOID *lpImageBase,
                               DWORD  cb,
                               PDWORD lpcbNeeded);

PPVOID WINAPI dbgDriverAddresses (PDWORD pdCount)
    {
    DWORD  dSize;
    DWORD  dCount = 0;
    PPVOID ppList = NULL;

    dSize = SIZE_MINIMUM * sizeof (PVOID);

    while ((ppList = dbgMemoryCreate (dSize)) != NULL)
        {
        if (EnumDeviceDrivers (ppList, dSize, &dCount) &&
            (dCount < dSize))
            {
            dCount /= sizeof (PVOID);
            break;
            }
        dCount = 0;
        ppList = dbgMemoryDestroy (ppList);
        if ((dSize <<= 1) > (SIZE_MAXIMUM * sizeof (PVOID))) break;
        }
    if (pdCount != NULL) *pdCount = dCount;
    return ppList;
    }
```

LISTING 1-3. *Enumerating System Module Addresses*

data are incomplete whenever the returned size is equal to the size of the array. The code starts out with a reasonable minimum size of 256 entries, represented by the constant `SIZE_MINIMUM`. This is usually enough, but, if not, the buffer size is doubled on every new trial until all pointers are retrieved or the maximum size of 65,536 entries (`SIZE_MAXIMUM`) would be exceeded. The memory buffer is allocated and freed by the helper functions `dbgMemoryCreate()` and `dbgMemoryDestroy()`, which are just fancy wrappers around the standard Win32 functions `LocalAlloc()` and `LocalFree()`, and therefore aren't reprinted here.

Listing 1-4 shows a possible implementation of `EnumDeviceDrivers()`. Note that this is *not* the original source code from `psapi.dll`. It is a random sequence of characters that happens to yield equivalent binary code if fed to a C compiler. To keep things clear and simple, I have omitted some distracting details found in the original code, such as Structured Exception Handling (SEH) clauses, for example. At

```
BOOL WINAPI EnumDeviceDrivers (PVOID *lpImageBase,
                               DWORD  cb,
                               DWORD *lpcbNeeded)
    {
    SYSTEM_MODULE_INFORMATION_N(1) smi;
    PSYSTEM_MODULE_INFORMATION     psmi;
    DWORD                          dSize, i;
    NTSTATUS                       ns;
    BOOL                           fOk = FALSE;

    ns = NtQuerySystemInformation (SystemModuleInformation,
                                   &smi, sizeof (smi), NULL);

    if ((ns == STATUS_SUCCESS) ||
        (ns == STATUS_INFO_LENGTH_MISMATCH))
        {
        dSize = sizeof (SYSTEM_MODULE_INFORMATION) +
                (smi.dCount * sizeof (SYSTEM_MODULE));

        if ((psmi = LocalAlloc (LMEM_FIXED, dSize)) != NULL)
            {
            ns = NtQuerySystemInformation (SystemModuleInformation,
                                           psmi, dSize, NULL);

            if (ns == STATUS_SUCCESS)
                {
                for (i = 0; (i < psmi->dCount) &&
                            (i < cb / sizeof (DWORD)); i++)
                    {
                    lpImageBase [i] = psmi->aModules [i].pImageBase;
                    }
                *lpcbNeeded = i * sizeof (DWORD);
                fOk         = TRUE;
                }
            LocalFree (psmi);

            if (!fOk) SetLastError (RtlNtStatusToDosError (ns));
            }
        }
    else
        {
        SetLastError (RtlNtStatusToDosError (ns));
        }
    return fOk;
    }
```

LISTING 1-4. *Sample Implementation of* `EnumDeviceDrivers()`

the heart of Listing 1-4, you can see the `NtQuerySystemInformation()` call that does the hard work. This is one of my favorite Windows 2000 functions, because it gives access to various kinds of important data structures, such as driver, process, thread, handle, and LPC port lists, plus many more. The internals of this powerful function and its friend `NtSetSystemInformation()` have been documented for the first time in my article "Inside Windows NT System Data," published in the November 1999 issue of *Dr. Dobb's Journal* (Schreiber 1999). Another comprehensive description of these functions can be looked up in Gary Nebbett's indispensable *Windows NT/ 2000 Native API Reference* (Nebbett 2000).

Don't worry too much about the various implementation details of the `EnumDeviceDrivers()` function in Listing 1-4. I have added this code snippet just to illustrate an interesting aspect of this function that runs like a red thread through `psapi.dll`. After obtaining the complete list of drivers in the second `NtQuerySystemInformation()` call by specifying the information class `SystemModuleInformation`, the code loops through the driver module array and copies all `pImageBase` members to the caller's pointer array named `lpImageBase[]`. This might seem OK, as long as you aren't aware of the other data contained in the module array supplied by `NtQuerySystemInformation()`. This data structure is undocumented, but I can tell you right now that it also specifies the sizes of the modules in memory, their paths and names, load counts, and some flags. Even the offset of the file name token inside the path is readily available! `EnumDeviceDrivers()` is mercilessly throwing away all of this valuable information, retaining nothing but the bare image base addresses.

This drama gets even weirder if you try to obtain more information about the modules referenced by the returned pointers. Guess what `psapi.dll` does if you are calling its API function `GetDeviceDriverFileName()` to obtain the image file path corresponding to an image base address. It runs through a code sequence similar to the one in Listing 1-4, again requesting the complete driver list, and again looping through its entries in search of the given address. If it finds a matching entry, it copies the path stored there to the caller's buffer. That's very efficient, isn't it? Why didn't `EnumDeviceDrivers()` copy the paths while it was scanning the driver list for the first time? It wouldn't have been very difficult to implement the function in this way. Besides the efficiency consideration, this design has another potential problem: What if the module in question has been unloaded right before the invocation of `GetDeviceDriverFileName()`? This entry would be missing from the second driver list, and `GetDeviceDriverFileName()` would fail. I don't understand why Microsoft has released a DLL that cripples the data returned by a powerful API function until it is almost useless.

ENUMERATING ACTIVE PROCESSES

Another typical task for `psapi.dll` is the enumeration of processes currently running in the system. To this end, the `EnumProcesses()` function is provided. It works quite similar to `EnumDeviceDrivers()`, but returns process IDs instead of virtual addresses. Again, there is no indication of the required buffer size if the output buffer is too small, so the usual trial-and-error loop must be used, as demonstrated in Listing 1-5. Actually, this code is nearly identical to Listing 1-3, except for slightly different symbol and type names.

A process ID is a global numeric tag that uniquely identifies a process within the entire system. Process and thread IDs are drawn from the same pool of numbers, starting at zero with the so-called Idle process. None of the running processes and threads have the same IDs at the same time. However, after a process terminates, it is possible that another process reuses some of the IDs previously assigned to the ceased

```
BOOL WINAPI EnumProcesses (DWORD *lpidProcess,
                           DWORD  cb,
                           DWORD *lpcbNeeded);

PDWORD WINAPI dbgProcessIds (PDWORD pdCount)
    {
    DWORD  dSize;
    DWORD  dCount = 0;
    PDWORD pdList = NULL;

    dSize = SIZE_MINIMUM * sizeof (DWORD);

    while ((pdList = dbgMemoryCreate (dSize)) != NULL)
        {
        if (EnumProcesses (pdList, dSize, &dCount) &&
            (dCount < dSize))
            {
            dCount /= sizeof (DWORD);
            break;
            }
        dCount = 0;
        pdList = dbgMemoryDestroy (pdList);
        if ((dSize <<= 1) > (SIZE_MAXIMUM * sizeof (DWORD))) break;
        }
    if (pdCount != NULL) *pdCount = dCount;
    return pdList;
    }
```

LISTING 1-5. *Enumerating Process IDs*

process and its threads. Therefore, a process ID obtained at time X might refer to a completely different process at time Y. It also might be undefined at the time it is used, or it might be assigned to a thread. Thus, a plain list of process IDs as returned by `EnumProcesses()` does not represent a faithful snapshot of the process activity in the system. This design flaw is even less pardonable if the implementation of this function is considered. Listing 1-6 is another `psapi.dll` function clone, outlining the basic actions taken by `EnumProcesses()`. Like `EnumDeviceDrivers()`, it relies on `NtQuerySystemInformation()`, but specifies the information class `SystemProcessInformation` instead of `SystemModuleInformation`. Please note the loop in the middle of Listing 1-6, where the `lpidProcess[]` array is filled with data from a `SYSTEM_PROCESS_INFORMATION` structure. It is not surprising that this structure is undocumented.

After having seen how wasteful `EnumDeviceDrivers()` is with the data it receives from `NtQuerySystemInformation()`, odds are that `EnumProcesses()` is of a similar kind. In fact, it is even worse! The available process information is much more exhaustive than the driver module information, because along with process data it also includes details about every thread in the system. While I am writing this text, my system runs 37 processes, and calling `NtQuerySystemInformation()` yields a data block of no less than 24,488 bytes! All that is left after `EnumProcesses()` has finished processing the data are 148 bytes, required for the 37 process IDs.

```
BOOL WINAPI EnumProcesses (PDWORD lpidProcess,
                           DWORD  cb,
                           PDWORD lpcbNeeded)
    {
    PSYSTEM_PROCESS_INFORMATION pspi, pspiNext;
    DWORD                       dSize, i;
    NTSTATUS                    ns;
    BOOL                        fOk = FALSE;

    for (dSize  = 0x8000;
         ((pspi = LocalAlloc (LMEM_FIXED, dSize)) != NULL);
         dSize += 0x8000)
        {
        ns = NtQuerySystemInformation (SystemProcessInformation,
                                       pspi, dSize, NULL);

        if (ns == STATUS_SUCCESS)
            {
            pspiNext = pspi;

            for (i = 0; i < cb / sizeof (DWORD); i++)
                {
```

```
                lpidProcess [i] = pspiNext->dUniqueProcessId;

                pspiNext = (PSYSTEM_PROCESS_INFORMATION)
                           ((PBYTE) pspiNext + pspiNext->dNext);
                }
            *lpcbNeeded = i * sizeof (DWORD);
            fOk         = TRUE;
            }
        LocalFree (pspi);

        if (fOk || (ns != STATUS_INFO_LENGTH_MISMATCH))
            {
            if (!fOk) SetLastError (RtlNtStatusToDosError (ns));
            break;
            }
        }
    return fOk;
    }
```

LISTING 1-6. *Sample Implementation of* EnumProcesses()

Although `EnumDeviceDrivers()` makes me somewhat sad, `EnumProcesses()` really breaks my heart. If you need justification for using undocumented API functions, these two functions are the best arguments. Why use less efficient functions such as these if the real thing is just one step away? Why not call `NtQuerySystemInformation()` yourself and get all that interesting system information for free? Many system administration utilities supplied by Microsoft rely on `NtQuerySystemInformation()` rather than `psapi.dll` functions, so why settle for less?

ENUMERATING PROCESS MODULES

Once you have found a process ID of interest in the process list returned by `EnumProcesses()`, you might want to know which modules are currently loaded into its virtual address space. `psapi.dll` provides yet another API function for this purpose, called `EnumProcessModules()`. Unlike `EnumDeviceDrivers()` and `EnumProcesses()`, this function requires four arguments (see top of Listing 1-7). Whereas these two functions return global system lists, `EnumProcessModules()` retrieves a process-specific list, so the process must be uniquely identified by an additional argument. However, instead of a process ID, this function requires a process `HANDLE`. To obtain a process handle given an ID, the `OpenProcess()` function must be called.

```
BOOL WINAPI EnumProcessModules (HANDLE   hProcess,
                                HMODULE *lphModule,
                                DWORD    cb,
                                DWORD   *lpcbNeeded);

PHMODULE WINAPI dbgProcessModules (HANDLE hProcess,
                                   PDWORD pdCount)
    {
    DWORD    dSize;
    DWORD    dCount = 0;
    PHMODULE phList = NULL;

    if (hProcess != NULL)
        {
        dSize = SIZE_MINIMUM * sizeof (HMODULE);

        while ((phList = dbgMemoryCreate (dSize)) != NULL)
            {
            if (EnumProcessModules (hProcess, phList, dSize,
                                    &dCount))
                {
                if (dCount <= dSize)
                    {
                    dCount /= sizeof (HMODULE);
                    break;
                    }
                }
            else
                {
                dCount = 0;
                }
            phList = dbgMemoryDestroy (phList);
            if (!(dSize = dCount)) break;
            }
        }
    if (pdCount != NULL) *pdCount = dCount;
    return phList;
    }
```

LISTING 1-7. *Enumerating Process Modules*

`EnumProcessModules()` returns references to the modules of a process by specifying their module handles. On Windows 2000, an `HMODULE` is simply the image base address of a module. In the Platform SDK header file `windef.h`, it is defined as an alias for `HINSTANCE`, which in turn is a `HANDLE` type. Microsoft has probably chosen this type assignment to point out that a module handle is an opaque quantity, and no assumptions should be made about its value. However, an `HMODULE` is not a handle in the strict sense. Usually, handles are indexes into a table managed by the system, where properties of objects are looked up. Each handle returned by the system increments an object-specific handle count, and an object instance cannot be removed from memory until all handles have been returned to the system. The Win32 API provides the `CloseHandle()` function for the latter purpose. Its equivalent in the context of the Native API is called `NtClose()`. The important thing about `HMODULE`s is that these "handles" need *not* be closed.

Another confusing thing is the fact that module handles are not generally guaranteed to remain valid. The remarks on the `GetModuleHandle()` function in the Platform SDK documentation state clearly that special care must be taken in multithreaded applications, because one thread might invalidate an `HMODULE` used by another thread by unloading the module to which this handle refers. The same is true in a multitasking environment in which an application (e.g., a debugger) wants to use a module handle of another application. This makes `HMODULE`s appear fairly useless, doesn't it? However, there are two situations in which an `HMODULE` remains valid long enough:

1. A `HMODULE` returned by `LoadLibrary()` or `LoadLibraryEx()` remains valid until the process calls `FreeLibrary()`, because these functions involve a module reference count. This prevents the module from being unloaded unexpectedly even in a multithreaded application design.
2. An `HMODULE` from a different process remains valid if it refers to a module that is permanently loaded. For example, all Windows 2000 kernel components (not including kernel-mode device drivers) are mapped to the same fixed addresses in each process and remain there for the lifetime of the process.

Unfortunately, neither of these situations applies to the module handles returned by the `psapi.dll` function `EnumProcessModules()`, at least not generally. The `HMODULE` values copied to the caller's buffer reflect the image base addresses that were in effect at the time the process snapshot was taken. A second later, the process might have called `FreeLibrary()` for one of the modules, removing it from memory and invalidating its handle. It is even possible that the process calls `LoadLibrary()` for a different DLL immediately afterward, and the new module is mapped to the address that has just been freed. If this looks familiar, you are right. This is the same problem encountered with the `EnumDeviceDrivers()` pointer array and the `EnumProcesses()` ID array. However, this problem is not inevitable. The undocumented API functions called by `psapi.dll` to collect the data work around these data integrity issues by returning a complete snapshot of the requested objects, including all properties of interest. It is not necessary to call other functions at a later time to obtain additional information. In my opinion, the design of `psapi.dll` is poor because of its ignorance of data integrity, which is why I would not use this DLL as a basis for a professional debugging application.

The `EnumProcessModules()` function is a better citizen than `EnumDeviceDrivers()` and `EnumProcesses()`, because it indicates exactly how many bytes are missing if the output data doesn't fit into the caller's array. Note that Listing 1-7 doesn't contain a loop where the buffer size is increased until it is large enough. However, a trial-and error loop is still required because the required size reported by `EnumProcessModules()` might be invalid at the next call if the process in question has loaded another module in the meantime. Therefore, the code in Listing 1-7 keeps on enumerating modules until `EnumProcessModules()` reports that the required buffer size is less than or equal to the available size or an error occurs.

I won't describe an equivalent implementation of `EnumProcessModules()`, because this function is slightly more complex than `EnumDeviceDrivers()` and `EnumProcesses()` and involves several undocumented data structures. Basically, it calls `NtQueryInformationProcess()` (it is undocumented, of course) to get the address of the target Process Environment Block (PEB), where it retrieves a pointer to a module information list. Because neither the PEB nor this list are "visible" in the caller's address space, `EnumProcessModules()` calls the Win32 API function `ReadProcessMemory()` (this one is documented) to take a peek at the target address space. By the way, the layout of the PEB structure is discussed later in Chapter 7, and also appears in the structure definition section of Appendix C.

Adjusting Process Privileges

Recall the earlier discussion about the process handle required by `EnumProcessModules()`. Usually, you will begin with a process ID—probably one of those returned by `EnumProcesses()`. The Win32 API provides the `OpenProcess()` function to get a handle to a process if its ID is known. This function expects an access flag mask as its first argument. Assuming that the process ID is stored in the `DWORD` variable `dId`, and you are calling `OpenProcess (PROCESS_ALL_ACCESS, FALSE, dId)` to obtain a handle with maximum access rights, you will get an error code for several processes with low ID numbers. This is not a bug—it is a security feature! These processes are system services that keep the system alive. A normal user process is not allowed to execute all possible operations on system services. For example, it is not a good idea to allow all processes to kill any other process in the system. If an application accidentally terminates a system service, the entire system crashes. Therefore, certain access rights can only be used by a process that has the appropriate privileges.

You can always bump up the privilege level of an application by claiming that it is a debugger. For obvious reasons, a debugger must have a large number of access rights to do its job. Changing the privileges of a process is essentially a straightforward sequence of three steps:

1. First, the so-called access token of the process must be opened, using the Win32 `advapi32.dll` function `OpenProcessToken()`.
2. If this call succeeds, the next step is to prepare a `TOKEN_PRIVILEGES` structure that contains information about the requested privilege. This task is facilitated by another `advapi32.dll` function named `LookupPrivilegeValue()`. The privilege is specified by name. The Platform SDK file `winnt.h` defines 27 privilege names and assigns symbols to them. For example, the debugging privilege has the symbol `SE_DEBUG_NAME`, which evaluates to the string `"SeDebugPrivilege"`.
3. If this call succeeds as well, `AdjustTokenPrivileges()` can be called with the token handle of the process and the initialized `TOKEN_PRIVILEGES` structure. Again, this function is exported by `advapi32.dll`.

Remember to close the token handle afterward if `OpenProcessToken()` succeeds. `w2k_dbg.dll` contains the API function `dbgPrivilegeSet()` that combines these steps, as shown in Listing 1-8. At the bottom of this listing, another `w2k_dbg.dll` function is included. `dbgPrivilegeDebug()` is a simple but convenient `dbgPrivilegeSet()` wrapper that specifically requests the debugging privilege. By the way, this trick is also employed by the wonderful `kill.exe` utility contained in Microsoft's Windows NT Server Resource Kit. `kill.exe` needs the debugging privilege to be able to kick starved services from memory. This is an indispensable tool for NT server administrators who want to restart a dead system service that doesn't respond to service control calls anymore, circumventing a full reboot. Anyone who runs Microsoft Internet Information Server (IIS) on the Web or in an intranet or extranet probably has this nifty tool in the emergency toolbox and issues a `kill inetinfo.exe` command every now and then.

```
BOOL WINAPI dbgPrivilegeSet (PWORD pwName)
    {
    HANDLE           hToken;
    TOKEN_PRIVILEGES tp;
    BOOL             fOk = FALSE;

    if ((pwName != NULL)
        &&
        OpenProcessToken (GetCurrentProcess (),
                          TOKEN_ADJUST_PRIVILEGES,
                          &hToken))
        {
        if (LookupPrivilegeValue (NULL, pwName,
                                  &tp.Privileges->Luid))
            {
            tp.Privileges->Attributes = SE_PRIVILEGE_ENABLED;
            tp.PrivilegeCount         = 1;
```

(continued)

```
            fOk = AdjustTokenPrivileges (hToken, FALSE, &tp,
                                         0, NULL, NULL)
                  &&
                  (GetLastError () == ERROR_SUCCESS);
            }
        CloseHandle (hToken);
        }
    return fOk;
    }

// -----------------------------------------------------------------

BOOL WINAPI dbgPrivilegeDebug (void)
    {
    return dbgPrivilegeSet (SE_DEBUG_NAME);
    }
```

LISTING 1-8. *Requesting a Privilege for a Process*

ENUMERATING SYMBOLS

After having bashed psapi.dll without mercy, it's time for a few more positive words. psapi.dll might be a flop, but on the other hand, imagehlp.dll is a true pearl! I came across this fine piece of software while searching for more information about the internal structure of Windows 2000 symbol files. Finally, a 3-year-old article of the world's best Windows surgeon Matt Pietrek (Pietrek 1997b) convinced me—at least for now—that it is absolutely unnecessary to know the layout of symbol files, because imagehlp.dll readily dissects them for me. This magic is done by its API function SymEnumerateSymbols(), whose prototype is shown in the upper half of Listing 1-9. Meanwhile, I have learned a lot about the most essential internals of the Windows NT 4.0 and Windows 2000 symbol files, so I no longer depend on imagehlp.dll. I will cover this information in the next section of this chapter.

The hProcess argument is usually a handle to the calling process, so it can be set to the result of GetCurrentProcess(). Note that GetCurrentProcess() doesn't return a real process handle. Instead, it returns a constant value of 0xFFFFFFFF called a *pseudo handle*, which is accepted by all API functions that expect a process handle. 0xFFFFFFFE is another pseudo handle that is interpreted as a handle to the current thread and is analogously returned by the API function GetCurrentThread().

BaseOfDll is defined as a DWORD, although it is actually sort of a HMODULE or HINSTANCE. I guess Microsoft has chosen this data type to express that this value need not be a valid HMODULE, although it frequently is. SymEnumerateSymbols() calculates the base addresses of all enumerated symbols relative to this value. It is absolutely OK to query the symbols of a DLL that isn't currently loaded into any process address space, so BaseOfDll can be chosen arbitrarily.

```
BOOL IMAGEAPISymEnumerateSymbols
        (HANDLE        hProcess,
        DWORD          BaseOfDll,
        PSYM_ENUMSYMBOLS_CALLBACK Callback,
        PVOID          UserContext);

typedef BOOL (CALLBACK *PSYM_ENUMSYMBOLS_CALLBACK)
        (PTSTR         SymbolName,
        DWORD          SymbolAddress,
        DWORD          SymbolSize,
        PVOID          UserContext);
```

LISTING 1-9. SymEnumerateSymbols() *and its Callback Function*

The `Callback` argument is a pointer to a user-defined callback function that is invoked for every symbol. The lower half of Listing 1-9 provides information about its arguments. The callback function receives a zero-terminated symbol name string, the base address of the symbol with respect to the `BaseOfDll` argument of `SymEnumerateSymbols()` and the estimated size of the item tagged by the symbol. `SymbolName` is defined as a `PTSTR`, which means that its actual type depends on whether the ANSI or Unicode version of `SymEnumerateSymbols()` has been called. The Platform SDK documentation explicitly states that `SymbolSize` is a "best-guess value," and can be zero. I have found that `SymbolAddress` might be zero as well, and that `SymbolSize` can assume the two's complement of `SymbolAddress`, that is, adding both values yields zero. It is a good idea to filter out these special cases if you are only interested in symbols that refer to real code or data.

`UserContext` is an arbitrary pointer that can be used by the caller to keep track of the enumeration sequence. For example, it might point to a memory block where the symbol information has accumulated. This pointer is identical to the `UserContext` argument passed to the `Callback` function. The callback function can cancel the enumeration any time by returning the value `FALSE`. This action is typically taken when an unrecoverable error occurs or the caller has received the information for which it was waiting.

Listing 1-10 demonstrates a typical application of `SymEnumerateSymbols()`, again taken from the source code of `w2k_dbg.dll`. To enumerate the symbols of a specified module, the following steps have to be taken:

1. Before anything else, `SymInitialize()` must be called to initialize the symbol handler. Listing 1-11 shows the prototypes of this and other functions discussed here. The `hProcess` argument can be a handle to any active process in the system. Debuggers that maintain symbolic information for several processes use this parameter to identify the target process. Applications that simply wish to enumerate symbols offline may

```
PDBG_LIST WINAPI dbgSymbolList (PWORD pwPath,
                                PVOID pBase)
    {
    PLOADED_IMAGE pli;
    HANDLE        hProcess = GetCurrentProcess ();
    PDBG_LIST     pdl      = NULL;

    if ((pwPath != NULL) &&
        SymInitialize (hProcess, NULL, FALSE))
        {
        if ((pli = dbgSymbolLoad (pwPath, pBase, hProcess)) != NULL)
            {
            if ((pdl = dbgListCreate ()) != NULL)
                {
                SymEnumerateSymbols (hProcess, (DWORD_PTR) pBase,
                                     dbgSymbolCallback, &pdl);
                }
            dbgSymbolUnload (pli, pBase, hProcess);
            }
        SymCleanup (hProcess);
        }
    return dbgListFinish (pdl);
    }
```

LISTING 1-10. *Creating a Symbol List*

pass in the value of `GetCurrentProcess()`. The resources allocated by `SymInitialize()` must be freed later by calling `SymCleanup()`.

2. To obtain accurate information about the module for which symbols will be enumerated, it is advisable to call `ImageLoad()` now. Note that this function is specific to `imagehlp.dll`—it is not exported by the redistributable component `dbghelp.dll`. `ImageLoad()` returns a pointer to a `LOADED_IMAGE` structure containing very detailed information about the loaded module (see Listing 1-11). This structure must be deallocated later using `ImageUnload()`.

3. The last step before `SymEnumerateSymbols()` can be called is to load the symbol table of the target module by invoking `SymLoadModule()`. If `ImageLoad()` has been called before, the `hFile` and `SizeOfImage` members of the returned `LOADED_IMAGE` structure can be passed in as the respective arguments. Otherwise, you have to set `hFile` to NULL and `SizeOfImage` to zero. In this case, `SymLoadModule()` attempts to obtain the image size from the symbol file, which is not guaranteed to be accurate. The symbol table must be unloaded later by calling `SymUnloadModule()`.

```
BOOL IMAGEAPI SymInitialize (HANDLE hProcess,
                             PSTR   UserSearchPath,
                             BOOL   fInvadeProcess);

BOOL IMAGEAPI SymCleanup (HANDLE hProcess);

DWORD IMAGEAPI SymLoadModule (HANDLE hProcess,
                              HANDLE hFile,
                              PSTR   ImageName,
                              PSTR   ModuleName,
                              DWORD  BaseOfDll,
                              DWORD  SizeOfDll);

BOOL IMAGEAPI SymUnloadModule (HANDLE hProcess,
                               DWORD  BaseOfDll);

PLOADED_IMAGE IMAGEAPI ImageLoad (PSTR DllName,
                                  PSTR DllPath);

BOOL IMAGEAPI ImageUnload (PLOADED_IMAGE LoadedImage);

typedef struct _LOADED_IMAGE
    {
    PSTR                  ModuleName;
    HANDLE                hFile;
    PUCHAR                MappedAddress;
    PIMAGE_NT_HEADERS     FileHeader;
    PIMAGE_SECTION_HEADER LastRvaSection;
    ULONG                 NumberOfSections;
    PIMAGE_SECTION_HEADER Sections;
    ULONG                 Characteristics;
    BOOLEAN               fSystemImage;
    BOOLEAN               fDOSImage;
    LIST_ENTRY            Links;
    ULONG                 SizeOfImage;
    }
    LOADED_IMAGE, *PLOADED_IMAGE;
```

LISTING 1-11. *Various* `imagehlp.dll` *API Prototypes*

In Listing 1-10, the `SymInitialize()`, `SymEnumerateSymbols()`, and `SymCleanup()` calls are clearly discernible. Please ignore the `dbgListCreate()` and `dbgListFinish()` calls—they refer to `w2k_dbg.dll` API functions that help build object lists in memory. The other `imagehlp.dll` function references mentioned above are hidden inside the `w2k_dbg.dll` API functions `dbgSymbolLoad()` and `dbgSymbolUnload()`, shown in Listing 1-12. Note that `dbgSymbolLoad()` uses `dbgStringAnsi()` to convert the module path string from Unicode to ANSI, because `imagehlp.dll` doesn't export a Unicode variant of `ImageLoad()`.

```
PLOADED_IMAGE WINAPI dbgSymbolLoad (PWORD  pwPath,
                                    PVOID  pBase,
                                    HANDLE hProcess)
    {
    WORD          awPath [MAX_PATH];
    PBYTE         pbPath;
    DWORD         dPath;
    PLOADED_IMAGE pli = NULL;

    if ((pbPath = dbgStringAnsi (pwPath, NULL)) != NULL)
        {
        if (((pli = ImageLoad (pbPath, NULL)) == NULL)         &&
            (dPath = dbgPathDriver (pwPath, awPath, MAX_PATH)) &&
            (dPath < MAX_PATH))
            {
            dbgMemoryDestroy (pbPath);

            if ((pbPath = dbgStringAnsi (awPath, NULL)) != NULL)
                {
                pli = ImageLoad (pbPath, NULL);
                }
            }
        if ((pli != NULL)
            &&
            (!SymLoadModule (hProcess, pli->hFile, pbPath, NULL,
                             (DWORD_PTR) pBase, pli->SizeOfImage)))
            {
            ImageUnload (pli);
            pli = NULL;
            }
        dbgMemoryDestroy (pbPath);
        }
    return pli;
    }

// -----------------------------------------------------------------

PLOADED_IMAGE WINAPI dbgSymbolUnload (PLOADED_IMAGE pli,
                                      PVOID         pBase,
                                      HANDLE        hProcess)
    {
    if (pli != NULL)
        {
        SymUnloadModule (hProcess, (DWORD_PTR) pBase);
        ImageUnload     (pli);
        }
    return NULL;
    }

// -----------------------------------------------------------------
```

```
PDBG_LIST WINAPI dbgSymbolList (PWORD pwPath,
                                PVOID pBase)
    {
    PLOADED_IMAGE pli;
    HANDLE        hProcess = GetCurrentProcess ();
    PDBG_LIST     pdl      = NULL;

    if ((pwPath != NULL) &&
        SymInitialize (hProcess, NULL, FALSE))
        {
        if ((pli = dbgSymbolLoad (pwPath, pBase, hProcess)) != NULL)
            {
            if ((pdl = dbgListCreate ()) != NULL)
                {
                SymEnumerateSymbols (hProcess, (DWORD_PTR) pBase,
                                     dbgSymbolCallback, &pdl);
                }
            dbgSymbolUnload (pli, pBase, hProcess);
            }
        SymCleanup (hProcess);
        }
    return dbgListFinish (pdl);
    }
```

LISTING 1-12. *Loading and Unloading Symbol Information*

`ImageLoad()` does a very good job locating the specified module, even if only its name is given, without any path information. However, it fails on kernel-mode drivers residing in the `\winnt\system32\drivers` directory, because it is usually not part of the system's search path list. In this case, `dbgSymbolLoad()` asks the `dbgPathDriver()` function for help and retries the `LoadImage()` call. `dbgPathDriver()` simply prefixes the specified path with the string "driver\" if the path consists of a bare file name only. If either of the `ImageLoad()` calls returns a valid `LOADED_IMAGE` pointer, `dbgSymbolLoad()` fulfills its mission by loading the module's symbol table via `SymLoadModule()` and returns the `LOADED_IMAGE` structure if successful. Its counterpart `dbgSymbolUnload()` is almost trivial—it unloads the symbol table and then destroys the `LOADED_IMAGE` structure.

In Listing 1-10, `SymEnumerateSymbols()` is instructed to use the `w2k_dbg.dll` function `dbgSymbolCallback()` for the callbacks. I am not including its source code here because it isn't relevant to `imagehlp.dll`. It just uses the symbol information it receives (see the definition of `PSYM_ENUMSYMBOLS_CALLBACK` in Listing 1-9) and adds it to a memory block passed in as its `UserContext` pointer. Although the list, index, and sorting functions featured by `w2k_dbg.dll` are interesting in their own right, they are beyond the scope of this book. Please consult the source files of `w2k_dbg.dll` and `w2k_sym.exe` on the CD if you need more information.

A Windows 2000 Symbol Browser

`w2k_sym.exe` is a sample client application of `w2k_dbg.dll` running in Win32 console mode. If you invoke it without arguments, it identifies itself as the Windows 2000 Symbol Browser and displays the help screen shown in Example 1-5. The program recognizes several command line switches that determine the actions it should take. The four basic options are `/p` (list processes), `/m` (list process modules), `/d` (list drivers and system modules), or the path of a module for which symbol information is requested. The default behavior can be altered by adding various display mode, sorting, and filtering switches. For example, if you want to see a list of all `ntoskrnl.exe`

```
// w2k_sym.exe
// SBS Windows 2000 Symbol Browser V1.00
// 08-27-2000 Sven B. Schreiber
// sbs@orgon.com

Usage: w2k_sym { <mode> [ /f | /F <filter> ] <operation> }

<mode> is a series of options for the next <operation>:

       /a : sort by address
       /s : sort by size
       /i : sort by ID (process/module lists only)
       /n : sort by name
       /c : sort by name (case-sensitive)
       /r : reverse order
       /l : load  checkpoint file (see below)
       /w : write checkpoint file (see below)
       /e : display end address instead of size
       /v : verbose mode

/f <filter> applies a case-insensitive search pattern.
/F <filter> works analogous, but case-sensitive.
In <filter>, the wildcards * and ? are allowed.

<operation> is one of the following:

       /p : display processes      - checkpoint: processes.dbgl
       /m : display modules        - checkpoint: modules.dbgl
       /d : display drivers        - checkpoint: drivers.dbgl
    <file> : display <file> symbols - checkpoint: symbols.dbgl

<file> is a file name, a relative path, or a fully qualified path.
Checkpoint files are loaded from and written to the current directory.
A checkpoint is an on-disk image of a DBG_LIST structure (see w2k_dbg.h).
```

Example 1-5. *The Command Help of* `w2k_sym.exe`

symbols sorted by name, issue the command `w2k_sym /n/v ntoskrnl.exe`. The `/n` switch selects sort-by-name mode, and `/v` tells the program to be verbose, displaying the complete symbol list—otherwise, only summary information would be visible.

As an additional option, `w2k_sym.exe` allows reading and writing checkpoint files. A checkpoint is simply a one-to-one copy of an object list written to a disk file. You can use checkpoints to save the state of your system for later comparison. A checkpoint file contains a CRC32 field that is used to validate the contents of the file when it is loaded. `w2k_sym.exe` maintains four checkpoints in the current directory, corresponding to the four basic program options mentioned earlier, that is, process, module, driver, and symbol lists.

MICROSOFT SYMBOL FILE INTERNALS

It is great that Microsoft provides a standard interface to access the Windows 2000 symbol files, no matter what internal format they are using. Sometimes, however, you may wish to have direct access to their internals, just to gain more control of the data. This section shows you how the data in symbol files of type `.dbg` and `.pdb` are structured, and presents a DLL with a sample client application that allows you to look up and browse symbolic information buried inside them. Yes, this is going to be another symbol browser application, but don't worry—I won't bore you with a simple rehash of familiar code. The alternative symbol browser is quite different from the one discussed in the previous section.

SYMBOL DECORATION

Microsoft symbol files store the names of symbols in their so-called decorated form, which means that the symbol name might be prefixed and postfixed by additional character sequences that carry information about the type and usage of the symbol. Table 1-4 lists the most common forms of decorations. Symbols generated by C code usually have a leading underscore or `@` character, depending on the calling convention. An `@` character indicates a `__fastcall` function, and an underscore indicates `__stdcall` and `__cdecl` functions. Because the `__fastcall` and `__stdcall` conventions leave the task of cleaning up the argument stack to the called function, the symbols assigned to functions of this type also include the number of argument bytes put on the stack by the caller. This information is appended to the symbol name in decimal notation, separated by an `@` character. In this scenario, global variables are treated like `__cdecl` functions—that is, their symbols start with an underscore and have no trailing argument stack information.

TABLE 1-4. *Symbol Decoration Categories*

EXAMPLE	DESCRIPTION
symbol	Undecorated symbol (might have been declared in an ASM module)
_*symbol*	__*cdecl* function or global variable
_*symbol*@N	__*stdcall* function with *N* argument bytes
@*symbol*@N	__*fastcall* function with *N* argument bytes
__imp__*symbol*	import thunk of a __*cdecl* function or variable
__imp__*symbol*@N	import thunk of a __*stdcall* function with *N* argument bytes
__imp_@*symbol*@N	import thunk of a __*fastcall* function with *N* argument bytes
?*symbol*	C++ symbol with embedded argument type information
___@@_PchSym_*symbol*	PCH symbol

Some symbol names have a prefix of `__imp__` or `__imp_@`. These symbols are assigned to import thunks, which are pointers to functions or variables in other modules. Import thunks facilitate dynamic linking to symbols exported by other components at runtime, regardless of the actual load address of the target module. When a module is loaded, the loader mechanism fixes up the thunk pointers to refer to the actual entry point addresses. The benefit of import thunks is that the fixup for each imported function or variable has to be done only once per symbol—all references to this external symbol are routed through its thunk. It should be noted that import thunks are not a requirement. It is up to the compiler to decide whether it wants to minimize fixups by adding thunks or minimize memory usage by saving the space required for the thunks. As Table 1-4 shows, the same prefix/postfix rules apply to local and imported symbols, except that import thunks have an additional `__imp_` prefix (with two leading underscores!).

The undecoration problems of `imagehlp.dll` can easily be demonstrated with the help of the `w2k_sym.exe` sample application from the previous section, because it ultimately relies on the `imagehlp.dll` API via the `w2k_dbg.dll` library. If you issue the command `w2k_sym /v/n/f __* ntoskrnl.exe`, instructing `w2k_sym.exe` to display a sorted list of names starting with two underscore characters, you will see something that should look like the list in Example 1-6. What's strange is the pile of `__` symbols at the top of the table. Entering a command such as `ln 8047F798` in the Kernel Debugger yields the result `ntoskrnl!__`, which isn't any better. The original decorated name of the symbol at address `0x8047F798` is actually `___@@_PchSym_@00@UmgUkirezgvUmglhUlyUfkUlyqUrDIGUlykOlyq@ob`, so it seems that `imagehlp.dll` simply has stripped all characters except for two of the three leading underscores.

```
      #  ADDRESS       SIZE NAME
    -----------------------------------------------------------------
    6870: 8047F798        4 __
    6871: 80480B8C       14 __
    6872: 8047E724        4 __
    6873: 80471FE0        4 __
    6874: 804733B8       28 __
    6875: 804721D0       20 __
    6876: 804759A4        4 __
    6877: 80480004       1C __
    6878: 8047DA8C       14 __
    6879: 8047238C        4 __
    6880: 8047E6D4        4 __
    6881: 804755D4        4 __
    6882: 80471700        4 __decimal_point
    6883: 80471704        4 __decimal_point_length
    6884: 80471FC0        8 __fastflag
    ...
```

EXAMPLE 1-6. *Results of the Command* `w2k_sym /v/n/f __* ntoskrnl.exe`

An even better example is the command `w2k_sym /v/n/f _imp_* ntoskrnl.exe` that displays all symbols starting with the character sequence `_imp_`. The resulting list, excerpted in Example 1-7, comprises the import thunks of `ntoskrnl.exe`. Again, the list starts with a long sequence of ambiguous names, and again the Kernel Debugger isn't helpful, because it reports the same names for these addresses. If I tell you now that the original name of the symbol at address `0x804005A4` is `__imp_@ExReleaseFastMutex@4`, what do you think? Obviously, one leading underscore has gotten lost, and the entire tail string starting at the first `@` character is missing. It seems that the undecoration algorithm inside `imagehlp.dll` has a problem with `@` characters. The reason for this strange behavior is that `@` is not only the prefix of `__fastcall` function names but also the separator for the argument stack size trailer of `__fastcall` and `__stdcall` functions. Obviously, the applied undecoration algorithm is satisfied to find a leading underscore and an `@` character, erroneously assuming that the remaining trailer specifies the number of bytes on the caller's argument stack. Therefore, the lengthy PCH symbols are stripped down to two underscores, and the `__fastcall` import thunks are reduced to `_imp_`. In both cases, the first leading underscore is removed and the first `@` plus all characters following it are discarded as well.

```
   #  ADDRESS      SIZE NAME
-------------------------------------------------------------
6761: 804005A4        4 _imp_
6762: 80400584        4 _imp_
6763: 80400594        4 _imp_
6764: 80400524        4 _imp_
6765: 8040059C        4 _imp_
6766: 80400534        4 _imp_
6767: 80400590        4 _imp_
6768: 804004EC        4 _imp_
6769: 80400554        4 _imp_
6770: 80400598        4 _imp_
6771: 80400520        4 _imp__HalAllocateAdapterChannel
6772: 804004C0        4 _imp__HalAllocateCommonBuffer
6773: 804004E8        4 _imp__HalAllProcessorsStarted
...
```

EXAMPLE 1-7. *Results of the Command* `w2k_sym /v/n/f _imp_* ntoskrnl.exe`

The above examples are two potential reasons why you might lose patience and say: "Hey, I'm going to do it my own way!" The problem is that the internals of the Microsoft symbol file format are only scarcely documented, and some parts of the symbolic information—most notably the structure of Program Database (PDB) files—are completely undocumented. The Microsoft Knowledge Base even contains an article that clearly states:

> *"The Program Database File Format also known as PDB file format is not documented. This information is Microsoft proprietary." (Microsoft 2000d.)*

This sounds as if any attempts to roll your own symbol information parser must fail. However, you can bet that I'd never dare to add a section to this book that would end with the words "... but unfortunately, I can't tell you more because the internals of PDB files are unknown to me." Of course, I will tell you how PDB files are structured. But first, we will have to examine to the internals of `.dbg` files, because this is where the entire story starts.

THE INTERNAL STRUCTURE OF .dbg FILES

The symbolic information of the Windows NT 4.0 components is packed into files whose names end with a `.dbg` extension. The file names and the subdirectories hosting these files can be immediately derived from the component file name. Assuming that the symbol root directory of a system is d:\winnt\symbols, the full path of the symbol file of the component filename.ext is d:\winnt\symbols\ext\filename.dbg. For example, the kernel symbols can be found in the file d:\winnt\symbols\exe\ntoskrnl.dbg. Windows 2000 comes with .dbg files, too. However, the symbolic information has been moved to separate .pdb files. Therefore, each Windows 2000 component has an associated ext\filename.dbg and an additional ext\filename.pdb file in the symbol root directory. Aside from this difference, the contents of the Windows NT 4.0 and 2000 .dbg files are quite similar.

Fortunately, the internals of .dbg files are at least partially documented. The Win32 Platform SDK header file winnt.h provides important constant and type definitions of the core parts, and the Microsoft Developer Network (MSDN) Library contains some very helpful articles about this file format. Certainly the most enlightening article is Matt Pietrek's March 1999 edition of his "Under the Hood" column in *Microsoft Systems Journal (MSJ)*, renamed *MSDN Magazine* (Pietrek 1999). Basically, a .dbg file consists of a header and a data section. Both sections have variable size and are further subdivided. The header part comprises four major subsections:

1. An IMAGE_SEPARATE_DEBUG_HEADER structure, starting with the two-letter signature "DI" (top section of Listing 1-13).
2. An array of IMAGE_SECTION_HEADER structures, one for each section in the component's PE file (middle section of Listing 1-13). The number of entries is specified by the NumberOfSections member of the IMAGE_SEPARATE_DEBUG_HEADER.
3. A sequence of zero-terminated 8-bit ANSI strings, comprising all exported symbols in undecorated form. The size of this subsection is specified by the ExportedNamesSize member of the IMAGE_SEPARATE_DEBUG_HEADER. If the module doesn't export any symbols, the ExportedNamesSize is zero, and the subsection is not present.
4. An array of IMAGE_DEBUG_DIRECTORY structures, describing the locations and formats of the subsequent data in the file (bottom section of Listing 1-13). The size of this subsection is specified by the DebugDirectorySize member of the IMAGE_SEPARATE_DEBUG_HEADER.

```
#define IMAGE_SEPARATE_DEBUG_SIGNATURE 0x4944 // "DI"
typedef struct _IMAGE_SEPARATE_DEBUG_HEADER
    {
    WORD  Signature;
    WORD  Flags;
    WORD  Machine;
    WORD  Characteristics;
    DWORD TimeDateStamp;
    DWORD CheckSum;
    DWORD ImageBase;
    DWORD SizeOfImage;
    DWORD NumberOfSections;
    DWORD ExportedNamesSize;
    DWORD DebugDirectorySize;
    DWORD SectionAlignment;
    DWORD Reserved[2];
    }
    IMAGE_SEPARATE_DEBUG_HEADER, *PIMAGE_SEPARATE_DEBUG_HEADER;

// -----------------------------------------------------------------

#define IMAGE_SIZEOF_SHORT_NAME 8

typedef struct _IMAGE_SECTION_HEADER
    {
    BYTE  Name[IMAGE_SIZEOF_SHORT_NAME];
    union
        {
        DWORD PhysicalAddress;
        DWORD VirtualSize;
        } Misc;
    DWORD VirtualAddress;
    DWORD SizeOfRawData;
    DWORD PointerToRawData;
    DWORD PointerToRelocations;
    DWORD PointerToLinenumbers;
    WORD  NumberOfRelocations;
    WORD  NumberOfLinenumbers;
    DWORD Characteristics;
    }
    IMAGE_SECTION_HEADER, *PIMAGE_SECTION_HEADER;

// -----------------------------------------------------------------

#define IMAGE_DEBUG_TYPE_UNKNOWN        0
#define IMAGE_DEBUG_TYPE_COFF           1
#define IMAGE_DEBUG_TYPE_CODEVIEW       2
#define IMAGE_DEBUG_TYPE_FPO            3
#define IMAGE_DEBUG_TYPE_MISC           4
#define IMAGE_DEBUG_TYPE_EXCEPTION      5
#define IMAGE_DEBUG_TYPE_FIXUP          6
```

```
#define IMAGE_DEBUG_TYPE_OMAP_TO_SRC    7
#define IMAGE_DEBUG_TYPE_OMAP_FROM_SRC  8
#define IMAGE_DEBUG_TYPE_BORLAND        9
#define IMAGE_DEBUG_TYPE_RESERVED10    10
#define IMAGE_DEBUG_TYPE_CLSID         11

typedef struct _IMAGE_DEBUG_DIRECTORY
    {
    DWORD Characteristics;
    DWORD TimeDateStamp;
    WORD  MajorVersion;
    WORD  MinorVersion;
    DWORD Type;
    DWORD SizeOfData;
    DWORD AddressOfRawData;
    DWORD PointerToRawData;
    }
    IMAGE_DEBUG_DIRECTORY, *PIMAGE_DEBUG_DIRECTORY;
```

LISTING 1-13. *Header Structures of a* `.dbg` *File*

Because of the variable size of the header subsections, their absolute positions within the `.dbg` file must be computed from the size of the preceding subsections, respectively. A `.dbg` file parser usually applies the following algorithm:

- The `IMAGE_SEPARATE_DEBUG_HEADER` is always located at the beginning of the file.
- The first `IMAGE_SECTION_HEADER` immediately follows the `IMAGE_SEPARATE_DEBUG_HEADER`, so it is always found at file offset `0x30`.
- The offset of the first exported name is determined by multiplying the size of the `IMAGE_SECTION_HEADER` structure by the number of sections and adding it to the offset of the first section header. Thus, the first string is located at offset `0x30 + (NumberOfSections * 0x28)`.
- The location of the first `IMAGE_DEBUG_DIRECTORY` entry is determined by adding the `ExportedNamesSize` to the offset of the exported-names subsection.
- The offsets of the remaining data items in the `.dbg` file are determined by the `IMAGE_DEBUG_DIRECTORY` entries. The offsets and sizes of the associated data blocks are specified by the `PointerToRawData` and `SizeOfData` members, respectively.

The IMAGE_DEBUG_TYPE_* definitions in Listing 1-13 reflect the various data formats a .dbg file can comprise. However, the Windows NT 4.0 symbol files typically contain only four of them: IMAGE_DEBUG_TYPE_COFF, IMAGE_DEBUG_TYPE_CODEVIEW, IMAGE_DEBUG_TYPE_FPO, and IMAGE_DEBUG_TYPE_MISC. The Windows 2000 .dbg files usually add IMAGE_DEBUG_TYPE_OMAP_TO_SRC, IMAGE_DEBUG_TYPE_OMAP_FROM_SRC, and an undocumented type with ID 0x1000 to this list. If you are interested only in resolving or browsing symbols, the only required directory entries are IMAGE_DEBUG_TYPE_CODEVIEW, IMAGE_DEBUG_TYPE_OMAP_TO_SRC, and IMAGE_DEBUG_TYPE_OMAP_FROM_SRC.

The companion CD of this book contains a sample DLL named w2k_img.dll that parses .dbg and .pdb files and exports several interesting functions for developers of debugging tools. The source code of this DLL is found in the \src\w2k_img tree of the CD. One important property of w2k_img.dll is that it is designed to run on *all* Win32 platforms. This not only includes Windows 2000 and Windows NT 4.0 but also Windows 95 and 98. Like all good citizens in the Win32 world, this DLL comes with separate entry points for ANSI and Unicode strings. By default, a client application uses the ANSI functions. If the application includes the line #define UNICODE in its source code, the Unicode entry points are selected transparently. Client applications that run on Win32 platforms should use ANSI exclusively. Applications specific to Windows 2000/NT can switch to Unicode for better performance.

The sample CD also contains an example application called SBS Windows 2000 CodeView Decompiler, whose Microsoft Visual C/C++ project files are found in the \src\w2k_cv tree. It is a very simple application that dissects .dbg and .pdb files and dumps the contents of their sections to a console window. You can use it while reading this section to see live examples of the data structures discussed here. w2k_cv.exe makes heavy use of several w2k_img.dll API functions.

Listing 1-14 shows one of the basic data structures defined in w2k_img.h. The IMG_DBG structure is essentially a concatenation of the first two .dbg file header sections, that is, the fixed-size basic header and the array of PE section headers. The actual size of the structure, given the number of sections, is computed by the macro IMG_DBG__(). Its result specifies the file offset of the exported-names subsection.

Several w2k_img.dll API functions expect a pointer to an initialized IMG_DBG structure. The imgDbgLoad() function (not reprinted here) allocates and returns a properly initialized IMG_DBG structure containing the data of the specified .dbg file. imgDbgLoad() performs very strict sanity checks on the data to verify that the file is valid and complete. The returned IMG_DBG structure can be passed to several parsing functions that return the linear addresses of the most frequently used .dbg file components. For example, the imgDbgExports() function in Listing 1-15 computes the linear address of the sequence of exported names following the IMAGE_SECTION_HEADER array. It also counts the number of available names by scanning the string sequence up to the end of the subsection and optionally writes this value to the variable pointed to by the pdCount argument.

```
typedef struct _IMG_DBG
    {
    IMAGE_SEPARATE_DEBUG_HEADER Header;
    IMAGE_SECTION_HEADER        aSections [];
    }
    IMG_DBG, *PIMG_DBG, **PPIMG_DBG;

#define IMG_DBG_ sizeof (IMG_DBG)
#define IMG_DBG__(_n) (IMG_DBG_ + ((_n) * IMAGE_SECTION_HEADER_))

#define IMG_DBG_DATA(_p,_d) \
        ((PVOID) ((PBYTE) (_p) + (_d)->PointerToRawData))
```

LISTING 1-14. *The* `IMG_DBG` *Structure and Related Macros*

```
PBYTE WINAPI imgDbgExports (PIMG_DBG pid,
                            PDWORD   pdCount)
    {
    DWORD i, j;
    DWORD dCount    = 0;
    PBYTE pbExports = NULL;

    if (pid != NULL)
        {
        pbExports = (PBYTE) pid->aSections
                    + (pid->Header.NumberOfSections
                       * IMAGE_SECTION_HEADER_);

        for (i = 0; i < pid->Header.ExportedNamesSize; i = j)
            {
            if (!pbExports [j = i]) break;

            while ((j < pid->Header.ExportedNamesSize) &&
                   pbExports [j++]);

            if ((j > i) && (!pbExports [j-1])) dCount++;
            }
        }
    if (pdCount != NULL) *pdCount = dCount;
    return pbExports;
    }
```

LISTING 1-15. *The* `imgDbgExports()` *API Function*

Listing 1-16 defines two more API functions that locate debug directory entries by their `IMAGE_DEBUG_TYPE_*` IDs. `imgDbgDirectories()` returns the base address of the `IMAGE_DEBUG_DIRECTORY` array, whereas `imgDbgDirectory()` returns a pointer to the first directory entry with the specified type ID or returns `NULL` if no such entry exists.

```
PIMAGE_DEBUG_DIRECTORY WINAPI imgDbgDirectories (PIMG_DBG pid,
                                                 PDWORD   pdCount)
    {
    DWORD                  dCount = 0;
    PIMAGE_DEBUG_DIRECTORY pidd   = NULL;

    if (pid != NULL)
        {
        pidd   = (PIMAGE_DEBUG_DIRECTORY)
                 ((PBYTE) pid
                  + IMG_DBG__ (pid->Header.NumberOfSections)
                  + pid->Header.ExportedNamesSize);

        dCount = pid->Header.DebugDirectorySize
                 / IMAGE_DEBUG_DIRECTORY_;
        }
    if (pdCount != NULL) *pdCount = dCount;
    return pidd;
    }

// -----------------------------------------------------------------

PIMAGE_DEBUG_DIRECTORY WINAPI imgDbgDirectory (PIMG_DBG pid,
                                               DWORD    dType)
    {
    DWORD                  dCount, i;
    PIMAGE_DEBUG_DIRECTORY pidd = NULL;

    if ((pidd = imgDbgDirectories (pid, &dCount)) != NULL)
        {
        for (i = 0; i < dCount; i++, pidd++)
            {
            if (pidd->Type == dType) break;
            }
        if (i == dCount) pidd = NULL;
        }
    return pidd;
    }
```

LISTING 1-16. *The* `imgDbgDirectories()` *and* `imgDbgDirectory()` *API Functions*

The `imgDbgDirectory()` function can be used to look up the CodeView data in the `.dbg` file. This is done by the `imgDbgCv()` function in Listing 1-17. It calls `imgDbgDirectory()` with the `IMAGE_DEBUG_TYPE_CODEVIEW` type ID, and invokes the `IMG_DBG_DATA()` macro shown in Listing 1-14 to convert the data offset supplied by the `IMAGE_DEBUG_DIRECTORY` entry to an absolute linear address. This macro simply adds the offset to the base address of the `IMG_DBG` structure and typecasts it to a `PVOID` pointer. `imgDbgCv()` copies the size of the CodeView subsection to `*pdSize` if the `pdSize` argument is not `NULL`. The internals of the CodeView data are discussed below.

The API functions for the other data subsections look quite similar. Listing 1-18 shows the `imgDbgOmapToSrc()` and `imgDbgOmapFromSrc()` functions along with the `OMAP_TO_SRC` and `OMAP_FROM_SRC` structures on which they operate. Later, we will need these structures to compute the linear addresses of a symbol from its CodeView data. Because the OMAP data are an array of fixed-length structures, both API functions don't return the plain subsection size, but compute the number of entries in the array by simply dividing the overall size by the size of an entry. The result is copied to `*pdCount` if the `pdCount` argument is not `NULL`.

```
PCV_DATA WINAPI imgDbgCv (PIMG_DBG pid,
                          PDWORD   pdSize)
    {
    PIMAGE_DEBUG_DIRECTORY pidd;
    DWORD                  dSize = 0;
    PCV_DATA               pcd   = NULL;

    if ((pidd = imgDbgDirectory (pid, IMAGE_DEBUG_TYPE_CODEVIEW))
        != NULL)
        {
        pcd   = IMG_DBG_DATA (pid, pidd);
        dSize = pidd->SizeOfData;
        }
    if (pdSize != NULL) *pdSize = dSize;
    return pcd;
    }
```

LISTING 1-17. *The* `imgDbgCv()` *API Function*

```
typedef struct _OMAP_TO_SRC
    {
    DWORD dTarget;
    DWORD dSource;
    }
    OMAP_TO_SRC, *POMAP_TO_SRC, **PPOMAP_TO_SRC;

#define OMAP_TO_SRC_ sizeof (OMAP_TO_SRC)
// ----------------------------------------------------------------
```

(continued)

```
// ----------------------------------------------------------------

typedef struct _OMAP_FROM_SRC
    {
    DWORD dSource;
    DWORD dTarget;
    }
    OMAP_FROM_SRC, *POMAP_FROM_SRC, **PPOMAP_FROM_SRC;

#define OMAP_FROM_SRC_ sizeof (OMAP_FROM_SRC)

// ----------------------------------------------------------------

POMAP_TO_SRC WINAPI imgDbgOmapToSrc (PIMG_DBG pid,
                                     PDWORD   pdCount)
    {
    PIMAGE_DEBUG_DIRECTORY pidd;
    DWORD                  dCount = 0;
    POMAP_TO_SRC           pots   = NULL;

    if ((pidd = imgDbgDirectory (pid,
                                 IMAGE_DEBUG_TYPE_OMAP_TO_SRC))
        != NULL)
        {
        pots   = IMG_DBG_DATA (pid, pidd);
        dCount = pidd->SizeOfData / OMAP_TO_SRC_;
        }
    if (pdCount != NULL) *pdCount = dCount;
    return pots;
    }

// ----------------------------------------------------------------

POMAP_FROM_SRC WINAPI imgDbgOmapFromSrc (PIMG_DBG pid,
                                         PDWORD   pdCount)
    {
    PIMAGE_DEBUG_DIRECTORY pidd;
    DWORD                  dCount = 0;
    POMAP_FROM_SRC         pofs   = NULL;

    if ((pidd = imgDbgDirectory (pid,
                                 IMAGE_DEBUG_TYPE_OMAP_FROM_SRC))
        != NULL)
        {
        pofs   = IMG_DBG_DATA (pid, pidd);
        dCount = pidd->SizeOfData / OMAP_FROM_SRC_;
        }
    if (pdCount != NULL) *pdCount = dCount;
    return pofs;
    }
```

LISTING 1-18. *The* `imgDbgOmapToSrc()` *and* imgDbgOmapFromSrc() *API Function*

CodeView Subsections

CodeView is Microsoft's own debugging information format. It has undergone various metamorphoses through the years of the evolution of the Microsoft C/C++ compiler and linker. The internals of some CodeView versions differ radically from each other. However, all CodeView versions share a 32-bit signature at the beginning of the data that uniquely identifies the data format. The Windows NT 4.0 symbol files use the `NB09` format, which has been introduced by CodeView 4.10. The Windows 2000 files contain `NB10` CodeView data, which is merely a referral to a separate `.pdb` file, as I will demonstrate later.

`NB09` CodeView data is subdivided into a directory and subordinate entries. As Matt Pietrek points out in his *MSJ* article about `.dbg` files, most of the basic CodeView structures are defined in a set of sample header files coming with the Platform SDK. If you have installed the SDK samples, you will find a group of highly interesting files in the directory `\Program Files\Microsoft Platform SDK\Samples\SdkTools\Image\Include`. The files you need for CodeView parsing are named `cvexefmt.h` and `cvinfo.h`. Unfortunately, these files haven't been updated for a long time, as their file date 09-07-1994 indicates. It is striking that all structure names defined in `cvexefmt.h` start with the letters OMF, which is the acronym for Object Module Format. OMF is the standard file format used by 16-bit DOS and Windows `.obj` and `.lib` files. Starting with the Win32 versions of Microsoft's development tools, this format has been superseded by the Common Object File Format (COFF, see Gircys 1988 for details).

Although the original OMF format is obsolete today, it must be acknowledged that it was a clever file format. One of its objectives is to waste as little memory and disk space as possible. Another important property is that this format can be successfully parsed by applications even if they do not fully understand all parts of the file. The basic OMF data structure is the tagged record, starting with a tag byte identifying the type of data contained in the record, and a 16-bit length word specifying the number of subsequent bytes. This design makes it possible for an OMF reader to skip from record to record, picking out the record types in which it is interested. Microsoft has adopted this paradigm for its CodeView format, which explains the OMF prefix of the CodeView structure names in `cvexefmt.h`. Although the CodeView records have very few things in common with the original OMF records, the basic property that the format can be read without understanding all contents still remains.

Listing 1-19 comprises the definitions of various basic CodeView structures, taken from `w2k_img.h`. Some of them loosely correspond to structures found in `cvexefmt.h` and `cvinfo.h`, but are tweaked to the requirements of the `w2k_img.dll` API functions. The `CV_HEADER` structure is present in all CodeView data, regardless of the format version. The `Signature` is a 32-bit format version ID, like `CV_SIGNATURE_NB09` or `CV_SIGNATURE_NB10`. The `lOffset` member specifies the offset of the CodeView directory relative to the header address. In `NB09`-formatted Windows NT

4.0 symbol files, its value seems to be always equal to eight, indicating that the directory follows immediately after the header. The Windows 2000 symbol files contain `NB10` data with `lOffset` set to zero. This data format will be discussed in detail later in this chapter.

```
#define CV_SIGNATURE_NB   'BN'
#define CV_SIGNATURE_NB09 '90BN'
#define CV_SIGNATURE_NB10 '01BN'

// -----------------------------------------------------------------

typedef union _CV_SIGNATURE
    {
    WORD  wMagic;      // 'BN'
    DWORD dVersion;    // 'xxBN'
    BYTE  abText [4]; // "NBxx"
    }
    CV_SIGNATURE, *PCV_SIGNATURE, **PPCV_SIGNATURE;

#define CV_SIGNATURE_ sizeof (CV_SIGNATURE)

// -----------------------------------------------------------------

typedef struct _CV_HEADER
    {
    CV_SIGNATURE Signature;
    LONG         lOffset;
    }
    CV_HEADER, *PCV_HEADER, **PPCV_HEADER;

#define CV_HEADER_ sizeof (CV_HEADER)

// -----------------------------------------------------------------

typedef struct _CV_DIRECTORY
    {
    WORD  wSize;       // in bytes, including this member
    WORD  wEntrySize; // in bytes
    DWORD dEntries;
    LONG  lOffset;
    DWORD dFlags;
    }
    CV_DIRECTORY, *PCV_DIRECTORY, **PPCV_DIRECTORY;

#define CV_DIRECTORY_ sizeof (CV_DIRECTORY)

// -----------------------------------------------------------------
```

```
#define sstModule      0x0120 // CV_MODULE
#define sstGlobalPub   0x012A // CV_PUBSYM
#define sstSegMap      0x012D // SV_SEGMAP

// -----------------------------------------------------------------

typedef struct _CV_ENTRY
    {
    WORD  wSubSectionType;    // sst*
    WORD  wModuleIndex;       // -1 if not applicable
    LONG  lSubSectionOffset;  // relative to CV_HEADER
    DWORD dSubSectionSize;    // in bytes, not including padding
    }
    CV_ENTRY, *PCV_ENTRY, **PPCV_ENTRY;

#define CV_ENTRY_ sizeof (CV_ENTRY)

// -----------------------------------------------------------------

typedef struct _CV_NB09 // CodeView 4.10
    {
    CV_HEADER    Header;
    CV_DIRECTORY Directory;
    CV_ENTRY     Entries [];
    }
    CV_NB09, *PCV_NB09, **PPCV_NB09;

#define CV_NB09_ sizeof (CV_NB09)
```

LISTING 1-19. *CodeView Data Structures*

The CodeView `NB09` directory consists of a single `CV_DIRECTORY` structure followed by an array of `CV_ENTRY` items. This is reflected by the `CV_NB09` structure defined at the end of Listing 1-19. It comprises the CodeView header, directory, and entry array. The size of the `Entries[]` array is determined by the `dEntries` member of the `CV_DIRECTORY`. Each `CV_ENTRY` refers to a CodeView subsection of the type specified by the `wSubSectionType` member. `cvexefmt.h` defines no fewer than 21 subsection types. However, the Windows NT 4.0 symbol files make use of only 3 of them: `sstModule (0x0120)`, `sstGlobalPub (0x012A)`, and `sstSegMap (0x012D)`. You will usually see several `sstModule` subsections in a symbol file, but the `sstGlobalPub` and `sstSegMap` subsections are unique. As the name suggests, `sstGlobalPub` is where we will find the global public symbol information of the corresponding module.

The w2k_img.dll API function imgCvEntry() shown in Listing 1-20 allows easy look up of CodeView directory entries by type. Its pc09 argument points to a CV_NB09 structure, that is, to the NB09 signature of the CodeView data block inside a .dbg file. The dType argument specifies one of the CodeView subsection type IDs sst*, and the dIndex value selects a specific subsection instance in cases of multiple subsections of the same type. Therefore, setting dIndex to a value other than zero makes sense only if dType indicates sstModule.

```
PCV_ENTRY WINAPI imgCvEntry (PCV_NB09 pc09,
                             DWORD    dType,
                             DWORD    dIndex)
    {
    DWORD     i, j;
    PCV_ENTRY pce = NULL;

    if ((pc09 != NULL) &&
        (pc09->Header.Signature.dVersion == CV_SIGNATURE_NB09))
        {
        for (i = j = 0; i < pc09->Directory.dEntries; i++)
            {
            if ((pc09->Entries [i].wSubSectionType == dType) &&
                (j++ == dIndex))
                {
                pce = pc09->Entries + i;
                break;
                }
            }
        }
    return pce;
    }

// ----------------------------------------------------------------

PCV_PUBSYM WINAPI imgCvSymbols (PCV_NB09 pc09,
                                PDWORD   pdCount,
                                PDWORD   pdSize)
    {
    PCV_ENTRY  pce;
    PCV_PUBSYM pcp1;
    DWORD      i;
    DWORD      dCount = 0;
    DWORD      dSize  = 0;
    PCV_PUBSYM pcp    = NULL;

    if ((pce = imgCvEntry (pc09, sstGlobalPub, 0)) != NULL)
        {
        pcp = CV_PUBSYM_DATA ((PBYTE) pc09
                              + pce->lSubSectionOffset);
        dSize = pce->dSubSectionSize;
```

```
        for (i  = 0; dSize - i >= CV_PUBSYM_;
             i += CV_PUBSYM_SIZE (pcp1))
            {
            pcp1 = (PCV_PUBSYM) ((PBYTE) pcp + i);
            if (dSize - i < CV_PUBSYM_SIZE (pcp1)) break;
            if (pcp1->Header.wRecordType == CV_PUB32) dCount++;
            }
        }
    if (pdCount != NULL) *pdCount = dCount;
    if (pdSize  != NULL) *pdSize  = dSize;
    return pcp;
    }
```

LISTING 1-20. *The* `imgCvEntry()` *and* `imgCvSymbols()` *API Functions*

CodeView Symbols

The lower half of Listing 1-20 shows the `imgCvSymbols()` function that returns a pointer to the first CodeView symbol record. The `sstGlobalPub` subsection consists of a fixed-length `CV_SYMHASH` header, followed by a sequence of variable-length `CV_PUBSYM` records. The definitions of both types are included in Listing 1-21. First, `imgCvSymbols()` calls `imgCvEntry()` to find the `CV_ENTRY` that has its `wSubSectionType` member set to `sstGlobalPub`. If available, it uses the `CV_PUBSYM_DATA()` macro included at the bottom of Listing 1-4 to skip over the leading `CV_SYMHASH` structure. Finally, `imgCvSymbols()` counts the number of symbols by walking through the list of `CV_PUBSYM` records, using the `CV_PUBSYM_SIZE()` macro in Listing 1-21 to compute the size of each record.

The `CV_PUBSYM` sequence bears some resemblance to the contents of an OMF object file. As already noted, an OMF data stream consists of variable-length records, each starting with a tag byte and a length word. `CV_PUBSYM` records are similar. They start with an `OMF_HEADER` that comprises `wRecordSize` and `wRecordType` members. This is just a variant of the OMF principle, different only in that the length word comes first and the tag byte has been extended to 16 bits. The last part of the `CV_PUBSYM` structure is the symbol name, specified in PASCAL format, as is usual in an OMF record. A PASCAL string consists of a leading length byte, followed by 0 to 255 8-bit characters. Contrary to C strings, no terminating zero byte is appended. The `CV_PUBSYM` record ends after the last `Name` character. However, the record is stuffed with filler bytes up to the next 32-bit boundary. This padding is accounted for by the `wRecordSize` value in the `OMF_HEADER`. Note that the `wRecordSize` specifies the size of the `CV_PUBSYM` record, *excluding* the `wRecordSize` member itself. That's why the `CV_PUBSYM_SIZE()` macro in Listing 1-21 adds `sizeof (WORD)` to the `wRecordSize` value to yield the total record size.

```
typedef struct _CV_SYMHASH
    {
    WORD  wSymbolHashIndex;
    WORD  wAddressHashIndex;
    DWORD dSymbolInfoSize;
    DWORD dSymbolHashSize;
    DWORD dAddressHashSize;
    }
    CV_SYMHASH, *PCV_SYMHASH, **PPCV_SYMHASH;

#define CV_SYMHASH_ sizeof (CV_SYMHASH)

// ----------------------------------------------------------------

typedef struct _OMF_HEADER
    {
    WORD wRecordSize; // in bytes, not including this member
    WORD wRecordType;
    }
    OMF_HEADER, *POMF_HEADER, **PPOMF_HEADER;

#define OMF_HEADER_ sizeof (OMF_HEADER)

// ----------------------------------------------------------------

typedef struct _OMF_NAME
    {
    BYTE bLength;      // in bytes, not including this member
    BYTE abName [];
    }
    OMF_NAME, *POMF_NAME, **PPOMF_NAME;

#define OMF_NAME_ sizeof (OMF_NAME)

// ----------------------------------------------------------------


#define S_PUB32  0x0203
#define S_ALIGN  0x0402

#define CV_PUB32 S_PUB32

// ----------------------------------------------------------------

typedef struct _CV_PUBSYM
    {
    OMF_HEADER Header;
    DWORD      dOffset;
```

```
    WORD        wSegment;     // 1-based section index     WORD        wTypeIndex;  // 0
    OMF_NAME    Name;         // zero-padded to next DWORD
    }
    CV_PUBSYM, *PCV_PUBSYM, **PPCV_PUBSYM;

#define CV_PUBSYM_ sizeof (CV_PUBSYM)

#define CV_PUBSYM_DATA(_p) \
        ((PCV_PUBSYM) ((PBYTE) (_p) + CV_SYMHASH_))

#define CV_PUBSYM_SIZE(_p) \
        ((DWORD) (_p)->Header.wRecordSize + sizeof (WORD))

#define CV_PUBSYM_NEXT(_p) \
        ((PCV_PUBSYM) ((PBYTE) (_p) + CV_PUBSYM_SIZE (_p)))
```

LISTING 1-21. *The* `CV_SYMHASH` *and* `CV_PUBSYM` *Structures*

If you are scanning the `CV_PUBSYM` stream, you typically will encounter two record types: `S_PUB32 (0x0203)` or `S_ALIGN (0x0402)`. The latter can be safely ignored because it is only padding. The `S_PUB32` records carry the real symbol information. Besides the symbol `Name`, the `wSegment` and `dOffset` members are of interest. `wSegment` specifies a one-based index that identifies the PE file section that contains the symbol. This value minus one can be used as an index into the `IMAGE_SECTION_HEADER` array at the beginning of the `.dbg` file. `dOffset` is the symbol's address relative to the beginning of its PE section. In this context, a symbol address is the entry point of the function or the base address of the global variable associated with the symbol. Normally, the `dOffset` value can simply be added to the `VirtualAddress` of the corresponding `IMAGE_SECTION_HEADER` to yield the address of the symbol relative to the module's base address. However, if the `.dbg` file includes `IMAGE_DEBUG_TYPE_OMAP_TO_SRC` and `IMAGE_DEBUG_TYPE_OMAP_FROM_SRC` subsections, the `dOffset` must pass through an additional conversion layer. The usage of OMAP tables will be discussed later, after introduction of the PDB file format.

The order of the symbols in a CodeView `sstGlobalPub` subsection appears somewhat random. I don't know what principle underlies it. However, I can say for sure that the symbols are *not* sorted by section number, offset, or name. Don't rely on assumptions about the order—if your applications need a specific sorting sequence, you have to sort the symbol records yourself. The `w2k_img.dll` sample library found on the companion CD provides three default symbol orders: by address, by name with case sensitivity, and by name ignoring the character case.

The Internal Structure of .pdb Files

After installing the Windows 2000 symbol files, the first striking observation is usually that each module now has *two* associated files: one with the `.dbg` extension, as usual, and an additional one with an extension of `.pdb`. Peeking into one of the `.pdb` files reveals the string "Microsoft C/C++ program database 2.00" at its very beginning. So PDB is obviously the acronym of Program Database. Searching for details about the internal PDB structure in the MSDN Library or on the Internet doesn't reveal anything useful, except for a Microsoft Knowledge Base article that classifies this format as Microsoft proprietary (Microsoft Corporation, 2000d). Even Windows guru Matt Pietrek admits:

> *"The format of PDB symbol tables isn't publicly documented. (Even I don't know the exact format, especially as it continues to evolve with each new release of Visual C++.)" (Pietrek 1997a)*

Well, it *might* evolve with each Visual C/C++ release, but for the current version of Windows 2000, I can tell you exactly how its PDB symbol files are structured. This is probably the first time the PDB format has been publicly documented. But first, let's examine how the `.dbg` and `.pdb` files are linked together.

One remarkable property of the Windows 2000 `.dbg` files is that they contain just a very tiny, almost negligible CodeView subsection. Example 1-8 shows the entire CodeView data included in the `ntoskrnl.dbg` file, generated by the `w2k_dump.exe` utility in the `\src\w2k_dump` directory tree of the sample CD. That's all—just those 32 bytes. As usual, the subsection starts with a `CV_HEADER` structure containing the CodeView version signature. This time, it is `NB10`. The MSDN Library (Microsoft 2000a) really doesn't tell us much about this special version:

> *"NB10 The signature for an executable with the debug information stored in a separate PDB file. Corresponds with the formats set forth in NB09 or NB11." (MSDN Library—April 2000 \ Specifications \ Technologies and Languages \ Visual C++ 5.0 Symbolic Debug Information Specification \ Debug Information Format).*

I don't know the internals of the `NB11` format, but the PDB format has almost nothing in common with the `NB09` format discussed above! The first sentence clearly states why the `NB10` data block is that small. All relevant information is moved to a separate file, so the main purpose of this CodeView section is to provide a link to the real data. As Example 1-8 suggests, the symbol information must be sought in the `ntoskrnl.pdb` file in the Windows 2000 symbol setup.

```
Address  | 00 01 02 03-04 05 06 07 : 08 09 0A 0B-0C 0D 0E 0F | 0123456789ABCDEF
---------|-------------------------:-------------------------|-----------------
00006590 | 4E 42 31 30-00 00 00 00 : 20 7D 23 38-54 00 00 00 | NB10.... }#8T...
000065A0 | 6E 74 6F 73-6B 72 6E 6C : 2E 70 64 62-00 00 00 00 | ntoskrnl.pdb....
```

EXAMPLE 1-8. *Hex Dump of a PDB CodeView Subsection*

If you are wondering what purpose the remaining data in Example 1-8 serves, Listing 1-22 should satisfy your curiosity. The `CV_HEADER` is self-explanatory. The next two members at offset `0x8` and `0xC` are named `dSignature` and `dAge` and play an important role in the linkage of `.dbg` and `.pdb` files. `dSignature` is a 32-bit UNIX-style time stamp, specifying the build date and time of the debug information in seconds since 01-01-1970. The `w2k_img.dll` sample library provides the API functions `imgTimeUnpack()` and `imgTimePack()` to convert this Windows-untypical date/time format back and forth. The purpose of the `dAge` member isn't entirely clear to me. However, it appears that its value is initially set to one and incremented each time the PDB data is rewritten. The `dSignature` and `dAge` values together constitute a 64-bit ID that can be used by debuggers to verify that a given PDB file matches the `.dbg` file referring to it. The PDB file contains duplicates of both values in one of its data streams, so a debugger can refuse processing a `.dbg/.pdb` pair of files with unmatched `dSignature` and `dAge` information.

Whenever you are faced with an unknown data format, the first thing to do is to run some examples of it through a hex dump viewer. The `w2k_dump.exe` utility on this book's companion CD does a good job in this respect. Examining the hex dump of a Windows 2000 PDB file such as `ntoskrnl.pdb` or `ntfs.pdb` reveals some interesting properties:

- The file seems to be divided into blocks of fixed size—typically `0x400` bytes.
- Some blocks consist of long runs of 1-bits, occasionally interrupted by shorter sequences of 0-bits.
- The information in the file is not necessarily contiguous. Sometimes, the data end abruptly at a block boundary, but continue somewhere else in the file.
- Some data blocks appear repeatedly within the file.

```
typedef struct _CV_NB10 // PDB reference
    {
    CV_HEADER     Header;
    DWORD         dSignature;    // seconds since 01-01-1970
    DWORD         dAge;          // 1++
    BYTE          abPdbName []; // zero-terminated
    }
    CV_NB10, *PCV_NB10, **PPCV_NB10;

#define CV_NB10_ sizeof (CV_NB10)
```

LISTING 1-22. *The CodeView* NB10 *Subsection*

It took some time for me to finally realize that these are typical properties of a compound file. A compound file is a small file system packaged into a single file. The "file system" metaphor readily explains some of the above observations:

- A file system subdivides a disk into *sectors* of fixed size and groups the sectors into *files* of variable size. The sectors representing a file can be located anywhere on the disk and don't need to be contiguous—the file/sector assignments are defined in a *file directory.*
- A compound file subdivides a raw disk file into *pages* of fixed size and groups the pages into *streams* of variable size. The pages representing a file can be located anywhere in the raw disk file and don't need to be contiguous—the stream/page assignments are defined in a *stream directory.*

Obviously, almost any assertions about file systems can be mapped to compound files by simply replacing "sector" by "page," and "file" by "stream." The file system metaphor explains why a PDB file is organized in fixed-size blocks. It also explains why the blocks are not necessarily contiguous. What about the pages with the masses of 1-bits? Actually, this type of data is something very common in file systems. To keep track of used and unused sectors on the disk, many file systems maintain an allocation bit array that provides one bit for each sector (or sector cluster). If a sector is unused, its bit is set. Whenever the file system allocates space for a file, it searches for unused sectors by scanning the allocation bits. After adding a sector to a file, its allocation bit is set to zero. The same procedure is applied to the pages and streams of a compound file. The long runs of 1-bits represent unused pages, and the 0-bits are assigned to existing streams.

The only thing that remains is the observation that some data blocks reoccur within a PDB file. The same thing happens with sectors on a disk. When a file in a file system is rewritten a couple of times, each write operation may use different sectors to store the data. Thus, it can happen that the disk contains free sectors with older duplicates of the file information. This doesn't constitute a problem for the file system. If the sector is marked free in the allocation bit array, it is unimportant what data it contains. As soon as the sector is reclaimed for another file, the data will be overwritten anyway. Applying the file system metaphor once more to compound files, this means that the observed duplicate pages are usually left over from earlier versions of a stream that has been rewritten to different pages in the compound file. They can be safely ignored; all we have to care for are the pages that are referred to by the stream directory. The remaining unassigned pages should be regarded as garbage.

With the basic paradigm of PDB files being introduced now, we can step to the more interesting task of examining their basic building blocks. Listing 1-23 shows the layout of the PDB header. The `PDB_HEADER` starts with a lengthy signature that specifies the PDB version as a text string. The text is terminated with an end-of-file (EOF) character (ASCII code `0x1A`) and supplemented with the magic number `0x0000474A`, or `"JG\0\0"` if interpreted as a string. Maybe these are the initials of the designer of the PDB format. The embedded EOF character has the nice effect that an unknowledgeable user can issue a command such as `type ntoskrnl.pdb` in a console window without getting garbage on the screen. The only thing that will be displayed is the message `Microsoft C/C++ program database 2.00\r\n`. All Windows 2000 symbol files are shipped as PDB 2.00 files. Apparently, a PDB 1.00 format exists as well, but it seems to be structured quite differently.

```
#define PDB_SIGNATURE_200 \
        "Microsoft C/C++ program database 2.00\r\n\x1AJG\0"

#define PDB_SIGNATURE_TEXT 40

// -----------------------------------------------------------------

typedef struct _PDB_SIGNATURE
    {
    BYTE abSignature [PDB_SIGNATURE_TEXT+4]; // PDB_SIGNATURE_nnn
    }
    PDB_SIGNATURE, *PPDB_SIGNATURE, **PPPDB_SIGNATURE;

#define PDB_SIGNATURE_ sizeof (PDB_SIGNATURE)

// -----------------------------------------------------------------

#define PDB_STREAM_FREE -1

// -----------------------------------------------------------------
```

(continued)

```
typedef struct _PDB_STREAM
    {
    DWORD dStreamSize;   // in bytes, -1 = free stream
    PWORD pwStreamPages; // array of page numbers
    }
    PDB_STREAM, *PPDB_STREAM, **PPPDB_STREAM;

#define PDB_STREAM_ sizeof (PDB_STREAM)

// -----------------------------------------------------------------

#define PDB_PAGE_SIZE_1K   0x0400 // bytes per page
#define PDB_PAGE_SIZE_2K   0x0800
#define PDB_PAGE_SIZE_4K   0x1000

#define PDB_PAGE_SHIFT_1K  10     // log2 (PDB_PAGE_SIZE_*)
#define PDB_PAGE_SHIFT_2K  11
#define PDB_PAGE_SHIFT_4K  12

#define PDB_PAGE_COUNT_1K  0xFFFF // page number < PDB_PAGE_COUNT_*
#define PDB_PAGE_COUNT_2K  0xFFFF
#define PDB_PAGE_COUNT_4K  0x7FFF

// -----------------------------------------------------------------

typedef struct _PDB_HEADER
    {
    PDB_SIGNATURE Signature;      // PDB_SIGNATURE_200
    DWORD         dPageSize;      // 0x0400, 0x0800, 0x1000
    WORD          wStartPage;     // 0x0009, 0x0005, 0x0002
    WORD          wFilePages;     // file size / dPageSize
    PDB_STREAM    RootStream;     // stream directory
    WORD          awRootPages []; // pages containing PDB_ROOT
    }
    PDB_HEADER, *PPDB_HEADER, **PPPDB_HEADER;

#define PDB_HEADER_ sizeof (PDB_HEADER)
```

LISTING 1-23. *The PDB File Header*

Following the signature at offset `0x2C` is a `DWORD` named `dPageSize` that specifies the size of the compound file pages in bytes. Legal values are `0x0400` (1 KB), `0x0800` (2 KB), and `0x1000` (4 KB). The `wFilePages` member reflects the total number of pages used by the PDB file image. The result of multiplying this value by the page size should always exactly match the file size in bytes. `wStartPage` is a zero-based page number that points to the first data page. The byte offset of this page can be computed by multiplying the page number by the page size. Typical values are *9* for 1-KB pages (byte offset `0x2400`), *5* for 2-KB pages (byte offset `0x2800`), or *2* for 4-KB pages (byte offset

0x2000). The pages between the PDB_HEADER and the first data page are reserved for the allocation bit array of the compound file, always starting at the beginning of the second page. This means that the PDB file maintains 0x2000 bytes with 0x10000 allocation bits if the page size is 1 or 2 KB, and 0x1000 bytes with 0x8000 allocation bits if the page size is 4 KB. In turn, this implies that the maximum amount of data a PDB file can manage is 64 MB in 1-KB page mode, and 128 MB in 2-KB or 4-KB page mode.

The RootStream and awRootPages[] members concluding the PDB_HEADER describe the location of the stream directory within the PDB file. As already noted, the PDB file is conceptually a collection of variable-length streams that carry the actual data. The locations and compositions of the streams are managed in a single stream directory. Odd as it may seem, the stream directory itself is stored in a stream. I have called this special stream the "root stream." The root stream holding the stream directory can be located anywhere in the PDB file. Its location and size are supplied by the RootStream and awRootPages[] members of the PDB_HEADER. The dStreamSize member of the PDB_STREAM substructure specifies the number of pages occupied by the stream directory, and the entries in the awRootPages[] array point to the pages containing the data.

Let's illustrate this with a simple example. The hex dump excerpt in Example 1-9 shows the PDB_HEADER of the ntoskrnl.pdb file. The values referenced are underlined. Obviously, this PDB file uses a page size of 0x0400 bytes and comprises 0x02D1 pages, resulting in a file size of 0xB4400 (738,304 in decimal notation). A quick check with the dir command shows that this value is correct. The root stream size is 0x5B0 bytes. With a page size of 0x400 bytes, this means that the awRootPages[] array contains two entries, found at the file offsets 0x3C and 0x3E. The values in these slots are page numbers that need to be multiplied by the page size to yield the corresponding byte offsets. In this case, the results are 0xB2000 and 0xB2800.

The bottom line of this computation is that the stream directory of the ntoskrnl.exe PDB file is located in two file pages, extending from 0xB2000 to 0xB23FF and 0xB2800 to 0xB29AF, respectively. Parts of these ranges are shown in Example 1-10.

```
Address  | 00 01 02 03-04 05 06 07 : 08 09 0A 0B-0C 0D 0E 0F | 0123456789ABCDEF
---------|-------------------------:-------------------------|-----------------
00000000 | 4D 69 63 72-6F 73 6F 66 : 74 20 43 2F-43 2B 2B 20 | Microsoft C/C++
00000010 | 70 72 6F 67-72 61 6D 20 : 64 61 74 61-62 61 73 65 | program database
00000020 | 20 32 2E 30-30 0D 0A 1A : 4A 47 00 00-00 04 00 00 |  2.00...JG......
00000030 | 09 00 D1 02-B0 05 00 00 : 5C 00 78 00-C8 02 CA 02 | ..Ñ.°...\.x.È.Ê.
```

EXAMPLE 1-9. *A Sample PDB Header*

```
Address   | 00 01 02 03-04 05 06 07 : 08 09 0A 0B-0C 0D 0E 0F | 0123456789ABCDEF
----------|-------------------------:-------------------------|-----------------
000B2000  | 08 00 00 00-B0 05 00 00 : 98 22 28 00-3A 00 00 00 | ....°...?"(.:...
000B2010  | 88 57 26 00-38 00 00 00 : 78 57 26 00-A9 02 04 00 | ?W&.8...xW&.©...
000B2020  | F8 BA E9 00-00 00 00 00 : 68 57 26 00-04 40 00 00 | øºé.....hW&..@..
000B2030  | C8 29 28 00-B4 9E 01 00 : 08 90 ED 00-3C DF 04 00 | È)(.´?...•í.<ß..
000B2040  | 08 BD E9 00-12 00 C9 02 : C7 02 13 00-C6 02 C6 01 | .½é...É.Ç...Æ.Æ.
000B2050  | C7 01 C8 01-C9 01 CA 01 : CB 01 CC 01-CD 01 CE 01 | Ç.È.É.Ê.Ë.Ì.Í.Î.
...
000B23A0  | BD 00 BE 00-BF 00 C0 00 : C1 00 C2 00-C3 00 C4 00 | ½.¾.¿.À.Á.Â.Ã.Ä.
000B23B0  | C5 00 C6 00-C7 00 C8 00 : C9 00 CA 00-CB 00 CC 00 | Å.Æ.Ç.È.É.Ê.Ë.Ì.
000B23C0  | CD 00 CE 00-CF 00 D0 00 : D1 00 D2 00-D3 00 D4 00 | Í.Î.Ï.Ð.Ñ.Ò.Ó.Ô.
000B23D0  | D5 00 D6 00-D7 00 D8 00 : D9 00 DA 00-DB 00 DC 00 | Õ.Ö.×.Ø.Ù.Ú.Û.Ü.
000B23E0  | DD 00 DE 00-DF 00 E0 00 : E1 00 E2 00-E3 00 E4 00 | _.Þ.ß.à.á.â.ã.ä.
000B23F0  | E5 00 E6 00-E7 00 E8 00 : E9 00 EA 00-EB 00 EC 00 | å.æ.ç.è.é.ê.ë.ì.
----------|-------------------------:-------------------------|-----------------
000B2800  | ED 00 EE 00-EF 00 F0 00 : F1 00 F2 00-F3 00 F4 00 | í.î.ï.ð.ñ.ò.ó.ô.
000B2810  | F5 00 F6 00-F7 00 F8 00 : F9 00 FA 00-FB 00 FC 00 | õ.ö.÷.ø.ù.ú.û.ü.
000B2820  | FD 00 FE 00-FF 00 00 01 : 01 01 02 01-03 01 04 01 | ý.þ.ÿ...........
000B2830  | 05 01 06 01-07 01 08 01 : 09 01 0A 01-0B 01 0C 01 | ................
000B2840  | 0D 01 0E 01-0F 01 10 01 : 11 01 12 01-13 01 14 01 | ................
000B2850  | 15 01 16 01-17 01 18 01 : 19 01 1A 01-1B 01 1C 01 | ................
...
000B2950  | 95 01 96 01-97 01 98 01 : 99 01 9A 01-9B 01 9C 01 | ?.?.?.?.?.?.?.?.
000B2960  | 9D 01 9E 01-9F 01 A0 01 : A1 01 A2 01-A3 01 A4 01 | •.?.?. .¡.¢.£.¤.
000B2970  | A5 01 A6 01-A7 01 A8 01 : A9 01 AA 01-AB 01 AC 01 | ¥.¦.§.¨.©.ª.«.¬.
000B2980  | AD 01 AE 01-AF 01 B0 01 : B1 01 B2 01-B3 01 B4 01 | =.®.¯.°.±.².³.´.
000B2990  | B5 01 B6 01-B7 01 B8 01 : B9 01 BA 01-BB 01 BC 01 | µ.¶.·.¸.¹.º.».¼.
000B29A0  | BD 01 BE 01-BF 01 C0 01 : C1 01 C2 01-C3 01 C4 01 | ½.¾.¿.À.Á.Â.Ã.Ä.
```

EXAMPLE 1-10. *Excerpts from a Sample PDB Stream Directory*

The stream directory is composed of two sections: a header part in the form of a `PDB_ROOT` structure, as defined in Listing 1-24, and a data part consisting of an array of 16-bit page numbers. The `wCount` member of the `PDB_ROOT` section specifies the number of streams stored in the PDB compound file. The `aStreams[]` array contains a `PDB_STREAM` entry (see Listing 1-23) for each stream, and the page number slots follow immediately after the last `aStreams[]` entry. In Example 1-10, the number of streams is eight, as the underlined value at offset `0xB2000` indicates. The subsequent eight `PDB_STREAM` structures define streams of size `0x5B0, 0x3A, 0x38, 0x402A9, 0x0, 0x4004, 0x19EB4,` and `0x4DF3C,` respectively. These values are underlined in Example 1-10, too. Expressed in 1-KB pages, the stream sizes are `0x2, 0x1, 0x1, 0x101, 0x0, 0x11, 0x68,` and `0x138,` yielding a total of `0x2B6` pages used by the streams. The first underlined value after the `PDB_STREAM` array is the first slot of the page number list. Counting two bytes per page number, and taking into account that the page directory is interrupted by one page that belongs somewhere else, the next offset after the page numbers should be `0xB2044 + 0x400 + (0x2B6 * 2) = 0xB29B0,` which fits perfectly into the picture.

```
#define PDB_STREAM_DIRECTORY 0
#define PDB_STREAM_PDB       1
#define PDB_STREAM_PUBSYM    7

// -----------------------------------------------------------------

typedef struct _PDB_ROOT
    {
    WORD        wCount;      // < PDB_STREAM_MAX
    WORD        wReserved;   // 0
    PDB_STREAM aStreams []; // stream #0 reserved for stream table
    }
    PDB_ROOT, *PPDB_ROOT, **PPPDB_ROOT;

#define PDB_ROOT_ sizeof (PDB_ROOT)
```

LISTING 1-24. *The PDB Stream Directory*

Finding the page number block associated with a given stream is somewhat tricky, because the page directory does not provide any cues except the stream size. If you are interested in stream 3, you have to compute the number of pages occupied by streams 1 and 2 to get the desired start index within the page number array. Once the stream's page number list is located, reading the stream data is simple. Just walk through the list and multiply each page number by the page size to yield the file offset, and read pages from the computed offsets until the end of the stream is reached. On first look, parsing a PDB file seemed rather tough. But it turns out that it is actually quite simple—probably much simpler than parsing a `.dbg` file. The compound-file nature of the PDB format with its clear-cut random access to stream pages reduces the task of reading a stream to a mere concatenation of fixed-sized pages. I'm amazed at this elegant data access mechanism!

An even greater benefit of the PDB format becomes apparent when updating an existing PDB file. Inserting data into a file with a sequential structure usually means reshuffling large portions of the contents. The PDB file's random-access structure borrowed from file systems allows addition and deletion of data with minimal effort, just as files can be modified with ease on a file system media. Only the stream directory has to be reshuffled when a stream grows or shrinks across a page boundary. This important property facilitates incremental updating of PDB files. Microsoft states the following in a Knowledge Base article titled "INFO: PDB and DBG Files—What They Are and How They Work":

> *"The .PDB extension stands for 'program database.' It holds the new format for storing debugging information that was introduced in Visual C++ version 1.0. In the future, the .PDB file will also hold other project state information.*

> *One of the most important motivations for the change in format was to allow incremental linking of debug versions of programs, a change first introduced in Visual C++ version 2.0" (Microsoft Corporation 2000e).*

Now that the internal format of PDB files is clear, the next problem is to identify the contents of their streams. After examining various PDB files, I have come to the conclusion that each stream number serves a predefined purpose. The first stream seems to always contain a stream directory, and the second one contains information about the PDB file that can be used to verify that the file matches an associated `.dbg` file. For example, the latter stream contains `dSignature` and `dAge` members that should have the same values as the corresponding members of an `NB10` CodeView section, as outlined in Listing 1-22. The eighth stream is most interesting in the context of this chapter because it hosts the CodeView symbol information we have been seeking. The meaning of the other streams is still unclear to me and is another area for future research.

I am not going to include PDB reader sample code here because this would exceed the scope of this chapter. Instead, I encourage you to peek into the `w2k_img.c` and `w2k_img.h` source files on the sample CD. Look for functions named `imgPdb*()` and data items called `PDB_*` for extensive code and data. By the way, the CD contains a ready-to-run PDB stream reader with full source code. You already know this program—it is the `w2k_dump.exe` utility that I have used to create some of the hex dump examples above. This simple console-mode utility provides a `+p` command line option that enables PDB stream decomposition. If the specified file is not a valid PDB file, the program falls back to sequential hex dump mode. The Visual C/C++ project files of `w2k_dump.exe` are found on the CD in the `\src\w2k_dump` directory tree.

PDB Symbols

After this long but hopefully interesting detour through the PDB format, it is time to return to our initial mission: the extraction of CodeView symbol information. Fortunately, this task is quite similar to the enumeration of public symbols in an `NB09` CodeView subsection. Once the stream containing the symbols is located, we are again faced with a sequence of OMF-like records of variable size. Unfortunately, the `NB09` and `NB10` record formats differ somewhat, but the deviations are only marginal. Listing 1-25 shows the layout of the `PDB_PUBSYM` structure. Compared with the corresponding `CV_PUBSYM` structure of the NB09 format, included in Listing 1-21, the `dOffset` and `wSegment` members have moved a bit toward the end. This and the fact that the tag value of PDB symbols is `0x1009` instead of `0x0203` are the most remarkable differences.

```
#define PDB_PUB32 0x1009

// ----------------------------------------------------------------

typedef struct _PDB_PUBSYM
    {
    OMF_HEADER Header;
    DWORD      dReserved;
    DWORD      dOffset;
    WORD       wSegment;     // 1-based section index
    OMF_NAME   Name;         // zero-padded to next DWORD
    }
    PDB_PUBSYM, *PPDB_PUBSYM, **PPPDB_PUBSYM;

#define PDB_PUBSYM_ sizeof (PDB_PUBSYM)

#define PDB_PUBSYM_SIZE(_p) \
        ((DWORD) (_p)->Header.wRecordSize + sizeof (WORD))

#define PDB_PUBSYM_NEXT(_p) \
        ((PPDB_PUBSYM) ((PBYTE) (_p) + PDB_PUBSYM_SIZE (_p)))
```

LISTING 1-25. *The* `PDB_PUBSYM` *Structure*

The `IMG_PUBSYM` union in Listing 1-26 is a convenient means to reference symbol records regardless of their type. This union can be interpreted in three ways:

1. `OMF_HEADER`: This point of view should be assumed unless the symbol type is known. The header provides just enough information to identify the symbol type or to skip to the next record.
2. `CV_PUBSYM`: This interpretation is valid only if the `wRecordType` of the `OMF_HEADER` is set to `CV_PUB32 (0x0203)`.
3. `PDB_PUBSYM`: This interpretation is valid only if the `wRecordType` of the `OMF_HEADER` is set to `PDB_PUB32 (0x1009)`.

The `IMG_PUBSYM_SIZE()` and `IMG_PUBSYM_NEXT()` macros found at the end of Listing 1-26 allow type-independent determination of the size of the current record and the address of the subsequent one, respectively.

SYMBOL ADDRESS COMPUTATION

The `wSegment` and `dOffset` members of the `CV_PUBSYM` and `PDB_PUBSYM` symbol records, together with the `IMAGE_SECTION_HEADER` array at the beginning of the `.dbg` file, supply necessary information for the computation of the address of a symbol relative to the beginning of the module's base address. If the `.dbg` file

```
typedef union _IMG_PUBSYM
    {
    OMF_HEADER Header;     // CV_PUB32 or PDB_PUB32
    CV_PUBSYM  CvPubSym;
    PDB_PUBSYM PdbPubSym;
    }
    IMG_PUBSYM, *PIMG_PUBSYM, **PPIMG_PUBSYM;

#define IMG_PUBSYM_ sizeof (IMG_PUBSYM)

#define IMG_PUBSYM_SIZE(_p) \
        ((DWORD) (_p)->Header.wRecordSize + sizeof (WORD))

#define IMG_PUBSYM_NEXT(_p) \
        ((PIMG_PUBSYM) ((PBYTE) (_p) + IMG_PUBSYM_SIZE (_p)))
```

LISTING 1-26. *The* `IMG_PUBSYUM` *Union*

doesn't contain any OMAP data in the form of `IMAGE_DEBUG_TYPE_OMAP_TO_SRC` and `IMAGE_DEBUG_TYPE_OMAP_FROM_SRC` subsections, the address computation algorithm is straightforward:

- Read the `wSegment` value of the symbol record and decrement it by one.
- Use the resulting index to look up the `IMAGE_SECTION_HEADER` of the target section where the symbol resides.
- Retrieve the `VirtualAddress` of this `IMAGE_SECTION_HEADER`.
- Add the `dOffset` value of the symbol record.

In case the load address of the module is known, the absolute linear address of the symbol can be determined by simply adding the computed relative address to the base address. The `ImageBase` member of the `IMAGE_SEPARATE_DEBUG_HEADER` at the very beginning of the `.dbg` file specifies the module's preferred load address. Unfortunately, this address isn't very helpful because many kernel modules are actually loaded to completely different addresses. For example, `ntoskrnl.dbg` reports a preferred load address of `0x00400000`, which is certainly wrong because this address is far outside the kernel memory range. Therefore, the `w2k_img.dll` provides the `imgModuleBase()` API function that attempts to locate kernel modules in memory. It uses the undocumented `NtQuerySystemInformation()` function exported by `ntdll.dll` to retrieve a list of modules currently found in memory. However, this function works on Windows 2000/NT only. For Windows 9x compatibility, `imgModuleBase()` loads `ntdll.dll` dynamically, so `w2k_img.dll` won't blow up immediately with a dynalink error while it is being loaded. Therefore, it always returns a `NULL` pointer on Windows 9x. This is the same value that you will get on Windows 2000 and Windows NT 4.0 if the specified module is not present in memory.

OMAP ADDRESS CONVERSION

Several Windows 2000 symbol files contain OMAP subsections, identified by `IMAGE_DEBUG_DIRECTORY` entries with `Type` IDs of `IMAGE_DEBUG_TYPE_OMAP_TO_SRC` and `IMAGE_DEBUG_TYPE_OMAP_FROM_SRC`. OMAP is yet another undocumented feature of the Microsoft development tools, so the reasons for its existence are still somewhat speculative. The OMAP data inside a `.dbg` file consist of two arrays of `OMAP_TO_SRC` and `OMAP_FROM_SRC` structures, as outlined in Listing 1-27, and this information is used in the computation of symbol addresses from the offset values stored in `CV_PUBSYM` or `PDB_PUBSYM` records.

In one of his fine *MSJ* "Under the Hood" articles about Microsoft debug information, Matt Pietrek writes his thoughts about OMAP:

> *Yet another form of debug information is relatively new and undocumented, except for a few obscure references in WINNT.H and the Win32 SDK help. This type of information is known as OMAP. Apparently, as part of Microsoft's internal build procedure, small fragments of code in EXEs and DLLs are moved around to put the most commonly used code at the beginning of the code section. This presumably keeps the process memory working set as small as possible. However, when shifting around the blocks of code, the corresponding debug information isn't updated. Instead, OMAP information is created. It lets symbol table code translate between the original address in a symbol table and the modified address where the variable or line of code really exists in memory. (Pietrek 1997a)*

```
typedef struct _OMAP_TO_SRC
    {
    DWORD dTarget;
    DWORD dSource;
    }
    OMAP_TO_SRC, *POMAP_TO_SRC, **PPOMAP_TO_SRC;

#define OMAP_TO_SRC_ sizeof (OMAP_TO_SRC)

// -----------------------------------------------------------------

typedef struct _OMAP_FROM_SRC
    {
    DWORD dSource;
    DWORD dTarget;
    }
    OMAP_FROM_SRC, *POMAP_FROM_SRC, **PPOMAP_FROM_SRC;

#define OMAP_FROM_SRC_ sizeof (OMAP_FROM_SRC)
```

LISTING 1-27. *The* `OMAP_TO_SRC` *and* `OMAP_FROM_SRC` *Table Entries*

And more than 2 years later, *MSJ* columnist John Robbins elaborates on this assumption in the October 1997 "Bugslayer":

> *The undocumented OMAP information is interesting because it appears to have something to do with basic block relocations. (Fellow* MSJ *colleague Matt Pietrek briefly discussed this in the May 1997 "Under the Hood" column.) My guess is that Microsoft has some sort of internal tool that packs the binary so that the most common code is pushed up to the front and the rest is put in the rear so that the working set is much smaller. Consequently, this binary rearrangement makes the program faster because it will not have to page in as much of the program. (Robbins 1999)*

Although the working set argument is striking, the fact that the `ntoskrnl.exe` module makes heavy use of OMAP seems to be at odds with it. As I will show in Chapter 4, the entire `ntoskrnl.exe` module is mapped to a single 4-MB memory page that is always present in memory, so splitting the code into more frequently and more rarely used fractions shouldn't be of benefit with respect to paging. My assumption is that this split is supposed to aid the processor's instruction prefetch. Examination of the OMAP tables reveals that the addresses they contain typically point to the beginning of a function, to an instruction that immediately follows a jump or call, or to unused filler code. This suggests that the OMAP data is used to reshuffle the branches of `if/else` instructions. Obviously, the Windows 2000 kernel developers at Microsoft can somehow tell the compiler whether the `if` or `else` branch is executed more frequently, so the code fraction that is run less frequently can be moved out of the way. Normally, a compiler tends to keep the code of a function in a monolithic block, and doesn't split up `if/else` branches. In the Windows 2000 kernel modules, however, it can be easily observed that large functions with numerous `if/else` clauses are heavily fragmented. The fact that the OMAP code atoms correspond to conditional branches leads me to the assumption that OMAP has something to do with branch prediction. If less frequently executed branches are separated from the more frequently used ones, the CPU can perform more effective instruction prefetch.

The `OMAP_TO_SRC` table converts a real instruction offset to a source offset, for example, the real offset of the `ExInterlockedAddLargeInteger()` API function relative to the base address of `ntoskrnl.exe` is `0x0000231E`. To verify this, enter the command `u ExInterlockedAddLargeInteger` at the Kernel Debugger prompt—it will unassemble a couple of lines, starting at the linear address `0x8040231E`. Subtracting the `ntoskrnl.exe` load address `0x80400000` yields `0x0000231E`, as expected. If you scan the `OMAP_TO_SRC` table inside `ntoskrnl.dbg`, you will find an entry whose `dTarget` member is set to this offset, and the corresponding `dSource` offset is `0x0005E7E4`. The `ExInterlockedAddLargeInteger()` function is located in the `.text` section, and the offset of this section relative to the image base address is

0x000004C0 according to its IMAGE_SECTION_HEADER. Subtracting the section offset from the source offset yields a raw symbol offset of 0x0005E324, and this is exactly the dOffset value of the PDB_PUBSYM record that defines the ExInterlockedAddLargeInteger symbol. That's easy, isn't it? Well, not really.

The OMAP_TO_SRC entries are always sorted in ascending order with respect to the target address. This is a good idea, because it facilitates the lookup of addresses by binary searching. The OMAP_FROM_SRC table is essentially a replica of the OMAP_TO_SRC table, but with all source and target addresses swapped and resorted by source address. This dual-table approach allows easy address translation in both directions.

An OMAP problem that puzzled me for several days is that you cannot make immediate use of the VirtualAddress values stored in the IMAGE_SECTION_HEADER array of the .dbg file while converting from source to target addresses via the OMAP_FROM_SRC table. In all PE sections except for the first one, this will result in target addresses that are too high. The reason for this strange effect is that the VirtualAddress values are valid in the target address world only. On the source address side, different section addresses apply. The main problem is now to find out the source addresses of the PE sections. After scanning the .dbg and .pdb files repeatedly—but without success—for any tables that might perform this translation, I eventually ended up with a trick that works fine, although I'm not sure whether it is legal. To determine the source address of a section, I simply enumerate all OMAP_TO_SRC entries that belong to this section and compute the minimum of their source addresses. This procedure is based on the assumption that OMAP is just a permutation of code fractions, so minimizing the source addresses of a section means finding the snippet that has been bumped to the top of the section. This address should correspond to the source address of the section. I have applied this technique to numerous Windows 2000 symbol files, and thus far, it has not failed.

If it sounds appealing to implement a symbol file parser based on the above information, just do it! Or, you can use the w2k_img.dll on the sample CD as is or rip out code from it. This DLL contains everything you need to take .dbg and .pdb files apart and much more. The most powerful API function set it exports is the imgTable*() group. It comprises the three functions listed in Table 1-5, whose prototypes are shown in Listing 1-28. They are intended for use by debugger or disassembler writers. With the imgTableLookup() API function, an application can display symbols instead of raw addresses, and the imgTableResolve() function can be used as a basis for a symbol search option. Both functions are carefully optimized for speed, which is of great benefit to applications that browse large amounts of symbol information. The sample symbol browser presented below is based on w2k_img.dll and is able to dump a sorted list of all ntoskrnl.exe symbols with lots of additional information to a file in less than 2 seconds.

TABLE 1-5. *Symbol Table Management Functions Exported by* `w2k_img.dll`

NAME	DESCRIPTION
imgTableLoad()	Builds an `IMG_TABLE` symbol table from a `.dbg` or `.pdb` file
imgTableLookup()	Finds an `IMG_ENTRY` symbol table entry matching a symbol address
imgTableResolve()	Finds an `IMG_ENTRY` symbol table entry matching a symbol name

```
PIMG_TABLE WINAPI imgTableLoad (PTBYTE ptPath,
                               PVOID  pBase);

PIMG_ENTRY WINAPI imgTableLookup (PIMG_TABLE pit,
                                 PVOID      pAddress,
                                 PDWORD     dOffset);

PIMG_ENTRY WINAPI imgTableResolve (PIMG_TABLE pit,
                                  PBYTE      pbSymbol);
```

LISTING 1-28. *Prototypes of the Symbol Table Management Functions*

Listing 1-29 is a compilation of the structures on which the `imgTable*()` functions operate. Apparently, they don't resemble the CodeView and PDB structures discussed above. In fact, the symbol table management functions inside `w2k_img.dll` completely rearrange the information found in the symbol files, allowing easier and faster processing. The most fundamental structure is the `IMG_TABLE`, which comprises the entire symbol information. It is composed of a fixed-size header, an array of `IMG_ENTRY` structures, and three `IMG_INDEX` arrays. Because the arrays are of variable size depending on the number of symbols, the `IMG_TABLE` also contains three pointers to the `IMG_INDEX` base addresses. As indicated by the comments in Listing 1-29, the indexes are sorted by address, by name considering character case, and by name ignoring character case. These indexes are not only convenient for applications that output symbol lists, but also for the `imgTableLookup()` and `imgTableResolve()` functions because they allow them to perform fast binary searches for addresses and names.

One particularly nice feature of the `IMG_ENTRY` structure is that it specifies the calling convention assigned to a symbol. This information is derived directly from the symbol decoration, based on the rules in Table 1-4. This nontrivial task is done by the `imgSymbolUndecorate()` function shown in Listing 1-30. First, it tries to identify one of the common prefixes, listed in the `apbPrefixes[]` array. In the next step, the code looks for a stack size trailer consisting of an `@` character and a decimal number. The calling convention is detected along the way by testing for special prefix/trailer combinations. `w2k_img.dll` undecorates symbols with high reliability. Actually, it correctly handles all `__fastcall` import thunks that `imagehlp.dll` is unable to manage. `imgSymbolUndecorate()`, however, does not attempt to undecorate C++ and PCH symbols. Maybe I will add this feature in a future version of `w2k_img.dll`.

```
#define IMG_CONVENTION_UNDEFINED    0
#define IMG_CONVENTION_STDCALL      1
#define IMG_CONVENTION_CDECL        2
#define IMG_CONVENTION_FASTCALL     3

// -----------------------------------------------------------------

typedef struct _IMG_ENTRY
    {
    DWORD dSection;          // 1-based section number
    PVOID pAddress;          // symbol address
    DWORD dConvention;       // calling convention IMG_CONVENTION_*
    DWORD dStack;            // number of argument stack bytes
    BOOL  fExported;         // TRUE if exported symbol
    BOOL  fSpecial;          // TRUE if special symbol
    BYTE  abSection   [IMAGE_SIZEOF_SHORT_NAME+4]; // section name
    BYTE  abSymbol    [256]; // undecorated symbol name
    BYTE  abDecorated [256]; // decorated symbol name
    }
    IMG_ENTRY, *PIMG_ENTRY, **PPIMG_ENTRY;

#define IMG_ENTRY_ sizeof (IMG_ENTRY)

// -----------------------------------------------------------------

typedef struct _IMG_INDEX
    {
    PIMG_ENTRY apEntries [1];
    }
    IMG_INDEX, *PIMG_INDEX, **PPIMG_INDEX;

#define IMG_INDEX_ sizeof (IMG_INDEX)
#define IMG_INDEX__(_n) ((_n) * IMG_INDEX_)

// -----------------------------------------------------------------

typedef struct _IMG_TABLE
    {
    DWORD      dSize;      // table size in bytes
    DWORD      dSections;  // number of sections
    DWORD      dSymbols;   // number of symbols
    DWORD      dTimeStamp; // module time stamp (sec since 1-1-1970)
    DWORD      dCheckSum;  // module checksum
    PVOID      pBase;      // module base address
    PIMG_INDEX piiAddress; // entries sorted by address
    PIMG_INDEX piiName;    // entries sorted by name
    PIMG_INDEX piiNameIC;  // entries sorted by name (ignore case)
    BOOL       fUnicode;   // character format
    union
        {
```

(continued)

```
        TBYTE atPath [MAX_PATH]; // .dbg file path
        BYTE  abPath [MAX_PATH]; // .dbg file path (ANSI)
        WORD  awPath [MAX_PATH]; // .dbg file path (Unicode)
        };
    IMG_ENTRY  aEntries []; // symbol info array
    }
    IMG_TABLE, *PIMG_TABLE, **PPIMG_TABLE;

#define IMG_TABLE_ sizeof (IMG_TABLE)

#define IMG_TABLE__(_n) \
        (IMG_TABLE_ + ((_n) * IMG_ENTRY_) + (3 * IMG_INDEX__ (_n)))
```

LISTING 1-29. *Symbol Table Management Structures*

```
DWORD WINAPI imgSymbolUndecorate (PBYTE  pbSymbol,
                                  PBYTE  pbBuffer,
                                  PDWORD pdConvention)
    {
    PBYTE apbPrefixes [] = {"__imp__", "__imp_@", "__imp_",
                            "_", "@", "\x7F",
                            NULL};

    BYTE  abBuffer [256] = "";
    DWORD i, j, k, l;
    DWORD dConvention = IMG_CONVENTION_UNDEFINED;
    DWORD dStack      = -1;

    if (pbSymbol != NULL)
        {
        // skip common prefixes
        for (i = j = 0; apbPrefixes [i] != NULL; i++)
            {
            for (j = 0; apbPrefixes [i] [j]; j++)
                {
                if (apbPrefixes [i] [j] != pbSymbol [j]) break;
                }
            if (!apbPrefixes [i] [j]) break;
            j = 0;
            }
        // test for multiple '@'
        for (k = j, l = 0; (l < 2) && pbSymbol [k]; k++)
            {
            if (pbSymbol [k] == '@') l++;
            }
```

```
// don't undecorate if multiple '@', or C++ symbol
if ((l == 2) || (pbSymbol [0] == '?'))
    {
    j = 0;          // keep prefix
    k = MAXDWORD; // keep length
    }
else
    {
    // search for next '@'
    for (k = j; pbSymbol [k] && (pbSymbol [k] != '@'); k++);

    // read number of argument stack bytes if '@' found
    if (pbSymbol [k] == '@')
        {
        dStack = 0;

        for (l = k + 1; (pbSymbol [l] >= '0') &&
                        (pbSymbol [l] <= '9'); l++)
            {
            dStack *= 10;
            dStack += pbSymbol [l] - '0';
            }
        // don't undecorate if non-numeric or empty trailer
        if (pbSymbol [l] || (l == k + 1))
            {
            dStack = -1;  // no stack size info

            j = 0;          // keep prefix
            k = MAXDWORD; // keep length
            }
        }
    }
// determine calling convention if single-char prefix
if (j == 1)
    {
    switch (pbSymbol [0])
        {
        case '@':
            {
            dConvention = IMG_CONVENTION_FASTCALL;
            break;
            }
        case '_':
            {
```

(continued)

```
                    dConvention = (dStack != -1
                                   ? IMG_CONVENTION_STDCALL
                                   : IMG_CONVENTION_CDECL);
                    break;
                    }
                }
            }
        // copy selected name portion
        k = min (k - j, sizeof (abBuffer) - 1);
        lstrcpynA (abBuffer, pbSymbol + j, k + 1);
        }
    if (pbBuffer != NULL)
        {
        lstrcpyA (pbBuffer, abBuffer);
        }
    if (pdConvention != NULL) *pdConvention = dConvention;
    return dStack;
    }
```

LISTING 1-30. *The* `imgSymbolUndecorate()` *API Function*

Note that the `imgTableResolve()` function ignores all symbols with undefined calling convention. This restriction safely excludes all import thunk, C++, and PCH symbols. Unfortunately, it also excludes some of the "good" symbols that don't have standard decorations. I don't think, however, that this is a big problem, because these symbols are not among those most frequently used.

The basic framework of a `w2k_img.dll` client application is outlined in Listing 1-31. The application first loads the symbol table from the `.dbg` file specified by the `ptPath` argument, using the `imgTableLoad()` API function. If the file contains an `NB10` CodeView subsection, the associated PDB file is loaded seamlessly. If the returned pointer is valid, the symbol entries can be enumerated in four ways, described by the comments inside the `for()` loop. Basically, the client can use the original order of the symbols as they appear in the `.dbg` or `.pdb` file, or it can choose one of the predefined sort indexes. When the symbol processing is finished, the application has to destroy the symbol table by calling `imgMemoryDestroy()`. That's all! The application doesn't need any intimate knowledge about the internals of symbol files. All information it needs is stored in the `IMG_TABLE` and `IMG_ENTRY` structures set up by `imgTableLoad()`.

```
VOID WINAPI SymbolProcessor (PTBYTE ptPath)
    {
    PIMG_TABLE pit;
    PIMG_ENTRY pie;
    PVOID      pBase;
    DWORD      i;

    pBase = imgModuleBase (ptPath); // get current module load address

    if ((pit = imgTableLoad (ptPath, pBase)) != NULL)
        {
        for (i = j = 0; i < pit->dSymbols; i++)
            {
            // Option #1: default symbol order
            // pie = pit->aEntries + i;

            // Option #2: symbols sorted by address
            // pie = pit->piiAddress->apEntries [i];

            // Option #3: symbols sorted by name (case sensitive)
            // pie = pit->piiName->apEntries [i];

            // Option #4: symbols sorted by name (ignore case)
            // pie = pit->piiNameIC->apEntries [i];

            // Now, pie points to the IMG_ENTRY of the next symbol!
            // Do something useful with it ...

            }
        imgMemoryDestroy (pit);
        }
    return;
    }
```

LISTING 1-31. *Using the Symbol Table Management Functions*

A typical client application of `w2k_img.dll` will be presented in the next subsection. Note that I will return to this powerful utility DLL in Chapter 6, where it serves a rather unusual purpose: It looks up addresses of internal `ntoskrnl.exe` symbols that are neither documented nor exported, and a companion DLL uses this information to call into or read from these addresses. This trick sounds odd, but it works fine and can solve some tough programming and debugging problems. Stay tuned!

ANOTHER WINDOWS 2000 SYMBOL BROWSER

The sample application that shall demonstrate the usage of `w2k_img.dll` is an alternative version of the symbol browser presented in the previous section. It is named `w2k_sym2.exe`, but despite the name similarity, it is not just a rehash of `w2k_sym.exe`. The sample applications have quite different features and command options—just compare their command help screens, shown in Examples 1-5 and 1-11. The source code of `w2k_sym2.exe` is found on the CD accompanying this book in the `\src\w2k_sym2` directory tree.

Example 1-12 shows some sample output, generated by the command `w2k_sym2 +nu beep.sys`. The `+n` option selects sorting by name without consideration of the character case, and the `+u` option forces inclusion of symbols with unknown calling convention. The symbols with `CDECL` or `STDCALL` in the `ARGUMENTS` column refer to addresses of functions or global variables. The remaining rows in Example 1-12 are mostly import thunks into `ntoskrnl.exe` or `hal.dll`.

```
// w2k_sym2.exe
// SBS Windows 2000 Symbol Browser V1.00
// 08-27-2000 Sven B. Schreiber
// sbs@orgon.com

Usage: w2k_sym2 { [+-anNiprdxusz] [:<sections>] [/<symbols>] <path> }

       +   enable subsequent options
       -   disable subsequent option
       a   sort by address
       n   sort by name
       N   sort by name (case sensitive)
       i   ignore case in filter strings
       p   force preferred load address
       r   display relative addresses
       d   display decorated symbols
       x   display exported symbols only
       u   include symbols with unknown calling convention
       s   include special symbols
       z   include zero-address symbols

<sections> and <symbols> are filter expressions,
optionally containing the wildcards * and ?.
```

EXAMPLE 1-11. *The Command Help of* `w2k_sym2.exe`

```
// w2k_sym2.exe
// SBS Windows 2000 Symbol Browser V1.00
// 08-27-2000 Sven B. Schreiber
// sbs@orgon.com

Module name:    beep.sys
Time stamp:     Wednesday, 10-20-1999, 22:18:59
Base address:   0xF09CF000
Check sum:      0x0000C54F
Symbol file:    E:\WINNT\Symbols\sys\beep.dbg
Symbol table:   23520 bytes
Symbol filter:  *
Sections:       *

   # INDEX ADDRESS  SECTION    ARGUMENTS   X NAME
-------------------------------------------------------------------
   1     0 F09CF70C  2 .rdata              _allmul
   2     1 F09CF6B2  1 .text       CDECL     _allmul
   3     2 F09CF7B4  3 INIT        CDECL     _IMPORT_DESCRIPTOR_HAL
   4     3 F09CF7A0  3 INIT        CDECL     _IMPORT_DESCRIPTOR_ntoskrnl
   5     4 F09CF7C8  3 INIT        CDECL     _NULL_IMPORT_DESCRIPTOR
   6     5 F09CF34C  1 .text     8 STDCALL   BeepCancel
   7     6 F09CF39E  1 .text     8 STDCALL   BeepCleanup
   8     7 F09CF50E  1 .text     8 STDCALL   BeepClose
   9     8 F09CF456  1 .text     8 STDCALL   BeepDeviceControl
  10     9 F09CF4C0  1 .text     8 STDCALL   BeepOpen
  11    10 F09CF572  1 .text     8 STDCALL   BeepStartIo
  12    11 F09CF660  1 .text    10 STDCALL   BeepTimeOut
  13    12 F09CF67E  1 .text     4 STDCALL   BeepUnload
  14    13 F09CF29A  1 .text     8 STDCALL   DriverEntry
  15    14 F09CF6C0  2 .rdata    4           ExAcquireFastMutex
  16    15 F09CF6C4  2 .rdata    4           ExReleaseFastMutex
  17    16 F09CF6D4  2 .rdata                HAL_NULL_THUNK_DATA
  18    17 F09CF6D0  2 .rdata    4           HalMakeBeep
  19    18 F09CF724  2 .rdata    4           InterlockedDecrement
  20    19 F09CF6E0  2 .rdata    8           InterlockedExchange
  21    20 F09CF708  2 .rdata    4           InterlockedIncrement
  22    21 F09CF6E8  2 .rdata    4           IoAcquireCancelSpinLock
  23    22 F09CF714  2 .rdata   1C           IoCreateDevice
  24    23 F09CF710  2 .rdata    4           IoDeleteDevice
  25    24 F09CF6F4  2 .rdata    8           IofCompleteRequest
  26    25 F09CF6F8  2 .rdata    4           IoReleaseCancelSpinLock
  27    26 F09CF700  2 .rdata    8           IoStartNextPacket
  28    27 F09CF6EC  2 .rdata   10           IoStartPacket
  29    28 F09CF728  2 .rdata    4           KeCancelTimer
  30    29 F09CF718  2 .rdata    C           KeInitializeDpc
```

(continued)

```
 31    30 F09CF720  2 .rdata    C          KeInitializeEvent
 32    31 F09CF71C  2 .rdata    4          KeInitializeTimer
 33    32 F09CF6E4  2 .rdata    4          KeRemoveDeviceQueue
 34    33 F09CF6DC  2 .rdata    8          KeRemoveEntryDeviceQueue
 35    34 F09CF704  2 .rdata   10          KeSetTimer
 36    35 F09CF6CC  2 .rdata    4          KfLowerIrql
 37    36 F09CF6C8  2 .rdata    4          KfRaiseIrql
 38    37 F09CF6F0  2 .rdata    4          MmLockPagableDataSection
 39    38 F09CF6FC  2 .rdata    4          MmUnlockPagableImageSection
 40    39 F09CF72C  2 .rdata               ntoskrnl_NULL_THUNK_DATA
 41    40 F09CF6D8  2 .rdata    8          RtlInitUnicodeString
-----------------------------------------------------------------
 13 non-NULL symbols
  0 exported symbols
```

Example 1-12. *Sample Output of* w2k_sym2.exe

Note that the `_allmul` symbol appears twice in the list. The first one is an import thunk for the `_allmul()` function exported by `ntoskrnl.exe`; the other one is a simple function call forwarder that jumps through this thunk. If you add the `+d` switch to the command to view the symbols with full decoration, you can see that the `_allmul` import thunk is really called `__imp___allmul`, whereas the original name of the forwarder is `__allmul`. Obviously, those decorations *do* serve some useful purpose, even though they are sometimes quite distracting.

This chapter has presented extensive information. Maybe you didn't expect that there is so much to say about Windows 2000 debuggers, debugging APIs, and symbol files. Most Windows programming books don't dedicate much space to this kind of information. However, I believe that this essential background knowledge will help you in writing your own debugging utilities.

CHAPTER 2

The Windows 2000 Native API

This introductory chapter about the Windows 2000 Native API focuses on the relationships among the operating system modules that form the environment of this basic programming interface. Emphasis is on the central interrupt gate mechanism employed by Windows 2000 to route kernel service requests from user-mode to kernel-mode and back. Additionally, the Win32K interface and some of the major runtime libraries associated with the Native API will be presented, along with some of the most frequently used data types. The chapter closes with hints for those who want to write applications that interface to the Native API via the `ntdll.dll` library.

The architecture of Windows 2000 has been described in detail elsewhere. Many things written about Windows NT also apply to Windows 2000, so both editions of *Inside Windows NT* (Custer 1993, Solomon 1998) are good introductory books, as is the follow-up volume *Inside Windows 2000* (Solomon and Russinovich 2000).

THE NT*() AND ZW*() FUNCTION SETS

One of the most interesting facts about the architecture of Windows 2000 is that it can emulate various operating systems. Windows 2000 comes with three built-in subsystems for Win32, POSIX, and OS/2 applications. The Win32 subsystem is clearly the most popular, and therefore it is frequently regarded by application developers as *the* operating system itself. They cannot really be blamed for this misconception—this point of view is correct for legacy operating systems such as Windows 95 or 98, with which the Win32 interface implementation is actually a fundamental part of the system. However, Windows 2000 is designed quite differently. Although the Win32 subsystem contains a system module named `kernel32.dll`, this is actually not the real operating system kernel. Instead, it is just one of the basic components of the Win32 subsystem. In many programming books, software development for Windows

NT and 2000 is reduced to the task of interfacing to the Win32 Application Programming Interface (API), concealing the fact that the NT platform exposes yet another more basic interface called the *Native API*. Developers writing kernel-mode device or file system drivers are already familiar with the Native API, because kernel-mode modules are located on a low system level where the subsystems are invisible. However, you don't have to go down to the driver level to access this interface—even ordinary Win32 applications can call down to the Native API at any time. There's no technical restriction—it's just that Microsoft doesn't support this kind of application development. Thus, little information has been available on this topic, and neither the Windows Platform Software Development Kit (SDK) nor the Windows 2000 Device Drive Kit (DDK) make the Native API available to Win32 applications. So this work has been left to others, and this book is another piece of the puzzle.

LEVELS OF "UNDOCUMENTEDNESS"

Much of the material presented in this book refers to so-called undocumented information. In its global sense, this means that this information isn't published by Microsoft. However, there are several grades of "undocumentedness" because of the large amount of information that could possibly be published about a huge operating system such as Windows 2000. My personal category system looks as follows:

- *Officially documented:* The information is available in one of Microsoft's books, papers, or development kits. The most prominent information sources are the SDK, DDK, and the Microsoft Developer Network (MSDN) Library.
- *Semidocumented:* Although not officially documented, the information can be extracted from files officially distributed by Microsoft. For example, many Windows 2000 functions and structures aren't mentioned in the SDK or DDK documentation, but appear in some header files or sample programs. For Windows 2000, the most important sources of semidocumentation are the header files `ntddk.h` and `ntdef.h`, which are part of the DDK.
- *Undocumented, but not hidden:* The information in question is neither found in the official documentation nor included in any form in the developer products, but parts of it are available for debugging tools. All symbolic information contained in executable or symbol files belongs to this category. The best examples are the `!processfields` and `!threadfields` commands of the Kernel Debugger, which dump the names and offsets of the undocumented `EPROCESS` and `ETHREAD` structures (see Chapter 1).

- *Completely undocumented:* Some information bits are so well hidden by Microsoft, that they can be unveiled only by reverse engineering and inference. This class contains many implementation-specific details that nobody except the Windows 2000 developers should care about, but it also includes information that might be invaluable for system programmers, particularly developers of debugging software. Unveiling system internals such as this is extremely difficult, but also incredibly interesting, for someone who loves puzzles of a million pieces.

The Windows 2000 internals discussed in this book are equally distributed on levels two, three, and four of this category system, so there should be something for everyone.

The System Service Dispatcher

The relationship between the Win32 subsystem API and the Native API is best explained by showing the dependencies between the Win32 core modules and the Windows 2000 kernel. Figure 2-1 illustrates the module relationships, using boxes for modules and arrows for dependencies. If an arrow points from module A to module B, this means that A depends on B, that is, module A calls functions inside module B. Modules connected by double arrows are mutually dependent on each other. In Figure 2-1, the modules `user32.dll`, `advapi32.dll`, `gdi32.dll`, `rpcrt4.dll`, and `kernel32.dll` represent the basic Win32 API providers. Of course, there are other DLLs that contribute to this API, such as `version.dll`, `shell32.dll`, and `comctl32.dll`, but for clarity, I have omitted them. An interesting property illustrated in Figure 2-1 is that all Win32 API calls are ultimately routed through `ntdll.dll`, which forwards them to `ntoskrnl.exe`.

The `ntdll.dll` module is the operating system component that hosts the Native API. To be more exact, `ntdll.dll` is the user-mode front end of the Native API. The "real" interface is implemented in `ntoskrnl.exe`. The file name already suggests that this is the *NT Operating System Kernel*. In fact, kernel mode drivers call into this module most of the time if they require operating system services. The main role of `ntdll.dll` is to make a certain subset of kernel functions available to applications running in user mode, including the Win32 subsystem DLLs. In Figure 2-1, the arrow pointing from `ntdll.dll` to `ntoskrnl.exe` is labeled `INT 2Eh` to indicate that Windows 2000 uses an interrupt gate to switch the CPU's privilege level from user mode to kernel mode. Kernel-mode programmers view user-mode code as offensive, buggy, and dangerous. Therefore, this kind of code must be kept away from kernel functions. Switching the privilege level from user mode to kernel mode and back in the course of an API call is one way to handle this problem in a controlled manner. The calling application never really touches any kernel bytes—it can only look at them.

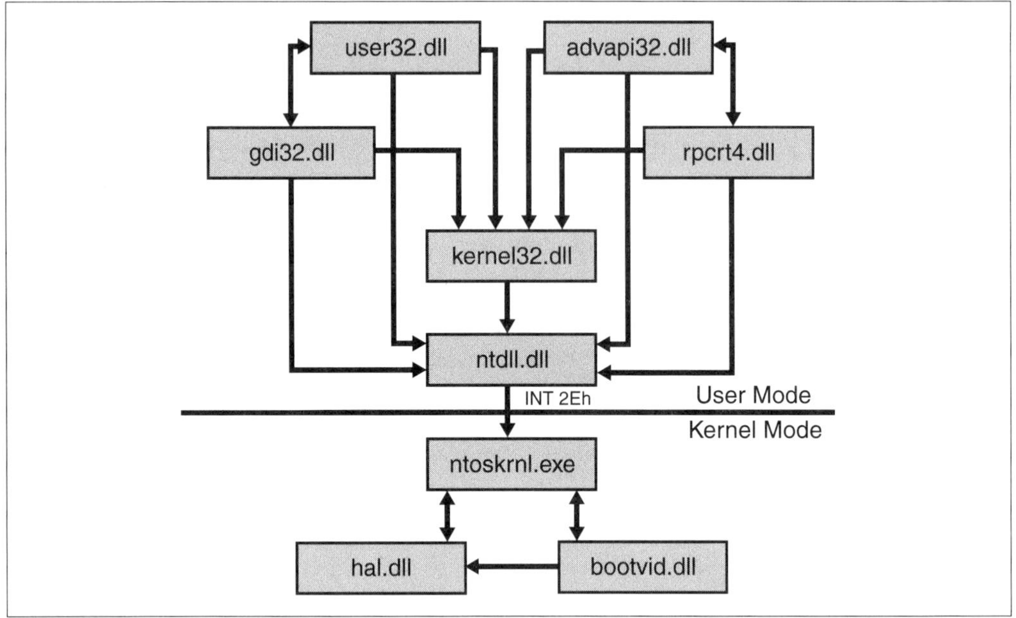

FIGURE 2-1. *System Module Dependencies*

For example, the Win32 API function `DeviceIoControl()` exported by `kernel32.dll` eventually calls the `ntdll.dll` export `NtDeviceIoControlFile()`. Disassembling this function reveals a surprisingly simple implementation, shown in Example 2-1. First, CPU register `EAX` is loaded with the magic number `0x38`, which is a dispatch ID. Next, register `EDX` is set up to point into the stack. The target address is the current value of the stack pointer `ESP` plus four, so `EDX` will point right behind the stack slot of the return address that has been saved on the stack immediately before entering `NtDeviceIoControlFile()`. Of course, this is the place where the arguments passed to the function are temporarily stored. The next instruction is a simple `INT 2Eh`, which branches to the interrupt handler stored in slot `0x2E` of the Interrupt Descriptor Table (IDT). Doesn't that look familiar? In fact, this code looks quite a bit like an old DOS `INT 21h` API call. However, the `INT 2Eh` interface of Windows 2000 is much more than a simple API call dispatcher—it serves as the main gate from user mode to kernel mode. Please note that this implementation of the mode switch is Intel i386 CPU specific. On the Alpha platform, different tricks are employed to achieve this transition.

```
NtDeviceIoControlFile:
        mov     eax, 38h
        lea     edx, [esp+4]
        int     2Eh
        ret     28h
```

EXAMPLE 2-1. *Implementation of* `ntdll.NtDeviceIoControlFile()`

The Windows 2000 Native API comprises 248 functions that are handled this way. That's 37 more than in Windows NT 4.0. You can easily recognize them by the function name prefix `Nt` in the `ntdll.dll` export list. There are 249 symbols of this kind exported by `ntdll.dll`. The reason for this mismatch is that one of the functions, `NtCurrentTeb()`, is a pure user-mode function and therefore isn't passed to the kernel. Table B-1 in Appendix B lists all available Native API functions, along with their `INT 2Eh` dispatch IDs, if any. The table also indicates which functions are exported by `ntoskrnl.exe`. Surprisingly, only a subset of the Native API can be called from kernel-mode modules. On the other hand, `ntoskrnl.exe` exports two `Nt*` symbols not provided by `ntdll.dll`, namely `NtBuildNumber` and `NtGlobalFlag`. Neither symbol refers to a function. Instead, they are pointers to `ntoskrnl.exe` variables that can be imported by a driver module using the C compiler's `extern` keyword. The Windows 2000 kernel exports many more variables in this manner, and the sample code following later will make use of some of them.

You may wonder why Table B-1 provides two columns for `ntdll.dll` and `ntoskrnl.exe`, respectively, labeled `ntdll.Nt*`, `ntdll.Zw*`, `ntoskrnl.Nt*`, and `ntoskrnl.Zw*`. The reason is that both modules export two sets of related Native API symbols. One of them comprises all names involving the `Nt` prefix, as listed in the leftmost column of Table B-1. The other set contains similar names, but with `Nt` replaced by `Zw`. Disassembly of `ntdll.dll` shows that each pair of symbols refers to exactly the same code. This may appear to be a waste of memory. However, if you disassemble `ntoskrnl.exe`, you will find that the `Nt*` symbols point to real code and the `Zw*` variants refer to `INT 2Eh` stubs such as the one shown in Example 2-1. This means that the `Zw*` function set is routed through the user-to-kernel-mode gate, and the `Nt*` symbols point directly to the code that is executed after the mode transition.

Two more things in Table B-1 should be noted. First, the function `NtCurrentTeb()` doesn't have a `Zw*` counterpart. This is not a big problem because the `Nt*` and `Zw*` functions exported by `ntdll.dll` are the same anyway. Second, `ntoskrnl.exe` doesn't consistently export `Nt/Zw` function pairs. Some of them come in either `Nt*` or `Zw*` versions only. I do not know the reason for this—I suppose that `ntoskrnl.exe` exports only the functions documented in the Windows 2000 DDK plus those required by other operating system modules. Note that the remaining Native API functions are nevertheless implemented inside `ntoskrnl.exe`. They don't feature a public entry point, but of course they may be reached from outside through the `INT 2Eh` gate.

THE SERVICE DESCRIPTOR TABLES

The disassembled code in Example 2-1 has shown that `INT 2Eh` is invoked with two parameters passed in the CPU registers `EAX` and `EDX`. I have already mentioned that the magic number in `EAX` is a dispatch ID. Because all Native API calls except `NtCurrentTeb()` are squeezed through the same hole, the code handling the `INT 2Eh` must determine which call should be dispatched to which function. That's why the dispatch ID is provided. The interrupt handler inside `ntoskrnl.exe` uses the value in `EAX` as an index into a lookup table, where it finds the information required to route the call to its ultimate destination. This table is called a System Service Table (SST), and the corresponding C structure `SYSTEM_SERVICE_TABLE` is defined in Listing 2-1. This listing also comprises the definition of a structure named `SERVICE_DESCRIPTOR_TABLE`, which is a four-member array of SSTs, the first two of which serve special purposes.

Although both tables are fundamental data types, they are not documented in the Windows 2000 DDK, which leads to the following important statement: Many code snippets reprinted in this book contain undocumented data types and functions. Therefore, there's no guarantee that this information is authentic. This is true for all symbolic information, such as structure names, structure members, and arguments. When creating symbols, I attempt to use appropriate names, based on the naming scheme apparent through the small subset of known symbols (including those available from the symbol files). However, this heuristic approach is likely to fail on many occasions. Only the original source code contains the full information, but I don't have access to it. Actually, I don't *want* to see the source code, because this would require a Non-Disclosure Agreement (NDA) with Microsoft, and the ties of an NDA would make it quite difficult to write a book about undocumented information.

So let's return to the secrets of the Service Descriptor Table (SDT). Its definition in Listing 2-1 shows that the first pair of slots is reserved for `ntoskrnl.exe` and the kernel-mode part of the Win32 subsystem buried inside the `win32k.sys` module. The calls dispatched through the `win32k` SST originate from `gdi32.dll` and `user32.dll`. `ntoskrnl.exe` exports a pointer to its main SDT via the symbol `KeServiceDescriptorTable`. The kernel maintains an alternative SDT named `KeServiceDescriptorTableShadow`, but this one is not exported. It is very simple to access the main SDT from a kernel-mode module—you need only two C instructions, as shown in Listing 2-2. The first is a simple variable declaration preceded by the `extern` keyword, which tells the linker that this variable is not part of the module and the corresponding symbol cannot be resolved at link time. All references to this symbol are linked dynamically as soon as the module is loaded into the address space of a process. The second C instruction in Listing 2-2 is such a reference. Assigning `KeServiceDescriptorTable` to a variable of type `PSERVICE_DESCRIPTOR_TABLE` causes the creation of a dynamic link to `ntoskrnl.exe`, similar to an API call into a DLL module.

```
typedef NTSTATUS (NTAPI *NTPROC) ();
typedef NTPROC *PNTPROC;
#define NTPROC_ sizeof (NTPROC)

// --------------------------------------------------------------

typedef struct _SYSTEM_SERVICE_TABLE
    {
    PNTPROC ServiceTable;           // array of entry points
    PDWORD  CounterTable;           // array of usage counters
    DWORD   ServiceLimit;           // number of table entries
    PBYTE   ArgumentTable;          // array of byte counts
    }
        SYSTEM_SERVICE_TABLE,
      * PSYSTEM_SERVICE_TABLE,
    **PPSYSTEM_SERVICE_TABLE;

// --------------------------------------------------------------

typedef struct _SERVICE_DESCRIPTOR_TABLE
    {
    SYSTEM_SERVICE_TABLE ntoskrnl;  // ntoskrnl.exe (native api)
    SYSTEM_SERVICE_TABLE win32k;    // win32k.sys (gdi/user support)
    SYSTEM_SERVICE_TABLE Table3;    // not used
    SYSTEM_SERVICE_TABLE Table4;    // not used
    }
        SERVICE_DESCRIPTOR_TABLE,
      * PSERVICE_DESCRIPTOR_TABLE,
    **PPSERVICE_DESCRIPTOR_TABLE;
```

LISTING 2-1. *Structure of the Service Descriptor Table*

```
// Import SDT pointer
extern PSERVICE_DESCRIPTOR_TABLE KeServiceDescriptorTable;

// Create SDT reference
PSERVICE_DESCRIPTOR_TABLE psdt = KeServiceDescriptorTable;
```

LISTING 2-2. *Accessing the Service Descriptor Table*

The `ServiceTable` member of each SST contained in an SDT points to an array of function pointers of type `NTPROC`, which is a convenient placeholder for the Native API functions, similar to the `PROC` type used in Win32 programming. `NTPROC` is defined at the top of Listing 2-1. Native API functions typically return an `NTSTATUS` code and use the `NTAPI` calling convention, which is synonymous to `__stdcall`. The `ServiceLimit` member holds the number of entries found in the `ServiceTable` array. On Windows 2000, its default value is 248. The `ArgumentTable` is an array of `BYTEs`, each one corresponding to a `ServiceTable` slot and indicating the number of argument bytes (!) available on the caller's stack. This information, along with the pointer supplied in register `EDX`, is required by the kernel when it copies the arguments from the caller's stack to its own, as described below. The `CounterTable` member is not used in the free build of Windows 2000. In the debug build, this member points to an array of `DWORDs` that represent usage counters for each function. This information can be used for profiling purposes.

It is easy to display the contents of the SDT using the Windows 2000 Kernel Debugger. Please refer to Chapter 1 if you haven't yet set up this very useful application. In Example 2-2, I have first issued the command `dd KeServiceDescriptorTable`. The debugger resolves this public symbol to `0x8046AB80` and displays a hex dump of the next 32 `DWORDs` at this address. Only the first four rows are significant, corresponding to the four `SDT` members in Listing 2-1. For better readability, they are printed in boldface. If you take a closer look, you will see that the fifth row looks exactly like the first—could this be another SDT? This is a great occasion for a test of the Kernel Debugger's `ln` command (List Nearest Symbols). In Example 2-2. right after the hex dump of `KeServiceDescriptorTable`, I have entered the command `ln 8046abc0`. Obviously, the debugger knows the address `0x8046abc0` well and converts it to the symbol `KeServiceDescriptorTableShadow`, proving that this is indeed the second SDT maintained by the kernel. The obvious difference between the SDTs is that the latter contains entries for `win32k.sys`, whereas the former doesn't. In both tables, the members `Table3` and `Table4` are empty. `ntoskrnl.exe` provides a convenient API function named `KeAddSystemServiceTable()` to fill these slots.

```
kd> dd KeServiceDescriptorTable
dd KeServiceDescriptorTable
8046ab80  804704d8 00000000 000000f8 804708bc
8046ab90  00000000 00000000 00000000 00000000
8046aba0  00000000 00000000 00000000 00000000
8046abb0  00000000 00000000 00000000 00000000
8046abc0  804704d8 00000000 000000f8 804708bc
8046abd0  a01859f0 00000000 0000027f a0186670
```

```
8046abe0  00000000 00000000 00000000 00000000
8046abf0  00000000 00000000 00000000 00000000
kd> ln 8046abc0
ln 8046abc0
(8047b3a0)   ntoskrnl!KeServiceDescriptorTableShadow

kd> ln 804704d8
ln 804704d8
(8046cd00)   ntoskrnl!KiServiceTable

kd> ln 804708bc
ln 804708bc
(8046d0e4)   ntoskrnl!KiArgumentTable

kd> ln a01859f0
ln a01859f0
(a016d8c0)   win32k!W32pServiceTable

kd> ln a0186670
ln a0186670
(a016e544)   win32k!W32pArgumentTable

kd> dd KiServiceTable
dd KiServiceTable
804704d8  804ab3bf 804ae86b 804bdef3 8050b034
804704e8  804c11f4 80459214 8050c2ff 8050c33f
804704f8  804b581c 80508874 8049860a 804fc7e2
80470508  804955f7 8049c8a6 80448472 804a8d50
80470518  804b6bfb 804f0cef 804fcb95 8040189a
80470528  804d06cb 80418f66 804f69d4 8049e0cc
80470538  8044c422 80496f58 804ab849 804aa9da
80470548  80465250 804f4bd5 8049bc80 804ca7a5

kd> db KiArgumentTable
db KiArgumentTable
804708bc  18 20 2c 2c 40 2c 40 44-0c 18 18 08 04 04 0c 10  . ,,@,@D........
804708cc  18 08 08 0c 08 08 04 04-04 0c 04 20 08 0c 14 0c  ........... ....
804708dc  2c 10 0c 1c 20 10 38 10-14 20 24 1c 14 10 20 10  ,.... .8.. $... .
804708ec  34 14 08 04 04 04 0c 08-28 04 1c 18 18 18 08 18  4.......(.......
804708fc  0c 08 0c 04 10 00 0c 10-28 08 08 10 00 1c 04 08  ........(.......
8047090c  0c 04 10 00 08 04 08 0c-28 10 04 0c 0c 28 24 28  ........(....($(
8047091c  30 0c 0c 0c 18 0c 0c 0c-0c 30 10 0c 0c 0c 0c 10  0........0......
8047092c  10 0c 0c 14 0c 14 18 14-08 14 08 08 04 2c 1c 24  .............,.$

kd> ln 8044c422
ln 8044c422
(80449c90)   ntoskrnl!NtClose
```

EXAMPLE 2-2. *Examination of the Service Descriptor Tables*

Note that I have truncated the output lines of the `ln` command, to demonstrate only the essential information.

At address `0x8046AB88` of the `KeServiceDescriptorTable` hex dump, where the `ServiceLimit` member should be located, the value `0xF8`—248 in decimal notation—shows up, as expected. The values of `ServiceTable` and `ArgumentTable` are pointers to the addresses `0x804704d8` and `0x804708bc`, respectively. This is another case for the `ln` command, revealing the names `KiServiceTable` and `KiArgumentTable`, respectively. None of these symbols is exported by `ntoskrnl.exe`, but the debugger recognizes them by looking into the Windows 2000 symbol files. The `ln` command can also be applied to the pointers in the `win32k` SST. For the `ServiceTable` and `ArgumentTable` members, the debugger reports `W32pServiceTable` and `W32pArgumentTable`, respectively. Both symbols are taken from the symbol file of `win32k.sys`. If the debugger refuses to resolve these addresses, issue the `.reload` command to force a reload of all available symbol files and try again.

The remaining parts of Example 2-2 are hex dumps of the first 128 bytes of `KiServiceTable` and `KiArgumentTable`. If the things I said about the Native API so far are correct, then the `NtClose()` function should be addressed by slot 24 of `KiServiceTable`, located at address `0x80470538`. The value found there is `0x8044c422`, marked boldface in the results of the `dd KiServiceTable` command. Applying the `ln` command to this address yields `NtClose()`. As a final test, let's examine slot 24 of `KiArgumentTable` at address `0x804708d4`. In the Windows 2000 DDK, `ZwClose()` is documented as receiving a single argument of type `HANDLE`, so the number of argument bytes on the caller's stack should amount to four. It doesn't come as a big surprise that this is exactly the value found in the argument table, marked boldface in the results of the `db KiArgumentTable` command.

THE INT 2Eh SYSTEM SERVICE HANDLER

The interrupt handler lurking at the kernel-mode side of the `INT 2Eh` gate is labeled `KiSystemService()`. Again, this is an internal symbol not exported by `ntoskrnl.exe`, but contained in the Windows 2000 symbol files. Therefore, the Kernel Debugger can resolve it without problem. Essentially, `KiSystemService()` performs the following steps:

1. Retrieve the SDT pointer from the current thread's control block.
2. Determine which one of the four SSTs in the SDT should be used. This is done by testing bits 12 and 13 of the dispatch ID in register `EAX` and selecting the corresponding SDT member. IDs in the range `0x0000-0x0FFF` are mapped to the `ntoskrnl` table; the range `0x1000-0x1FFF` is assigned to

the win32k table. The remaining ranges 0x2000-0x2FFF and 0x3000-0x3FFF are reserved for the additional SDT members Table3 and Table4. If an ID exceeds 0x3FFF, the unwanted bits are masked off before dispatching.

3. Check bits 0 to 11 of the dispatch ID in register EAX against the ServiceLimit member of the selected SST. If the ID is out of range, an error code of STATUS_INVALID_SYSTEM_SERVICE is returned. In an unused SST, this member is zero, yielding an error code for all possible dispatch IDs.
4. Check the argument stack pointer in register EDX against the value of MmUserProbeAddress. This is a public variable exported from ntoskrnl.exe and usually evaluates to 0x7FFF0000. If the argument pointer is not below this address, STATUS_ACCESS_VIOLATION is returned.
5. Look up the number of argument stack bytes in the ArgumentTable referenced by the SST, and copy all function arguments from the caller's stack to the current kernel-mode stack.
6. Look up the service function pointer in the ServiceTable referenced by the SST, and call this function.
7. Transfer control to the internal function KiServiceExit() after returning from the service call.

It is interesting to see that the INT 2Eh handler doesn't use the global SDT addressed by KeServiceDescriptorTable, but uses a thread-specific pointer instead. Obviously, threads can have different SDTs associated to them. On thread initialization, KeInitializeThread() writes the KeServiceDescriptorTable pointer to the thread control block. However, this default setting may be changed later to a different value, such as KeServiceDescriptorTableShadow, for example.

THE WIN32 KERNEL-MODE INTERFACE

The discussion of the SDT in the previous section has shown that a second main kernel-mode interface exists along with the Native API. This interface connects the Graphics Device Interface (GDI) and the Window Manager (USER) of the Win32 subsystem to a kernel-mode component called Win32K, introduced with Windows NT 4.0, and residing in the file win32k.sys. This component has been added to overcome an inherent performance limit of the Win32 display engine, caused by the original Windows NT subsystem design. On Windows NT 3.x, the client-server model imposed on the Win32 subsystem and the kernel involved frequent switches from user-mode to kernel-mode and back. By moving considerable parts of the display engine to the kernel-mode module win32k.sys, much of this overhead could be eliminated.

WIN32K DISPATCH IDS

Now that `win32k.sys` has entered the scene, it's time for an update of Figure 2-1. Figure 2-2 is based on the original drawing, but with a `win32k.sys` box added to the left of `ntoskrnl.exe`. I have also added arrows pointing from `gdi32.dll` and `user32.dll` to `win32k.sys`. Of course, this is not 100 percent correct, because the `INT 2Eh` calls inside these modules are actually directed to `ntoskrnl.exe`, which owns the interrupt handler. However, the calls are ultimately handled by `win32k.sys`, and this is what the arrows should indicate.

As pointed out earlier, the Win32K interface is also based on the `INT 2Eh` dispatcher, much like the Native API. The only difference is that Win32K uses a different range of dispatch IDs. Although all Native API calls involve dispatch IDs that range from `0x0000` to `0x0FFF`, Win32K dispatch IDs are numbers between `0x1000` and `0x1FFF`. As Figure 2-2 demonstrates, the primary Win32K clients are `gdi32.dll` and `user32.dll`. Therefore, it should be possible to find out the symbolic names associated to the Win32K dispatch IDs by disassembling these modules. As it turns out, only a small subset of `INT 2Eh` calls has public names in their export sections, so it is again time for a Kernel Debugger session. In Example 2-3, I have issued the command `dd W32pServiceTable`. To be sure that the `win32k.sys` symbols are available, it is preceded by a `.reload` command.

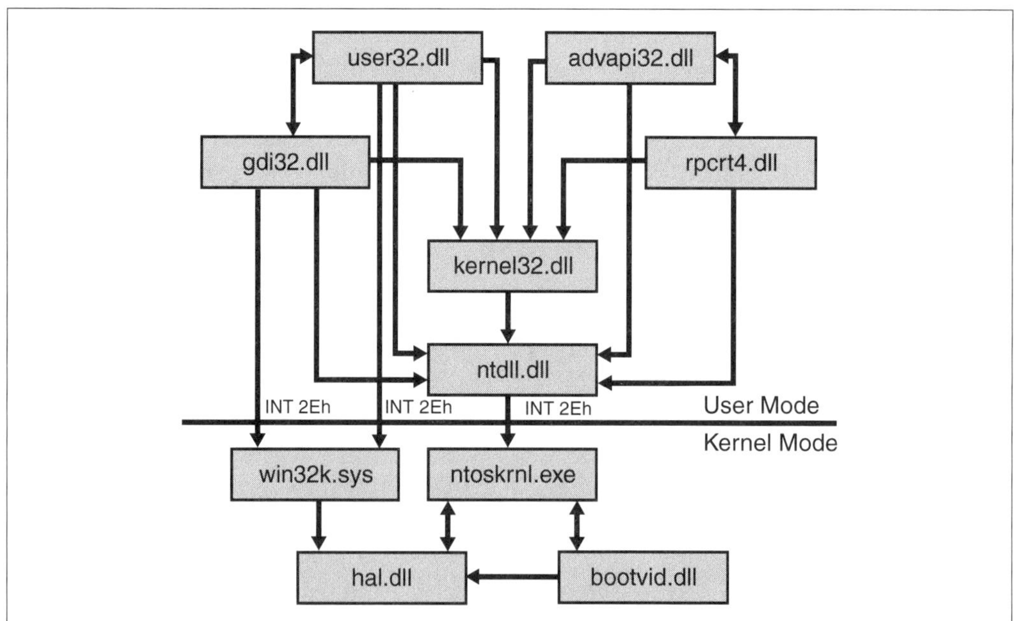

FIGURE 2-2. *System Module Dependencies, including* `win32k.sys`

```
kd> .reload
.reload
Loading Kernel Symbols...
Unable to read image header for fdc.sys at f0798000 - status c0000001
Unable to read image header for ATMFD.DLL at beaaf000 - status c0000001
Loading User Symbols...
Unable to read selector for PCR for Processor 0
PPEB is NULL (Addr= 0000018c)

kd> dd W32pServiceTable
dd W32pServiceTable
a01859f0  a01077f0 a011f59e a000788a a01141e1
a0185a00  a0121264 a0107e05 a01084df a010520b
a0185a10  a0120a6f a008c9eb a00befa2 a007cb5c
a0185a20  a0085c9b a001e4e7 a0120fd1 a0122d19
a0185a30  a0085d0c a0122e73 a0027671 a006d1f0
a0185a40  a0043fe0 a009baeb a007eb9b a009eb05
a0185a50  a0043392 a007c14f a01229cc a0027470
a0185a60  a001ad09 a00af751 a004e9f5 a004ef53

kd> ln a01077f0
ln a01077f0
(a00b316e)   win32k!NtGdiAbortDoc   |  (a00ba173)      win32k!IsRectEmpty
```

EXAMPLE 2-3. *Examination of the Win32K System Services*

In the last three lines of Example 2-3, I have applied the `ln` command to the first entry in the `W32pServiceTable` hex dump. So the Win32K function with dispatch ID zero is obviously called `NtGdiAbortDoc()`. You can repeat this procedure for all 639 dispatch IDs, but it is better to automate the symbol lookup. I have done this for you, and the results are collected in Appendix B, Table B-2. The symbol mapping from `gdi32.dll` and `user32.dll` to `win32k.sys` is simple: A GDI symbol is converted to a Win32K symbol by adding the prefix `NtGdi`, and a USER symbol is converted by adding `NtUser`. However, there are some minor exceptions. For example, if a GDI symbol starts out with `Gdi`, the prefix is reduced to `Nt`, probably to avoid the character sequence `NtGdiGdi`. In some other instances, the character case is different (e.g., `EnableEUDC()` and `NtGdiEnableEudc()`), or a trailing W marking a Unicode function is missing (e.g., `CopyAcceleratorTableW()` and `NtUserCopyAcceleratorTable()`).

Documenting the complete Win32K API in detail would be a tremendous effort. The function set is almost three times larger than the Native API. Maybe someday someone will pick up the pieces and write a great reference handbook, like Gary Nebbett did for the Native API (Nebbett 2000). For the scope of this book, the above information should suffice, however.

THE WINDOWS 2000 RUNTIME LIBRARY

The Nt*() and Zw*() functions making up the Native API are an essential, but nevertheless minor, part of the code found inside ntdll.dll. This DLL exports no fewer than 1179 symbols. 249/248 of them belong to the Nt*()/Zw*() sets, so there are still 682 functions left that are not routed through the INT 2Eh gate. Obviously, this large group of functions doesn't rely on the Windows 2000 kernel. So what purpose do they serve?

THE C RUNTIME LIBRARY

If you study the symbols in the export section of ntdll.dll, you will find many lowercase function names that look quite familiar to a C programmer. These well-known names, such as memcpy(), sprintf(), and qsort(), are members of the C Runtime Library incorporated into ntdll.dll. The same is true for ntoskrnl.exe, which features a similar set of C Runtime functions, although these sets are not identical. Table B-3 in Appendix B lists the union of both sets and points out which ones are available from which module.

You can link to these functions by simply adding the file ntdll.lib from the Windows 2000 DDK to the list of import libraries that should be scanned by the linker during symbol resolution. If you prefer using dialogs, you can choose the **Settings...** entry from the **Project** menu of Visual C/C++, click the **Link** tab, select the category **General,** and append ntdll.dll to the **Object/library modules** list. Alternatively, you can add the line #pragma comment (linker, "/defaultlib:ntdll.lib") somewhere to your source code. This has the same effect, but has the advantage that other developers can rebuild your project with default Visual C/C++ settings.

Disassembling the code of some of the C Runtime functions available from both ntdll.dll and ntoskrnl.exe shows that ntdll.dll does not rely on ntoskrnl.exe here, like it did with respect to the Native API functions. Instead, both modules implement the functions separately. The same applies to all other functions presented in this section. Note that some of these functions in Table B-3 aren't intended for import by name. For example, if you are using the shift operators >> and << on 64-bit LARGE_INTEGER numbers in a kernel-mode driver, the compiler and linker will automatically import the _allshr() and _allshl() functions from ntoskrnl.exe, respectively.

THE EXTENDED RUNTIME LIBRARY

Along with the standard C Runtime, Windows 2000 provides an extended set of runtime functions. Again, both ntdll.dll and ntoskrnl.exe implement them separately, and, again, the implemented sets overlap, but don't match exactly. The functions belonging to this group share the common name prefix `Rtl` (for Runtime Library). Table B-4 in Appendix B lists them all, using the same layout as Table B-3. The Windows 2000 Runtime Library contains helper functions for common tasks that go beyond the capabilities of C Runtime. For example, some of them handle security issues, others manipulate Windows 2000–specific data structures, and still others support memory management. It is hard to understand why Microsoft documents just 115 out of these 406 extremely useful functions in the Windows 2000 DDK.

THE FLOATING-POINT EMULATOR

I'll conclude this gallery of API functions with another function set provided by `ntdll.dll`, just to show how many interesting functions are buried inside this goldmine. Table 2-1 lists a set of names that should look somewhat familiar to assembly language programmers. Take one of the names starting with `__e` and strip this prefix—you get an assembly language mnemonic of the floating-point unit (FPU) built into the i386-compatible CPUs. In fact, `ntdll.dll` contains a full-fledged floating-point emulator, represented by the functions in Table 2-1. This proves again that this DLL is an immense repository of code and almost invites a system spelunker to disassembly.

TABLE 2-1. *The Floating Point Emulator Interface of* ntdll.dll

FUNCTION NAMES			
__eCommonExceptions	__eFIST32	__eFLD64	__eFSTP32
__eEmulatorInit	__eFISTP16	__eFLD80	__eFSTP64
__eF2XM1	__eFISTP32	__eFLDCW	__eFSTP80
__eFABS	__eFISTP64	__eFLDENV	__eFSTSW
__eFADD32	__eFISUB16	__eFLDL2E	__eFSUB32
__eFADD64	__eFISUB32	__eFLDLN2	__eFSUB64
__eFADDPreg	__eFISUBR16	__eFLDPI	__eFSUBPreg
__eFADDreg	__eFISUBR32	__eFLDZ	__eFSUBR32
__eFADDtop	__eFLD1	__eFMUL32	__eFSUBR64
__eFCHS	__eFIDIVR16	__eFMUL64	__eFSUBreg
__eFCOM	__eFIDIVR32	__eFMULPreg	__eFSUBRPreg
__eFCOM32	__eFILD16	__eFMULreg	__eFSUBRreg
__eFCOM64	__eFILD32	__eFMULtop	__eFSUBRtop
__eFCOMP	__eFILD64	__eFPATAN	__eFSUBtop
__eFCOMP32	__eFIMUL16	__eFPREM	__eFTST

(continued)

TABLE 2-1. *(continued)*

FUNCTION NAMES			
__eFCOMP64	__eFIMUL32	__eFPREM1	__eFUCOM
__eFCOMPP	__eFINCSTP	__eFPTAN	__eFUCOMP
__eFCOS	__eFINIT	__eFRNDINT	__eFUCOMPP
__eFDECSTP	__eFIST16	__eFRSTOR	__eFXAM
__eFIDIVR16	__eFIST32	__eFSAVE	__eFXCH
__eFIDIVR32	__eFISTP16	__eFSCALE	__eFXTRACT
__eFILD16	__eFISTP32	__eFSIN	__eFYL2X
__eFILD32	__eFISTP64	__eFSQRT	__eFYL2XP1
__eFILD64	__eFISUB16	__eFST	__eGetStatusWord
__eFIMUL16	__eFISUB32	__eFST32	NPXEMULATORTABLE
__eFIMUL32	__eFISUBR16	__eFST64	RestoreEm87Context
__eFINCSTP	__eFISUBR32	__eFSTCW	SaveEm87Context
__eFINIT	__eFLD1	__eFSTENV	
__eFIST16	__eFLD32	__eFSTP	

For more information about the floating-point instruction set, please consult the original documentation of the Intel CPUs 80386 and up. For example, the Pentium manuals can be downloaded in PDF format from Intel's Web site at http://developer.intel.com/design/pentium/manuals/. The manual explaining the machine code instruction set is called *Intel Architecture Software Developer's Manual. Volume 2: Instruction Set Reference* (Intel 1999b). Another great reference book with detailed FPU information is Robert L. Hummel's aged but still applicable i486 handbook (Hummel 1992).

OTHER API FUNCTION CATEGORIES

Along with the functions listed explicitly in Appendix B and Table 2-1, `ntdll.dll` and `ntoskrnl.exe` export numerous other functions specific to various components of the kernel. Rather than add more lengthy tables to this book, I'm including a short one that lists the available function name prefixes with their associated categories (Table 2-2). The `ntdll.dll` and `ntoskrnl.exe` columns contain the entry N/A (not applicable) for modules that do not export functions of this category.

TABLE 2-2. *Function Prefix to Function Category Mapping*

PREFIX	ntdll.dll	ntoskrnl.exe	CATEGORY
__e		N/A	Floating-point emulator
Cc	N/A		Cache manager
Csr		N/A	Client-server runtime library
Dbg			Debugging support
Ex	N/A		Executive support
FsRtl	N/A		File system runtime library
Hal	N/A		Hardware Abstraction Layer (HAL) dispatcher
Inbv	N/A		System initialization/VGA boot driver (bootvid.dll)
Init	N/A		System initialization
Interlocked	N/A		Thread-safe variable manipulation
Io	N/A		I/O manager
Kd	N/A		Kernel Debugger support
Ke	N/A		Kernel routines
Ki			Kernel interrupt handling
Ldr			Image loader
Lpc	N/A		Local Procedure Call (LPC) facility
Lsa	N/A		Local Security Authority (LSA)
Mm	N/A		Memory manager
Nls			National Language Support (NLS)
Nt			NT Native API
Ob	N/A		Object manager
Pfx			Prefix handling
Po	N/A		Power manager
Ps	N/A		Process support
READ_REGISTER_	N/A		Read from register address
Rtl			Windows 2000 runtime library
Se	N/A		Security handling
WRITE_REGISTER_	N/A		Write to register address
Zw			Alternative Native API
<other>			Helper functions and C runtime library

N/A, Not applicable.

Many kernel functions use a uniform naming scheme of type `PrefixOperationObject()`. For example, the function `NtQueryInformationFile()` belongs to the Native API because of its `Nt` prefix, and obviously it executes a `QueryInformation operation on a File object`. Not all functions obey this rule, but many do, so it is usually easy to guess what a function does by simply parsing its name.

FREQUENTLY USED DATA TYPES

When writing software that interacts with the Windows 2000 kernel—whether in user-mode via `ntdll.dll` or in kernel-mode via `ntoskrnl.exe`—you will have to deal with a couple of basic data types that are rarely seen in the Win32 world. Many of them appear repeatedly in this book. The following section outlines the most frequently used types.

INTEGRAL TYPES

Traditionally, integral data types come in several different variations. Neither the Win32 Platform SDK header files nor the SDK documentation commit themselves to a special nomenclature—they mix fundamental C/C++ types with several derived types. Table 2-3 lists the commonly used integral types, showing their equivalence relationships. In the "MASM" column, the assembly language type names expected by the Microsoft Macro Assembler (MASM) are shown. The Win32 Platform SDK defines `BYTE`, `WORD`, and `DWORD` as aliases for the corresponding fundamental C/C++ data types. The columns "Alias #1" and "Alias #2" contain other frequently used aliases. For example, `WCHAR` represents the basic Unicode character type. The last column, "Signed," lists the usual aliases of the corresponding signed data types. It is important to keep in mind that ANSI characters of type `CHAR` are signed quantities, whereas the Unicode `WCHAR` is unsigned. This inconsistency can lead to unexpected side effects when the compiler converts these types to other integral values in arithmetic or logical expressions.

The MASM `TBYTE` type (read "10-byte") in the last row of Table 2-3 is an 80-bit floating-point number used in high-precision floating-point unit (FPU) operations. Microsoft Visual C/C++ doesn't offer an appropriate fundamental data type to Win32 programs—the 80-bit *long double* type featured by Microsoft's 16-bit compilers is now treated like a *double,* that is, i.e. a signed 64-bit number with an 11-bit exponent and a 52-bit mantissa, according to the IEEE `real*8` specification. Please note that the MASM `TBYTE` type has nothing to do with the Win32 `TBYTE` (read "text byte"), which is a convenient macro that can define a `CHAR` or `WCHAR` type, depending on the absence or presence of a `#define UNICODE` line in the source code.

TABLE 2-3. *Equivalent Integral Data Types*

BITS	MASM	FUNDAMENTAL	ALIAS #1	ALIAS #2	SIGNED
8	BYTE	unsigned char	UCHAR		CHAR
16	WORD	unsigned short	USHORT	WCHAR	SHORT
32	DWORD	unsigned long	ULONG		LONG
32	DWORD	unsigned int	UINT		INT
64	QWORD	unsigned __int64	ULONGLONG	DWORDLONG	LONGLONG
80	TBYTE	N/A			

The Windows 2000 Device Driver Kit (DDK) is more consistent in its use of aliases. You will usually come across the type names in the "Alias #1" and "Signed" columns throughout the header files and documentation. As a long-term assembly language programmer, I've grown accustomed to using the MASM types. Therefore, you will frequently find the names listed in the "MASM" column in the header files on the companion CD of this book.

Because 64-bit integer handling is somewhat awkward in a 32-bit programming environment, Windows 2000 usually does not employ the fundamental `__int64` type and its derivatives. Instead, the DDK header file `ntdef.h` defines a neat union/structure combination that allows different interpretations of a 64-bit quantity as either a pair of 32-bit chunks or a 64-bit monolith. Listing 2-3 shows the definition of the `LARGE_INTEGER` and `ULARGE_INTEGER` types, representing signed and unsigned integers, respectively. The sign is controlled by using `LONGLONG/ULONGLONG` for the 64-bit QuadPart member or `LONG/ULONG` for the 32-bit HighPart member.

STRINGS

In Win32 programming, the basic types `PSTR` and `PWSTR` are commonly used for ANSI and Unicode strings. `PSTR` is defined as `CHAR*`, and `PWSTR` is a `WCHAR*` (see Table 2-3). Depending on the absence or presence of the `#define UNICODE` directive in the source code, the additional `PTSTR` pseudo-type evaluates to `PSTR` or `PWSTR`, respectively, allowing maintenance of ANSI and Unicode versions of an application with a single set of source files. Basically, these strings are simply pointers to zero-terminated `CHAR` or `WCHAR` arrays. If you are working with the Windows 2000 kernel, you have to deal with quite different string representations. The most common type is the UNICODE_STRING, which is a three-part structure defined in Listing 2-4.

```
typedef union _LARGE_INTEGER
    {
    struct
        {
        ULONG LowPart;
        LONG HighPart;
        };
    LONGLONG QuadPart;
    }
    LARGE_INTEGER, *PULARGE_INTEGER;

typedef union _ULARGE_INTEGER
    {
    struct
        {
        ULONG LowPart;
        ULONG HighPart;
        };
    ULONGLONG QuadPart;
    }
   U LARGE_INTEGER, *PULARGE_INTEGER;
```

LISTING 2-3. `LARGE_INTEGER` *and* `ULARGE_INTEGER`

```
typedef struct _UNICODE_STRING
    {
    USHORT Length;
    USHORT MaximumLength;
    PWSTR  Buffer;
    }
    UNICODE_STRING, *PUNICODE_STRING;

typedef struct _STRING
    {
    USHORT Length;
    USHORT MaximumLength;
    PCHAR  Buffer;
    }
    STRING, *PSTRING;

typedef STRING ANSI_STRING, *PANSI_STRING;
typedef STRING OEM_STRING,  *POEM_STRING;
```

LISTING 2-4. *Structured String Types*

The Length member specifies the current length of the string in bytes—not characters! The MaximumLength member indicates the size of the memory block addressed by the Buffer member where the string data resides, again in bytes, not characters. Because Unicode characters are 16 bits wide, the Length is always twice the number of string characters. Usually, the string pointed to by the Buffer member is zero-terminated. However, some kernel-mode modules might rely entirely on the Length value and won't take care of adding the terminating zero character, so be careful in case of doubt.

The ANSI version of the Windows 2000 string structure is simply called STRING, as shown in Listing 2-4. For convenience, ntdef.h also defines the ANSI_STRING and OEM_STRING aliases to distinguish 8-byte strings containing characters of different code pages (default ANSI code page: 1252; default OEM code page: 437). However, the predominant string type of the Windows 2000 kernel is the UNICODE_STRING. You will come across 8-bit strings only occasionally.

In Figure 2-3, I have drawn two typical UNICODE_STRING examples. The sample on the left-hand side consists of two independent memory blocks: a UNICODE_STRING structure and an array of 16-bit PWCHAR Unicode characters. This is probably the most common string type found inside the Windows 2000 data areas. On the right-hand side, I have added a frequently occurring special case, in which both the UNICODE_STRING and the PWCHAR are part of the same memory block. Several kernel functions, including some inside the Native API, return structured system information in contiguous memory blocks. If the data includes strings, they are often stored as embedded UNICODE_STRINGs, as shown in the right half of Figure 2-3. For example, the NtQuerySystemInformation() function used in the sample code of Chapter 1 makes heavy use of this special string representation.

These string structures don't need to be manipulated manually. ntdll.dll and ntoskrnl.exe export a rich set of runtime API functions such as RtlCreatUnicodeString(), RtlInitUnicodeString(), RtlCopyUnicodeString(), and the like. Usually, an equivalent function is available for the STRING and ANSI_STRING types as well. Many of these functions are officially documented in the DDK, but some are not. However, it is usually easy to guess what the undocumented string functions do and what arguments they take. The main advantage of UNICODE_STRING and its siblings is the implicit specification of the size of the buffer containing the string. If you are passing a UNICODE_STRING to a function that converts its value in place, possibly increasing its length, this function simply has to examine the MaximumLength member to find out whether enough space is left for the result.

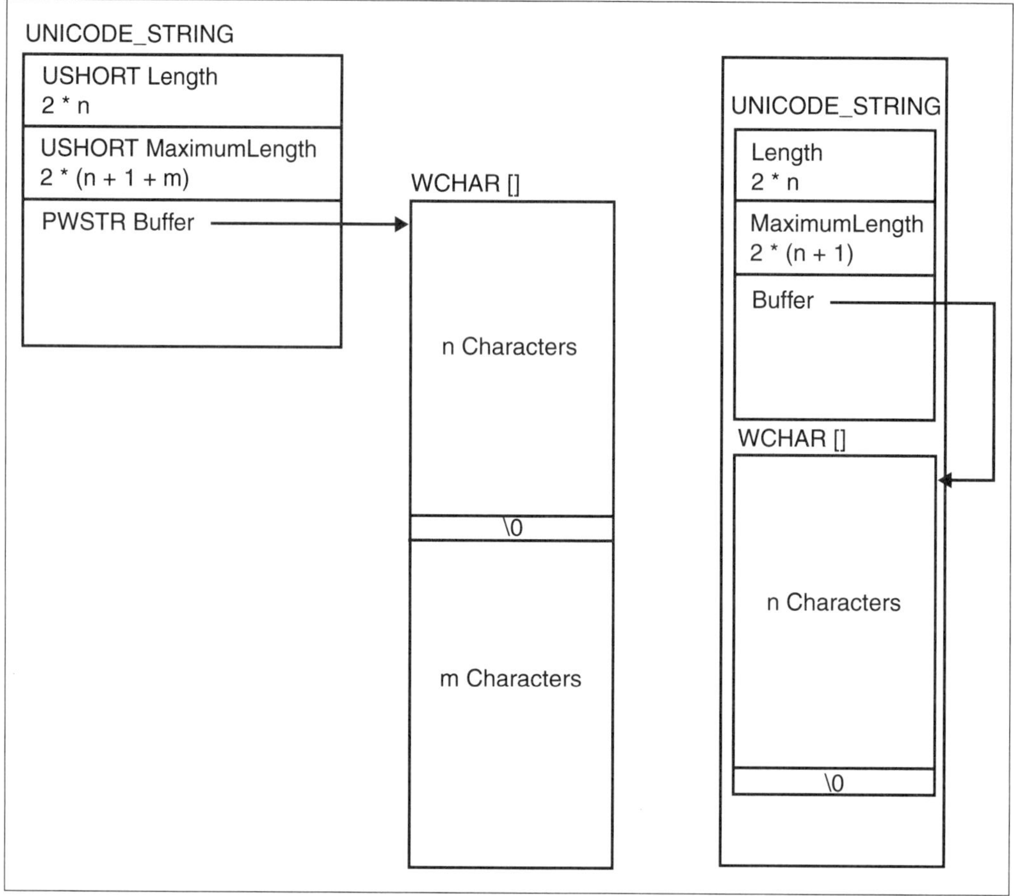

FIGURE 2-3. *Examples of* `UNICODE_STRINGs`

STRUCTURES

Several kernel API functions that work with objects expect them to be specified by an appropriately filled `OBJECT_ATTRIBUTES` structure, outlined in Listing 2-5. For example, the `NtOpenFile()` function doesn't have a `PWSTR` or `PUNICODE_STRING` argument for the path of the file to be opened. Instead, the `ObjectName` member of an `OBJECT_ATTRIBUTES` structure indicates the path. Usually, the setup of this structure is trivial. Along with the `ObjectName`, the `Length` and `Attributes` members are required. The `Length` must be set to `sizeof (OBJECT_ATTRIBUTES)`, and the `Attributes` are a combination of `OBJ_*` values from `ntdef.h`, for example, `OBJ_CASE_INSENSITIVE` if the object name should be matched without regard to character case. Of course, the `ObjectName` is a `UNICODE_STRING` pointer, not a plain `PWSTR`. The remaining members can be set to `NULL` as long as they aren't needed.

Whereas the OBJECT_ATTRIBUTES structure specifies details about the input data of an API function, the IO_STATUS_BLOCK structure in Listing 2-6 provides information about the outcome of the requested operation. This structure is quite simple—the Status member contains an NTSTATUS code, which can assume the value STATUS_SUCCESS or any of the error codes defined in the DDK header file ntstatus.h. The Information member provides additional request-specific data in case of success. For example, if the function has returned a data block, this member is typically set to the size of this block.

Another ubiquitous Windows 2000 data type is the LIST_ENTRY structure, shown in Listing 2-7. The kernel uses this simple structure to arrange objects in doubly linked lists. It is quite common that one object is part of several lists, resulting in multiple LIST_ENTRY structures used in the object's definition. The Flink member is the forward link, pointing to the next item, and the Blink member is the backward link, addressing the previous one. The links always point to another LIST_ENTRY, not to the owner object itself. Usually, the linked lists are circular, that is, the last Flink points to the first LIST_ENTRY in the chain, and the first Blink points to the end of the list. This makes it easy to traverse a linked list in both directions from either end or even from a list item somewhere in the middle. If a program walks down a list of objects, it has to save the address of the starting point to find out when it is time to stop. If a list contains just a single entry, its LIST_ENTRY must reference itself—that is, both the Flink and Blink members point to their own LIST_ENTRY.

```
typedef struct _OBJECT_ATTRIBUTES
    {
    ULONG           Length;
    HANDLE          RootDirectory;
    PUNICODE_STRING ObjectName;
    ULONG           Attributes;
    PVOID           SecurityDescriptor;
    PVOID           SecurityQualityOfService;
    }
    OBJECT_ATTRIBUTES, *POBJECT_ATTRIBUTES;
```

LISTING 2-5. *The* OBJECT_ATTRIBUTES *structure*

```
typedef struct _IO_STATUS_BLOCK
    {
    NTSTATUS Status;
    ULONG    Information;
    }
    IO_STATUS_BLOCK, *PIO_STATUS_BLOCK;
```

LISTING 2-6. *The* IO_STATUS_BLOCK *structure*

```
typedef struct _LIST_ENTRY
 {
 struct _LIST_ENTRY *Flink;
 struct _LIST_ENTRY *Blink;
 }
 LIST_ENTRY, *PLIST_ENTRY;
```

LISTING 2-7. *The* `LIST_ENTRY` *Structure*

Figure 2-4 illustrates the relationships between the members of object lists. Objects A1, A2, and A3 are part of a three-item list. Note how `A3.Flink` points back to A1 and `A1.Blink` points to A3. Object B1 on the right-hand side is the only member of an orphaned list. Hence, its `Flink` and `Blink` members point to the same address inside Object B1. Typical examples of doubly linked lists are process and thread lists. The internal variable `PsActiveProcessHead` is a `LIST_ENTRY` structure inside the `.data` section of `ntoskrnl.exe` that addresses the first (and—by virtue of its `Blink` pointer—also the last) member of the system's process list. You can walk down this list in a Kernel Debugger console window by first issuing the command `dd PsActiveProcessHead`, and then using copy and paste to set up subsequent `dd` commands for the `Flink` or `Blink` values. Of course, this is an annoying way of exploring Windows 2000 processes, but it might help gaining insight into the basic system architecture. The Windows 2000 Native API features much more convenient ways of enumerating processes, such as `NTQuerySystemInformation()` function.

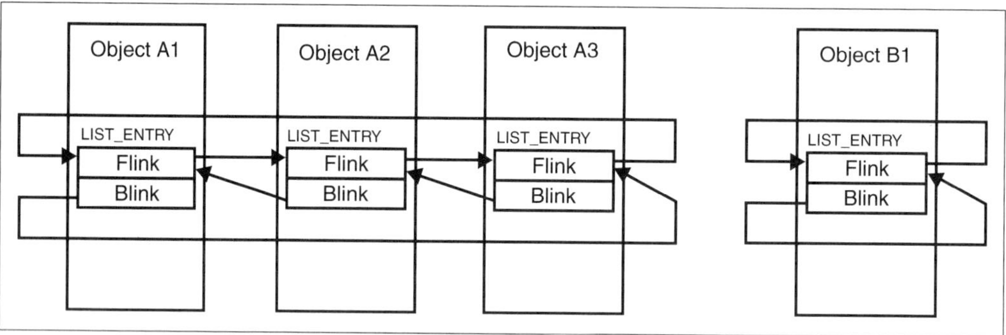

FIGURE 2-4. *Examples of Doubly Linked Lists*

API functions operating on processes and threads, such as `NtOpenProcess()` and `NtOpenThread()`, use the `CLIENT_ID` structure shown in Listing 2-8 to jointly specify process and thread IDs. Although defined as `HANDLE` types, the `UniqueProcess` and `UniqueThread` members aren't handles in the strict sense. Instead, they are integral process and thread IDs, as returned by the standard Win32 API functions `GetCurrentProcessId()` and `GetCurrentThreadId()`, which have `DWORD` return values.

The `CLIENT_ID` structure is also used by the Windows 2000 Executive to globally identify a thread in the system. For example, if you are issuing the Kernel Debugger's `!thread` command to display the parameters of the current thread, it will list its `CLIENT_ID` in the first output line as "Cid ppp.ttt," where "ppp" is the value of the `UniqueProcess` member, and "ttt" is the `UniqueThread` ID.

INTERFACING TO THE NATIVE API

For kernel-mode drivers, interfacing to the Native API is normal, just as calling Win32 API functions is in a user-mode application. The header and library files provided by the Windows 2000 DDK contain everything needed to call into the Native API exposed by `ntoskrnl.exe`. On the other hand, the Win32 Platform SDK contains almost no support for applications that want to use Native API functions exported by `ntdll.dll`. I say "almost" because one important item is actually included: It is the import library `ntdll.lib`, supplied in the `\Program Files\Microsoft Platform SDK\Lib` directory. Without the library, it would be difficult to call functions exported by `ntdll.dll`.

ADDING THE NTDLL.DLL IMPORT LIBRARY TO A PROJECT

Before you can successfully compile and link user-mode code that uses `ntdll.dll` API functions, you must consider the following four important points:

1. The Platform SDK header files don't contain prototypes for these functions.
2. Several basic data structures used by these functions are missing from the SDK files.

```
typedef struct _CLIENT_ID
    {
    HANDLE UniqueProcess;
    HANDLE UniqueThread;
    }
    CLIENT_ID, *PCLIENT_ID;
```

LISTING 2-8. *The* `CLIENT_ID` *Structure*

3. The SDK and DDK header files are incompatible—you cannot add `#include <ntddk.h>` to your Win32 C source files.
4. `ntdll.lib` is not included in the default list of import libraries offered by Visual C/C++.

The last problem is easily solved. Just edit the project settings of your application, or add the line `#pragma comment (linker, "/defaultlib:ntdll.lib")` to your source code, as explained in the section The Windows 200 Runtime Library earlier in this chapter. This linker pragma adds `ntdll.lib` to the `/defaultlib` settings of the linker command at compile time. The problem with the missing definitions is much more difficult. Because it is not possible to merge the SDK and DDK header files in programs written in plain C, the least expensive solution is to write a custom header file that contains just as many definitions as needed to call the required `ntdll.dll` API functions. Fortunately, you don't have to start from scratch. The `w2k_def.h` file in the `\src\common\include` directory of the sample CD contains much of the basic information you may need. This header file will play an important role in Chapters 6 and 7. Because it is designed to be compatible to both user-mode and kernel-mode projects, you must insert the line `#define _USER_MODE_` somewhere before the `#include <w2k_def.h>` line in user-mode code to enable the definitions that are present in the DDK but missing from the SDK.

Considerable information about Native API programming has already been published elsewhere. Three good sources of detailed information on this topic are listed below in chronological order of publication:

- Mark Russinovich has published an article titled "Inside the Native API" on the *sysinternals.com* Web site, available for download at http://www.sysinternals.com/ntdll.htm (Russinovich 1998).
- The November 1999 issue of *Dr. Dobb's Journal* (DDJ) contains my article "Inside Windows NT System Data," which details, among other things, how to interface to `ntdll.dll` and provides lots of sample code that facilitates this task (Schreiber 1999). The sample code can be downloaded from the *DDJ* Web site at http://www.ddj.com/ftp/1999/1999_11/ntinfo.zip. Please note that this article targets Windows NT 4.0 only.
- Gary Nebbett's recently published Native API bible, *Windows NT/2000 Native API Reference* (Nebbett 2000), doesn't contain much sample code, but it does feature complete coverage of all Native API functions available in Windows NT 4.0 and Windows 2000, including the data structures and other definitions they require. It is an ideal complement to the above articles.

The `w2k_call.dll` sample library, introduced in Chapter 6, demonstrates the typical usage of `w2k_def.h`. Chapter 6 also discusses an alternative method to call into the Windows 2000 kernel from user-mode that isn't restricted to the Native API function set. Actually, this trick is not restricted to `ntoskrnl.exe`—it is applicable to *any* module loaded into kernel memory that either exports API functions or comes with matching `.dbg` or `.pdb` symbol files. As you see, there is plenty of interesting material waiting for you in the remaining chapters of this book. But, before we get there, we'll discuss some fundamental concepts and techniques.

CHAPTER 3

Writing Kernel-Mode Drivers

In the next chapters, we will frequently have to access system resources that are available in kernel-mode only. Large portions of the sample code are designed as kernel-mode driver routines. Therefore, some basic knowledge about the development of this type of software is required. Because I cannot assume that all readers already have this expertise, I will insert here a short introduction to kernel-mode programming that focuses on the usage of a driver wizard found on the accompanying CD.

This chapter also discusses the basics of the Windows 2000 Service Control Manager that allow loading, controlling, and unloading drivers at runtime, resulting in wonderfully short change-build-test turnaround cycles. The title of this chapter might be a bit misleading—the word *driver* is usually associated with low-level software that controls some piece of hardware. In fact, many kernel-mode programmers do just that all day long. However, the layered driver model of Windows 2000 allows much more than this. Kernel-mode drivers can do arbitrary complex tasks and might even act like high-level user-mode DLLs, except that they are running on a higher CPU privilege level and use a different programming interface. In this book, the driver paradigm will not be applied to any hardware. Instead, we will use this powerful programming technique to spy on Windows 2000 internals, using kernel-mode drivers as a shuttle to fly from the small world of user-mode to the outer space of the Windows 2000 kernel.

CREATING A DRIVER SKELETON

Even developers who have been writing Win32 applications or libraries for a long time tend to feel like absolute beginners as soon as they have to write their first kernel-mode driver. The reason for this is that kernel-mode code runs in a completely different operating system environment. A Win32 programmer works exclusively with a set of system components that belong to a subsystem of Windows 2000, named Win32. Other programmers might prefer to write POSIX or OS/2 applications, which are also supported by Windows 2000 by means of additional subsystems. Thanks to its subsystem concept, Windows 2000 acts like a chameleon—it can emulate various operating systems by exposing their application interfaces in the form of subsystems. Contrary to this, kernel-mode modules are located somewhere below this layer, using a more basic operating system interface. Because there are no more subsystems on this system level, kernel-mode code can "see" the real Windows 2000 operating system. The interface they are talking to is the "final frontier." Of course, it is not absolutely correct that the kernel-mode zone is free of subsystems. In Chapter 2, we saw that the `win32k.sys` module is a kernel-mode branch of the Win32 GUI and Window Manager, installed there for performance reasons. However, only a small part of the API functions exposed by `win32k.sys` reappear in `gdi32.dll` and `user32.dll` as Win32 API functions, so Win32K is more than just a Win32 foot on kernel-mode soil. It could be regarded as a high-performance display engine kernel as well.

The Windows 2000 Device Driver Kit

Because kernel-mode programming works on a different system interface, the usual header and import library files used in Win32 programming aren't of use here. For Win32 development, Microsoft provides the Platform Software Development Kit (SDK). For kernel-mode drivers, the Windows 2000 Device Driver Kit (DDK) is required. Along with documentation, the DDK provides special header files and import libraries needed to interface the Windows 2000 kernel modules. After installing the DDK, your next step should be to open Microsoft Visual C to add the DDK file paths to the directory lists of the compiler and linker. From the main menu, select **Tools** and **Options...**, then click on the **Directories** tab. From the **Show directories for:** drop-down list, select **Include files** and add the appropriate DDK path to the list, as shown in Figure 3-1. By default, the DDK is installed into a base directory named `\NTDDK`, and the included files are located in the `\NTDDK\inc` subdirectory. After entering the path, use the **up arrow** to move it to the position of your choice—preferably on Top Two right after the Platform SDK. Always keep the original Microsoft Visual Studio files at the end of the list, because many of them are superseded by more recent SDK and DDK files.

After adding the base directory of the DDK header files, do the same for the import libraries. The DDK comes with two sets of files, one for free (release) builds, and another one for checked (debug) builds. The corresponding subdirectories are `\NTDDK\libfre\i386` and `\NTDDK\libchk\i386`, respectively. Figure 3-2

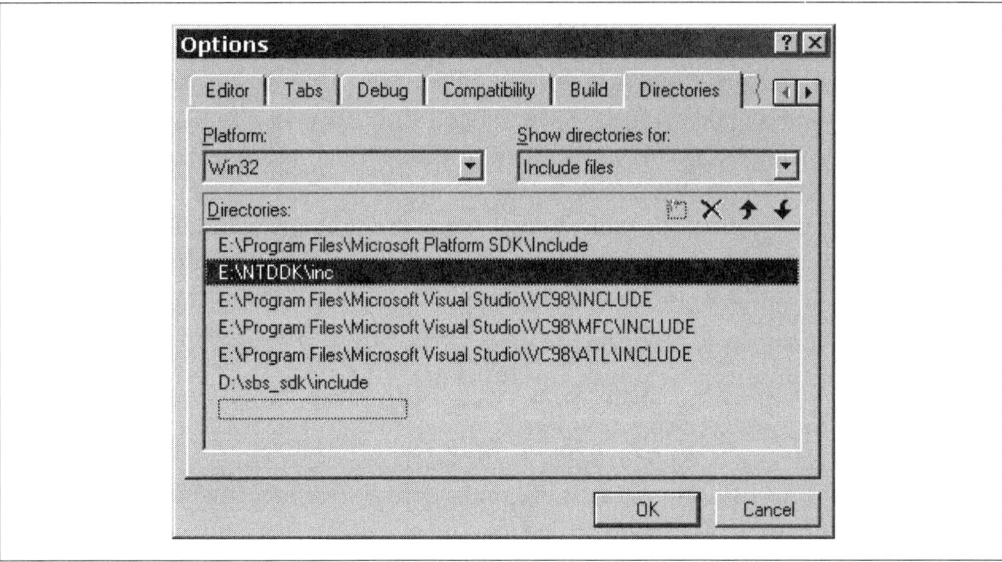

FIGURE 3-1. *Adding the DDK Header File Path*

FIGURE 3-2. *Adding the DDK Import Library Path*

shows an example. To enter the path, select **Library files** from the **Show directories for:** list first. After you are done, move this entry to an appropriate position using the **up arrow.**

The programming environment of the DDK differs somewhat from the Win32 model. The following list points out some of the most obvious differences:

- For Win32 programs, the main header file that has to be included is `windows.h`. In kernel-mode driver code, this file is not applicable. It is replaced by `ntddk.h`.
- The main entry point function is called `DriverEntry()`, not `WinMain()` or `main()`. Its prototype is shown in Listing 3-1.
- Be aware that some of the common Win32 data types, such as `BYTE`, `WORD`, and `DWORD`, are not available. The DDK prefers `UCHAR`, `USHORT`, `ULONG`, and the like. However, it is easy to define your favorite types, as done exemplary in Listing 3-2.

Three important differences between the Windows NT 4.0 and Windows 2000 versions of the DDK should be noted as well:

- Although the base directory of the Windows NT 4.0 DDK is called `\DDK` by default, the Windows 2000 DDK now uses the default name `\NTDDK`.
- In the Windows NT 4.0 DDK, the main header file `ntddk.h` resides in the base directory. In the Windows 2000 DDK, this file has moved to the subdirectory `ddk` of the base directory.
- The paths of the import library files have changed as well: `lib\i386\free` has become `libfre\i386`, and `lib\i386\checked` has been replaced by `libchk\i386`.

I am not sure whether this reshuffling and renaming was really necessary, but we do have to live with it now.

```
NTSTATUS DriverEntry (PDRIVER_OBJECT  pDriverObject,
                      PUNICODE_STRING pusRegistryPath);
```

LISTING 3-1. *Prototype of the* `DriverEntry()` *Function*

```
typedef UCHAR  BYTE,   *PBYTE;
typedef USHORT WORD,   *PWORD;
typedef ULONG  DWORD, *PDWORD;
```

LISTING 3-2. *Defining Common Win32 Data Types*

A CUSTOMIZABLE DRIVER WIZARD

The main problem with kernel-mode drivers is that Visual C/C++ doesn't provide a wizard for projects of this kind. None of the various project types offered by the **File/New** dialog is suited for drivers. Fortunately, the Microsoft Developer Network (MSDN) Library contains a series of great articles about Windows NT kernel-mode driver development, written between 1994 and 1995 by Ruediger R. Asche. Two of them give detailed instructions on how to add a custom driver wizard to Visual C/C++, with sample code and application notes (Asche 1995a, 1995b). These articles have been of immense help to me, and although the output of the original wizard didn't fit all my needs, it was an ideal starting point. The kernel-mode driver wizard I will present now is based on output files generated by Ruediger Asche's original wizard.

My driver wizard is included with full source code on the companion CD of this book in the directory tree `\src\w2k_wiz`. By reading the source files, you will find that its real title is "SBS Windows 2000 Code Wizard." In fact, this is a general-purpose Windows 2000 program skeleton generator that can produce several program types, including Win32 DLLs and applications. However, the configuration files on the CD are tailored to kernel-mode driver development. Essentially, my wizard is a file converter that reads in a set of files, converts them by applying some simple rules, and writes the results back to another set of files. The input files are templates, and the output files are C project files. By modifying the templates, the driver wizard can be turned into a DLL wizard, and so on. Up to seven templates can be supplied (if one is missing, a noncritical error is reported):

- Files with the extension `.tw` are workspace templates and will be saved as Microsoft Developer Studio Workspace Files with extension `.dsw`. You probably know this file type from the **File/Open Workspace...** menu command of Visual C/C++, which requests a `.dsw` file to be specified.
- Files with the extension `.tp` are project templates and will be saved as Microsoft Developer Studio Project Files with extension `.dsp`. Project files are referenced by the associated workspace files and contain all build settings of the project for all configurations (e.g., **Release** and **Debug**).

- Files with the extensions `.tc`, `.th`, `.tr`, and `.td` are C source files and will become files of type `.c`, `.h`, `.rc`, and `.def`. I am sure that everyone knows the purpose of these files.
- Files with the extension `.ti` are icon files and are saved unchanged with extension `.ico`. This template is just a dummy icon included with the wizard to prevent the resource compiler from reporting an error. You should edit or replace it by your own creation after running the wizard.

This seven-piece set of files is the minimum requirement of a new project. The `.def` file is a somewhat old-fashioned way of exporting API functions from a DLL, but I like it more than the `__declspec(dllexport)` method. Because drivers usually don't export functions, I have omitted the `.td` template, which results in a benign error reported by the wizard. I also could have omitted the resource script and the icon, but experience shows that both are nice to have. Moreover, the default `.rc` file output by the wizard contains a full-featured personalized version resource, constructed from your individual configuration settings. The applied conversion rules are simple, consisting of a short list of string substitutions. While scanning a template file, the converter looks for escape sequences consisting of character pairs in which the first one is a percent sign. If it detects one, it decides which action to take by evaluating the second character. Table 3-1 lists the recognized escape sequences.

TABLE 3-1. *The Wizard's String Substitution Rules*

INPUT	OUTPUT
%n	Project name (original notation)
%N	Project name (uppercase notation)
%s	Fully qualified path of the *w2k_wiz.ini* file
%d	Current day (always two digits)
%m	Current month (always two digits)
%y	Current year (always four digits)
%t	Default project description, as defined in *w2k_wiz.ini*
%c	Author's company name, as defined in *w2k_wiz.ini*
%a	Author's name, as defined in *w2k_wiz.ini*
%e	Author's email address, as defined in *w2k_wiz.ini*
%p	Default ProgID prefix, as defined in *w2k_wiz.ini*
%i	DDK header file path, as defined in *w2k_wiz.ini*
%l	DDK import library path (release configuration), as defined in *w2k_wiz.ini*
%L	DDK import library path (debug configuration), as defined in *w2k_wiz.ini*
%%	% (escapement for a single percent character)
%<other>	Copied unchanged to the output file

Table 3-1 contains several references to the configuration file w2k_wiz.ini. Its default contents are shown in Example 3-1. Before using the wizard, you should copy w2k_wiz.exe, w2k_wiz.ini, and all w2k_wiz.t* template files from the CD's \src\w2k_wiz\release directory to your hard disk and edit the configuration file, replacing the values in angular brackets with your personal settings. You should also set the Include, Free, and Checked values to match your DDK setup configuration. If you are using Visual C/C++ Version 6.0, the Root entry can remain unchanged. If not, set its value to the registry key where the base directory of your projects is stored. If this value ends with a backslash, it is interpreted as the default value of the specified registry key. Otherwise, the token following the last backslash should denote a named value of the key specified by the remaining character sequence. In Example 3-1, the key is HKEY_CURRENT_USER\Software\Microsoft\DevStudio\6.0\Directories, and its value WorkspaceDir stores the basic workspace directory.

Invocation of the wizard is: Just type w2k_wiz MyDriver, and it will generate a project folder named MyDriver in the current directory, containing the files MyDriver.dsw, MyDriver.dsp, MyDriver.c, MyDriver.h, MyDriver.rc, and MyDriver.ico. If you specify the project name with a preceding path, the project folder will be created at the specified location. Another legal command option is the asterisk, such as in w2k_wiz *MyDriver. In this case, the wizard will not create the project folder in the current directory, but queries the registry for the default base directory maintained by Visual C/C++, using the Root entry in w2k_wiz.ini. This is probably the most convenient command variant and is the one I usually use.

```
; w2k_wiz.ini
; 08-27-2000 Sven B. Schreiber
; sbs@orgon.com

[Settings]
Text    = <SBS Windows 2000 Code Wizard Project>
Company = <MyCompany>
Author  = <MyName>
Email   = <my@email>
Prefix  = <MyPrefix>
Include = E:\NTDDK\inc
Free    = E:\NTDDK\libfre\i386
Checked = E:\NTDDK\libchk\i386
Root    = HKEY_CURRENT_USER\Software\Microsoft\DevStudio\6.0\Directories\WorkspaceDir
```

EXAMPLE 3-1. *Personal Settings Supported by the Wizard*

The wizard always looks for its configuration and template files in the directory of the executable. Therefore, you can keep several copies of the wizard with different settings on your disk, provided that they reside in individual directories or have different base names. The files on the CD are preset for simple kernel-mode driver projects. You can customize all files to fit your needs, keeping separate copies for drivers, Win32 applications, DLLs, or whatever type of Windows 2000 code you write.

Running the Driver Wizard

Now it is time to try the driver wizard. The example below resulted from the command `w2k_wiz *TestDrv` entered at a Windows 2000 console prompt. This should create a project named `TestDrv` in the default workspace folder of Visual C/C++. Example 3-2 shows the status messages displayed by the program on the screen while it is converting files.

```
D:\>w2k_wiz *TestDrv

// w2k_wiz.exe
// SBS Windows 2000 Code Wizard V1.00
// 08-27-2000 Sven B. Schreiber
// sbs@orgon.com

Project D:\Program Files\DevStudio\MyProjects\TestDrv\

Loading D:\etc32\w2k_wiz.tc ... OK
Writing D:\Program Files\DevStudio\MyProjects\TestDrv\TestDrv.c ... OK

Loading D:\etc32\w2k_wiz.td ... ERROR

Loading D:\etc32\w2k_wiz.th ... OK
Writing D:\Program Files\DevStudio\MyProjects\TestDrv\TestDrv.h ... OK

Loading D:\etc32\w2k_wiz.ti ... OK
Writing D:\Program Files\DevStudio\MyProjects\TestDrv\TestDrv.ico ... OK

Loading D:\etc32\w2k_wiz.tp ... OK
Writing D:\Program Files\DevStudio\MyProjects\TestDrv\TestDrv.dsp ... OK

Loading D:\etc32\w2k_wiz.tr ... OK
Writing D:\Program Files\DevStudio\MyProjects\TestDrv\TestDrv.rc ... OK

Loading D:\etc32\w2k_wiz.tw ... OK
Writing D:\Program Files\DevStudio\MyProjects\TestDrv\TestDrv.dsw ... OK
```

Example 3-2. *Running the Windows 2000 Code Wizard*

Obviously, all operations were completed without error except for the `.td` to `.def` conversion, which is a benign error condition. The driver skeleton produced by the wizard doesn't require a `.def` file, so there is no need for a `.td` template. Now it should be possible to open the new workspace in Visual C/C++, using the **File/Open Workspace...** menu command. Indeed, there is a new folder named `TestDrv`, and it contains a workspace file named `TestDrv.dsw` that can be opened without problem. Next, you should select the active configuration for your builds. The `.dsp` file generated by the driver wizard defines the following two configurations:

1. Win2K kernel-mode driver (debug)
2. Win2K kernel-mode driver (release)

By default, the debug configuration is selected, but you can switch configurations at any time by choosing **Build/Set Active Configuration...** from the Visual C/C++ menu. Next, you should copy the file `\src\common\include\DrvInfo.h` from the CD to one of your header file directories, and open the `TestDrv.c`, `TestDrv.h`, and `TestDrv.rc` files for editing. When opening `TestDrv.rc`, be sure to open it as a text file (Figure 3-3), because it uses complex macros from `DrvInfo.h` that cause the resource editor to die with an exception. This nasty problem was introduced with Visual C/C++ 5.0, as far as I remember, and has not yet been fixed. Contrary to the editor, the resource compiler doesn't have problems with complex resource macros.

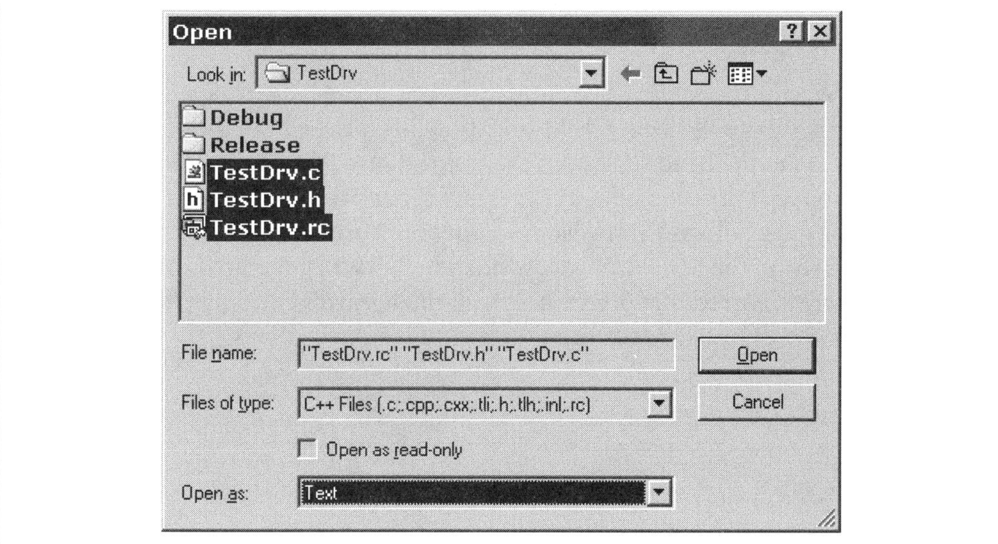

FIGURE 3-3. *Opening the Driver Source Files in Text Mode*

Now everything should be set up for the first build. In Example 3-3, I have attempted to build a release version of the new driver by selecting **Build/Rebuild All** from the Visual C/C++ menu, and it seems that everything works fine. By the way, the ellipses ending the first two lines of the build command output indicate that I have truncated them.

The linker creates an executable file named `TestDrv.sys` in the `Debug` or `Release` subdirectory of the project folder, depending on the chosen build configuration. The release version of the test driver is 5.5 KB in size, and the debug version is 8 KB. You can use the Multi-Format Visual Disassembler (MFVDasm) or the PE and COFF File Viewer (PEview) on the companion CD to verify that the resulting `TestDrv.sys` file contains valid code and data.

```
Deleting intermediate files and output files for project 'TestDrv - Win2K ...
-------- Configuration: TestDrv - Win2K kernel-mode driver (release) ...
Compiling resources...
Compiling...
TestDrv.c
Linking...

TestDrv.sys - 0 error(s), 0 warning(s)
```

EXAMPLE 3-3. *Building the Release Version of the Test Driver*

INSIDE THE DRIVER SKELETON

Listing 3-3 shows the `TestDrv.c` file emitted by the wizard. The associated header file `TestDrv.h` is shown in Listing 3-4. In Listing 3-3, please note the `<MyName>` and `<MyCompany>` tags in the heading and in the fourth line of the disclaimer. If the `Author` and `Company` entries in `w2k_wiz.ini` are set appropriately, your own name and company strings will go here. Also note that the current date appears in the heading, as well as in the revision history. (Listing 3-3 was generated on August 27, 2000, so the date is correct.) More values from the wizard's configuration file are found in the `PROGRAM IDENTIFICATION` section of Listing 3-4.

```
// TestDrv.c
// 08-27-2000 <MyName>
// Copyright © 2000 <MyCompany>

#define  _TESTDRV_SYS_
#include <ddk\ntddk.h>
#include "TestDrv.h"

// =================================================================
// DISCLAIMER
// =================================================================

/*

This software is provided "as is" and any express or implied
warranties, including, but not limited to, the implied warranties of
merchantability and fitness for a particular purpose are disclaimed.
In no event shall the author <MyName> be liable for any direct,
indirect, incidental, special, exemplary, or consequential
damages (including, but not limited to, procurement of substitute
goods or services; loss of use, data, or profits; or business
interruption) however caused and on any theory of liability, whether
in contract, strict liability, or tort (including negligence
or otherwise) arising in any way out of the use of this software,
even if advised of the possibility of such damage.

*/

// =================================================================
// REVISION HISTORY
// =================================================================

/*

// 08-27-2000 V1.00 Original version.

*/

// =================================================================
// GLOBAL DATA
// =================================================================

PRESET_UNICODE_STRING (usDeviceName,       CSTRING (DRV_DEVICE));
PRESET_UNICODE_STRING (usSymbolicLinkName, CSTRING (DRV_LINK  ));

PDEVICE_OBJECT  gpDeviceObject  = NULL;
PDEVICE_CONTEXT gpDeviceContext = NULL;

// =================================================================
// DISCARDABLE FUNCTIONS
// =================================================================
```

(continued)

```
NTSTATUS DriverInitialize (PDRIVER_OBJECT  pDriverObject,
                           PUNICODE_STRING pusRegistryPath);

NTSTATUS DriverEntry      (PDRIVER_OBJECT  pDriverObject,
                           PUNICODE_STRING pusRegistryPath);

// -----------------------------------------------------------------

#ifdef ALLOC_PRAGMA

#pragma alloc_text (INIT, DriverInitialize)
#pragma alloc_text (INIT, DriverEntry)

#endif

// =================================================================
// DEVICE REQUEST HANDLER
// =================================================================

NTSTATUS DeviceDispatcher (PDEVICE_CONTEXT pDeviceContext,
                           PIRP            pIrp)
    {
    PIO_STACK_LOCATION pisl;
    DWORD              dInfo = 0;
    NTSTATUS           ns    = STATUS_NOT_IMPLEMENTED;

    pisl = IoGetCurrentIrpStackLocation (pIrp);

    switch (pisl->MajorFunction)
        {
        case IRP_MJ_CREATE:
        case IRP_MJ_CLEANUP:
        case IRP_MJ_CLOSE:
            {
            ns = STATUS_SUCCESS;
            break;
            }
        }
    pIrp->IoStatus.Status      = ns;
    pIrp->IoStatus.Information = dInfo;

 IoCompleteRequest (pIrp, IO_NO_INCREMENT);
 return ns;
    }

// =================================================================
// DRIVER REQUEST HANDLER
// =================================================================

NTSTATUS DriverDispatcher (PDEVICE_OBJECT pDeviceObject,
                           PIRP           pIrp)
    {
```

```
    return (pDeviceObject == gpDeviceObject
            ? DeviceDispatcher (gpDeviceContext, pIrp)
            : STATUS_INVALID_PARAMETER_1);
    }

// -----------------------------------------------------------------

void DriverUnload (PDRIVER_OBJECT pDriverObject)
    {
    IoDeleteSymbolicLink (&usSymbolicLinkName);
    IoDeleteDevice       (gpDeviceObject);
    return;
    }

// =================================================================
// DRIVER INITIALIZATION
// =================================================================

NTSTATUS DriverInitialize (PDRIVER_OBJECT  pDriverObject,
                           PUNICODE_STRING pusRegistryPath)
    {
    PDEVICE_OBJECT pDeviceObject = NULL;
    NTSTATUS       ns = STATUS_DEVICE_CONFIGURATION_ERROR;

    if ((ns = IoCreateDevice (pDriverObject, DEVICE_CONTEXT_,
                              &usDeviceName, FILE_DEVICE_CUSTOM,
                              0, FALSE, &pDeviceObject))
        == STATUS_SUCCESS)
        {
        if ((ns = IoCreateSymbolicLink (&usSymbolicLinkName,
                                        &usDeviceName))
            == STATUS_SUCCESS)
            {
            gpDeviceObject  = pDeviceObject;
            gpDeviceContext = pDeviceObject->DeviceExtension;

            gpDeviceContext->pDriverObject = pDriverObject;
            gpDeviceContext->pDeviceObject = pDeviceObject;
            }
        else
            {
            IoDeleteDevice (pDeviceObject);
            }
        }
    return ns;
    }

// -----------------------------------------------------------------

NTSTATUS DriverEntry (PDRIVER_OBJECT  pDriverObject,
                      PUNICODE_STRING pusRegistryPath)
    {
```

(continued)

```
    PDRIVER_DISPATCH *ppdd;
    NTSTATUS          ns = STATUS_DEVICE_CONFIGURATION_ERROR;

    if ((ns = DriverInitialize (pDriverObject, pusRegistryPath))
        == STATUS_SUCCESS)
        {
        ppdd = pDriverObject->MajorFunction;

        ppdd [IRP_MJ_CREATE                   ] =
        ppdd [IRP_MJ_CREATE_NAMED_PIPE        ] =
        ppdd [IRP_MJ_CLOSE                    ] =
        ppdd [IRP_MJ_READ                     ] =
        ppdd [IRP_MJ_WRITE                    ] =
        ppdd [IRP_MJ_QUERY_INFORMATION        ] =
        ppdd [IRP_MJ_SET_INFORMATION          ] =
        ppdd [IRP_MJ_QUERY_EA                 ] =
        ppdd [IRP_MJ_SET_EA                   ] =
        ppdd [IRP_MJ_FLUSH_BUFFERS            ] =
        ppdd [IRP_MJ_QUERY_VOLUME_INFORMATION] =
        ppdd [IRP_MJ_SET_VOLUME_INFORMATION  ] =
        ppdd [IRP_MJ_DIRECTORY_CONTROL        ] =
        ppdd [IRP_MJ_FILE_SYSTEM_CONTROL      ] =
        ppdd [IRP_MJ_DEVICE_CONTROL           ] =
        ppdd [IRP_MJ_INTERNAL_DEVICE_CONTROL ] =
        ppdd [IRP_MJ_SHUTDOWN                 ] =
        ppdd [IRP_MJ_LOCK_CONTROL             ] =
        ppdd [IRP_MJ_CLEANUP                  ] =
        ppdd [IRP_MJ_CREATE_MAILSLOT          ] =
        ppdd [IRP_MJ_QUERY_SECURITY           ] =
        ppdd [IRP_MJ_SET_SECURITY             ] =
        ppdd [IRP_MJ_POWER                    ] =
        ppdd [IRP_MJ_SYSTEM_CONTROL           ] =
        ppdd [IRP_MJ_DEVICE_CHANGE            ] =
        ppdd [IRP_MJ_QUERY_QUOTA              ] =
        ppdd [IRP_MJ_SET_QUOTA                ] =
        ppdd [IRP_MJ_PNP                      ] = DriverDispatcher;
        pDriverObject->DriverUnload             = DriverUnload;
        }
    return ns;
    }

// =================================================================
// END OF PROGRAM
// =================================================================
```

LISTING 3-3. *The Source Code of the Driver Skeleton*

The C code of the driver skeleton in Listings 3-3 and 3-4 contains some common boilerplate code that is shared by all kernel-mode drivers I have written so far. I have designed the wizard to be as customizable as possible. Feel free to change the

```
// TestDrv.h
// 08-27-2000 <MyName>
// Copyright © 2000 <MyCompany>

// ================================================================
// PROGRAM IDENTIFICATION
// ================================================================

#define DRV_BUILD           1
#define DRV_VERSION_HIGH    1
#define DRV_VERSION_LOW     0

//  ----------------------------------------------------------------

#define DRV_DAY             27
#define DRV_MONTH           08
#define DRV_YEAR            2000

// ----------------------------------------------------------------

// Customize these settings by editing the configuration file
// D:\etc32\w2k_wiz.ini

#define DRV_MODULE          TestDrv
#define DRV_NAME            <SBS Windows 2000 Code Wizard Project>
#define DRV_COMPANY         <MyCompany>
#define DRV_AUTHOR          <MyName>
#define DRV_EMAIL           <my@email>
#define DRV_PREFIX          <MyPrefix>

// ================================================================
// HEADER FILES
// ================================================================

#include <drvinfo.h>        // defines more DRV_* items

////////////////////////////////////////////////////////////////////
#ifndef _RC_PASS_
////////////////////////////////////////////////////////////////////

// ================================================================
// CONSTANTS
// ================================================================

#define FILE_DEVICE_CUSTOM      0x8000

// ================================================================
// STRUCTURES
// ================================================================

typedef struct _DEVICE_CONTEXT
    {
```

(continued)

```
    PDRIVER_OBJECT pDriverObject;
    PDEVICE_OBJECT pDeviceObject;
    }
    DEVICE_CONTEXT, *PDEVICE_CONTEXT, **PPDEVICE_CONTEXT;

#define DEVICE_CONTEXT_ sizeof (DEVICE_CONTEXT)

////////////////////////////////////////////////////////////////////
#endif // #ifndef _RC_PASS_
////////////////////////////////////////////////////////////////////

// =================================================================
// END OF FILE
// =================================================================
```

LISTING 3-4. *The Header File of the Driver Skeleton*

wizard's templates. For those who want to keep the code for now, the following section is a short description of its internals.

The main entry point of the driver module is `DriverEntry()`. Like all Windows 2000 module entry points, this name is not a requirement. You can choose any symbol you like, but you must tell the linker the name of the entry point by adding the `/entry` switch to its command line. For this test driver, the wizard has already taken care of this task. Inside the `w2k_wiz.tp` template or the resulting `TestDrv.dsp` file, you will find two occurrences of the string `/entry:"DriverEntry@8"` in the linker command line, one for each build configuration. The `@8` suffix indicates that `DriverEntry()` receives eight argument bytes on the stack, which is in perfect congruence with its prototype definition in Listing 3-1: two pointer arguments, each of them 32 bits wide, yield 64 bits, or 8 bytes.

The first thing `DriverEntry()` does is call `DriverInitialize()`, which will create a device object and a symbolic link that you will probably need later to communicate with the device from user-mode applications. It is a bit difficult to find out which names are used in the `IoCreateDevice()` and `IoCreateSymbolicLink()` calls, because they are constructed by macros defined in the common header file `DrvInfo.h`, found in the `\src\common\include` directory of the CD. This file is a header file that compiles various sorts of program information from a couple of basic customizable strings. If you want to know more about this trick, go to the `PROGRAM IDENTIFICATION` section in `TestDrv.h` (see top of Listing 3-4) and trace the `DRV_*` definitions as they are grouped in various ways inside `DrvInfo.h`. For example, a full-fledged `VERSIONINFO` resource is constructed from several pieces. Among other things, the constants `DRV_DEVICE` and `DRV_LINK` are defined, which evaluate to

\Device\TestDrv and \DosDevices\TestDrv here, respectively. Note that many kernel API functions, such as IoCreateDevice() and IoCreateSymbolicLink(), don't accept strings as plain zero-terminated character sequences, but rather expect them to be packed into a special UNICODE_STRING structure, introduced in Chapter 2 and repeated in Listing 3-5. The macro PRESET_UNICODE_STRING, defined in DrvInfo.h and applied in the GLOBAL DATA section of TestDrv.c in Listing 3-3, creates a static UNICODE_STRING structure from a simple Unicode string literal. This is a convenient shorthand notation for the definition of UNICODE_STRINGs that remain unchanged throughout the lifetime of a program instance.

After successfully creating the device object and its symbolic link, DriverInitialize() stores pointers to the device object and the device context in static global variables. The device context is a private structure of the device that can have arbitrary size and shape. The driver skeleton attaches a simple DEVICE_CONTEXT structure, defined in TestDrv.h, to its device. This structure contains nothing but pointers to the device and driver objects. You can extend this structure if you need persistent device-specific storage for any private data of your driver. The device context will be supplied by the system with every I/O Request Packet (IRP) the driver receives.

After DriverInitialize() returns and reports success, DriverEntry() sets up an important array, passed in by the system as part of the driver object structure pDriverObject. This array contains slots for all IRPs the driver can expect, and DriverEntry() has to write callback function pointers to the slots of all request types it wishes to handle. The driver skeleton defers this decision and saves a single DriverDispatcher() pointer to all 28 available slots, listed in Table 3-2. Later on, DriverDispatcher() will decide which IRP types are of interest, returning STATUS_NOT_IMPLEMENTED for all unhandled IRPs. Note that there are subtle differences between the Windows NT 4.0 and Windows 2000 layouts of the IRP handler array. In Table 3-2, the differing slots are marked boldface.

```
typedef struct _UNICODE_STRING
    {
    WORD  Length;
    WORD  MaximumLength;
    PWORD Buffer;
    }
    UNICODE_STRING, *PUNICODE_STRING;
```

LISTING 3-5. *An Ubiquitous Windows 2000 Structure:* UNICODE_STRING

TABLE 3-2. *I/O Request Packet Slots Compared*

SLOT	WINDOWS NT 4.0	WINDOWS 2000
0x00	IRP_MJ_CREATE	IRP_MJ_CREATE
0x01	IRP_MJ_CREATE_NAMED_PIPE	IRP_MJ_CREATE_NAMED_PIPE
0x02	IRP_MJ_CLOSE	IRP_MJ_CLOSE
0x03	IRP_MJ_READ	IRP_MJ_READ
0x04	IRP_MJ_WRITE	IRP_MJ_WRITE
0x05	IRP_MJ_QUERY_INFORMATION	IRP_MJ_QUERY_INFORMATION
0x06	IRP_MJ_SET_INFORMATION	IRP_MJ_SET_INFORMATION
0x07	IRP_MJ_QUERY_EA	IRP_MJ_QUERY_EA
0x08	IRP_MJ_SET_EA	IRP_MJ_SET_EA
0x09	IRP_MJ_FLUSH_BUFFERS	IRP_MJ_FLUSH_BUFFERS
0x0A	IRP_MJ_QUERY_VOLUME_INFORMATION	IRP_MJ_QUERY_VOLUME_INFORMATION
0x0B	IRP_MJ_SET_VOLUME_INFORMATION	IRP_MJ_SET_VOLUME_INFORMATION
0x0C	IRP_MJ_DIRECTORY_CONTROL	IRP_MJ_DIRECTORY_CONTROL
0x0D	IRP_MJ_FILE_SYSTEM_CONTROL	IRP_MJ_FILE_SYSTEM_CONTROL
0x0E	IRP_MJ_DEVICE_CONTROL	IRP_MJ_DEVICE_CONTROL
0x0F	IRP_MJ_INTERNAL_DEVICE_CONTROL	IRP_MJ_INTERNAL_DEVICE_CONTROL
0x10	IRP_MJ_SHUTDOWN	IRP_MJ_SHUTDOWN
0x11	IRP_MJ_LOCK_CONTROL	IRP_MJ_LOCK_CONTROL
0x12	IRP_MJ_CLEANUP	IRP_MJ_CLEANUP
0x13	IRP_MJ_CREATE_MAILSLOT	IRP_MJ_CREATE_MAILSLOT
0x14	IRP_MJ_QUERY_SECURITY	IRP_MJ_QUERY_SECURITY
0x15	IRP_MJ_SET_SECURITY	IRP_MJ_SET_SECURITY
0x16	**IRP_MJ_QUERY_POWER**	**IRP_MJ_POWER**
0x17	**IRP_MJ_SET_POWER**	**IRP_MJ_SYSTEM_CONTROL**
0x18	IRP_MJ_DEVICE_CHANGE	IRP_MJ_DEVICE_CHANGE
0x19	IRP_MJ_QUERY_QUOTA	IRP_MJ_QUERY_QUOTA
0x1A	IRP_MJ_SET_QUOTA	IRP_MJ_SET_QUOTA
0x1B	**IRP_MJ_PNP_POWER**	**IRP_MJ_PNP**

As soon as the IRP array is complete, `DriverEntry()` writes a pointer to its `DriverUnload()` callback function to the driver object structure. This allows the driver to be unloaded at runtime. `DriverUnload()` simply destroys all objects created by `DriverInitialize()`, that is, the symbolic link and the device. After that, the driver can be safely removed from the system.

The `DriverDispatcher()` function is invoked whenever a module requests a response from the driver. Because a driver can host several devices, the dispatcher first checks which device should handle the request. The driver skeleton maintains just a single device, so the only thing needed is a sanity check to verify that the device object pointer is identical to the one received from `IoCreateDevice()` during initialization. If it is, `DriverDispatcher()` forwards the received IRP to the `DeviceDispatcher()` function, along with the device context prepared by `DriverInitialize()`. When you extend the skeleton to a multidevice driver, you may have to write distinct IRP dispatchers for each device. The `DeviceDispatcher()` in Listing 3-3 is a trivial implementation that recognizes only three very common requests: `IRP_MJ_CREATE`, `IRP_MJ_CLEANUP`, and `IRP_MJ_CLOSE`. These requests are handled by returning a `STATUS_SUCCESS` code. This is the minimum requirement to allow the device to be opened and closed without error. Other requests cause a `STATUS_NOT_IMPLEMENTED` to be reported.

You may wonder about the purpose of the `#pragma alloc_text` lines in the `DISCARDABLE FUNCTIONS` section of Listing 3-3. `#pragma` directives are a powerful means to send commands to the compiler and linker while they are building a module. The `alloc_text` command instructs them to write the code of the specified function to a nondefault section inside the executable file. By default, all code goes into the `.text` section. However, the directive `#pragma alloc_text (INIT, DriverEntry)` causes the `DriverEntry()` code to be saved to a new file section called `INIT`. The driver loader recognizes this special section and discards it after initialization. `DriverEntry()` and its helper function `DriverInitialize()` are called only once while the driver starts up; therefore, they can be safely removed from memory after having done their work.

The remaining ingredient of the driver skeleton is the resource script `TestDrv.rc`, shown in Listing 3-6. This file is trivial because it consists of references to macros from `DrvInfo.h` only. `DRV_RC_VERSION` creates a `VERSIONINFO` resource with various items compiled from data contributed by the wizard, and `DRV_RC_ICON` evaluates to a simple `ICON` resource statement that adds `TestDrv.ico` to the resource section of `TestDrv.sys`.

Device I/O Control

As mentioned in the introductory remarks of this chapter, we won't build hardware drivers in this book. Instead, we will use the powerful capabilities of kernel-mode drivers to investigate Windows 2000 secrets. The power of the drivers results from the fact that these modules run at the highest possible CPU privilege level. This means that a kernel-mode driver has access to all system resources, can read all memory, and is allowed to execute privileged CPU instructions, such as reading the

```
// TestDrv.rc
// 08-27-2000 <MyName>
// Copyright © 2000 <MyCompany>

#define  _RC_PASS_
#define  _TESTDRV_SYS_
#include "TestDrv.h"

// ================================================================
// STANDARD RESOURCES
// ================================================================

DRV_RC_VERSION
DRV_RC_ICON

// ================================================================
// END OF FILE
// ================================================================
```

LISTING 3-6. *The Resource Script of the Driver Skeleton*

current values of the CPU's control registers. User-mode applications will be aborted immediately if they try to read a single byte from kernel memory or try to execute an assembly language instruction such as `MOV EAX, CR3`. However, the downside of this power is that a driver can trash the entire system with a snap. Even the smallest error is answered by the system with a Blue Screen, so a kernel-mode programmer must be far more concerned about bugs than is a Win32 application or DLL developer. Remember the Windows 2000 killer device we used in Chapter 1 to get a crash dump of the system? All it did was touch the virtual memory address `0x00000000`—and boom! Be aware that you will boot your machine much more frequently when developing kernel-mode drivers.

The driver code I will present in the following chapters will employ a technique called Device I/O Control (IOCTL) to allow user-mode code some degree of "remote control." If an application needs access to some system resources that are unreachable from user-mode, a kernel-mode driver will do the job, and IOCTL will be the bridge between the two. Actually, IOCTL is neither new nor specific to Windows 2000. Even ancient operating systems such as DOS 2.11 had this capability—`Function 0x44` with its various subfunctions has been the IOCTL workhorse of DOS. Basically, IOCTL is a means to communicate with a device on a control channel, which is logically separated from its data channel. Imagine a hard disk device that transfers disk sector contents through its main data channel. If a client wants information about the media currently used by the device, it has to use a different channel. For example, DOS function `0x44`, subfunction `0x0D`, sub-subfunction `0x66` is the DOS IOCTL call that reads the 32-bit serial number of a disk drive (see Brown and Kyle 1991, 1993).

Device I/O Control can be implemented in various ways, depending on the device to be controlled. In its general form, IOCTL has the following characteristics:

- A client controls a device through a special entry point. On DOS, this has been `INT 21h`, function `0x44`. On Windows 2000, it is the Win32 `DeviceIoControl()` function exported by `kernel32.dll`.
- The client provides a device identifier, a control code, an input data buffer, and an output data buffer upon calling the IOCTL entry point. On Windows 2000, the device identifier is a `HANDLE` to a successfully opened device.
- The control code tells the target device's IOCTL dispatcher which control function is requested by the client.
- The input buffer contains any additional data that the device might need to fulfill the request.
- If the request generates any data, it is returned in the client's output buffer.
- The overall result of the IOCTL operation is reported to the client by means of a status code.

It is obvious that this is a powerful general-purpose mechanism that can cover a wide range of control requests. For example, an application might want to have access to forbidden kernel memory. Because the application would throw an exception as soon as it touched the first byte, it could work around this problem by loading a kernel-mode driver to delegate this task. Both modules would have to agree on an IOCTL protocol to manage the data transfer. For example, the application might send the control code `0x80002000` to the driver if it wanted to read memory or `0x80002001` if it wanted to write to it. In a read request, the IOCTL input buffer would probably specify the base address and the number of bytes to read. The kernel-mode driver could pick up requests and distinguish read and write operations by evaluating the control code. In a read request, it would copy the requested memory range to the caller's output buffer and report success if the output buffer is large enough to hold the data. In a write request, the driver would copy data from the input buffer to a memory location that has been specified in the input buffer as well. In Chapter 4, I will provide sample code for such a memory spy.

By now, it should be obvious that IOCTL is a sort of backdoor that Win32 applications can use to perform almost any action that is usually allowed to privileged modules only. Of course, this involves writing such a privileged module in the first place, but once you have such a spy module running in the system, everything else is easy. Two aims of this book are to demonstrate in detail how to write such code and to provide a sample driver that is capable of doing lots of amazing things.

THE WINDOWS 2000 KILLER DEVICE

Before stepping to more advanced driver projects, let's take a look at a very simple driver. In Chapter 1, I introduced the Windows 2000 killer device `w2k_kill.sys`, which is designed to cause a benign system crash. This driver doesn't require most of the code in Listing 3-3 because it will tear down the system before it had an opportunity to receive the first I/O request packet. Listing 3-7 shows its apparently trivial implementation. The file `w2k_kill.h` is not reprinted here because it doesn't contain any code of interest.

The code in Listing 3-7 does not attempt to perform initialization inside its `DriverEntry()` function. The system will stop before `DriverEntry()` returns, so extra work is unnecessary.

LOADING AND UNLOADING DRIVERS

After writing a kernel-mode driver, you probably want to run it immediately. How is this done? Typically, drivers are loaded and started at system boot time, so do you have to reboot the system every time you have updated your driver? Fortunately, this is not necessary. Windows 2000 features a Win32 interface that allows loading and unloading drivers at runtime. This is done by the Service Control (SC) Manager, and the following section details its use.

THE SERVICE CONTROL MANAGER

The name "Service Control Manager" is a bit misleading because it suggests that this component manages services only. Services are a class of powerful Windows 2000 modules well suited to run applications in the background, independent of the user interface shell. That is, a service is a Win32 process that can keep running in the system even if no user is logged in. Although service development is an exciting topic, it is beyond the scope of this book. For further reading on service development, refer to Paula Tomlinson's excellent tutorial in *Windows Developer's Journal (WDJ)* (Tomlinson 1996a), as well as her follow-up treatises on services in her *WDJ* column "Understanding NT" (Tomlinson 1996b and follow-up articles).

```
#define  _W2K_KILL_SYS_
#include <ddk\ntddk.h>
#include "w2k_kill.h"

// =================================================================
// DISCARDABLE FUNCTIONS
// =================================================================

NTSTATUS DriverEntry (PDRIVER_OBJECT  pDriverObject,
                      PUNICODE_STRING pusRegistryPath);

#ifdef ALLOC_PRAGMA
#pragma alloc_text (INIT, DriverEntry)
#endif

// =================================================================
// DRIVER INITIALIZATION
// =================================================================

NTSTATUS DriverEntry (PDRIVER_OBJECT  pDriverObject,
                      PUNICODE_STRING pusRegistryPath)
    {
    return *((NTSTATUS *) 0);
    }

// =================================================================
// END OF PROGRAM
// =================================================================
```

LISTING 3-7. *A Tiny System Crasher*

The SC Manager can handle both services and drivers. For reasons of simplicity, I will use the term "service" here to refer to all objects controlled by the SC Manager, including services in the strict sense of the word and kernel-mode drivers. The SC interface is made available to Win32 applications by the Win32 subsystem component `advapi32.dll`, which hosts an interesting collection of API functions. The names of the main API functions required to load, control, and unload services are listed in Table 3-3, along with short descriptions. Before you can load or access any services, you must obtain a handle to the SC Manager by calling `OpenSCManager()`. In the following discussion, this will be called a *manager handle.* This handle is required in all `CreateService()` and `OpenService()` calls. In turn, these functions return handles that will be called *service handles* here. This type of handle can be specified in all calls that refer to a specific service, such as `ControlService()`, `DeleteService()`, and `StartService()`. Both types of SC handles are released by the `CloseServiceHandle()` function.

TABLE 3-3. *Essential Service Control API Functions*

NAME	DESCRIPTION
CloseServiceHandle	Close handle obtained from `OpenSCManager()`, `CreateService()`, or `OpenService()`
ControlService	Stop, pause, continue, interrogate, or notify a loaded service/driver
CreateService	Load a service/driver
DeleteService	Unload a service/driver
OpenSCManager	Obtain a handle to the SC Manager
OpenService	Obtain a handle to a loaded service/driver
QueryServiceStatus	Query the properties and the current state of a service/driver
StartService	Start a loaded service/driver

Loading and running a service involves the following typical sequence of steps:

1. Call `OpenSCManager()` to obtain a manager handle.
2. Call `CreateService()` to add the service to the system.
3. Call `StartService()` to set the service to the running state.
4. Call `CloseServiceHandle()` to release the manager and service handles.

Be sure to rewind all previous successful actions if an error occurs somewhere in this sequence. For example, you should call `DeleteService()` if the SC Manager reports an error on `StartService()`. Otherwise, the service will remain loaded in an undesired state. Another stumbling stone of the SC Manager API is that the `CreateService()` function insists on receiving a fully qualified path to the executable file. If you specify a relative path, the function will fail—it will not be looking for the file in the current directory. Therefore, you should normalize all file specifications passed to `CreateService()` using the Win32 function `GetFullPathName()` unless they are guaranteed to be fully qualified.

HIGH-LEVEL DRIVER MANAGEMENT FUNCTIONS

To make interaction with the SC Manager easier, the CD accompanying this book contains high-level wrapper functions that hide most of its peculiarities. These functions are part of the large Windows 2000 Utility Library found on the CD in the directory tree `\src\w2k_lib`. All functions exported by `w2k_lib.dll` have a global name prefix of `w2k`, and the service and driver management functions are discernible by the group name prefix `w2kService`. Listing 3-8 shows the implementation of the library functions that load, control, and unload services and drivers.

```
SC_HANDLE WINAPI w2kServiceConnect (void)
    {
    return OpenSCManager (NULL, NULL, SC_MANAGER_ALL_ACCESS);
    }

// -----------------------------------------------------------------

SC_HANDLE WINAPI w2kServiceDisconnect (SC_HANDLE hManager)
    {
    if (hManager != NULL) CloseServiceHandle (hManager);
    return NULL;
    }

// -----------------------------------------------------------------

SC_HANDLE WINAPI w2kServiceManager (SC_HANDLE  hManager,
                                    PSC_HANDLE phManager,
                                    BOOL       fOpen)
    {
    SC_HANDLE hManager1 = NULL;

    if (phManager != NULL)
        {
        if (fOpen)
            {
            if (hManager == NULL)
                {
                *phManager = w2kServiceConnect ();
                }
            else
                {
                *phManager = hManager;
                }
            }
        else
            {
            if (hManager == NULL)
                {
                *phManager = w2kServiceDisconnect (*phManager);
                }
            }
        hManager1 = *phManager;
        }
    return hManager1;
    }

// -----------------------------------------------------------------

SC_HANDLE WINAPI w2kServiceOpen (SC_HANDLE hManager,
                                 PWORD     pwName)
    {
    SC_HANDLE hManager1;
```

(continued)

```
    SC_HANDLE hService = NULL;

    w2kServiceManager (hManager, &hManager1, TRUE);

    if ((hManager1 != NULL) && (pwName != NULL))
        {
        hService = OpenService (hManager1, pwName,
                                SERVICE_ALL_ACCESS);
        }
    w2kServiceManager (hManager, &hManager1, FALSE);
    return hService;
    }

// -----------------------------------------------------------------

BOOL WINAPI w2kServiceClose (SC_HANDLE hService)
    {
    return (hService != NULL) && CloseServiceHandle (hService);
    }

// -----------------------------------------------------------------

BOOL WINAPI w2kServiceAdd (SC_HANDLE hManager,
                           PWORD     pwName,
                           PWORD     pwInfo,
                           PWORD     pwPath)
    {
    SC_HANDLE hManager1, hService;
    PWORD     pwFile;
    WORD      awPath [MAX_PATH];
    DWORD     n;
    BOOL      fOk = FALSE;

    w2kServiceManager (hManager, &hManager1, TRUE);

    if ((hManager1 != NULL) && (pwName != NULL) &&
        (pwInfo    != NULL) && (pwPath != NULL) &&
        (n = GetFullPathName (pwPath, MAX_PATH, awPath, &pwFile)) &&
        (n < MAX_PATH))
        {
        if ((hService = CreateService (hManager1, pwName, pwInfo,
                                       SERVICE_ALL_ACCESS,
                                       SERVICE_KERNEL_DRIVER,
                                       SERVICE_DEMAND_START,
                                       SERVICE_ERROR_NORMAL,
                                       awPath, NULL, NULL,
                                       NULL, NULL, NULL))
            != NULL)
            {
            w2kServiceClose (hService);
            fOk = TRUE;
```

```
            }
        else
            {
            fOk = (GetLastError () ==
                   ERROR_SERVICE_EXISTS);
            }
        }
    w2kServiceManager (hManager, &hManager1, FALSE);
    return fOk;
    }

// -----------------------------------------------------------------

BOOL WINAPI w2kServiceRemove (SC_HANDLE hManager,
                              PWORD     pwName)
    {
    SC_HANDLE hService;
    BOOL      fOk = FALSE;

    if ((hService = w2kServiceOpen (hManager, pwName)) != NULL)
        {
        if (DeleteService (hService))
            {
            fOk = TRUE;
            }
        else
            {
            fOk = (GetLastError () ==
                   ERROR_SERVICE_MARKED_FOR_DELETE);
            }
        w2kServiceClose (hService);
        }
    return fOk;
    }

// -----------------------------------------------------------------

BOOL WINAPI w2kServiceStart (SC_HANDLE hManager,
                             PWORD     pwName)
    {
    SC_HANDLE hService;
    BOOL      fOk = FALSE;

    if ((hService = w2kServiceOpen (hManager, pwName)) != NULL)
        {
        if (StartService (hService, 1, &pwName))
            {
            fOk = TRUE;
            }
        else
            {
```

(continued)

```
            fOk = (GetLastError () ==
                   ERROR_SERVICE_ALREADY_RUNNING);
            }
        w2kServiceClose (hService);
        }
    return fOk;
    }

// -----------------------------------------------------------------

BOOL WINAPI w2kServiceControl (SC_HANDLE hManager,
                               PWORD     pwName,
                               DWORD     dControl)
    {
    SC_HANDLE      hService;
    SERVICE_STATUS ServiceStatus;
    BOOL           fOk = FALSE;

    if ((hService = w2kServiceOpen (hManager, pwName)) != NULL)
        {
        if (QueryServiceStatus (hService, &ServiceStatus))
            {
            switch (ServiceStatus.dwCurrentState)
                {
                case SERVICE_STOP_PENDING:
                case SERVICE_STOPPED:
                    {
                    fOk = (dControl == SERVICE_CONTROL_STOP);
                    break;
                    }
                case SERVICE_PAUSE_PENDING:
                case SERVICE_PAUSED:
                    {
                    fOk = (dControl == SERVICE_CONTROL_PAUSE);
                    break;
                    }
                case SERVICE_START_PENDING:
                case SERVICE_CONTINUE_PENDING:
                case SERVICE_RUNNING:
                    {
                    fOk = (dControl == SERVICE_CONTROL_CONTINUE);
                    break;
                    }
                }
            }
        fOk = fOk ||
              ControlService (hService, dControl, &ServiceStatus);

        w2kServiceClose (hService);
        }
```

```
    return fOk;
    }

// -----------------------------------------------------------------

BOOL WINAPI w2kServiceStop (SC_HANDLE hManager,
                            PWORD     pwName)
    {
    return w2kServiceControl (hManager, pwName,
                              SERVICE_CONTROL_STOP);
    }

// -----------------------------------------------------------------

BOOL WINAPI w2kServicePause (SC_HANDLE hManager,
                             PWORD     pwName)
    {
    return w2kServiceControl (hManager, pwName,
                              SERVICE_CONTROL_PAUSE);
    }

// -----------------------------------------------------------------

BOOL WINAPI w2kServiceContinue (SC_HANDLE hManager,
                                PWORD     pwName)
    {
    return w2kServiceControl (hManager, pwName,
                              SERVICE_CONTROL_CONTINUE);
    }

// -----------------------------------------------------------------

SC_HANDLE WINAPI w2kServiceLoad (PWORD pwName,
                                 PWORD pwInfo,
                                 PWORD pwPath,
                                 BOOL  fStart)
    {
    BOOL      fOk;
    SC_HANDLE hManager = NULL;

    if ((hManager = w2kServiceConnect ()) != NULL)
        {
        fOk = w2kServiceAdd (hManager, pwName, pwInfo, pwPath);

        if (fOk && fStart)
            {
            if (!(fOk = w2kServiceStart (hManager, pwName)))
                {
                w2kServiceRemove (hManager, pwName);
                }
            }
```

(continued)

```
        if (!fOk)
            {
            hManager = w2kServiceDisconnect (hManager);
            }
        }
    return hManager;
    }

// -----------------------------------------------------------------

SC_HANDLE WINAPI w2kServiceLoadEx (PWORD pwPath,
                                   BOOL  fStart)
    {
    PVS_VERSIONDATA pvvd;
    PWORD           pwPath1, pwInfo;
    WORD            awName [MAX_PATH];
    DWORD           dName, dExtension;
    SC_HANDLE       hManager = NULL;

    if (pwPath != NULL)
        {
        dName = w2kPathName (pwPath, &dExtension);

        lstrcpyn (awName, pwPath + dName,
                  min (MAX_PATH, dExtension - dName + 1));

        pwPath1 = w2kPathEvaluate (pwPath,  NULL);
        pvvd    = w2kVersionData  (pwPath1, -1);

        pwInfo  = ((pvvd != NULL) && pvvd->awFileDescription [0]
                   ? pvvd->awFileDescription
                   : awName);

        hManager = w2kServiceLoad (awName, pwInfo, pwPath1, fStart);

        w2kMemoryDestroy (pvvd);
        w2kMemoryDestroy (pwPath1);
        }
    return hManager;
    }

// -----------------------------------------------------------------

BOOL WINAPI w2kServiceUnload (PWORD     pwName,
                              SC_HANDLE hManager)
    {
    SC_HANDLE hManager1 = hManager;
    BOOL      fOk       = FALSE;

    if (pwName != NULL)
        {
```

```
        if (hManager1 == NULL)
            {
            hManager1 = w2kServiceConnect ();
            }
        if (hManager1 != NULL)
            {
            w2kServiceStop (hManager1, pwName);
            fOk = w2kServiceRemove (hManager1, pwName);
            }
        }
    w2kServiceDisconnect (hManager1);
    return fOk;
    }

// -----------------------------------------------------------------

BOOL WINAPI w2kServiceUnloadEx (PWORD     pwPath,
                                SC_HANDLE hManager)
    {
    DWORD dName, dExtension;
    WORD  awName [MAX_PATH];
    PWORD pwName = NULL;

    if (pwPath != NULL)
        {
        dName = w2kPathName (pwPath, &dExtension);

        lstrcpyn (pwName = awName, pwPath + dName,
                  min (MAX_PATH, dExtension - dName + 1));
        }
    return w2kServiceUnload (pwName, hManager);
    }
```

LISTING 3-8. *Service and Driver Management Library Functions*

In Table 3-4, the functions defined in Listing 3-8 are listed, along with short descriptions. Some function names, such as `w2kServiceStart()` and `w2kServiceControl()`, are similar to certain SC Manager API functions—`StartService()` and `ControlService()`, in this case. This isn't coincidence—the respective functions are in fact found at the heart of these wrappers. The main difference is that `StartService()` and `ControlService()` operate on service handles, whereas `w2kServiceStart()` and `w2kServiceControl()` accept service names. The names are seamlessly converted to handles by internally calling `w2kServiceOpen()` and `w2kServiceClose()`, which in turn call `OpenService()` and `CloseServiceHandle()`.

TABLE 3-4. *SC Manager Wrappers Provided by* `w2k_lib.dll`

NAME	DESCRIPTION
w2kServiceAdd	Add a service/driver to the system
w2kServiceClose	Close a service handle
w2kServiceConnect	Connect to the Service Control Manager
w2kServiceContinue	Resume a paused service/driver
w2kServiceControl	Stop, pause, continue, interrogate, or notify a loaded service/driver
w2kServiceDisconnect	Disconnect from the Service Control Manager
w2kServiceLoad	Load and optionally start a service/driver
w2kServiceLoadEx	Load and optionally start a service/driver (automatic name generation)
w2kServiceManager	Open/close a temporary Service Control Manager handle
w2kServiceOpen	Obtain a handle to a loaded service/driver
w2kServicePause	Pause a running service/driver
w2kServiceRemove	Remove a service/driver from the system
w2kServiceStart	Start a loaded service/driver
w2kServiceStop	Stop a running service/driver
w2kServiceUnload	Stop and unload a service/driver
w2kServiceUnloadEx	Stop and unload a service/driver (automatic name generation)

The typical usage of the library functions in Table 3-4 is along the following guidelines:

- To load a service, call `w2kServiceLoad()` or `w2kServiceLoadEx()`. The latter generates the service and display names automatically from the file's path and version resource. The Boolean `fStart` argument decides whether the service should be started automatically after a successful load. On success, the function returns a manager handle for further requests. No error is reported if the service is already loaded or if `fStart` is `TRUE` and the service is already running. If an error occurs, the service is automatically unloaded, if necessary.
- To unload a service, call `w2kServiceUnload()` or `w2kServiceUnloadEx()`, using the manager handle returned by `w2kServiceLoad()` or `w2kServiceLoadEx()`. `w2kServiceUnloadEx()` generates the service name automatically from the file's path. If you have already closed this handle,

obtain a new one from `w2kServiceConnect()` or simply pass in `NULL` to work with a temporary handle. The manager handle will be closed automatically by `w2kServiceUnload()`. No error is reported if the service is already marked for deletion but cannot be deleted because open device handles are still existing.

- To control a service, call `w2kServiceStart()`, `w2kServiceStop()`, `w2kServicePause()`, or `w2kServiceContinue()`, using a manager handle returned by `w2kServiceLoad()` or `w2kServiceConnect()`. If you supply `NULL` for the manager handle, a temporary handle is used. No error is reported if the service is already in the requested state.
- To close a manager handle, call `w2kServiceDisconnect()`. You can request another manager handle at any time by calling `w2kServiceConnect()`.

`w2kServiceLoadEx()` is a very powerful function. It builds all parameters needed to load the service automatically, expecting nothing but the path of the executable file. The service name requested by the SC Manager's `CreateService()` function is derived from the file name by stripping the extension. To build an appropriate display name for a newly created service, `w2kServiceLoadEx()` attempts to read the value of the `FileDescription` string from the file version information. If no version resource is included in the executable, or the `FileDescription` string is not available, the service name is used by default. Unlike `w2kServiceLoad()`, `w2kServiceLoadEx()` evaluates environment variables embedded in the path. That is, if the path string contains substrings such as `%SystemRoot%` or `%TEMP%`, they are replaced by the current values of the corresponding environment variables. `w2kServiceUnloadEx()` is the counterpart of `w2kServiceLoadEx()`—it extracts the service name from the supplied path, as explained above, and passes it to `w2kServiceUnload()`. Both functions are ideally suited for applications that have to load and unload third-party device drivers on behalf of the user, knowing nothing about them but their executable paths. A sample application of this kind is included on the CD accompanying this book. The console-mode utility `w2k_load.exe` is a general-purpose kernel-mode device driver (un)loader that provides a simple command line interface for `w2kServiceLoadEx()` and `w2kServiceUnloadEx()`. The source files can be found on the CD in the directory tree `\src\w2k_load`. The relevant code is shown in Listing 3-9, proving that this utility is almost trivial because all the hard work is done inside `w2k_lib.dll` by the `w2kServiceLoadEx()` and `w2kServiceUnloadEx()` functions.

```
// =================================================================
// GLOBAL STRINGS
// =================================================================

WORD awUsage  [] =
    L"\r\n"
    L"Usage: " SW(MAIN_MODULE) L" <driver path>\r\n"
    L"        " SW(MAIN_MODULE) L" <driver path> %s\r\n"
    L"        " SW(MAIN_MODULE) L" <driver name> %s\r\n";

WORD awUnload [] = L"/unload";

WORD awOk     [] = L"OK\r\n";
WORD awError  [] = L"ERROR\r\n";

// =================================================================
// COMMAND HANDLERS
// =================================================================

BOOL WINAPI DriverLoad (PWORD pwPath)
    {
    SC_HANDLE hManager;
    BOOL      fOk = FALSE;

    _printf (L"\r\nLoading \"%s\" ... ", pwPath);

    if ((hManager = w2kServiceLoadEx (pwPath, TRUE)) != NULL)
        {
        w2kServiceDisconnect (hManager);
        fOk = TRUE;
        }
    _printf (fOk ? awOk : awError);
    return fOk;
    }

// -----------------------------------------------------------------

BOOL WINAPI DriverUnload (PWORD pwPath)
    {
    BOOL fOk = FALSE;

    _printf (L"\r\nUnloading \"%s\" ... ", pwPath);

    fOk = w2kServiceUnloadEx (pwPath, NULL);
    _printf (fOk ? awOk : awError);
    return fOk;
    }

// =================================================================
// MAIN PROGRAM
// =================================================================
```

```
DWORD Main (DWORD argc, PTBYTE *argv, PTBYTE *argp)
    {
    if (argc == 2)
        {
        DriverLoad (argv [1]);
        }
    else
        {
        if ((argc == 3) && (!lstrcmpi (argv [2], awUnload)))
            {
            DriverUnload (argv [1]);
            }
        else
            {
            _printf (awUsage, awUnload, awUnload);
            }
        }
    return 0;
    }

// =================================================================
// END OF PROGRAM
// =================================================================
```

LISTING 3-9. *Loading and Unloading Device Drivers*

The remaining library functions listed in Table 3-4 are working on a lower level and are used internally by `w2k_lib.dll`. Of course, you can call them from your applications, if you like. Their usage should be obvious from the source code in Listing 3-8.

ENUMERATING SERVICES AND DRIVERS

From time to time it might be necessary to know which services and drivers are currently loaded inside the system and what state they are in. For this purpose, the SC Manager provides another powerful function named `EnumServicesStatus()`. This function requires a manager handle, as usual, and fills an array of `ENUM_SERVICE_STATUS` structures with information about each currently loaded service or driver. The list can be filtered by service/driver type and state. If the buffer supplied by the caller isn't large enough to hold all entries at once, the function can be called repeatedly until all items have been retrieved. It is difficult to compute the required buffer size in advance because the buffer has to provide extra space of unknown size for the strings that are referenced by the members of the `ENUM_SERVICE_STATUS` structures. Fortunately, `EnumServicesStatus()` returns the number of bytes needed to return the remaining entries, so the correct buffer size can be determined by trial and error. Listing 3-10 shows the definitions of the `SERVICE_STATUS` and `ENUM_SERVICE_STATUS` structures, which are declared in the Win32 header file `WinSvc.h`.

```
typedef struct _SERVICE_STATUS
    {
    DWORD dwServiceType;
    DWORD dwCurrentState;
    DWORD dwControlsAccepted;
    DWORD dwWin32ExitCode;
    DWORD dwServiceSpecificExitCode;
    DWORD dwCheckPoint;
    DWORD dwWaitHint;
    }
    SERVICE_STATUS, *LPSERVICE_STATUS;

typedef struct _ENUM_SERVICE_STATUS
    {
    LPTSTR         lpServiceName;
    LPTSTR         lpDisplayName;
    SERVICE_STATUS ServiceStatus;
    }
    ENUM_SERVICE_STATUS;
```

LISTING 3-10. *Definition of* `ENUM_SERVICE_STATUS` *and* `SERVICE_STATUS`

The `w2kServiceList()` function in Listing 3-11 is another goodie from the `w2k_lib.dll` utility library on the companion CD. It hides the required actions mentioned above and returns a ready-to-use structure with all requested data plus a couple of extras. It returns a pointer to a `W2K_SERVICES` structure, defined in `w2k_lib.h` and included at the top of Listing 3-11. Along with the `ENUM_SERVICE_STATUS` array `aess[]`, this structure contains four additional members. dEntries indicates how many entries have been copied to the status array, and `dBytes` specifies the total size of the returned `W2K_SERVICES` structure. `dDisplayName` and `dServiceName` are set to the maximum lengths of the `lpDisplayName` and `lpServiceName` strings in `aess[]`, respectively. These values are very convenient if you are writing a console-mode application that outputs a service/driver list to the screen with proper alignment of the name columns.

To report an accurate snapshot of the system, `w2kServiceList()` attempts to retrieve all entries in a single call to `EnumServicesStatus()`. To this end, it starts out with a zero-length buffer, which will usually yield an `ERROR_MORE_DATA` status. In this case, `EnumServicesStatus()` returns the required buffer size. After allocating an appropriately sized buffer, `w2kServiceList()` tries again. This time, `EnumServicesStatus()` should succeed. However, a small probability exists that another entry has been added to the list in the meantime, so this procedure is repeated in a loop until everything is correct or an error other than `ERROR_MORE_DATA` is returned.

```
typedef struct _W2K_SERVICES
    {
    DWORD                dEntries;     // number of entries in aess[]
    DWORD                dBytes;       // overall number of bytes
    DWORD                dDisplayName; // maximum display name length
    DWORD                dServiceName; // maximum service name length
    ENUM_SERVICE_STATUS aess [];       // service/driver status array
    }
    W2K_SERVICES, *PW2K_SERVICES, **PPW2K_SERVICES;

#define W2K_SERVICES_ sizeof (W2K_SERVICES)

PW2K_SERVICES WINAPI w2kServiceList (BOOL fDriver,
                                     BOOL fWin32,
                                     BOOL fActive,
                                     BOOL fInactive)
    {
    SC_HANDLE     hManager;
    DWORD         dType, dState, dBytes, dResume, dName, i;
    PW2K_SERVICES pws = NULL;

    if ((pws = w2kMemoryCreate (W2K_SERVICES_)) != NULL)
        {
        pws->dEntries     = 0;
        pws->dBytes       = 0;
        pws->dDisplayName = 0;
        pws->dServiceName = 0;

        if ((fDriver || fWin32) && (fActive || fInactive))
            {
            if ((hManager = w2kServiceConnect ()) != NULL)
                {
                dType   = (fDriver ? SERVICE_DRIVER : 0) |
                          (fWin32  ? SERVICE_WIN32  : 0);

                dState  = (fActive && fInactive
                           ? SERVICE_STATE_ALL
                           : (fActive
                              ? SERVICE_ACTIVE
                              : SERVICE_INACTIVE));

                dBytes  = pws->dBytes;
                while (pws != NULL)
                    {
                    pws->dEntries     = 0;
                    pws->dBytes       = dBytes;
                    pws->dDisplayName = 0;
                    pws->dServiceName = 0;

                    dResume = 0;
```

(continued)

```
                if (EnumServicesStatus (hManager, dType, dState,
                                        pws->aess, pws->dBytes,
                                        &dBytes, &pws->dEntries,
                                        &dResume))
                    break;

                dBytes += pws->dBytes;
                pws     = w2kMemoryDestroy (pws);

                if (GetLastError () != ERROR_MORE_DATA) break;

                pws = w2kMemoryCreate (W2K_SERVICES_ + dBytes);
                }
            w2kServiceDisconnect (hManager);
            }
        else
            {
            pws = w2kMemoryDestroy (pws);
            }
        }
    if (pws != NULL)
        {
        for (i = 0; i < pws->dEntries; i++)
            {
            dName = lstrlen (pws->aess [i].lpDisplayName);
            pws->dDisplayName = max (pws->dDisplayName, dName);

            dName = lstrlen (pws->aess [i].lpServiceName);
            pws->dServiceName = max (pws->dServiceName, dName);
            }
        }
    }
return pws;
}
```

LISTING 3-11. *Enumerating Services and Drivers*

w2kServiceList() expects four Boolean arguments determining the contents of the returned list. With the fDriver and fWin32 arguments, you can choose the inclusion of drivers and services, respectively. If both flags are set, the list will contain both drivers and services. The fActive and fInactive flags impose a state filter onto the list. If fActive is set, the list contains all modules that currently are in the running or paused state. The fInactive parameter selects the remaining modules, that is, those that are currently loaded but stopped. If all four arguments are FALSE, the function returns a W2K_SERVICES structure with an empty status array. The sample code CD contains a simple service and driver browser, designed as a Win32 console-mode application and based on the w2kServiceList() function of w2k_lib.dll. It uses the dDisplayName and dServiceName members of the returned W2K_SERVICES structure (see Listing 3-11) for proper horizontal alignment of all names. You can find the source code of this utility in the CD's directory tree `\src\w2k_svc`. The program can be run from the CD by executing `\bin\w2k_svc.exe`. Example 3-4 resulted from running it on my machine, requesting a list of all active kernel-mode drivers by specifying the command switches `/drivers /active`.

```
D:\> w2k_svc /drivers /active

// w2k_svc.exe
// SBS Windows 2000 Service List V1.00
// 08-27-2000 Sven B. Schreiber
// sbs@orgon.com

Found 29 active drivers:

    1. Alerter . . . . . . . . . . . . . . . . . . . . . . . . . Alerter
    2. Computer Browser  . . . . . . . . . . . . . . . . . . . . Browser
    3. Creative Service for CDROM Access . . . . . . . . . . . . Creative Service
    4. DHCP Client . . . . . . . . . . . . . . . . . . . . . . . Dhcp
    5. Logical Disk Manager  . . . . . . . . . . . . . . . . . . dmserver
    6. DNS Client . . . . . . . . . . . . . . . . . . . . . . . . Dnscache
    7. Event Log  . . . . . . . . . . . . . . . . . . . . . . . . Eventlog
    8. COM+ Event System  . . . . . . . . . . . . . . . . . . . . EventSystem
    9. Server . . . . . . . . . . . . . . . . . . . . . . . . . . lanmanserver
   10. Workstation  . . . . . . . . . . . . . . . . . . . . . . . lanmanworkstation
   11. TCP/IP NetBIOS Helper Service . . . . . . . . . . . . . . LmHosts
   12. Messenger  . . . . . . . . . . . . . . . . . . . . . . . . Messenger
   13. Network Connections . . . . . . . . . . . . . . . . . . . Netman
   14. Removable Storage  . . . . . . . . . . . . . . . . . . . . NtmsSvc
   15. Plug and Play  . . . . . . . . . . . . . . . . . . . . . . PlugPlay
   16. IPSEC Policy Agent . . . . . . . . . . . . . . . . . . . . PolicyAgent
   17. Protected Storage  . . . . . . . . . . . . . . . . . . . . ProtectedStorage
   18. Remote Access Connection Manager  . . . . . . . . . . . . RasMan
   19. Remote Registry Service . . . . . . . . . . . . . . . . . RemoteRegistry
   20. Remote Procedure Call (RPC) . . . . . . . . . . . . . . . RpcSs
   21. Security Accounts Manager . . . . . . . . . . . . . . . . SamSs
   22. Task Scheduler  . . . . . . . . . . . . . . . . . . . . . Schedule
   23. RunAs Service  . . . . . . . . . . . . . . . . . . . . . . seclogon
   24. System Event Notification . . . . . . . . . . . . . . . . SENS
   25. Print Spooler  . . . . . . . . . . . . . . . . . . . . . . Spooler
   26. Telephony  . . . . . . . . . . . . . . . . . . . . . . . . TapiSrv
   27. Distributed Link Tracking Client  . . . . . . . . . . . . TrkWks
   28. Windows Management Instrumentation  . . . . . . . . . . . WinMgmt
   29. Windows Management Instrumentation Driver Extensions . Wmi
```

EXAMPLE 3-4. *Running the Service List Utility* `w2k_svc.exe`

In the next chapter, we will start developing a real-world kernel-mode driver that spies on kernel memory and cracks essential memory management data structures. This project accompanies you while reading Chapters 4, 5, and 6, and the driver is enhanced incrementally in each chapter. The final result is a versatile Windows 2000 kernel spy, complemented by several nice client applications.

CHAPTER 4

Exploring Windows 2000 Memory

Memory management is one of the most important and most difficult duties of an operating system. This chapter presents a comprehensive overview of Windows 2000 memory management and the structure of the 4-GB linear address space. In this context, the virtual memory addressing and paging capabilities of the Intel i386 CPU family are explained, focusing on how the Windows 2000 kernel exploits them. To aid the exploration of memory, this chapter features a pair of sample programs: a kernel-mode device driver that collects information about the system, and a user-mode client application that queries this data from the driver via device I/O control and displays it in a console window. The "spy driver" module will be reused in the remaining chapters for several other interesting tasks that require execution of kernel-mode code. This chapter—especially the first section—is tough reading because it puts your hands directly on the CPU hardware. Nevertheless I hope you won't skip it, because virtual memory management is an exciting topic, and understanding how it works provides insight into the mechanics of a complex operating system such as Windows 2000.

INTEL i386 MEMORY MANAGEMENT

The Windows 2000 kernel makes heavy use of the protected-mode virtual memory management mechanisms of the Intel i386 CPU class. To get a better understanding of how Windows 2000 manages its main memory, it is important to be at least minimally familiar with some architectural issues of the i386 CPU. The term *i386* might look somewhat anachronistic because the 80386 CPU dates back to the early days of Windows computing. Windows 2000 is designed for Pentium CPUs and above. However, even these newer processors rely on the memory management model originally designed for the 80386 CPU, with some important enhancements, of course. Therefore, Microsoft usually labels the Windows NT and 2000 versions built for

Intel processors “i386” or even “x86.” Don’t be confused about that—whenever you read the numbers 86 or 386 in this book, keep in mind that the corresponding information refers to a specific CPU *architecture,* not a specific processor release.

Basic Memory Layout

Windows 2000 uses a very straightforward memory layout for application and system code. The 4-GB virtual memory space offered by the 32-bit Intel CPUs is divided into two equal parts. Memory addresses below *0x80000000* are assigned to user-mode modules, including the Win32 subsystem, and the remaining 2 GB are reserved for the kernel. Windows 2000 Advanced Server also supports an alternative memory model commonly called *4GT RAM Tuning,* which has been introduced with Windows NT 4.0 Server Enterprise Edition. This model features 3-GB address space for user processes, and 1-GB space for the kernel. It is enabled by adding the `/3GB` switch to the bootstrap command line in the boot manager configuration file `boot.ini`.

The Advanced Server and Datacenter variants of Windows 2000 support yet another memory option named *Physical Address Extension (PAE)* enabled by the `boot.ini` switch `/PAE`. This option exploits a feature of some Intel CPUs (e.g., the Pentium Pro processor) that allows physical memory larger than 4 GB to be mapped into the 32-bit address space. In this Chapter, I will ignore these special configurations. You can read more about them in Microsoft’s Knowledge Base article Q171793 (Microsoft 2000c), Intel’s Pentium manuals (Intel 1999a, 1999b, 1999c), and the Windows 2000 Device Driver Kit (DDK) documentation (Microsoft 2000f).

Memory Segmentation and Demand Paging

Before delving into the technical details of the i386 architecture, let’s travel back in time to the year 1978, when Intel released the mother of all PC processors: the 8086. I want to restrict this discussion to the most significant milestones. If you want to know more, Robert L. Hummel’s 80486 programmer’s reference is an excellent starting point (Hummel 1992). It is a bit outdated now because it doesn’t cover the new features of the Pentium family; however, this leaves more space for important information about the basic i386 architecture. Although the 8086 was able to address 1 MB of Random Access Memory (RAM), an application could never “see” the entire physical address space because of the restriction of the CPU’s address registers to 16 bits. This means that applications were able to access a contiguous linear address space of only 64 KB, but this memory window could be shifted up and down in the physical space with the help of a set of 16-bit segment registers. Each segment register defined a base address in 16-byte increments, and the linear addresses in the 64-KB logical space were added as offsets to this base, effectively resulting in 20-bit addresses. This archaic memory model is still supported even by the latest Pentium CPUs, and it is called *Real-Address Mode,* commonly referred to as *Real Mode.*

An alternative mode was introduced with the 80286 CPU, referred to as *Protected Virtual Address Mode,* or simply *Protected Mode.* It featured a memory model where physical addresses were not generated by simply adding a linear address to a segment base. To retain backward compatibility with the 8086 and 80186, the 80286 still used segment registers, but they did not contain physical segment addresses after the CPU had been switched to Protected Mode. Instead, they provided a selector, comprising an index into a descriptor table. The target entry defined a 24-bit physical base address, allowing access to 16 MB of RAM, which seemed like an incredible amount then. However, the 80286 was still a 16-bit CPU, so the limitation of the linear address space to 64 KB tiles still applied.

The breakthrough came in 1985 with the 80386 CPU. This chip finally cut the ties of 16-bit addressing, pushing up the linear address space to 4 GB by introducing 32-bit linear addresses while retaining the basic selector/descriptor architecture of its predecessor. Fortunately, the 80286 descriptor structure contained some spare bits that could be reclaimed. While moving from 16- to 32-bit addresses, the size of the CPU's data registers was doubled as well, and new powerful addressing modes were added. This radical shift to 32-bit data and addresses was a real benefit for programmers—at least theoretically. Practically, it took several years longer before the Microsoft Windows platform was ready to fully support the 32-bit model. The first version of Windows NT was released on July 26th, 1993, constituting the very first incarnation of the Win32 API. Whereas Windows 3.x programmers still had to deal with memory tiles of 64 KB with separate code and data segments, Windows NT provided a flat linear address space of 4 GB, where all code and data could be addressed by simple 32-bit pointers, without segmentation. Internally, of course, segmentation was still active, as I will show later in this chapter, but the entire responsibility for managing segments finally had been moved to the operating system.

Another essential new 80386 feature was the hardware support for paging, or, more precisely, demand-paged virtual memory. This is a technique that allows memory to be backed up by a storage medium other than RAM—a hard disk, for example. With paging enabled, the CPU can access more memory than physically available by swapping out the least recently accessed memory contents to backup storage, making space for new data. Theoretically, up to 4 GB of contiguous linear memory can be accessed this way, provided that the backup media is large enough—even if the installed physical RAM amounts to just a small fraction of the memory. Of course, paging is not the fastest way to access memory. It is always good to have as much physical RAM as possible. But it is an excellent way to work with large amounts of data that would otherwise exceed the available memory. For example, graphics and database applications require a large amount of working memory, and some wouldn't be able to run on a low-end PC system if paging weren't available.

In the paging scheme of the 80386, memory is subdivided into pages of 4-KB or 4-MB size. The operating system designer is free to choose between these two options, and it is even possible to mix pages of both sizes. Later I will show that Windows 2000 uses such a mixed page design, keeping the operating system in 4-MB pages and using 4-KB pages for the remaining code and data. The pages are managed by means of a hierarchically structured page-table tree that indicates for each page where it is currently located in physical memory. This management structure also contains information on whether the page is actually in physical memory in the first place. If a page has been swapped out to the hard disk, and some module touches an address within this page, the CPU generates a page fault, similar to an interrupt generated by a peripheral hardware device. Next, the page fault handler inside the operating system kernel will attempt to swap back this page to physical memory, possibly writing other memory contents to disk to make space. Usually, the system will apply a least-recently-used (LRU) schedule to decide which pages qualify to be swapped out. By now it should be clear why this procedure is sometimes referred to as *demand* paging: Physical memory contents are moved to the backup storage and back on software demand, based on statistics of the memory usage of the operating system and its applications.

The address indirection layer represented by the page-tables has two interesting implications. First, there is no predetermined relationship between the addresses used by a program and the addresses found on the physical address bus of the CPU chip. If you know that a data structure of your application is located at the address, say, `0x00140000`, you still don't know anything about the physical address of your data unless you examine the page-table tree. It is up to the operating system to decide what this address mapping looks like. Even more, the address translation currently in effect is unpredictable, in part because of the probabilistic nature of the paging mechanism. Fortunately, knowledge of physical addresses isn't required in most application cases. This is something left for developers of hardware drivers. The second implication of paging is that the address space is not necessarily contiguous. Depending on the page-table contents, the 4-GB space can comprise large "holes" where neither physical nor backup memory is mapped. If an application tries to read to or write from such an address, it will be aborted immediately by the system. Later in this chapter, I will show in detail how Windows 2000 spreads its available memory over the 4-GB address space.

The 80486 and Pentium CPUs use the very same i386 segmentation and paging mechanisms introduced with the 80386, except for some exotic addressing features such as the Physical Address Extension (PAE) of the Pentium Pro. Along with higher clock frequencies, these newer models contain optimizations in other areas. For example, the Pentium features a dual instruction pipeline that enables it to execute two operations at the same time, as long as these instructions don't depend on each other. For example, if instruction A modifies a register value, and the consecutive instruction B uses the modified value for a computation, B cannot be executed before A has finished. But if instruction B involves a different register, the CPU can execute A and B simultaneously without adverse effects. This and other Pentium optimizations have opened a wide field for compiler optimization. If this topic looks interesting, see Rick Booth's *Inner Loops* (Booth 1997).

In the context of i386 memory management, three sorts of addresses must be distinguished, termed *logical, linear,* and *physical* addresses in Intel's system programming manual for the Pentium (Intel 1999c).

1. *Logical addresses:* This is the most precise specification of a memory location, usually written in hexadecimal form as `XXXX:YYYYYYYY`, where `XXXX` is a selector, and `YYYYYYYY` is a linear offset into the segment addressed by the selector. Instead of a numeric `XXXX` value, it is also possible to specify the name of a segment register holding the selector, such as `CS` (code segment), `DS` (data segment), `ES` (extra segment), `FS` (additional data segment #1), `GS` (additional data segment #2), and `SS` (stack segment). This notation is borrowed from the old "segment:offset" style of specifying "far pointers" in 8086 Real-Mode.
2. *Linear addresses:* Most applications and many kernel-mode drivers disregard virtual addresses. More precisely, they are just interested in the offset part of a virtual address, which is referred to as a *linear address*. An address of this type assumes a default segmentation model, determined by the current values of the CPU's segment registers. Windows 2000 uses flat segmentation, with the `CS`, `DS`, `ES`, and `SS` registers pointing to the same linear address space; therefore, programs can safely assume that all code, data, and stack pointers can be cast among one another. For example, a stack location can be cast to a data pointer at any time without concern about the values of the corresponding segment registers.
3. *Physical addresses:* This address type is of interest only if the CPU works in paging mode. Basically, a physical address is the voltage pattern measurable at the address bus pins of the CPU chip. The operating system maps linear addresses to physical addresses by setting up page-tables. The layout of the Windows 2000 page-tables, which has some very interesting properties for debugging software developers, will be discussed later in this chapter.

The distinction between virtual and linear addresses is somewhat artificial, and some documentation uses both terms interchangeably. I will do my best to use this nomenclature consistently. It is important to note that Windows 2000 assumes physical addresses to be 64 bits wide. This might seem odd on Intel i386 systems, which usually have a 32-bit address bus. However, some Pentium systems can address more than 4 GB of physical memory. For example, the Physical Address Extension (PAE) mode of the Pentium Pro CPU extends the physical address space to 36 bits, allowing access to 64 GB of RAM (Intel 1999c). Therefore, the Windows 2000 API functions involving physical addresses usually rely on the data type `PHYSICAL_ADDRESS`, which is just an alias name for the `LARGE_INTEGER` structure, as shown in Listing 4-1. Both types are defined in the DDK header file `ntdef.h`. The `LARGE_INTEGER` is a structural representation of a 64-bit signed integer, allowing interpretation as a concatenation of two 32-bit quantities (`LowPart` and `HighPart`) or a single 64-bit number (`QuadPart`). The `LONGLONG` type is equivalent to the native Visual C/C++ type `__int64`. Its unsigned sibling is called `ULONGLONG` or `DWORDLONG` and is based on the native `unsigned __int64` type.

Figure 4-1 outlines the i386 memory segmentation model, showing the relationship between logical and linear addresses. For clarity, I have drawn the descriptor table and the segment as small, nonoverlapping boxes. However, this isn't a requirement. Actually, a 32-bit operating system usually applies a segmentation layout as shown in Figure 4-2. This so-called flat memory model is based on segments that span the entire 4-GB address space. As a side effect, the descriptor table becomes part of the segment and can be accessed by all code that has sufficient access rights.

```
typedef LARGE_INTEGER PHYSICAL_ADDRESS, *PPHYSICAL_ADDRESS;

typedef union _LARGE_INTEGER
    {
    struct
        {
        ULONG LowPart;
        LONG  HighPart;
        };
    LONGLONG QuadPart;
    }
    LARGE_INTEGER, *PLARGE_INTEGER;
```

LISTING 4-1. *Definition of* `PHYSICAL_ADDRESS` *and* `LARGE_INTEGER`

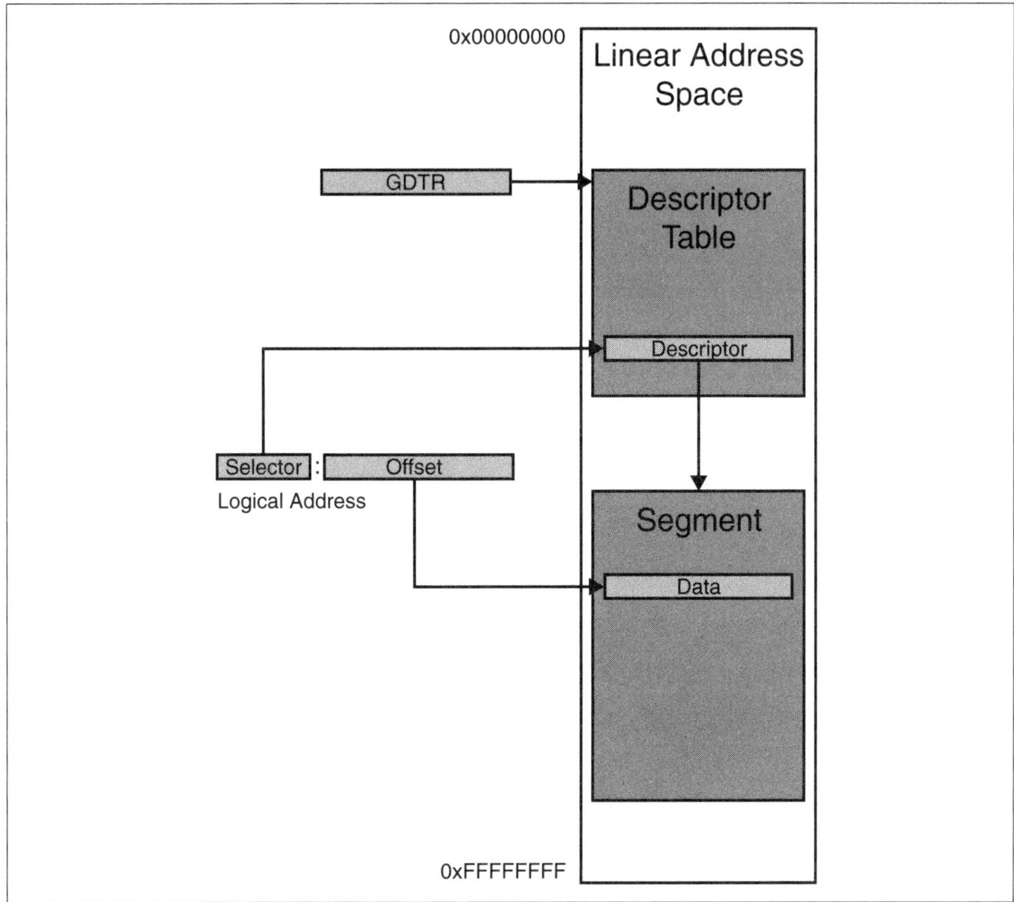

FIGURE 4-1. *i386 Memory Segmentation*

The memory model in Figure 4-2 is adopted by Windows 2000 for the standard code, data, and stack segments, that is, all logical addresses that involve the `CS`, `DS`, `ES`, and `SS` segment registers. The `FS` and `GS` segments are treated differently. `GS` is not used by Windows 2000, and `FS` addresses special system data areas inside the linear address space. Therefore, its base address is greater than zero and its size is less than 4 GB. Interestingly, Windows 2000 maintains different `FS` segments in user-mode and kernel-mode. More on this topic follows later in this chapter.

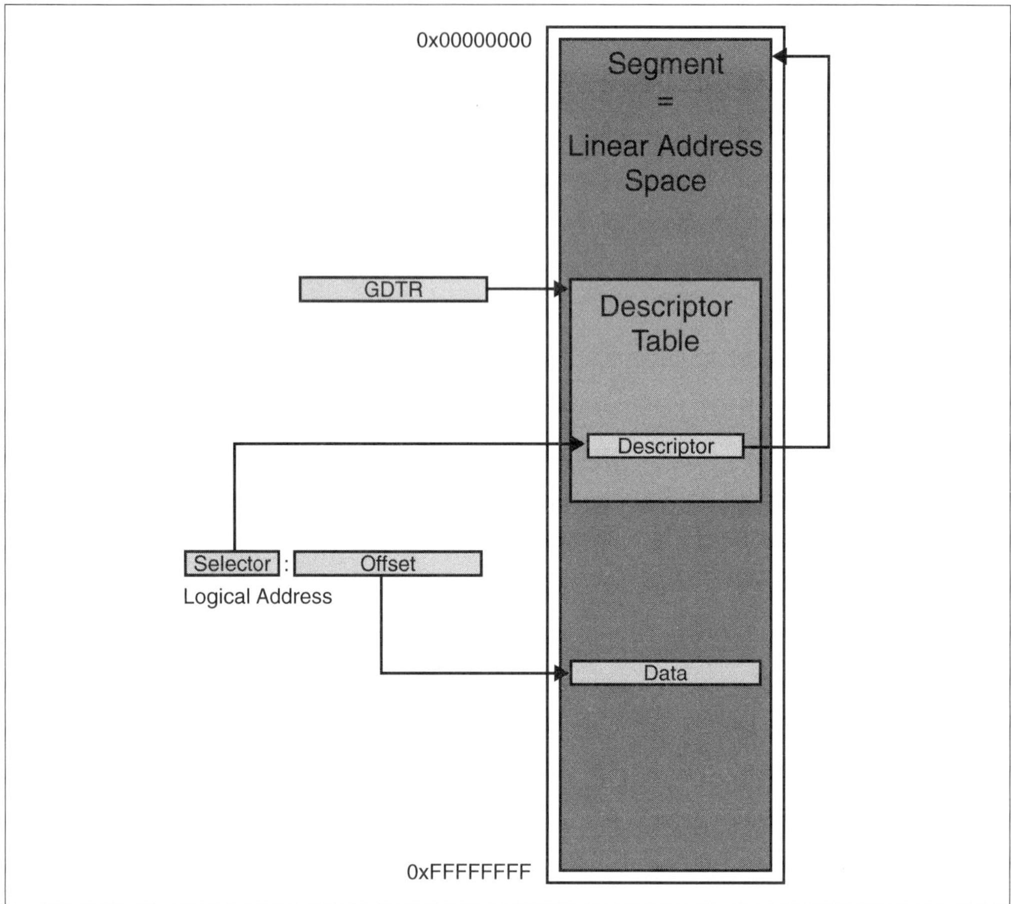

FIGURE 4-2. *Flat 4-GB Memory Segmentation*

In Figures 4-1 and 4-2, the selector portion of the logical address is shown to point into a descriptor table determined by a register termed `GDTR`. This is the CPU's Global Descriptor Table Register, which can be set by the operating system to any suitable linear address. The first entry of the Global Descriptor Table (GDT) is reserved, and the corresponding selector called "null segment selector" is intended as an initial value for unused segment registers. Windows 2000 keeps its GDT at address `0x80036000`. The GDT can hold up to 8,192 64-bit entries, resulting in a maximum size of 64 KB. Windows 2000 uses only the first 128 entries, restricting the GDT size to 1,024 bytes. Along with the GDT, the i386 CPU provides a Local Descriptor Table (LDT) and an Interrupt Descriptor Table (IDT), addressed by the `LDTR` and `IDTR` registers, respectively. Whereas the `GDTR` and `IDTR` values are unique and apply to all tasks executed by the CPU, the `LDTR` value is task-specific, and, if used, contains a 16-bit GDT selector.

Figure 4-3 demonstrates the complex mechanism of linear-to-physical address translation applied by the i386 memory management unit if demand paging is enabled in 4-KB page mode. The Page-Directory Base Register (PDBR) in the upper left corner contains the physical base address of the page-directory. The PDBR is identical to the i386 CR3 register. Only the upper 20 bits are used for addressing. Therefore, the page-directory is always located on a page boundary. The remaining PDBR bits are either flags or reserved for future extensions. The page-directory occupies exactly one 4-KB page, structured as an array of 1,024 32-bit page-directory entries (PDEs). Similar to the PDBR, each PDE can be divided into a 20-bit page-frame number (PFN) addressing a page-table, and an array of bit flags. Each page-table is page-aligned and spans 4 KB, comprising 1,024 page-table entries (PTEs). Again, the

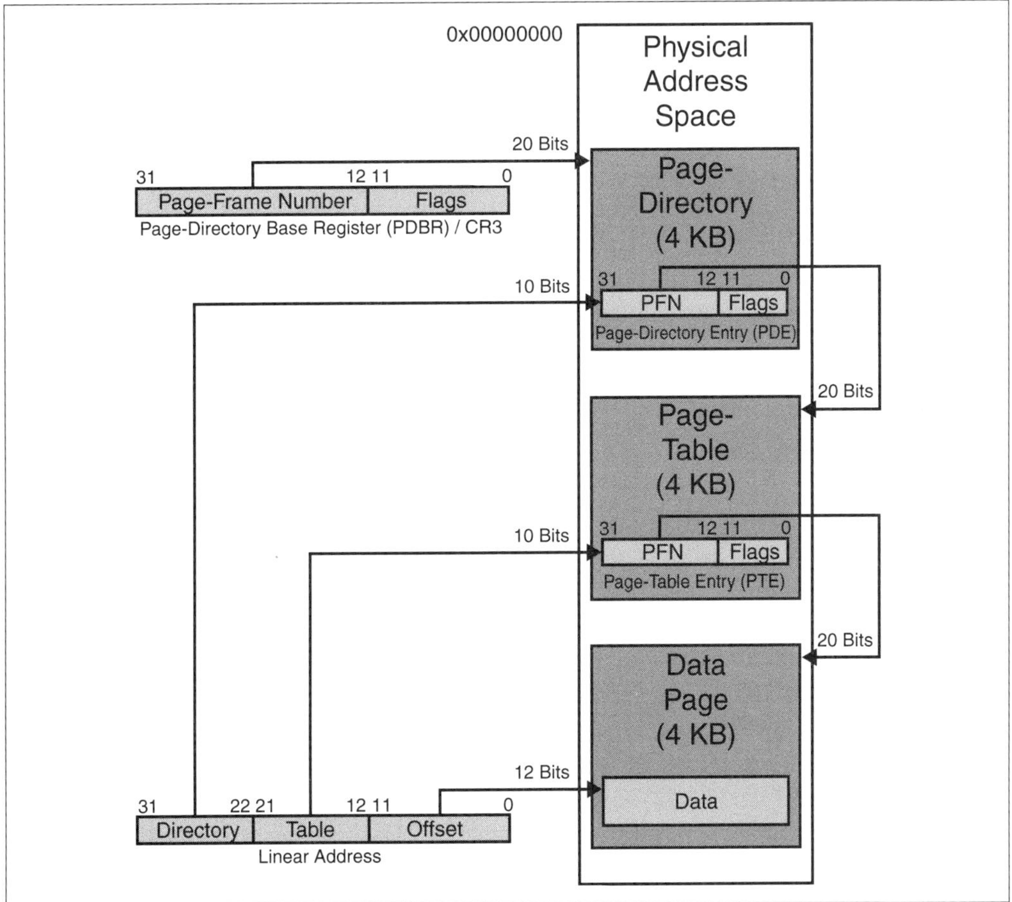

FIGURE 4-3. *Double-Layered Paging with 4-KB Pages*

upper 20 bits are extracted from a PTE to form a pointer to a 4-KB data page. Address translation takes place by breaking a linear address into three parts: The upper 10 bits select a PDE out of the page-directory, the next lower 10 bits select a PTE out of the page-table addressed by the PDE, and, finally, the lower 12 bits specify an offset into the data page addressed by the PTE.

In the 4-KB paging scheme, the 4-GB linear address space is addressable by means of a double-layered indirection mechanism. In the worst case, 1,048,576 PTEs are required to cover the entire range. Because each page-table holds 1,024 PTEs, this amounts to 1,024 page-tables, which is the number of PDEs the page-directory contains. With the page-directory and each page-table consuming 4 KB, the maximum memory management overhead in this paging model is 4 KB plus 4 MB, or 4,100 KB. That's a reasonable price for a subdivision of the entire 4-GB space into 4-KB tiles that can be mapped to any linear address.

In 4-MB paging mode, things are much simpler because one indirection layer is eliminated, as shown in Figure 4-4. Again, the PDBR points to the page-directory, but now only the upper 10 bits of the PDE are used, resulting in 4-MB alignment of the target address. Because no page-tables are used, this address is already the base address of a 4-MB data page. Consequently, the linear address now consists of two parts only: 10 bits for PDE selection and 22 offset bits. The 4-MB memory scheme requires no more than 4 KB overhead, because only the page-directory consumes additional memory. Each of its 1,024 PDEs can address one 4-MB page. This is just enough to cover the entire 4-GB address space. Thus, 4-MB pages have the advantage of keeping the memory management overhead low, but for the price of a more coarse addressing granularity.

Both the 4-KB and 4-MB paging modes have advantages and disadvantages. Fortunately, operating system designers don't have to decide for one of them, but can run the CPU in mixed mode. For example, Windows 2000 works with 4-MB pages in the memory range `0x80000000` to `0x9FFFFFFF`, where the kernel modules `hal.dll` and `ntoskrnl.exe` are loaded. The remaining linear address blocks are managed in 4-KB tiles. This mixed design is recommended by Intel for improved system performance, because 4-KB and 4-MB page entries are cached in different Translation Lookaside Buffers (TLBs) inside the i386 CPU (Intel 1999c, pp. 3-22f). The operating system kernel is usually large and is always resident in memory, so storing it in several 4-KB pages would permanently use up valuable TLB space.

Note that all address translation steps are carried out in physical memory. The PDBR and all PDEs and PTEs contain physical address pointers. The only linear address found in Figures 4-3 and 4-4 is the box in the lower left corner specifying the address to be converted to an offset inside a physical page. On the other hand, applications must work with linear addresses and are ignorant of physical addresses. However, it is possible to fill this gap by mapping the page-directory and all of its subordinate page-tables into the linear address space. On Windows 2000 and Windows NT 4.0, all

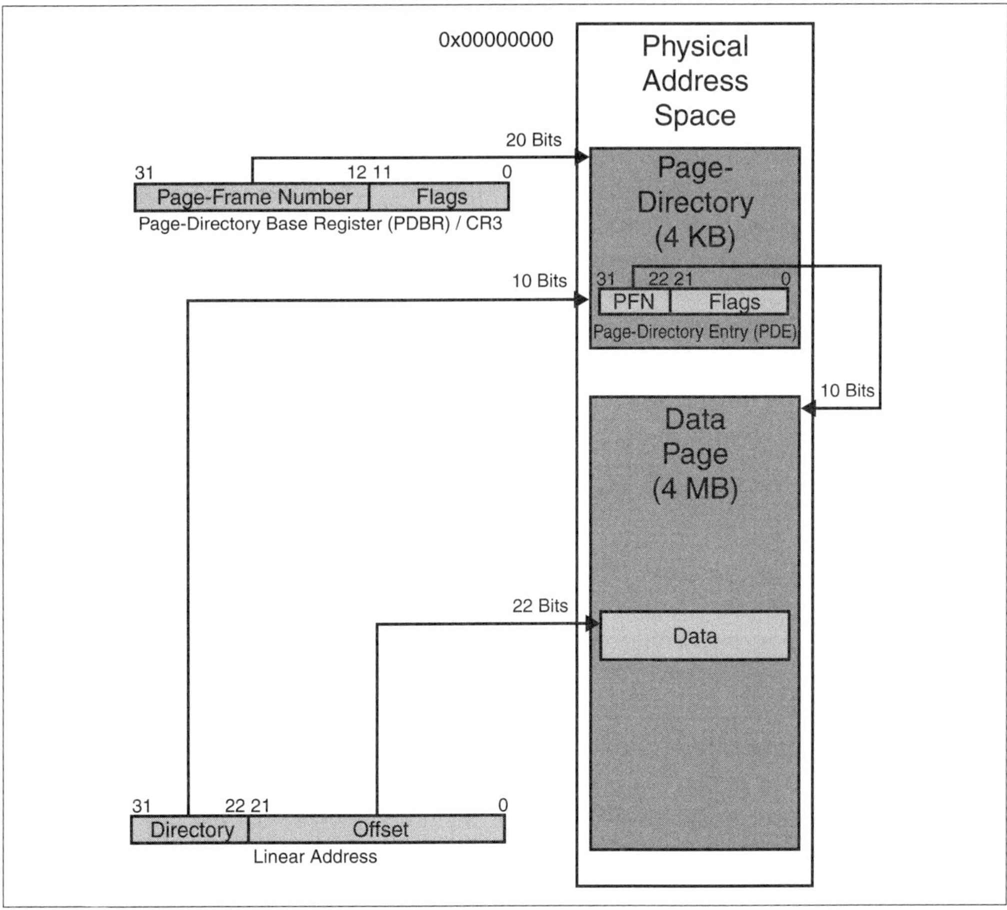

FIGURE 4-4. *Single-Layered Paging with 4-MB Pages*

PDEs and PTEs are accessible in the address range `0xC0000000` to `0xC03FFFFF`. This is a linear memory area of 4-MB size. This is obviously the maximum amount of memory consumed by the page-table layer in 4-KB paging mode. The PTE associated to a linear address can be looked up by simply using its most significant 20 bits as an index into the array of 32-bit PTEs starting at `0xC0000000`. For example, the PTE of address `0x00000000` is located at `0xC0000000`. The PTE index of address `0x80000000` is computed by shifting it right by 12 bits to get at the upper 20 bits, yielding `0x80000`. Because each PTE takes four bytes, the target PTE is found at `0xC0000000 + (4 * 0x80000) = 0xC0200000`. This result looks interesting—obviously, the address that divides the 4-GB address space in two equal halves is mapped to a PTE address that divides the PTE array in two equal halves.

Now let's go one more step ahead and compute the entry address of the PTE array itself. The general mapping formula is `((LinearAddress >> 12) * 4) + 0xC0000000`. Setting `LinearAddress` to `0xC0000000` yields `0xC0300000`. Let's pause for a moment: The entry at linear address `0xC0300000` points to the beginning of the PTE array in physical memory. Now look back to Figure 4-3. The 1,024 entries starting at address `0xC0300000` must be the page-directory! This special PDE and PTE arrangement is exploited by various memory management functions implemented in `ntoskrnl.exe`. For example, the (documented) API functions `MmIsAddressValid()` and `MmGetPhysicalAddress()` take a 32-bit linear address, look up its PDE and, if applicable, its PTE, and examine their contents. `MmIsAddressValid()` simply checks out whether the target page is currently present in physical memory. If the test fails, the linear address is either invalid or it refers to a page that has been flushed to backup storage, represented by the set of system pagefiles. `MmGetPhysicalAddress()` first extracts the page-frame number (PFN) corresponding to a linear address, which is the base address of its associated physical page divided by the page size. Next, it computes the offset into this page by extracting the least significant 12 bits of the linear address, and adds the offset to the physical base address determined by the PFN.

More thorough examination of the implementation of `MmGetPhysicalAddress()` reveals another interesting property of the Windows 2000 memory layout. Before anything else, the code tests whether the linear address is within the range `0x80000000` to `0x9FFFFFFF`. As already mentioned, this is the home of `hal.dll` and `ntoskrnl.exe`, and it is also the address block where Windows 2000 uses 4-MB pages. The interesting thing is that `MmGetPhysicalAddress()` doesn't care at all for PDEs or PTEs if the address is within this range. Instead, it simply sets the top three bits to zero, adds the byte offset, as usual, and returns the result as the physical address. This means that the physical address range `0x00000000` to `0x1FFFFFFF` is mapped 1:1 to the linear addresses `0x80000000` to `9FFFFFFF`! Knowing that `ntoskrnl.exe` is always loaded to the linear address `0x80400000`, this means that the Windows 2000 kernel is always found at physical address `0x00400000`, which happens to be the base address of the second 4-MB page in physical memory. In fact, examination of these memory regions proves that the above assumptions are correct. You will have the opportunity to see this with the memory spy presented in this chapter.

DATA STRUCTURES

Some portions of the sample code following in this chapter are concerned with low-level memory management and peek inside the mechanisms outlined above. For convenience, I have defined several C data structures that make this task easier. Because many data items inside the i386 CPU are concatenations of single bits or bit groups, C bit-fields come in handy. Bit-fields are an efficient way to access individual bits of or extract contiguous bit groups from larger data words. Microsoft Visual C/C++

generates quite clever code for bit-field operations. Listing 4-2 is part one of a series of CPU data type definitions, containing the following items:

- `X86_REGISTER` is a basic unsigned 32-bit integral type that can represent various CPU registers. This comprises all general-purpose, index, pointer, control, debug, and test registers.
- `X86_SELECTOR` represents a 16-bit segment selector, as stored in the segment registers `CS`, `DS`, `ES`, `FS`, `GS`, and `SS`. In Figures 4-1 and 4-2, selectors are depicted as the upper third of a logical 48-bit address, serving as an index into a descriptor table. For computational convenience, the 16-bit selector value is extended to 32 bits, with the upper half marked "reserved." Note that the `X86_SELECTOR` structure is a union of two structures. The first one specifies the selector value as a packed 16-bit `WORD` named `wValue`, and the second breaks it up into bit-fields. The `RPL` field specifies the Requested Privilege Level, which is either 0 (kernel-mode) or 3 (user-mode) on Windows 2000. The `TI` bit switches between the Global and Local Descriptor Tables (GDT/LDT).
- `X86_DESCRIPTOR` defines the format of a table entry pointed to by a selector. It is a 64-bit quantity with a very convoluted structure resulting from its historic evolution. The linear base address defining the start location of the associated segment is scattered among three bit-fields named `Base1`, `Base2`, and `Base3`, with `Base1` being the least significant part. The segment limit specifying the segment size minus one is divided into the pair `Limit1` and `Limit2`, with the former representing the least significant half. The remaining bit-fields store various segment properties (cf. Intel 1999c, pp. 3-11). For example, the `G` bit defines the segment granularity. If zero, the segment limit is specified in bytes; otherwise, the limit value has to be multiplied by 4 KB. Like `X86_SELECTOR`, the `X86_DESCRIPTOR` structure is composed of a union to allow different interpretations of its value. The `dValueLow` and `dValueHigh` members are helpful if you have to copy descriptors without regard to their internal structure.
- `X86_GATE` looks somewhat similar to `X86_DESCRIPTOR`. In fact, the structures are related: `X86_DESCRIPTOR` is a GDT entry and describes the memory properties of a segment, and `X86_GATE` is an entry inside the Interrupt Descriptor Table (IDT) and describes the memory properties of an interrupt handler. The IDT can contain task, interrupt, and trap gates. (No, Bill Gates is *not* stored in the IDT!) The `X86_GATE` structure matches all three types, with the Type bit-field determining the identity. Type 5

identifies a task gate; types 6 and 14, interrupt gates; and types 7 and 15, trap gates. The most significant type bit specifies the size of the gate: 16-bit gates have this bit set to zero; otherwise it is a 32-bit gate.

- X86_TABLE is a tricky structure that is used to read the values of the GDTR or IDTR by means of the assembly language instructions SGDT (store GDT register) and SIDT (store IDT register) respectively (cf. Intel 1999b, pp. 3-636). Both instructions require a 48-bit memory operand, where the limit and base address values will be stored. To maintain DWORD alignment for the 32-bit base address, X86_TABLE starts out with the 16-bit dummy member wReserved. Depending on whether the SGDT or SIDT instruction is applied, the base address must be interpreted as a descriptor or gate pointer, as suggested by the union of PX86_DESCRIPTOR and PX86_GATE types. The wLimit member is the same for both table types.

```
// =================================================================
// INTEL X86 STRUCTURES, PART 1 OF 3
// =================================================================

typedef DWORD X86_REGISTER, *PX86_REGISTER, **PPX86_REGISTER;

// -----------------------------------------------------------------

typedef struct _X86_SELECTOR
    {
    union
        {
        struct
            {
            WORD wValue;            // packed value
            WORD wReserved;
            };
        struct
            {
            unsigned RPL      :  2; // requested privilege level
            unsigned TI       :  1; // table indicator: 0=gdt, 1=ldt
            unsigned Index    : 13; // index into descriptor table
            unsigned Reserved : 16;
            };
        };
    }
    X86_SELECTOR, *PX86_SELECTOR, **PPX86_SELECTOR;
```

```
#define X86_SELECTOR_ sizeof (X86_SELECTOR)

// ----------------------------------------------------------------

typedef struct _X86_DESCRIPTOR
    {
    union
        {
        struct
            {
            DWORD dValueLow;        // packed value
            DWORD dValueHigh;
            };
        struct
            {
            unsigned Limit1   : 16; // bits 15..00
            unsigned Base1    : 16; // bits 15..00
            unsigned Base2    :  8; // bits 23..16
            unsigned Type     :  4; // segment type
            unsigned S        :  1; // type (0=system, 1=code/data)
            unsigned DPL      :  2; // descriptor privilege level
            unsigned P        :  1; // segment present
            unsigned Limit2   :  4; // bits 19..16
            unsigned AVL      :  1; // available to programmer
            unsigned Reserved :  1;
            unsigned DB       :  1; // 0=16-bit, 1=32-bit
            unsigned G        :  1; // granularity (1=4KB)
            unsigned Base3    :  8; // bits 31..24
            };
        };
    }
    X86_DESCRIPTOR, *PX86_DESCRIPTOR, **PPX86_DESCRIPTOR;

#define X86_DESCRIPTOR_ sizeof (X86_DESCRIPTOR)

// ----------------------------------------------------------------

typedef struct _X86_GATE
    {
    union
        {
        struct
            {
            DWORD dValueLow;          // packed value
            DWORD dValueHigh;
            };
        struct
            {
            unsigned Offset1    : 16; // bits 15..00
            unsigned Selector   : 16; // segment selector
            unsigned Parameters :  5; // parameters
            unsigned Reserved   :  3;
```

(continued)

```
            unsigned Type       :  4; // gate type and size
            unsigned S          :  1; // always 0
            unsigned DPL        :  2; // descriptor privilege level
            unsigned P          :  1; // segment present
            unsigned Offset2    : 16; // bits 31..16
            };
        };
    }
    X86_GATE, *PX86_GATE, **PPX86_GATE;

#define X86_GATE_ sizeof (X86_GATE)

// -----------------------------------------------------------------

typedef struct _X86_TABLE
    {
    WORD wReserved;                   // force 32-bit alignment
    WORD wLimit;                      // table limit
    union
        {
        PX86_DESCRIPTOR pDescriptors; // used by sgdt instruction
        PX86_GATE       pGates;       // used by sidt instruction
        };
    }
    X86_TABLE, *PX86_TABLE, **PPX86_TABLE;

#define X86_TABLE_ sizeof (X86_TABLE)

// =================================================================
```

LISTING 4-2. *i386 Registers, Selectors, Descriptors, Gates, and Tables*

The next set of i386 memory management structures, collected in Listing 4-3, relates to demand paging and contains several items illustrated in Figures 4-3 and 4-4:

- `X86_PDBR` is, of course, a structural representation of the CPU's `CR3` register, also known as the *page-directory base register (PDBR)*. The upper 20 bits contain the PFN, which is an index into the array of physical 4-KB pages. `PFN=0` corresponds to physical address `0x00000000`, `PFN=1` to `0x00001000`, and so forth. Twenty bits are just enough to cover the entire 4-GB address space. The PFN in the PDBR is the index of the physical page that holds the page-directory. Most of the remaining bits are reserved, except for bit #3, controlling page-level write-through (PWT), and bit #4, disabling page-level caching if set.

- `X86_PDE_4M` and `X86_PDE_4K` are alternative incarnations of page-directory entries (PDEs) for 4-MB and 4-KB pages, respectively. A page-directory contains a maximum of 1,024 PDEs. Again, PFN is the page-frame number, pointing to the subordinate page. For a 4-MB PDE, the PFN bit-field is only 10 bits wide, addressing a 4-MB data page. The 20-bit PFN of 4-KB PDE points to a page-table that ultimately selects the physical data pages. The remaining bits define various properties. The most interesting ones are the "Page Size" bit `PS`, controlling the page size (0 = 4-KB, 1 = 4-MB), and the "Present" bit `P`, indicating whether the subordinate data page (4-MB mode) or page-table (4-KB mode) is present in physical memory.
- `X86_PTE_4K` defines the internal structure of a page-table entry (PTE) contained in a page-table. Like a page-directory, a page-table can contain up to 1,024 entries. The only difference between `X86_PTE_4K` and `X86_PDE_4K` is that the former lacks the `PS` bit, which is not required because the page size must be 4-KB, as determined by the PDE's `PS` bit. Note that there is no such thing as a 4-MB PTE, because the 4-MB memory model doesn't require an intermediate page-table layer.
- `X86_PNPE` represents a "page-not-present entry" (PNPE), that is, a PDE or PTE in which the `P` bit is zero. According to the Intel manuals, the remaining 31 bits are "available to operating system or executive" (Intel 1999c, pp. 3-28). If a linear address maps to a PNPE, this means either that this address is unused or that it points to a page that is currently swapped out to one of the pagefiles. Windows 2000 uses the 31 unassigned bits of the PNPE to store status information of the page. The structure of this information is undocumented, but it seems that bit #10, named `PageFile` in Listing 4-3, is set if the page is swapped out. In this case, the `Reserved1` and `Reserved2` bit-fields contain values that enable the system to locate the page in the pagefiles, so it can be swapped in as soon as one of its linear addresses is touched by a memory read/write instruction.
- `X86_PE` is included for convenience. It is merely a union of all possible forms a page entry can take, comprising the PDBR contents, 4-MB and 4-KB PDEs, PTEs, and PNPEs.

```
// =================================================================
// INTEL X86 STRUCTURES, PART 2 OF 3
// =================================================================

typedef struct _X86_PDBR // page-directory base register (cr3)
    {
    union
        {
        struct
            {
            DWORD dValue;            // packed value
            };
        struct
            {
            unsigned Reserved1 :  3;
            unsigned PWT       :  1; // page-level write-through
            unsigned PCD       :  1; // page-level cache disabled
            unsigned Reserved2 :  7;
            unsigned PFN       : 20; // page-frame number
            };
        };
    }
    X86_PDBR, *PX86_PDBR, **PPX86_PDBR;

#define X86_PDBR_ sizeof (X86_PDBR)

// -----------------------------------------------------------------

typedef struct _X86_PDE_4M // page-directory entry (4-MB page)
    {
    union
        {
        struct
            {
            DWORD dValue;            // packed value
            };
        struct
            {
            unsigned P         :  1; // present (1 = present)
            unsigned RW        :  1; // read/write
            unsigned US        :  1; // user/supervisor
            unsigned PWT       :  1; // page-level write-through
            unsigned PCD       :  1; // page-level cache disabled
            unsigned A         :  1; // accessed
            unsigned D         :  1; // dirty
            unsigned PS        :  1; // page size (1 = 4-MB page)
            unsigned G         :  1; // global page
            unsigned Available :  3; // available to programmer
            unsigned Reserved  : 10;
            unsigned PFN       : 10; // page-frame number
            };
```

```
        };
    }
    X86_PDE_4M, *PX86_PDE_4M, **PPX86_PDE_4M;

#define X86_PDE_4M_ sizeof (X86_PDE_4M)

// -----------------------------------------------------------------

typedef struct _X86_PDE_4K // page-directory entry (4-KB page)
    {
    union
        {
        struct
            {
            DWORD dValue;           // packed value
            };
        struct
            {
            unsigned P         :  1; // present (1 = present)
            unsigned RW        :  1; // read/write
            unsigned US        :  1; // user/supervisor
            unsigned PWT       :  1; // page-level write-through
            unsigned PCD       :  1; // page-level cache disabled
            unsigned A         :  1; // accessed
            unsigned Reserved  :  1; // dirty
            unsigned PS        :  1; // page size (0 = 4-KB page)
            unsigned G         :  1; // global page
            unsigned Available :  3; // available to programmer
            unsigned PFN       : 20; // page-frame number
            };
        };
    }
    X86_PDE_4K, *PX86_PDE_4K, **PPX86_PDE_4K;

#define X86_PDE_4K_ sizeof (X86_PDE_4K)

// -----------------------------------------------------------------

typedef struct _X86_PTE_4K // page-table entry (4-KB page)
    {
    union
        {
        struct
            {
            DWORD dValue;           // packed value
            };
        struct
            {
            unsigned P         :  1; // present (1 = present)
            unsigned RW        :  1; // read/write
            unsigned US        :  1; // user/supervisor
```

(continued)

```
            unsigned PWT       :  1; // page-level write-through
            unsigned PCD       :  1; // page-level cache disabled
            unsigned A         :  1; // accessed
            unsigned D         :  1; // dirty
            unsigned Reserved  :  1;
            unsigned G         :  1; // global page
            unsigned Available :  3; // available to programmer
            unsigned PFN       : 20; // page-frame number
            };
        };
    }
    X86_PTE_4K, *PX86_PTE_4K, **PPX86_PTE_4K;

#define X86_PTE_4K_ sizeof (X86_PTE_4K)

// -----------------------------------------------------------------

typedef struct _X86_PNPE // page not present entry
    {
    union
        {
        struct
            {
            DWORD dValue;            // packed value
            };
        struct
            {
            unsigned P         :  1; // present (0 = not present)
            unsigned Reserved1 :  9;
            unsigned PageFile  :  1; // page swapped to pagefile
            unsigned Reserved2 : 21;
            };
        };
    }
    X86_PNPE, *PX86_PNPE, **PPX86_PNPE;

#define X86_PNPE_ sizeof (X86_PNPE)

// -----------------------------------------------------------------

typedef struct _X86_PE // general page entry
    {
    union
        {
        DWORD      dValue; // packed value
        X86_PDBR   pdbr;   // page-directory Base Register
        X86_PDE_4M pde4M;  // page-directory entry (4-MB page)
        X86_PDE_4K pde4K;  // page-directory entry (4-KB page)
        X86_PTE_4K pte4K;  // page-table entry (4-KB page)
        X86_PNPE   pnpe;   // page not present entry
        };
```

```
    }
    X86_PE, *PX86_PE, **PPX86_PE;

#define X86_PE_ sizeof (X86_PE)

// =================================================================
```

LISTING 4-3. *i386 PDBR, PDE, PTE, and PNPE Values*

In Listing 4-4, I have added structural representations of linear addresses. These structures are formal definitions of the "Linear Address" boxes in Figures 4-3 and 4-4:

- `X86_LINEAR_4M` is the format of linear addresses that point into a 4-MB data page, as shown in Figure 4-4. The page-directory index `PDI` is an index into the page-directory currently addressed by the PDBR, selecting one of its PDEs. The 22-bit `Offset` member points to the target address within the corresponding 4-MB physical page.
- `X86_LINEAR_4K` is the 4-KB variant of a linear address. As outlined in Figure 4-3, it is composed of three bit-fields: Like in a 4-MB address, the upper 10 `PDI` bits select a PDE. The page-table index `PTI` has a similar duty, pointing to a PTE inside the page-table addressed by this PDE. The remaining 12 bits are the offset into the resulting 4-KB physical page.
- `X86_LINEAR` is another convenience structure that simply unites `X86_LINEAR_4M` and `X86_LINEAR_4K` in a single data type.

MACROS AND CONSTANTS

The definitions in Listing 4-5 are supplements to the structures in Listings 4-2 to 4-4 and make the work with i386 memory management easier. They can be subdivided into three main groups. The first group handles linear addresses:

1. `X86_PAGE_MASK`, `X86_PDI_MASK`, and `X86_PTI_MASK` are bit masks that isolate the constituent parts of linear addresses. They are based on the constants `PAGE_SHIFT (12)`, `PDI-SHIFT (22)`, and `PTI-SHIFT (12)`, defined in the Windows 2000 DDK header file `ntddk.h`. `X86_PAGE_MASK` evaluates to `0xFFFFF000`, effectively masking off the 4-KB offset part of a linear address (cf. `X86_LINEAR_4K`). `X86_PDI_MASK` is equal to `0xFFC00000` and obviously extracts the 10 topmost PDI bits of a linear address (cf. `X86_LINEAR_4M` and `X86_LINEAR_4K`). `X86_PTI_MASK` evaluates to `0x003FF0000` and masks off all bits except for the page-table index (PTI) bits of a linear address (cf. `X86_LINEAR_4K`).

```
// =================================================================
// INTEL X86 STRUCTURES, PART 3 OF 3
// =================================================================

typedef struct _X86_LINEAR_4M // linear address (4-MB page)
    {
    union
        {
        struct
            {
            PVOID pAddress;       // packed address
            };
        struct
            {
            unsigned Offset : 22; // offset into page
            unsigned PDI    : 10; // page-directory index
            };
        };
    }
    X86_LINEAR_4M, *PX86_LINEAR_4M, **PPX86_LINEAR_4M;

#define X86_LINEAR_4M_ sizeof (X86_LINEAR_4M)

// -----------------------------------------------------------------

typedef struct _X86_LINEAR_4K // linear address (4-KB page)
    {
    union
        {
        struct
            {
            PVOID pAddress;       // packed address
            };
        struct
            {
            unsigned Offset : 12; // offset into page
            unsigned PTI    : 10; // page-table index
            unsigned PDI    : 10; // page-directory index
            };
        };
    }
    X86_LINEAR_4K, *PX86_LINEAR_4K, **PPX86_LINEAR_4K;

#define X86_LINEAR_4K_ sizeof (X86_LINEAR_4K)

// -----------------------------------------------------------------

typedef struct _X86_LINEAR // general linear address
    {
    union
        {
```

```
        PVOID          pAddress; // packed address
        X86_LINEAR_4M linear4M; // linear address (4-MB page)
        X86_LINEAR_4K linear4K; // linear address (4-KB page)
        };
    }
    X86_LINEAR, *PX86_LINEAR, **PPX86_LINEAR;

#define X86_LINEAR_ sizeof (X86_LINEAR)

// =================================================================
```

LISTING 4-4. *i386 Linear Addresses*

2. `X86_PAGE()`, `X86_PDI()`, and `X86_PTI()` use the above constants to compute the page index, PDI, or PTI of a given linear address. `X86_PAGE()` is typically used to read a PTE from the Windows 2000 PTE array starting at address `0xC0000000`. `X86_PDI()` and `X86_PTI()` simply apply `X86_PDI_MASK` or `X86_PTI_ MASK` to the supplied pointer and shift the resulting index to the rightmost bit position.
3. `X86_OFFSET_4M()` and `X86_OFFSET_4K()` extract the offset portion of a 4-MB or 4-KB linear address, respectively.
4. `X86_PAGE_4M` and `X86_PAGE_4K` compute the sizes of 4-MB and 4-KB pages from the DDK constants `PDI_SHIFT` and `PTI_SHIFT`, resulting in `X86_PAGE_4M` = 4,194,304 and `X86_PAGE_4K` = 4,096. Note that `X86_PAGE_4K` is equivalent to the DDK constant `PAGE_SIZE`, also defined in `ntddk.h`.
5. `X86_PAGES_4M` and `X86_PAGES_4K` state the number of 4-MB or 4-KB pages fitting into the 4-GB linear address space. `X86_PAGES_4M` evaluates to 1,024, and `X86_PAGES_4K` to 1,048,576.

The second group of macros and constants relates to the Windows 2000 PDE and PTE arrays. Unlike several other system addresses, the base addresses of these arrays are not available as global variables set up at boot time, but are defined as constants. This can be proved easily by disassembling the memory manager API functions `MmGetPhysicalAddress()` or `MmIsAddressValid()`, where these addresses appear as "magic numbers." These constants are not included in the DDK header files, but Listing 4-5 shows how they might have been defined.

- `X86_PAGES` is a hard-coded address and points, of course, to `0xC0000000`, where the Windows 2000 PTE array starts.

- `X86_PTE_ARRAY` is equal to `X86_PAGES`, but typecasts the value to `PX86_PE`, that is, a pointer to an array of `X86_PE` page entry structures, as defined in Listing 4-2.
- `X86_PDE_ARRAY` is a tricky definition that computes the base address of the PDE array from the PTE array location, using the `PTI_SHIFT` constant. As explained earlier, the general formula for mapping a linear address to a PTE address is `((LinearAddress >> 12) * 4) + 0xC0000000`, and the page-directory is located by setting `LinearAddress` to `0xC0000000`. Nothing else is done by the definition of `X86_PDE_ARRAY`.

```
// =================================================================
// INTEL X86 MACROS & CONSTANTS
// =================================================================

#define X86_PAGE_MASK (0 - (1 << PAGE_SHIFT))
#define X86_PAGE(_p)   (((DWORD) (_p) & X86_PAGE_MASK) >> PAGE_SHIFT)

#define X86_PDI_MASK   (0 - (1 << PDI_SHIFT))
#define X86_PDI(_p)    (((DWORD) (_p) & X86_PDI_MASK) >> PDI_SHIFT)

#define X86_PTI_MASK   ((0 - (1 << PTI_SHIFT)) & ~X86_PDI_MASK)
#define X86_PTI(_p)    (((DWORD) (_p) & X86_PTI_MASK) >> PTI_SHIFT)

#define X86_OFFSET_4M(_p) ((_p) & ~(X86_PDI_MASK               ))
#define X86_OFFSET_4K(_p) ((_p) & ~(X86_PDI_MASK | X86_PTI_MASK))

#define X86_PAGE_4M    (1 << PDI_SHIFT)
#define X86_PAGE_4K    (1 << PTI_SHIFT)

#define X86_PAGES_4M   (1 << (32 - PDI_SHIFT))
#define X86_PAGES_4K   (1 << (32 - PTI_SHIFT))

// -----------------------------------------------------------------

#define X86_PAGES          0xC0000000
#define X86_PTE_ARRAY      ((PX86_PE) X86_PAGES)
#define X86_PDE_ARRAY      (X86_PTE_ARRAY + (X86_PAGES >> PTI_SHIFT))

// -----------------------------------------------------------------

#define X86_SELECTOR_RPL             0x0003
#define X86_SELECTOR_TI              0x0004
#define X86_SELECTOR_INDEX           0xFFF8
#define X86_SELECTOR_SHIFT           3
```

```
#define X86_SELECTOR_LIMIT          (X86_SELECTOR_INDEX >> \
                                     X86_SELECTOR_SHIFT)

// -----------------------------------------------------------------

#define X86_DESCRIPTOR_SYS_TSS16A       0x1
#define X86_DESCRIPTOR_SYS_LDT          0x2
#define X86_DESCRIPTOR_SYS_TSS16B       0x3
#define X86_DESCRIPTOR_SYS_CALL16       0x4
#define X86_DESCRIPTOR_SYS_TASK         0x5
#define X86_DESCRIPTOR_SYS_INT16        0x6
#define X86_DESCRIPTOR_SYS_TRAP16       0x7
#define X86_DESCRIPTOR_SYS_TSS32A       0x9
#define X86_DESCRIPTOR_SYS_TSS32B       0xB
#define X86_DESCRIPTOR_SYS_CALL32       0xC
#define X86_DESCRIPTOR_SYS_INT32        0xE
#define X86_DESCRIPTOR_SYS_TRAP32       0xF

// -----------------------------------------------------------------

#define X86_DESCRIPTOR_APP_ACCESSED     0x1
#define X86_DESCRIPTOR_APP_READ_WRITE   0x2
#define X86_DESCRIPTOR_APP_EXECUTE_READ 0x2
#define X86_DESCRIPTOR_APP_EXPAND_DOWN  0x4
#define X86_DESCRIPTOR_APP_CONFORMING   0x4
#define X86_DESCRIPTOR_APP_CODE         0x8

// =================================================================
```

LISTING 4-5. *Additional i386 Memory Management Definitions*

The last two sections of Listing 4-5 handle selectors and special types of descriptors, and are complementary to Listing 4-2:

- `X86_SELECTOR_RPL`, `X86_SELECTOR_TI`, and `X86_SELECTOR_INDEX` are bit masks corresponding to the `RPL`, `TI`, and `Index` members of the `X86_SELECTOR` structures defined in Listing 4-2.
- `X86_SELECTOR_SHIFT` is a right-shift factor that right-aligns the value of the selector's `Index` member.
- `X86_SELECTOR_LIMIT` defines the maximum index value a selector can hold and is equal to 8,191. This value determines the maximum size of a descriptor table. Each selector index points to a descriptor, and each descriptor consists of 64 bits or 8 bytes (cf. `X86_DESCRIPTOR` in Listing 4-2), so the maximum descriptor table size amounts to 8,192 * 8 = 64 KB.

- The list of X86_DESCRIPTOR_SYS_* constants define values of a descriptor's Type member if its S-bit is zero, identifying it as a system descriptor. Please refer to Listing 4-2 for the bit-field layout of a descriptor, determined by the structure X86_DESCRIPTOR. The system descriptor types are described in detail in the Intel manuals (Intel 1999c, pp. 3-15f) and summarized in Table 4-1.

The X86_DESCRIPTOR_APP_* constants concluding Listing 4-5 apply to a descriptor's Type member if it is an application descriptor referring to a code or data segment, identified by a nonzero S-bit. Because application descriptor types can be characterized by independent properties reflected by the four type bits, the X86_DESCRIPTOR_APP_* constants are defined as single-bit masks, in which some bits are interpreted differently for data and code segments:

- X86_DESCRIPTOR_APP_ACCESSED is set if the segment has been accessed.
- X86_DESCRIPTOR_APP_READ_WRITE decides whether a data segment allows read-only or read/write access.
- X86_DESCRIPTOR_APP_EXECUTE_READ decides whether a code segment allows execute-only or execute/read access.
- X86_DESCRIPTOR_APP_DOWN is set for expand-down data segments, which is a property commonly exposed by stack segments.
- X86_DESCRIPTOR_APP_CONFORMING indicates whether a code segment is conforming, that is, whether it can be called by less privileged code (cf. Intel 1999c, pp. 4-13ff).
- X86_DESCRIPTOR_APP_CODE distinguishes code and data segments. Note that stack segments belong to the data segment category and must always be writable.

We will revisit system descriptors later when the memory spy application presented in the next sections is up and running. Table 4-1 also concludes a short introduction to i386 memory management. For more information on this topic, please refer to the original Intel Pentium manuals (Intel 1999a, 1999b, 1999c) or one of the secondary readings, such as Robert L. Hummel's great 80486 reference handbook (Hummel 1992).

TABLE 4-1. *System Descriptor Types*

NAME	VALUE	DESCRIPTION
X86_DESCRIPTOR_SYS_TSS16A	0x1	16-bit Task State Segment (Available)
X86_DESCRIPTOR_SYS_LDT	0x2	Local Descriptor Table
X86_DESCRIPTOR_SYS_TSS16B	0x3	16-bit Task State Segment (Busy)
X86_DESCRIPTOR_SYS_CALL16	0x4	16-bit Call Gate
X86_DESCRIPTOR_SYS_TASK	0x5	Task Gate
X86_DESCRIPTOR_SYS_INT16	0x6	16-bit Interrupt Gate
X86_DESCRIPTOR_SYS_TRAP16	0x7	16-bit Trap Gate
X86_DESCRIPTOR_SYS_TSS32A	0x9	32-bit Task State Segment (Available)
X86_DESCRIPTOR_SYS_TSS32B	0xB	32-bit Task State Segment (Busy)
X86_DESCRIPTOR_SYS_CALL32	0xC	32-bit Call Gate
X86_DESCRIPTOR_SYS_INT32	0xE	32-bit Interrupt Gate
X86_DESCRIPTOR_SYS_TRAP32	0xF	32-bit Trap Gate

A SAMPLE MEMORY SPY DEVICE

One of the frequently recurring Microsoft statements about Windows NT and 2000 is that it is a *secure* operating system. Along with user authentication issues in networking environments, this also includes robustness against bad applications that might compromise the system's integrity by misusing pointers or writing outside the bounds of a memory data structure. This has always been a nasty problem on Windows 3.x, in which the system and all applications shared a single memory space. Windows NT has introduced a clear separation between system and application memory and between concurrent processes. Each process gets its own 4-GB address space, as depicted in Figure 4-2. Whenever a task switch occurs, the current address space is switched out and another one is mapped in by selecting different values for the segment registers, page tables, and other memory management data specific to a process. This design prevents applications from inadvertently tampering with memory of other applications. Each process also requires access to system resources, so the 4-GB space always contains some system code and data. To protect these memory regions from being overwritten by hostile application code, a different trick is employed.

Windows 2000 Memory Segmentation

Windows 2000 has inherited the basic memory segmentation scheme of Windows NT 4.0, which divides the 4-GB process address space in two equal parts by default. The lower half, comprising the range `0x00000000` to `0x7FFFFFFF`, contains application data and code running in user-mode, which is equivalent to Privilege Level 3 or "Ring 3" in Intel's terminology (Intel 1999a, pp. 4-8ff; Intel 1999c, pp. 4-8ff). The upper half, ranging from `0x80000000` to `0xFFFFFFFF`, is reserved for the system, which is running in kernel-mode, also known as Intel's Privilege Level 0 or "Ring 0." The privilege level determines what operations may be executed and which memory locations can be accessed by the code. Especially, this means that certain CPU instructions are forbidden and certain memory regions are inaccessible, for low-privileged code. For example, if a user-mode application touches any address in the upper half of the 4-GB address space, the system will throw an exception and terminate the application process without giving it another chance.

Figure 4-5 demonstrates what happens if an application attempts to read from address `0x80000000`. This strict access limitation is good for the integrity of the system but bad for debugging tools that should be able to show the contents of all valid memory regions. Fortunately, an easy workaround exists: Like the system itself, kernel-mode drivers run on the highest privilege level and therefore are allowed to execute all CPU instructions and to see all memory locations. The trick is to inject a spy driver into the system that reads the requested memory and sends the contents to a companion application waiting in user-mode. Of course, even a kernel-mode driver cannot read from virtual memory addresses that aren't backed up by physical or page file memory. Therefore, such a driver must check all addresses carefully before accessing them in order to avoid the dreaded Blue Screen Of Death (BSOD). Contrary to an application exception, which terminates the problem application only, a driver exception stops the entire system and forces a full reboot.

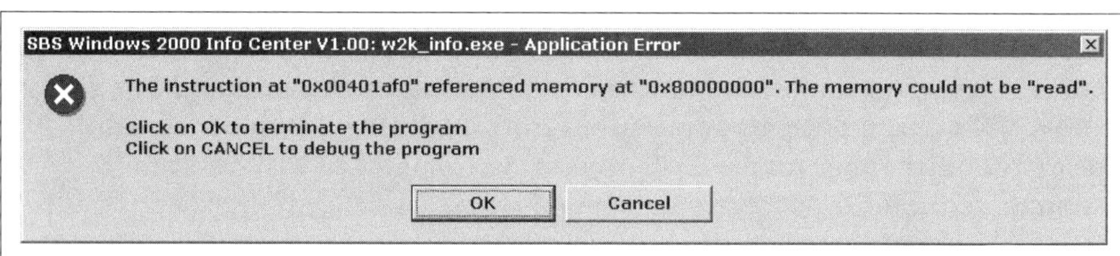

FIGURE 4-5. *Addresses Starting at* 0x80000000 *Are Not Accessible in User-mode*

The Device I/O Control Dispatcher

The companion CD of this book contains the source code of a versatile spy device implemented as a kernel-mode driver, which can be found in the `\src\w2k_spy` directory tree. This device is based on a driver skeleton generated by the driver wizard introduced in Chapter 3. The user-mode interface of w2k_spy.sys is based on Win32 Device I/O Control (IOCTL), briefly described in the same chapter. The spy driver defines a device named \Device\w2k_spy and a symbolic link, \DosDevices\w2k_spy, required to make the device reachable from user-mode. It is funny that the namespace of symbolic links is called \DosDevices. We are certainly not working with DOS device drivers here. This name has historic roots and is now set in stone. With the symbolic link installed, the driver can be opened by any user-mode module via the standard Win32 API function CreateFile(), using the path \\.\w2k_spy. The character sequence \\.\ is a general escape for local devices. For example, \\.\C: refers to hard disk C: of the local system. See the CreateFile() documentation in the Microsoft Platform SDK for more details.

Parts of the driver's header file w2k_spy.h are included above as Listings 4-2 to 4-5. This file is somewhat similar to a DLL header file: It contains definitions required by the module itself during compilation, but it also provides enough information for a client application that needs to interface to it. Both the DLL/driver and the client application include the same header file, and each module picks out the definitions it needs for proper operation. However, this Janus-headed nature of the header file creates many more problems for a kernel-mode driver than for a DLL because of the special development environment Microsoft provides for drivers. Unfortunately, the header files contained in the DDK are not compatible with the Win32 files in the Platform SDK. The header files cannot be mixed, at least not in C language projects, resulting in a deadlocked situation in which the kernel-mode driver has access to constants, macros, and data types not available to the client application, and vice versa. Therefore, w2k_spy.c defines a flag constant named _W2K_SPY_SYS_, and w2k_spy.h checks the presence or absence of this constant to define items that are missing in one or the other environment, using #ifdef...#else...#endif clauses. This means that all definitions found in the #ifdef _W2K_SPY_SYS_ branch are "seen" by the driver code only, whereas the definitions in the #else branch are evaluated exclusively by the client application. All parts of w2k_spy.h outside these conditional clauses apply to both modules.

In Chapter 3, in the discussion of my driver wizard, I presented the driver skeleton code provided by the wizard in Listing 3-3. The starting point of any new driver project created by this wizard is usually the DeviceDispatcher() function. It receives a device context pointer and a pointer to the I/O Request Packet (IRP) that is to be dispatched. The wizard's boilerplate code already handles the basic I/O requests IRP_MJ_CREATE, IRP_MJ_CLEANUP, and IRP_MJ_CLOSE, sent to the device when it is opened or closed by a client. The DeviceDispatcher() simply returns STATUS_SUCCESS for these requests, so the device can be opened and closed without error. For some devices, this behavior is sufficient, but others require more or less complex initialization and cleanup code here. All remaining requests return STATUS_NOT_IMPLEMENTED. The first step in the extension of the code is to change this default behavior by handling more requests. As already noted, one of the main tasks of `w2k_spy.sys` is to send data unavailable in user-mode to a Win32 application by means of IOCTL calls, so the work starts with the addition of an `IRP_MJ_DEVICE_CONTROL` case to the `DeviceDispatcher()` function. Listing 4-6 shows the updated code, as it appears in `w2k_spy.c`.

```
NTSTATUS DeviceDispatcher (PDEVICE_CONTEXT pDeviceContext,
                           PIRP            pIrp)
    {
    PIO_STACK_LOCATION pisl;
    DWORD              dInfo = 0;
    NTSTATUS           ns    = STATUS_NOT_IMPLEMENTED;

    pisl = IoGetCurrentIrpStackLocation (pIrp);

    switch (pisl->MajorFunction)
        {
        case IRP_MJ_CREATE:
        case IRP_MJ_CLEANUP:
        case IRP_MJ_CLOSE:
            {
            ns = STATUS_SUCCESS;
            break;
            }
        case IRP_MJ_DEVICE_CONTROL:
            {
            ns = SpyDispatcher (pDeviceContext,

                                pisl->Parameters.DeviceIoControl
                                                .IoControlCode,

                                pIrp->AssociatedIrp.SystemBuffer,
                                pisl->Parameters.DeviceIoControl
                                                .InputBufferLength,

                                pIrp->AssociatedIrp.SystemBuffer,
                                pisl->Parameters.DeviceIoControl
                                                .OutputBufferLength,
                                &dInfo);
            break;
            }
        }
    pIrp->IoStatus.Status      = ns;
    pIrp->IoStatus.Information = dInfo;

    IoCompleteRequest (pIrp, IO_NO_INCREMENT);
    return ns;
    }
```

LISTING 4-6. *Adding an* `IRP_MJ_DEVICE_CONTROL` *Case to the Dispatcher*

The IOCTL handler in Listing 4-6 is fairly simple—it just calls `SpyDispatcher()` with parameters it extracts from the IRP structure and the current I/O stack location embedded in it. The `SpyDispatcher()`, shown in Listing 4-7, requires the following arguments:

- `pDeviceContext` is the driver's device context. The basic `Device_Context` structure provided by the driver wizard contains the driver and device object pointers only (see Listing 3-4). The spy driver adds a couple of members to it for private use.
- `dCode` specifies the IOCTL code that determines the command to be executed by the spy device. An IOCTL code is a 32-bit integer consisting of 4 bit-fields, as illustrated by Figure 4-6.
- `pInput` points to the buffer providing the IOCTL input data.
- `dInput` is the size of the input buffer.
- `pOutput` points to the buffer receiving the IOCTL output data.
- `dOutput` is the size of the output buffer.
- `pdInfo` points to a `DWORD` variable that should receive the number of bytes written to the output buffer.

Depending on the IOCTL method used, the input and output buffers are passed differently from the system to the driver. The spy device uses buffered I/O, directing the system to copy the input data to a safe buffer allocated automatically by the system, and to copy a specified amount of data from the same system buffer to the caller's output buffer on return. It is important to keep in mind that the input and output buffers overlap in this case, so the IOCTL handler must save any input data it might need later before it writes any output data to the buffer. The pointer to this I/O buffer is stored in the `SystemBuffer` member of the `AssociatedIrp` union inside the `IRP` structure (cf. `ntddk.h`). The input and output buffer sizes are stored in a completely different location of the `IRP`—they are part of the `DeviceIoControl` member of the `Parameters` union inside the `IRP's` current stack location, named `InputBufferLength` and `OutputBufferLength`, respectively. The `DeviceIoControl` substructure also provides the IOCTL code via its `IoControlCode` member. More information about the Windows NT/2000 IOCTL methods and how they pass data in and out can be found in my article "A Spy Filter Driver for Windows NT" in *Windows Developer's Journal* (Schreiber 1997).

```
NTSTATUS SpyDispatcher (PDEVICE_CONTEXT pDeviceContext,
                        DWORD           dCode,
                        PVOID           pInput,
                        DWORD           dInput,
                        PVOID           pOutput,
                        DWORD           dOutput,
                        PDWORD          pdInfo)
    {
    SPY_MEMORY_BLOCK smb;
    SPY_PAGE_ENTRY   spe;
    SPY_CALL_INPUT   sci;
    PHYSICAL_ADDRESS pa;
    DWORD            dValue, dCount;
    BOOL             fReset, fPause, fFilter, fLine;
    PVOID            pAddress;
    PBYTE            pbName;
    HANDLE           hObject;
    NTSTATUS         ns = STATUS_INVALID_PARAMETER;

    MUTEX_WAIT (pDeviceContext->kmDispatch);

    *pdInfo = 0;

    switch (dCode)
        {
        case SPY_IO_VERSION_INFO:
            {
            ns = SpyOutputVersionInfo (pOutput, dOutput, pdInfo);
            break;
            }
        case SPY_IO_OS_INFO:
            {
            ns = SpyOutputOsInfo (pOutput, dOutput, pdInfo);
            break;
            }
        case SPY_IO_SEGMENT:
            {
            if ((ns = SpyInputDword (&dValue,
                                     pInput, dInput))
                == STATUS_SUCCESS)
                {
                ns = SpyOutputSegment (dValue,
                                       pOutput, dOutput, pdInfo);
                }
            break;
            }
        case SPY_IO_INTERRUPT:
            {
            if ((ns = SpyInputDword (&dValue,
                                     pInput, dInput))
                == STATUS_SUCCESS)
                {
```

```
            ns = SpyOutputInterrupt (dValue,
                                     pOutput, dOutput, pdInfo);
            }
        break;
        }
    case SPY_IO_PHYSICAL:
        {
        if ((ns = SpyInputPointer (&pAddress,
                                   pInput, dInput))
            == STATUS_SUCCESS)
            {
            pa = MmGetPhysicalAddress (pAddress);

            ns = SpyOutputBinary (&pa, PHYSICAL_ADDRESS_,
                                  pOutput, dOutput, pdInfo);
            }
        break;
        }
    case SPY_IO_CPU_INFO:
        {
        ns = SpyOutputCpuInfo (pOutput, dOutput, pdInfo);
        break;
        }
    case SPY_IO_PDE_ARRAY:
        {
        ns = SpyOutputBinary (X86_PDE_ARRAY, SPY_PDE_ARRAY_,
                              pOutput, dOutput, pdInfo);
        break;
        }
    case SPY_IO_PAGE_ENTRY:
        {
        if ((ns = SpyInputPointer (&pAddress,
                                   pInput, dInput))
            == STATUS_SUCCESS)
            {
            SpyMemoryPageEntry (pAddress, &spe);

            ns = SpyOutputBinary (&spe, SPY_PAGE_ENTRY_,
                                  pOutput, dOutput, pdInfo);
            }
        break;
        }
    case SPY_IO_MEMORY_DATA:
        {
        if ((ns = SpyInputMemory (&smb,
                                  pInput, dInput))
            == STATUS_SUCCESS)
            {
            ns = SpyOutputMemory (&smb,
                                  pOutput, dOutput, pdInfo);
            }
```

(continued)

```
            break;
            }
        case SPY_IO_MEMORY_BLOCK:
            {
            if ((ns = SpyInputMemory (&smb,
                                      pInput, dInput))
                == STATUS_SUCCESS)
                {
                ns = SpyOutputBlock (&smb,
                                     pOutput, dOutput, pdInfo);
                }
            break;
            }
        case SPY_IO_HANDLE_INFO:
            {
            if ((ns = SpyInputHandle (&hObject,
                                      pInput, dInput))
                == STATUS_SUCCESS)
                {
                ns = SpyOutputHandleInfo (hObject,
                                          pOutput, dOutput, pdInfo);
                }
            break;
            }
        case SPY_IO_HOOK_INFO:
            {
            ns = SpyOutputHookInfo (pOutput, dOutput, pdInfo);
            break;
            }
        case SPY_IO_HOOK_INSTALL:
            {
            if (((ns = SpyInputBool (&fReset,
                                     pInput, dInput))
                 == STATUS_SUCCESS)
                &&
                ((ns = SpyHookInstall (fReset, &dCount))
                 == STATUS_SUCCESS))
                {
                ns = SpyOutputDword (dCount,
                                     pOutput, dOutput, pdInfo);
                }
            break;
            }
        case SPY_IO_HOOK_REMOVE:
            {
            if (((ns = SpyInputBool (&fReset,
                                     pInput, dInput))
                 == STATUS_SUCCESS)
                &&
                ((ns = SpyHookRemove (fReset, &dCount))
                 == STATUS_SUCCESS))
                {
```

```
            ns = SpyOutputDword (dCount,
                                 pOutput, dOutput, pdInfo);
            }
        break;
        }
    case SPY_IO_HOOK_PAUSE:
        {
        if ((ns = SpyInputBool (&fPause,
                                pInput, dInput))
            == STATUS_SUCCESS)
            {
            fPause = SpyHookPause (fPause);

            ns = SpyOutputBool (fPause,
                                pOutput, dOutput, pdInfo);
            }
        break;
        }
    case SPY_IO_HOOK_FILTER:
        {
        if ((ns = SpyInputBool (&fFilter,
                                pInput, dInput))
            == STATUS_SUCCESS)
            {
            fFilter = SpyHookFilter (fFilter);

            ns = SpyOutputBool (fFilter,
                                pOutput, dOutput, pdInfo);
            }
        break;
        }
    case SPY_IO_HOOK_RESET:
        {
        SpyHookReset ();
        ns = STATUS_SUCCESS;
        break;
        }
    case SPY_IO_HOOK_READ:
        {
        if ((ns = SpyInputBool (&fLine,
                                pInput, dInput))
            == STATUS_SUCCESS)
            {
            ns = SpyOutputHookRead (fLine,
                                    pOutput, dOutput, pdInfo);
            }
        break;
        }
    case SPY_IO_HOOK_WRITE:
        {
        SpyHookWrite (pInput, dInput);
```

(continued)

```
            ns = STATUS_SUCCESS;
            break;
            }
        case SPY_IO_MODULE_INFO:
            {
            if ((ns = SpyInputPointer (&pbName,
                                       pInput, dInput))
                == STATUS_SUCCESS)
                {
                ns = SpyOutputModuleInfo (pbName,
                                          pOutput, dOutput, pdInfo);
                }
            break;
            }
        case SPY_IO_PE_HEADER:
            {
            if ((ns = SpyInputPointer (&pAddress,
                                       pInput, dInput))
                == STATUS_SUCCESS)
                {
                ns = SpyOutputPeHeader (pAddress,
                                        pOutput, dOutput, pdInfo);
                }
            break;
            }
        case SPY_IO_PE_EXPORT:
            {
            if ((ns = SpyInputPointer (&pAddress,
                                       pInput, dInput))
                == STATUS_SUCCESS)
                {
                ns = SpyOutputPeExport (pAddress,
                                        pOutput, dOutput, pdInfo);
                }
            break;
            }
        case SPY_IO_PE_SYMBOL:
            {
            if ((ns = SpyInputPointer (&pbName,
                                       pInput, dInput))
                == STATUS_SUCCESS)
                {
                ns = SpyOutputPeSymbol (pbName,
                                        pOutput, dOutput, pdInfo);
                }
            break;
            }
        case SPY_IO_CALL:
            {
            if ((ns = SpyInputBinary (&sci, SPY_CALL_INPUT_,
                                      pInput, dInput))
                == STATUS_SUCCESS)
```

```
            {
            ns = SpyOutputCall (&sci,
                                pOutput, dOutput, pdInfo);
            }
        break;
        }
    }
MUTEX_RELEASE (pDeviceContext->kmDispatch);
return ns;
}
```

LISTING 4-7. *The Spy Driver's Internal Command Dispatcher*

The main DDK header file `ntddk.h`, as well as the Win32 file `winioctl.h` in the Platform SDK, define the simple but highly convenient `CTL_CODE()` macro shown in Listing 4-8 to build IOCTL codes according to the diagram in Figure 4-6. The four parts serve the following purposes:

1. `DeviceType` is a 16-bit device type ID. `ntddk.h` lists a couple of predefined types, symbolized by the constants `FILE_DEVICE_*`. Microsoft reserves the range `0x0000` to `0x7FFF` for internal use, while the range `0x8000` to `0xFFFF` is available to developers. The spy driver defines its own device ID `FILE_DEVICE_SPY` and sets it to `0x8000`.
2. `Access` specifies the 2-bit access check value determining the required access rights for the IOCTL operation. Possible values are `FILE_ANY_ACCESS` (0), `FILE_READ_ACCESS` (1), `FILE_WRITE_ACCESS` (2), and the combination of the latter two, `FILE_READ_ACCESS | FILE_WRITE_ACCESS` (3). See `ntddk.h` for more details.
3. `Function` is a 12-bit ID that selects the operation to be performed by the device. Microsoft reserves the values `0x000` to `0x7FF` for internal use, and leaves range `0x800` to `0xFFF` for developers. The IOCTL function IDs recognized by the spy device are drawn from the latter number pool.
4. `Method` consists of 2 bits, selecting one of four available I/O transfer methods named `METHOD_BUFFERED` (0), `METHOD_IN_DIRECT` (1), `METHOD_OUT_DIRECT` (2), and `METHOD_NEITHER` (3), found in `ntddk.h`. The spy device uses `METHOD_BUFFERED` for all requests, which is a highly secure but also somewhat sluggish method because of the data copying between the client and system buffers. Because the I/O of the memory spy is not time-critical, it is a good idea to opt for security. If you want to know more about the other methods, please refer to my spy filter article mentioned on p.191. (Schreiber 1997).

```
#define CTL_CODE (DeviceType, Function, Method, Access) \
        (((DeviceType) << 16) | ((Access) << 14) | ((Function) << 2) (Method))
```

LISTING 4-8. *The* `CTL_CODE()` *Macro Builds I/O Control Codes*

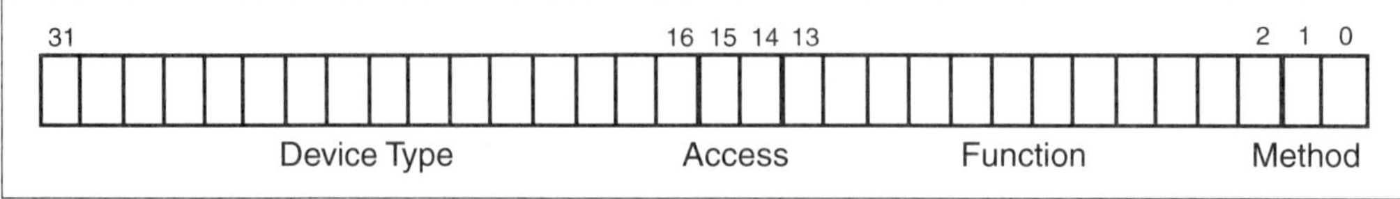

FIGURE 4-6. *Structure of a Device I/O Control Code*

Table 4-2 summarizes all IOCTL functions supported by `w2k_spy.sys`. The functions with IDs in the range 0 to 10 are memory exploration primitives that are sufficient to cover a wide range of tasks; they are discussed later in this chapter. The remaining functions with IDs of 11 and up belong to different IOCTL groups that will be described in detail in the next chapters, where Native API hooks and kernel calls from user-mode are discussed. Note that some IOCTL codes require the write access right, indicated by bit #15 being set (see Figure 4-6). That is, all IOCTL commands with a code of `0x80006nnn` can be issued via a read-only device handle, and a code of `0x8000Ennn` requires a read/write handle. The access rights are typically requested in the `CreateFile()` call that opens the device by specifying a combination of the `GENERIC_READ` and `GENERIC_WRITE` flags for the `dwDesiredAccess` argument.

The function names in the leftmost column of Table 4-2 also appear as cases of the large switch/case statement of the `SpyDispatcher()` function in Listing 4-7. This function first obtains the device's dispatcher mutex to guarantee that only a single request is executed at a time if more than one client or a multithreaded application communicates with the device. `MUTEX_WAIT()` is a wrapper macro for `KeWaitForMutexObject()`, which takes no less than five arguments. `KeWaitForMutexObject()` is a macro itself, forwarding its arguments to `KeWaitForSingleObject()`. `MUTEX_WAIT()`, along with its friends `MUTEX_RELEASE()` and `MUTEX_INITIALIZE()`, is shown in Listing 4-9. After the mutex object becomes signaled, `SpyDispatcher()` branches to various short code sequences, depending on the received IOCTL code. At the end, it releases the mutex and returns a status code to the caller.

The `SpyDispatcher()` uses a couple of helper functions to read input parameters, obtain the requested data, and write the data to the caller's output buffer. As already mentioned, a kernel-mode driver must be overly fussy with any user-mode

TABLE 4-2. *IOCTL Functions Supported by the Spy Device*

FUNCTION NAME	ID	IOCTL CODE	DESCRIPTION
SPY_IO_VERSION_INFO	0	0x80006000	Returns spy version information
SPY_IO_OS_INFO	1	0x80006004	Returns operating system information
SPY_IO_SEGMENT	2	0x80006008	Returns the properties of a segment
SPY_IO_INTERRUPT	3	0x8000600C	Returns the properties of an interrupt gate
SPY_IO_PHYSICAL	4	0x80006010	Linear-to-physical address translation
SPY_IO_CPU_INFO	5	0x80006014	Returns the values of special CPU registers
SPY_IO_PDE_ARRAY	6	0x80006018	Returns the PDE array at 0xC0300000
SPY_IO_PAGE_ENTRY	7	0x8000601C	Returns the PDE or PTE of a linear address
SPY_IO_MEMORY_DATA	8	0x80006020	Returns the contents of a memory block
SPY_IO_MEMORY_BLOCK	9	0x80006024	Returns the contents of a memory block
SPY_IO_HANDLE_INFO	10	0x80006028	Looks up object properties from a handle
SPY_IO_HOOK_INFO	11	0x8000602C	Returns info about Native API hooks
SPY_IO_HOOK_INSTALL	12	0x8000E030	Installs Native API hooks
SPY_IO_HOOK_REMOVE	13	0x8000E034	Removes Native API hooks
SPY_IO_HOOK_PAUSE	14	0x8000E038	Pauses/resumes the hook protocol
SPY_IO_HOOK_FILTER	15	0x8000E03C	Enables/disables the hook protocol filter
SPY_IO_HOOK_RESET	16	0x8000E040	Clears the hook protocol
SPY_IO_HOOK_READ	17	0x80006044	Reads data from the hook protocol
SPY_IO_HOOK_WRITE	18	0x8000E048	Writes data to the hook protocol
SPY_IO_MODULE_INFO	19	0x8000604C	Returns information about loaded system modules
SPY_IO_PE_HEADER	20	0x80006050	Returns `IMAGE_NT_HEADERS` data
SPY_IO_PE_EXPORT	21	0x80006054	Returns `IMAGE_EXPORT_DIRECTORY` data
SPY_IO_PE_SYMBOL	22	0x80006058	Returns the address of an exported system symbol
SPY_IO_CALL	23	0x8000E05C	Calls a function inside a loaded module

parameters it receives. From a driver's perspective, all user-mode code is evil and has no other thing on its mind but to trash the system. This somewhat paranoid view is not absurd—just the slightest slip brings the whole system to an immediate stop, with the appearance of a BlueScreen. So, if a client application says: "Here's my buffer—it can take up to 4,096 bytes," the driver does not accept it—neither that the buffer

```
#define MUTEX_INITIALIZE(_mutex) \
        KeInitializeMutex \
            (&(_mutex), 0)

#define MUTEX_WAIT(_mutex) \
        KeWaitForMutexObject \
            (&(_mutex), Executive, KernelMode, FALSE, NULL)

#define MUTEX_RELEASE(_mutex) \
        KeReleaseMutex \
            (&(_mutex), FALSE)
```

LISTING 4-9. *Kernel-Mutex Management Macros*

points to valid memory, nor that the buffer size is correct. In an IOCTL situation with buffered I/O (i.e., if the `Method` portion of the IOCTL code indicates `METHOD_BUFFERED`), the system takes care of the sanity checks and allocates a buffer that is large enough to hold both the input and output data. However, the other I/O transfer methods, most notably `METHOD_NEITHER`, where the driver receives original user-mode buffer pointers, require more foresight.

Although the spy device uses buffered I/O, it has to check the input and output parameters for validity. It might be that the client application passes in less data than is required or provides an output buffer that is not large enough for the output data. The system cannot catch these semantic problems, because it doesn't know what kind of data is transferred in an IOCTL transaction. Therefore, `SpyDispatcher()` calls the `SpyInput*()` and `SpyOutput*()` helper functions to copy data from or to the I/O buffers. These functions execute the requested operation only if the buffer size matches the requirements of the operation. Listing 4-10 shows the basic input functions, and Listing 4-11 shows the basic output functions. `SpyInputBinary()` and `SpyOutputBinary()` are the workhorses. They test the buffer size, and, if it is OK, they copy the requested amount of data using the Windows 2000 Runtime Library function `RtlCopyMemory()`. The remaining functions are simple wrappers for the common data types `DWORD`, `BOOL`, `PVOID`, and `HANDLE`. Additionally, `SpyOutputBlock()` copies the data block specified by the caller in a `SPY_MEMORY_BLOCK` structure after verifying that all bytes in the indicated range are readable. The `SpyInput*()` functions return `STATUS_INVALID_BUFFER_SIZE` if incomplete input data is passed in, and the `SpyOutput*()` functions return `STATUS_ BUFFER_TOO_SMALL` if the output buffer is smaller than required.

```
NTSTATUS SpyInputBinary (PVOID  pData,
                         DWORD  dData,
                         PVOID  pInput,
                         DWORD  dInput)
    {
    NTSTATUS ns = STATUS_OBJECT_TYPE_MISMATCH;

    if (dData <= dInput)
        {
        RtlCopyMemory (pData, pInput, dData);
        ns = STATUS_SUCCESS;
        }
    return ns;
    }

// -----------------------------------------------------------------

NTSTATUS SpyInputDword (PDWORD pdValue,
                        PVOID  pInput,
                        DWORD  dInput)
    {
    return SpyInputBinary (pdValue, DWORD_, pInput, dInput);
    }

// -----------------------------------------------------------------

NTSTATUS SpyInputBool (PBOOL  pfValue,
                       PVOID  pInput,
                       DWORD  dInput)
    {
    return SpyInputBinary (pfValue, BOOL_, pInput, dInput);
    }

// -----------------------------------------------------------------

NTSTATUS SpyInputPointer (PPVOID ppAddress,
                          PVOID  pInput,
                          DWORD  dInput)
    {
    return SpyInputBinary (ppAddress, PVOID_, pInput, dInput);
    }

// -----------------------------------------------------------------

NTSTATUS SpyInputHandle (PHANDLE phObject,
                         PVOID   pInput,
                         DWORD   dInput)
    {
    return SpyInputBinary (phObject, HANDLE_, pInput, dInput);
    }
```

LISTING 4-10. *Reading Input Data from an IOCTL Buffer*

```
NTSTATUS SpyOutputBinary (PVOID  pData,
                          DWORD  dData,
                          PVOID  pOutput,
                          DWORD  dOutput,
                          PDWORD pdInfo)
    {
    NTSTATUS ns = STATUS_BUFFER_TOO_SMALL;

    *pdInfo = 0;

    if (dData <= dOutput)
        {
        RtlCopyMemory (pOutput, pData, *pdInfo = dData);
        ns = STATUS_SUCCESS;
        }
    return ns;
    }

// -----------------------------------------------------------------

NTSTATUS SpyOutputBlock (PSPY_MEMORY_BLOCK psmb,
                         PVOID             pOutput,
                         DWORD             dOutput,
                         PDWORD            pdInfo)
    {
    NTSTATUS ns = STATUS_INVALID_PARAMETER;

    if (SpyMemoryTestBlock (psmb->pAddress, psmb->dBytes))
        {
        ns = SpyOutputBinary (psmb->pAddress, psmb->dBytes,
                              pOutput, dOutput, pdInfo);
        }
    return ns;
    }

// -----------------------------------------------------------------

NTSTATUS SpyOutputDword (DWORD  dValue,
                         PVOID  pOutput,
                         DWORD  dOutput,
                         PDWORD pdInfo)
    {
    return SpyOutputBinary (&dValue, DWORD_,
                            pOutput, dOutput, pdInfo);
    }

// -----------------------------------------------------------------

NTSTATUS SpyOutputBool (BOOL   fValue,
                        PVOID  pOutput,
                        DWORD  dOutput,
                        PDWORD pdInfo)
    {
```

```
    return SpyOutputBinary (&fValue, BOOL_,
                            pOutput, dOutput, pdInfo);
    }

// ---------------------------------------------------------------

NTSTATUS SpyOutputPointer (PVOID  pValue,
                           PVOID  pOutput,
                           DWORD  dOutput,
                           PDWORD pdInfo)
    {
    return SpyOutputBinary (&pValue, PVOID_,
                            pOutput, dOutput, pdInfo);
    }
```

LISTING 4-11. *Writing Output Data to an IOCTL Buffer*

You might have noticed that the `SpyDispatcher()` in Listing 4-7 contains references to a few more `SpyInput*()` and `SpyOutput*()` functions. Although ultimately based on `SpyInputBinary()` and `SpyOutputBinary()`, they are slightly more complex than the basic functions in Listings 4-10 and 4-11 and, therefore, are discussed separately a little later in this chapter. So let's start at the beginning of `SpyDispatcher()` and work through the switch/case statement step by step.

THE IOCTL FUNCTION SPY_IO_VERSION_INFO

The IOCTL `SPY_IO_VERSION_INFO` function fills a caller-supplied `SPY_VERSION_INFO` structure with data about the spy driver itself. It doesn't require input parameters and uses the `SpyOutputVersionInfo()` helper function. This function, included in Listing 4-12 together with the `SPY_VERSION_INFO` structure, is trivial. It sets the `dVersion` member to the constant `SPY_VERSION` (currently 100, indicating V1.00) defined in `w2k_spy.h`, and copies the driver's name symbolized by the string constant `DRV_NAME` ("SBS Windows 2000 Spy Device") to the `awName` member. The major version number is obtained by dividing `dVersion` by 100. The remainder yields the minor version number.

```
typedef struct _SPY_VERSION_INFO
    {
    DWORD dVersion;
    WORD  awName [SPY_NAME_];
    }
    SPY_VERSION_INFO, *PSPY_VERSION_INFO, **PPSPY_VERSION_INFO;
```

(continued)

```
#define SPY_VERSION_INFO_ sizeof (SPY_VERSION_INFO)

// ---------------------------------------------------------------

NTSTATUS SpyOutputVersionInfo (PVOID  pOutput,
                               DWORD  dOutput,
                               PDWORD pdInfo)
    {
    SPY_VERSION_INFO svi;

    svi.dVersion = SPY_VERSION;

    wcscpyn (svi.awName, USTRING (CSTRING (DRV_NAME)), SPY_NAME_);

    return SpyOutputBinary (&svi, SPY_VERSION_INFO_,
                            pOutput, dOutput, pdInfo);
    }
```

LISTING 4-12. *Obtaining Version Information About the Spy Driver*

THE IOCTL FUNCTION SPY_IO_OS_INFO

The IOCTL `SPY_IO_OS_INFO` function is much more interesting than the preceding one. It is another output-only function, expecting no input arguments and filling a caller-supplied `SPY_OS_INFO` structure with the values of several internal operating system parameters. Listing 4-13 shows the definition of this structure and the helper function `SpyOutputOsInfo()` called by the dispatcher. Some of the structure members are simply set to constants drawn from the DDK header files and `w2k_spy.h`; others receive "live" values read out from several internal kernel variables and structures. In Chapter 2, you became acquainted with the variables `NtBuildNumber` and `NtGlobalFlag`, exported by `ntoskrnl.exe` (see Table B-1 in Appendix B). Other than the other exported `Nt*` symbols, these don't point to API functions, but to variables in the kernel's `.data` section. In the Win32 world, it is quite uncommon to export variables. However, several Windows 2000 kernel modules make use of this technique. `ntoskrnl.exe` exports no fewer than 55 variables, `ntdll.dll` provides 4, and `hal.dll` provides 1. Of the set of `ntoskrnl.exe` variables, `SpyOutputOsInfo()` copies `MmHighestUserAddress`, `MmUserProbeAddress`, `MmSystemRangeStart`, `NtGlobalFlag`, `KeI386MachineType`, `KeNumberProcessors`, and `NtBuildNumber` to the output buffer.

When a module imports data from another module, it has to instruct the compiler and linker accordingly by using the `extern` keyword. This will cause the linker to generate an entry in the module's import section instead of trying to resolve the symbol to a fixed address. Some `extern` declarations are already included in `ntddk.h`. Those that are missing are included in Listing 4-13.

```
typedef struct _SPY_OS_INFO
    {
    DWORD    dPageSize;
    DWORD    dPageShift;
    DWORD    dPtiShift;
    DWORD    dPdiShift;
    DWORD    dPageMask;
    DWORD    dPtiMask;
    DWORD    dPdiMask;
    PX86_PE  PteArray;
    PX86_PE  PdeArray;
    PVOID    pLowestUserAddress;
    PVOID    pThreadEnvironmentBlock;
    PVOID    pHighestUserAddress;
    PVOID    pUserProbeAddress;
    PVOID    pSystemRangeStart;
    PVOID    pLowestSystemAddress;
    PVOID    pSharedUserData;
    PVOID    pProcessorControlRegion;
    PVOID    pProcessorControlBlock;
    DWORD    dGlobalFlag;
    DWORD    dI386MachineType;
    DWORD    dNumberProcessors;
    DWORD    dProductType;
    DWORD    dBuildNumber;
    DWORD    dNtMajorVersion;
    DWORD    dNtMinorVersion;
    WORD     awNtSystemRoot [MAX_PATH];
    }
    SPY_OS_INFO, *PSPY_OS_INFO, **PPSPY_OS_INFO;

#define SPY_OS_INFO_ sizeof (SPY_OS_INFO)

// -----------------------------------------------------------------
```

(continued)

```
extern PWORD  NlsAnsiCodePage;
extern PWORD  NlsOemCodePage;
extern PWORD  NtBuildNumber;
extern PDWORD NtGlobalFlag;
extern PDWORD KeI386MachineType;

// -----------------------------------------------------------------

NTSTATUS SpyOutputOsInfo (PVOID  pOutput,
                          DWORD  dOutput,
                          PDWORD pdInfo)
    {
    SPY_SEGMENT     ss;
    SPY_OS_INFO     soi;
    NT_PRODUCT_TYPE NtProductType;
    PKPCR           pkpcr;

    NtProductType = (SharedUserData->ProductTypeIsValid
                     ? SharedUserData->NtProductType
                     : 0);

    SpySegment (X86_SEGMENT_FS, 0, &ss);
    pkpcr = ss.pBase;

    soi.dPageSize                =  PAGE_SIZE;
    soi.dPageShift               =  PAGE_SHIFT;
    soi.dPtiShift                =  PTI_SHIFT;
    soi.dPdiShift                =  PDI_SHIFT;
    soi.dPageMask                =  X86_PAGE_MASK;
    soi.dPtiMask                 =  X86_PTI_MASK;
    soi.dPdiMask                 =  X86_PDI_MASK;
    soi.PteArray                 =  X86_PTE_ARRAY;
    soi.PdeArray                 =  X86_PDE_ARRAY;
    soi.pLowestUserAddress       =  MM_LOWEST_USER_ADDRESS;
    soi.pThreadEnvironmentBlock  =  pkpcr->NtTib.Self;
    soi.pHighestUserAddress      = *MmHighestUserAddress;
    soi.pUserProbeAddress        =  (PVOID) *MmUserProbeAddress;
    soi.pSystemRangeStart        = *MmSystemRangeStart;
    soi.pLowestSystemAddress     =  MM_LOWEST_SYSTEM_ADDRESS;
    soi.pSharedUserData          =  SharedUserData;
    soi.pProcessorControlRegion  =  pkpcr;
    soi.pProcessorControlBlock   =  pkpcr->Prcb;
    soi.dGlobalFlag              = *NtGlobalFlag;
    soi.dI386MachineType         = *KeI386MachineType;
    soi.dNumberProcessors        = *KeNumberProcessors;
    soi.dProductType             =  NtProductType;
    soi.dBuildNumber             = *NtBuildNumber;
    soi.dNtMajorVersion          =  SharedUserData->NtMajorVersion;
    soi.dNtMinorVersion          =  SharedUserData->NtMinorVersion;
```

```
    wcscpyn (soi.awNtSystemRoot, SharedUserData->NtSystemRoot,
             MAX_PATH);

    return SpyOutputBinary (&soi, SPY_OS_INFO_,
                            pOutput, dOutput, pdInfo);
    }
```

LISTING 4-13. *Obtaining Information About the Operating System*

The remaining members of the SPY_OS_INFO structure are filled with values from system data structures lying around in memory. For example, SpyOutputOsInfo() assigns the base address of the Kernel's Processor Control Region (KPCR) to the pProcessorControlRegion member. This is a very important data structure that contains lots of frequently used thread-specific data items, and therefore is placed in its own memory segment addressed by the CPU's FS register. Both Windows NT 4.0 and Windows 2000 set up FS to point to the linear address 0xFFDFF000 in kernel-mode. SpyOutputOsInfo() calls the SpySegment() function discussed later to query the base address of the FS segment in the linear address space. This segment also comprises the Kernel's Processor Control Block (KPRCB), pointed to by the Prcb member of the KPCR, immediately followed by a CONTEXT structure containing low-level CPU status information of the current thread. The definitions of the KPCR, KPRCB, and CONTEXT structures can be looked up in the ntddk.h header file. More on this topic follows later in this chapter.

Another internal data structure referenced in Listing 4-13 is SharedUserData. It is actually nothing but a "well-known address," typecast to a structure pointer. Listing 4-14 shows the definition as it appears in ntddk.h. Well-known addresses are locations within the linear address space that are set at compile time, and hence do not vary over time or with the configuration. Obviously, SharedUserData is a pointer to a KUSER_SHARED_DATA structure found at the fixed linear address 0xFFDF0000. This memory area is shared by the user-mode application and the system, and it contains such interesting things as the operating system's version number, which SpyOutputOsInfo() copies to the dNtMajorVersion and dNtMinorVersion members of the caller's SPY_OS_INFO structure. As I will show later, the KUSER_SHARED_DATA structure is mirrored to address 0x7FFE0000, where user-mode code can access it.

Following the explanation of the spy device's IOCTL functions is a demo application that displays the returned data on the screen.

```
#define KI_USER_SHARED_DATA 0xffdf0000
#define SharedUserData ((KUSER_SHARED_DATA * const) KI_USER_SHARED_DATA)
```

LISTING 4-14. *Definition of* SharedUserData

THE IOCTL FUNCTION SPY_IO_SEGMENT

Now this discussion becomes really interesting. The `SPY_IO_SEGMENT` function does some very-low-level operations to query the properties of a segment, given a selector. `SpyDispatcher()` first calls `SpyInputDword()` to get the selector value passed in by the calling application. You might recall that selectors are 16-bit quantities. However, I try to avoid 16-bit data types whenever possible because the native word size of the i386 CPUs in 32-bit mode is the 32-bit `DWORD`. Therefore, I have extended the selector argument to a `DWORD` where the upper 16 bits are always zero. If `SpyInputDword()` reports success, the `SpyOutputSegment()` function shown in Listing 4-15 is called. This function simply returns to the caller whatever the `SpySegment()` helper function, included in Listing 4-15, returns. Basically, `SpySegment()` fills a `SPY_SEGMENT` structure, defined at the top of Listing 4-15. It comprises the selector's value in the form of a `X86_SELECTOR` structure (see Listing 4-2), along with its 64-bit `X86_DESCRIPTOR` (Listing 4-2, again), the corresponding segment's linear base address, the segment limit (i.e., the segment size minus one), and a flag named `fOk` indicating whether the data in the `SPY_SEGMENT` structure is valid. The latter is required in the context of other functions (e.g., `SPY_IO_CPU_INFO`) that return the properties of several segments at once. In this case, the `fOk` member enables the caller to sort out any invalid segments contained in the output data.

```
typedef struct _SPY_SEGMENT
    {
    X86_SELECTOR    Selector;
    X86_DESCRIPTOR Descriptor;
    PVOID           pBase;
    DWORD           dLimit;
    BOOL            fOk;
    }
    SPY_SEGMENT, *PSPY_SEGMENT, **PPSPY_SEGMENT;

#define SPY_SEGMENT_ sizeof (SPY_SEGMENT)

// -----------------------------------------------------------------

NTSTATUS SpyOutputSegment (DWORD  dSelector,
                           PVOID  pOutput,
                           DWORD  dOutput,
                           PDWORD pdInfo)
    {
    SPY_SEGMENT ss;

    SpySegment (X86_SEGMENT_OTHER, dSelector, &ss);
```

```
    return SpyOutputBinary (&ss, SPY_SEGMENT_,
                            pOutput, dOutput, pdInfo);
    }

// -----------------------------------------------------------------

BOOL SpySegment (DWORD        dSegment,
                 DWORD        dSelector,
                 PSPY_SEGMENT pSegment)
    {
    BOOL fOk = FALSE;

    if (pSegment != NULL)
        {
        fOk = TRUE;

        if (!SpySelector   (dSegment, dSelector,
                            &pSegment->Selector))
            {
            fOk = FALSE;
            }
        if (!SpyDescriptor (&pSegment->Selector,
                            &pSegment->Descriptor))
            {
            fOk = FALSE;
            }
        pSegment->pBase  =
            SpyDescriptorBase  (&pSegment->Descriptor);

        pSegment->dLimit =
            SpyDescriptorLimit (&pSegment->Descriptor);

        pSegment->fOk = fOk;
        }
    return fOk;
    }
```

LISTING 4-15. *Querying Segment Properties*

`SpySegment()` relies on several other helper functions that provide the parts that make up the resulting `SPY_SEGMENT` structure. First, `SpySelector()` copies a selector value to the passed-in `X86_SELECTOR` structure (Listing 4-16). If the first argument, `dSegment`, is set to `X86_SEGMENT_OTHER`, the `dSelector` argument is assumed to specify a valid selector value, so this value is simply assigned to the `wValue` member of the output structure. Otherwise, `dSelector` is ignored, and `dSegment` is used in a switch/case construct that selects one of the CPU's segment registers or its task register `TR`. Note that this requires a little bit of inline assembly—the C language doesn't provide a standard means for accessing processor-specific features such as segment registers.

```
#define X86_SEGMENT_OTHER           0
#define X86_SEGMENT_CS              1
#define X86_SEGMENT_DS              2
#define X86_SEGMENT_ES              3
#define X86_SEGMENT_FS              4
#define X86_SEGMENT_GS              5
#define X86_SEGMENT_SS              6
#define X86_SEGMENT_TSS             7

// -----------------------------------------------------------------

BOOL SpySelector (DWORD         dSegment,
                  DWORD         dSelector,
                  PX86_SELECTOR pSelector)
    {
    X86_SELECTOR Selector = {0, 0};
    BOOL         fOk      = FALSE;

    if (pSelector != NULL)
        {
        fOk = TRUE;

        switch (dSegment)
            {
            case X86_SEGMENT_OTHER:
                {
                if (fOk = ((dSelector >> X86_SELECTOR_SHIFT)
                           <= X86_SELECTOR_LIMIT))
                    {
                    Selector.wValue = (WORD) dSelector;
                    }
                break;
                }
            case X86_SEGMENT_CS:
                {
                __asm mov Selector.wValue, cs
                break;
                }
            case X86_SEGMENT_DS:
                {
                __asm mov Selector.wValue, ds
                break;
                }
            case X86_SEGMENT_ES:
                {
                __asm mov Selector.wValue, es
                break;
                }
            case X86_SEGMENT_FS:
                {
                __asm mov Selector.wValue, fs
                break;
```

```
                }
            case X86_SEGMENT_GS:
                {
                __asm mov Selector.wValue, gs
                break;
                }
            case X86_SEGMENT_SS:
                {
                __asm mov Selector.wValue, ss
                break;
                }
            case X86_SEGMENT_TSS:
                {
                __asm str Selector.wValue
                break;
                }
            default:
                {
                fOk = FALSE;
                break;
                }
            }
        RtlCopyMemory (pSelector, &Selector, X86_SELECTOR_);
        }
    return fOk;
    }
```

LISTING 4-16. *Obtaining Selector Values*

`SpyDescriptor()` reads in the 64-bit descriptor pointed to by the segment selector (Listing 4-17). As you might recall, all selectors contain a Table Indicator (`TI`) bit that decides whether the selector refers to a descriptor in the Global Descriptor Table (GDT, `TI`=0) or Local Descriptor Table (LDT, `TI`=1). The upper half of Listing 4-17 handles the LDT case. First, the assembly language instructions `SLDT` and `SGDT` are used to read the LDT selector value and the segment limit and base address of the GDT, respectively. Remember that the linear base address of the GDT is specified explicitly, whereas the LDT is referenced indirectly via a selector that points into the GDT. Therefore, `SpyDescriptor()` first validates the LDT selector value. If it is not the null segment selector and does not point beyond the GDT limit, the `SpyDescriptorType()`, `SpyDescriptorLimit()`, and `SpyDescriptorBase()` functions attached to the bottom of Listing 4-17 are called to obtain the basic properties of the LDT:

- `SpyDescriptorType()` returns the values of a descriptor's `Type` and *S* bit-fields (cf. Listing 4-2). The LDT selector must point to a system descriptor of type `X86_DESCRIPTOR_SYS_LDT` (2).

- `SpyDescriptorLimit()` compiles the segment limit from the `Limit1` and `Limit2` bit-fields of a descriptor. If its *G* flag indicates a granularity of 4-KB, the value is shifted left by 12 bits, shifting in 1-bits from the right end.
- `SpyDescriptorBase()` simply arranges the `Base1, Base2,` and `Base3` bit-fields of a descriptor properly to yield a 32-bit linear address.

```
BOOL SpyDescriptor (PX86_SELECTOR   pSelector,
                    PX86_DESCRIPTOR pDescriptor)
    {
    X86_SELECTOR     ldt;
    X86_TABLE        gdt;
    DWORD            dType, dLimit;
    BOOL             fSystem;
    PX86_DESCRIPTOR pDescriptors = NULL;
    BOOL             fOk          = FALSE;

    if (pDescriptor != NULL)
        {
        if (pSelector != NULL)
            {
            if (pSelector->TI) // ldt descriptor
                {
                __asm
                    {
                    sldt ldt.wValue
                    sgdt gdt.wLimit
                    }
                if ((!ldt.TI) && ldt.Index &&
                    ((ldt.wValue & X86_SELECTOR_INDEX)
                     <= gdt.wLimit))
                    {
                    dType  = SpyDescriptorType  (gdt.pDescriptors +
                                                 ldt.Index,
                                                 &fSystem);

                    dLimit = SpyDescriptorLimit (gdt.pDescriptors +
                                                 ldt.Index);

                    if ((dType == X86_DESCRIPTOR_SYS_LDT)
                        &&
                        ((DWORD) (pSelector->wValue
                                  & X86_SELECTOR_INDEX)
                         <= dLimit))
                        {
                        pDescriptors =
```

```
                        SpyDescriptorBase (gdt.pDescriptors +
                                           ldt.Index);
                    }
                }
            }
        else // gdt descriptor
            {
            if (pSelector->Index)
                {
                __asm
                    {
                    sgdt gdt.wLimit
                    }
                if ((pSelector->wValue & X86_SELECTOR_INDEX)
                    <= gdt.wLimit)
                    {
                    pDescriptors = gdt.pDescriptors;
                    }
                }
            }
        }
    if (pDescriptors != NULL)
        {
        RtlCopyMemory (pDescriptor,
                       pDescriptors + pSelector->Index,
                       X86_DESCRIPTOR_);
        fOk = TRUE;
        }
    else
        {
        RtlZeroMemory (pDescriptor,
                       X86_DESCRIPTOR_);
        }
    }
return fOk;
}

// -----------------------------------------------------------------

PVOID SpyDescriptorBase (PX86_DESCRIPTOR pDescriptor)
    {
    return (PVOID) ((pDescriptor->Base1      ) |
                    (pDescriptor->Base2 << 16) |
                    (pDescriptor->Base3 << 24));
    }

// -----------------------------------------------------------------

DWORD SpyDescriptorLimit (PX86_DESCRIPTOR pDescriptor)
    {
    return (pDescriptor->G ? (pDescriptor->Limit1 << 12) |
                             (pDescriptor->Limit2 << 28) | 0xFFF
```

(continued)

```
                              : (pDescriptor->Limit1       ) |
                                (pDescriptor->Limit2 << 16));
    }

// -----------------------------------------------------------------

DWORD SpyDescriptorType (PX86_DESCRIPTOR pDescriptor,
                         PBOOL           pfSystem)
    {
    if (pfSystem != NULL) *pfSystem = !pDescriptor->S;
    return pDescriptor->Type;
    }
```

LISTING 4-17. *Obtaining Descriptor Values*

If the selector's `TI` bit indicates a GDT descriptor, things are much simpler. Again, the `SGDT` instruction is used to get the size and location of the GDT in linear memory, and if the descriptor index specified by the selector is within the proper range, the `pDescriptors` variable is set to point to the GDT base address. In both the LDT and GDT cases, the `pDescriptor` variable is non-NULL if the caller has passed in a valid selector. In this case, the 64-bit descriptor value is copied to the caller's `X86_DESCRIPTOR` structure. Otherwise, all members of this structure are set to zero with the kind help of `RtlZeroMemory()`.

We are still in the discussion of the `SpySegment()` function shown in Listing 4-15. The `SpySelector()` and `SpyDescriptor()` calls have been handled. Only the concluding `SpyDescriptorBase()` and `SpyDescriptorLimit()` invocations are left, but you already know what these functions do (see Listing 4-17). If `SpySelector()` and `SpyDescriptor()` succeed, the data returned in the `SPY_SEGMENT` structure is valid. `SpyDescriptorBase()` and `SpyDescriptorLimit()` don't return error flags because they cannot fail—they just might return meaningless data if the supplied descriptor is invalid.

THE IOCTL FUNCTION SPY_IO_INTERRUPT

`SPY_IO_INTERRUPT` is similar to `SPY_IO_SEGMENT`, except that this function works on interrupt descriptors stored in the system's Interrupt Descriptor Table (IDT), rather than on LDT or GDT descriptors. The IDT contains up to 256 descriptors that can represent task, interrupt, or trap gates (cf. Intel 1999c, pp. 5-11ff). By the way, interrupts and traps are quite similar in nature, differing in a tiny detail only: An interrupt handler is always entered with interrupts disabled, whereas the interrupt flag is left unchanged upon entering a trap handler. The `SPY_IO_INTERRUPT` caller supplies an interrupt number between 0 and 256 in its input buffer and a `SPY_INTERRUPT` structure as output buffer, which will contain the properties of the corresponding interrupt handler on successful return. The `SpyOutputInterrupt()` helper function invoked by the dispatcher is a simple wrapper that calls `SpyInterrupt()` and copies the returned data to the output buffer. Both functions, as well as the `SPY_INTERRUPT` structure they operate on, are shown in Listing 4-18. The latter is filled by `SpyInterrupt()` with the following items:

- `Selector` specifies the selector of a Task-State Segment (TSS, see Intel 1999c, pp. 6-4ff) or a code segment. A code segment selector determines the segment where an interrupt or trap handler is located.
- `Gate` is the 64-bit task, interrupt, or trap gate descriptor addressed by the selector.
- `Segment` contains the properties of the segment addressed by the gate.
- `pOffset` specifies the offset of the interrupt or trap handler's entry point relative to the base address of the surrounding code segment. Because task gates don't comprise an offset value, this member must be ignored if the input selector refers to a TSS.
- `fOk` is a flag that indicates whether the data in the `SPY_INTERRUPT` structure is valid.

A TSS is typically used to guarantee that an error situation is handled by a valid task. It is a special system segment type that holds 104 bytes of processor state information needed to restore a task after a task switch has occurred, as outlined in Table 4-3. The CPU always forces a task switch and saves all CPU registers to the TSS when an interrupt associated with a TSS occurs. Windows 2000 stores task gates in the interrupt slots `0x02` (Nonmaskable Interrupt [NMI]), `0x08` (Double Fault), and `0x12` (Stack-Segment Fault). The remaining entries point to interrupt handlers. Unused interrupts are handled by dummy routines named `KiUnexpectedInterruptNNN()`, where "`NNN`" is a decimal ordinal number. These handlers branch to the internal function `KiEndUnexpectedRange()`, which in turn branches to `KiUnexpectedInterruptTail()`, passing in the number of the unhandled interrupt.

```
typedef struct _SPY_INTERRUPT
    {
    X86_SELECTOR Selector;
    X86_GATE     Gate;
    SPY_SEGMENT  Segment;
    PVOID        pOffset;
    BOOL         fOk;
    }
    SPY_INTERRUPT, *PSPY_INTERRUPT, **PPSPY_INTERRUPT;
```

(continued)

```
#define SPY_INTERRUPT_ sizeof (SPY_INTERRUPT)

// -----------------------------------------------------------------

NTSTATUS SpyOutputInterrupt (DWORD  dInterrupt,
                             PVOID  pOutput,
                             DWORD  dOutput,
                             PDWORD pdInfo)
    {
    SPY_INTERRUPT si;

    SpyInterrupt (dInterrupt, &si);

    return SpyOutputBinary (&si, SPY_INTERRUPT_,
                            pOutput, dOutput, pdInfo);
    }

// -----------------------------------------------------------------

BOOL SpyInterrupt (DWORD          dInterrupt,
                   PSPY_INTERRUPT pInterrupt)
    {
    BOOL fOk = FALSE;

    if (pInterrupt != NULL)
        {
        if (dInterrupt <= X86_SELECTOR_LIMIT)
            {
            fOk = TRUE;

            if (!SpySelector (X86_SEGMENT_OTHER,
                              dInterrupt << X86_SELECTOR_SHIFT,
                              &pInterrupt->Selector))
                {
                fOk = FALSE;
                }
            if (!SpyIdtGate  (&pInterrupt->Selector,
                              &pInterrupt->Gate))
                {
                fOk = FALSE;
                }
            if (!SpySegment  (X86_SEGMENT_OTHER,
                              pInterrupt->Gate.Selector,
                              &pInterrupt->Segment))
                {
                fOk = FALSE;
                }
            pInterrupt->pOffset = SpyGateOffset (&pInterrupt->Gate);
            }
        else
            {
```

```
            RtlZeroMemory (pInterrupt, SPY_INTERRUPT_);
            }
        pInterrupt->fOk = fOk;
        }
    return fOk;
    }

// ----------------------------------------------------------------

PVOID SpyGateOffset (PX86_GATE pGate)
    {
    return (PVOID) (pGate->Offset1 | (pGate->Offset2 << 16));
    }
```

LISTING 4-18. *Querying Interrupt Properties*

TABLE 4-3. *CPU Status Fields in the Task State Segment (TSS)*

OFFSET	BITS	ID	DESCRIPTION
0x00	16		Previous Task Link
0x04	32	ESP0	Stack Pointer Register for Privilege Level 0
0x08	16	SS0	Stack Segment Register for Privilege Level 0
0x0C	32	ESP1	Stack Pointer Register for Privilege Level 1
0x10	16	SS1	Stack Segment Register for Privilege Level 1
0x14	32	ESP2	Stack Pointer Register for Privilege Level 2
0x18	16	SS2	Stack Segment Register for Privilege Level 2
0x1C	32	CR3	Page-Directory Base Register (PDBR)
0x20	32	EIP	Instruction Pointer Register
0x24	32	EFLAGS	Processor Flags Register
0x28	32	EAX	General-Purpose Register EAX
0x2C	32	ECX	General-Purpose Register ECX
0x30	32	EDX	General-Purpose Register EDX
0x34	32	EBX	General-Purpose Register EDX
0x38	32	ESP	Stack Pointer Register
0x3C	32	EBP	Base Pointer Register
0x40	32	ESI	Source Index Register
0x44	32	EDI	Destination Index Register
0x48	16	ES	Extra Segment Register
0x4C	16	CS	Code Segment Register
0x50	16	SS	Stack Segment Register

(continued)

TABLE 4-3. *(continued)*

OFFSET	BITS	ID	DESCRIPTION
0x54	16	DS	Data Segment Register
0x58	16	FS	Additional Data Segment Register #1
0x5C	16	GS	Additional Data Segment Register #2
0x60	16	LDT	Local Descriptor Table Segment Selector
0x64	1	T	Debug Trap Flag
0x66	16		I/O Map Base Address
0x68	—		End of CPU State Information

The `SpySegment()` and `SpySelector()` functions called by `SpyInterrupt()` have already been presented in Listings 4-15 and 4-16. `SpyGateOffset()`, included at the end of Listing 4-18, works analogous to `SpyDescriptorBase()` and `SpyDescriptorLimit()`, picking up the `Offset1` and `Offset2` bit-fields of an `X86_GATE` structure and arranging them properly to yield a 32-bit address. `SpyIdtGate()` is defined in Listing 4-19. It bears a strong similarity to `SpyDescriptor()` in Listing 4-17 if the LDT clause would be omitted. The assembly language instruction `SIDT` stores the 48-bit contents of the CPU's IDT register, comprising the 16-bit table limit and the 32-bit linear base address of the IDT. The remaining code in Listing 4-19 compares the descriptor index of the supplied selector to the IDT limit, and, if it is valid, the corresponding interrupt descriptor is copied to the caller's `X86_GATE` structure. Otherwise, all gate structure members are set to zero.

```
BOOL SpyIdtGate (PX86_SELECTOR pSelector,
                 PX86_GATE     pGate)
    {
    X86_TABLE idt;
    PX86_GATE pGates = NULL;
    BOOL      fOk    = FALSE;

    if (pGate != NULL)
        {
        if (pSelector != NULL)
            {
            __asm
                {
                sidt idt.wLimit
                }
            if ((pSelector->wValue & X86_SELECTOR_INDEX)
```

```
                <= idt.wLimit)
                {
                pGates = idt.pGates;
                }
            }
        if (pGates != NULL)
            {
            RtlCopyMemory (pGate,
                           pGates + pSelector->Index,
                           X86_GATE_);
            fOk = TRUE;
            }
        else
            {
            RtlZeroMemory (pGate, X86_GATE_);
            }
        }
    return fOk;
    }
```

LISTING 4-19. *Obtaining IDT Gate Values*

THE IOCTL FUNCTION SPY_IO_PHYSICAL

The IOCTL `SPY_IO_PHYSICAL` function is simple, because it relies entirely on the `MmGetPhysicalAddress()` function exported by `ntoskrnl.exe`. The IOCTL function handler simply calls `SpyInputPointer()` (see Listing 4-10) to get the linear address to be converted, lets `MmGetPhysicalAddress()` look up the corresponding physical address, and returns the resulting `PHYSICAL_ADDRESS` value to the caller. Note that `PHYSICAL_ADDRESS` is a 64-bit `LARGE_INTEGER`. On most i386 systems, the upper 32 bits will be always zero. However, on systems with Physical Address Extension (PAE) enabled and more than 4 GB of memory installed, these bits can assume nonzero values.

`MmGetPhysicalAddress()` uses the PTE array starting at linear address `0xC0000000` to find out the physical address. The basic mechanism works as follows:

- If the linear address is within the range `0x80000000` to `0x9FFFFFFF`, the three most significant bits are set to zero, yielding a physical address in the range `0x00000000` to `0x1FFFFFFF`.
- Otherwise, the upper 20 bits are used as an index into the PTE array at address `0xC0000000`.

- If the `P` bit of the target PTE is set, indicating that the corresponding page is present in physical memory, all PTE bits except for the 20-bit PFN are stripped, and the least significant 12 bits of the linear address are added, resulting in a proper 32-bit physical address.
- If the physical page is not present, `MmGetPhysicalAddress()` returns zero.

It is interesting to see that `MmGetPhysicalAddress()` assumes 4-KB pages for all linear addresses outside the kernel memory range `0x80000000` to `0x9FFFFFFF`. Other functions, such as `MmIsAddressValid()`, first load the PDE of the linear address and check its `PS` bit to find out whether the page size is 4 KB or 4 MB. This is a much more general approach that can cope with arbitrary memory configurations. Both functions return correct results, because Windows 2000 happens to use 4-MB pages in the `0x80000000` to `0x9FFFFFFF` memory area only. Some kernel API functions, however, are apparently designed to be more flexible than others.

The IOCTL Function SPY_IO_CPU_INFO

Several CPU instructions are available only to code running on privilege level zero, which is the most privileged of the four available levels. In Windows 2000 terminology, this means kernel-mode. Among the forbidden instructions are those that read the contents of the control registers `CR0`, `CR2`, and `CR3`. Because these registers contain interesting information, an application might wish to find a way to access them, and the `SPY_IO_CPU_INFO` function is the solution. As Listing 4-20 shows, the `SpyOutputCpuInfo()` function invoked by the IOCTL handler uses some ASM inline code to read the control registers, along with other valuable information, such as the contents of the IDT, GDT, and LDT registers and the segment selectors stored in the registers `CS`, `DS`, `ES`, `FS`, `GS`, `SS`, and `TR`. The Task Register `TR` contains a selector that refers to the TSS of the current task.

```
typedef struct _SPY_CPU_INFO
    {
    X86_REGISTER cr0;
    X86_REGISTER cr2;
    X86_REGISTER cr3;
    SPY_SEGMENT  cs;
    SPY_SEGMENT  ds;
    SPY_SEGMENT  es;
    SPY_SEGMENT  fs;
    SPY_SEGMENT  gs;
    SPY_SEGMENT  ss;
    SPY_SEGMENT  tss;
    X86_TABLE    idt;
    X86_TABLE    gdt;
```

```
    X86_SELECTOR ldt;
    }
    SPY_CPU_INFO, *PSPY_CPU_INFO, **PPSPY_CPU_INFO;

#define SPY_CPU_INFO_ sizeof (SPY_CPU_INFO)

// -----------------------------------------------------------------

NTSTATUS SpyOutputCpuInfo (PVOID  pOutput,
                           DWORD  dOutput,
                           PDWORD pdInfo)
    {
    SPY_CPU_INFO  sci;
    PSPY_CPU_INFO psci = &sci;

    __asm
        {
        push    eax
        push    ebx
        mov     ebx, psci

        mov     eax, cr0
        mov     [ebx.cr0], eax

        mov     eax, cr2
        mov     [ebx.cr2], eax

        mov     eax, cr3
        mov     [ebx.cr3], eax

        sidt    [ebx.idt.wLimit]
        mov     [ebx.idt.wReserved], 0
        sgdt    [ebx.gdt.wLimit]
        mov     [ebx.gdt.wReserved], 0
        sldt    [ebx.ldt.wValue]
        mov     [ebx.ldt.wReserved], 0

        pop     ebx
        pop     eax
        }
    SpySegment (X86_SEGMENT_CS,  0, &sci.cs);
    SpySegment (X86_SEGMENT_DS,  0, &sci.ds);
    SpySegment (X86_SEGMENT_ES,  0, &sci.es);
    SpySegment (X86_SEGMENT_FS,  0, &sci.fs);
    SpySegment (X86_SEGMENT_GS,  0, &sci.gs);
    SpySegment (X86_SEGMENT_SS,  0, &sci.ss);
    SpySegment (X86_SEGMENT_TSS, 0, &sci.tss);

    return SpyOutputBinary (&sci, SPY_CPU_INFO_,
                            pOutput, dOutput, pdInfo);
    }
```

LISTING 4-20. *Querying CPU State Information*

The segment selectors are obtained with the help of the `SpySegment()` function discussed earlier. See Listing 4-15 for details.

THE IOCTL FUNCTION SPY_IO_PDE_ARRAY

`SPY_IO_PDE_ARRAY` is another trivial function that simply copies the entire page-directory from address `0xC0300000` to the caller's output buffer. This buffer has to take the form of a `SPY_PDE_ARRAY` structure shown in Listing 4-21. As you might have guessed, this structure's size is exactly 4 KB, and it comprises 1,024 32-bit PDE values. The `X86_PE` structure used here, which represents a generalized page entry, can be found in Listing 4-3, and the constant `X86_PAGES_4M` is defined in Listing 4-5. Because the items in a `SPY_PDE_ARRAY` are always page-directory entries, the embedded `X86_PE` structures are either of type `X86_PDE_4M` or `X86_PDE_4K`, depending on the value of the page size bit `PS`.

It usually is not a good idea to copy memory contents without ensuring that the source page is currently present in physical memory. However, the page-directory is one of the few exceptions. The page-directory of the current task is always present in physical memory while the task is running (Intel 1999c, pp. 3-23). It cannot be swapped out to a pagefile unless another task is switched in. That's why the CPU's Page-Directory Base Register (PDBR) doesn't have a *P* (present) bit, like the PDEs and PTEs. Please refer to the definition of the `X86_PDBR` structure in Listing 4-3 to verify this.

```
typedef struct _SPY_PDE_ARRAY
    {
    X86_PE apde [X86_PAGES_4M];
    }
    SPY_PDE_ARRAY, *PSPY_PDE_ARRAY, **PPSPY_PDE_ARRAY;

#define SPY_PDE_ARRAY_ sizeof (SPY_PDE_ARRAY)
```

LISTING 4-21. *Definition of* `SPY_PDE_ARRAY`

THE IOCTL FUNCTION SPY_IO_PAGE_ENTRY

If you are interested in the page entry of a given linear address, this is the function of choice. Listing 4-22 shows the internals of the `SpyMemoryPageEntry()` function that handles this IOCTL request. The `SPY_PAGE_ENTRY` structure it returns is basically a `X86_PE` page entry, as defined in Listing 4-3, plus two convenient additions: The `dSize` member indicates the page size in bytes, which is either `X86_PAGE_4K`

(4,096 bytes) or X86_PAGE_4M (4,194,304 bytes), and the fPresent member indicates whether the page is present in physical memory. This flag must be contrasted to the return value of SpyMemoryPageEntry() itself, which can be TRUE even if fPresent is FALSE. In this case, the supplied linear address is valid, but points to a page currently swapped out to a pagefile. This situation is indicated by bit #10 of the page entry—referred to as PageFile in Listing 4-22—being set while the *P* bit is clear. Please refer to the introduction to the X86_PNPE structure earlier in this chapter for details. X86_PNPE represents a page-not-present entry and is defined in Listing 4-3.

SpyMemoryPageEntry() first assumes that the target page is a 4-MB page, and, therefore, copies the PDE of the specified linear address from the system's PDE array at address 0xC0300000 to the pe member of the SPY_PAGE_ENTRY structure. If the *P* bit is set, the subordinate page or page-table is present, so the next test checks the *PS* bit for the page size. If it is set, the PDE addresses a 4-MB page, and the work is done—SpyMemoryPageEntry() returns TRUE, and the fPresent member of the SPY_PAGE_ENTRY structure is set to TRUE as well. If the PS bit is zero, the PDE refers to a PTE, so the code extracts this PTE from the array at address 0xC0000000 and checks its *P* bit. If set, the 4-KB page comprising the linear address is present, and both SpyMemoryPageEntry() and fPresent report TRUE. Otherwise, the retrieved value must be a page-not-present entry, so fPresent is FALSE, and SpyMemoryPageEntry() returns TRUE only if the PageFile bit of the page entry is set.

```
typedef struct _SPY_PAGE_ENTRY
    {
    X86_PE pe;
    DWORD  dSize;
    BOOL   fPresent;
    }
    SPY_PAGE_ENTRY, *PSPY_PAGE_ENTRY, **PPSPY_PAGE_ENTRY;

#define SPY_PAGE_ENTRY_ sizeof (SPY_PAGE_ENTRY)

// -----------------------------------------------------------------

BOOL SpyMemoryPageEntry (PVOID           pVirtual,
                         PSPY_PAGE_ENTRY pspe)
    {
    SPY_PAGE_ENTRY spe;
    BOOL           fOk = FALSE;

    spe.pe       = X86_PDE_ARRAY [X86_PDI (pVirtual)];
    spe.dSize    = X86_PAGE_4M;
    spe.fPresent = FALSE;
```

(continued)

```
if (spe.pe.pde4M.P)
    {
    if (spe.pe.pde4M.PS)
        {
        fOk = spe.fPresent = TRUE;
        }
    else
        {
        spe.pe    = X86_PTE_ARRAY [X86_PAGE (pVirtual)];
        spe.dSize = X86_PAGE_4K;

        if (spe.pe.pte4K.P)
            {
            fOk = spe.fPresent = TRUE;
            }
        else
            {
            fOk = (spe.pe.pnpe.PageFile != 0);
            }
        }
    }
if (pspe != NULL) *pspe = spe;
return fOk;
}
```

LISTING 4-22. *Querying PDEs and PTEs*

Note that `SpyMemoryPageEntry()` does not identify swapped-out 4-MB pages. If a 4-MB PDE refers to an absent page, there is no indication whether the linear address is invalid or the page is currently kept in a pagefile. 4-MB pages are used in the kernel memory range `0x80000000` to `0x9FFFFFFF` only. I have never seen one of these pages swapped out, even in extreme low-memory situations, so I was not able to examine any associated page-not-present entries.

THE IOCTL FUNCTION SPY_IO_MEMORY_DATA

The `SPY_IO_MEMORY_DATA` function is certainly one of the most important ones, because it copies arbitrary amounts of memory data to a buffer supplied by the caller. As you might recall, user-mode applications are readily passed in invalid addresses. Therefore, this function is very cautious and verifies the validity of all source addresses before touching them. Remember, the Blue Screen is lurking everywhere in kernel-mode.

The calling application requests the contents of a memory block by passing in a `SPY_MEMORY_BLOCK` structure—shown at the top of Listing 4-23—that specifies its address and size. For convenience, the address is defined as a union, allowing interpretation as a byte array `(PBYTE pbAddress)` or an arbitrary pointer `(PVOID pAddress)`.

The `SpyInputMemory()` function in Listing 4-23 copies this structure from the IOCTL input buffer. The companion function `SpyOutputMemory()`, concluding Listing 4-23, is a wrapper around `SpyMemoryReadBlock()`, which is shown in Listing 4-24. The main duty of `SpyOutputMemory()` is to return the appropriate `NTSTATUS` values while `SpyMemoryReadBlock()` provides the data.

`SpyMemoryReadBlock()` returns the memory contents in a `SPY_MEMORY_DATA` structure, defined in Listing 4-25. I have chosen a different approach than in the previous definitions because `SPY_MEMORY_DATA` is a data type of variable size. Essentially, it consists of a `SPY_MEMORY_BLOCK` structure named `smb`, followed by an array of `WORD`s called `awData[]`. The length of the array is determined by the `dBytes` member of `smb`. To allow easy definition of `SPY_MEMORY_DATA` instances as global or local variables of a predetermined size, this structure's definition is based on the macro `SPY_MEMORY_DATA_N()`. The single argument of this macro specifies the size of the `awData[]` array. The actual structure definition follows the macro definition, providing `SPY_MEMORY_DATA` with a zero-length `awData[]` array. The `SPY_MEMORY_DATA__()` macro computes the overall size of a `SPY_MEMORY_DATA` structure given the size of its data array, and the remaining definitions allow packing and unpacking the data `WORD`s in the array. Obviously, the lower half of each `WORD` contains the memory data byte and the upper half specifies flags. Currently, only bit #8 has a meaning, indicating whether the data byte in bits #0 to #7 is valid.

```
typedef struct _SPY_MEMORY_BLOCK
    {
    union
        {
        PBYTE pbAddress;
        PVOID pAddress;
        };
    DWORD dBytes;
    }
    SPY_MEMORY_BLOCK, *PSPY_MEMORY_BLOCK, **PPSPY_MEMORY_BLOCK;

#define SPY_MEMORY_BLOCK_ sizeof (SPY_MEMORY_BLOCK)

// -----------------------------------------------------------------

NTSTATUS SpyInputMemory (PSPY_MEMORY_BLOCK psmb,
                         PVOID             pInput,
                         DWORD             dInput)
    {
    return SpyInputBinary (psmb, SPY_MEMORY_BLOCK_, pInput, dInput);
    }
```

(continued)

```
// ----------------------------------------------------------------

NTSTATUS SpyOutputMemory (PSPY_MEMORY_BLOCK psmb,
                          PVOID             pOutput,
                          DWORD             dOutput,
                          PDWORD            pdInfo)
    {
    NTSTATUS ns = STATUS_BUFFER_TOO_SMALL;

    if (*pdInfo = SpyMemoryReadBlock (psmb, pOutput, dOutput))
        {
        ns = STATUS_SUCCESS;
        }
    return ns;
    }
```

LISTING 4-23. *Handling Memory Blocks*

```
DWORD SpyMemoryReadBlock (PSPY_MEMORY_BLOCK psmb,
                          PSPY_MEMORY_DATA  psmd,
                          DWORD             dSize)
    {
    DWORD i;
    DWORD n = SPY_MEMORY_DATA__ (psmb->dBytes);

    if (dSize >= n)
        {
        psmd->smb = *psmb;

        for (i = 0; i < psmb->dBytes; i++)
            {
            psmd->awData [i] =
                (SpyMemoryTestAddress (psmb->pbAddress + i)
                 ? SPY_MEMORY_DATA_VALUE (psmb->pbAddress [i], TRUE)
                 : SPY_MEMORY_DATA_VALUE (0, FALSE));
            }
        }
    else
        {
        if (dSize >= SPY_MEMORY_DATA_)
            {
            psmd->smb.pbAddress = NULL;
            psmd->smb.dBytes    = 0;
            }
        n = 0;
        }
    return n;
    }
```

```
// -----------------------------------------------------------------

BOOL SpyMemoryTestAddress (PVOID pVirtual)
    {
    return SpyMemoryPageEntry (pVirtual, NULL);

// -----------------------------------------------------------------

BOOL SpyMemoryTestBlock (PVOID pVirtual,
                         DWORD dBytes)
    {
    PBYTE pbData;
    DWORD dData;
    BOOL  fOk = TRUE;

    if (dBytes)
        {
        pbData = (PBYTE) ((DWORD_PTR) pVirtual & X86_PAGE_MASK);
        dData  = (((dBytes + X86_OFFSET_4K (pVirtual) - 1)
                   / PAGE_SIZE) + 1) * PAGE_SIZE;
        do  {
            fOk = SpyMemoryTestAddress (pbData);
            pbData += PAGE_SIZE;
            dData  -= PAGE_SIZE;
            }
        while (fOk && dData);
        }
    return fOk;
    }
```

LISTING 4-24. *Copying Memory Block Contents*

The validity of a data byte is determined by the function `SpyMemoryTest Address()`, which is called by `SpyMemoryReadBlock()` for the address of each byte before it is copied to the buffer. `SpyMemoryTestAddress()`, included in the lower half of Listing 4-24, simply calls `SpyMemoryPageEntry()` with the second argument set to `NULL`. The latter function has just been introduced in the course of the discussion of the IOCTL function `SPY_IO_PAGE_ENTRY` (Listing 4-22). Setting its `PSPY_PAGE_ENTRY` pointer argument to `NULL` means that the caller is not interested in the page entry of the supplied linear address, so all that remains is the function's return value, which is `TRUE` if the linear address is valid. In the context of `SpyMemoryPageEntry()`, an address is valid if the page it is contained in is either present in physical memory or resident in one of the system's pagefiles. Note that this behavior is not compatible with the `ntoskrnl.exe` API function `MmIsAddressValid()`, which will always return `FALSE` if the page is not present, even if it is a valid page currently kept in a pagefile. Also included in Listing 4-24 is the function

```
#define SPY_MEMORY_DATA_N(_n) \
        struct _SPY_MEMORY_DATA_##_n \
            { \
            SPY_MEMORY_BLOCK smb; \
            WORD             awData [_n]; \
            }

typedef SPY_MEMORY_DATA_N (0)
        SPY_MEMORY_DATA, *PSPY_MEMORY_DATA, **PPSPY_MEMORY_DATA;

#define SPY_MEMORY_DATA_ sizeof (SPY_MEMORY_DATA)
#define SPY_MEMORY_DATA__(_n) (SPY_MEMORY_DATA_ + ((_n) * WORD_))

#define SPY_MEMORY_DATA_BYTE  0x00FF
#define SPY_MEMORY_DATA_VALID 0x0100

#define SPY_MEMORY_DATA_VALUE(_b,_v) \
        ((WORD) (((_b) & SPY_MEMORY_DATA_BYTE      ) | \
                 ((_v) ? SPY_MEMORY_DATA_VALID : 0)))
```

LISTING 4-25. *Definition of* `SPY_MEMORY_DATA`

`SpyMemoryTestBlock()`, which is an enhanced version of `SpyMemoryTestAddress()`. It tests a memory range for validity by walking across the specified block in 4,096-byte steps, testing whether all pages it spans are accessible.

Accepting swapped-out pages as valid address ranges has the important advantage that the page will be pulled back into physical memory as soon as `SpyMemoryReadBlock()` tries to access one of its bytes. The sample memory dump utility presented later would not be quite useful if it relied on `MmIsAddressValid()`. It would sometimes refuse to display the contents of certain address ranges, even if it was able to display them 5 minutes before, because the underlying page recently would have been transferred to a pagefile.

THE IOCTL FUNCTION SPY_IO_MEMORY_BLOCK

The `SPY_IO_MEMORY_BLOCK` function is related to `SPY_IO_MEMORY_DATA` in that it also copies data blocks from arbitrary addresses to a caller-supplied buffer. The main difference is that `SPY_IO_MEMORY_DATA` attempts to copy all bytes that are accessible, whereas `SPY_IO_MEMORY_BLOCK` fails if the requested range comprises any invalid addresses. This function will be needed in Chapter 6 to deliver the contents of data structures living in kernel memory to a user-mode application. It is obvious that this function must be very restrictive. A structure that contains inaccessible bytes cannot be copied safely—the copy would be lacking parts of the data.

Like SPY_IO_MEMORY_DATA, the SPY_IO_MEMORY_BLOCK function expects input in the form of a SPY_MEMORY_BLOCK structure that specifies the base address and size of the memory range to be copied. The returned copy is a faithful 1:1 reproduction of the original data. The output buffer must be large enough to hold the entire copy. Otherwise, an error is reported, and no data is sent back.

THE IOCTL FUNCTION SPY_IO_HANDLE_INFO

Like the SPY_IO_PHYSICAL function introduced above, this function allows a user-mode application to call kernel-mode API functions that are otherwise unreachable. A kernel-mode driver can always get a pointer to an object represented by a handle by simply calling the ntoskrnl.exe function ObReferenceObjectByHandle(). There is no equivalent function in the Win32 API. However, the application can instruct the spy device to execute the function call on its behalf and to return the object pointer afterward. Listing 4-26 shows the SpyOutputHandleInfo() function called by the SpyDispatcher() after obtaining the input handle via SpyInputHandle(), defined in Listing 4-10.

The SPY_HANDLE_INFO structure at the beginning of Listing 4-26 receives the pointer to the body of the object associated with the handle and the handle attributes, both returned by ObReferenceObjectByHandle(). It is important to call ObDereferenceObject() if ObReferenceObjectByHandle() reports success to reset the object's pointer reference count to its previous value. Failing to do so constitutes an "object reference leak."

```
typedef struct _SPY_HANDLE_INFO
    {
    PVOID pObjectBody;
    DWORD dHandleAttributes;
    }
    SPY_HANDLE_INFO, *PSPY_HANDLE_INFO, **PPSPY_HANDLE_INFO;

#define SPY_HANDLE_INFO_ sizeof (SPY_HANDLE_INFO)

// -----------------------------------------------------------------

NTSTATUS SpyOutputHandleInfo (HANDLE hObject,
                              PVOID  pOutput,
                              DWORD  dOutput,
                              PDWORD pdInfo)
    {
    SPY_HANDLE_INFO           shi;
    OBJECT_HANDLE_INFORMATION ohi;
    NTSTATUS                  ns = STATUS_INVALID_PARAMETER;
```

(continued)

```
    if (hObject != NULL)
        {
        ns = ObReferenceObjectByHandle (hObject,
                                        STANDARD_RIGHTS_READ,
                                        NULL, KernelMode,
                                        &shi.pObjectBody, &ohi);
        }
    if (ns == STATUS_SUCCESS)
        {
        shi.dHandleAttributes = ohi.HandleAttributes;

        ns = SpyOutputBinary (&shi, SPY_HANDLE_INFO_,
                              pOutput, dOutput, pdInfo);

        ObDereferenceObject (shi.pObjectBody);
        }
    return ns;
    }
```

LISTING 4-26. *Referencing an Object by Its Handle*

A SAMPLE MEMORY DUMP UTILITY

Now that you have worked through the complex and possibly confusing IOCTL function handler code of the memory spy device driver, you probably want to see these functions in action. Therefore, I have created a sample console-mode utility named "SBS Windows 2000 Memory Spy" that loads the spy driver and calls various IOCTL functions, depending on the parameters passed in on the command line. This application resides in the executable file `w2k_mem.exe`, and its source code is included on the CD accompanying this book, in the directory `\src\w2k_mem`.

COMMAND LINE FORMAT

You can run the memory spy utility from the CD by invoking `d:\bin\w2k_mem.exe`, where `d:` should be replaced by the drive letter of your CD-ROM drive. If `w2k_mem.exe` is started without arguments, the lengthy command info screen shown in Example 4-1 is displayed. The basic command philosophy of `w2k_mem` is that a command consists of one or more data requests, each providing at least a linear base address where the memory dump should start. Optionally, the memory block size can be specified as well—otherwise, the default size 256 is used. The memory size must be prefixed by the "#" character. Several option switches may be added that modify the default behavior of the command. An option consists of a single-character option ID and a "+" or "–" prefix that determines whether the option is switched on or off. By default, all options are turned off.

```
// w2k_mem.exe
// SBS Windows 2000 Memory Spy V1.00
// 08-27-2000 Sven B. Schreiber
// sbs@orgon.com

Usage: w2k_mem { { [+option|-option] [/<path>] } [#[[0]x]<size>] [[0]x]<base> }

<path> specifies a module to be loaded into memory.
Use the +x/-x switch to enable/disable its startup code.
If <size> is missing, the default size is 256 bytes.

Display address options (mutually exclusive):
   +z -z   zero-based display         on / OFF
   +r -r   physical RAM addresses     on / OFF

Display mode options (mutually exclusive):

   +w -w   WORD  data formatting      on / OFF
   +d -d   DWORD data formatting      on / OFF
   +q -q   QWORD data formatting      on / OFF

Addressing options (mutually exclusive):

   +t -t   TEB-relative addressing    on / OFF
   +f -f   FS-relative  addressing    on / OFF
   +u -u   user-mode   FS:[<base>]    on / OFF
   +k -k   kernel-mode FS:[<base>]    on / OFF
   +h -h   handle/object resolution   on / OFF
   +a -a   add bias  to  last base    on / OFF
   +s -s   sub bias from last base    on / OFF
   +p -p   pointer  from last block   on / OFF

System status options (cumulative):

   +o -o   display OS  information    on / OFF
   +c -c   display CPU information    on / OFF
   +g -g   display GDT information    on / OFF
   +i -i   display IDT information    on / OFF
   +b -b   display contiguous blocks  on / OFF

Other options (cumulative):

   +x -x   execute DLL startup code   on / OFF

Example: The following command displays the first 64
bytes of the current Process Environment Block (PEB)
in zero-based DWORD format, assuming that a pointer to
the PEB is located at offset 0x30 inside the current
Thread Environment Block (TEB):

   w2k_mem +t #0 0 +pzd #64 0x30

Note: Specifying #0 after +t causes the TEB to be
addressed without displaying its contents.
```

EXAMPLE 4-1. *Help Screen of the Memory Spy Utility*

A data request is executed for each command line token that cannot be identified as an option, a data block size specification, a path, or any other command modifier. Each plain number on the command line is assumed to specify a linear address and triggers a hex dump, starting at this address. Numbers are interpreted as decimal by default or hexadecimal if prefixed by "0x" or simply "x."

Complex command line option models like the one employed by `w2k_mem.exe` are much easier to grasp if some simple examples are provided. Here is a short compilation:

- **`w2k_mem 0x80400000`** displays the first 256 bytes of memory at linear address `0x80400000`, yielding something that should look similar to Example 4-2. By the way, this is the DOS header of the `ntoskrnl.exe` module (note the "MZ" ID at the beginning).
- **`w2k_mem #0x40 0x80400000`** displays the same data block, but stops after 64 bytes, as demanded by the block size specification `#0x40`.
- **`w2k_mem +d #0x40 0x80400000`** is another variant, this time packing the bytes into 32-bit `DWORD` chunks because of the `+d` option. This option remains in effect until reset by `–d` or overridden by a competing option such as `+w` or `+q`.
- **`w2k_mem +wz #0x40 0x10000 +d –z 0x20000`** contains two data requests. First, the linear address range `0x10000` to `0x1003F` is shown in 16-bit `WORD` format, followed by the range `0x20000` to `0x2003F` in `DWORD` format (Example 4-3). The first request also includes the `+z` switch, which forces the numbers in the "Address" column to start at zero. In the second request, the zero-based display mode is turned off by adding a `-z` switch.
- **`w2k_mem +rd #4096 0xC0300000`** displays the system's page-directory at address `0xC0300000` in `DWORD` format. The `+r` option enables the display of physical RAM addresses in the "Address" column instead of linear ones.

By now, you should have a basic understanding of how the command line format works. In the following subsections, some of the more exotic options and features are discussed in more detail. Most of them alter the interpretation of the address parameter they precede. In default mode, the specified address is a linear base address where the memory dump starts. The options `+t`, `+f`, `+u`, `+k`, `+h`, `+a`, `+s`, and `+p` change this default interpretation in various ways.

```
E:\>w2k_mem 0x80400000

// w2k_mem.exe
// SBS Windows 2000 Memory Spy V1.00
// 08-27-2000 Sven B. Schreiber
// sbs@orgon.com

Loading "SBS Windows 2000 Spy Device" (w2k_spy) ...
Driver: "D:\Program Files\DevStudio\MyProjects\w2k_mem\Release\w2k_spy.sys"
Opening "\\.\w2k_spy" ...

SBS Windows 2000 Spy Device V1.00 ready

80400000..804000FF: 256 valid bytes

Address  | 00 01 02 03-04 05 06 07 : 08 09 0A 0B-0C 0D 0E 0F | 0123456789ABCDEF
---------|-------------------------:-------------------------|-----------------
80400000 | 4D 5A 90 00-03 00 00 00 : 04 00 00 00-FF FF 00 00 | MZ•.........ÿÿ..
80400010 | B8 00 00 00-00 00 00 00 : 40 00 00 00-00 00 00 00 | ¸.......@.......
80400020 | 00 00 00 00-00 00 00 00 : 00 00 00 00-00 00 00 00 | ................
80400030 | 00 00 00 00-00 00 00 00 : 00 00 00 00-C8 00 00 00 | ............È...
80400040 | 0E 1F BA 0E-00 B4 09 CD : 21 B8 01 4C-CD 21 54 68 | ..º..´.Í!¸.LÍ!Th
80400050 | 69 73 20 70-72 6F 67 72 : 61 6D 20 63-61 6E 6E 6F | is program canno
80400060 | 74 20 62 65-20 72 75 6E : 20 69 6E 20-44 4F 53 20 | t be run in DOS 
80400070 | 6D 6F 64 65-2E 0D 0D 0A : 24 00 00 00-00 00 00 00 | mode....$.......
80400080 | 50 7A C4 CE-14 1B AA 9D : 14 1B AA 9D-14 1B AA 9D | PzÄÎ..ª•..ª•..ª•
80400090 | 14 1B AB 9D-53 1B AA 9D : 18 3B A4 9D-5B 1B AA 9D | ..«•S.ª•.;¤•[.ª•
804000A0 | 42 13 AC 9D-15 1B AA 9D : 14 1B AA 9D-1A 19 AA 9D | B.¬•..ª•..ª•..ª•
804000B0 | 4D 38 B9 9D-12 1B AA 9D : 52 69 63 68-14 1B AA 9D | M8¹•..ª•Rich..ª•
804000C0 | 00 00 00 00-00 00 00 00 : 50 45 00 00-4C 01 13 00 | ........PE..L...
804000D0 | 17 9B 4D 38-00 00 00 00 : 00 00 00 00-E0 00 0E 03 | .?M8........à...
804000E0 | 0B 01 05 0C-C0 2D 14 00 : 80 D6 04 00-00 00 00 00 | ....À-..?Ö......
804000F0 | 20 D1 00 00-C0 04 00 00 : 80 73 06 00-00 00 40 00 |  Ñ..À...?s....@.

       256 bytes requested
       256 bytes received

Closing the spy device ...
```

EXAMPLE 4-2. *A Sample Data Request*

```
E:\>w2k_mem +wz #0x40 0x10000 +d -z 0x20000

// w2k_mem.exe
// SBS Windows 2000 Memory Spy V1.00
// 08-27-2000 Sven B. Schreiber
// sbs@orgon.com

Loading "SBS Windows 2000 Spy Device" (w2k_spy) ...
```

(continued)

```
Driver: "D:\Program Files\DevStudio\MyProjects\w2k_mem\Release\ w2k_spy.sys"
Opening "\\.\w2k_spy" ...
SBS Windows 2000 Spy Device V1.00 ready

00010000..0001003F: 64 valid bytes

Address  | 0000 0002-0004 0006 : 0008 000A-000C 000E | 00 02 04 06 08 0A 0C 0E
---------|---------------------:---------------------|------------------------
00000000 | 003D 0044-003A 003D : 0044 003A-005C 0050 | .= .D .: .= .D .: .\ .P
00000010 | 0072 006F-0067 0072 : 0061 006D-0020 0046 | .r .o .g .r .a .m .  .F
00000020 | 0069 006C-0065 0073 : 005C 0044-0065 0076 | .i .l .e .s .\ .D .e .v
00000030 | 0053 0074-0075 0064 : 0069 006F-005C 004D | .S .t .u .d .i .o .\ .M

00020000..0002003F: 64 valid bytes

Address  | 00000000 - 00000004 : 00000008 - 0000000C | 0000 0004 0008 000C
---------|---------------------:---------------------|--------------------
00020000 | 00001000 - 00000880 : 00000001 - 00000000 | .... ...? .... ....
00020010 | 02B20001 - 00000000 : 00000003 - 00000007 | .².. .... .... ....
00020020 | 0000000B - 0208006C : 00020290 - 00000018 | .... ...l ...• ....
00020030 | 02A0029E - 00020498 : 00840082 - 00020738 | . .? ...? .?.? ...8

       128 bytes requested
       128 bytes received

Closing the spy device ...
```

EXAMPLE 4-3. *Displaying Data in Special Formats*

TEB-RELATIVE ADDRESSING

Each thread in a process has its own Thread Environment Block (`TEB`) where the system keeps frequently used thread-specific data. In user-mode, the `TEB` of the current thread is located in a separate 4-KB segment accessible via the processor's `FS` register. In kernel-mode, `FS` points to a different segment, as will be explained below. All `TEB`s of a process are stacked up in linear memory at linear address `0x7FFDE000`, expanding down in 4-KB steps as needed. That is, the `TEB` of the second thread is found at address `0x7FFDD000`, the `TEB` of the third thread at `0x7FFDC000`, and so on. The contents of the `TEB`s and the Process Environment Block (`PEB`) address `0x7FFDF000` will be discussed in more detail in Chapter 7 (see Listings 7-18 and 7-19). Here it should suffice to take note that `TEB`s exist and that they are addressed by the `FS` register.

If the `+t` switch precedes an address on the command line, `w2k_mem.exe` adds the base address of the `FS` segment to it, effectively applying a bias of `0x7FFDE000` bytes. Example 4-4 shows the output of the command **`w2k_mem +dt #0x38 0`** on my system. This time I have omitted the banner and status messages issued by `w2k_mem.exe`. The omissions are marked by [...].

```
E:\>w2k_mem +dt #0x38 0
[...]
7FFDE000..7FFDE037: 56 valid bytes

Address   | 00000000 - 00000004 : 00000008 - 0000000C | 0000 0004 0008 000C
---------|---------------------:---------------------|--------------------
7FFDE000 | 0012FA58 - 00130000 : 0012E000 - 00000000 | ..úX .... ..à. ....
7FFDE010 | 00001E00 - 00000000 : 7FFDE000 - 00000000 | .... .... .ýà. ....
7FFDE020 | 000002C0 - 000002C8 : 00000000 - 00000000 | ...À ...È .... ....
7FFDE030 | 7FFDF000 - 00000000 :          -          | .ýô. ....
[...]
```

EXAMPLE 4-4. *Displaying the first Thread Environment Block* (TEB)

FS-RELATIVE ADDRESSING

I have already mentioned that the `FS` refers to different segments in user- and kernel-mode. Whereas the `+t` switch selects the user-mode `FS` address as the reference point, the `+f` switch uses the `FS` base address that is in effect in kernel-mode. Of course, a Win32 application has no way to get at this value, so once again the spy device is required. `w2k_mem.exe` calls the IOCTL function `SPY_IO_CPU_INFO`, introduced in the previous section, to read CPU status information that includes the kernel-mode values of all segment registers. From there, everything goes on just the same as with the `+t` switch.

The kernel-mode `FS` points to another thread-specific structure frequently accessed by the Windows 2000 kernel, named the Kernel's Processor Control Region (`KPCR`). This structure has already been mentioned in the course of the discussion of the IOCTL function `SPY_IO_OS_INFO` and will be revisited in Chapter 7 (see Listing 7-16). Again, suffice it to note for now that this structure exists at linear address `0xFFDFF000`, and that the `+f` switch gives easy access to it. In Example 4-5, I have issued the command **`w2k_mem +df #0x54 0`** to demonstrate that the `+f` switch in fact applies a bias of `0xFFDFF000` bytes to the specified memory address.

```
E:\>w2k_mem +df #0x54 0
[...]
FFDFF000..FFDFF053: 84 valid bytes

Address   | 00000000 - 00000004 : 00000008 - 0000000C | 0000 0004 0008 000C
---------|---------------------:---------------------|--------------------
FFDFF000 | BECD9CF0 - BECD9DF0 : BECD6000 - 00000000 | ¾í?ô ¾í•õ ¾í`. ....
FFDFF010 | 00000000 - 00000000 : 7FFDE000 - FFDFF000 | .... .... .ýà. ÿßõ.
FFDFF020 | FFDFF120 - 00000000 : 00000000 - 00000000 | ÿßñ  .... .... ....
FFDFF030 | FFFF20C0 - 00000000 : 80036400 - 80036000 | ÿÿ À .... ?.d. ?.`.
FFDFF040 | 80244000 - 00010001 : 00000001 - 000000C9 | ?$@. .... .... ...É
FFDFF050 | 00000000 -          :          -          | ....
[...]
```

EXAMPLE 4-5. *Displaying the Kernel's Processor Control Region* (KPCR)

FS:[<bASE>] ADDRESSING

When examining Windows 2000 kernel code, you will frequently come across instructions such as `MOV EAX,` and `FS:[18h]`. These instructions retrieve member values of the `TEB`, `KPCR`, or other structures contained in the `FS` segment. Many of them are pointers to other internal structures. The command line switches `+u` and `+k` allow you to follow this indirection with ease. `+u` retrieves a pointer from the user-mode `FS` segment; `+k` does the same in kernel-mode. For example, the command **`w2k_mem +du #0x1E8 0x30`** (see Example 4-6) dumps 488 bytes of the memory block addressed by `FS:[30h]` in user-mode, which happens to be a pointer to the Process Environment Block `(PEB)` of `w2k_mem.exe`. The command **`w2k_mem +dk #0x1C 0x20`** (see Example 4-7) displays the first 28 bytes of memory pointed to by `FS:[20h]` in kernel-mode, which is a pointer to the Kernel's Processor Control Block `(KPRCB)`, briefly mentioned earlier in the discussion of the IOCTL function `SPY_IO_OS_INFO` and also discussed in Chapter 7 (see Listing 7-15). Don't worry if you don't know what a `PEB` or `KPRCB` is—you *will* know it after having read this book.

```
E:\>w2k_mem +du #0x1E8 0x30
[...]
7FFDF000..7FFDF1E7: 488 valid bytes

Address  | 00000000 - 00000004 : 00000008 - 0000000C | 0000 0004 0008 000C
---------|---------------------:---------------------|--------------------
7FFDF000 | 00000000 - FFFFFFFF : 00400000 - 00131E90 | .... ÿÿÿÿ .@.. ...•
7FFDF010 | 00020000 - 00000000 : 00130000 - 77FCD170 | .... .... .... wüÑp
7FFDF020 | 77F8AA4C - 77F8AA7D : 00000001 - 77E33E58 | wøªL wøª} .... wã>X
7FFDF030 | 00000000 - 00000000 : 00000000 - 00000000 | .... .... .... ....
7FFDF040 | 77FCD1A8 - 0000007F : 00000000 - 7F6F0000 | wüÑ¨ .... .... .o..
7FFDF050 | 7F6F0000 - 7F6F0688 : 7FFB0000 - 7FFC1000 | .o.. .o.? .û.. .ü..
7FFDF060 | 7FFD2000 - 00000001 : 00000000 - 00000000 | .ý . .... .... ....
7FFDF070 | 079B8000 - FFFFE86D : 00100000 - 00002000 | .??. ÿÿèm .... .. .
7FFDF080 | 00010000 - 00001000 : 00000003 - 00000010 | .... .... .... ....
7FFDF090 | 77FCE380 - 00410000 : 00000000 - 00000014 | wüã? .A.. .... ....
7FFDF0A0 | 77FCD348 - 00000005 : 00000000 - 00000893 | wüÓH .... .... ...?
7FFDF0B0 | 00000002 - 00000003 : 00000004 - 00000000 | .... .... .... ....
7FFDF0C0 | 00000000 - 00000000 : 00000000 - 00000000 | .... .... .... ....
7FFDF0D0 | 00000000 - 00000000 : 00000000 - 00000000 | .... .... .... ....
7FFDF0E0 | 00000000 - 00000000 : 00000000 - 00000000 | .... .... .... ....
7FFDF0F0 | 00000000 - 00000000 : 00000000 - 00000000 | .... .... .... ....
7FFDF100 | 00000000 - 00000000 : 00000000 - 00000000 | .... .... .... ....
7FFDF110 | 00000000 - 00000000 : 00000000 - 00000000 | .... .... .... ....
7FFDF120 | 00000000 - 00000000 : 00000000 - 00000000 | .... .... .... ....
7FFDF130 | 00000000 - 00000000 : 00000000 - 00000000 | .... .... .... ....
7FFDF140 | 00000000 - 00000000 : 00000000 - 00000000 | .... .... .... ....
7FFDF150 | 77FCDCC0 - 00000000 : 00000000 - 00000000 | wüÜÀ .... .... ....
7FFDF160 | 00000000 - 00000000 : 00000000 - 00000000 | .... .... .... ....
```

```
7FFDF170 | 00000000 - 00000000 : 00000000 - 00000000 | .... .... .... ....
7FFDF180 | 00000000 - 00000000 : 00000000 - 00000000 | .... .... .... ....
7FFDF190 | 00000000 - 00000000 : 00000000 - 00000000 | .... .... .... ....
7FFDF1A0 | 00000000 - 00000000 : 00000000 - 00000000 | .... .... .... ....
7FFDF1B0 | 00000000 - 00000000 : 00000000 - 00000000 | .... .... .... ....
7FFDF1C0 | 00000000 - 00000000 : 00000000 - 00000000 | .... .... .... ....
7FFDF1D0 | 00000000 - 00000000 : 00000000 - 00020000 | .... .... .... ....
7FFDF1E0 | 7F6F06C2 - 00000000 :          -          | .o.Â ....
[...]
```

EXAMPLE 4-6. *Displaying the Process Environment Block* (PEB)

```
E:\>w2k_mem +dk #0x1C 0x20
[...]
FFDFF120..FFDFF13B: 28 valid bytes

Address   | 00000000 - 00000004 : 00000008 - 0000000C | 0000 0004 0008 000C
---------|---------------------:---------------------|-------------------
FFDFF120 | 00010001 - 86BBA820 : 00000000 - 8046BDF0 | .... ?»¨  .... ?F½ó
FFDFF130 | 00020000 - 00000001 : 05010106 -          | .... .... ....
[...]
```

EXAMPLE 4-7. *Displaying the Kernel's Processor Control Block* (KPRCB)

HANDLE/OBJECT RESOLUTION

Suppose you have an object `HANDLE` and want to see what the corresponding object looks like in memory. This is an almost trivial task if you use the `+h` switch, which simply calls the spy device's `SPY_IO_HANDLE_INFO` function (Listing 4-26) to look up the object body of the given handle. The world of Windows 2000 objects is an amazing topic that will be treated in depth in Chapter 7. So let's forget about it for now.

RELATIVE ADDRESSING

Sometimes it might be useful to display a series of memory blocks that are spaced out by the same number of bytes. This might be, for example, an array of structures, like the stack of `TEB`s in a multithreaded application. The `+a` and `+s` switches enable this kind of relative addressing by changing the interpretation of the specified address to an offset. The difference between these options is that `+a` ("add bias") yields a positive offset, whereas `+s` ("subtract bias") yields a negative one. Example 4-8 shows the output of the command **`w2k_mem +d #32 0xC0000000 +a 4096 4096`** on my system. It samples the first 32 bytes of three consecutive 4-KB pages, starting at address `0xC0000000`, where the system's page-tables are located. Note the `+a` switch near the end of the command. It causes the following "4096" tokens to be interpreted as offsets

```
E:\>w2k_mem +d #32 0xC0000000 +a 4096 4096
[...]
C0000000..C000001F: 32 valid bytes

Address  | 00000000 - 00000004 : 00000008 - 0000000C | 0000 0004 0008 000C
---------|--------------------:--------------------|--------------------
C0000000 | 00000000 - 00000000 : 00000000 - 00000000 | .... .... .... ....
C0000010 | 00000000 - 00000000 : 00000000 - 00000000 | .... .... .... ....

C0001000..C000101F: 32 valid bytes

Address  | 00000000 - 00000004 : 00000008 - 0000000C | 0000 0004 0008 000C
---------|--------------------:--------------------|--------------------
C0001000 | 037D1025 - 03324025 : 0329D025 - 04DDE025 | .}.% .2@% .)Ð% .Ýà%
C0001010 | 06F17067 - 03297225 : 05115067 - 00000000 | .ñpg .)r% ..Pg ....

C0002000..C000201F: 0 valid bytes

Address  | 00000000 - 00000004 : 00000008 - 0000000C | 0000 0004 0008 000C
---------|--------------------:--------------------|--------------------
C0002000 |          -          :          -          |
C0002010 |          -          :          -          |

        96 bytes requested
        64 bytes received
[...]
```

EXAMPLE 4-8. *Sampling Page-Tables*

to be added to the previous base address. The `+a` and `+s` switches remain in effect until switched off explicitly by specifying `–a` or `-s` or overridden by any of the other switches that change the interpretation of the address parameter.

Example 4-8 also shows what happens if an invalid linear address is passed in. Obviously, the first pair of page-tables referring to the 4-MB address ranges `0x00000000` to `0x003F0000` and `0x00400000` to `0x007F0000` were valid, and the third one was not. `w2k_mem.exe` reflects this fact by displaying an empty hex dump table. The program knows which address ranges are valid because the spy device's `SPY_IO_MEMORY_DATA` function puts this information into the resulting `SPY_MEMORY_DATA` structure (cf. Listing 4-25).

INDIRECT ADDRESSING

One of my favorite command options is `+p`, because it saved a lot of typing while I was preparing this book. This option works similar to `+u` and `+k`, but doesn't use the `FS` segment as reference, but rather uses the previously displayed data block. This is a great feature if you want to chase down a linked list of objects, for example. Instead of displaying the first list member, reading out the address of the next member, typing a new command with this address, and so on, simply append `+p` to the command and a series of offsets that specify where the link to the next object is located in the previous hex dump panel.

In Example 4-9, I have used this option to walk down the list of active processes. First, I have asked the Kernel Debugger to give me the address of the internal variable `PsActiveProcessHead`, which is a `LIST_ENTRY` structure marking the beginning of the process list. A `LIST_ENTRY` consists of a `Flink` (forward link) member at offset 0 and a `Blink` (backward link) member at offset 4 (cf. Listing 2-7). The command **`w2k_mem #8 +d 0x8046a180 +p 0 0 0 0`** first dumps the `LIST_ENTRY` of `PsActiveProcessHead`, and then it switches to indirect addressing on behalf of the `+p` switch. The four zeros tell `w2k_mem.exe` to extract the value at offset zero of the previous data block, which is, of course, the `Flink` member of each `LIST_ENTRY`. Note that the `Blink` members in Example 4-9, located at offset 4, do in fact point back to the previous `LIST_ENTRY`, as expected.

If enough zero-valued parameters would be appended to the command, the hex dump would eventually return to `PsActiveProcessHead`, which marks the beginning *and* the end of the process list. As explained in Chapter 2, the doubly-linked lists maintained by Windows 2000 are usually circular; that is, the `Flink` of the last list member points to the first one, and the `Blink` of the first list member points to the last one.

```
E:\>w2k_mem #8 +d 0x8046a180 +p 0 0 0 0
[...]
8046A180..8046A187: 8 valid bytes

Address   | 00000000 - 00000004 : 00000008 - 0000000C | 0000 0004 0008 000C
---------|---------------------:---------------------|--------------------
8046A180 | 8149D900 - 840D2BE0 :          -          | •IÙ.  ?.+à

8149D900..8149D907: 8 valid bytes

Address   | 00000000 - 00000004 : 00000008 - 0000000C | 0000 0004 0008 000C
---------|---------------------:---------------------|--------------------
8149D900 | 8131A4A0 - 8046A180 :          -          |  •1¤  ?F¡?

8131A4A0..8131A4A7: 8 valid bytes

Address   | 00000000 - 00000004 : 00000008 - 0000000C | 0000 0004 0008 000C
---------|---------------------:---------------------|--------------------
8131A4A0 | 812FFDE0 - 8149D900 :          -          | •/ýà •IÙ.

812FFDE0..812FFDE7: 8 valid bytes
```

(continued)

```
Address   | 00000000 - 00000004 : 00000008 - 0000000C | 0000 0004 0008 000C
---------|---------------------:---------------------|--------------------
812FFDE0 | 812FA460 - 8131A4A0 :          -           | •/¤` •1¤

812FA460..812FA467: 8 valid bytes

Address   | 00000000 - 00000004 : 00000008 - 0000000C | 0000 0004 0008 000C
---------|---------------------:---------------------|--------------------
812FA460 | 812E30C0 - 812FFDE0 :          -           | •.0À •/ýà
[...]
```

EXAMPLE 4-9. *Walking Down the Active-Process List*

LOADING MODULES ON THE FLY

Sometimes you might want to dump the memory image of a module, but the module is not mapped into the linear address space of the `w2k_mem.exe` process. This problem can be solved by loading the module explicitly using the `/<path>` and `+x` command options. Every command token prefixed by a slash character is interpreted as a module path, and `w2k_mem.exe` attempts to load this module from this path using the Win32 API function `LoadLibraryEx()`. By default, the load option `DONT_RESOLVE_DLL_REFERENCES` is used, causing the module to be loaded without initializing it. For a DLL, this means that its `DllMain()` entry point is not called. Also, none of the dependent modules specified in the import section is loaded. However, if you specify the `+x` switch before the path, the module is loaded and fully initialized. Note that some modules might refuse initialization in the context of the `w2k_mem.exe` process. For example, kernel-mode device drivers should not be loaded with this option turned on.

Loading and displaying a module is typically a two-step operation, as shown in Example 4-10. First you should load the module without displaying any data, to find out the base address assigned to it by the system. Fortunately, load addresses are deterministic as long as no other modules are added to the process in the meantime, so the next attempt to load the module will yield the same base address. In Example 4-10, I have loaded the kernel-mode device driver `nwrdr.sys`, which is the Microsoft's NetWare redirector. I'm not using IPX/SPX on my machine, so this driver is not yet loaded. Obviously, `LoadLibraryEx()` succeeds, and the hex dumps of the reported load address `0x007A0000` preceding and following this API call prove that this memory region is initially unused but contains a DOS header afterward.

```
E:\>w2k_mem /e:\winnt\system32\drivers\nwrdr.sys
[...]
You didn't request any data!
```

```
LoadLibrary (e:\winnt\system32\drivers\nwrdr.sys) = 0x007A0000
[...]
E:\>w2k_mem 0x007A0000 /e:\winnt\system32\drivers\nwrdr.sys 0x007A0000
[...]
007A0000..007A00FF: 0 valid bytes

Address  | 00 01 02 03-04 05 06 07 : 08 09 0A 0B-0C 0D 0E 0F | 0123456789ABCDEF
---------|-------------------------:-------------------------|-----------------
007A0000 |            -            :            -            |
007A0010 |            -            :            -            |
007A0020 |            -            :            -            |
007A0030 |            -            :            -            |
007A0040 |            -            :            -            |
007A0050 |            -            :            -            |
007A0060 |            -            :            -            |
007A0070 |            -            :            -            |
007A0080 |            -            :            -            |
007A0090 |            -            :            -            |
007A00A0 |            -            :            -            |
007A00B0 |            -            :            -            |
007A00C0 |            -            :            -            |
007A00D0 |            -            :            -            |
007A00E0 |            -            :            -            |
007A00F0 |            -            :            -            |

LoadLibrary (e:\winnt\system32\drivers\nwrdr.sys) = 0x007A0000

007A0000..007A00FF: 256 valid bytes

Address  | 00 01 02 03-04 05 06 07 : 08 09 0A 0B-0C 0D 0E 0F | 0123456789ABCDEF
---------|-------------------------:-------------------------|-----------------
007A0000 | 4D 5A 90 00-03 00 00 00 : 04 00 00 00-FF FF 00 00 | MZ•.........ÿÿ..
007A0010 | B8 00 00 00-00 00 00 00 : 40 00 00 00-00 00 00 00 | ¸.......@.......
007A0020 | 00 00 00 00-00 00 00 00 : 00 00 00 00-00 00 00 00 | ................
007A0030 | 00 00 00 00-00 00 00 00 : 00 00 00 00-D0 00 00 00 | ............Ð...
007A0040 | 0E 1F BA 0E-00 B4 09 CD : 21 B8 01 4C-CD 21 54 68 | ..º..´.Í!¸.LÍ!Th
007A0050 | 69 73 20 70-72 6F 67 72 : 61 6D 20 63-61 6E 6E 6F | is program canno
007A0060 | 74 20 62 65-20 72 75 6E : 20 69 6E 20-44 4F 53 20 | t be run in DOS
007A0070 | 6D 6F 64 65-2E 0D 0D 0A : 24 00 00 00-00 00 00 00 | mode....$.......
007A0080 | 61 14 4B C1-25 75 25 92 : 25 75 25 92-25 75 25 92 | a.KÁ%u%?%u%?%u%?
007A0090 | 29 55 2B 92-27 75 25 92 : 7C 56 36 92-22 75 25 92 | )U+?'u%?|V6?"u%?
007A00A0 | 25 75 24 92-BF 75 25 92 : 0F 7D 23 92-24 75 25 92 | %u$?¿u%?.}#?$u%?
007A00B0 | 25 75 25 92-14 75 25 92 : 52 69 63 68-25 75 25 92 | %u%?.u%?Rich%u%?
007A00C0 | 00 00 00 00-00 00 00 00 : 00 00 00 00-00 00 00 00 | ................
007A00D0 | 50 45 00 00-4C 01 09 00 : 66 EC 08 38-00 00 00 00 | PE..L...fì.8....
007A00E0 | 00 00 00 00-E0 00 0E 03 : 0B 01 05 0C-00 2D 02 00 | ....à........-..
007A00F0 | 40 3A 00 00-00 00 00 00 : 3E 14 01 00-40 03 00 00 | @:......>...@...
[...]
```

EXAMPLE 4-10. *Loading and Displaying a Module Image*

Oddly, you can even load the .exe file of another application into memory using the /<path> option. However, this module probably will be loaded to an unusual address, because its preferred load address is usually occupied by w2k_mem.exe. Moreover, you cannot get the loaded application to run—the +x switch applies to DLLs only and has no effect on other module types.

DEMAND-PAGING IN ACTION

In the discussion of the spy device function SPY_IO_MEMORY_DATA, I mentioned that this function is able to read the contents of memory pages that are flushed out to a pagefile. Now is the time to prove this claim. First, it is necessary to maneuver the system into a severe low-memory situation, forcing it to swap to the pagefiles anything that isn't urgently needed. My favorite method goes as follows:

1. Copy the Windows 2000 desktop to the clipboard by pressing the Print key.
2. Paste this bitmap into a graphics application.
3. Inflate the bitmap to an enormous size.

Now watch out what the command **w2k_mem +d #16 0xC0280000 0xA0000000 0xA0001000 0xA0002000 0xC0280000** yields on the screen. You might wonder what this command is supposed to do. Well, it simply takes a snapshot of some PTEs before and after touching the pages they refer to. The four PTEs found at address 0xC0280000 are associated with the linear address range 0xA0000000 to 0xA0003FFF, which is part of the image of the kernel module win32k.sys. As Example 4-11 shows, this address range has been swapped out because of the bitmap operation I had performed just before. How do I know? Because the four DWORDs at address 0xC0280000 are even numbers, meaning that their least significant bit—the P bit of a PTE—is zero, indicating a nonpresent page. The next three hex dump panels belong to the command parameters 0xA0000000, 0xA0001000, and 0xA0002000, requesting data from three of the four pages currently under examination. As it turns out, w2k_mem.exe has no problems accessing these pages—the system simply swaps them in on demand. However, the final test is still to come: What do the four PTEs look like afterward? The answer is given by the last panel of Example 4-11: The first three PTEs have the P bit set, and the fourth still indicates "not present."

```
E:\>w2k_mem +d #16 0xC0280000 0xA0000000 0xA0001000 0xA0002000 0xC0280000
[...]
C0280000..C028000F: 16 valid bytes

Address  | 00000000 - 00000004 : 00000008 - 0000000C | 0000 0004 0008 000C
---------|---------------------:---------------------|--------------------
C0280000 | 056A14E0 - 056A14E2 : 056A14E4 - 056A14E6 | .j.à .j.â .j.ä .j.æ

A0000000..A000000F: 16 valid bytes

Address  | 00000000 - 00000004 : 00000008 - 0000000C | 0000 0004 0008 000C
---------|---------------------:---------------------|--------------------
A0000000 | 00905A4D - 00000003 : 00000004 - 0000FFFF | .•ZM .... .... ..ÿÿ

A0001000..A000100F: 16 valid bytes

Address  | 00000000 - 00000004 : 00000008 - 0000000C | 0000 0004 0008 000C
---------|---------------------:---------------------|--------------------
A0001000 | 000000A6 - FF0C75FF : 1738B415 - F8458BA0 | ...¦ ÿ.uÿ .8´. øE?

A0002000..A000200F: 16 valid bytes

Address  | 00000000 - 00000004 : 00000008 - 0000000C | 0000 0004 0008 000C
---------|---------------------:---------------------|--------------------
A0002000 | 89A018E0 - F685D875 : 468D1A74 - 458D5020 | ? .à ö?Øu F•.t E•P

C0280000..C028000F: 16 valid bytes

Address  | 00000000 - 00000004 : 00000008 - 0000000C | 0000 0004 0008 000C
---------|---------------------:---------------------|--------------------
C0280000 | 0556B123 - 028C2121 : 05AD1121 - 056A14E6 | .V±# .?!! .-.! .j.æ
[...]
```

EXAMPLE 4-11. *Watching PTEs Change Their States*

Before stepping to the next section, please study the first hex dump panel of Example 4-11 once more. The four PTEs at address `0xC0280000` all look quite similar. In fact, they differ only in the three least-significant bits. If you examine more of these PNPES that refer to pages in the pagefiles, you find that they all have bit #10 set. That's why I assigned the name `PageFile` to this bit in Listing 4-3. If it is set, the remaining bits—except for the `P` flag, of course—apparently specify the location of this page in the pagefiles.

MORE COMMAND OPTIONS

Some of the most interesting command options listed in Example 4-1 have not yet been explained. For example the "System status options" `+o`, `+c`, `+g`, `+i`, and `+b` are missing, although they sound promising. I will return to them in the last section of this chapter, where several secrets of the Windows 2000 memory system will be revealed.

INTERFACING TO THE SPY DEVICE

Now that you know how `w2k_mem.exe` is used, it's time to see how it works. Rather than discuss command line parsing and dispatching, let's see how this application communicates with the spy device inside `w2k_spy.sys`.

DEVICE I/O CONTROL REVISITED

The kernel-mode side of IOCTL communication has already been shown in Listings 4-6 and 4-7. The spy device simply sits waiting for I/O Request Packets (IRPs) and handles some of them, especially those tagged `IRP_MJ_DEVICE_CONTROL`, which request some forbidden actions to be executed, at least forbidden in the context of the user-mode application that sends these requests. It does so by calling the Win32 API function `DeviceIoControl()`, prototyped in Listing 4-27. The `dwIoControlCode`, `lpInBuffer`, `nInBufferSize`, `lpOutBuffer`, `nOutBufferSize`, and `lpBytesReturned` arguments should look familiar to you. In fact, they correspond 1:1 to the `dCode`, `pInput`, `dInput`, `pOutput`, `dOutput`, and `pdInfo` arguments of the `SpyDispatcher()` function in Listing 4-7. The remaining arguments are explained quickly. `hDevice` is the handle to the spy device, and `lpOverlapped` optionally points to an `OVERLAPPED` structure required for asynchronous IOCTL. We are not going to send asynchronous requests, so this argument will always be `NULL`.

Listing 4-28 is a collection of wrapper functions that perform basic IOCTL operations. The most basic function is `IoControl()`, which calls `DeviceIoControl()` and tests the reported output data size. Because `w2k_mem.exe` sizes its output buffers accurately, the number of output bytes should always be equal to the buffer size. `ReadBinary()` is a simplified version of `IoControl()` for IOCTL functions that don't require input data. `ReadCpuInfo()`, `ReadSegment()`, and `ReadPhysical()` are specifically tailored to the spy functions `SPY_IO_CPU_INFO`, `SPY_IO_SEGMENT`, and `SPY_IO_PHYSICAL`, because these are the most frequently used IOCTL functions. Encapsulating them in C functions makes the code much more readable.

```
BOOL WINAPI DeviceIoControl (HANDLE      hDevice,
                             DWORD       dwIoControlCode,
                             PVOID       lpInBuffer,
                             DWORD       nInBufferSize,
                             PVOID       lpOutBuffer,
                             DWORD       nOutBufferSize,
                             PDWORD      lpBytesReturned,
                             POVERLAPPED lpOverlapped);
```

LISTING 4-27. *Prototype of* `DeviceIoControl()`

```
BOOL WINAPI IoControl (HANDLE hDevice,
                       DWORD  dCode,
                       PVOID  pInput,
                       DWORD  dInput,
                       PVOID  pOutput,
                       DWORD  dOutput)
    {
    DWORD dData = 0;

    return DeviceIoControl (hDevice, dCode,
                            pInput,  dInput,
                            pOutput, dOutput,
                            &dData,  NULL)
           &&
           (dData == dOutput);
    }

// -----------------------------------------------------------------

BOOL WINAPI ReadBinary (HANDLE hDevice,
                        DWORD  dCode,
                        PVOID  pOutput,
                        DWORD  dOutput)
    {
    return IoControl (hDevice, dCode, NULL, 0, pOutput, dOutput);
    }

// -----------------------------------------------------------------

BOOL WINAPI ReadCpuInfo (HANDLE        hDevice,
                         PSPY_CPU_INFO psci)
    {
    return IoControl (hDevice, SPY_IO_CPU_INFO,
                      NULL,    0,
                      psci,    SPY_CPU_INFO_);
    }
```

(continued)

```
// -----------------------------------------------------------------

BOOL WINAPI ReadSegment (HANDLE       hDevice,
                         DWORD        dSelector,
                         PSPY_SEGMENT pss)
    {
    return IoControl (hDevice,    SPY_IO_SEGMENT,
                      &dSelector, DWORD_,
                      pss,        SPY_SEGMENT_);
    }

// -----------------------------------------------------------------

BOOL WINAPI ReadPhysical (HANDLE             hDevice,
                          PVOID              pLinear,
                          PPHYSICAL_ADDRESS ppa)
    {
    return IoControl (hDevice,  SPY_IO_PHYSICAL,
                      &pLinear, PVOID_,
                      ppa,      PHYSICAL_ADDRESS_)
           &&
           (ppa->LowPart || ppa->HighPart);
    }
```

LISTING 4-28. *Various IOCTL Wrappers*

All functions shown so far in this section require a spy device handle. It's time that I show how to obtain it. It is actually a quite simple Win32 operation, similar to opening a file. Listing 4-29 shows the implementation of the command handler inside `w2k_mem.exe`. This code uses the API functions `w2kFilePath()`, `w2kServiceLoad()`, and `w2kServiceUnload()`, exported by the "SBS Windows 2000 Utility Library" `w2k_lib.dll`, included on the companion CD of this book. If you have read the section about the Windows 2000 Service Control Manager in Chapter 3, you already know `w2kServiceLoad()` and `w2kServiceUnload()` from Listing 3-8. These powerful functions load and unload kernel-mode device drivers on the fly and handle benign error situations, such as gracefully loading a driver that is already loaded. `w2kFilePath()` is a helpful utility function that derives a file path from a base path, given a file name or file extension. `w2k_mem.exe` calls it to obtain a fully qualified path to the spy driver executable that matches its own path.

```
WORD awSpyFile      [] = SW(DRV_FILENAME);
WORD awSpyDevice    [] = SW(DRV_MODULE);
WORD awSpyDisplay   [] = SW(DRV_NAME);
WORD awSpyPath      [] = SW(DRV_PATH);
```

```
// ----------------------------------------------------------------

void WINAPI Execute (PPWORD ppwArguments,
                     DWORD  dArguments)
    {
    SPY_VERSION_INFO svi;
    DWORD            dOptions, dRequest, dReceive;
    WORD             awPath [MAX_PATH] = L"?";
    SC_HANDLE        hControl          = NULL;
    HANDLE           hDevice           = NULL;
    _printf (L"\r\nLoading \"%s\" (%s) ...\r\n",
             awSpyDisplay, awSpyDevice);

    if (w2kFilePath (NULL, awSpyFile, awPath, MAX_PATH))
        {
        _printf (L"Driver: \"%s\"\r\n",
                 awPath);

        hControl = w2kServiceLoad (awSpyDevice, awSpyDisplay,
                                   awPath, TRUE);
        }
    if (hControl != NULL)
        {
        _printf (L"Opening \"%s\" ...\r\n",
                 awSpyPath);

        hDevice = CreateFile (awSpyPath, GENERIC_READ,
                              FILE_SHARE_READ | FILE_SHARE_WRITE,
                              NULL, OPEN_EXISTING,
                              FILE_ATTRIBUTE_NORMAL, NULL);
        }
    if (hDevice != INVALID_HANDLE_VALUE)
        {
        if (ReadBinary (hDevice, SPY_IO_VERSION_INFO,
                        &svi, SPY_VERSION_INFO_))
            {
            _printf (L"\r\n%s V%lu.%02lu ready\r\n",
                     svi.awName,
                     svi.dVersion / 100, svi.dVersion % 100);
            }
        dOptions = COMMAND_OPTION_NONE;
        dRequest = CommandParse (hDevice, ppwArguments, dArguments,
                                 TRUE, &dOptions);

        dOptions = COMMAND_OPTION_NONE;
        dReceive = CommandParse (hDevice, ppwArguments, dArguments,
                                 FALSE, &dOptions);
        if (dRequest)
            {
            _printf (awSummary,
                     dRequest, (dRequest == 1 ? awByte : awBytes),
```

(continued)

```
                    dReceive, (dReceive == 1 ? awByte : awBytes));
            }
        _printf (L"\r\nClosing the spy device ...\r\n");
        CloseHandle (hDevice);
        }
    else
        {
        _printf (L"Spy device not available.\r\n");
        }
    if ((hControl != NULL) && gfSpyUnload)
        {
        _printf (L"Unloading the spy device ...\r\n");
        w2kServiceUnload (hControl, awSpyDevice);
        }
    return;
    }
```

LISTING 4-29. *Controlling the Spy Device*

Please note the four global string definitions at the top of Listing 4-29. The constants `DRV_FILENAME`, `DRV_MODULE`, `DRV_NAME`, and `DRV_PATH` are drawn from the header file of the spy device driver, `w2k_spy.h`. Table 4-4 lists their current values. You will not find device-specific definitions in the source files of `w2k_mem.exe`. `w2k_spy.h` provides everything a client application needs. This is very important: If any device-specific definitions change in the future, there is no need to update any application files. Just rebuild the application with the updated spy header file, and everything will fall into place.

The `w2kFilePath()` call near the beginning of Listing 4-29 guarantees that the `w2k_spy.sys` file specified by the global string `awSpyFile` (cf. Table 4-4) is always loaded from the directory where `w2k_mem.exe` resides. Next, the code in Listing 4-29 passes the global strings `awSpyDevice` and `awSpyDisplay` (cf. Table 4-4) to `w2kServiceLoad()`, attempting to load and start the spy device driver. If the driver was not loaded yet, these strings will be stored in the driver's property list and can be retrieved by other applications; otherwise, the current property settings are retained. Although the `w2kServiceLoad()` call in Listing 4-29 returns a handle, this is *not* a handle that can be used in any IOCTL calls. To get a handle to the spy device, the Win32 multipurpose function `CreateFile()` must be used. This function opens or creates almost anything that can be opened or created on Windows 2000. You certainly have called this function a million times to get a file handle. `CreateFile()` can also open kernel-mode devices if the symbolic link name of the device is supplied in the format `\\.\<SymbolicLink>` for the `lpFileName` argument. The symbolic link of the spy device is named `w2k_spy`, so the first `CreateFile()` argument must be `\\.\w2k_spy`, which is the value of the global string variable `awSpyPath` according to Table 4-4.

TABLE 4-4. *Device-Specific String Definitions*

w2k_spy CONSTANT	w2k_mem VARIABLE	VALUE
DRV_FILENAME	awSpyFile	w2k_spy.sys
DRV_MODULE	awSpyDevice	w2k_spy
DRV_NAME	awSpyDisplay	SBS Windows 2000 Spy Device
DRV_PATH	awSpyPath	\\.\w2k_spy

If `CreateFile()` succeeds, it returns a device handle that can be passed to `DeviceIoControl()`. The `Execute()` function in Listing 4-29 uses this handle immediately to query the version information of the spy device, which it displays on the screen if the IOCTL call succeeds. Next, the `CommandParse()` function is invoked twice with a different `BOOL` value for the fourth argument. The first call simply checks the command line for invalid parameters and displays any errors, and the second call actually executes all commands. I do not want to discuss in detail the command parser. The remaining code in Listing 4-29 is cleanup code that closes handles and optionally unloads the spy drives. The source code of `w2k_mem.exe` contains other interesting code snippets, but I will not discuss them here. Please see the files `w2k_mem.c` and `w2k_mem.h` in the `\src\w2k_mem` directory on the sample CD for further details.

The only notable thing left is the `gfSpyUnload` flag tested before unloading the spy driver. I have set this global flag to `FALSE`, so the driver will not be unloaded automatically. This enhances the performance of `w2k_mem.exe` and other `w2k_spy.sys` clients because loading a driver takes some time. The first client has to take the loading overhead, but all successors will benefit from having the driver already in memory. This setting also avoids conflict situations involving competitive clients, in which one client attempts to unload the driver while another one is still using it. Of course, Windows 2000 will not unload the driver unless all handles to its devices are closed, but it will put it into a `STOP_PENDING` state that will not allow new clients to access the device. However, if you don't run `w2k_spy.sys` in a multiclient environment, and you are updating the device driver frequently, you should probably set the `gfSpyUnload` flag to `TRUE`.

WINDOWS 2000 MEMORY INTERNALS

Along with the global separation of the 4-GB address space into user-mode and kernel-mode portions, these two halves are subdivided into various smaller blocks. As you might have guessed, most of them contain undocumented structures that serve undocumented purposes. It would be easy to forget about them if they were uninteresting. However, that's not the case—some of them are a real gold mine for anyone developing system diagnosis or debugging software.

Basic Operating System Information

Now the time has come to introduce one of the postponed command line options of the memory spy application `w2k_mem.exe`. If you take a look at the lower half of the program's help screen in Example 4-1, you will see a section titled "System Status Options." Let's try the option `+o`, named "display OS information." Example 4-12 shows a sample run on my machine. The data displayed here are the contents of the `SPY_OS_INFO` structure, defined in Listing 4-13 and set up by the spy device function `SpyOutputOsInfo()`, also included in Listing 4-13. In Example 4-12, you can already see some characteristic addresses within the 4-GB linear memory space of a process. For example, the valid user address range is reported to be `0x00010000` to `0x7FFEFFFF`. You have probably read in other programming books about Windows NT or Windows 2000 that the first and last 64 KB of the user-mode half of linear memory are "no-access regions" that are there to catch wild pointers produced by common programming errors (cf. Solomon 1998, Chapter 5). The output of `w2k_mem.exe` proves that this is correct.

```
E:\>w2k_mem +o
[...]
OS information:
---------------

Memory page size          : 4096 bytes
Memory page shift         : 12 bits
Memory PTI  shift         : 12 bits
Memory PDI  shift         : 22 bits
Memory page mask          : 0xFFFFF000
Memory PTI  mask          : 0x003FF000
Memory PDI  mask          : 0xFFC00000
Memory PTE  array         : 0xC0000000
Memory PDE  array         : 0xC0300000

Lowest user address       : 0x00010000
Thread environment block  : 0x7FFDE000
Highest user address      : 0x7FFEFFFF
User probe address        : 0x7FFF0000
System range start        : 0x80000000
Lowest system address     : 0xC0800000
Shared user data          : 0xFFDF0000
Processor control region  : 0xFFDFF000
Processor control block   : 0xFFDFF120
```

```
Global flag                 : 0x00000000
i386 machine type           : 0
Number of processors        : 1
Product type                : Windows NT Workstation (1)
Version & Build number      : 5.00.2195
System root                 : "E:\WINNT"
[...]
```

EXAMPLE 4-12. *Displaying Operating System Information*

The last three lines of Example 4-12 contain interesting information about the system, mostly extracted from the `SharedUserData` area at address `0xFFDF0000`. The data structure maintained there by the system is called `KUSER_SHARED_DATA` and is defined in the DDK header file `ntddk.h`.

WINDOWS 2000 SEGMENTS AND DESCRIPTORS

Another fine option of `w2k_mem.exe` is `+c`, which displays and interprets the contents of the processor's segment registers and descriptor tables. Example 4-13 shows the typical output. The contents of the `CS`, `DS`, and `ES` segment registers clearly demonstrate that Windows 2000 provides each process with a flat 4-GB address space: These basic segments start at offset `0x00000000` and have a limit of `0xFFFFFFFF`.

The flag characters in the rightmost column indicate the segment type as defined by its descriptor's Type member. The type attributes of code and data segments are symbolized by combinations of the characters "cra" and "ewa," respectively. A dash means that the corresponding attribute is not set. A Task State Segment (TSS) can have the attributes "a" (available) and "b" (busy) only. All applicable attributes are summarized in Table 4-5. Example 4-13 shows that the Windows 2000 `CS` segments are nonconforming and allow execute/read access, whereas the `DS`, `ES`, `FS`, and `SS` segments are of expand-up type and allow read/write access. Another inconspicuous but important detail is the different DPL of the `CS`, `FS`, and `SS` segments in user- and kernel-mode. DPL is the Descriptor Privilege Level. For nonconforming code segments, the DPL specifies the privilege level a caller must be on in order to be able to call into this segment (cf. Intel 1999c, pp. 4-8f). In user-mode, the required level is three; in kernel-mode, it is zero. For data segments, the DPL is the lowest privilege level required to be able to access the segment. This means that the `FS` and `SS` segments are accessible from all privilege levels in user-mode, whereas only level-0 accesses are allowed in kernel-mode.

```
E:\>w2k_mem +c
[...]
CPU information:
----------------

User mode segments:

CS  : Selector = 001B, Base = 00000000, Limit = FFFFFFFF, DPL3, Type = CODE -ra
DS  : Selector = 0023, Base = 00000000, Limit = FFFFFFFF, DPL3, Type = DATA -wa
ES  : Selector = 0023, Base = 00000000, Limit = FFFFFFFF, DPL3, Type = DATA -wa
FS  : Selector = 0038, Base = 7FFDE000, Limit = 00000FFF, DPL3, Type = DATA -wa
SS  : Selector = 0023, Base = 00000000, Limit = FFFFFFFF, DPL3, Type = DATA -wa
TSS : Selector = 0028, Base = 80244000, Limit = 000020AB, DPL0, Type = TSS32 b

Kernel mode segments:

CS  : Selector = 0008, Base = 00000000, Limit = FFFFFFFF, DPL0, Type = CODE -ra
DS  : Selector = 0023, Base = 00000000, Limit = FFFFFFFF, DPL3, Type = DATA -wa
ES  : Selector = 0023, Base = 00000000, Limit = FFFFFFFF, DPL3, Type = DATA -wa
FS  : Selector = 0030, Base = FFDFF000, Limit = 00001FFF, DPL0, Type = DATA -wa
SS  : Selector = 0010, Base = 00000000, Limit = FFFFFFFF, DPL0, Type = DATA -wa
TSS : Selector = 0028, Base = 80244000, Limit = 000020AB, DPL0, Type = TSS32 b

IDT : Limit    = 07FF, Base = 80036400
GDT : Limit    = 03FF, Base = 80036000
LDT : Selector = 0000

CR0 : Contents = 8001003B
CR2 : Contents = 00401050
CR3 : Contents = 06F70000
[...]
```

EXAMPLE 4-13. *Displaying CPU Information*

The contents of the IDT and GDT registers show that the GDT spans from linear address `0x80036000` to `800363FF`, immediately followed by the IDT, occupying the address range `0x80036400` to `0x80036BFF`. With each descriptor taking 64 bits, the GDT and IDT contain 128 and 256 entries, respectively. Note that the GDT could comprise as many as 8,192 entries, but Windows 2000 uses only a small fraction of them.

The `w2k_mem.exe` utility features two more options—`+g` and `+i`—that display more details about the GDT and IDT. Example 4-14 demonstrates the output of the `+g` option. It is similar to the "kernel-mode segments:" section of Example 4-13, but lists all segment selectors available in kernel-mode, not just those that are stored in segment registers. `w2k_mem.exe` compiles this list by looping through the entire GDT,

TABLE 4-5. *Code and Data Segment Type Attributes*

SEGMENT	ATTRIBUTE	DESCRIPTION
CODE	c	Conforming segment (may be entered by less privileged code)
CODE	r	Read-access allowed (as opposed to execute-only access)
CODE	a	Segment has been accessed
DATA	e	Expand-down segment (typical attribute for stack segments)
DATA	w	Write-access allowed (as opposed to read-only access)
DATA	a	Segment has been accessed
TSS32	a	Task State Segment is available
TSS32	b	Task State Segment is busy

querying the spy device for segment information by means of the IOCTL function `SPY_IO_SEGMENT`. Only valid selectors are displayed. It is interesting to compare Examples 4-13 and 4-14 with the GDT selector definitions in `ntddk.h`, summarized in Table 4-6. Obviously, they are in accordance with the details reported by `w2k_mem.exe`.

```
E:\>w2k_mem +g
[...]
GDT information:
----------------

001 : Selector = 0008, Base = 00000000, Limit = FFFFFFFF, DPL0, Type = CODE -ra
002 : Selector = 0010, Base = 00000000, Limit = FFFFFFFF, DPL0, Type = DATA -wa
003 : Selector = 0018, Base = 00000000, Limit = FFFFFFFF, DPL3, Type = CODE -ra
004 : Selector = 0020, Base = 00000000, Limit = FFFFFFFF, DPL3, Type = DATA -wa
005 : Selector = 0028, Base = 80244000, Limit = 000020AB, DPL0, Type = TSS32 b
006 : Selector = 0030, Base = FFDFF000, Limit = 00001FFF, DPL0, Type = DATA -wa
007 : Selector = 0038, Base = 7FFDE000, Limit = 00000FFF, DPL3, Type = DATA -wa
008 : Selector = 0040, Base = 00000400, Limit = 0000FFFF, DPL3, Type = DATA -wa
009 : Selector = 0048, Base = E2E6A000, Limit = 00000177, DPL0, Type = LDT
00A : Selector = 0050, Base = 80470040, Limit = 00000068, DPL0, Type = TSS32 a
00B : Selector = 0058, Base = 804700A8, Limit = 00000068, DPL0, Type = TSS32 a
00C : Selector = 0060, Base = 00022AB0, Limit = 0000FFFF, DPL0, Type = DATA -wa
00D : Selector = 0068, Base = 000B8000, Limit = 00003FFF, DPL0, Type = DATA -w-
00E : Selector = 0070, Base = FFFF7000, Limit = 000003FF, DPL0, Type = DATA -w-
00F : Selector = 0078, Base = 80400000, Limit = 0000FFFF, DPL0, Type = CODE -r-
010 : Selector = 0080, Base = 80400000, Limit = 0000FFFF, DPL0, Type = DATA -w-
011 : Selector = 0088, Base = 00000000, Limit = 00000000, DPL0, Type = DATA -w-
```

(continued)

```
014 : Selector = 00A0, Base = 814985A8, Limit = 00000068, DPL0, Type = TSS32 a
01C : Selector = 00E0, Base = F0430000, Limit = 0000FFFF, DPL0, Type = CODE cra
01D : Selector = 00E8, Base = 00000000, Limit = 0000FFFF, DPL0, Type = DATA -w-
01E : Selector = 00F0, Base = 8042DCE8, Limit = 000003B7, DPL0, Type = CODE --
01F : Selector = 00F8, Base = 00000000, Limit = 0000FFFF, DPL0, Type = DATA -w-
020 : Selector = 0100, Base = F0440000, Limit = 0000FFFF, DPL0, Type = DATA -wa
021 : Selector = 0108, Base = F0440000, Limit = 0000FFFF, DPL0, Type = DATA -wa
022 : Selector = 0110, Base = F0440000, Limit = 0000FFFF, DPL0, Type = DATA -wa
[...]
```

EXAMPLE 4-14. *Displaying GDT Descriptors*

TABLE 4-6. *GDT Selectors Defined in* ntddk.h

SYMBOL	VALUE	COMMENTS
KGDT_NULL	0x0000	Null segment selector (invalid)
KGDT_R0_CODE	0x0008	*CS* register in kernel-mode
KGDT_R0_DATA	0x0010	*SS* register in kernel-mode
KGDT_R3_CODE	0x0018	*CS* register in user-mode
KGDT_R3_DATA	0x0020	*DS, ES,* and *SS* register in user-mode, *DS* and *ES* register in kernel-mode
KGDT_TSS	0x0028	Task State Segment in user- and kernel-mode
KGDT_R0_PCR	0x0030	*FS* register in kernel-mode (Processor Control Region)
KGDT_R3_TEB	0x0038	*FS* register in user-mode (Thread Environment Block)
KGDT_VDM_TILE	0x0040	Base 0x00000400, limit 0x0000FFFF (Virtual DOS Machine)
KGDT_LDT	0x0048	Local Descriptor Table
KGDT_DF_TSS	0x0050	*ntoskrnl.exe* variable *KiDoubleFaultTSS*
KGDT_NMI_TSS	0x0058	*ntoskrnl.exe* variable *KiNMITSS*

The selectors in Example 4-14 that are not listed in Table 4-6 can in part be identified by looking for familiar base addresses or memory contents, and by using the Kernel Debugger to look up the symbols for some of the base addresses. Table 4-7 comprises the selectors that I have identified so far.

The `+i` option of `w2k_mem.exe` dumps the gate descriptors stored in the IDT. Example 4-15 is an excerpt from this rather long list, comprising only the first 20 entries that have a predefined meaning assigned by Intel (Intel 1999c, pp. 5-6). Interrupts `0x14` to `0x1F` are reserved for Intel; the remaining range `0x20` to `0xFF` is available to the operating system.

In Table 4-8, I have summarized all interrupts that refer to identifiable and non-trivial interrupt, trap, and task gates. Most of the user defined interrupts point to dummy handlers named `KiUnexpectedInterruptNNN()`, as explained earlier in this chapter. Some interrupt handlers are located at addresses that can't be resolved to symbols by the Kernel Debugger.

TABLE 4-7. *More GDT Selectors*

VALUE	BASE	DESCRIPTION
0x0078	0x80400000	*ntoskrnl.exe* code segment
0x0080	0x80400000	*ntoskrnl.exe* data segment
0x00A0	0x814985A8	TSS (EIP member points to *HalpMcaExceptionHandlerWrapper*)
0x00E0	0xF0430000	ROM BIOS code segment
0x00F0	0x8042DCE8	*ntoskrnl.exe* function *KiI386CallAbios*
0x0100	0xF0440000	ROM BIOS data segment
0x0108	0xF0440000	ROM BIOS data segment
0x0110	0xF0440000	ROM BIOS data segment

```
E:\>w2k_mem +i
[...]
IDT information:
----------------

00 : Pointer = 0008:804625E6, Base = 00000000, Limit = FFFFFFFF, Type = INT32
01 : Pointer = 0008:80462736, Base = 00000000, Limit = FFFFFFFF, Type = INT32
02 : TSS     = 0058,          Base = 804700A8, Limit = 00000068, Type = TASK
03 : Pointer = 0008:80462A0E, Base = 00000000, Limit = FFFFFFFF, Type = INT32
04 : Pointer = 0008:80462B72, Base = 00000000, Limit = FFFFFFFF, Type = INT32
05 : Pointer = 0008:80462CB6, Base = 00000000, Limit = FFFFFFFF, Type = INT32
06 : Pointer = 0008:80462E1A, Base = 00000000, Limit = FFFFFFFF, Type = INT32
07 : Pointer = 0008:80463350, Base = 00000000, Limit = FFFFFFFF, Type = INT32
08 : TSS     = 0050,          Base = 80470040, Limit = 00000068, Type = TASK
09 : Pointer = 0008:8046370C, Base = 00000000, Limit = FFFFFFFF, Type = INT32
0A : Pointer = 0008:80463814, Base = 00000000, Limit = FFFFFFFF, Type = INT32
0B : Pointer = 0008:80463940, Base = 00000000, Limit = FFFFFFFF, Type = INT32
0C : Pointer = 0008:80463C44, Base = 00000000, Limit = FFFFFFFF, Type = INT32
0D : Pointer = 0008:80463E50, Base = 00000000, Limit = FFFFFFFF, Type = INT32
0E : Pointer = 0008:804648A4, Base = 00000000, Limit = FFFFFFFF, Type = INT32
0F : Pointer = 0008:80464C3F, Base = 00000000, Limit = FFFFFFFF, Type = INT32
10 : Pointer = 0008:80464D47, Base = 00000000, Limit = FFFFFFFF, Type = INT32
11 : Pointer = 0008:80464E6B, Base = 00000000, Limit = FFFFFFFF, Type = INT32
12 : TSS     = 00A0,          Base = 814985A8, Limit = 00000068, Type = TASK
13 : Pointer = 0008:80464C3F, Base = 00000000, Limit = FFFFFFFF, Type = INT32
[...]
```

EXAMPLE 4-15. *Displaying IDT Gate Descriptors*

TABLE 4-8. *Windows 2000 Interrupt, Trap, and Task Gates*

INT	INTEL DESCRIPTION	OWNER	HANDLER/TSS
0x00	Divide Error (DE)	ntoskrnl.exe	KiTrap00
0x01	Debug (DB)	ntoskrnl.exe	KiTrap01
0x02	NMI Interrupt	ntoskrnl.exe	KiNMITSS
0x03	Breakpoint (BP)	ntoskrnl.exe	KiTrap03
0x04	Overflow (OF)	ntoskrnl.exe	KiTrap04
0x05	BOUND Range Exceeded (BR)	ntoskrnl.exe	KiTrap05
0x06	Undefined Opcode (UD)	ntoskrnl.exe	KiTrap06
0x07	No Math Coprocessor (NM)	ntoskrnl.exe	KiTrap07
0x08	Double Fault (DF)	ntoskrnl.exe	KiDouble
0x09	Coprocessor Segment Overrun	ntoskrnl.exe	KiTrap09
0x0A	Invalid TSS (TS)	ntoskrnl.exe	KiTrap0A
0x0B	Segment Not Present (NP)	ntoskrnl.exe	KiTrap0B
0x0C	Stack-Segment Fault (SS)	ntoskrnl.exe	KiTrap0C
0x0D	General Protection (GP)	ntoskrnl.exe	KiTrap0D
0x0E	Page Fault (PF)	ntoskrnl.exe	KiTrap0E
0x0F	(Intel reserved)	ntoskrnl.exe	KiTrap0F
0x10	Math Fault (MF)	ntoskrnl.exe	KiTrap10
0x11	Alignment Check (AC)	ntoskrnl.exe	KiTrap11
0x12	Machine Check (MC)	?	?
0x13	Streaming SIMD Extensions	ntoskrnl.exe	KiTrap0F
0x14-0x1F	(Intel reserved)	ntoskrnl.exe	KiTrap0F
0x2A	User Defined	ntoskrnl.exe	KiGetTickCount
0x2B	User Defined	ntoskrnl.exe	KiCallbackReturn
0x2C	User Defined	ntoskrnl.exe	KiSetLowWaitHighThread
0x2D	User Defined	ntoskrnl.exe	KiDebugService
0x2E	User Defined	ntoskrnl.exe	KiSystemService
0x2F	User Defined	ntoskrnl.exe	KiTrap0F
0x30	User Defined	hal.dll	HalpClockInterrupt
0x38	User Defined	hal.dll	HalpProfileInterrupt

WINDOWS 2000 MEMORY AREAS

The last `w2k_mem.exe` option that remains to be discussed is the `+b` switch. It generates an enormously long list of contiguous memory regions within the 4-GB linear address space. `w2k_mem.exe` builds this list by walking through the entire PTE array at address `0xC0000000`, using the spy device's IOCTL function `SPY_IO_PAGE_ENTRY`.

The `dSize` member contained in each resulting `SPY_PAGE_ENTRY` structure is added to the linear address associated with the PTE to get the linear address of the next PTE to be retrieved. Listing 4-30 shows the implementation of this option.

```
DWORD WINAPI DisplayMemoryBlocks (HANDLE hDevice)
    {
    SPY_PAGE_ENTRY spe;
    PBYTE          pbPage, pbBase;
    DWORD          dBlock, dPresent, dTotal;
    DWORD          n = 0;

    pbPage   = 0;
    pbBase   = INVALID_ADDRESS;
    dBlock   = 0;
    dPresent = 0;
    dTotal   = 0;

    n += _printf (L"\r\nContiguous memory blocks:"
                  L"\r\n-------------\r\n\r\n");

    do  {
        if (!IoControl (hDevice, SPY_IO_PAGE_ENTRY,
                        &pbPage, PVOID_,
                        &spe,    SPY_PAGE_ENTRY_))
            {
            n += _printf (L" !!! Device I/O error !!!\r\n");
            break;
            }
        if (spe.fPresent)
            {
            dPresent += spe.dSize;
            }
        if (spe.pe.dValue)
            {
            dTotal += spe.dSize;

            if (pbBase == INVALID_ADDRESS)
                {
                n += _printf (L"%5lu : 0x%08lX ->",
                              ++dBlock, pbPage);

                pbBase = pbPage;
                }
            }
        else
            {
            if (pbBase != INVALID_ADDRESS)
                {
                n += _printf (L" 0x%08lX (0x%08lX bytes)\r\n",
                              pbPage-1, pbPage-pbBase);
```

(continued)

```
                    pbBase = INVALID_ADDRESS;
                    }
                }
            }
        while (pbPage += spe.Size);

        if (pbBase != INVALID_ADDRESS)
            {
            n += _printf (L"0x%08lX\r\n", pbPage-1);
            }
        n += _printf (L"\r\n"
                      L" Present bytes: 0x%08lX\r\n"
                      L" Total   bytes: 0x%08lX\r\n",
                      dPresent, dTotal);
        return n;
        }
```

LISTING 4-30. *Finding Contiguous Linear Memory Blocks*

Example 4-16 is an excerpt from a sample run on my machine, showing some of the more interesting regions. Some very obvious addresses are `0x00400000`, where the image of `w2k_mem.exe` starts (block #13), and `0x10000000`, where the image of `w2k_lib.dll` is located (block #23). The TEB and PEB pages also are clearly discernible (block #104), as are the `hal.dll`, `ntoskrnl.exe`, and `win32k.sys` areas (blocks #105 and 106). Blocks #340 to 350 are, of course, the valid fragments of the system's PTE array, featuring the page-directory as part of block #347. Block #2122 contains the `SharedUserData` area, and #2123 comprises the `KPCR`, `KPRCB`, and `CONTEXT` structures containing thread and processor status information.

```
E:\>w2k_mem +b
[...]
Contiguous memory blocks:
-------------------------

    1 : 0x00010000 -> 0x00010FFF (0x00001000 bytes)
    2 : 0x00020000 -> 0x00020FFF (0x00001000 bytes)
    3 : 0x0012D000 -> 0x00138FFF (0x0000C000 bytes)
    4 : 0x00230000 -> 0x00230FFF (0x00001000 bytes)
    5 : 0x00240000 -> 0x00241FFF (0x00002000 bytes)
    6 : 0x00247000 -> 0x00247FFF (0x00001000 bytes)
    7 : 0x0024F000 -> 0x00250FFF (0x00002000 bytes)
```

```
     8 : 0x00260000 -> 0x00260FFF (0x00001000 bytes)
     9 : 0x00290000 -> 0x00290FFF (0x00001000 bytes)
    10 : 0x002E0000 -> 0x002E0FFF (0x00001000 bytes)
    11 : 0x002E2000 -> 0x002E3FFF (0x00002000 bytes)
    12 : 0x003B0000 -> 0x003B1FFF (0x00002000 bytes)
    13 : 0x00400000 -> 0x00404FFF (0x00005000 bytes)
    14 : 0x00406000 -> 0x00406FFF (0x00001000 bytes)
    15 : 0x00410000 -> 0x00410FFF (0x00001000 bytes)
    16 : 0x00419000 -> 0x00419FFF (0x00001000 bytes)
    17 : 0x0041B000 -> 0x0041BFFF (0x00001000 bytes)
    18 : 0x00450000 -> 0x00450FFF (0x00001000 bytes)
    19 : 0x00760000 -> 0x00760FFF (0x00001000 bytes)
    20 : 0x00770000 -> 0x00770FFF (0x00001000 bytes)
    21 : 0x00780000 -> 0x00783FFF (0x00004000 bytes)
    22 : 0x00790000 -> 0x00791FFF (0x00002000 bytes)
    23 : 0x10000000 -> 0x10003FFF (0x00004000 bytes)
    24 : 0x10005000 -> 0x10005FFF (0x00001000 bytes)
    25 : 0x1000E000 -> 0x10016FFF (0x00009000 bytes)
    26 : 0x759B0000 -> 0x759B1FFF (0x00002000 bytes)
[...]
   103 : 0x7FFD2000 -> 0x7FFD3FFF (0x00002000 bytes)
   104 : 0x7FFDE000 -> 0x7FFE0FFF (0x00003000 bytes)
   105 : 0x80000000 -> 0xA01A5FFF (0x201A6000 bytes)
   106 : 0xA01B0000 -> 0xA01F2FFF (0x00043000 bytes)
   107 : 0xA0200000 -> 0xA02C7FFF (0x000C8000 bytes)
   108 : 0xA02F0000 -> 0xA03FFFFF (0x00110000 bytes)
   109 : 0xA4000000 -> 0xA4001FFF (0x00002000 bytes)
   110 : 0xBE63B000 -> 0xBE63CFFF (0x00002000 bytes)
[...]
   340 : 0xC0000000 -> 0xC0001FFF (0x00002000 bytes)
   341 : 0xC0040000 -> 0xC0040FFF (0x00001000 bytes)
   342 : 0xC01D6000 -> 0xC01D6FFF (0x00001000 bytes)
   343 : 0xC01DA000 -> 0xC01DAFFF (0x00001000 bytes)
   344 : 0xC01DD000 -> 0xC01E0FFF (0x00004000 bytes)
   345 : 0xC01FD000 -> 0xC01FDFFF (0x00001000 bytes)
   346 : 0xC01FF000 -> 0xC0280FFF (0x00082000 bytes)
   347 : 0xC0290000 -> 0xC0301FFF (0x00072000 bytes)
   348 : 0xC0303000 -> 0xC0386FFF (0x00084000 bytes)
   349 : 0xC0389000 -> 0xC038CFFF (0x00004000 bytes)
   350 : 0xC039E000 -> 0xC03FFFFF (0x00062000 bytes)
[...]
  2121 : 0xFFC00000 -> 0xFFD0FFFF (0x00110000 bytes)
  2122 : 0xFFDF0000 -> 0xFFDF0FFF (0x00001000 bytes)
  2123 : 0xFFDFF000 -> 0xFFDFFFFF (0x00001000 bytes)
[...]
 Present bytes: 0x22AA9000
 Total   bytes: 0x2B8BA000
[...]
```

EXAMPLE 4-16. *A Sample List of Contiguous Memory Blocks*

The odd thing about the +b option of w2k_mem.exe is that it reports an amount of used memory that is far beyond any reasonable value. Note the summary lines at the end of Example 4-16. Am I really using 700 MB of memory now? The Windows 2000 Task Manager indicates 150 MB—so what's going on here? This strange effect comes from memory block #105, which is reported to range from 0x80000000 to 0xA01A5FFF, spanning 0x201A6000 bytes, which equals *538,599,424* bytes. This is obviously nonsense. The problem is that the entire linear address range from 0x80000000 to 0x9FFFFFFF is mapped to the physical address range 0x00000000 to 0x1FFFFFFF, as already noted earlier in this chapter. All 4-MB pages in this range have valid PDEs in the page-directory at address 0xC0300000, which can be proved by issuing the command **w2k_mem +d #0x200 0xC0300800** (Example 4-17). Because all PDEs in the resulting list are odd numbers, the corresponding pages must be present; however, they are not necessarily backed up by physical memory. In fact, large portions of this memory range are really "holes" and seem to be filled with 0xFF bytes if copied to a buffer. Therefore, you shouldn't take the memory usage summary displayed by w2k_mem.exe too seriously.

```
E:\>w2k_mem +d #0x200 0xC0300800
[...]
C0300800..C03009FF: 512 valid bytes

Address  | 00000000 - 00000004 : 00000008 - 0000000C | 0000 0004 0008 000C
---------|---------------------:---------------------|-------------------
C0300800 | 000001E3 - 004001E3 : 008001E3 - 00C001E3 | ...ã .@.ã .?.ã .À.ã
C0300810 | 010001E3 - 014001E3 : 018001E3 - 01C001E3 | ...ã .@.ã .?.ã .À.ã
C0300820 | 020001E3 - 024001E3 : 028001E3 - 02C001E3 | ...ã .@.ã .?.ã .À.ã
C0300830 | 030001E3 - 034001E3 : 038001E3 - 03C001E3 | ...ã .@.ã .?.ã .À.ã
C0300840 | 040001E3 - 044001E3 : 048001E3 - 04C001E3 | ...ã .@.ã .?.ã .À.ã
C0300850 | 050001E3 - 054001E3 : 058001E3 - 05C001E3 | ...ã .@.ã .?.ã .À.ã
C0300860 | 060001E3 - 064001E3 : 068001E3 - 06C001E3 | ...ã .@.ã .?.ã .À.ã
C0300870 | 070001E3 - 074001E3 : 078001E3 - 07C001E3 | ...ã .@.ã .?.ã .À.ã
C0300880 | 080001E3 - 084001E3 : 088001E3 - 08C001E3 | ...ã .@.ã .?.ã .À.ã
C0300890 | 090001E3 - 094001E3 : 098001E3 - 09C001E3 | ...ã .@.ã .?.ã .À.ã
C03008A0 | 0A0001E3 - 0A4001E3 : 0A8001E3 - 0AC001E3 | ...ã .@.ã .?.ã .À.ã
C03008B0 | 0B0001E3 - 0B4001E3 : 0B8001E3 - 0BC001E3 | ...ã .@.ã .?.ã .À.ã
C03008C0 | 0C0001E3 - 0C4001E3 : 0C8001E3 - 0CC001E3 | ...ã .@.ã .?.ã .À.ã
C03008D0 | 0D0001E3 - 0D4001E3 : 0D8001E3 - 0DC001E3 | ...ã .@.ã .?.ã .À.ã
C03008E0 | 0E0001E3 - 0E4001E3 : 0E8001E3 - 0EC001E3 | ...ã .@.ã .?.ã .À.ã
C03008F0 | 0F0001E3 - 0F4001E3 : 0F8001E3 - 0FC001E3 | ...ã .@.ã .?.ã .À.ã
C0300900 | 100001E3 - 104001E3 : 108001E3 - 10C001E3 | ...ã .@.ã .?.ã .À.ã
```

```
C0300910 | 110001E3 - 114001E3 : 118001E3 - 11C001E3 | ...ã .@.ã .?.ã .À.ã
C0300920 | 120001E3 - 124001E3 : 128001E3 - 12C001E3 | ...ã .@.ã .?.ã .À.ã
C0300930 | 130001E3 - 134001E3 : 138001E3 - 13C001E3 | ...ã .@.ã .?.ã .À.ã
C0300940 | 140001E3 - 144001E3 : 148001E3 - 14C001E3 | ...ã .@.ã .?.ã .À.ã
C0300950 | 150001E3 - 154001E3 : 158001E3 - 15C001E3 | ...ã .@.ã .?.ã .À.ã
C0300960 | 160001E3 - 164001E3 : 168001E3 - 16C001E3 | ...ã .@.ã .?.ã .À.ã
C0300970 | 170001E3 - 174001E3 : 178001E3 - 17C001E3 | ...ã .@.ã .?.ã .À.ã
C0300980 | 180001E3 - 184001E3 : 188001E3 - 18C001E3 | ...ã .@.ã .?.ã .À.ã
C0300990 | 190001E3 - 194001E3 : 198001E3 - 19C001E3 | ...ã .@.ã .?.ã .À.ã
C03009A0 | 1A0001E3 - 1A4001E3 : 1A8001E3 - 1AC001E3 | ...ã .@.ã .?.ã .À.ã
C03009B0 | 1B0001E3 - 1B4001E3 : 1B8001E3 - 1BC001E3 | ...ã .@.ã .?.ã .À.ã
C03009C0 | 1C0001E3 - 1C4001E3 : 1C8001E3 - 1CC001E3 | ...ã .@.ã .?.ã .À.ã
C03009D0 | 1D0001E3 - 1D4001E3 : 1D8001E3 - 1DC001E3 | ...ã .@.ã .?.ã .À.ã
C03009E0 | 1E0001E3 - 1E4001E3 : 1E8001E3 - 1EC001E3 | ...ã .@.ã .?.ã .À.ã
C03009F0 | 1F0001E3 - 1F4001E3 : 1F8001E3 - 1FC001E3 | ...ã .@.ã .?.ã .À.ã
[...]
```

EXAMPLE 4-17. *The PDEs of the Address Range* `0x80000000` *to* `0x9FFFFFFF`

THE WINDOWS 2000 MEMORY MAP

The last part of this chapter is dedicated to the general layout of the 4-GB linear address space as it is "seen" by a Windows 2000 process. Table 4-9 lists the address ranges of various essential data structures. The big holes between them are used for several purposes, such as load areas for process modules and device drivers, memory pools, working set lists, and the like. Note that some addresses and block sizes might vary considerably from system to system, depending on the memory and hardware configuration, the process properties, and several other variables. Therefore, use this list only as a rough sketch, not as an accurate roadmap.

Some physical memory blocks appear twice or more in the linear address space. For example, the `SharedUserData` area at linear address `0xFFDF0000` is mirrored at address `0x7FFE0000`. Both refer to the same page in physical memory—writing a byte to `0xFFDF0000+n` mysteriously changes the value of the byte at `0x7FFE0000+n`. This is the world of virtual memory—a physical address can be mapped anywhere into the linear address space, even to several addresses at the same time. It's just a matter of setting up the page-directory and page-tables appropriately. Please recall Figures 4-3 and 4-4, which clearly show that linear addresses are fake. Their `Directory` and `Table` bit fields are just pointers to structures that determine the real location of the data. And if the PFNs of two PTEs happen to be identical, the corresponding linear addresses refer to the same physical memory location.

TABLE 4-9. *Identifiable Memory Regions in the Address Space of a Process*

START	END	HEX SIZE	TYPE/DESCRIPTION
0x00000000	0x0000FFFF	10000	Lower guard block
0x00010000	0x0001FFFF	10000	WCHAR[]/Environment strings, allocated in 4-KB pages
0x00020000	0x0002FFFF	10000	PROCESS_PARAMETERS/allocated in 4-KB pages
0x00030000	0x0012FFFF	100000	DWORD [4000]/Process stack (default: 1 MB)
0x7FFDD000	0x7FFDDFFF	1000	TEB/Thread Environment Block of thread #2
0x7FFDE000	0x7FFDEFFF	1000	TEB/Thread Environment Block of thread #1
0x7FFDF000	0x7FFDFFFF	1000	PEB/Process Environment Block
0x7FFE0000	0x7FFE02D7	2D8	KUSER_SHARED_DATA/SharedUserData in user-mode
0x7FFF0000	0x7FFFFFFF	10000	Upper guard block
0x80000000	0x800003FF	400	IVT/Interrupt Vector Table
0x80036000	0x800363FF	400	KGDTENTRY[80]/Global Descriptor Table
0x80036400	0x80036BFF	800	KIDTENTRY[100]/Interrupt Descriptor Table
0x800C0000	0x800FFFFF	40000	VGA/ROM BIOS
0x80244000	0x802460AA	20AB	KTSS/user/kernel Task State Segment (busy)
0x8046AB80	0x8046ABBF	40	KeServiceDescriptorTable
0x8046ABC0	0x8046ABFF	40	KeServiceDescriptorTableShadow
0x80470040	0x804700A7	68	KTSS/KiDoubleFaultTSS
0x804700A8	0x8047010F	68	KTSS/KiNMITSS
0x804704D8	0x804708B7	3E0	PROC[F8]/KiServiceTable
0x804708B8	0x804708BB	4	DWORD/KiServiceLimit
0x804708BC	0x804709B3	F8	BYTE[F8]/KiArgumentTable
0x814C6000	0x82CC5FFF	1800000	PFN[100000]/MmPfnDatabase (max. for 4 GB)
0xA01859F0	0xA01863EB	9FC	PROC[27F]/W32pServiceTable
0xA0186670	0xA01868EE	27F	BYTE[27F]/W32pArgumentTable
0xC0000000	0xC03FFFFF	400000	X86_PE[100000]/page-directory and page-tables
0xC1000000	0xE0FFFFFF	20000000	System Cache (MmSystemCacheStart, MmSystemCacheEnd)
0xE1000000	0xE77FFFFF	6800000	Paged Pool (MmPagedPoolStart, MmPagedPoolEnd)
0xF0430000	0xF043FFFF	10000	ROM BIOS code segment
0xF0440000	0xF044FFFF	10000	ROM BIOS data segment

TABLE 4-9. *(continued)*

START	END	HEX SIZE	TYPE/DESCRIPTION
0xFFDF0000	0xFFDF02D7	2D8	KUSER_SHARED_DATA/SharedUserData in kernel-mode
0xFFDFF000	0xFFDFF053	54	KPCR/Processor Control Region (kernel-mode FS segment)
0xFFDFF120	0xFFDFF13B	1C	KPRCB/Processor Control Block
0xFFDFF13C	0xFFDFF407	2CC	CONTEXT/Thread Context (CPU state)
0xFFDFF620	0xFFDFF71F	100	Lookaside list directories

CHAPTER 5

Monitoring Native API Calls

Intercepting operating system calls is an all-time favorite of programmers everywhere. The motivations for this public interest are numerous: code profiling and optimization, reverse engineering, user activity logging, and the like. All of these share a common intention: to pass control to a special piece of code whenever an application calls a system service, making it possible to find out which service was called, what parameters it received, what results it returned, and how long it took to execute. Based on a technique originally proposed by Mark Russinovich and Bryce Cogswell (Russinovich and Cogswell 1997), this chapter presents a general framework for implanting hooks into arbitrary Native API functions. The approach used here is completely data-driven, so it can be easily extended and adapted to other Windows 2000/NT versions. The data gathered from the API calls of all processes in the system are written to a circular buffer that can be read by a client application via device I/O control. The protocol data are formatted as a simple line-oriented ANSI text stream that obeys strict formatting rules, making automated postprocessing by an application easy. To demonstrate the basic outline of such a client application, this chapter also presents a sample protocol data viewer running in a console window.

PATCHING THE SERVICE DESCRIPTOR TABLE

Whereas "primitive" operating systems such as DOS or Windows 3.xx offered little resistance to programmers who wanted to apply hooks to their Application Programming Interfaces (APIs), Win32 systems such as Windows 2000, Windows NT, and Windows 9x are much harder to handle, because they use clever protection mechanisms to separate unrelated pieces of code from each other. Setting a system-wide hook on a Win32 API is not a small task. Fortunately, we have Win32 wizards such as Matt Pietrek (Pietrek 1996e) and Jeffrey Richter (Richter 1997), who have put much work into showing us how it can be done, despite the fact that there's no simple and elegant solution. In 1997, Russinovich and Cogswell presented a completely different approach to system-wide hooks for Windows NT, intercepting the system at a much lower level (Russinovich and Cogswell 1997). They proposed to inject the logging mechanism into the Native API dispatcher, just below the frontier between user-mode and kernel-mode, where Windows NT exposes a "bottleneck" that all user-mode threads must pass through to be serviced by the operating system kernel.

Service and Argument Tables

As discussed in Chapter 2, the doorway through which all Native API calls originating in user-mode must pass is the `INT 2Eh` interface that provides an i386 interrupt gate for the privilege level change. You might recall as well that all `INT 2Eh` calls are handled in kernel-mode by the internal function `KiSystemService()`, which uses the system's Service Descriptor Table (SDT) to look up the entry points of the Native API handlers. In Figure 5-1, the interrelations of the basic components of this dispatching mechanism are outlined. The formal definitions of the `SERVICE_DESCRIPTOR_TABLE` structure and its subtypes from Chapter 2 (Listing 2-1) are repeated in Listing 5-1.

`KiSystemService()` is called with two arguments, passed in by the `INT 2Eh` caller in the CPU registers `EAX` and `EDX`. `EAX` contains a zero-based index into an array of API handler function pointers, and `EDX` points to the caller's argument stack. `KiSystemService()` retrieves the base address of the function array by reading the value of the `ServiceTable` member of a public `ntoskrnl.exe` data structure named `KeServiceDescriptorTable`, shown on the left-hand side of Figure 5-1. Actually, `KeServiceDescriptorTable` points to an array of four service table parameter structures, but only the first one contains valid entries by default. `KiSystemService()` looks up the address of the function that should handle the API call by using `EAX` as an index into the internal `KiServiceTable` structure. Before calling the target function, `KiSystemService()` queries the `KiArgumentTable` structure in much the same way to find out how many bytes were passed in by the caller on the argument stack, and uses this value to copy the arguments to the current kernel-mode stack. After that, a simple assembly language `CALL` instruction is required to invoke the API handler. Everything is then set up as a normal `__stdcall` C function would expect.

Windows 2000 provides another service descriptor table parameter block named `KeServiceDescriptorTableShadow`. Whereas `KeServiceDescriptorTable` is publicly exported by `ntoskrnl.exe` so kernel-mode drivers can readily access it, `KeServiceDescriptorTableShadow` is not. On Windows 2000, `KeServiceDescriptorTableShadow` follows immediately after `KeServiceDescriptorTable`, but you should not count on that—this rule does not hold on Windows NT 4.0, and it is possible that it won't hold on future updates of Windows 2000. The difference between both parameter blocks is that in `KeServiceDescriptorTableShadow` the second slot

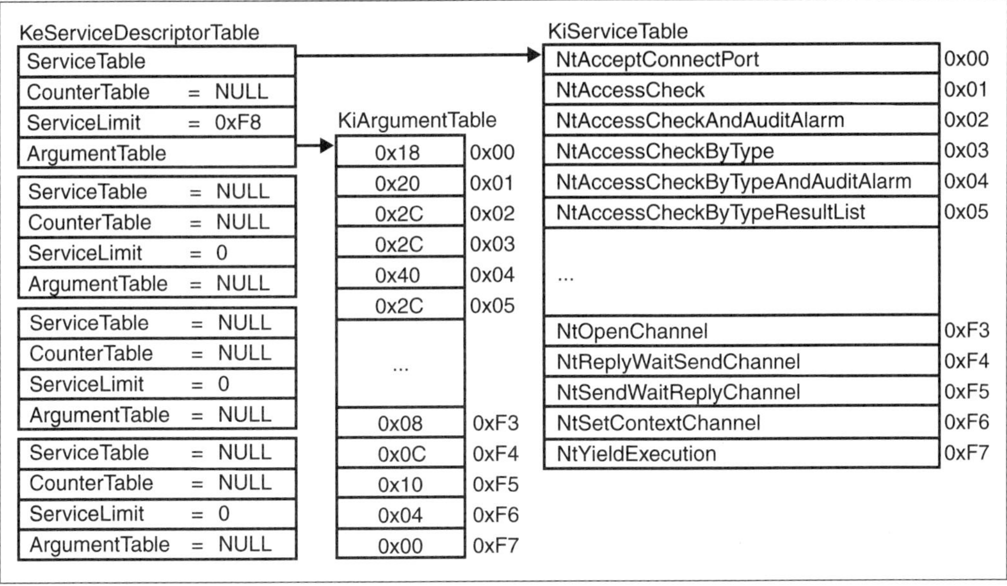

FIGURE 5-1. *Structure of the* `KeServiceDescriptorTable`

```
typedef NTSTATUS (NTAPI *NTPROC) ();
typedef NTPROC *PNTPROC;
#define NTPROC_ sizeof (NTPROC)

// ----------------------------------------------------------------

typedef struct _SYSTEM_SERVICE_TABLE
    {
    PNTPROC ServiceTable;          // array of entry points
    PDWORD  CounterTable;          // array of usage counters
    DWORD   ServiceLimit;          // number of table entries
    PBYTE   ArgumentTable;         // array of byte counts
    }
        SYSTEM_SERVICE_TABLE,
     * PSYSTEM_SERVICE_TABLE,
    **PPSYSTEM_SERVICE_TABLE;

// ----------------------------------------------------------------

typedef struct _SERVICE_DESCRIPTOR_TABLE
    {
    SYSTEM_SERVICE_TABLE ntoskrnl;  // ntoskrnl.exe (native api)
```

(continued)

```
    SYSTEM_SERVICE_TABLE win32k;      // win32k.sys (gdi/user support)
    SYSTEM_SERVICE_TABLE Table3;      // not used
    SYSTEM_SERVICE_TABLE Table4;      // not used
    }
        SERVICE_DESCRIPTOR_TABLE,
      * PSERVICE_DESCRIPTOR_TABLE,
    **PPSERVICE_DESCRIPTOR_TABLE;
```

LISTING 5-1. *Definition of the* `SERVICE_DESCRIPTOR_TABLE` *Structure*

is used by the system, too. It contains references to the internal `w32pServiceTable` and `w32pArgumentTable` structures that are used by the Win32 kernel-mode component `win32k.sys` to dispatch its own API calls, as shown in Figure 5-2. `KiSystemService()` knows that it is handling a `win32k.sys` API call by examining bits #12 and 13 of the function index in register `EAX`. If both bits are zero, it is a Native API call handled by `ntoskrnl.exe`, so `KiSystemService()` uses the first SDT slot. If bit #12 is set and bit #13 is zero, `KiSystemService()` uses the second slot. The remaining two bit combinations are assigned to the last pair of slots, which are currently not used by the system. This means that the index numbers of Native API calls potentially range from `0x0000` to `0x0FFF`, and `win32k.sys` calls involve index numbers in the range `0x1000` to `0x1FFF`. Consequently, the ranges `0x2000` to `0x2FFF` and `0x3000` to `0x3FFF` are assigned to the reserved tables. On Windows 2000, the Native API service table contains 248 entries and the `win32k.sys` table contains 639 entries.

The ingenious idea of Russinovich and Cogswell was to hook API calls by simply putting a different handler into the `KiServiceTable` array. This handler would ultimately call the original handler inside `ntoskrnl.exe`, but it had the opportunity to take a peek at the input and output parameters of the called function. This approach is extremely powerful but also very simple. Because all user-mode threads have to pass through this needle's eye in order to get their Native API requests serviced, a simple exchange of function pointers installs a global hook that continues to work reliably even after new processes and threads have been started. There is no need for a notification mechanism that signals the addition or removal of processes and threads.

Unfortunately, the system service pointer tables are subject to nontrivial changes across Windows NT versions. Table 5-1 compares the `KiServiceTable` entries of Windows 2000 and Windows NT 4.0. It is obvious that not only has the number of handlers been increased from 211 to 248 but the new handlers haven't been appended to the end of the list. They were inserted somewhere in between! Thus, a service function index of, say, `0x20` refers to `NtCreateFile()` on Windows 2000 but is associated with `NtCreateProfile()` on Windows NT 4.0. Consequently,

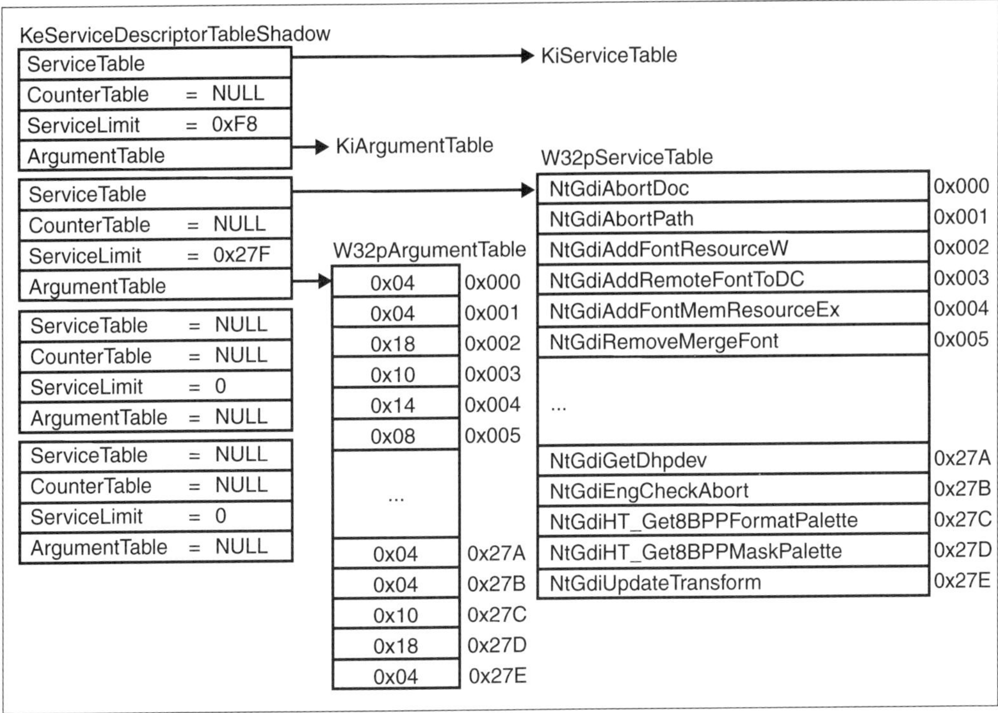

FIGURE 5-2. *Structure of* `KeServiceDescriptorTableShadow`

an API call monitor that installs a hook by manipulating the entries in the service function table must carefully check the Windows NT version it is running on. This can be done in several ways:

- One possibility is to check the public `NtBuildNumber` variable exported by `ntoskrnl.exe`, as Russinovich and Cogswell did in their original article (Russinovich and Cogswell 1997). Windows NT 4.0 exposes a build number of 1,381 for all service packs. The build number of Windows 2000 is currently 2,195. Hopefully, this number will remain as stable as it did in the previous Windows NT versions.
- Another possibility is to check the `NtMajorVersion` and `NtMinorVersion` members of the `SharedUserData` structure defined in the Windows 2000 header file `ntddk.h`. All Windows NT 4.0 service packs set `SharedUserData->NtMajorVersion` to four and `SharedUserData->NtMinorVersion` to zero. Windows 2000 currently indicates a Windows NT version of 5.0.

- The code presented in this chapter uses yet another alternative—it tests whether the `ServiceLimit` member of the SDT entry matches its expectations, which is 211 (`0xD3`) for Windows NT 4.0 and 248 (`0xF8`) for Windows 2000.

TABLE 5-1. *Windows 2000 and NT 4.0 Service Table Comparison*

WINDOWS 2000	INDEX	WINDOWS NT 4.0
NtAcceptConnectPort	0x00	NtAcceptConnectPort
NtAccessCheck	0x01	NtAccessCheck
NtAccessCheckAndAuditAlarm	0x02	NtAccessCheckAndAuditAlarm
NtAccessCheckByType	0x03	NtAddAtom
NtAccessCheckByTypeAndAuditAlarm	0x04	NtAdjustGroupsToken
NtAccessCheckByTypeResultList	0x05	NtAdjustPrivilegesToken
NtAccessCheckByTypeResultListAndAuditAlarm	0x06	NtAlertResumeThread
NtAccessCheckByTypeResultListAndAuditAlarmByHandle	0x07	NtAlertThread
NtAddAtom	0x08	NtAllocateLocallyUniqueId
NtAdjustGroupsToken	0x09	NtAllocateUuids
NtAdjustPrivilegesToken	0x0A	NtAllocateVirtualMemory
NtAlertResumeThread	0x0B	NtCallbackReturn
NtAlertThread	0x0C	NtCancelIoFile
NtAllocateLocallyUniqueId	0x0D	NtCancelTimer
NtAllocateUserPhysicalPages	0x0E	NtClearEvent
NtAllocateUuids	0x0F	NtClose
NtAllocateVirtualMemory	0x10	NtCloseObjectAuditAlarm
NtAreMappedFilesTheSame	0x11	NtCompleteConnectPort
NtAssignProcessToJobObject	0x12	NtConnectPort
NtCallbackReturn	0x13	NtContinue
NtCancelIoFile	0x14	NtCreateDirectoryObject
NtCancelTimer	0x15	NtCreateEvent
NtCancelDeviceWakeupRequest	0x16	NtCreateEventPair
NtClearEvent	0x17	NtCreateFile
NtClose	0x18	NtCreateIoCompletion
NtCloseObjectAuditAlarm	0x19	NtCreateKey
NtCompleteConnectPort	0x1A	NtCreateMailslotFile
NtConnectPort	0x1B	NtCreateMutant
NtContinue	0x1C	NtCreateNamedPipeFile
NtCreateDirectoryObject	0x1D	NtCreatePagingFile
NtCreateEvent	0x1E	NtCreatePort
NtCreateEventPair	0x1F	NtCreateProcess
NtCreateFile	0x20	NtCreateProfile
NtCreateIoCompletion	0x21	NtCreateSection

TABLE 5-1. *(continued)*

WINDOWS 2000	INDEX	WINDOWS NT 4.0
NtCreateJobObject	0x22	NtCreateSemaphore
NtCreateKey	0x23	NtCreateSymbolicLinkObject
NtCreateMailslotFile	0x24	NtCreateThread
NtCreateMutant	0x25	NtCreateTimer
NtCreateNamedPipeFile	0x26	NtCreateToken
NtCreatePagingFile	0x27	NtDelayExecution
NtCreatePort	0x28	NtDeleteAtom
NtCreateProcess	0x29	NtDeleteFile
NtCreateProfile	0x2A	NtDeleteKey
NtCreateSection	0x2B	NtDeleteObjectAuditAlarm
NtCreateSemaphore	0x2C	NtDeleteValueKey
NtCreateSymbolicLinkObject	0x2D	NtDeviceIoControlFile
NtCreateThread	0x2E	NtDisplayString
NtCreateTimer	0x2F	NtDuplicateObject
NtCreateToken	0x30	NtDuplicateToken
NtCreateWaitablePort	0x31	NtEnumerateKey
NtDelayExecution	0x32	NtEnumerateValueKey
NtDeleteAtom	0x33	NtExtendSection
NtDeleteFile	0x34	NtFindAtom
NtDeleteKey	0x35	NtFlushBuffersFile
NtDeleteObjectAuditAlarm	0x36	NtFlushInstructionCache
NtDeleteValueKey	0x37	NtFlushKey
NtDeviceIoControlFile	0x38	NtFlushVirtualMemory
NtDisplayString	0x39	NtFlushWriteBuffer
NtDuplicateObject	0x3A	NtFreeVirtualMemory
NtDuplicateToken	0x3B	NtFsControlFile
NtEnumerateKey	0x3C	NtGetContextThread
NtEnumerateValueKey	0x3D	NtGetPlugPlayEvent
NtExtendSection	0x3E	NtGetTickCount
NtFilterToken	0x3F	NtImpersonateClientOfPort
NtFindAtom	0x40	NtImpersonateThread
NtFlushBuffersFile	0x41	NtInitializeRegistry
NtFlushInstructionCache	0x42	NtListenPort
NtFlushKey	0x43	NtLoadDriver
NtFlushVirtualMemory	0x44	NtLoadKey
NtFlushWriteBuffer	0x45	NtLoadKey2
NtFreeUserPhysicalPages	0x46	NtLockFile
NtFreeVirtualMemory	0x47	NtLockVirtualMemory
NtFsControlFile	0x48	NtMakeTemporaryObject

(continued)

TABLE 5-1. *(continued)*

WINDOWS 2000	INDEX	WINDOWS NT 4.0
NtGetContextThread	0x49	NtMapViewOfSection
NtGetDevicePowerState	0x4A	NtNotifyChangeDirectoryFile
NtGetPlugPlayEvent	0x4B	NtNotifyChangeKey
NtGetTickCount	0x4C	NtOpenDirectoryObject
NtGetWriteWatch	0x4D	NtOpenEvent
NtImpersonateAnonymousToken	0x4E	NtOpenEventPair
NtImpersonateClientOfPort	0x4F	NtOpenFile
NtImpersonateThread	0x50	NtOpenIoCompletion
NtInitializeRegistry	0x51	NtOpenKey
NtInitiatePowerAction	0x52	NtOpenMutant
NtIsSystemResumeAutomatic	0x53	NtOpenObjectAuditAlarm
NtListenPort	0x54	NtOpenProcess
NtLoadDriver	0x55	NtOpenProcessToken
NtLoadKey	0x56	NtOpenSection
NtLoadKey2	0x57	NtOpenSemaphore
NtLockFile	0x58	NtOpenSymbolicLinkObject
NtLockVirtualMemory	0x59	NtOpenThread
NtMakeTemporaryObject	0x5A	NtOpenThreadToken
NtMapUserPhysicalPages	0x5B	NtOpenTimer
NtMapUserPhysicalPagesScatter	0x5C	NtPlugPlayControl
NtMapViewOfSection	0x5D	NtPrivilegeCheck
NtNotifyChangeDirectoryFile	0x5E	NtPrivilegedServiceAuditAlarm
NtNotifyChangeKey	0x5F	NtPrivilegeObjectAuditAlarm
NtNotifyChangeMultipleKeys	0x60	NtProtectVirtualMemory
NtOpenDirectoryObject	0x61	NtPulseEvent
NtOpenEvent	0x62	NtQueryInformationAtom
NtOpenEventPair	0x63	NtQueryAttributesFile
NtOpenFile	0x64	NtQueryDefaultLocale
NtOpenIoCompletion	0x65	NtQueryDirectoryFile
NtOpenJobObject	0x66	NtQueryDirectoryObject
NtOpenKey	0x67	NtQueryEaFile
NtOpenMutant	0x68	NtQueryEvent
NtOpenObjectAuditAlarm	0x69	NtQueryFullAttributesFile
NtOpenProcess	0x6A	NtQueryInformationFile
NtOpenProcessToken	0x6B	NtQueryIoCompletion
NtOpenSection	0x6C	NtQueryInformationPort
NtOpenSemaphore	0x6D	NtQueryInformationProcess
NtOpenSymbolicLinkObject	0x6E	NtQueryInformationThread

TABLE 5-1. *(continued)*

WINDOWS 2000	INDEX	WINDOWS NT 4.0
NtOpenThread	0x6F	NtQueryInformationToken
NtOpenThreadToken	0x70	NtQueryIntervalProfile
NtOpenTimer	0x71	NtQueryKey
NtPlugPlayControl	0x72	NtQueryMultipleValueKey
NtPowerInformation	0x73	NtQueryMutant
NtPrivilegeCheck	0x74	NtQueryObject
NtPrivilegedServiceAuditAlarm	0x75	NtQueryOleDirectoryFile
NtPrivilegeObjectAuditAlarm	0x76	NtQueryPerformanceCounter
NtProtectVirtualMemory	0x77	NtQuerySection
NtPulseEvent	0x78	NtQuerySecurityObject
NtQueryInformationAtom	0x79	NtQuerySemaphore
NtQueryAttributesFile	0x7A	NtQuerySymbolicLinkObject
NtQueryDefaultLocale	0x7B	NtQuerySystemEnvironmentValue
NtQueryDefaultUILanguage	0x7C	NtQuerySystemInformation
NtQueryDirectoryFile	0x7D	NtQuerySystemTime
NtQueryDirectoryObject	0x7E	NtQueryTimer
NtQueryEaFile	0x7F	NtQueryTimerResolution
NtQueryEvent	0x80	NtQueryValueKey
NtQueryFullAttributesFile	0x81	NtQueryVirtualMemory
NtQueryInformationFile	0x82	NtQueryVolumeInformationFile
NtQueryInformationJobObject	0x83	NtQueueApcThread
NtQueryIoCompletion	0x84	NtRaiseException
NtQueryInformationPort	0x85	NtRaiseHardError
NtQueryInformationProcess	0x86	NtReadFile
NtQueryInformationThread	0x87	NtReadFileScatter
NtQueryInformationToken	0x88	NtReadRequestData
NtQueryInstallUILanguage	0x89	NtReadVirtualMemory
NtQueryIntervalProfile	0x8A	NtRegisterThreadTerminatePort
NtQueryKey	0x8B	NtReleaseMutant
NtQueryMultipleValueKey	0x8C	NtReleaseSemaphore
NtQueryMutant	0x8D	NtRemoveIoCompletion
NtQueryObject	0x8E	NtReplaceKey
NtQueryOpenSubKeys	0x8F	NtReplyPort
NtQueryPerformanceCounter	0x90	NtReplyWaitReceivePort
NtQueryQuotaInformationFile	0x91	NtReplyWaitReplyPort
NtQuerySection	0x92	NtRequestPort
NtQuerySecurityObject	0x93	NtRequestWaitReplyPort
NtQuerySemaphore	0x94	NtResetEvent

(continued)

TABLE 5-1. *(continued)*

WINDOWS 2000	INDEX	WINDOWS NT 4.0
NtQuerySymbolicLinkObject	0x95	NtRestoreKey
NtQuerySystemEnvironmentValue	0x96	NtResumeThread
NtQuerySystemInformation	0x97	NtSaveKey
NtQuerySystemTime	0x98	NtSetIoCompletion
NtQueryTimer	0x99	NtSetContextThread
NtQueryTimerResolution	0x9A	NtSetDefaultHardErrorPort
NtQueryValueKey	0x9B	NtSetDefaultLocale
NtQueryVirtualMemory	0x9C	NtSetEaFile
NtQueryVolumeInformationFile	0x9D	NtSetEvent
NtQueueApcThread	0x9E	NtSetHighEventPair
NtRaiseException	0x9F	NtSetHighWaitLowEventPair
NtRaiseHardError	0xA0	NtSetHighWaitLowThread
NtReadFile	0xA1	NtSetInformationFile
NtReadFileScatter	0xA2	NtSetInformationKey
NtReadRequestData	0xA3	NtSetInformationObject
NtReadVirtualMemory	0xA4	NtSetInformationProcess
NtRegisterThreadTerminatePort	0xA5	NtSetInformationThread
NtReleaseMutant	0xA6	NtSetInformationToken
NtReleaseSemaphore	0xA7	NtSetIntervalProfile
NtRemoveIoCompletion	0xA8	NtSetLdtEntries
NtReplaceKey	0xA9	NtSetLowEventPair
NtReplyPort	0xAA	NtSetLowWaitHighEventPair
NtReplyWaitReceivePort	0xAB	NtSetLowWaitHighThread
NtReplyWaitReceivePortEx	0xAC	NtSetSecurityObject
NtReplyWaitReplyPort	0xAD	NtSetSystemEnvironmentValue
NtRequestDeviceWakeup	0xAE	NtSetSystemInformation
NtRequestPort	0xAF	NtSetSystemPowerState
NtRequestWaitReplyPort	0xB0	NtSetSystemTime
NtRequestWakeupLatency	0xB1	NtSetTimer
NtResetEvent	0xB2	NtSetTimerResolution
NtResetWriteWatch	0xB3	NtSetValueKey
NtRestoreKey	0xB4	NtSetVolumeInformationFile
NtResumeThread	0xB5	NtShutdownSystem
NtSaveKey	0xB6	NtSignalAndWaitForSingleObject
NtSaveMergedKeys	0xB7	NtStartProfile
NtSecureConnectPort	0xB8	NtStopProfile
NtSetIoCompletion	0xB9	NtSuspendThread
NtSetContextThread	0xBA	NtSystemDebugControl
NtSetDefaultHardErrorPort	0xBB	NtTerminateProcess

TABLE 5-1. *(continued)*

WINDOWS 2000	INDEX	WINDOWS NT 4.0
NtSetDefaultLocale	0xBC	NtTerminateThread
NtSetDefaultUILanguage	0xBD	NtTestAlert
NtSetEaFile	0xBE	NtUnloadDriver
NtSetEvent	0xBF	NtUnloadKey
NtSetHighEventPair	0xC0	NtUnlockFile
NtSetHighWaitLowEventPair	0xC1	NtUnlockVirtualMemory
NtSetInformationFile	0xC2	NtUnmapViewOfSection
NtSetInformationJobObject	0xC3	NtVdmControl
NtSetInformationKey	0xC4	NtWaitForMultipleObjects
NtSetInformationObject	0xC5	NtWaitForSingleObject
NtSetInformationProcess	0xC6	NtWaitHighEventPair
NtSetInformationThread	0xC7	NtWaitLowEventPair
NtSetInformationToken	0xC8	NtWriteFile
NtSetIntervalProfile	0xC9	NtWriteFileGather
NtSetLdtEntries	0xCA	NtWriteRequestData
NtSetLowEventPair	0xCB	NtWriteVirtualMemory
NtSetLowWaitHighEventPair	0xCC	NtCreateChannel
NtSetQuotaInformationFile	0xCD	NtListenChannel
NtSetSecurityObject	0xCE	NtOpenChannel
NtSetSystemEnvironmentValue	0xCF	NtReplyWaitSendChannel
NtSetSystemInformation	0xD0	NtSendWaitReplyChannel
NtSetSystemPowerState	0xD1	NtSetContextChannel
NtSetSystemTime	0xD2	NtYieldExecution
NtSetThreadExecutionState	0xD3	N/A
NtSetTimer	0xD4	N/A
NtSetTimerResolution	0xD5	N/A
NtSetUuidSeed	0xD6	N/A
NtSetValueKey	0xD7	N/A
NtSetVolumeInformationFile	0xD8	N/A
NtShutdownSystem	0xD9	N/A
NtSignalAndWaitForSingleObject	0xDA	N/A
NtStartProfile	0xDB	N/A
NtStopProfile	0xDC	N/A
NtSuspendThread	0xDD	N/A
NtSystemDebugControl	0xDE	N/A
NtTerminateJobObject	0xDF	N/A
NtTerminateProcess	0xE0	N/A
NtTerminateThread	0xE1	N/A
NtTestAlert	0xE2	N/A

(continued)

TABLE 5-1. *(continued)*

WINDOWS 2000	INDEX	WINDOWS NT 4.0
NtUnloadDriver	0xE3	N/A
NtUnloadKey	0xE4	N/A
NtUnlockFile	0xE5	N/A
NtUnlockVirtualMemory	0xE6	N/A
NtUnmapViewOfSection	0xE7	N/A
NtVdmControl	0xE8	N/A
NtWaitForMultipleObjects	0xE9	N/A
NtWaitForSingleObject	0xEA	N/A
NtWaitHighEventPair	0xEB	N/A
NtWaitLowEventPair	0xEC	N/A
NtWriteFile	0xED	N/A
NtWriteFileGather	0xEE	N/A
NtWriteRequestData	0xEF	N/A
NtWriteVirtualMemory	0xF0	N/A
NtCreateChannel	0xF1	N/A
NtListenChannel	0xF2	N/A
NtOpenChannel	0xF3	N/A
NtReplyWaitSendChannel	0xF4	N/A
NtSendWaitReplyChannel	0xF5	N/A
NtSetContextChannel	0xF6	N/A
NtYieldExecution	0xF7	N/A

The most important step taken by Russinovich and Cogswell was to write a kernel-mode device driver that installs and maintains the Native API hooks, because user-mode modules do not have the appropriate privileges to modify the system at this low system level. Like the spy driver in Chapter 4, this is a somewhat unusual driver, because it does not perform the usual I/O request processing. It just exposes a simple Device I/O Control (IOCTL) interface to give user-mode code access to the data it collects. The main task of this driver is to manipulate the `KiServiceTable` and intercept and log selected calls to the Windows 2000 Native API. Although this method is simple and elegant, it is also somewhat alarming. Its simplicity reminds me of the old DOS days when hooking a system service was as simple as modifying a pointer in the processor's interrupt vector table. Anyone who knows how to write a basic Windows 2000 kernel-mode driver can hook any NT system service without much effort.

Russinovich and Cogswell used their technique to develop a very useful Windows NT registry monitor. While adapting their code for other spying tasks, I quickly became annoyed by the requirement of writing an individual hook function for each API function on which I wanted to spy. To avoid having to write extensive stereotypic code, I wanted to find a way to force all API functions I was interested in through a single hook function. This turned out to be a task that took considerable time and showed me all possible variants of Blue Screens. However, this resulted in a general-purpose solution that enabled me to vary the set of hooked API functions with minimum effort.

Assembly Language to the Rescue

The main obstacle to a general-purpose solution was the typical parameter passing mechanism of the C language. As you may know, C usually passes function arguments on the CPU stack before calling the function's entry point. Depending on the number of arguments a function requires, the size of the argument stack varies considerably. The 248 Native API functions of Windows 2000 involve argument stack sizes between zero and 68 bytes. Given the diligent type checking of C, this makes writing a unique hook function a tough job. Microsoft Visual C/C++ comes with a versatile integrated assembly language (ASM) compiler that is capable of processing moderately complex code. Ironically, the advantage of ASM in this situation is exactly what is commonly regarded as one of its biggest drawbacks: ASM doesn't provide a strict type checking mechanism. As long as the number of bits is OK, you can store almost anything in any register and you can call any address without concern for what is currently on the stack. Although this is a dangerous feature in application programming, it comes in quite handy here: In ASM, it is easy to call a common entry point with different arguments on the stack, and this feature will be exploited in the API hook dispatcher introduced in a moment.

The Microsoft Visual C/C++ inline assembler is invoked by putting ASM code into delimited blocks tagged by the keyword `__asm`. It lacks the macro definition and evaluation capabilities of Microsoft's big Macro Assembler (MASM), but this doesn't severely restrict its usefulness. The best feature of the inline assembler is that it has access to all C variables and type definitions, so it is quite easy to mix C and ASM code. However, when ASM code is included in a C function, some important basic conventions of the C compiler must be obeyed to avoid interference with the compiled C code:

- The caller of a C function assumes that the CPU registers `EBP`, `EBX`, `ESI`, and `EDI` are preserved.
- If the ASM code is mixed with C code in a single function, be careful to preserve all intermediate values the C code might hold in registers. It is always a good idea to save and restore all registers used inside an `__asm` clause.
- 8-bit function results (`CHAR`, `BYTE`, etc.) are returned in register `AL`.
- 16-bit function results (`SHORT`, `WORD`, etc.) are returned in register `AX`.

- 32-bit function results (`INT, LONG, DWORD,` pointers, etc.) are returned in register `EAX`.
- 64-bit function results (`__int64, LONGLONG, DWORDLONG,` etc.) are returned in register pair `EDX:EAX`. Register `EAX` contains bits #0 to 31, and `EDX` holds bits #32 to 63.
- Functions with a fixed number of arguments usually pass arguments according to the `__stdcall` convention. From the caller's perspective, this means that the arguments must be pushed onto the stack in reverse order before the call, and the callee is responsible for removing them from the stack before returning. From the perspective of the called function, this means that the stack pointer `ESP` points to the caller's return address, followed by the arguments in their original order. The original order is retained because the stack grows downward, from high linear addresses to lower ones. Therefore, the argument pushed last by the caller (i.e., argument #1) appears as the first argument in the array pointed to by `ESP`.
- Some API functions with fixed arguments, most notably the C Runtime Library functions exported by `ntdll.dll` and `ntoskrnl.exe,` traditionally employ the `__cdecl` calling convention, which involves the same argument ordering as `__stdcall,` but forces the caller to clean up the argument stack.
- Functions with a variable number of arguments are always of the `__cdecl` type, because only the caller knows exactly how many arguments were passed to the callee. Therefore, the responsibility of removing the arguments from the stack is left to the caller.
- Functions declared with the `__fastcall` modifier expect the first two arguments in the CPU registers `ECX` and `EDX`. If more arguments are required, they are passed in on the stack in reverse order, and the callee cleans up the stack, as in the `__stdcall` scheme.
- Many C compilers build a stack frame for the function arguments immediately after entering the function, using the CPU's base pointer register `EBP`. This code, shown in Listing 5-2, is frequently referred to as a function's "prologue" and "epilogue." Some compilers use the more elegant i386 `ENTER` and `LEAVE` operations that integrate this `EBP/ESP` shuffling into single instructions (cf. Intel 1999b). After the prologue has

```
SomeFunction:
```

```
; this is the function's prologue
push    ebp                       ; save current value of ebp
mov     ebp, esp                  ; set stack frame base address
sub     esp, SizeOfLocalStorage ; create local storage area
...
; this is the function's epilogue
mov     esp, ebp                  ; destroy local storage area
pop     ebp                       ; restore value of ebp
ret
```

LISTING 5-2. *Stack frame, prologue, and epilogue*

been executed, the stack appears as shown in Figure 5-3. The value of the `EBP` register is the unique point of reference that splits the function's parameter stack into (1) the local storage area containing all local variables defined within the scope of the function and (2) the caller's argument stack, including the `EBP` backup slot and the return address. Note that the latest versions of Microsoft Visual C/C++ don't use stack frames by default. Instead, the code accesses the values on the stack through register `ESP`, specifying the offset of the variable relative to the current top of the stack. Code of this kind is extremely difficult to read, because each `PUSH` and `POP` instruction affects the `ESP` value and, consequently, all parameter offsets. Because `EBP` isn't required in this scenario, it is used as an additional general-purpose register.

- Be extremely careful when accessing C variables. One of the most frequent inline ASM bugs is that you are loading the address of a variable to a register instead of its value, and vice versa. In case of potential ambiguity, use the `ptr` and `offset` address operators. For example, the instruction `mov eax, dword ptr SomeVariable` loads the `DWORD`-type value of `SomeVariable` to register `EAX`, whereas `mov eax, offset SomeVariable` loads its linear address (i.e., a pointer to its value) to `EAX`.

THE HOOK DISPATCHER

The code that follows is extremely difficult. It took many hours to write, and produced an incredible number of Blue Screens in the process. My original approach involved a separate module, written in native ASM language and assembled with Microsoft's MASM. However, this design created problems on the linker level, so I changed to inline ASM inserted into the main C module. Instead of creating another kernel-mode driver, I decided to integrate the hook code into the spy device

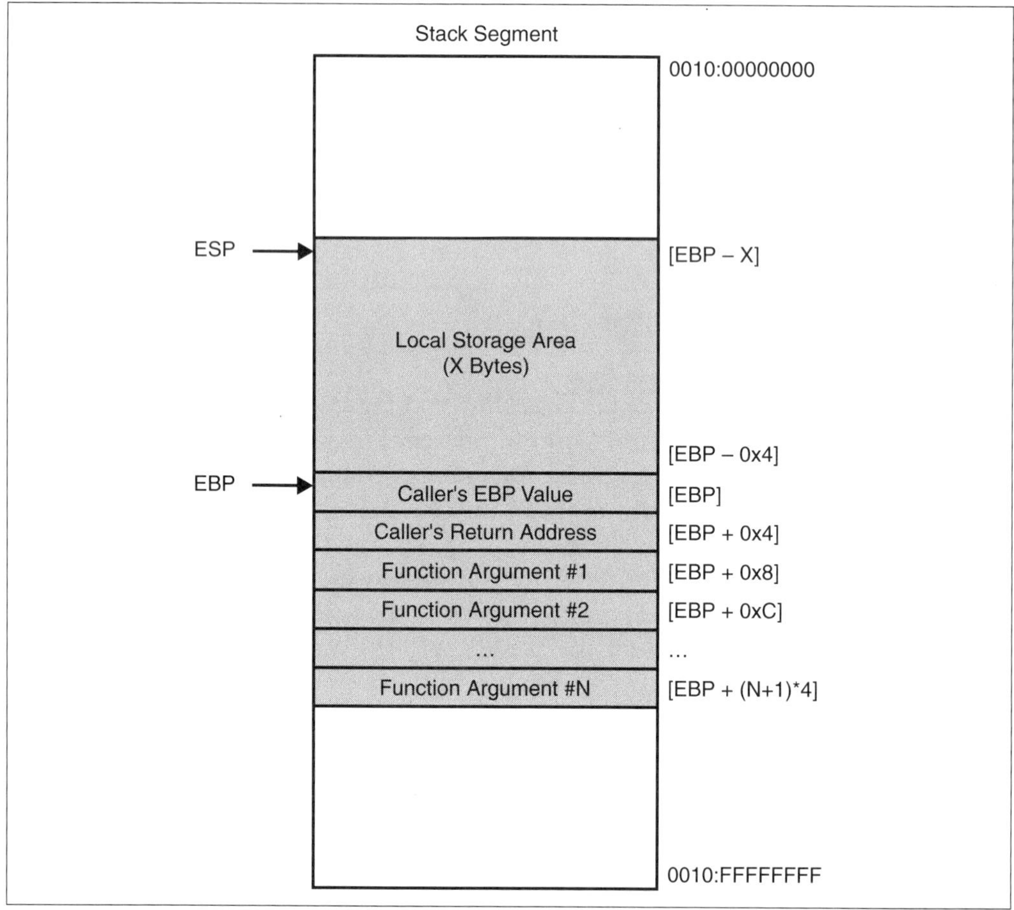

FIGURE 5-3. *Typical Layout of a Stack Frame*

introduced in Chapter 4. Remember the `SPY_IO_HOOK_*` IOCTL functions listed at the bottom of Table 4-2? Now is the time to take a closer look at them. The next section of sample code is taken from the source files `w2k_spy.c` and `w2k_spy.h`, found on the CD accompanying this book, in the `\src\w2k_spy` directory.

In Listing 5-3, the core parts of the Native API hook mechanism are shown. The listing starts with a couple of constant and structure definitions referenced by the code and is followed by the definition of the array `aSpyHooks[]`. Following this array is a macro that evaluates to three important lines of inline assembly language that will be investigated in a moment. The last part of Listing 5-3 is made up of the function `SpyHookInitializeEx()`. On first sight, it is difficult to grasp what this function is supposed to do. This function is a combination of two functions:

1. The "outer" part of `SpyHookInitializeEx()` consists of C code that simply populates the `aSpyHooks[]` array with pointers to the spy device's hook functions and their associated protocol format strings. This function is split in two sections. The first ends inside the first `__asm` clause at the `jmp SpyHook9` instruction. It is obvious that the second section must start at an ASM label named `SpyHook9`, which can be found near the end of the second `__asm` block.
2. The "inner" part of `SpyHookInitializeEx()` comprises everything between the two C sections of the code. It starts with an extensive repetition of `SpyHook` macro invocations and is followed by a large and complex ASM code section. As you may have guessed, this code is the common hook handler mentioned earlier.

```
#define SPY_CALLS            0x00000100 // max api call nesting level
#define SDT_SYMBOLS_NT4      0xD3
#define SDT_SYMBOLS_NT5      0xF8
#define SDT_SYMBOLS_MAX      SDT_SYMBOLS_NT5

// -------------------------------------------------------------------

typedef struct _SPY_HOOK_ENTRY
    {
    NTPROC Handler;
    PBYTE  pbFormat;
    }
    SPY_HOOK_ENTRY, *PSPY_HOOK_ENTRY, **PPSPY_HOOK_ENTRY;

#define SPY_HOOK_ENTRY_ sizeof (SPY_HOOK_ENTRY)

// -------------------------------------------------------------------

typedef struct _SPY_CALL
    {
    BOOL            fInUse;               // set if used entry
    HANDLE          hThread;              // id of calling thread
    PSPY_HOOK_ENTRY pshe;                 // associated hook entry
    PVOID           pCaller;              // caller's return address
    DWORD           dParameters;          // number of parameters
    DWORD           adParameters [1+256]; // result and parameters
    }
    SPY_CALL, *PSPY_CALL, **PPSPY_CALL;

#define SPY_CALL_ sizeof (SPY_CALL)

// -------------------------------------------------------------------
```

(continued)

```
SPY_HOOK_ENTRY aSpyHooks [SDT_SYMBOLS_MAX];

// -----------------------------------------------------------------

// The SpyHook macro defines a hook entry point in inline assembly
// language. The common entry point SpyHook2 is entered by a call
// instruction, allowing the hook to be identified by its return
// address on the stack. The call is executed through a register to
// remove any degrees of freedom from the encoding of the call.

#define SpyHook                              \
        __asm   push    eax                  \
        __asm   mov     eax, offset SpyHook2 \
        __asm   call    eax

// -----------------------------------------------------------------

// The SpyHookInitializeEx() function initializes the aSpyHooks[]
// array with the hook entry points and format strings. It also
// hosts the hook entry points and the hook dispatcher.

void SpyHookInitializeEx (PPBYTE ppbSymbols,
                          PPBYTE ppbFormats)
    {
    DWORD dHooks1, dHooks2, i, j, n;

    __asm
        {
        jmp     SpyHook9
        ALIGN   8
SpyHook1:       ; start of hook entry point section
        }

// the number of entry points defined in this section
// must be equal to SDT_SYMBOLS_MAX (i.e. 0xF8)

SpyHook SpyHook SpyHook SpyHook SpyHook SpyHook SpyHook SpyHook //08
SpyHook SpyHook SpyHook SpyHook SpyHook SpyHook SpyHook SpyHook //10
SpyHook SpyHook SpyHook SpyHook SpyHook SpyHook SpyHook SpyHook //18
SpyHook SpyHook SpyHook SpyHook SpyHook SpyHook SpyHook SpyHook //20
SpyHook SpyHook SpyHook SpyHook SpyHook SpyHook SpyHook SpyHook //28
SpyHook SpyHook SpyHook SpyHook SpyHook SpyHook SpyHook SpyHook //30
SpyHook SpyHook SpyHook SpyHook SpyHook SpyHook SpyHook SpyHook //38
SpyHook SpyHook SpyHook SpyHook SpyHook SpyHook SpyHook SpyHook //40
SpyHook SpyHook SpyHook SpyHook SpyHook SpyHook SpyHook SpyHook //48
SpyHook SpyHook SpyHook SpyHook SpyHook SpyHook SpyHook SpyHook //50
SpyHook SpyHook SpyHook SpyHook SpyHook SpyHook SpyHook SpyHook //58
SpyHook SpyHook SpyHook SpyHook SpyHook SpyHook SpyHook SpyHook //60
SpyHook SpyHook SpyHook SpyHook SpyHook SpyHook SpyHook SpyHook //68
SpyHook SpyHook SpyHook SpyHook SpyHook SpyHook SpyHook SpyHook //70
SpyHook SpyHook SpyHook SpyHook SpyHook SpyHook SpyHook SpyHook //78
SpyHook SpyHook SpyHook SpyHook SpyHook SpyHook SpyHook SpyHook //80
SpyHook SpyHook SpyHook SpyHook SpyHook SpyHook SpyHook SpyHook //88
```

```
SpyHook SpyHook SpyHook SpyHook SpyHook SpyHook SpyHook SpyHook //90
SpyHook SpyHook SpyHook SpyHook SpyHook SpyHook SpyHook SpyHook //98
SpyHook SpyHook SpyHook SpyHook SpyHook SpyHook SpyHook SpyHook //A0
SpyHook SpyHook SpyHook SpyHook SpyHook SpyHook SpyHook SpyHook //A8
SpyHook SpyHook SpyHook SpyHook SpyHook SpyHook SpyHook SpyHook //B0
SpyHook SpyHook SpyHook SpyHook SpyHook SpyHook SpyHook SpyHook //B8
SpyHook SpyHook SpyHook SpyHook SpyHook SpyHook SpyHook SpyHook //C0
SpyHook SpyHook SpyHook SpyHook SpyHook SpyHook SpyHook SpyHook //C8
SpyHook SpyHook SpyHook SpyHook SpyHook SpyHook SpyHook SpyHook //D0
SpyHook SpyHook SpyHook SpyHook SpyHook SpyHook SpyHook SpyHook //D8
SpyHook SpyHook SpyHook SpyHook SpyHook SpyHook SpyHook SpyHook //E0
SpyHook SpyHook SpyHook SpyHook SpyHook SpyHook SpyHook SpyHook //E8
SpyHook SpyHook SpyHook SpyHook SpyHook SpyHook SpyHook SpyHook //F0
SpyHook SpyHook SpyHook SpyHook SpyHook SpyHook SpyHook SpyHook //F8

    __asm
        {
SpyHook2:       ; end of hook entry point section
        pop     eax                     ; get stub return address
        pushfd
        push    ebx
        push    ecx
        push    edx
        push    ebp
        push    esi
        push    edi
        sub     eax, offset SpyHook1    ; compute entry point index
        mov     ecx, SDT_SYMBOLS_MAX
        mul     ecx
        mov     ecx, offset SpyHook2
        sub     ecx, offset SpyHook1
        div     ecx
        dec     eax
        mov     ecx, gfSpyHookPause     ; test pause flag
        add     ecx, -1
        sbb     ecx, ecx
        not     ecx
        lea     edx, [aSpyHooks + eax * SIZE SPY_HOOK_ENTRY]
        test    ecx, [edx.pbFormat]     ; format string == NULL?
        jz      SpyHook5
        push    eax
        push    edx
        call    PsGetCurrentThreadId    ; get thread id
        mov     ebx, eax
        pop     edx
        pop     eax
        cmp     ebx, ghSpyHookThread    ; ignore hook installer
        jz      SpyHook5
        mov     edi, gpDeviceContext
        lea     edi, [edi.SpyCalls]     ; get call context array
        mov     esi, SPY_CALLS          ; get number of entries
```

(continued)

```
SpyHook3:
        mov     ecx, 1                  ; set in-use flag
        xchg    ecx, [edi.fInUse]
        jecxz   SpyHook4                ; unused entry found
        add     edi, SIZE SPY_CALL      ; try next entry
        dec     esi
        jnz     SpyHook3
        mov     edi, gpDeviceContext
        inc     [edi.dMisses]           ; count misses
        jmp     SpyHook5                ; array overflow
SpyHook4:
        mov     esi, gpDeviceContext
        inc     [esi.dLevel]            ; set nesting level
        mov     [edi.hThread], ebx      ; save thread id
        mov     [edi.pshe], edx         ; save PSPY_HOOK_ENTRY
        mov     ecx, offset SpyHook6    ; set new return address
        xchg    ecx, [esp+20h]
        mov     [edi.pCaller], ecx      ; save old return address
        mov     ecx, KeServiceDescriptorTable
        mov     ecx, [ecx].ntoskrnl.ArgumentTable
        movzx   ecx, byte ptr [ecx+eax] ; get argument stack size
        shr     ecx, 2
        inc     ecx                     ; add 1 for result slot
        mov     [edi.dParameters], ecx  ; save number of parameters
        lea     edi, [edi.adParameters]
        xor     eax, eax                ; initialize result slot
        stosd
        dec     ecx
        jz      SpyHook5                ; no arguments
        lea     esi, [esp+24h]          ; save argument stack
        rep     movsd
SpyHook5:
        mov     eax, [edx.Handler]      ; get original handler
        pop     edi
        pop     esi
        pop     ebp
        pop     edx
        pop     ecx
        pop     ebx
        popfd
        xchg    eax, [esp]              ; restore eax and...
        ret                             ; ...jump to handler
SpyHook6:
        push    eax
        pushfd
        push    ebx
        push    ecx
        push    edx
        push    ebp
        push    esi
        push    edi
        push    eax
```

```
        call    PsGetCurrentThreadId    ; get thread id
        mov     ebx, eax
        pop     eax
        mov     edi, gpDeviceContext
        lea     edi, [edi.SpyCalls]     ; get call context array
        mov     esi, SPY_CALLS          ; get number of entries
SpyHook7:
        cmp     ebx, [edi.hThread]      ; find matching thread id
        jz      SpyHook8
        add     edi, SIZE SPY_CALL      ; try next entry
        dec     esi
        jnz     SpyHook7
        push    ebx                     ; entry not found ?!?
        call    KeBugCheck
SpyHook8:
        push    edi                     ; save SPY_CALL pointer
        mov     [edi.adParameters], eax ; store NTSTATUS
        push    edi
        call    SpyHookProtocol
        pop     edi                     ; restore SPY_CALL pointer
        mov     eax, [edi.pCaller]
        mov     [edi.hThread], 0        ; clear thread id
        mov     esi, gpDeviceContext
        dec     [esi.dLevel]            ; reset nesting level
        dec     [edi.fInUse]            ; clear in-use flag
        pop     edi
        pop     esi
        pop     ebp
        pop     edx
        pop     ecx
        pop     ebx
        popfd
        xchg    eax, [esp]              ; restore eax and...
        ret                             ; ...return to caller
SpyHook9:
        mov     dHooks1, offset SpyHook1
        mov     dHooks2, offset SpyHook2
        }
    n = (dHooks2 - dHooks1) / SDT_SYMBOLS_MAX;

    for (i = j = 0; i < SDT_SYMBOLS_MAX; i++, dHooks1 += n)
        {
        if ((ppbSymbols     != NULL) && (ppbFormats != NULL) &&
            (ppbSymbols [j] != NULL))
            {
            aSpyHooks [i].Handler  = (NTPROC) dHooks1;
            aSpyHooks [i].pbFormat =
                SpySearchFormat (ppbSymbols [j++], ppbFormats);
            }
        else
            {
```

(continued)

```
            aSpyHooks [i].Handler  = NULL;
            aSpyHooks [i].pbFormat = NULL;
            }
        }
    return;
    }
```

LISTING 5-3. *Implementation of the Hook Dispatcher*

So what is the `SpyHook` macro all about? Inside `SpyHookInitializeEx()`, this macro is repeated exactly 248 (`0xF8`) times, which matches the number of Windows 2000 Native API functions. At the top of Listing 5-3, this number is assigned to the constant `SDT_SYMBOLS_MAX`, which is the maximum of `SDT_SYMBOLS_NT4` and `SDT_SYMBOLS_NT5`. Yes, that's right—I am going to support Windows NT 4.0 as well! Back to the `SpyHook` macro: This sequence of invocations produces the ASM code shown in Listing 5-4. Each `SpyHook` entry produces three lines of code:

1. First, the current contents of the `EAX` register are saved on the stack.
2. Next, the linear address of the label `SpyHook2` is stored in `EAX`.
3. Finally, a `CALL` to the address in `EAX` is performed.

You might wonder what will happen when this `CALL` returns. Would the next group of `SpyHook` code lines be invoked? No—this `CALL` is not supposed to return, because the return address of this call is removed immediately from the stack after reaching the destination label `SpyHook2`, as the `POP EAX` instruction at the end of Listing 5-4 proves. This apparently senseless code is a trick of the old ASM programming days that has fallen into disuse in today's world of high-level object-oriented application development. This trick was applied by ASM gurus when they had to build an array of homogenous entry points to be dispatched to individual functions. Using almost identical code for all entry points guarantees equal spacing, so the index of the entry point used by a client could easily be calculated from the return address of the `CALL` instruction, the base address and total size of the array, and the number of entries, using a simple rule of three.

```
SpyHook1:
        push    eax
        mov     eax, offset SpyHook2
        call    eax
        push    eax
        mov     eax, offset SpyHook2
        call    eax
; 244 boring repetitions omitted
        push    eax
```

```
        mov     eax, offset SpyHook2
        call    eax
        push    eax
        mov     eax, offset SpyHook2
        call    eax
SpyHook2:
        pop     eax
```

LISTING 5-4. *Expansion of the SpyHook Macro Invocations*

For example, the return address of the first `CALL EAX` instruction in Listing 5-4 is the address of the second entry point. Generally, the return address of the `N`-th `CALL EAX` is equal to the address of entry `N+1`, except for the last one, which, of course, would return to `SpyHook2`. Thus, the zero-based array index of all entry points can be computed by the general formula in Figure 5-4. The underlying rule of three is as follows: `SDT_SYMBOLS_MAX` entry points fit into the memory block `SpyHook2–SpyHook1`. How many entry points fit into `ReturnAddress–SpyHook1`? Because the result of this computation is a number between one and `SDT_SYMBOLS_MAX`, it must be decremented by one to get the zero-based index.

The implementation of the formula in Figure 5-4 can be found in Listing 5-3, right after the ASM label `SpyHook2`. It is also included in the lower left corner of Figure 5-5, which presents the basic mechanics of the hook dispatch mechanism. Note that the i386 `MUL` instruction yields a 64-bit result in registers `EDX:EAX`, while the `DIV` instruction expects a 64-bit dividend in `EDX:EAX`, so there is no danger of an integer overflow. In the upper left corner, the `KiServiceTable` is depicted, which will be patched with the addresses of the entry points generated by the `SpyHook` macro. The middle section shows again the expanded macro code from Listing 5-4. The linear addresses of the entry points are shown on the right-hand side. By pure coincidence, the size of each entry point is 8 bytes, so the address is computed by multiplying the `KiServiceTable` index of each function by 8 and adding it to the address of `SpyHook1`.

Actually, I was just kidding—it's *not* pure coincidence that each entry is 8 bytes long. In reality, I spent a considerable amount of time figuring out the ideal implementation of the hook entries. Although not strictly necessary, aligning code on 32-bit boundaries is never a bad idea, because it speeds up performance. Of course, the performance gain is marginal here. You may wonder why I perform an indirect `CALL` to label `SpyHook2` through register `EAX`—wouldn't a simple middle-of-the-road `CALL SpyHook2` instruction have been much more efficient? Right! However, the problem with the i386 call (and jump) instructions is that they can be implemented in several ways that have the same effect but yield different instruction sizes. Just consult Intel's *Instruction Set Reference* of the Pentium CPU family (Intel 1999b).

$$\text{Index} = \frac{(\text{ReturnAddress} - \text{SpyHook1}) * \text{SDT\_SYMBOLS\_MAX}}{\text{SpyHook2} - \text{SpyHook1}} - 1$$

FIGURE 5-4. *Identifying Hook Entry Points by their Return Addresses*

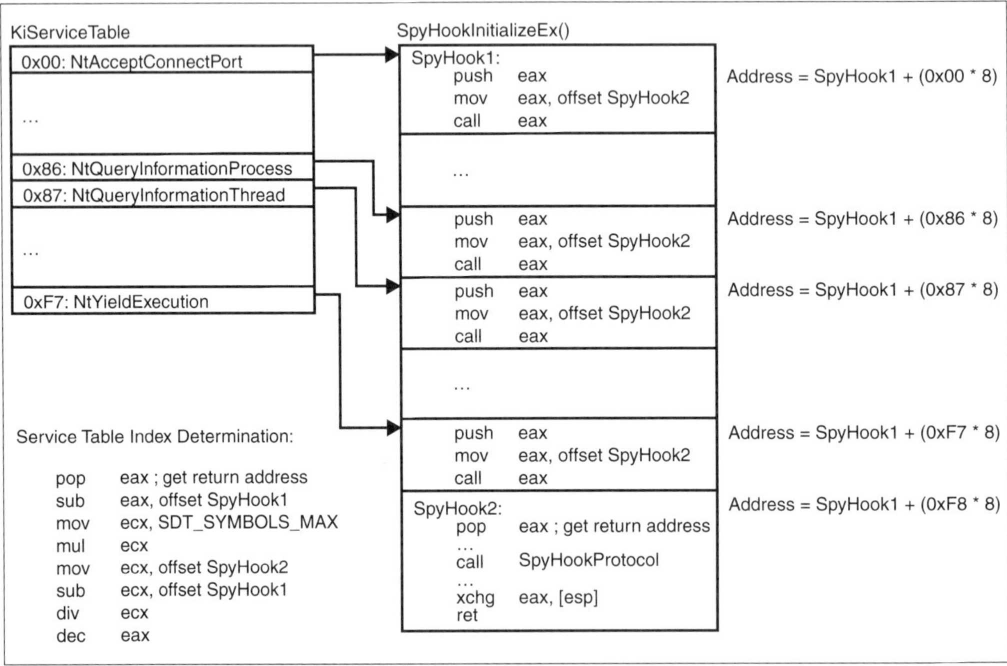

FIGURE 5-5. *Functional Principle of the Hook Dispatcher*

Because the choice of variant used is up to the compiler/assembler, there would be no guarantee that all entry points would end up in the same encoding. On the other hand, a `MOV EAX` with a constant 32-bit operand is always encoded in the same way, and so is the `CALL EAX` instruction.

Other points in Listing 5-3 should be clarified. Let's start with the final C code section starting after the label `SpyHook9`. The ASM code at this label has preset the C variables `dHook1` and `dHook2` with the linear addresses of the labels `SpyHook1` and `SpyHook2`. Next, the variable `n` is set to the size of each hook entry point by dividing the size of the entry point array by the number of entries. Of course, this will yield eight. The remaining part of Listing 5-3 is a loop that initializes all entries of the global `aSpyHooks[]` array. This array consists of `SPY_HOOK_ENTRY` structures defined in the top half of Listing 5-3, and each entry is associated with a Native API function. To understand how their `Handler` and `pbFormat` members are set up, it is necessary to know more about the arguments `ppbSymbols` and `ppbFormats` passed to `SpyHookInitializeEx()`. Listing 5-5 shows the wrapper function `SpyHookInitialize()` that calls `SpyHookInitializeEx()` with arguments appropriate for the operating system (OS) version currently running. As noted earlier, the code doesn't test the OS version or the build number directly, but rather compares the `ServiceLimit` member of the SDT entry assigned to `ntoskrnl.exe` with the constants `SDT_SYMBOLS_NT4` and `SDT_SYMBOLS_NT5`. If none of them matches, the spy device will initialize all `aSpyHooks[]` entries with `NULL` pointers, effectively disabling the entire Native API hook mechanism.

```
BOOL SpyHookInitialize (void)
    {
    BOOL fOk = TRUE;

    switch (KeServiceDescriptorTable->ntoskrnl.ServiceLimit)
        {
        case SDT_SYMBOLS_NT4:
            {
            SpyHookInitializeEx (apbSdtSymbolsNT4, apbSdtFormats);
            break;
            }
        case SDT_SYMBOLS_NT5:
            {
            SpyHookInitializeEx (apbSdtSymbolsNT5, apbSdtFormats);
            break;
            }
        default:
            {
            SpyHookInitializeEx (NULL, NULL);
            fOk = FALSE;
            break;
            }
        }
    return fOk;
    }
```

LISTING 5-5. SpyHookInitialize() *Chooses the Symbol Table Matching the OS Version*

The global arrays `apbSdtSymbolsNT4[]` and `apbSdtSymbolsNT5[]` passed into `SpyHookInitializeEx()` as first argument `ppbSymbols` are simply string tables that contain all Windows NT 4.0 and Windows 2000 Native API function names, sorted by their `KiServiceTable` index, and terminated by a `NULL` pointer. The string array `apbSdtFormats[]` is shown in Listing 5-6. This format string list is one of the most important parts of the hook mechanism because it determines which Native API calls are logged and the appearance of each log entry. Obviously, the structure of these strings is borrowed from the `printf()` function of the C Runtime Library but specifically tailored to the most frequently used argument types of the Native API. Table 5-2 is a complete list of format IDs recognized by the API logger.

```
PBYTE apbSdtFormats [] =
    {
    "%s=NtCancelIoFile(%!,%i)",
    "%s=NtClose(%-)",
    "%s=NtCreateFile(%+,%n,%o,%i,%l,%n,%n,%n,%n,%p,%n)",
    "%s=NtCreateKey(%+,%n,%o,%n,%u,%n,%d)",
    "%s=NtDeleteFile(%o)",
    "%s=NtDeleteKey(%-)",
    "%s=NtDeleteValueKey(%!,%u)",
    "%s=NtDeviceIoControlFile(%!,%p,%p,%p,%i,%n,%p,%n,%p,%n)",
    "%s=NtEnumerateKey(%!,%n,%n,%p,%n,%d)",
    "%s=NtEnumerateValueKey(%!,%n,%n,%p,%n,%d)",
    "%s=NtFlushBuffersFile(%!,%i)",
    "%s=NtFlushKey(%!)",
    "%s=NtFsControlFile(%!,%p,%p,%p,%i,%n,%p,%n,%p,%n)",
    "%s=NtLoadKey(%o,%o)",
    "%s=NtLoadKey2(%o,%o,%n)",
    "%s=NtNotifyChangeKey(%!,%p,%p,%p,%i,%n,%b,%p,%n,%b)",
    "%s=NtNotifyChangeMultipleKeys(%!,%n,%o,%p,%p,%p,%i,%n,%b,%p,%n,%b)",
    "%s=NtOpenFile(%+,%n,%o,%i,%n,%n)",
    "%s=NtOpenKey(%+,%n,%o)",
    "%s=NtOpenProcess(%+,%n,%o,%c)",
    "%s=NtOpenThread(%+,%n,%o,%c)",
    "%s=NtQueryDirectoryFile(%!,%p,%p,%p,%i,%p,%n,%n,%b,%u,%b)",
    "%s=NtQueryInformationFile(%!,%i,%p,%n,%n)",
    "%s=NtQueryInformationProcess(%!,%n,%p,%n,%d)",
    "%s=NtQueryInformationThread(%!,%n,%p,%n,%d)",
    "%s=NtQueryKey(%!,%n,%p,%n,%d)",
    "%s=NtQueryMultipleValueKey(%!,%p,%n,%p,%d,%d)",
    "%s=NtQueryOpenSubKeys(%o,%d)",
    "%s=NtQuerySystemInformation(%n,%p,%n,%d)",
    "%s=NtQuerySystemTime(%l)",
    "%s=NtQueryValueKey(%!,%u,%n,%p,%n,%d)",
    "%s=NtQueryVolumeInformationFile(%!,%i,%p,%n,%n)",
    "%s=NtReadFile(%!,%p,%p,%p,%i,%p,%n,%l,%d)",
    "%s=NtReplaceKey(%o,%!,%o)",
    "%s=NtSetInformationKey(%!,%n,%p,%n)",
```

```
"%s=NtSetInformationFile(%!,%i,%p,%n,%n)",
"%s=NtSetInformationProcess(%!,%n,%p,%n)",
"%s=NtSetInformationThread(%!,%n,%p,%n)",
"%s=NtSetSystemInformation(%n,%p,%n)",
"%s=NtSetSystemTime(%l,%l)",
"%s=NtSetValueKey(%!,%u,%n,%n,%p,%n)",
"%s=NtSetVolumeInformationFile(%!,%i,%p,%n,%n)",
"%s=NtUnloadKey(%o)",
"%s=NtWriteFile(%!,%p,%p,%p,%i,%p,%n,%l,%d)",
NULL
};
```

LISTING 5-6. *Format Strings Used by the Native API Logger*

It's important to note that each format string must contain the function correctly spelled. `SpyHookInitializeEx()` walks though the list of Native API symbols it receives via its `ppbSymbols` argument and attempts to find a format string in the `ppbFormats` list that contains a matching function name. The comparison is performed by the helper function `SpySearchFormat()`, invoked in the `if` clause at the end of Listing 5-3. Because many string search operations must be performed for all `aSpyHooks[]` entries to be set up, I am using a highly optimized search engine based on the ingenious "Shift/And Search Algorithm." If you want to learn more about its implementation, please check out the `SpySearch*()` function group in the source file `\src\w2k_spy\w2k_spy.c` on the companion CD. As soon as `SpyHookInitializeEx()` exits the loop, all `Handler` members in the `aSpyHooks[]` array point to the appropriate hook entry points, and the `pbFormat` members provide the matching format string, if any. With Windows NT 4.0, both members of the entries in the index range `0xD3` to `0xF8` are set to `NULL`, because they are undefined for this version.

TABLE 5-2. *Recognized Format Control IDs*

ID	NAME	DESCRIPTION
%+	Handle (register)	Logs a handle and object name and adds them to the handle table
%!	Handle (retrieve)	Logs a handle and retrieves its object name from the handle table
%-	Handle (unregister)	Logs a handle and object name and removes them from the handle table
%a	ANSI string	Logs a string of 8-bit ANSI characters
%b	BOOLEAN	Logs an 8-bit BOOLEAN value
%c	CLIENT_ID *	Logs the members of a CLIENT_ID structure

(continued)

TABLE 5-2. *(continued)*

ID	NAME	DESCRIPTION
%d	DWORD *	Logs the value of the addressed DWORD
%i	IO_STATUS_BLOCK *	Logs the members of an IO_STATUS_BLOCK structure
%l	LARGE_INTEGER *	Logs the value of a LARGE_INTEGER structure
%n	Number (DWORD)	Logs the value of an unsigned 32-bit number
%o	OBJECT_ATTRIBUTES *	Logs the *ObjectName* of an object
%p	Pointer	Logs the target address of a pointer
%s	Status (NTSTATUS)	Logs a NT status code
%u	UNICODE_STRING *	Logs the *Buffer* member of an UNICODE_STRING structure
%w	Wide character string	Logs a string of 16-bit Unicode characters
%%	Percent escape	Logs a single '%' character

The most notable property of this hook mechanism design is that it is completely data driven. The hook dispatcher can be adapted to a new Windows 2000 release by simply adding a new API symbol table. Moreover, the logging of additional API functions can be enabled at any time by adding new format strings to the `apbSdtFormats[]` array. There is no need to write any additional code—the actions of the API spy are completely determined by a set of character strings! However, care must be taken while defining format strings. Never forget that `w2k_spy.sys` runs as a kernel-mode driver. On this system level, errors are not handled very gracefully. Giving an invalid argument to a Win32 API is not a problem—you will get an error window, and the application will be terminated. In kernel-mode, the tiniest access violation will cause a Blue Screen. So be careful—an improper or missing format control ID at the right place can easily tear down your system. Even a simple character string *sometimes* can be deadly!

The only thing left to discuss is the large ASM block inside `SpyHookInitializeEx()`, enclosed by the ASM labels `SpyHook2` and `SpyHook9`. One interesting property of this code is that it is never executed when `SpyHookInitializeEx()` is called. On entry, the function code simply jumps across this entire section and resumes execution at the label `SpyHook9`, shortly before the C section containing the `aSpyHooks[]` array initialization starts. This code can only be entered via the `Handler` members of this array. Later, I will show how these entry points are linked to the SDT.

One of my foremost aims in designing this code was to make it absolutely nonintrusive. Intercepting operating system calls is dangerous because you never know whether the called code relies on some unknown properties of the calling context. Theoretically, it should suffice to obey the `__stdcall` convention, but it is possible that problems may occur. I have chosen to put the original Native API function handler into almost exactly the same environment it would find if no hooks were present. This means that the function should run on the original argument stack and see all CPU registers as they are passed in by the caller. Of course, a minimal degree of intrusion must be accepted—otherwise, no monitoring would be possible. Here, the most significant intervention is the manipulation of the return address on the stack. If you flip back to Figure 5-3, you see that the caller's return address is on top of the argument stack on entry of the function. The hook dispatcher inside `SpyHookInitializeEx()` grabs this address and puts its own `SpyHook6` label address there. Thus, the original Native API function handler will branch to this location after terminating, enabling the hook dispatcher to inspect its arguments and returned values.

Before calling the original handler, the dispatcher sets up a `SPY_CALL` control block (see top section of Listing 5-3) containing parameters it needs later. Some of them are required for proper API call logging, whereas others provide information about the caller so the dispatcher can return control to it after writing the log entry, just as if nothing had happened. The spy device maintains an array of `SPY_CALL` structures in its global `DEVICE_CONTEXT` block, accessible via the global variable `gpDeviceContext` in `w2k_spy.c`. The hook dispatcher searches for a free `SPY_CALL` slot by examining their `fInUse` members. It uses the CPU's `XCHG` instruction to load and set this member in a single operation. This is very important because this code runs in a multithreaded environment, where read/write accesses to global data must be protected against race conditions. If a free slot is available, the dispatcher stores the caller's thread ID obtained from `PsGetCurrentThreadId()`, the address of the `SPY_HOOK_ ENTRY` associated with the current API function, the return address of the caller, and the entire argument stack. The number of argument bytes to be copied is taken from the `KiArgumentTable` array stored in the system's SDT. If all `SPY_CALL` entries are in use, the original API function handler is invoked without logging it.

The necessity of a `SPY_CALL` array comes again from the multithreading nature of Windows 2000. It happens quite frequently that a Native API function is suspended, and another thread gains control, invoking another Native API function during its time slice. This means that the spy device's hook dispatcher can be reentered at any time and at any execution point. If the hook dispatcher would have a single global `SPY_CALL` storage area, it would be overwritten by the running thread before the waiting thread has finished using it. This situation is an ideal candidate for a Blue Screen. To gain a better sense of the nesting level typically occurring within the Native API, I have added the `dLevel` and `dMisses` members to the spy's `DEVICE_CONTEXT` structure. Whenever the hook dispatcher is reentered (i.e., whenever a new `SPY_CALL` slot is occupied) `dLevel` is increased by one. If the maximum nesting level is exceeded (i.e., if no more `SPY_CALL` structures are available), `dMisses` is increased, indicating that a log entry is missing. My observations have shown that in practical situations, nesting levels of up to four are easily observable. It is possible that the Native API is reentered even more frequently in heavy-load situations, so I set the upper limit generously to 256.

Before invoking the original API handler, the hook dispatcher restores all CPU registers including the `EFLAGS`, and branches to the function's entry point. This is done immediately before the `SpyHook6` label in Listing 5-3. At this time, `SpyHook6` is on top of the stack, followed by the caller's arguments. As soon as the API handler exits, control is passed back to the hook dispatcher at the `SpyHook6` label. The code executed from there on is also designed to be as nonintrusive as possible. This time, the main objective is to allow the caller to see the call context almost exactly as it was set up by the original API function handler. The main problem of the dispatcher is now to find the `SPY_CALL` entry where it has stored the information about the current API call. The only reliable cue it has is the caller's thread ID, which has been saved to the `hThread` member of the `SPY_CALL` structure. Therefore, the dispatcher loops through the entire `SPY_CALL` array trying to find a matching thread ID. Note that the code is not concerned about the value of the `fInUse` flag; this is not necessary because all unused entries have `hThread` set to zero, which is the thread ID of the system idle thread. The loop should *always* terminate before the end of the array is reached. Otherwise, the dispatcher cannot return control to the caller, which is fatal. In this case, the code has few options, so it runs into a `KeBugCheck()` that results in a controlled system shutdown. This situation should never occur, but if it does, something terrible must have happened to the system, so the shutdown is probably the best solution.

If the matching `SPY_CALL` slot can be found, the hook dispatcher has almost finished its job. The last major action is the invocation of the logging function `SpyHookProtocol()`, passing in a pointer to the `SPY_CALL` structure. Everything the logger needs is stored there. After `SpyHookProtocol()` returns, the dispatcher frees its `SPY_CALL` slot, restores all CPU registers, and returns to the caller.

THE API HOOK PROTOCOL

A good API spy should look at the arguments *after* the original function has been called, because the function might return additional data in buffers passed in by reference. Therefore, the main logging function `SpyHookProtocol()` is called at the end of the hook handler, just before the API function returns to the caller. Before discussing secrets of its implementation, examine the following two sample protocols for a foretaste of what's to come. Figure 5-6 is a snapshot of the logged file operations performed in the context of the console command **dir c:**.

Please compare the log entries listed in Figure 5-6 with the protocol format strings contained in Listing 5-6. In Example 5-1, the format strings of `NtOpenFile()` and `NtClose()` are contrasted to the first and fourth protocol lines in Figure 5-6, respectively. The similarities are striking; for each format control ID preceded by a percent character (cf. Table 5-2), an associated parameter value entry is generated in the protocol. However, the protocol obviously contains some additional information that is not part of the format strings. I'll reveal the reason for this discrepancy in a moment.

The general format of a protocol entry is shown in Example 5-2. Each entry consists of a fixed number of fields with intermittent separators. The separators allow the entries to be easily parsed by a program. The fields are constructed on the basis of the following set of simple rules:

- All numeric quantities are stated in hexadecimal notation without leading zeros and without the usual leading "0x."
- Function arguments are separated by commas.
- String arguments are enclosed in double quotes.
- If a pointer argument is `NULL`, its value is omitted.
- The values of structure members are separated by dots.

```
18:s0=NtOpenFile(+46C.18,n100001,o"\??\C:\",i0.1,n3,n4021)1BFEE5AE05B6710,278,2
19:s0=NtQueryInformationFile(!46C.18="\??\C:\",i0.6,p12E21C,n210,n9)1BFEE5AE05B6710,278,2
1A:s0=NtQueryVolumeInformationFile(!46C.18="\??\C:\",i0.12,p1321C8,n21C,n5)1BFEE5AE05B6710,278,2
1B:s0=NtClose(-46C.18="\??\C:\")1BFEE5AE05B6710,278,1
1C:s0=NtOpenFile(+46C.18,n100001,o"\??\C:\",i0.1,n3,n4021)1BFEE5AE05B6710,278,2
1D:s0=NtQueryInformationFile(!46C.18="\??\C:\",i0.6,p12E664,n210,n9)1BFEE5AE05B6710,278,2
1E:s0=NtQueryVolumeInformationFile(!46C.18="\??\C:\",i0.26,p1321C8,n220,n1)1BFEE5AE05B6710,278,2
1F:s0=NtClose(-46C.18="\??\C:\")1BFEE5AE05B6710,278,1
20:s0=NtOpenFile(+46C.18,n100001,o"\??\c:\",i0.1,n3,n4021)1BFEE5AE05FFCA0,278,2
21:s0=NtQueryDirectoryFile(!46C.18="\??\c:\",p,p,p,i0.68,p12E994,n268,n3,bTRUE,u"*",bFALSE)1BFEE5AE05FFCA0,278,2
22:s0=NtQueryDirectoryFile(!46C.18="\??\c:\",p,p,p,i0.9FE,p139128,n1000,n3,bFALSE,u,bFALSE)1BFEE5AE05FFCA0,278,2
23:s80000006=NtQueryDirectoryFile(!46C.18="\??\c:\",p,p,p,i80000006.0,p139128,n1000,n3,bFALSE,u,bFALSE)1BFEE5AE0661960,278,2
24:s0=NtClose(-46C.18="\??\c:\")1BFEE5AE0661960,278,1
25:s0=NtOpenFile(+46C.18,n100001,o"\??\c:\",i0.1,n3,n800021)1BFEE5AE0661960,278,2
26:s0=NtQueryVolumeInformationFile(!46C.18="\??\c:\",i0.20,p12ED10,n20,n7)1BFEE5AE0661960,278,2
27:s0=NtClose(-46C.18="\??\c:\")1BFEE5AE0661960,278,1
```

FIGURE 5-6. *Sample Protocol of the Command* dir c:\

```
"%s=NtOpenFile(%+,%n,%o,%i,%n,%n)"
18:s0=NtOpenFile(+46C.18,n100001,o"\??\C:\",i0.1,n3,n4021)1BFEE5AE05B6710,278,2

"%s=NtClose(%-)"
1B:s0=NtClose(-46C.18="\??\C:\")1BFEE5AE05B6710,278,1
```

EXAMPLE 5-1. *Comparing Format Strings to Protocol Entries*

```
<#>:<status>=<function>(<arguments>)<time>,<thread>,<handles>
```

EXAMPLE 5-2. *General Protocol Entry Format*

- Object names associated with a handle are appended to the handle's value with a separating "=" character.
- The date/time stamp is specified in 1/10 microsecond since 01-01-1601—the basic system time format of Windows 2000.
- The thread ID indicates the unique numeric identifier of the thread that called the API function.
- The handle count states the number of handles currently registered in the spy device's handle list. This list allows the protocol function to look up the object names associated with handles.

Figure 5-7 is another API spy protocol resulting from the command **type c:\boot.ini** issued in a console window. The following is the semantic interpretation of some selected log entries:

- In line `0x31`, `NtCreateFile()` is called to open the file `\??\c:\boot.ini`. `(o"\??\c:\boot.ini")` The function returned an `NTSTATUS` code of zero `(s0)`, that is, `STATUS_SUCCESS`, and allocated a new file handle with value `0x18`, owned by process `0x46C` `(+46C.18)`. Consequently, the handle count rises from one to two.
- In line `0x36`, the **type** command reads in the first 512 bytes `(n200)` from file `\??\c:\boot.ini` to a buffer at the linear address `0x0012F5B4` `(p12F5B4)`, passing the handle obtained from `NtCreateFile()` `(!46C.18="\??\c:\boot.ini")` to `NtReadFile()`. The system successfully returns 512 bytes `(i0.200)`.

```
2D:s0=NtOpenFile(+46C.18,n100001,o"\??\c:\",i0.1,n3,n4021)1BFEE5B075EE890,278,2
2E:s0=NtQueryDirectoryFile(!46C.18="\??\c:\",p,p,p,i0.6E,p12F4DC,n268,n3,bTRUE,u"boot.ini",bFALSE)1BFEE5B075EE890,278,2
2F:s80000006=NtQueryDirectoryFile(!46C.18="\??\c:\",p,p,p,i80000006.0,p1389F0,n1000,n3,bFALSE,u,bFALSE)1BFEE5B07606FC0,278,2
30:s0=NtClose(-46C.18="\??\c:\")1BFEE5B07606FC0,278,1
31:s0=NtCreaterFile(+46C.18,n80100080,o"\??\c:\boot.ini",i0.1,l,n80,n3,n1n60,p,n0)1BFEE5B07606FC0,278,2
32:s0=NtQueryVolumeInformationFile(!46C.18="\??\c:\boot.ini",i0.8,p12E728,n8,n4)1BFEE5B07606FC0,278,2
33:s0=NtQueryVolumeInformationFile(!46C.18="\??\c:\boot.ini",i0.8,p12E778,n8,n4)1BFEE5B07606FC0,278,2
34:s0=NtQueryInformationFile(!46C.18="\??\c:\boot.ini",i0.18,p12E758,n18,n5)1BFEE5B07606FC0,278,2
35:s0=NtSetInformationFile(!46C.18="\??\c:\boot.ini",i0.0,p12E780,n8,nE)1BFEE5B07606FC0,278,2
36:s0=NtReadFile(!46C.18="\??\c:\boot.ini",p,p,p,i0.200,p12F5B4,n200,l,d)1BFEE5B07606FC0,278,2
37:s0=NtQueryInformationFile(!46C.18="\??\c:\boot.ini",i0.8,p12E780,n8,nE)1BREE5B07650550,278,2
38:s0=NtSetInformationFile(!46C.18="\??\c:\boot.ini",i0.0,p12E780,n8,nE)1BFEE5B07650550,278,2
39:s0=NtReadFile(!46C.18="\??\c:\boot.ini",p,p,p,i0.4B,p12F5B4,n200,l,d)1BFEE5B07650550,278,2
3A:s0=NtQueryInformationFile(!46C.18="\??\c:\boot.ini",i0.8,p12E780,n8,nE)1BFEE5B07650550,278,2
3B:s0=NtSetInformationFile(!46C.18="\??\c:\boot.ini",i0.0,p12E780,n8,nE)1BFEE5B07650550,278,2
3C:s0=NtClose(-46C.18="\??\c:\boot.ini")1BFEE5B07650550,278,1
```

FIGURE 5-7. *Sample Protocol of the Command* `type c:\boot.ini`

- In line `0x39`, another file block of 512 bytes is ordered `(n200)`. This time, however, the end of the file is reached, so `NtReadFile()` returns 75 bytes only `(i0.4B)`. Obviously, the size of my `boot.ini` file is 512 + 75 = 587 bytes, which is correct.
- In line `0x3C`, the file handle to `\??\c:\boot.ini` is successfully released by `NtClose() (-46C.18="\??\c:\boot.ini")`, so the handle count drops from two to one.

By now, you should have an idea of how the API spy protocol is structured, which will help you grasp the details of the protocol generation mechanism, to be discussed next. As already noted, the main API call logging function is called `SpyHookProtocol()`. This function, shown in Listing 5-7, uses the data in the `SPY_CALL` structure it receives from the hook dispatcher to write a protocol record for each API function call to a circular buffer. A spy device client can read this protocol via IOCTL calls. Each record is a text line terminated by a single line-feed character (`'\n'` in C notation). Access to the protocol buffer is serialized by means of the kernel mutex `KMUTEX kmProtocol`, located in the global `DEVICE_CONTEXT` structure of the spy device. The functions `SpyHookWait()` and `SpyHookRelease()` in Listing 5-7 acquire and release this mutex object. All accesses to the protocol buffer must be preceded by `SpyHookWait()` and followed `SpyHookRelease()`, as demonstrated by the `SpyHookProtocol()` function.

```
NTSTATUS SpyHookWait (void)
    {
    return MUTEX_WAIT (gpDeviceContext->kmProtocol);
    }

// ----------------------------------------------------------------

LONG SpyHookRelease (void)
    {
    return MUTEX_RELEASE (gpDeviceContext->kmProtocol);
    }

// ----------------------------------------------------------------

// <#>:<status>=<function>(<arguments>)<time>,<thread>,<handles>

void SpyHookProtocol (PSPY_CALL psc)
    {
    LARGE_INTEGER liTime;
    PSPY_PROTOCOL psp = &gpDeviceContext->SpyProtocol;

    KeQuerySystemTime (&liTime);

    SpyHookWait ();

    if (SpyWriteFilter (psp, psc->pshe->pbFormat,
                             psc->adParameters,
                             psc->dParameters))
        {
        SpyWriteNumber (psp, 0, ++(psp->sh.dCalls));   // <#>:
        SpyWriteChar   (psp, 0, ':');
                                                  // <status>=
        SpyWriteFormat (psp, psc->pshe->pbFormat, //  <function>
                             psc->adParameters);  //   (<arguments>)

        SpyWriteLarge  (psp, 0, &liTime);              // <time>,
        SpyWriteChar   (psp, 0, ',');

        SpyWriteNumber (psp, 0, (DWORD) psc->hThread); // <thread>,
        SpyWriteChar   (psp, 0, ',');

        SpyWriteNumber (psp, 0, psp->sh.dHandles);     // <handles>
        SpyWriteChar   (psp, 0, '\n');
        }
    SpyHookRelease ();
    return;
    }
```

LISTING 5-7. *The Main Hook Protocol Function* SpyHookProtocol()

If you compare the main body of `SpyHookProtocol()` in Listing 5-7 with the general protocol entry layout in Example 5-2, it is obvious which statement generates which entry field. It also becomes clear why the protocol strings in Listing 5-6 don't account for the entire entry data—some function-independent data are added by `SpyHookProtocol()` without the help of the format string. It's the `SpyWriteFormat()` call at the heart of `SpyHookProtocol()` that generates the `<status>=<function>(<arguments>)` part, based on the format string associated with the currently logged API function. Consult the source files `w2k_spy.c` and `w2k_spy.h` in directory `\src\w2k_spy` of the accompanying sample CD for more information about the implementation of the various `SpyWrite*()` functions inside the spy device driver.

Note that this code is somewhat critical. This code was written in 1997 for Windows NT 4.0, and it worked like a charm then. After porting the program to Windows 2000, occasional Blue Screens occurred when the hooks remained installed for a longer time interval. Worse yet, some special operations reliably produced an instant Blue Screen, for example, navigating to "My Computer" in the **File \ Open** dialog of my favorite text editor. Analyzing numerous crash dumps, I found that the crashes were the result of invalid non-`NULL` pointers passed to some API functions. As soon as the spy device attempted to follow one of these pointers in order to log the data it referenced, the system crashed. Typical candidates were pointers to `IO_STATUS_BLOCK` structures, and invalid string pointers inside `UNICODE_STRING` and `OBJECT_ATTRIBUTES` structures. I also found some `UNICODE_STRING`s with `Buffer` members that were not zero-terminated. Therefore, I emphasize again that you should not assume that all `UNICODE_STRING`s are zero-terminated. In case of doubt, the `Length` member always tells the number of valid bytes you can expect at the `Buffer` address.

To remedy this problem, I have added pointer validation to all logging functions that have to follow client pointers. To this end, I use the `SpyMemoryTestAddress()` function discussed in Chapter 4 that checks out whether a linear address points to a valid page-table entry (PTE). See Listings 4-22 and 4-24 for details. Another alternative possibility would have been the addition of Structured Exception Handling (SEH) clauses (`__try` / `__except`).

HANDLING HANDLES

It is important to note that `SpyHookProtocol()` logs an API function call only if the `SpyWriteFilter()` function in its `if` clause condition returns `TRUE`. This is a trick that helps to suppress garbage in the hook protocol. For example, moving the mouse across the screen triggers a distracting series of `NtReadFile()` calls. Another source of garbage has an interesting equivalent in physics: If you are measuring a physical effect in an experimental situation, the act of measurement itself interferes with the measured effect and leads to distortion of the results. This also can happen in API logging. Note that the `NtDeviceIoControlFile()` function is also included in the format string array in Listing 5-6. However, a client of the spy device uses device I/O control calls to read the API hook protocol. This means that the client will find its own `NtDeviceIoControlFile()` calls in the protocol data. Depending on the frequency of the IOCTL transactions, the desired data might easily get lost in self-made noise. The spy device works around this problem by remembering the ID of the thread that installed the API hooks to be able to ignore all API calls originating from this thread.

`SpyWriteFilter()` eliminates garbage by ignoring all API calls involving handles if the call that generated the handle has not been logged. If the spy device observes that a handle is closed or otherwise returned to the system, any subsequent functions using this handle value are discarded as well. Effectively, this trick suppresses all API calls that involve long-term handles created by the system or other processes before the start of the API hook protocol. Of course, filtering can be enabled or disabled on behalf of the client by means of IOCTL. You can easily test the usefulness of the filter mechanism with the sample client application introduced later in this chapter. You will be surprised how great this simple "noise filter" works!

In Listing 5-6, the functions that generate handles are `NtCreateFile()`, `NtCreateKey()`, `NtOpenFile()`, `NtOpenKey()`, `NtOpenProcess()`, and `NtOpenThread()`. All of these functions contain a `%+` control token in their format strings, which is identified as "Handle (register)" in Table 5-2. Functions that close or invalidate handles are `NtClose()` and `NtDeleteKey()`. Both include a `%-` token in their format strings, labeled "Handle (unregister)" in Table 5-2. Other functions that simply use a handle without creating or releasing it feature a `%!` format control ID. Basically, a handle is a number that uniquely identifies an object in the context of a process. Physically, it provides an index into a handle table that contains the properties of the associated object. When a new handle is issued by an API function, the client usually has to pass in an `OBJECT_ATTRIBUTES` structure that contains, among other things, the name of the object it wishes to access. Later, this name is no longer required because the system can look up all object properties it needs using the object handle and the handle table. This is unfortunate for the user of an API spy because it necessitates wading through countless protocol entries containing meaningless numbers instead of symbolic names. Therefore, my spy device registers all object names together with the respective handle values and the IDs of the owning processes, updating this list whenever a new handle appears. When one of the registered handle/process pairs reappears later, the API logger retrieves the original symbolic name from the list and adds it to the protocol.

A handle remains registered until it is explicitly closed by an API function or reappears in an API call that generates a new handle. With Windows 2000, I frequently observed that the same handle value is returned several times by the system, although the protocol doesn't contain any call that has closed this handle before. I don't remember having seen this with Windows NT 4.0. A registered handle that reappears with different object attributes has obviously been closed somehow, so it must be unregistered. Otherwise, the handle directory of the spy device eventually would run into an overflow situation.

The `SpyWriteFilter()` function called by `SpyHookProtocol()` in Listing 5-7 is an essential part of this handle tracking mechanism. Every call to any of the hooked API functions has to pass through it. The implementation is shown in Listing 5-8.

```
BOOL SpyWriteFilter (PSPY_PROTOCOL psp,
                     PBYTE         pbFormat,
```

```
                     PVOID         pParameters,
                     DWORD         dParameters)
    {
    PHANDLE            phObject = NULL;
    HANDLE             hObject  = NULL;
    POBJECT_ATTRIBUTES poa      = NULL;
    PDWORD             pdNext;
    DWORD              i, j;

    pdNext = pParameters;
    i = j  = 0;

    while (pbFormat [i])
        {
        while (pbFormat [i] && (pbFormat [i] != '%')) i++;

        if (pbFormat [i] && pbFormat [++i])
            {
            j++;

            switch (pbFormat [i++])
                {
                case 'b':
                case 'a':
                case 'w':
                case 'u':
                case 'n':
                case 'l':
                case 's':
                case 'i':
                case 'c':
                case 'd':
                case 'p':
                    {
                    break;
                    }
                case 'o':
                    {
                    if (poa == NULL)
                        {
                        poa = (POBJECT_ATTRIBUTES) *pdNext;
```

(continued)

```
                    }
                break;
                }
            case '+':
                {
                if (phObject == NULL)
                    {
                    phObject = (PHANDLE) *pdNext;
                    }
                break;
                }
            case '!':
            case '-':
                {
                if (hObject == NULL)
                    {
                    hObject = (HANDLE) *pdNext;
                    }
                break;
                }
            default:
                {
                j--;
                break;
                }
            }
        pdNext++;
        }
    }
return // number of arguments ok
       (j == dParameters)
       &&
        // no handles involved
       (((phObject == NULL) && (hObject == NULL))
        ||
        // new handle, successfully registered
        ((phObject != NULL) &&
         SpyHandleRegister (psp, PsGetCurrentProcessId (),
                            *phObject, OBJECT_NAME (poa)))
        ||
        // registered handle
        SpyHandleSlot (psp, PsGetCurrentProcessId (), hObject)
        ||
        // filter disabled
        (!gfSpyHookFilter));
}
```

LISTING 5-8. `SpyWriteFilter()` *Excludes Undesired API Calls from the Protocol*

Basically, `SpyWriteFilter()` scans a protocol format string for occurrences of `%o` (object attributes), `%+` (new handle), `%!` (open handle), and `%-` (closed handle) and takes special actions for certain combinations, as follows:

- If no handles are involved, the API call is always logged. This concerns all API functions with format strings that don't contain the format control IDs `%+, %!,` and `%-`.
- If `%+` is included in the format string, indicating that this function allocates a new handle, this handle is registered and associated with the name of the first `%o` item in the format string using the helper function `SpyHandleRegister()`. If no such item exists, the handle is registered with an empty string. If the registration succeeds, the call is logged.
- If `%!` or `%-` occur in the format string, the called function uses or closes an open handle. In this case, `SpyWriteFilter()` tests whether this handle is registered by querying its slot number via `SpyHandleSlot()`. If this function succeeds, the API call is logged.
- In all other cases, the call is logged only if the filter mechanism is disabled, as indicated by the global Boolean variable `gfSpyHookFilter`.

The handle directory is part of the `SPY_PROTOCOL` structure, included in the global `DEVICE_CONTEXT` structure of the spy device `w2k_spy.sys` and defined in Listing 5-9, along with its `SPY_HEADER` substructure. Following the structure definitions is the source code of the four handle management functions `SpyHandleSlot()`, `SpyHandleName()`, `SpyHandleUnregister()`, and `SpyHandleRegister()`. A handle is registered by appending its value to the current end of the `ahObjects[]` array. At the same time, the ID of the owning process is added to the `ahProcesses[]` array, the object name is copied to the `awNames[]` buffer, and the start offset of the name is stored in the `adNames[]` array. When a handle is unregistered, these actions are undone, shifting left all subsequent array members to ensure that none of the arrays contains "holes." The constant definitions at the top of Listing 5-9 define the dimensions of the handle directory: It can take up to 4,096 handles, the name data limit is set to 1,048,576 Unicode characters (2 MB), and the protocol buffer size amounts to 1 MB.

```
#define SPY_HANDLES         0x00001000 // max number of handles
#define SPY_NAME_BUFFER     0x00100000 // object name buffer size
#define SPY_DATA_BUFFER     0x00100000 // protocol data buffer size

// -----------------------------------------------------------------

typedef struct _SPY_HEADER
    {
    LARGE_INTEGER liStart;  // start time
    DWORD         dRead;    // read data index
    DWORD         dWrite;   // write data index
    DWORD         dCalls;   // api usage count
    DWORD         dHandles; // handle count
    DWORD         dName;    // object name index
    }
    SPY_HEADER, *PSPY_HEADER, **PPSPY_HEADER;

#define SPY_HEADER_ sizeof (SPY_HEADER)

// -----------------------------------------------------------------

typedef struct _SPY_PROTOCOL
    {
    SPY_HEADER    sh;                             // protocol header
    HANDLE        ahProcesses [SPY_HANDLES];      // process id array
    HANDLE        ahObjects   [SPY_HANDLES];      // handle array
    DWORD         adNames     [SPY_HANDLES];      // name offsets
    WORD          awNames     [SPY_NAME_BUFFER];  // name strings
    BYTE          abData      [SPY_DATA_BUFFER];  // protocol data
    }
    SPY_PROTOCOL, *PSPY_PROTOCOL, **PPSPY_PROTOCOL;

#define SPY_PROTOCOL_ sizeof (SPY_PROTOCOL)

// -----------------------------------------------------------------

DWORD SpyHandleSlot (PSPY_PROTOCOL psp,
                     HANDLE        hProcess,
                     HANDLE        hObject)
    {
    DWORD dSlot = 0;

    if (hObject != NULL)
        {
        while ((dSlot < psp->sh.dHandles)
               &&
               ((psp->ahProcesses [dSlot] != hProcess) ||
                (psp->ahObjects   [dSlot] != hObject ))) dSlot++;
```

```
        dSlot = (dSlot < psp->sh.dHandles ? dSlot+1 : 0);
        }
    return dSlot;
    }

// ----------------------------------------------------------------

DWORD SpyHandleName (PSPY_PROTOCOL psp,
                     HANDLE        hProcess,
                     HANDLE        hObject,
                     PWORD         pwName,
                     DWORD         dName)
    {
    WORD  w;
    DWORD i;
    DWORD dSlot = SpyHandleSlot (psp, hProcess, hObject);

    if ((pwName != NULL) && dName)
        {
        i = 0;

        if (dSlot)
            {
            while ((i+1 < dName) &&
                   (w = psp->awNames [psp->adNames [dSlot-1] + i]))
                {
                pwName [i++] = w;
                }
            }
        pwName [i] = 0;
        }
    return dSlot;
    }

// ----------------------------------------------------------------

DWORD SpyHandleUnregister (PSPY_PROTOCOL psp,
                           HANDLE        hProcess,
                           HANDLE        hObject,
                           PWORD         pwName,
                           DWORD         dName)
    {
    DWORD i, j;
    DWORD dSlot = SpyHandleName (psp, hProcess, hObject,
                                 pwName, dName);
    if (dSlot)
        {
        if (dSlot == psp->sh.dHandles)
            {
            // remove last name entry
```

(continued)

```
            psp->sh.dName = psp->adNames [dSlot-1];
            }
        else
            {
            i = psp->adNames [dSlot-1];
            j = psp->adNames [dSlot  ];

            // shift left all remaining name entries
            while (j < psp->sh.dName)
                {
                psp->awNames [i++] = psp->awNames [j++];
                }
            j -= (psp->sh.dName = i);

            // shift left all remaining handles and name offsets
            for (i = dSlot; i < psp->sh.dHandles; i++)
                {
                psp->ahProcesses [i-1] = psp->ahProcesses [i];
                psp->ahObjects   [i-1] = psp->ahObjects   [i];
                psp->adNames     [i-1] = psp->adNames     [i] - j;
                }
            }
        psp->sh.dHandles--;
        }
    return dSlot;
    }

// -----------------------------------------------------------------

DWORD SpyHandleRegister (PSPY_PROTOCOL   psp,
                         HANDLE          hProcess,
                         HANDLE          hObject,
                         PUNICODE_STRING puName)
    {
    PWORD pwName;
    DWORD dName;
    DWORD i;
    DWORD dSlot = 0;

    if (hObject != NULL)
        {
        // unregister old handle with same value
        SpyHandleUnregister (psp, hProcess, hObject, NULL, 0);

        if (psp->sh.dHandles == SPY_HANDLES)
            {
```

```
            // unregister oldest handle if overflow
            SpyHandleUnregister (psp, psp->ahProcesses [0],
                                 psp->ahObjects [0], NULL, 0);
            }
        pwName = ((puName != NULL) && SpyMemoryTestAddress (puName)
                  ? puName->Buffer
                  : NULL);

        dName  = ((pwName != NULL) && SpyMemoryTestAddress (pwName)
                  ? puName->Length / WORD_
                  : 0);

        if (dName + 1 <= SPY_NAME_BUFFER - psp->sh.dName)
            {
            // append object to end of list
            psp->ahProcesses [psp->sh.dHandles] = hProcess;
            psp->ahObjects   [psp->sh.dHandles] = hObject;
            psp->adNames     [psp->sh.dHandles] = psp->sh.dName;

            for (i = 0; i < dName; i++)
                {
                psp->awNames [psp->sh.dName++] = pwName [i];
                }
            psp->awNames [psp->sh.dName++] = 0;

            psp->sh.dHandles++;
            dSlot = psp->sh.dHandles;
            }
        }
    return dSlot;
    }
```

LISTING 5-9. *Handle Management Structures and Functions*

CONTROLLING THE API HOOKS IN USER-MODE

A spy device client running in user-mode can control the Native API hook mechanism and the protocol it generates by means of a set of IOCTL functions. This set of functions with names of type `SPY_IO_HOOK_*` was mentioned in Chapter 4, where the memory spying functions of `w2k_spy.sys` were discussed (see Listing 4-7 and Table 4-2).

The relevant part of Table 4-2 is repeated below in Table 5-3. Listing 5-10 is an excerpt from Listing 4-7, demonstrating how the hook management functions are dispatched. Each of these functions is reviewed in the subsequent subsections.

TABLE 5-3. *IOCTL Hook Management Functions Supported by the Spy Device*

FUNCTION NAME	ID	IOCTL CODE	DESCRIPTION
SPY_IO_HOOK_INFO	11	0x8000602C	Returns info about Native API hooks
SPY_IO_HOOK_INSTALL	12	0x8000E030	Installs Native API hooks
SPY_IO_HOOK_REMOVE	13	0x8000E034	Removes Native API hooks
SPY_IO_HOOK_PAUSE	14	0x8000E038	Pauses/resumes the hook protocol
SPY_IO_HOOK_FILTER	15	0x8000E03C	Enables/disables the hook protocol filter
SPY_IO_HOOK_RESET	16	0x8000E040	Clears the hook protocol
SPY_IO_HOOK_READ	17	0x80006044	Reads data from the hook protocol
SPY_IO_HOOK_WRITE	18	0x8000E048	Writes data to the hook protocol

```
NTSTATUS SpyDispatcher (PDEVICE_CONTEXT pDeviceContext,
                        DWORD           dCode,
                        PVOID           pInput,
                        DWORD           dInput,
                        PVOID           pOutput,
                        DWORD           dOutput,
                        PDWORD          pdInfo)
    {
    SPY_MEMORY_BLOCK smb;
    SPY_PAGE_ENTRY   spe;
    SPY_CALL_INPUT   sci;
    PHYSICAL_ADDRESS pa;
    DWORD            dValue, dCount;
    BOOL             fReset, fPause, fFilter, fLine;
    PVOID            pAddress;
    PBYTE            pbName;
    HANDLE           hObject;
    NTSTATUS         ns = STATUS_INVALID_PARAMETER;

    MUTEX_WAIT (pDeviceContext->kmDispatch);

    *pdInfo = 0;

    switch (dCode)
        {
// ====================================================
// unrelated IOCTL functions omitted (cf. Listing 4-7)
// ====================================================
        case SPY_IO_HOOK_INFO:
            {
            ns = SpyOutputHookInfo (pOutput, dOutput, pdInfo);
            break;
            }
```

```
case SPY_IO_HOOK_INSTALL:
    {
    if (((ns = SpyInputBool (&fReset,
                             pInput, dInput))
         == STATUS_SUCCESS)
        &&
        ((ns = SpyHookInstall (fReset, &dCount))
         == STATUS_SUCCESS))
        {
        ns = SpyOutputDword (dCount,
                             pOutput, dOutput, pdInfo);
        }
    break;
    }
case SPY_IO_HOOK_REMOVE:
    {
    if (((ns = SpyInputBool (&fReset,
                             pInput, dInput))
         == STATUS_SUCCESS)
        &&
        ((ns = SpyHookRemove (fReset, &dCount))
         == STATUS_SUCCESS))
        {
        ns = SpyOutputDword (dCount,
                             pOutput, dOutput, pdInfo);
        }
    break;
    }
case SPY_IO_HOOK_PAUSE:
    {
    if ((ns = SpyInputBool (&fPause,
                            pInput, dInput))
        == STATUS_SUCCESS)
        {
        fPause = SpyHookPause (fPause);

        ns = SpyOutputBool (fPause,
                            pOutput, dOutput, pdInfo);
        }
    break;
    }
case SPY_IO_HOOK_FILTER:
    {
    if ((ns = SpyInputBool (&fFilter,
                            pInput, dInput))
        == STATUS_SUCCESS)
        {
        fFilter = SpyHookFilter (fFilter);

        ns = SpyOutputBool (fFilter,
                            pOutput, dOutput, pdInfo);
        }
```

(continued)

```
            break;
            }
        case SPY_IO_HOOK_RESET:
            {
            SpyHookReset ();
            ns = STATUS_SUCCESS;
            break;
            }
        case SPY_IO_HOOK_READ:
            {
            if ((ns = SpyInputBool (&fLine,
                                    pInput, dInput))
                == STATUS_SUCCESS)
                {
                ns = SpyOutputHookRead (fLine,
                                        pOutput, dOutput, pdInfo);
                }
            break;
            }
        case SPY_IO_HOOK_WRITE:
            {
            SpyHookWrite (pInput, dInput);
            ns = STATUS_SUCCESS;
            break;
            }
// =======================================================
// unrelated IOCTL functions omitted (cf. Listing 4-7)
// =======================================================
        }
    MUTEX_RELEASE (pDeviceContext->kmDispatch);
    return ns;
    }
```

LISTING 5-10. *Excerpt from the Spy Driver's Hook Command Dispatcher*

THE IOCTL FUNCTION SPY_IO_HOOK_INFO

The IOCTL Function `SPY_IO_HOOK_INFO` function fills a `SPY_HOOK_INFO` structure with information about the current state of the hook mechanism, as well as the system's SDT. This structure (Listing 5-11) contains or references various other structures introduced earlier:

- The `SERVICE_DESCRIPTOR_TABLE` is defined in Listing 5-1.
- `SPY_CALL` and `SPY_HOOK_ENTRY` are defined in Listing 5-2.
- `SPY_HEADER` and `SPY_PROTOCOL` are defined in Listing 5-9.

```
typedef struct _SPY_HOOK_INFO
    {
    SPY_HEADER                 sh;
    PSPY_CALL                  psc;
    PSPY_PROTOCOL              psp;
    PSERVICE_DESCRIPTOR_TABLE psdt;
    SERVICE_DESCRIPTOR_TABLE  sdt;
    DWORD                      ServiceLimit;
    NTPROC                     ServiceTable  [SDT_SYMBOLS_MAX];
    BYTE                       ArgumentTable [SDT_SYMBOLS_MAX];
    SPY_HOOK_ENTRY             SpyHooks      [SDT_SYMBOLS_MAX];
    }
    SPY_HOOK_INFO, *PSPY_HOOK_INFO, **PPSPY_HOOK_INFO;

#define SPY_HOOK_INFO_ sizeof (SPY_HOOK_INFO)
```

LISTING 5-11. *Definition of the* `SPY_HOOK_INFO` *structure*

Be careful when evaluating the members of this structure. Some of them are pointers into kernel-mode memory that is not accessible from user-mode. However, you can use the spy device's `SPY_IO_MEMORY_DATA` function to examine the contents of these memory blocks.

THE IOCTL FUNCTION SPY_IO_HOOK_INSTALL

The IOCTL `SPY_IO_HOOK_INSTALL` function patches the service table of `ntoskrnl.exe` inside the system's SDT with the hook entry points stored in the global `aSpyHooks[]` array. This array is prepared by `SpyHookInitialize()` (Listing 5-5) and `SpyHookInitializeEx()` (Listing 5-3) during driver initialization. Each `aSpyHooks[]` entry comprises a hook entry point and a corresponding format string address, if available. The `SpyDispatcher()` calls the `SpyHookInstall()` helper function shown in Listing 5-12 to install the hooks. `SpyHookInstall()` in turn uses `SpyHookExchange()`, also included in Listing 5-12, to perform this task.

```
DWORD SpyHookExchange (void)
    {
    PNTPROC ServiceTable;
    BOOL    fPause;
    DWORD   i;
    DWORD   n = 0;

    fPause       = SpyHookPause (TRUE);
    ServiceTable = KeServiceDescriptorTable->ntoskrnl.ServiceTable;

    for (i = 0; i < SDT_SYMBOLS_MAX; i++)
```

(continued)

```
        {
        if (aSpyHooks [i].pbFormat != NULL)
            {
            aSpyHooks [i].Handler = (NTPROC)
                InterlockedExchange ((PLONG) ServiceTable+i,
                                     ( LONG) aSpyHooks [i].Handler);
            n++;
            }
        }
    gfSpyHookState = !gfSpyHookState;
    SpyHookPause (fPause);
    return n;
    }

// -----------------------------------------------------------------

NTSTATUS SpyHookInstall (BOOL   fReset,
                         PDWORD pdCount)
    {
    DWORD    n  = 0;
    NTSTATUS ns = STATUS_INVALID_DEVICE_STATE;

    if (!gfSpyHookState)
        {
        ghSpyHookThread = PsGetCurrentThreadId ();

        n = SpyHookExchange ();
        if (fReset) SpyHookReset ();

        ns = STATUS_SUCCESS;
        }
    *pdCount = n;
    return ns;
    }
```

LISTING 5-12. *Patching the System's API Service Table*

`SpyHookExchange()` is used both in the installation and removal of hooks, because it simply swaps the entries in the system's API service table and the `aSpyHooks[]` array. Therefore, calling this function twice restores the service table and the array to their original states. `SpyHookExchange()` loops through the `aSpyHooks[]` array and searches for entries that contain a format string pointer. The presence of such a string indicates that the function should be monitored. In this case, the API function pointer in the service table and the `Handler` member of the `aSpyHooks[]` entry are exchanged using the `ntoskrnl.exe` function `InterlockedExchange()`, which guarantees that no other thread can interfere in this operation. The protocol mechanism is temporarily paused until the entire service table is patched. `SpyHookInstall()` is merely a wrapper around `SpyHookExchange()` that performs some additional actions:

- The service table is not touched if the global `gfSpyHookState` flag indicates that the hooks are already installed.
- The thread ID of the caller is written to the global variable `ghSpyHookThread`. The hook dispatcher inside `SpyHookInitializeEx()` uses this information to suppress all API calls originating from this thread. Otherwise, the hook protocol would be interrupted with irrelevant and distracting material as a result of the interaction of the spy device and its user-mode client.
- On request of the client, the protocol is reset. This means that all buffer contents are discarded and the handle directory is reinitialized.

The `SPY_IO_HOOK_INSTALL` function receives a Boolean input parameter from the caller. If `TRUE`, the protocol is reset after the hooks have been installed. This is the most frequently used option. Passing in `FALSE` continues a protocol eventually left over from a previous hook session. The return value of the function tells you how many service table entries were patched. On Windows 2000, `SPY_IO_HOOK_INSTALL` reports a value of 44, which is the number of entries in the format string array `apbSdtFormats[]` in Listing 5-6. On Windows NT 4.0, only 42 hooks are installed, because the API functions `NtNotifyChangeMultipleKeys()` and `NtQueryOpenSubKeys()` are not supported by this operating system version.

THE IOCTL FUNCTION SPY_IO_HOOK_REMOVE

The IOCTL `SPY_IO_HOOK_REMOVE` function is similar to `SPY_IO_HOOK_INSTALL`, because it basically reverses the actions of the latter. The IOCTL input and output arguments are identical. However, the `SpyHookRemove()` helper function called inside the `SpyDispatcher()` deviates in some important respects from `SpyHookInstall()`, as a comparison of Listing 5-12 and 5-13 reveals:

- The call is ignored if the global `gfSpyHookState` flag indicates that no hooks are currently installed.
- After the service table has been restored to its original state, the thread ID of the client that installed the hooks is cleared by setting the global variable `ghSpyHookThread` to zero.

- The most important extra feature is the `do/while` loop in the middle of Listing 5-13. In this loop, `SpyHookRemove()` tests whether other threads are currently serviced by the hook dispatcher by testing the `fInUse` members of all `SPY_CALL` structures inside the global `DEVICE_CONTEXT` structure. This is necessary because a client might attempt to unload the spy driver immediately after uninstalling the hooks. If this happens while some other processes' API calls are still within the hook dispatcher, the system throws an exception, followed by a Blue Screen. These in-use tests are performed in 100-msec intervals to give the other threads time to exit the spy device.

```
NTSTATUS SpyHookRemove (BOOL   fReset,
                        PDWORD pdCount)
    {
    LARGE_INTEGER liDelay;
    BOOL          fInUse;
    DWORD         i;
    DWORD         n  = 0;
    NTSTATUS      ns = STATUS_INVALID_DEVICE_STATE;

    if (gfSpyHookState)
        {
        n = SpyHookExchange ();
        if (fReset) SpyHookReset ();

        do  {
            for (i = 0; i < SPY_CALLS; i++)
                {
                if (fInUse = gpDeviceContext->SpyCalls [i].fInUse)
                    break;
                }
            liDelay.QuadPart = -1000000;
            KeDelayExecutionThread (KernelMode, FALSE, &liDelay);
            }
        while (fInUse);

        ghSpyHookThread = 0;

        ns = STATUS_SUCCESS;
        }
    *pdCount = n;
    return ns;
    }
```

LISTING 5-13. *Restoring the System's API Service Table*

Note that a final 100-msec delay is added even if all `fInUse` flags are clear. This precaution is required because a tiny security hole exists inside the hook dispatcher, just between the instruction where the `fInUse` flag of the current `SPY_CALL` entry is reset and the `RET` instruction where the dispatcher returns control to the caller (cf. Listing 5-2 between the ASM labels `SpyHook8` and `SpyHook9`). If all `fInUse` flags are `FALSE`, there is a small probability that some threads have been suspended just before the `RET` instruction could be executed. Delaying the hook removal for another 100-msec interval should allow all threads time to leave this critical code sequence.

The IOCTL Function SPY_IO_HOOK_PAUSE

The IOCTL `SPY_IO_HOOK_PAUSE` function, shown in Listing 5-14, allows a client to temporarily disable and reenable the hook protocol function. Essentially, it sets the global variable `gfSpyHookPause` to the Boolean value supplied by the client and returns its previous value, using the `ntoskrnl.exe` API function `InterlockedExchange()`. By default, the protocol is enabled; that is, `gfSpyHookPause` is `FALSE`.

It is important to note that `SPY_IO_HOOK_PAUSE` works totally independent of `SPY_IO_HOOK_INSTALL` and `SPY_IO_HOOK_REMOVE`. If the protocol is paused while hooks are installed, the hooks remain in effect, but the hook dispatcher lets all API calls pass through without interference. You can also disable the protocol before installing the hooks, if you don't want the protocol to start automatically after `SPY_IO_HOOK_INSTALL` has patched the API service table. Note that the protocol is automatically reset when the protocol is resumed.

The IOCTL Function SPY_IO_HOOK_FILTER

The IOCTL function `SPY_IO_HOOK_FILTER` manipulates a global flag, as shown in Listing 5-15. Here, the global flag `gfSpyHookFilter` is set to the client-supplied value, and the previous setting is returned. The default value is `FALSE`; that is, the filter is disabled.

```
BOOL SpyHookPause (BOOL fPause)
    {
    BOOL fPause1 = (BOOL)
                   InterlockedExchange ((PLONG) &gfSpyHookPause,
                                        ( LONG) fPause);
    if (!fPause) SpyHookReset ();
    return fPause1;
    }
```

Listing 5-14. *Switching the Protocol On and Off*

```
BOOL SpyHookFilter (BOOL fFilter)
    {
    return (BOOL) InterlockedExchange ((PLONG) &gfSpyHookFilter,
                                       ( LONG) fFilter);
    }
```

LISTING 5-15. *Switching the Protocol Filter On and Off*

You already know the variable `gfSpyHookFilter` from the discussion of the `SpyWriteFilter()` function in Listing 5-8. If `gfSpyHookFilter` is `TRUE`, this function helps `SpyHookProtocol()` (see Listing 5-7) to drop all API calls that involve handles not previously registered by the spy device.

THE IOCTL FUNCTION SPY_IO_HOOK_RESET

The IOCTL `SPY_IO_HOOK_RESET` function resets the protocol mechanism to its original state, clearing the data buffer and discarding all registered handles. The `SpyHookReset()` function called by the `SpyDispatcher()` is merely a wrapper around `SpyWriteReset()`. Both functions are included in Listing 5-16. `SpyHookReset()` features additional serialization by means of the mutex calls `SpyHookWait()` and `SpyHookRelease()` (see Listing 5-7).

THE IOCTL FUNCTION SPY_IO_HOOK_READ

The API hook logger writes the protocol data to the `abData[]` buffer inside the global `SPY_PROTOCOL` structure shown in Listing 5-9. This byte array is designed as a circular buffer. That is, it features a pair of pointers for read and write access, respectively. Whenever one of the pointers moves past the end of the buffer, it is reset to the buffer base. The read pointer always tries to catch up with the write pointer, and if both point to the same location, the buffer is empty.

`SPY_IO_HOOK_READ` is by far the most important hook management function offered by the spy device. It reads arbitrary amounts of data from the protocol data buffer and adjusts the read pointer appropriately. This function should be called frequently while the protocol is enabled, to avoid buffer overflows. Listing 5-17 shows the function set handling this IOCTL request. The basic handlers are `SpyReadData()` and `SpyReadLine()`. The difference between them is that the former returns the requested amount of data, if available, whereas the latter retrieves single lines only. Line mode can be very convenient when the read data must be filtered by a client application. Callers of `SPY_IO_HOOK_READ` pass in a Boolean value that decides whether block mode (`FALSE`) or line mode (`TRUE`) is requested.

```
void SpyWriteReset (PSPY_PROTOCOL psp)
    {
    KeQuerySystemTime (&psp->sh.liStart);

    psp->sh.dRead    = 0;
    psp->sh.dWrite   = 0;
    psp->sh.dCalls   = 0;
    psp->sh.dHandles = 0;
    psp->sh.dName    = 0;
    return;
    }

// -----------------------------------------------------------------

void SpyHookReset (void)
    {
    SpyHookWait    ();
    SpyWriteReset  (&gpDeviceContext->SpyProtocol);
    SpyHookRelease ();
    return;
    }
```

LISTING 5-16. *Resetting the Protocol*

```
DWORD SpyReadData (PSPY_PROTOCOL psp,
                   PBYTE         pbData,
                   DWORD         dData)
    {
    DWORD i = psp->sh.dRead;
    DWORD n = 0;

    while ((n < dData) && (i != psp->sh.dWrite))
        {
        pbData [n++] = psp->abData [i++];
        if (i == SPY_DATA_BUFFER) i = 0;
        }
    psp->sh.dRead = i;
    return n;
    }

// -----------------------------------------------------------------

DWORD SpyReadLine (PSPY_PROTOCOL psp,
                   PBYTE         pbData,
                   DWORD         dData)
    {
    BYTE  b = 0;
```

(continued)

```
    DWORD i = psp->sh.dRead;
    DWORD n = 0;

    while ((b != '\n') && (i != psp->sh.dWrite))
        {
        b = psp->abData [i++];
        if (i == SPY_DATA_BUFFER) i = 0;
        if (n < dData) pbData [n++] = b;
        }
    if (b == '\n')
        {
        // remove current line from buffer
        psp->sh.dRead = i;
        }
    else
        {
        // don't return any data until full line available
        n = 0;
        }
    if (n)
        {
        pbData [n-1] = 0;
        }
    else
        {
        if (dData) pbData [0] = 0;
        }
    return n;
    }

// -----------------------------------------------------------------

DWORD SpyHookRead (PBYTE pbData,
                   DWORD dData,
                   BOOL  fLine)
    {
    DWORD n = 0;

    SpyHookWait ();

    n = (fLine ? SpyReadLine : SpyReadData)
            (&gpDeviceContext->SpyProtocol, pbData, dData);

    SpyHookRelease ();
    return n;
    }

// -----------------------------------------------------------------
```

```
NTSTATUS SpyOutputHookRead (BOOL   fLine,
                            PVOID  pOutput,
                            DWORD  dOutput,
                            PDWORD pdInfo)
    {
    *pdInfo = SpyHookRead (pOutput, dOutput, fLine);
    return STATUS_SUCCESS;
    }
```

LISTING 5-17. *Reading from the Protocol Buffer*

The `SpyOutputHookRead()` and `SpyHookRead()` functions are trivial. `SpyHookRead()` adds the usual mutex serialization and chooses between `SpyReadLine()` and `SpyReadData()`, and `SpyOutputHookRead()` postprocesses its results as demanded by the IOCTL framework.

THE IOCTL FUNCTION SPY_IO_HOOK_WRITE

The IOCTL `SPY_IO_HOOK_WRITE` function allows the client to write data to the protocol buffer. An application can use this feature to add separators or additional status information to the protocol. The implementation is shown in Listing 5-18. `SpyHookWrite()` is yet another wrapper with additional mutex serialization. The `SpyWriteData()` function it calls is the basic protocol generator of the spy device. All `SpyWrite*()` helper functions (e.g., the `SpyWriteFormat()`, `SpyWriteNumber()`, `SpyWriteChar()`, and `SpyWriteLarge()` functions used by `SpyHookProtocol()` in Listing 5-7) are ultimately built upon it.

```
DWORD SpyWriteData (PSPY_PROTOCOL psp,
                    PBYTE         pbData,
                    DWORD         dData)
    {
    BYTE  b;
    DWORD i = psp->sh.dRead;
    DWORD j = psp->sh.dWrite;
    DWORD n = 0;

    while (n < dData)
        {
        psp->abData [j++] = pbData [n++];
        if (j == SPY_DATA_BUFFER) j = 0;

        if (j == i)
            {
            // remove first line from buffer
```

(continued)

```
            do  {
                b = psp->abData [i++];
                if (i == SPY_DATA_BUFFER) i = 0;
                }
            while ((b != '\n') && (i != j));

            // remove half line only if single line
            if ((i == j) &&
                ((i += (SPY_DATA_BUFFER / 2)) >= SPY_DATA_BUFFER))
                {
                i -= SPY_DATA_BUFFER;
                }
            }
        }
    psp->sh.dRead  = i;
    psp->sh.dWrite = j;
    return n;
    }

// ----------------------------------------------------------------

DWORD SpyHookWrite (PBYTE pbData,
                    DWORD dData)
    {
    DWORD n = 0;

    SpyHookWait ();

    n = SpyWriteData
            (&gpDeviceContext->SpyProtocol, pbData, dData);

    SpyHookRelease ();
    return n;
    }
```

LISTING 5-18. *Writing to the Protocol Buffer*

Note how `SpyWriteData()` handles overflow situations. If the read pointer advances slowly, the write pointer may lap it. In this situation, two options are available:

1. Write access is disabled until the read pointer is advanced.
2. Buffered data is discarded to make space.

The spy device chooses the second option. If an overflow occurs, the entire protocol line at the current read pointer position is dropped by advancing the read pointer to the next line. If the buffer contains just a single line (which is highly improbable), only the first half of the line is discarded. The code handling these situations is marked in Listing 5-18 by appropriate comments.

A SAMPLE HOOK PROTOCOL READER

To help you write your own API hook client applications, I have added a very simple sample application that reads the hook protocol buffer and displays it in a console window. The pause, filter, and reset functions can be issued by pressing keys **P**, **F**, and **R** on the keyboard, and the output can be filtered according to a series of user-specified function name patterns. The application is called "SBS Windows 2000 API Hook Viewer," and its source code is available on the book's companion CD in the directory tree `\src\w2k_hook`.

CONTROLLING THE SPY DEVICE

For convenience, the `w2k_hook.exe` application uses a couple of simple wrappers for the various `SPY_IO_HOOK_*` IOCTL functions, summarized in Listing 5-19. These utility functions make the code much more readable and minimize the probability of parameter errors during the development of a spy device client application.

```
BOOL WINAPI SpyIoControl (HANDLE hDevice,
                          DWORD  dCode,
                          PVOID  pInput,
                          DWORD  dInput,
                          PVOID  pOutput,
                          DWORD  dOutput)
    {
    DWORD dInfo = 0;

    return DeviceIoControl (hDevice, dCode,
                            pInput,  dInput,
                            pOutput, dOutput,
                            &dInfo,  NULL)
           &&
           (dInfo == dOutput);
    }

// -----------------------------------------------------------------

BOOL WINAPI SpyVersionInfo (HANDLE            hDevice,
                            PSPY_VERSION_INFO psvi)
    {
    return SpyIoControl (hDevice, SPY_IO_VERSION_INFO,
                         NULL, 0,
```

(continued)

```
                         psvi, SPY_VERSION_INFO_);
    }

// ---------------------------------------------------------------

BOOL WINAPI SpyHookInfo (HANDLE         hDevice,
                         PSPY_HOOK_INFO pshi)
    {
    return SpyIoControl (hDevice, SPY_IO_HOOK_INFO,
                         NULL, 0,
                         pshi, SPY_HOOK_INFO_);
    }

// ---------------------------------------------------------------

BOOL WINAPI SpyHookInstall (HANDLE hDevice,
                            BOOL   fReset,
                            PDWORD pdCount)
    {
    return SpyIoControl (hDevice, SPY_IO_HOOK_INSTALL,
                         &fReset, BOOL_,
                         pdCount, DWORD_);
    }

// ---------------------------------------------------------------

BOOL WINAPI SpyHookRemove (HANDLE hDevice,
                           BOOL   fReset,
                           PDWORD pdCount)
    {
    return SpyIoControl (hDevice, SPY_IO_HOOK_REMOVE,
                         &fReset, BOOL_,
                         pdCount, DWORD_);
    }

// ---------------------------------------------------------------

BOOL WINAPI SpyHookPause (HANDLE hDevice,
                          BOOL   fPause,
                          PBOOL  pfPause)
    {
    return SpyIoControl (hDevice, SPY_IO_HOOK_PAUSE,
                         &fPause, BOOL_,
                         pfPause, BOOL_);
    }

// ---------------------------------------------------------------
```

```
BOOL WINAPI SpyHookFilter (HANDLE hDevice,
                           BOOL   fFilter,
                           PBOOL  pfFilter)
    {
    return SpyIoControl (hDevice, SPY_IO_HOOK_FILTER,
                         &fFilter, BOOL_,
                         pfFilter, BOOL_);
    }

// -----------------------------------------------------------------

BOOL WINAPI SpyHookReset (HANDLE hDevice)
    {
    return SpyIoControl (hDevice, SPY_IO_HOOK_RESET,
                         NULL, 0,
                         NULL, 0);
    }

// -----------------------------------------------------------------

DWORD WINAPI SpyHookRead (HANDLE hDevice,
                          BOOL   fLine,
                          PBYTE  pbData,
                          DWORD  dData)
    {
    DWORD dInfo;

    if (!DeviceIoControl (hDevice, SPY_IO_HOOK_READ,
                          &fLine, BOOL_,
                          pbData, dData,
                          &dInfo, NULL))
        {
        dInfo = 0;
        }
    return dInfo;
    }

// -----------------------------------------------------------------

BOOL WINAPI SpyHookWrite (HANDLE hDevice,
                          PBYTE  pbData)
    {
    return SpyIoControl (hDevice, SPY_IO_HOOK_WRITE,
                         pbData, lstrlenA (pbData),
                         NULL,   0);
    }
```

LISTING 5-19. *Device I/O Control Utility Functions*

Before the functions in Listing 5-19 can be used, the spy device must be loaded and started. This operation is much the same as that outlined in Chapter 4 in conjunction with the memory spy application `w2k_mem.exe`. Listing 5-20 shows the application's main function, `Execute()`, which loads and unloads the spy device driver, opens and closes a device handle, and interacts with the device via IOCTL. If you compare Listing 5-20 to Listing 4-29, the similarities at the beginning and end are obvious. Only the middle sections, where the application-dependent code is located, are different.

```
void WINAPI Execute (PPWORD ppwFilters,
                     DWORD  dFilters)
    {
    SPY_VERSION_INFO svi;
    SPY_HOOK_INFO    shi;
    DWORD            dCount, i, j, k, n;
    BOOL             fPause, fFilter, fRepeat;
    BYTE             abData [HOOK_MAX_DATA];
    WORD             awData [HOOK_MAX_DATA];
    WORD             awPath [MAX_PATH] = L"?";
    SC_HANDLE        hControl          = NULL;
    HANDLE           hDevice           = INVALID_HANDLE_VALUE;

    _printf (L"\r\nLoading \"%s\" (%s) ...\r\n",
             awSpyDisplay, awSpyDevice);

    if (w2kFilePath (NULL, awSpyFile, awPath, MAX_PATH))
        {
        _printf (L"Driver: \"%s\"\r\n",
                 awPath);

        hControl = w2kServiceLoad (awSpyDevice, awSpyDisplay,
                                   awPath, TRUE);
        }
    if (hControl != NULL)
        {
        _printf (L"Opening \"%s\" ...\r\n",
                 awSpyPath);

        hDevice = CreateFile (awSpyPath,
                              GENERIC_READ    | GENERIC_WRITE,
                              FILE_SHARE_READ | FILE_SHARE_WRITE,
                              NULL, OPEN_EXISTING,
                              FILE_ATTRIBUTE_NORMAL, NULL);
        }
    else
        {
```

```
        _printf (L"Unable to load the spy device driver.\r\n");
        }
    if (hDevice != INVALID_HANDLE_VALUE)
        {
        if (SpyVersionInfo (hDevice, &svi))
            {
            _printf (L"\r\n"
                     L"%s V%lu.%02lu ready\r\n",
                     svi.awName,
                     svi.dVersion / 100, svi.dVersion % 100);
            }
        if (SpyHookInfo (hDevice, &shi))
            {
            _printf (L"\r\n"
                     L"API hook parameters:       0x%08lX\r\n"
                     L"SPY_PROTOCOL structure:    0x%08lX\r\n"
                     L"SPY_PROTOCOL data buffer:  0x%08lX\r\n"
                     L"KeServiceDescriptorTable:  0x%08lX\r\n"
                     L"KiServiceTable:            0x%08lX\r\n"
                     L"KiArgumentTable:           0x%08lX\r\n"
                     L"Service table size:        0x%lX (%lu)\r\n",
                     shi.psc,
                     shi.psp,
                     shi.psp->abData,
                     shi.psdt,
                     shi.sdt.ntoskrnl.ServiceTable,
                     shi.sdt.ntoskrnl.ArgumentTable,
                     shi.ServiceLimit, shi.ServiceLimit);
            }
        SpyHookPause  (hDevice, TRUE, &fPause ); fPause  = FALSE;
        SpyHookFilter (hDevice, TRUE, &fFilter); fFilter = FALSE;

        if (SpyHookInstall (hDevice, TRUE, &dCount))
            {
            _printf (L"\r\n"
                     L"Installed %lu API hooks\r\n",
                     dCount);
            }
        _printf (L"\r\n"
                 L"Protocol control keys:\r\n"
                 L"\r\n"
                 L"P   -  pause  ON/off\r\n"
                 L"F   -  filter ON/off\r\n"
                 L"R   -  reset protocol\r\n"
                 L"ESC -  exit\r\n"
                 L"\r\n");

        for (fRepeat = TRUE; fRepeat;)
            {
```

(continued)

```
if (n = SpyHookRead (hDevice, TRUE,
                     abData, HOOK_MAX_DATA))
    {
    if (abData [0] == '-')
        {
        n = 0;
        }
    else
        {
        i = 0;
        while (abData [i] && (abData [i++] != '='));

        j = i;
        while (abData [j] && (abData [j] != '(')) j++;

        k = 0;
        while (i < j) awData [k++] = abData [i++];

        awData [k] = 0;

        for (i = 0; i < dFilters; i++)
            {
            if (PatternMatcher (ppwFilters [i], awData))
                {
                n = 0;
                break;
                }
            }
        }
    if (!n) _printf (L"%hs\r\n", abData);
    Sleep (0);
    }
else
    {
    Sleep (HOOK_IOCTL_DELAY);
    }
switch (KeyboardData ())
    {
    case 'P':
        {
        SpyHookPause (hDevice, fPause, &fPause);
        SpyHookWrite (hDevice, (fPause ? abPauseOff
                                       : abPauseOn));
        break;
        }
    case 'F':
        {
        SpyHookFilter (hDevice, fFilter, &fFilter);
        SpyHookWrite  (hDevice, (fFilter ? abFilterOff
                                         : abFilterOn));
```

```
                    break;
                    }
                case 'R':
                    {
                    SpyHookReset (hDevice);
                    SpyHookWrite (hDevice, abReset);
                    break;
                    }
                case VK_ESCAPE:
                    {
                    _printf (L"%hs\r\n", abExit);
                    fRepeat = FALSE;
                    break;
                    }
                }
            }
        if (SpyHookRemove (hDevice, FALSE, &dCount))
            {
            _printf (L"\r\n"
                     L"Removed %lu API hooks\r\n",
                     dCount);
            }
        _printf (L"\r\nClosing the spy device ...\r\n");
        CloseHandle (hDevice);
        }
    else
        {
        _printf (L"Unable to open the spy device.\r\n");
        }
    if ((hControl != NULL) && gfSpyUnload)
        {
        _printf (L"Unloading the spy device ...\r\n");
        w2kServiceUnload (awSpyDevice, hControl);
        }
    return;
    }
```

LISTING 5-20. *The Main Application Framework*

Note that the `Execute()` function in Listing 5-20 requests `GENERIC_READ` and `GENERIC_WRITE` access in the `CreateFile()` call, whereas the function in Listing 4-29 uses only `GENERIC_READ` access. The reason for this discrepancy is buried in the IOCTL codes used by these applications. Whereas the memory spy in Chapter 4 uses read-only functions throughout, the API hook viewer discussed here calls functions that modify system data and hence require a device handle with additional write access. If you examine the IOCTL codes in the third column of Table 5-3, you can see that most of them have the hex digit `E` at the fourth position from the right, whereas `SPY_IO_HOOK_INFO` and `SPY_IO_HOOK_READ` have the digit `6` there. According to Figure 4-6 in Chapter 4, this means that the latter pair of hook management functions require a device handle with read access, whereas the remaining ones require read/write rights. The designer of a device driver must decide which read/write access right combinations are demanded by the I/O requests handled by the device. Patching the system's API service table is a radical write operation, so urging a client to obtain a handle with write access is certainly appropriate.

Most of the remaining code in Listing 5-20 should be self-explaining. Following are features that are worth noting:

- The `SPY_IO_HOOK_READ` function is operated in line mode, as the second argument of the `SpyHookRead()` call at the beginning of the big `for` loop shows.
- The user of the application can specify a series of pattern strings with embedded wildcards `'*'` and `'?'` on the command line. These patterns are compared sequentially with the function name within each protocol line using the helper function `PatternMatcher()` shown in Listing 5-21. If no pattern matches the name, the line is suppressed. To view the hook protocol unfiltered, the command `w2k_hook` * must be issued.
- After handling a protocol line, the application returns the rest of its time slice to the system by calling `Sleep (0)`, so the time is available for other processes.
- If no protocol data is available, the application suspends itself for 10 msec (`HOOK_IOCTL_DELAY`) before polling the spy device again. This reduces the CPU load considerably in times with low usage of the Native API.
- In the main loop, the keyboard is polled as well. All keys except **P**, **F**, **R**, and **Esc** are ignored. **P** switches the pause mode on and off (default: on), **F** enables and disables filtering by handle (default: enabled), **R** resets the protocol, and **Esc** terminates the application.
- If one of the **P**, **F**, **R**, or **Esc** keys is pressed, a separator line is written to the hook protocol buffer using the `SPY_IO_HOOK_WRITE` function. This line indicates the state change resulting from the entered command. Writing the separator to the buffer is better than writing it directly to the console window because the state change might appear on the screen with some delay. For example, if the **P** key is pressed to halt the display, the application will continue to generate output until all data has been read from the protocol buffer. The separator generated by the **P** command will be appended after the last entry, so it appears at the correct location.
- Just like the `w2k_mem.exe` application in Chapter 4, `w2k_hook.exe` unloads the spy device only if the global flag `gfSpyUnload` is set. By default, it is *not* set—for the reasons explained in Chapter 4.

```
BOOL WINAPI PatternMatcher (PWORD pwFilter,
                            PWORD pwData)
    {
    DWORD i, j;

    i = j = 0;
    while (pwFilter [i] && pwData [j])
        {
        if (pwFilter [i] != '?')
            {
            if (pwFilter [i] == '*')
                {
                i++;
                if ((pwFilter [i] != '*') && (pwFilter [i] != '?'))
                    {
                    if (pwFilter [i])
                        {
                        while (pwData [j] &&
                               (!PatternMatcher (pwFilter + i,
                                                 pwData   + j)))
                            {
                            j++;
                            }
                        }
                    return (pwData [j]);
                    }
                }
            if ((WORD) CharUpperW ((PWORD) (pwFilter [i])) !=
                (WORD) CharUpperW ((PWORD) (pwData   [j])))
                {
                return FALSE;
                }
            }
        i++;
        j++;
        }
    if (pwFilter [i] == '*') i++;
    return !(pwFilter [i] || pwData [j]);
    }
```

LISTING 5-21. *A Simple String Pattern Matcher*

The examples shown in Figures 5-6 and 5-7 were generated by `w2k_hook.exe` with the name patterns `*file` and `ntclose` specified on the command line. This filters out all file management function calls plus `NtClose()`. It is important to keep in mind that the name patterns are applied to the protocol data *after* it has been generated, whereas the "garbage" filter of the spy device based on registered handles manipulates the protocol *before* it is written. If you exclude protocol entries by specifying name patterns on the `w2k_hook.exe` command line, this has absolutely no effect on the protocol data generator. The only effect is that protocol entries are thrown away after having been retrieved from the protocol buffer.

Highlights and Pitfalls

The API hooking mechanism of Russinovich and Cogswell (Russinovich and Cogswell 1997) adapted here is clearly ingenious and elegant. The following are its most notable advantages:

- Installing and uninstalling a hook in the system's API service table is a simple pointer exchange operation.
- After the hook is installed, it receives the Native API calls of all processes running in the system, even of new ones started after the hook installation.
- Because the hook device runs in kernel-mode, it has maximum access to all system resources. It is even allowed to execute privileged CPU instructions.

The following are problem areas I encountered during the development of my spy device:

- The hook device must be designed and written with extreme care. Because all traffic occurring on the Native API level will pass through in the context of various application threads, it must be as stable as the operating system kernel itself. The smallest oversight may immediately crash the system.
- Only a small part of the kernel's API traffic is logged. For example, API calls originating from other kernel-mode modules don't pass through the system's `INT 2Eh` gate and hence don't appear in the hook protocol. Also, many important functions exported by `ntdll.dll` and `ntoskrnl.exe` are not part of the Native API, so they cannot be hooked in the service table.

The incomplete API coverage is clearly more restrictive than the demand for stability. Anyway, it is amazing how much useful data can be gained about the internals of an application by tracing its Native API calls. For example, I was able to gain deep insight into the NetWare Core Protocol (NCP) operations performed by Microsoft's NetWare redirector `nwrdr.sys` by simply observing its `NtFsControlFile()` traffic. Therefore, this approach to API monitoring is certainly the most proficient of the alternatives available to date for Windows 2000.

CHAPTER 6

Calling Kernel API Functions from User-Mode

In Chapter 2, I explained how Windows 2000 allows user-mode applications to call a subset of its kernel API functions—the Native API—by means of an interrupt gate mechanism. Chapters 4 and 5 relied heavily on a mechanism referred to as Device I/O Control (IOCTL) to carry out additional tasks that aren't allowed in user-mode. Both the Native API and IOCTL are quite powerful, but think of the benefit of being able to call almost *any* kernel-mode function as if it were located in a normal user-mode DLL. This is generally considered impossible. However, I will demonstrate in this chapter that it is possible with the help of a couple of wacky programming tricks. Again, IOCTL will come to the rescue to solve a problem that seems impossible at first sight. This chapter is revolutionary because it builds a general-purpose bridge from user-mode to kernel-mode, allowing the Win32 application to call kernel API functions just as if they were part of the Win32 API. Even better, an application can call internal kernel functions that are not even available to kernel-mode drivers, with the help of the symbol files coming with the Windows 2000 debugging tools. This "kernel call interface" works seamlessly in the background, almost completely unnoticed by the calling application.

A GENERAL KERNEL CALL INTERFACE

In Chapter 4, we used a kernel-mode driver to call selected kernel API functions on behalf of a user-mode program. For example, the `SPY_IO_PHYSICAL` function offered by the spy driver `w2k_spy.sys` is merely a wrapper around the memory manager's `MmGetPhysicalAddress()` function. Another example is `SPY_IO_HANDLE_INFO`, which is built upon the object manager's `ObReferenceObjectByHandle()` and `ObDereferenceObject()` functions. Although this technique works fine, it is quite tedious and inefficient to design a custom IOCTL function for every kernel API function that should be made available to user-mode code. Therefore, I have added a general-purpose IOCTL function to the spy device inside the sample driver `w2k_spy.sys` that calls arbitrary kernel-mode functions, given a symbolic name or an entry point plus a list of arguments. This sounds like a lot of work, but you will be surprised how simple the necessary code actually is. The only difficulty is that again we will need a good deal of inline assembly language (ASM).

Designing a Gate to Kernel-Mode

If a program running in user-mode wants to call a kernel-mode function, it has to solve two problems. First, it must somehow jump across the barrier between user-mode and kernel-mode, and second, it must transfer data in and out. For the subset comprising the Native API, the `ntdll.dll` component takes over this duty, using an interrupt gate to accomplish the mode change and CPU registers to pass in a pointer to the caller's argument stack and to return the function's result to the caller. For kernel functions not included in the Native API, the operating system doesn't offer such a gate mechanism. Therefore, we will have to create our own. Part one of the problem is easily solved: The `w2k_spy.sys` driver introduced in Chapter 4 and extended in Chapter 5 crosses the user-to-kernel-mode border back and forth many times during its IOCTL transactions. And because IOCTL optionally allows passing data blocks in both directions, the date transfer problem is solved as well. In the end, the whole matter boils down to the following simple sequence of steps:

1. The user-mode application posts an IOCTL request, passing in information about the function to be called, as well as a pointer to its argument stack.
2. The kernel-mode driver dispatches the request, copies the arguments onto its own stack, calls the function, and passes the results back to the caller in the IOCTL output buffer.
3. The caller picks up the results of the IOCTL operation and proceeds as it would after a normal DLL function call.

The main problem with this scenario is that the kernel-mode module must cope with various data formats and calling conventions. Following is a list of situations the driver must be prepared for:

- The size of the argument stack depends on the target function. Because it is impractical to give the driver detailed knowledge about all functions it might possibly have to call, the caller must supply the size of the argument stack.

- Windows 2000 kernel API functions use three calling conventions: `__stdcall`, `__cdecl`, and `__fastcall`, which differ considerably in the way arguments are treated. `__stdcall` and `__cdecl` require all arguments to be passed in on the stack, whereas `__fastcall` aims at minimizing stack fumbling overhead by passing the first two arguments in the CPU registers `ECX` and `EDX`. On the other hand, `__stdcall` and `__fastcall` agree in the way arguments are removed from the stack, forcing the called code to take over the responsibility. `__cdecl`, however, leaves this task to the calling code. Although the stack cleanup problem can be easily solved by saving the stack pointer before the call and resetting it to its original position after returning, regardless of the calling convention, the driver is helpless with respect to the `__fastcall` convention. Therefore, the caller must specify on every call whether the `__fastcall` convention is in effect, to allow the driver to prepare the registers `ECX` and `EDX` if necessary.
- Windows 2000 kernel functions return results in various sizes, ranging from zero to 64 bits. The 64-bit register pair `EDX:EAX` transports the results back to the caller. Data is filled in from the least-significant end toward the most-significant end. For example, if a function returns a 16-bit `SHORT` data type, only register `AX` (comprising `AL` and `AH`) is significant. The upper half of `EAX` and the entire `EDX` contents are undefined. Because the driver is ignorant of the called function's I/O data, it must assume the worst case, which is 64-bits. Otherwise, the result may be truncated.
- The application might supply invalid arguments. In user-mode, this is usually benign. At worst, the application process is aborted with an error message box. Occasionally, this error results in system damage that requires a reboot for recovery. In kernel-mode, the most frequent programming error, known as "bad pointer," almost instantly results in a Blue Screen of Death, which might cause loss of user data. This problem can be addressed to a great extent by using the operating system's Structured Exception Handling (SEH) mechanism.

That said, let's examine how our spy driver handles function properties, arguments, and results. Listing 6-1 shows the involved IOCTL input and output structures, `SPY_CALL_INPUT` and `SPY_CALL_OUTPUT`. The latter is quite simple—it consists of a `ULARGE_INTEGER` structure that is used by Windows 2000 to represent a 64-bit value both as a single 64-bit integer and a pair of 32-bit halves. Please consult Listing 2-3 in Chapter 2 for the layout of this structure.

```
typedef struct _SPY_CALL_INPUT
    {
    BOOL  fFastCall;
    DWORD dArgumentBytes;
    PVOID pArguments;
    PBYTE pbSymbol;
    PVOID pEntryPoint;
    }
    SPY_CALL_INPUT, *PSPY_CALL_INPUT, **PPSPY_CALL_INPUT;

#define SPY_CALL_INPUT_ sizeof (SPY_CALL_INPUT)

// -----------------------------------------------------------------

typedef struct _SPY_CALL_OUTPUT
    {
    ULARGE_INTEGER uliResult;
    }
    SPY_CALL_OUTPUT, *PSPY_CALL_OUTPUT, **PPSPY_CALL_OUTPUT;

#define SPY_CALL_OUTPUT_ sizeof (SPY_CALL_OUTPUT)
```

LISTING 6-1. *Definition of* `SPY_CALL_INPUT` *and* `SPY_CALL_OUTPUT`

`SPY_CALL_INPUT` needs a bit more explanation. The purpose of the `fFastCall` member should be obvious. It signals to the spy driver that the function to be called obeys the `__fastcall` convention, so the first two arguments, if any, must not be passed in on the stack, but in CPU registers. `dArgumentBytes` specifies the number of bytes piled up on the argument stack, and `pArguments` points to the top of this stack. The remaining arguments, `pbSymbol` and `pEntryPoint`, are mutually exclusive, and tell the driver which function to execute. You can specify either a function name or a plain entry point address. The other member should always be set to `NULL`. If both values are non-`NULL`, `pbSymbol` takes precedence over `pEntryPoint`. Calling a function by name rather than by address adds an additional step, where the entry point of the specified symbolic name is determined. If it can be retrieved, the function is entered through this address. Passing in an entry point simply bypasses the symbol resolution step.

Finding the linear address associated with a symbol exported by a kernel-mode module sounds easier than it actually is. The powerful Win32 functions `GetModuleHandle()` and `GetProcAddress()`, which work fine with all components within the Win32 subsystem, do not recognize kernel-mode system modules and drivers. Implementing this part of the sample code was difficult, the details are covered in the next section of this chapter. For now, let's assume that a valid entry point is available, no matter how it has been supplied. Listing 6-2 shows the function `SpyCall()` that constitutes the core part of my kernel call interface. As you see, it is almost 100% assembly language. It is always unpleasant to resort to ASM in a C program, but some tasks simply can't be done in pure C. In this case, the problem is that `SpyCall()` needs total control of the stack and the CPU registers, and therefore it must bypass the C compiler and optimizer, which use the stack and registers as they see fit.

Before delving into the details of Listing 6-2, let me describe another special feature of the `SpyCall()` function that obscures the code. As explained in Chapter 2, the Windows 2000 system modules export some of their variables by name. Typical examples are `NtBuildNumber` and `KeServiceDescriptorTable`. The Portable Executable (PE) file format of Windows 2000/NT/9x provides a general-purpose mechanism for attaching symbols to addresses, regardless of whether an address points to code or data. Therefore, a Windows 2000 module is free to attach exported symbols to its global variables at will. A client module can dynamically link to them like it links to function symbols, and it is able to use these variables as if they were located in its own global data section. Of course, my kernel call interface would not be complete if it were not able to cope with this kind of symbol as well, so I decided that negative values of the `dArgumentBytes` member inside the `SPY_CALL_INPUT` structure should indicate that data is to be copied from the entry point instead of calling it. Valid values range from `-1` to `-9`, where `-1` means that the entry point address itself is copied to the `SPY_CALL_OUTPUT` buffer. For the remaining values, their one's complement states the number of bytes copied from the entry point, that is, `-2` copies a single `BYTE` or `CHAR`; `-3`, a 16-bit `WORD` or `SHORT`; `-5`, a 32-bit `DWORD` or `LONG`; and `-9` a 64-bit `DWORDLONG` or `LONGLONG`. You may wonder why it should be necessary to copy the entry point itself. Well, some kernel symbols, such as `KeServiceDescriptorTable` point to structures that exceed the 64-bit return value limit, so it is wiser to return the plain pointer rather than truncating the value to 64 bits.

```
void SpyCall (PSPY_CALL_INPUT  psci,
              PSPY_CALL_OUTPUT psco)
    {
    PVOID pStack;

    __asm
        {
        pushfd
        pushad
        xor     eax, eax
        mov     ebx, psco              ; get output parameter block
        lea     edi, [ebx.uliResult]   ; get result buffer
        mov     [edi  ], eax           ; clear result buffer (lo)
        mov     [edi+4], eax           ; clear result buffer (hi)
        mov     ebx, psci              ; get input parameter block
        mov     ecx, [ebx.dArgumentBytes]
```

(continued)

```
        cmp     ecx, -9                 ; call or store/copy?
        jb      SpyCall2
        mov     esi, [ebx.pEntryPoint]  ; get entry point
        not     ecx                     ; get number of bytes
        jecxz   SpyCall1                ; 0 -> store entry point
        rep     movsb                   ; copy data from entry point
        jmp     SpyCall5
SpyCall1:
        mov     [edi], esi              ; store entry point
        jmp     SpyCall5
SpyCall2:
        mov     esi, [ebx.pArguments]
        cmp     [ebx.fFastCall], eax    ; __fastcall convention?
        jz      SpyCall3
        cmp     ecx, 4                  ; 1st argument available?
        jb      SpyCall3
        mov     eax, [esi]              ; eax = 1st argument
        add     esi, 4                  ; remove argument from list
        sub     ecx, 4
        cmp     ecx, 4                  ; 2nd argument available?
        jb      SpyCall3
        mov     edx, [esi]              ; edx = 2nd argument
        add     esi, 4                  ; remove argument from list
        sub     ecx, 4
SpyCall3:
        mov     pStack, esp             ; save stack pointer
        jecxz   SpyCall4                ; no (more) arguments
        sub     esp, ecx                ; copy argument stack
        mov     edi, esp
        shr     ecx, 2
        rep     movsd
SpyCall4:
        mov     ecx, eax                ; load 1st __fastcall arg
        call    [ebx.pEntryPoint]       ; call entry point
        mov     esp, pStack             ; restore stack pointer
        mov     ebx, psco               ; get output parameter block
        mov     [ebx.uliResult.LowPart ], eax   ; store result (lo)
        mov     [ebx.uliResult.HighPart], edx   ; store result (hi)
SpyCall5:
        popad
        popfd
        }
    return;
    }
```

LISTING 6-2. *The Core Function of the Kernel Call Interface*

With the special case of accessing exported variables kept in mind, Listing 6-2 shouldn't be too difficult to understand. First, the 64-bit result buffer is cleared, guaranteeing that unused bits are always zero. Next, the `dArgumentBytes` member of the input data is compared with `-9` to find out whether the client requested a function call or a data copying operation. The function call handler starts at the label `SpyCall2`. After setting register `ESI` to the top of the argument stack by evaluating the `pArguments` member, it is time to check the calling convention. If `__fastcall` is required and there is at least one 32-bit value on the stack, `SpyCall()` removes it and stores it temporarily in `EAX`. If another 32-bit value is available, it is removed as well and stored in `EDX`. Any remaining arguments remain on the stack. Meanwhile, the label `SpyCall3` is reached. Now the current top-of-stack address is saved to the local variable `pStack`, and the argument stack (minus the arguments removed in the `__fastcall` case) is copied to the spy driver's stack using the fast i386 `REP MOVSD` instruction. Note that the direction flag that determines whether `MOVSD` proceeds upward or downward in memory can be assumed to be clear by default; that is, `ESI` and `EDI` are incremented after each copying step. The only thing left to do before executing the `CALL` instruction is to copy the first `__fastcall` argument from its preliminary location `EAX` to its final destination `ECX`. `SpyCall()` blindly copies `EAX` to `ECX` because this operation doesn't create havoc if the calling convention is `__stdcall` or `__cdecl`. The `MOV ECX, EAX` instruction is so fast that executing it in vain is much more efficient than jumping around it after testing the value of the `fFastCall` member.

After the call to the function's entry point returns, `SpyCall()` resets the stack pointer to the location saved off to the variable `pStack`. This takes care of the different stack cleanup policy of `__stdcall` and `__fastcall` versus `__cdecl`. A `__cdecl` function returns to the caller, with the `ESP` register pointing to the top of the argument stack, whereas an `__stdcall` or a `__fastcall` function resets it to its original address before the call. Forcing `ESP` to a previously backed-up address always cleans up the stack properly, no matter which calling convention is used. The last few ASM lines of `SpyCall()` store the function result returned in `EDX:EAX` to the caller's `SPY_CALL_OUTPUT` structure. No attempt is made to find out the correct result size. This is unnecessary because the caller knows exactly how many valid result bits it can expect. Copying too many bits does no harm—they are simply ignored by the caller.

One thing that should be noted about the code in Listing 6-2 is that it contains absolutely no provisions for invalid arguments. It does not even check the validity of the stack pointer itself. In kernel-mode, this is equivalent to playing with fire. However, how could the spy driver verify all arguments? A 32-bit value on the stack could be a counter value, a bit-field array, or maybe a pointer. Only the caller and the called target function know the argument semantics. The `SpyCall()` function is a simple pass-through layer that has no knowledge about the type of data it forwards. Adding context-sensitive argument checking to this function would amount to rewriting large parts of the operating system. Fortunately, Windows 2000 offers an easy way out of this dilemma: Structured Exception Handling (SEH).

SEH is an easy-to-use framework that enables a program to catch exceptions that would otherwise crash the system. An exception is an abnormal situation that forces the CPU to stop whatever it is currently doing. Typical operations that generate exceptions are reading from or writing to linear addresses that don't map to physical or paged-out memory, writing data to a code segment, attempting to execute instructions in a data segment, or dividing a number by zero. Some exceptions are benign. For example, accessing a memory location that has been swapped to a pagefile generates an exception that the system can handle by bringing the target page back to physical memory. However, most exceptions are fatal, because the operating system has no idea how to recover from the exception, so the system simply shuts down. This reaction might seem harsh, but sometimes it is better to halt an imminent catastrophe before things become worse. With SEH, the program that caused the exception is granted a second chance. Using the Microsoft-specific C construct `__try /__except`, an arbitrary sequence of instructions can be guarded against exceptions. If an exception puts the system into a critical state, a custom handler inside the program is invoked, allowing the programmer to provide a more useful reaction than just triggering a Blue Screen.

Obviously, SEH is also able to work around the parameter validation problem of our spy device. Listing 6-3 shows a wrapper that puts the `SpyCall()` function into a SEH frame. The guarded code is enclosed in the braces of the `__try` clause. Of course, not only the `SpyCall()` instruction is protected; all subordinate code that is executed in the context of the call is protected as well. If an exception is thrown, the code inside the `__except` clause is entered, as demanded by the filter expression `EXCEPTION_EXECUTE_HANDLER`. The exception handler in Listing 6-3 is trivial. It just causes `SpyCallEx()` to return the status code `STATUS_ACCESS_VIOLATION` instead of `STATUS_SUCCESS`, which will in turn result in failure of the `DeviceIoControl()` call on the user-mode side. No Blue Screen appears; the only problem remaining after the exception is that the results of the called function are undefined, but this is something the caller should be prepared for anyway.

```
NTSTATUS SpyCallEx (PSPY_CALL_INPUT  psci,
                    PSPY_CALL_OUTPUT psco)
    {
    NTSTATUS ns = STATUS_SUCCESS;

    __try
        {
        SpyCall (psci, psco);
        }
    __except (EXCEPTION_EXECUTE_HANDLER)
        {
        ns = STATUS_ACCESS_VIOLATION;
        }
    return ns;
    }
```

LISTING 6-3. *Adding Structured Exception Handling to the Kernel Call Interface*

Although SEH catches the most common parameter errors, you should not expect it to be a remedy against any garbage a client application might possibly deliver to a kernel API function. Some bad function arguments silently wreck the system without causing an exception. For example, a function that copies a string can easily overwrite vital parts of system memory if the destination buffer pointer is set to the wrong address. This kind of bug might remain undetected for a long time, until the system suddenly and unexpectedly breaks down when the program execution eventually rushes into the modified memory area. While testing the spy driver, I occasionally managed to get the test application hung in its IOCTL call to the spy device. The application didn't respond anymore and even refused to be removed from memory. Even worse, the system became unable to shut down. This is almost as annoying as a Blue Screen!

LINKING TO SYSTEM MODULES AT RUNTIME

After implementing the basic kernel call interface, the next problem is to resolve symbolic function names to linear addresses required in the ASM CALL instruction in Listing 6-2. This step is very important because you cannot be sure that the entry points of the various kernel API functions remain unchanged over a longer period. Whenever possible, functions should be called by name. Calling a system function by address is certainly exceptional, typically restricted to functions that are not exported by the target module. In most cases, it is more desirable to use the symbolic name, which is provided somewhere in the module's export section.

Looking Up Names Exported by a PE Image

For a Win32 programmer, linking at runtime to a function exported by a DLL is an everyday task. For example, if you want to write a DLL that uses the enhanced features of Windows 2000, but also runs on legacy systems such as Windows 95 or 98 with reduced functionality, you should link to the special functions at runtime, silently falling back to default behavior if these functions aren't available. In this case, you would just call `GetModuleHandle()` if the DLL is already in memory and is guaranteed to stay there long enough, or `LoadLibrary()` if it has to be loaded or must be protected against premature unloading. The returned module handle can in turn be used in a sequence of `GetProcAddress()` calls that retrieve the entry points of all DLL functions the application wants to call. So it seems only logical to try the same with kernel functions exported by `ntoskrnl.exe`, `hal.dll`, or other system modules. However, neither of the above functions works in this situation! `GetModuleHandle()` reports that no such module is loaded, and `GetProcAddress()` returns `NULL` all the time if you pass in a hard-coded module handle, for example, `(HMODULE) 0x80400000` for `ntoskrnl.exe`. On second thought, this seems reasonable; these functions are designed for Win32 components that run in user-mode and therefore are loaded into the lower half of the 4-GB linear address space. Why should they care about kernel-mode components that are out of reach for Win32 applications anyway?

If the Win32 subsystem is ignorant about the modules in kernel memory, the next logical step is to let a kernel-mode driver do the work—the usual strategy applied throughout this book. The undocumented `MmGetSystemRoutineAddress()` function, exported by `ntoskrnl.exe`, obviously does the job, but, unfortunately, it isn't available on Windows NT 4.0. Because the main premise of this book's sample code is to remain compatible with the Windows 2000 predecessor to the greatest extent possible, I chose to reject this special feature looking up the function entries without the help of the system. The Windows 2000 runtime library provides some limited support for image file parsing, such as the undocumented `RtlImageNtHeader()` function, whose prototype is shown in Listing 6-4. This simple function takes the base address of a module image mapped to linear memory (i.e., a pointer to its `IMAGE_DOS_HEADER` structure, as defined in the Win32 SDK header file `winnt.h`) and returns a pointer to the `Portable PE` header referenced by the DOS header's `e_lfanew` member at file offset `0x3C`. This function must be used with care, because it performs only minimal sanity checks on the input pointer. It tests it for `NULL` and `0xFFFFFFFF` and verifies that the memory block it points to contains the `MZ` signature at the beginning. This means that if you pass in a bogus address that is neither `NULL` nor `0xFFFFFFFF`, a Blue Screen will be triggered immediately when `RtlImageNtHeader()` reads the DOS header signature. Oddly, Windows NT 4.0 runs this code in an SEH frame, whereas Windows 2000 doesn't.

```
PIMAGE_NT_HEADERS NTAPI RtlImageNtHeader (PVOID Base);
```

LISTING 6-4. *The Prototype of* RtlImageNtHeader()

Listing 6-4 shows that `RtlImageNtHeader()` returns a pointer to an `IMAGE_NT_HEADERS` structure. The entire set of PE file structures is defined in `winnt.h`. Unfortunately, the DDK header files do not have them, so it is necessary to add these definitions manually. My spy driver contains the structures it needs for symbol lookup (Listing 6-5) in its header file `w2k_spy.h`. `IMAGE_NT_HEADERS` is simply a concatenation of the PE signature "`PE\0\0`," an `IMAGE_FILE_HEADER`, and an `IMAGE_OPTIONAL_HEADER`. The latter ends with an array of `IMAGE_DATA_DIRECTORY` structures providing fast lookup of file sections with special duties. The first array entry, identified by the index `IMAGE_DIRECTORY_ENTRY_EXPORT` defined at the very beginning of Listing 6-5, points to the export section that contains the names and addresses of the functions exported by the module. This is the section where we must look up the function names passed to the kernel call interface.

```
#define IMAGE_DIRECTORY_ENTRY_EXPORT            0
#define IMAGE_DIRECTORY_ENTRY_IMPORT            1
#define IMAGE_DIRECTORY_ENTRY_RESOURCE          2
#define IMAGE_DIRECTORY_ENTRY_EXCEPTION         3
#define IMAGE_DIRECTORY_ENTRY_SECURITY          4
#define IMAGE_DIRECTORY_ENTRY_BASERELOC         5
#define IMAGE_DIRECTORY_ENTRY_DEBUG             6
#define IMAGE_DIRECTORY_ENTRY_COPYRIGHT         7
#define IMAGE_DIRECTORY_ENTRY_GLOBALPTR         8
#define IMAGE_DIRECTORY_ENTRY_TLS               9
#define IMAGE_DIRECTORY_ENTRY_LOAD_CONFIG      10
#define IMAGE_DIRECTORY_ENTRY_BOUND_IMPORT     11
#define IMAGE_DIRECTORY_ENTRY_IAT              12
#define IMAGE_DIRECTORY_ENTRY_DELAY_IMPORT     13
#define IMAGE_DIRECTORY_ENTRY_COM_DESCRIPTOR   14

#define IMAGE_NUMBEROF_DIRECTORY_ENTRIES       16

// -----------------------------------------------------------------

typedef struct _IMAGE_FILE_HEADER
    {
    WORD  Machine;
    WORD  NumberOfSections;
    DWORD TimeDateStamp;
    DWORD PointerToSymbolTable;
    DWORD NumberOfSymbols;
    WORD  SizeOfOptionalHeader;
    WORD  Characteristics;
    }
    IMAGE_FILE_HEADER, *PIMAGE_FILE_HEADER;
```

(continued)

```
// ----------------------------------------------------------------

typedef struct _IMAGE_DATA_DIRECTORY
    {
    DWORD VirtualAddress;
    DWORD Size;
    }
    IMAGE_DATA_DIRECTORY, *PIMAGE_DATA_DIRECTORY;

// ----------------------------------------------------------------

typedef struct _IMAGE_OPTIONAL_HEADER
    {
    WORD                 Magic;
    BYTE                 MajorLinkerVersion;
    BYTE                 MinorLinkerVersion;
    DWORD                SizeOfCode;
    DWORD                SizeOfInitializedData;
    DWORD                SizeOfUninitializedData;
    DWORD                AddressOfEntryPoint;
    DWORD                BaseOfCode;
    DWORD                BaseOfData;
    DWORD                ImageBase;
    DWORD                SectionAlignment;
    DWORD                FileAlignment;
    WORD                 MajorOperatingSystemVersion;
    WORD                 MinorOperatingSystemVersion;
    WORD                 MajorImageVersion;
    WORD                 MinorImageVersion;
    WORD                 MajorSubsystemVersion;
    WORD                 MinorSubsystemVersion;
    DWORD                Win32VersionValue;
    DWORD                SizeOfImage;
    DWORD                SizeOfHeaders;
    DWORD                CheckSum;
    WORD                 Subsystem;
    WORD                 DllCharacteristics;
    DWORD                SizeOfStackReserve;
    DWORD                SizeOfStackCommit;
    DWORD                SizeOfHeapReserve;
    DWORD                SizeOfHeapCommit;
    DWORD                LoaderFlags;
    DWORD                NumberOfRvaAndSizes;
    IMAGE_DATA_DIRECTORY DataDirectory
                         [IMAGE_NUMBEROF_DIRECTORY_ENTRIES];
    }
    IMAGE_OPTIONAL_HEADER, *PIMAGE_OPTIONAL_HEADER;

// ----------------------------------------------------------------

typedef struct _IMAGE_NT_HEADERS
    {
```

```
    DWORD                 Signature;
    IMAGE_FILE_HEADER     FileHeader;
    IMAGE_OPTIONAL_HEADER OptionalHeader;
    }
    IMAGE_NT_HEADERS, *PIMAGE_NT_HEADERS;

// -----------------------------------------------------------------

typedef struct _IMAGE_EXPORT_DIRECTORY
    {
    DWORD Characteristics;
    DWORD TimeDateStamp;
    WORD  MajorVersion;
    WORD  MinorVersion;
    DWORD Name;
    DWORD Base;
    DWORD NumberOfFunctions;
    DWORD NumberOfNames;
    DWORD AddressOfFunctions;
    DWORD AddressOfNames;
    DWORD AddressOfNameOrdinals;
    }
    IMAGE_EXPORT_DIRECTORY, *PIMAGE_EXPORT_DIRECTORY;
```

LISTING 6-5. *A Subset of the Basic PE File Structures*

The layout of the export section inside a PE file is governed by the `IMAGE_EXPORT_DIRECTORY` structure, found at the bottom of Listing 6-5. Basically, it consists of a header composed of the members of the `IMAGE_EXPORT_DIRECTORY`, plus three variable-length arrays and a sequence of zero-terminated ANSI strings. An export item is usually identified by the following three parameters:

1. A zero-terminated symbolic name, consisting of 8-bit ANSI characters
2. A 16-bit ordinal number
3. A 32-bit target offset relative to the beginning of the file image

The export mechanism is not restricted to functions. It is merely a means to assign a symbol to an address inside the PE image. For functions, the symbol is attached to its entry point. For public variables, the symbol references its base address. The assignments are achieved by filling three parallel arrays with the characteristic parameters of the symbols. In Figure 6-1, these arrays are referred to as Array of Target Addresses, Array of Name Offsets, and Array of Ordinal Numbers. They correspond to the `IMAGE_EXPORT_DIRECTORY` members `AddressOfFunctions`, `AddressOfNames`, and `AddressOfNameOrdinals`, respectively, which supply the array offsets relative to the image base address. The `Name` member contains the offset of a symbol string that names the PE file itself. If the executable file is renamed, this entry can be used to retrieve its original name. Figure 6-1 is just a common example of an export section arrangement—the order of the arrays and the symbol string subsection is not fixed. A PE file writer can shuffle them around to its liking, as long as the members of the `IMAGE_EXPORT_DIRECTORY` reference them correctly. The same is true for the string referenced by the `Name` member. Although it is usually located at the beginning of the name string sequence, this is not a requirement. Never rely on assumptions about the locations of the variable portions of the export section.

The `NumberOfFunctions` and `NumberOfNames` members of the `IMAGE_EXPORT_DIRECTORY` specify the number of entries in the `AddressOfFunctions` and `AddressOfNames` arrays, respectively. No count is specified for the `AddressOfNameOrdinals` array, because it always contains as many entries as the `AddressOfNames` array. The maintenance of separate entry counts for addresses and names suggests that it might be possible to build executables that export unnamed addresses. I have never seen such a file, but it is a good idea to keep this possibility in mind while accessing the arrays. Again, don't rely on assumptions!

The process of looking up the address of an exported function or variable by name requires the following steps, given a module base address (i.e., an `HMODULE` in Win32 lingo):

1. Call `RtlImageNtHeader()` with the module's base address to get at its `IMAGE_NT_HEADERS`. If this function returns `NULL`, the address does not reference a valid PE image.[*]
2. Use the constant `IMAGE_DIRECTORY_ENTRY_EXPORT` as an index into the `DataDirectory` of the `OptionalHeader` member to find out the offset of the export section.
3. Locate the name array inside the export section by evaluating the `AddressOfNames` member of the `IMAGE_EXPORT_DIRECTORY` header.
4. Enumerate the names until a match is found or the end of the array indicated by `NumberOfNames` is reached.
5. If a matching name is available, use the name array index to read the associated ordinal number from the array of ordinals. The values in this array are zero-based, so you can use the name's ordinal immediately as an index into the address array.
6. Add the module's base address to the offset retrieved from the address array.

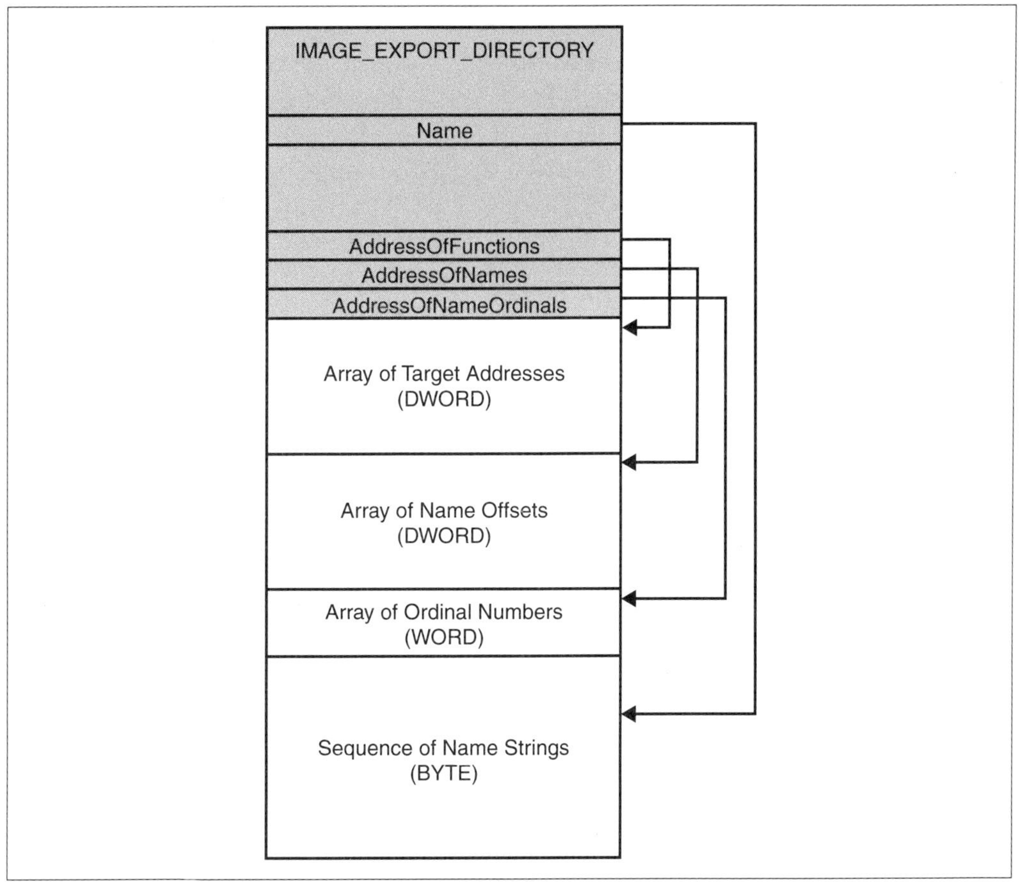

FIGURE 6-1. *Typical Layout of a PE File's Export Section*

This sequence of steps appears fairly simple. However, it contains one unknown quantity: the module base address. Whereas the above actions basically reflect the behavior of the Win32 `GetProcAddress()` function, finding the module address means mimicking the behavior of `GetModuleHandle()`. If you scan the function names exported by `ntoskrnl.exe`, you won't be able to find anything that sounds even remotely like a function that might do the trick. The reason is that the Windows 2000 kernel provides a comprehensive function for this and many other tasks that involve access to internal system data. This function is called `NtQuerySystemInformation()`.

LOCATING SYSTEM MODULES AND DRIVERS IN MEMORY

`NtQuerySystemInformation()` is one of the most essential API functions for Windows 2000 system programmers, and there is hardly any built-in administration utility that does not make use of it—yet you won't find it mentioned anywhere in the Device Driver Kit (DDK) documentation. There is a single mention in the comments to the `CONFIGURATION_INFORMATION` structure inside `ntddk.h`, proving that this function exists, but that's it. If an "undocumentedness coefficient" would exist that were defined as the usefulness of a function divided by its frequency of occurrence in the Microsoft documentation, `NtQuerySystemInformation()` would certainly be ranked at the top. Along with many other wonderful things, this function can return a list of loaded system modules, including all system core components and kernel-mode drivers.

The spy driver source files contain the bare minimum of code and type definitions required to obtain the loaded-module list from `NtQuerySystemInformation()`. From the caller's point of view, it is a simple function. It expects four arguments, as shown in Listing 6-6. The `SystemInformationClass` is a numeric zero-based value that specifies the type of information to be queried. The information—which can be of variable length, depending on the information class—is copied to the `System Information` buffer supplied by the caller. The buffer length is specified by the `SystemInformationLength` argument. On success, the actual number of bytes copied to the buffer is written to the variable pointed to by `ReturnLength`. The problem with this function is that it doesn't report how many bytes it wanted to copy if it finds out that the buffer is too small. Thus, the caller must apply a trial-and-error heuristic until the returned status code changes from `STATUS_INFO_LENGTH_MISMATCH` (`0xC0000004`) to `STATUS_SUCCESS` (`0x00000000`).

Listing 6-6 doesn't show `NtQuerySystemInformation()` itself, but rather its twin, `ZwQuerySystemInformation()`, which is identical except for the function name prefix. You might recall from Chapter 2 that the `Nt*` and `Zw*` variants of the Native API functions work exactly the same if called from user-mode. The interface module `ntdll.dll` routes each pair through the same `INT 2Eh` stub. In kernel-mode, however, things are different. In this case, Native API calls are handled by `ntoskrnl.exe`, using different execution paths for `Nt*` and `Zw*` functions. The `Zw*` variants are again routed through the `INT 2Eh` interrupt gate, exactly as `ntdll.dll`. The `Nt*` variants, however,

```
NTSTATUS NTAPI ZwQuerySystemInformation (DWORD  SystemInformationClass,
                                         PVOID  SystemInformation,
                                         DWORD  SystemInformationLength,
                                         PDWORD ReturnLength);
```

LISTING 6-6. *The Prototype of* `NtQuerySystemInformation()`

bypass this gate. In the glossary of the DDK documentation, Microsoft provides the following description for the `Zw*` function set (Microsoft 2000f):

> *"A set of entry points parallel to the executive's system services. A call to a* **ZwXxx** *entry point from kernel-mode code (including calls from other system services or drivers) supplies the corresponding system service, except the caller's access rights and the arguments to the* ***Zw*** *'alias' are not checked for validity, and the call does not cause the previous mode to be set to user mode."* (Windows 2000 DDK \ Kernel-Mode Drivers \ Design Guide \ Kernel-Mode Glossary \ Z \ Zw routines.)

The last passage about the "previous mode" is important. Peter G. Viscarola and W. Anthony Mason put it in different, more clarifying words:

> *"Although either variant of the function may typically be called from Kernel mode, the* Zw *variant is used in place of the* Nt *version to cause the previous mode (and hence the mode in which the request was issued) to be set to Kernel mode." (Viscarola and Mason 1999, p. 18).*

The side effect of this previous-mode handling is that calling `NtQuerySystemInformation()` from a kernel-mode driver without any additional provisions returns an error status of `STATUS_ACCESS_VIOLATION` (`0xC0000005`), whereas `ZwQuerySystemInformation()` succeeds or at least returns `STATUS_INFO_LENGTH_MISMATCH`.

In Listing 6-7, the constant and type definitions required for the `SystemModuleInformation` class are shown. The list of loaded modules is returned in the form of a `MODULE_LIST` structure, composed of a 32-bit module count and an array of `MODULE_INFO` structures, one for each module.

```
#define SystemModuleInformation 11 // SYSTEMINFOCLASS

// -----------------------------------------------------------------

typedef struct _MODULE_INFO
    {
    DWORD dReserved1;
    DWORD dReserved2;
    PVOID pBase;
    DWORD dSize;
    DWORD dFlags;
    WORD  wIndex;
    WORD  wRank;
    WORD  wLoadCount;
```

(continued)

```
    WORD  wNameOffset;
    BYTE  abPath [MAXIMUM_FILENAME_LENGTH];
    }
    MODULE_INFO, *PMODULE_INFO, **PPMODULE_INFO;

#define MODULE_INFO_ sizeof (MODULE_INFO)

// -----------------------------------------------------------------

typedef struct _MODULE_LIST
    {
    DWORD       dModules;
    MODULE_INFO aModules [];
    }
    MODULE_LIST, *PMODULE_LIST, **PPMODULE_LIST;

#define MODULE_LIST_ sizeof (MODULE_LIST)
```

LISTING 6-7. `SystemModuleInformation` *Definitions*

Now everything is set up for a `ZwQuerySystemInformation()` call. Listing 6-8 contains the `SpyModuleList()` function that implements the usual trial-and-error loop required for this API function, along with two simple memory management functions, `SpyMemoryCreate()` and `SpyMemoryDestroy()`, that internally call the Windows 2000 Executive functions `ExAllocatePoolWithTag()` and `ExFreePool()`. The code starts out with a 4,096-byte buffer and doubles its size if the status code says `STATUS_INFO_LENGTH_MISMATCH`. All other status codes break the loop. The optional arguments `pdData` and `pns` provide more information about the returned value. If `SpyModuleList()` yields `NULL`, indicating failure, the `NTSTATUS` buffer pointed to by `pns` receives an error status code and `*pdData` is set to zero. On success, `*pdData` specifies the number of bytes copied to the buffer, and `*pns` reports `STATUS_SUCCESS`.

```
#define SPY_TAG '>YPS' // SPY> read backwards

// -----------------------------------------------------------------

PVOID SpyMemoryCreate (DWORD dSize)
    {
    return ExAllocatePoolWithTag (PagedPool, max (dSize, 1),
                                  SPY_TAG);
    }

// -----------------------------------------------------------------
```

```
PVOID SpyMemoryDestroy (PVOID pData)
    {
    if (pData != NULL) ExFreePool (pData);
    return NULL;
    }

// -----------------------------------------------------------------

PMODULE_LIST SpyModuleList (PDWORD    pdData,
                            PNTSTATUS pns)
    {
    DWORD        dSize;
    DWORD        dData = 0;
    NTSTATUS     ns    = STATUS_INVALID_PARAMETER;
    PMODULE_LIST pml   = NULL;

    for (dSize = PAGE_SIZE; (pml == NULL) && dSize; dSize <<= 1)
        {
        if ((pml = SpyMemoryCreate (dSize)) == NULL)
            {
            ns = STATUS_NO_MEMORY;
            break;
            }
        ns = ZwQuerySystemInformation (SystemModuleInformation,
                                       pml, dSize, &dData);
        if (ns != STATUS_SUCCESS)
            {
            pml   = SpyMemoryDestroy (pml);
            dData = 0;

            if (ns != STATUS_INFO_LENGTH_MISMATCH) break;
            }
        }
    if (pdData != NULL) *pdData = dData;
    if (pns    != NULL) *pns    = ns;
    return pml;
    }
```

LISTING 6-8. *Obtaining a module list from* `ZwQuerySystemInformation()`

The remaining actions to be taken to retrieve the base address of a given module are quite simple. Listing 6-9 defines two more functions: `SpyModuleFind()` is an enhanced `SpyModuleList()` wrapper that scans the module list returned by `ZwQuerySystemInformation()` for a specified module file name, and `SpyModuleBase()` in turn wraps `SpyModuleFind()`, extracting just the base address of the module in question from its `MODULE_INFO` and discarding the rest. The `SpyModuleHeader()` function concluding Listing 6-9 calls `SpyModuleBase()` and passes the result to `RtlImageNtHeader()`. This function provides the first step to the export section of a loaded module.

```
PMODULE_LIST SpyModuleFind (PBYTE     pbModule,
                            PDWORD    pdIndex,
                            PNTSTATUS pns)
    {
    DWORD        i;
    DWORD        dIndex = -1;
    NTSTATUS     ns     = STATUS_INVALID_PARAMETER;
    PMODULE_LIST pml    = NULL;

    if ((pml = SpyModuleList (NULL, &ns)) != NULL)
        {
        for (i = 0; i < pml->dModules; i++)
            {
            if (!_stricmp (pml->aModules [i].abPath +
                           pml->aModules [i].wNameOffset,
                           pbModule))
                {
                dIndex = i;
                break;
                }
            }
        if (dIndex == -1)
            {
            pml = SpyMemoryDestroy (pml);
            ns  = STATUS_NO_SUCH_FILE;
            }
        }
    if (pdIndex != NULL) *pdIndex = dIndex;
    if (pns     != NULL) *pns     = ns;
    return pml;
    }

// ----------------------------------------------------------------

PVOID SpyModuleBase (PBYTE     pbModule,
                     PNTSTATUS pns)
    {
    PMODULE_LIST pml;
    DWORD        dIndex;
    NTSTATUS     ns    = STATUS_INVALID_PARAMETER;
    PVOID        pBase = NULL;

    if ((pml = SpyModuleFind (pbModule, &dIndex, &ns)) != NULL)
        {
        pBase = pml->aModules [dIndex].pBase;
        SpyMemoryDestroy (pml);
        }
    if (pns != NULL) *pns = ns;
    return pBase;
    }

// ----------------------------------------------------------------
```

```
PIMAGE_NT_HEADERS SpyModuleHeader (PBYTE     pbModule,
                                   PPVOID    ppBase,
                                   PNTSTATUS pns)
    {
    PVOID             pBase = NULL;
    NTSTATUS          ns    = STATUS_INVALID_PARAMETER;
    PIMAGE_NT_HEADERS pinh  = NULL;

    if (((pBase = SpyModuleBase (pbModule, &ns)) != NULL) &&
        ((pinh  = RtlImageNtHeader (pBase))      == NULL))
        {
        ns = STATUS_INVALID_IMAGE_FORMAT;
        }
    if (ppBase != NULL) *ppBase = pBase;
    if (pns    != NULL) *pns    = ns;
    return pinh;
    }
```

LISTING 6-9. *Looking Up Information About a Specified Module*

RESOLVING SYMBOLS OF EXPORTED FUNCTIONS AND VARIABLES

The previous subsections explained how a PE file image is searched for a symbolic name of an exported function or variable and how the base address of a loaded system module or driver can be determined. Now it is time to put the loose ends together. Essentially, looking up a symbol exported by a given module is a three-step procedure:

1. Find out the linear base address of the module.
2. Search the export section of this module for the symbol.
3. Add the symbol offset to the module address.

The first step was discussed at some length above. Listing 6-10 provides the implementation details concerning the remaining steps. `SpyModuleExport()` expects a file name, such as `ntoskrnl.exe`, `hal.dll`, `ntfs.sys`, or similar, for the `pbModule` argument, and returns a pointer to the module's `IMAGE_EXPORT_DIRECTORY` structure, provided that the module is present in kernel memory and features an export section. The optional `ppBase` and `pns` arguments return additional information: `*ppBase` returns the module base address on success, and `*pns` reports a diagnostic error status on failure. First, `SpyModuleExport()` calls `SpyModuleHeader()` to locate the `IMAGE_NT_HEADERS`; then it evaluates the PE `DataDirectory` that contains the characteristic parameters of the export section in its first slot. If the

VirtualAddress member of this IMAGE_DATA_DIRECTORY entry (cf. Listing 6-5) is non-*NULL*, and the Size member states a reasonable value, the PE image contains an export section. In this case, SpyModuleExport() uses the PTR_ADD() macro included at the top of Listing 6-10 to add the module base address to the VirtualAddress, yielding the absolute linear address of the IMAGE_EXPORT_DIRECTORY. Otherwise, it returns NULL and sets the status code to STATUS_DATA_ERROR (0xC000003E).

```
#define PTR_ADD(_base,_offset) \
        ((PVOID) ((PBYTE) (_base) + (DWORD) (_offset)))

// -----------------------------------------------------------------

PIMAGE_EXPORT_DIRECTORY SpyModuleExport (PBYTE     pbModule,
                                         PPVOID    ppBase,
                                         PNTSTATUS pns)
    {
    PIMAGE_NT_HEADERS       pinh;
    PIMAGE_DATA_DIRECTORY   pidd;
    PVOID                   pBase = NULL;
    NTSTATUS                ns    = STATUS_INVALID_PARAMETER;
    PIMAGE_EXPORT_DIRECTORY pied  = NULL;

    if ((pinh = SpyModuleHeader (pbModule, &pBase, &ns)) != NULL)
        {
        pidd = pinh->OptionalHeader.DataDirectory
               + IMAGE_DIRECTORY_ENTRY_EXPORT;

        if (pidd->VirtualAddress &&
            (pidd->Size >= IMAGE_EXPORT_DIRECTORY_))
            {
            pied = PTR_ADD (pBase, pidd->VirtualAddress);
            }
        else
            {
            ns = STATUS_DATA_ERROR;
            }
        }
    if (ppBase != NULL) *ppBase = pBase;
    if (pns    != NULL) *pns    = ns;
    return pied;
    }
```

```
// ----------------------------------------------------------------

PVOID SpyModuleSymbol (PBYTE     pbModule,
                       PBYTE     pbName,
                       PPVOID    ppBase,
                       PNTSTATUS pns)
    {
    PIMAGE_EXPORT_DIRECTORY pied;
    PDWORD                  pdNames, pdFunctions;
    PWORD                   pwOrdinals;
    DWORD                   i, j;
    PVOID                   pBase    = NULL;
    NTSTATUS                ns       = STATUS_INVALID_PARAMETER;
    PVOID                   pAddress = NULL;

    if ((pied = SpyModuleExport (pbModule, &pBase, &ns)) != NULL)
        {
        pdNames     = PTR_ADD (pBase, pied->AddressOfNames);
        pdFunctions = PTR_ADD (pBase, pied->AddressOfFunctions);
        pwOrdinals  = PTR_ADD (pBase, pied->AddressOfNameOrdinals);

        for (i = 0; i < pied->NumberOfNames; i++)
            {
            j = pwOrdinals [i];

            if (!strcmp (PTR_ADD (pBase, pdNames [i]), pbName))
                {
                if (j < pied->NumberOfFunctions)
                    {
                    pAddress = PTR_ADD (pBase, pdFunctions [j]);
                    }
                break;
                }
            }
        if (pAddress == NULL)
            {
            ns = STATUS_PROCEDURE_NOT_FOUND;
            }
        }
    if (ppBase != NULL) *ppBase = pBase;
    if (pns    != NULL) *pns    = ns;
    return pAddress;
    }
```

Listing 6-10. *Looking Up Symbols in a Module's Export Section*

SpyModuleSymbol() does the final work. Here you find the code that accesses the various items shown in Figure 6-1. After requesting an IMAGE_EXPORT_DIRECTORY pointer from SpyModuleExport(), the linear addresses of the address, name, and ordinal arrays are determined, again with the help of the PTR_ADD() macro. Fortunately, the PE file format specifies pointers to its internal data structures consistently as offsets from the base address of the image, so the PTR_ADD() macro constitutes a convenient general-purpose shortcut whenever a linear address must be computed from such an offset. It is important to note the role of the ordinal number array during address lookup. If the symbol has been found in the name array, the variable i contains the zero-based index of the array entry pointing to the symbol name. This value cannot be used as is to retrieve the associated address—it must be converted by means of the ordinal number array. The code line j = pwOrdinals [i]; does the trick. The resulting zero-based ordinal number j is the index that finally selects the correct address. Note that ordinal numbers are 16-bit quantities, whereas the other two arrays contain 32-bit numbers. If the symbol passed to SpyModuleSymbol() as its pbName argument cannot be resolved, a NULL pointer is returned, along with a status code of STATUS_PROCEDURE_NOT_FOUND (0xC000007A).

Although it looks like SpyModuleSymbol() provides everything we need to call kernel functions by name, I'm putting one more wrapper around it. Listing 6-11 shows the ultimate achievement: The function SpyModuleSymbolEx() takes a single string composed of a module/symbol pair in the form "module!symbol" and resolves it with the help of SpyModuleSymbol(). The largest part of the code is busy parsing the input string into a module name and a symbol. If no "!" separator is found, SpyModuleSymbolEx() assumes that ntoskrnl.exe is the target module, because this is certainly the most frequently used option.

```
PVOID SpyModuleSymbolEx (PBYTE      pbSymbol,
                         PPVOID     ppBase,
                         PNTSTATUS pns)
    {
    DWORD    i;
    BYTE     abModule [MAXIMUM_FILENAME_LENGTH] = "ntoskrnl.exe";
    PBYTE    pbName   = pbSymbol;
    PVOID    pBase    = NULL;
    NTSTATUS ns       = STATUS_INVALID_PARAMETER;
    PVOID    pAddress = NULL;

    for (i = 0; pbSymbol [i] && (pbSymbol [i] != '!'); i++);

    if (pbSymbol [i++])
        {
```

```
        if (i <= MAXIMUM_FILENAME_LENGTH)
            {
            strcpyn (abModule, pbSymbol, i);
            pbName = pbSymbol + i;
            }
        else
            {
            pbName = NULL;
            }
        }
    if (pbName != NULL)
        {
        pAddress = SpyModuleSymbol (abModule, pbName, &pBase, &ns);
        }
    if (ppBase != NULL) *ppBase = pBase;
    if (pns    != NULL) *pns    = ns;
    return pAddress;
    }
```

LISTING 6-11. *A Powerful Symbol Lookup Function*

THE BRIDGE TO USER-MODE

Now the evolution of the kernel call interface will slowly come to an end—at least as far as kernel-mode is concerned. Let me sum up what we have so far:

- A function named `SpyCallEx()` (Listing 6-3) that receives a `SPY_CALL_INPUT` control block containing a target address and some function arguments. It calls the specified address and returns any results in a `SPY_CALL_OUTPUT` control block.
- A mechanism to look up exported system functions and variables by name, represented by the function `SpyModuleSymbolEx()` (Listing 6-11).

So the last question is: "How do we make this stuff accessible to user-mode applications?" The answer is, of course: "Via Device I/O Control," as usual. To this end, the spy device provides a couple of IOCTL functions, summarized in Table 6-1. This is yet another excerpt from Table 4-2 in Chapter 4, which is a complete summary of all IOCTL functions offered by `w2k_spy.sys`. Listing 6-12 excerpts the relevant portions of the `SpyDispatcher()` function, which is shown in Listing 4-7 in Chapter 4.

The last row in Table 6-1 names the SPY_IO_CALL function that will serve as the bridge to user-mode. The remaining functions are there just for fun. I thought that once the spy device has access to this sort of valuable information, it would be nice to make it available to applications as well. As in Chapters 4 and 5, short descriptions of all newly introduced IOCTL functions follow.

TABLE 6-1. *IOCTL Functions Associated with the Kernel Call Interface*

FUNCTION NAME	ID	IOCTL CODE	DESCRIPTION
SPY_IO_MODULE_INFO	19	0x8000604C	Returns information about loaded system modules
SPY_IO_PE_HEADER	20	0x80006050	Returns IMAGE_NT_HEADERS data
SPY_IO_PE_EXPORT	21	0x80006054	Returns IMAGE_EXPORT_DIRECTORY data
SPY_IO_PE_SYMBOL	22	0x80006058	Returns the address of an exported system symbol
SPY_IO_CALL	23	0x8000E05C	Calls a function inside a loaded module

```
NTSTATUS SpyDispatcher (PDEVICE_CONTEXT pDeviceContext,
                        DWORD           dCode,
                        PVOID           pInput,
                        DWORD           dInput,
                        PVOID           pOutput,
                        DWORD           dOutput,
                        PDWORD          pdInfo)
    {
    SPY_MEMORY_BLOCK smb;
    SPY_PAGE_ENTRY   spe;
    SPY_CALL_INPUT   sci;
    PHYSICAL_ADDRESS pa;
    DWORD            dValue, dCount;
    BOOL             fReset, fPause, fFilter, fLine;
    PVOID            pAddress;
    PBYTE            pbName;
    HANDLE           hObject;
    NTSTATUS         ns = STATUS_INVALID_PARAMETER;

    MUTEX_WAIT (pDeviceContext->kmDispatch);

    *pdInfo = 0;

    switch (dCode)
        {
```

```
// ================================================
// unrelated IOCTL functions omitted (cf. Listing 4-7)
// ================================================
        case SPY_IO_MODULE_INFO:
            {
            if ((ns = SpyInputPointer (&pbName,
                                       pInput, dInput))
                == STATUS_SUCCESS)
                {
                ns = SpyOutputModuleInfo (pbName,
                                          pOutput, dOutput, pdInfo);
                }
            break;
            }
        case SPY_IO_PE_HEADER:
            {
            if ((ns = SpyInputPointer (&pAddress,
                                       pInput, dInput))
                == STATUS_SUCCESS)
                {
                ns = SpyOutputPeHeader (pAddress,
                                        pOutput, dOutput, pdInfo);
                }
            break;
            }
        case SPY_IO_PE_EXPORT:
            {
            if ((ns = SpyInputPointer (&pAddress,
                                       pInput, dInput))
                == STATUS_SUCCESS)
                {
                ns = SpyOutputPeExport (pAddress,
                                        pOutput, dOutput, pdInfo);
                }
            break;
            }
        case SPY_IO_PE_SYMBOL:
            {
            if ((ns = SpyInputPointer (&pbName,
                                       pInput, dInput))
                == STATUS_SUCCESS)
                {
                ns = SpyOutputPeSymbol (pbName,
                                        pOutput, dOutput, pdInfo);
                }
            break;
            }
        case SPY_IO_CALL:
            {
```

(continued)

```
            if ((ns = SpyInputBinary (&sci, SPY_CALL_INPUT_,
                                      pInput, dInput))
                == STATUS_SUCCESS)
                {
                ns = SpyOutputCall (&sci,
                                    pOutput, dOutput, pdInfo);
                }
            break;
            }
// =======================================================
// unrelated IOCTL functions omitted (cf. Listing 4-7)
// =======================================================
        }
    MUTEX_RELEASE (pDeviceContext->kmDispatch);
    return ns;
    }
```

LISTING 6-12. *Excerpt from the Spy Driver's Hook Command Dispatcher*

THE IOCTL FUNCTION SPY_IO_MODULE_INFO

The IOCTL `SPY_IO_MODULE_INFO` function receives a module base address and sends back a `SPY_MODULE_INFO` structure if the address points to a valid PE image. The definition of this structure plus the related `SpyOutputModuleInfo()` helper function called by the `SpyDispatcher()` in Listing 6-12 are shown in Listing 6-13. `SpyOutputModuleInfo()` is based on `SpyModuleFind()` (Listing 6-9), which returns `MODULE_INFO` data obtained from `ZwQuerySystemInformation()`. The `MODULE_INFO` is converted to `SPY_MODULE_INFO` format and sent off to the caller.

```
typedef struct _SPY_MODULE_INFO
    {
    PVOID pBase;
    DWORD dSize;
    DWORD dFlags;
    DWORD dIndex;
    DWORD dLoadCount;
    DWORD dNameOffset;
    BYTE  abPath [MAXIMUM_FILENAME_LENGTH];
    }
    SPY_MODULE_INFO, *PSPY_MODULE_INFO, **PPSPY_MODULE_INFO;

#define SPY_MODULE_INFO_ sizeof (SPY_MODULE_INFO)

// -----------------------------------------------------------------
```

```
NTSTATUS SpyOutputModuleInfo (PBYTE  pbModule,
                              PVOID  pOutput,
                              DWORD  dOutput,
                              PDWORD pdInfo)
    {
    SPY_MODULE_INFO smi;
    PMODULE_LIST    pml;
    PMODULE_INFO    pmi;
    DWORD           dIndex;
    NTSTATUS        ns = STATUS_INVALID_PARAMETER;

    if ((pbModule != NULL) && SpyMemoryTestAddress (pbModule) &&
        ((pml = SpyModuleFind (pbModule, &dIndex, &ns)) != NULL))
        {
        pmi = pml->aModules + dIndex;

        smi.pBase       = pmi->pBase;
        smi.dSize       = pmi->dSize;
        smi.dFlags      = pmi->dFlags;
        smi.dIndex      = pmi->wIndex;
        smi.dLoadCount  = pmi->wLoadCount;
        smi.dNameOffset = pmi->wNameOffset;

        strcpyn (smi.abPath, pmi->abPath, MAXIMUM_FILENAME_LENGTH);

        ns = SpyOutputBinary (&smi, SPY_MODULE_INFO_,
                              pOutput, dOutput, pdInfo);

        SpyMemoryDestroy (pml);
        }
    return ns;
    }
```

LISTING 6-13. *Implementation of* SPY_IO_MODULE_INFO

THE IOCTL FUNCTION SPY_IO_PE_HEADER

The IOCTL SPY_IO_PE_HEADER function is merely an IOCTL wrapper for the ntoskrnl.exe API function RtlImageNtHeader(), as Listing 6-14 proves. Like SPY_IO_MODULE_INFO, it expects a module base address. The returned data is the module's IMAGE_NT_HEADERS structure.

```
NTSTATUS SpyOutputPeHeader (PVOID  pBase,
                            PVOID  pOutput,
                            DWORD  dOutput,
                            PDWORD pdInfo)
```

(continued)

```
    {
    PIMAGE_NT_HEADERS pinh;
    NTSTATUS          ns = STATUS_INVALID_PARAMETER;

    if ((pBase != NULL) && SpyMemoryTestAddress (pBase) &&
        ((pinh = RtlImageNtHeader (pBase)) != NULL))
        {
        ns = SpyOutputBinary (pinh, IMAGE_NT_HEADERS_,
                              pOutput, dOutput, pdInfo);
        }
    return ns;
    }
```

LISTING 6-14. *Implementation of* `SPY_IO_PE_HEADER`

The IOCTL Function SPY_IO_PE_EXPORT

The IOCTL `SPY_IO_PE_EXPORT` function is more interesting than the previous one. In short, it returns the `IMAGE_EXPORT_DIRECTORY` associated with a module base address to the caller. A close look at its implementation in Listing 6-15 reveals a strong similarity to the `SpyModuleExport()` function in Listing 6-10. However, `SpyOutputPeExport()` does a lot of additional work. The reason for this is that the `IMAGE_EXPORT_DIRECTORY` contains relative addresses throughout, as explained earlier. The caller can't make much use of these offsets after the data has been copied to a separate buffer, because the base address to which the offsets relate has changed. Without additional address information from the PE header, it is impossible to compute a new matching base address. To save the caller from this excess work, `SpyOutputPeExport()` converts all offsets that point into the export section to offsets relative to the beginning of this section by subtracting its `VirtualAddress` specified in the `IMAGE_DATA_DIRECTORY`. The entries in the address array must be handled differently because they refer to other sections in the PE image. Therefore, `SpyOutputPeExport()` relocates them to absolute linear addresses by adding the image base address.

```
NTSTATUS SpyOutputPeExport (PVOID  pBase,
                            PVOID  pOutput,
                            DWORD  dOutput,
                            PDWORD pdInfo)
    {
    PIMAGE_NT_HEADERS       pinh;
    PIMAGE_DATA_DIRECTORY   pidd;
    PIMAGE_EXPORT_DIRECTORY pied;
    PVOID                   pData;
    DWORD                   dData, dBias, i;
```

```
    PDWORD                   pdData;
    NTSTATUS                 ns = STATUS_INVALID_PARAMETER;

    if ((pBase != NULL) && SpyMemoryTestAddress (pBase) &&
        ((pinh = RtlImageNtHeader (pBase)) != NULL))
        {
        pidd = pinh->OptionalHeader.DataDirectory
               + IMAGE_DIRECTORY_ENTRY_EXPORT;

        if (pidd->VirtualAddress &&
            (pidd->Size >= IMAGE_EXPORT_DIRECTORY_))
            {
            pData = (PBYTE) pBase + pidd->VirtualAddress;
            dData = pidd->Size;

            if ((ns = SpyOutputBinary (pData, dData,
                                       pOutput, dOutput, pdInfo))
                == STATUS_SUCCESS)
                {
                pied  = pOutput;
                dBias = pidd->VirtualAddress;

                pied->Name                  -= dBias;
                pied->AddressOfFunctions    -= dBias;
                pied->AddressOfNames        -= dBias;
                pied->AddressOfNameOrdinals -= dBias;

                pdData = PTR_ADD (pied, pied->AddressOfFunctions);

                for (i = 0; i < pied->NumberOfFunctions; i++)
                    {
                    pdData [i] += (DWORD) pBase;
                    }
                pdData = PTR_ADD (pied, pied->AddressOfNames);

                for (i = 0; i < pied->NumberOfNames; i++)
                    {
                    pdData [i] -= dBias;
                    }
                }
            }
        else
            {
            ns = STATUS_DATA_ERROR;
            }
        }
    return ns;
    }
```

LISTING 6-15. *Implementation of* `SPY_IO_PE_EXPORT`

THE IOCTL FUNCTION SPY_IO_PE_SYMBOL

The IOCTL SPY_IO_PE_SYMBOL function makes the symbol lookup engine of the kernel call interface accessible to user-mode applications. Its implementation, shown in Listing 6-16, isn't extraordinarily exciting, because it is an IOCTL wrapper for the SpyModuleSymbolEx() function in Listing 6-11. The caller must pass in a pointer to a string in the form "module!symbol," or simply "symbol" if the symbol should be looked up in the export section of ntoskrnl.exe, and gets back a pointer to the symbol's associated linear address, or NULL if the symbol is invalid or an error occurs.

THE IOCTL FUNCTION SPY_IO_CALL

Finally, this is the IOCTL SPY_IO_CALL function we have been waiting for. Listing 6-17 provides the implementation details. This function calls SpyModuleSymbolEx() if the passed-in symbol string address is OK, and continues with SpyCallEx() if the symbol could be resolved. Like SPY_IO_PE_SYMBOL, this function expects the symbol name to be specified as "module!symbol" or simply "symbol," with the latter variant defaulting to ntoskrnl.exe. This time, however, the symbol string must be supplied as part of a properly initialized SPY_CALL_INPUT structure. On success, SPY_IO_CALL returns a SPY_CALL_OUTPUT structure containing either the result of the function call if the symbol refers to an API function or the value of the target variable if the symbol specifies a public variable such as NtBuildNumber or KeServiceDescriptorTable.

If SPY_IO_CALL fails, no data is returned. The caller must be prepared to handle this situation properly. Ignoring this error would mean returning bogus data from a kernel function call. If this data is passed in turn to another kernel function, problems may occur. If you are lucky, the faulty data is caught by the exception handler inside SpyCallEx(). If you are not so lucky, the entire process may hang persistently inside the spy device IOCTL call. As usual, however, there is a probability of a Blue Screen. But don't worry—the next section shows how the kernel call interface is properly used in user-mode applications.

```
NTSTATUS SpyOutputPeSymbol (PBYTE  pbSymbol,
                            PVOID  pOutput,
                            DWORD  dOutput,
                            PDWORD pdInfo)
    {
    PVOID     pAddress;
    NTSTATUS ns = STATUS_INVALID_PARAMETER;

    if ((pbSymbol != NULL) && SpyMemoryTestAddress (pbSymbol)
        &&
```

```
        ((pAddress = SpyModuleSymbolEx (pbSymbol, NULL, &ns))
         != NULL))
        {
        ns = SpyOutputPointer (pAddress,
                               pOutput, dOutput, pdInfo);
        }
    return ns;
    }
```

LISTING 6-16. *Implementation of* `SPY_IO_PE_SYMBOL`

```
NTSTATUS SpyOutputCall (PSPY_CALL_INPUT psci,
                        PVOID           pOutput,
                        DWORD           dOutput,
                        PDWORD          pdInfo)
    {
    SPY_CALL_OUTPUT sco;
    NTSTATUS        ns = STATUS_INVALID_PARAMETER;

    if (psci->pbSymbol != NULL)
        {
        psci->pEntryPoint =
            (SpyMemoryTestAddress (psci->pbSymbol)
             ? SpyModuleSymbolEx  (psci->pbSymbol, NULL, &ns)
             : NULL);
        }
    if ((psci->pEntryPoint != NULL)              &&
        SpyMemoryTestAddress (psci->pEntryPoint) &&
        ((ns = SpyCallEx (psci, &sco)) == STATUS_SUCCESS))
        {
        ns = SpyOutputBinary (&sco, SPY_CALL_OUTPUT_,
                              pOutput, dOutput, pdInfo);
        }
    return ns;
    }
```

LISTING 6-17. *Implementation of* `SPY_IO_CALL`

ENCAPSULATING THE CALL INTERFACE IN A DLL

Although it is good news that `w2k_spy.sys` exports an IOCTL call interface for kernel functions, this interface is somewhat clumsy to operate. Suppose you want to call a simple function such as `MmGetPhysicalAddress()` or `MmIsAddressValid()`. First, you must fill a `SPY_CALL_INPUT` structure with information about the function and its arguments. Next, you must issue a Win32 `DeviceIoControl()` call. If this function reports `ERROR_SUCCESS`, the returned `SPY_CALL_OUTPUT` structure must be evaluated. Otherwise, the error must be handled properly. Doesn't sound very appealing, does it? Fortunately, we have DLLs, so the solution to this problem is to hide the IOCTL mechanism in a DLL that does the dirty work. That's the purpose of the `w2k_call.dll` project included on this book's sample CD. The code snippets reprinted in this section are excerpts from the files `w2k_call.c` and `w2k_call.h`, found on the CD in the `\src\w2k_call` directory.

HANDLING IOCTL FUNCTION CALLS

Before anything else, the `DeviceIoControl()` calls must be encapsulated in a convenient way, because this is the bottleneck through which all kernel function calls must pass. Listing 6-18 shows the wrapper function `w2kSpyControl()`, which contains a `DeviceIoControl()` invocation at its heart. Altogether, this function carries out the following tasks:

- Validates the input/output parameters
- Loads the spy device driver and opens the spy device, if not yet done
- Invokes `DeviceIoControl()`
- Tests the output data for the expected size
- Sets the Win32 last-error code appropriately

If successful, the system's last-error code, to be retrieved by the application via `GetLastError()`, is set to `ERROR_SUCCESS (0)`. Otherwise, it is set according to the following strategy:

- If the input or output parameters are invalid, the last-error value is `ERROR_INVALID_PARAMETER (87)`, indicating "The parameter is incorrect" according to the `winerror.h` header file in the Platform Software Development Kit (SDK).
- If the spy device can't be initialized, the last-error value is `ERROR_GEN_FAILURE (31)`, indicating "A device attached to the system is not functioning."
- If the size of the data returned by the spy device doesn't match the caller's buffer size, the last-error value is `ERROR_DATATYPE_MISMATCH`, indicating "Data supplied is of wrong type."
- In all other cases, `w2kSpyControl()` preserves the last-error value set by the `DeviceIoControl()` function, whatever it might be. Usually, it will be the `NTSTATUS` returned by the spy device, but mapped to a more or less appropriate Win32 status code.

```
BOOL WINAPI w2kSpyControl (DWORD dCode,
                           PVOID pInput,
                           DWORD dInput,
                           PVOID pOutput,
                           DWORD dOutput)
    {
    DWORD dInfo = 0;
    BOOL  fOk   = FALSE;

    SetLastError (ERROR_INVALID_PARAMETER);

    if (((pInput  != NULL) || (!dInput )) &&
        ((pOutput != NULL) || (!dOutput)))
        {
        if (w2kSpyStartup (FALSE, NULL))
            {
            if (DeviceIoControl (ghDevice, dCode,
                                 pInput,   dInput,
                                 pOutput,  dOutput,
                                 &dInfo,   NULL))
                {
                if (dInfo == dOutput)
                    {
                    SetLastError (ERROR_SUCCESS);
                    fOk = TRUE;
                    }
                else
                    {
                    SetLastError (ERROR_DATATYPE_MISMATCH);
                    }
                }
            }
        else
            {
            SetLastError (ERROR_GEN_FAILURE);
            }
        }
    return fOk;
    }
```

LISTING 6-18. *The Basic* `DeviceIoControl()` *Wrapper*

The `w2kSpyStartup()` call in Listing 6-18, issued immediately before `DeviceIo Control()`, deserves some more attention. Because `w2k_call.dll` relies on the services of a kernel-mode driver, this driver must somehow be brought into memory before the first IOCTL transaction. Moreover, a device handle must be opened, identifying the target device to be accessed via `DeviceIoControl()`. To keep the DLL as flexible as possible, I opted for a mixed model in which the caller can either take full control of the loading/unloading and opening/closing of the spy device or rely on a default mechanism, leaving the device management responsibilities to the DLL. This automatism is quite simple: Loading the driver and opening the device is delayed until the first IOCTL transaction is requested. As soon as the DLL is unloaded, it automatically closes the device handle, but keeps the kernel-mode driver in memory. The latter decision constitutes a defensive strategy. As long as the caller doesn't supply any information as to how the driver should be handled, `w2k_call.dll` assumes that other clients might use the driver as well, so it can't unload the driver without impairing the operation of the other applications. As explained in Chapter 4 in the context of the memory spy application, the problem candidates are `not` the processes that still have open handles to the spy device. The Windows 2000 service control manager will delay the driver shutdown until all handles have been closed. The problem is that it won't allow any new device handles to be opened.

A `w2k_call.dll` client application can control the state of the spy device by means of the API function pair `w2kSpyStartup()` and `w2kSpyCleanup()`, shown in Listing 6-19. Because these functions might be called concurrently in a multithreading scenario, they use a critical-section object for serialization. Only one thread at a time can load/open or close/unload the spy device. If, for example, two threads call `w2kSpyStartup()` at approximately the same time, only one of them will be admitted to open the device. The other one is suspended, and will find the device up and running after resuming execution.

```
BOOL WINAPI w2kSpyLock (void)
    {
    BOOL fOk = FALSE;

    if (gpcs != NULL)
    {
        EnterCriticalSection (gpcs);
        fOk = TRUE;
        }
    return fOk;
    }

// ------------------------------------------------------------------

BOOL WINAPI w2kSpyUnlock (void)
    {
    BOOL fOk = FALSE;

    if (gpcs != NULL)
        {
        LeaveCriticalSection (gpcs);
        fOk = TRUE;
```

```
        }
    return fOk;
    }

// -----------------------------------------------------------------

BOOL WINAPI w2kSpyStartup (BOOL      fUnload,
                           HINSTANCE hInstance)
    {
    HINSTANCE hInstance1;
    SC_HANDLE hControl;
    BOOL      fOk = FALSE;

    w2kSpyLock ();

    hInstance1 = (hInstance != NULL ? hInstance : ghInstance);

    if ((ghDevice == INVALID_HANDLE_VALUE) &&
        w2kFilePath (hInstance1, awSpyFile, awDriver, MAX_PATH)
        &&
        ((hControl = w2kServiceLoad (awSpyDevice, awSpyDisplay,
                                     awDriver, TRUE))
         != NULL))
        {
        ghDevice = CreateFile (awSpyPath,
                               GENERIC_READ    | GENERIC_WRITE,
                               FILE_SHARE_READ | FILE_SHARE_WRITE,
                               NULL, OPEN_EXISTING,
                               FILE_ATTRIBUTE_NORMAL, NULL);

        if ((ghDevice == INVALID_HANDLE_VALUE) && fUnload)
            {
            w2kServiceUnload (awSpyDevice, hControl);
            }
        else
            {
            w2kServiceDisconnect (hControl);
            }
        }
    fOk = (ghDevice != INVALID_HANDLE_VALUE);

    w2kSpyUnlock ();
    return fOk;
    }

// -----------------------------------------------------------------

BOOL WINAPI w2kSpyCleanup (BOOL fUnload)
    {
```

(continued)

```
    BOOL fOk = FALSE;

    w2kSpyLock ();

    if (ghDevice != INVALID_HANDLE_VALUE)
        {
        CloseHandle (ghDevice);
        ghDevice = INVALID_HANDLE_VALUE;
        }
    if (fUnload)
        {
        w2kServiceUnload (awSpyDevice, NULL);
        }
    w2kSpyUnlock ();
    return fOk;
    }
```

LISTING 6-19. *The Spy Device Management Functions*

TYPE-SPECIFIC CALL INTERFACE FUNCTIONS

The `DeviceIoControl()` calls and the spy device management automatism have now been stowed in a set of functions, with `w2kSpyControl()` constituting their main entry point. The next step is to provide functions that perform `SPY_IO_CALL`s to the spy device. Listing 6-20 shows the basic implementation of the user-mode side of the kernel call interface, represented by the functions `w2kCallExecute()`, `w2kCall()`, and `w2kCallV()`. Regarding its input arguments, the former is the user-mode equivalent of `SpyCallEx()`, shown in Listing 6-3. In fact, the implementation of `w2kCallExecute()` shows that it calls the spy device's `SPY_IO_CALL` function via `w2kSpyControl()` after ensuring that the input control block contains either a symbol name string or an entry point address. From Listing 6-12, we know that `SPY_IO_CALL` is implemented by `SpyOutputCall()` (Listing 6-17), which in turn relies on `SpyModuleSymbolEx()` and `SpyCallEx()`.

```
BOOL WINAPI w2kCallExecute (PSPY_CALL_INPUT  psci,
                            PSPY_CALL_OUTPUT psco)
    {
    BOOL fOk = FALSE;

    SetLastError (ERROR_INVALID_PARAMETER);

    if (psco != NULL)
        {
        psco->uliResult.QuadPart = 0;
```

```
        if ((psci != NULL)
            &&
            ((psci->pbSymbol     != NULL) ||
             (psci->pEntryPoint != NULL)))
            {
            fOk = w2kSpyControl (SPY_IO_CALL,
                                 psci, SPY_CALL_INPUT_,
                                 psco, SPY_CALL_OUTPUT_);
            }
        }
    return fOk;
    }

// -----------------------------------------------------------------

BOOL WINAPI w2kCall (PULARGE_INTEGER puliResult,
                     PBYTE           pbSymbol,
                     PVOID           pEntryPoint,
                     BOOL            fFastCall,
                     DWORD           dArgumentBytes,
                     PVOID           pArguments)
    {
    SPY_CALL_INPUT  sci;
    SPY_CALL_OUTPUT sco;
    BOOL            fOk = FALSE;

    sci.fFastCall      = fFastCall;
    sci.dArgumentBytes = dArgumentBytes;
    sci.pArguments     = pArguments;
    sci.pbSymbol       = pbSymbol;
    sci.pEntryPoint    = pEntryPoint;

    fOk = w2kCallExecute (&sci, &sco);

    if (puliResult != NULL) *puliResult = sco.uliResult;
    return fOk;
    }

// -----------------------------------------------------------------

BOOL WINAPI w2kCallV (PULARGE_INTEGER puliResult,
                      PBYTE           pbSymbol,
                      BOOL            fFastCall,
                      DWORD           dArgumentBytes,
                      ...)
    {
    return w2kCall (puliResult, pbSymbol, NULL, fFastCall,
                    dArgumentBytes, &dArgumentBytes + 1);
    }
```

LISTING 6-20. *The Basic Call Interface Functions*

The SpyCall() and w2kCallV() functions in Listing 6-20 are the core functions of the kernel call interface inside w2k_call.dll, serving as a basis for several more specific functions. The main purpose of w2kCall() is to put the values of its arguments into a SPY_CALL_INPUT structure before calling w2kCallExecute() and to return the resulting ULARGE_INTEGER value. As explained earlier, not all bits of the result must be valid, depending on the result type of the called kernel function. w2kCallV() is a simple w2kCall() wrapper, featuring a variable argument list (hence the trailing V in the function name). Because the argument list of w2kCall() is tailored to the general case of kernel API invocations, it is overkill for many common function types. The most common type is the __stdcall (or NTAPI) function that returns an NTSTATUS value. In this case, the fFastCall argument is always FALSE and only the lower half of the returned 64-bit ULARGE_INTEGER contains valid data. Therefore, the w2kCallNT() function in Listing 6-21 does a much better job here. Please note how w2kCallNT() handles errors reported by w2kCall(). If w2kCall() returns FALSE, this means that w2kSpyControl() failed, indicating that the result of the function call is invalid. In this case, it would be nonsense to retrieve the LowPart value of the uliResult structure, because it contains unpredictable garbage. Therefore, w2kCallNT() defaults to STATUS_IO_DEVICE_ERROR (0xC0000185). After all, the caller must be prepared for return values other than STATUS_SUCCESS (0x00000000), so reporting this error code appears to be a reasonable decision. Other kernel functions that don't return NTSTATUS codes require a much more cautious selection of default return values in case of failure.

Listing 6-22 is a collection of five additional interface functions for __stdcall API functions that return the basic data types BYTE, WORD, DWORD, DWORDLONG, and PVOID. A trailing number in the function name indicates the number of significant return value bits. w2kCallP() is equivalent to w2kCall32(), except that the 32-bit return value is typecast to a pointer. It is not necessary to provide separate functions for the signed versions of the basic data types or for pointers to various types,

```
NTSTATUS WINAPI w2kCallNT (PBYTE pbSymbol,
                           DWORD dArgumentBytes,
                           ...)
    {
    ULARGE_INTEGER uliResult;

    return (w2kCall (&uliResult, pbSymbol, NULL, FALSE,
                     dArgumentBytes, &dArgumentBytes + 1)

            ? uliResult.LowPart
            : STATUS_IO_DEVICE_ERROR);
    }
```

LISTING 6-21. *A Simplified Interface for* NTAPI/NTSTATUS *Function Types*

because these smallish differences will be addressed by the automatic typecasting performed by the compiler. Note that all functions in Listing 6-22 expect a default return value to be passed in as the first argument. This is necessary because the call interface has no idea what value would be best to be returned if the call into kernel-mode fails, so this responsibility is up to the caller.

```
BYTE WINAPI w2kCall08 (BYTE  bDefault,
                       PBYTE pbSymbol,
                       BOOL  fFastCall,
                       DWORD dArgumentBytes,
                       ...)
    {
    ULARGE_INTEGER uliResult;

    return (w2kCall (&uliResult, pbSymbol, NULL, fFastCall,
                     dArgumentBytes, &dArgumentBytes + 1)

            ? (BYTE) uliResult.LowPart
            : bDefault);
    }

// -----------------------------------------------------------------

WORD WINAPI w2kCall16 (WORD  wDefault,
                       PBYTE pbSymbol,
                       BOOL  fFastCall,
                       DWORD dArgumentBytes,
                       ...)
    {
    ULARGE_INTEGER uliResult;

    return (w2kCall (&uliResult, pbSymbol, NULL, fFastCall,
                     dArgumentBytes, &dArgumentBytes + 1)

            ? (WORD) uliResult.LowPart
            : wDefault);
    }

// -----------------------------------------------------------------

DWORD WINAPI w2kCall32 (DWORD dDefault,
                        PBYTE pbSymbol,
                        BOOL  fFastCall,
                        DWORD dArgumentBytes,
                        ...)
    {
    ULARGE_INTEGER uliResult;
```

(continued)

```
    return (w2kCall (&uliResult, pbSymbol, NULL, fFastCall,
                     dArgumentBytes, &dArgumentBytes + 1)

            ? uliResult.LowPart
            : dDefault);
    }

// -----------------------------------------------------------------

QWORD WINAPI w2kCall64 (QWORD qDefault,
                        PBYTE pbSymbol,
                        BOOL  fFastCall,
                        DWORD dArgumentBytes,
                        ...)
    {
    ULARGE_INTEGER uliResult;

    return (w2kCall (&uliResult, pbSymbol, NULL, fFastCall,
                     dArgumentBytes, &dArgumentBytes + 1)

            ? uliResult.QuadPart
            : qDefault);
    }

// -----------------------------------------------------------------

PVOID WINAPI w2kCallP (PVOID pDefault,
                       PBYTE pbSymbol,
                       BOOL  fFastCall,
                       DWORD dArgumentBytes,
                       ...)
    {
    ULARGE_INTEGER uliResult;

    return (w2kCall (&uliResult, pbSymbol, NULL, fFastCall,
                     dArgumentBytes, &dArgumentBytes + 1)

            ? (PVOID) uliResult.LowPart
            : pDefault);
    }
```

LISTING 6-22. *More Interface Functions for Common Function Types*

DATA-COPYING INTERFACE FUNCTIONS

Before we get to the more interesting task of defining substitutes for a couple of real kernel API functions, some more lines of boilerplate code are required. I mentioned earlier that the kernel call interface of the spy device can also handle public variables exported by the kernel modules. In the description of Listing 6-2, where the

`SpyCall()` function was shown, I explained that a negative value for the argument stack size, supplied via the `dArgumentBytes` member of the `SPY_CALL_INPUT` structure, is interpreted as the one's complement of the size of an exported variable. In this case, `SpyCall()` doesn't call the specified entry point, but copies the appropriate number of bytes from this address to the result buffer. If `dArgumentBytes` is set to `-1`, yielding a one's complement of zero, the entry point address itself is copied to the buffer.

Listing 6-23 shows the data-copying functions exported by `w2k_call.dll`. This function set closely corresponds to the set of call interface functions in Listing 6-22. However, these functions require fewer input arguments. Copying the value of an exported variable requires no more than the name of the variable—no input parameters are required and no calling convention applies.

```
BOOL WINAPI w2kCopy (PULARGE_INTEGER puliResult,
                     PBYTE           pbSymbol,
                     PVOID           pEntryPoint,
                     DWORD           dBytes)
    {
    return w2kCall (puliResult, pbSymbol, pEntryPoint, FALSE,
                    0xFFFFFFFF - dBytes, NULL);
    }

// ----------------------------------------------------------------

BYTE WINAPI w2kCopy08 (BYTE  bDefault,
                       PBYTE pbSymbol)
    {
    ULARGE_INTEGER uliResult;

    return (w2kCopy (&uliResult, pbSymbol, NULL, 1)
            ? (BYTE) uliResult.LowPart
            : bDefault);
    }

// ----------------------------------------------------------------

WORD WINAPI w2kCopy16 (WORD  wDefault,
                       PBYTE pbSymbol)
    {
    ULARGE_INTEGER uliResult;

    return (w2kCopy (&uliResult, pbSymbol, NULL, 2)
            ? (WORD) uliResult.LowPart
            : wDefault);
    }

// ----------------------------------------------------------------
```

(continued)

```
DWORD WINAPI w2kCopy32 (DWORD dDefault,
                        PBYTE pbSymbol)
    {
    ULARGE_INTEGER uliResult;

    return (w2kCopy (&uliResult, pbSymbol, NULL, 4)
            ? uliResult.LowPart
            : dDefault);
    }

// ----------------------------------------------------------------

QWORD WINAPI w2kCopy64 (QWORD qDefault,
                        PBYTE pbSymbol)
    {
    ULARGE_INTEGER uliResult;

    return (w2kCopy (&uliResult, pbSymbol, NULL, 8)
            ? uliResult.QuadPart
            : qDefault);
    }

// ----------------------------------------------------------------

PVOID WINAPI w2kCopyP (PVOID pDefault,
                       PBYTE pbSymbol)
    {
    ULARGE_INTEGER uliResult;

    return (w2kCopy (&uliResult, pbSymbol, NULL, 4)
            ? (PVOID) uliResult.LowPart
            : pDefault);
    }

// ----------------------------------------------------------------

PVOID WINAPI w2kCopyEP (PVOID pDefault,
                        PBYTE pbSymbol)
    {
    ULARGE_INTEGER uliResult;

    return (w2kCopy (&uliResult, pbSymbol, NULL, 0)
            ? (PVOID) uliResult.LowPart
            : pDefault);
    }
```

LISTING 6-23. *Data-Copying Interface Functions for the Basic Data Types*

In Listing 6-23, `w2kCopy()` is the main workhorse, much like the `w2kCall()` function in case of a function invocation. Again, `w2k_call.dll` provides separate functions for the basic data types `BYTE`, `WORD`, `DWORD`, `DWORDLONG`, and `PVOID`, with a trailing number in the function name indicating the number of significant return value bits. `w2kCopyP()` returns a pointer value, and `w2kCopyEP()` handles the special case of querying an entry point address. Calling `w2kCopyEP()` is equivalent to calling the spy device's `SPY_IO_PE_SYMBOL` function. Yes, this is redundant, but having two alternative ways home is always better than none at all, isn't it?

IMPLEMENTING KERNEL API THUNKS

Meanwhile, the basic framework for the simple and easy implementation of kernel API function substitutes is available. I call these substitutes "thunks," which is the usual term in Windows lingo for a short piece of code that serves as a front-end to a function implemented in a different part of the system. Another common term is "proxy," but it is too tightly associated with the Microsoft Component Object Model (COM), so that using it here might be distracting. Let's start with two very simple Windows 2000 Memory Manager functions that have been my primary test objects during the development of the `w2k_call.dll` module: `MmGetPhysicalAddress()` and `MmIsAddressValid()`. Listing 6-24 shows how their thunks are implemented with the help of `w2kCall64()` and `w2kCall08()`. To avoid confusion with the original target functions, I am prefixing all thunk names with an underscore character.

```
PHYSICAL_ADDRESS WINAPI
_MmGetPhysicalAddress (PVOID BaseAddress)
    {
    PHYSICAL_ADDRESS pa;

    pa.QuadPart = w2kCall64 (0, "MmGetPhysicalAddress", FALSE,
                             4, BaseAddress);
    return pa;
    }

// -----------------------------------------------------------------

BOOLEAN WINAPI
_MmIsAddressValid (PVOID VirtualAddress)
    {
    return w2kCall08 (FALSE, "MmIsAddressValid", FALSE,
                      4, VirtualAddress);
    }
```

LISTING 6-24. *Sample Thunks for* `MmGetPhysicalAddress()` *and* `MmIsAddressValid()`

MmGetPhysicalAddress() receives a 32-bit linear address and returns a 64-bit PHYSICAL_ADDRESS structure, which is nothing but an alias for LARGE_INTEGER. Therefore, the thunk code calls w2kCall64(), indicating that 4 bytes are passed in on the argument stack, and putting the BaseAddress parameter on the list of arguments. The default value, to be returned in case of a fatal IOCTL error, is zero, which is the value that the original function returns on error. Because MmGetPhysicalAddress() uses the __stdcall convention, fFastCall is set to FALSE. The implementation of the MmIsAddressValid() thunk is similar, except that only the eight least significant bits of the SpyCallEx() result, corresponding to a BOOLEAN data type, are returned. The default return value is set to FALSE, which is a defensive choice. MmIsAddressValid() is typically called immediately before a memory access to avoid a potential page fault. Therefore, returning TRUE when the actual result of the function is indeterminable because of an IOCTL error would increase the risk of a Blue Screen.

That was easy. Now let's see how exported variables can be accessed in this framework. In Listing 6-25, two thunks, _NtBuildNumber() and _KeServiceDescriptorTable(), are shown. NtBuildNumber is exported by ntoskrnl.exe as a 16-bit WORD type, so the appropriate w2k_call.dll interface function is w2kCopy16(). The thunk returns zero in case of an error (if you can think of a more suitable value, please let me know). The _KeServiceDescriptorTable() thunk is a bit different, because the original KeServiceDescriptorTable address exported by ntoskrnl.exe points to a structure that comprises more than 64 bits. In this case, the best of the available options is to return the address of the KeServiceDescriptorTable itself, rather than reading an incomplete portion of the data it refers to. Therefore, the thunk makes use of the w2kCopyEP() helper function included in Listing 6-23.

You can imagine how excited I was when I realized that these thunks actually work! Then I thought: I'll try calling some very-low-level functions—that bang directly onto the hardware—that read and write I/O ports or the like. Fortunately, I had designed

```
WORD WINAPI
_NtBuildNumber (VOID)
    {
    return w2kCopy16 (0, "NtBuildNumber");
    }

// ----------------------------------------------------------------

PSERVICE_DESCRIPTOR_TABLE WINAPI
_KeServiceDescriptorTable (VOID)
    {
    return w2kCopyEP (NULL, "KeServiceDescriptorTable");
    }
```

LISTING 6-25. *Sample Thunks for* NtBuildNumber *and* KeServiceDescriptorTable

the `SpyModuleSymbolEx()` function in Listing 6-11 in a way that allows resolving symbols in `any` system module, including kernel-mode drivers. My next task was to call some functions exported by the Windows 2000 Hardware Abstraction Layer (HAL). After scanning the list of symbols contained in the export section of `hal.dll`, I decided to try two simple functions that are guaranteed to talk directly to the hardware: `HalMakeBeep()` and `HalQueryRealTimeClock()`. The `HalMakeBeep()` function reminded me of the old DOS days when it was possible to let the PC speaker squeak in many creative ways by programming some of the hardware chips on the motherboard. Actually, the implementation of `HalMakeBeep()` looks much like one of my old assembly language programs from 1987 that was able to play long sequences of music, given an array of tone pitches and durations. Operating the PC speaker involves programming a timer and a parallel I/O (PIO) chip at the I/O addresses `0x0042`, `0x0043`, and `0x0061`, so `HalMakeBeep()` was an ideal candidate for a first test of a thunk to a hardware-dependent function that would also guarantee immediate audible feedback.

Listing 6-26 shows the implementation of the `_HalMakeBeep()` thunk, an extraordinarily simple piece of code thanks to the `w2kCall08()` helper function. `HalMakeBeep()` starts a beep tone on the speaker with the requested pitch. If the pitch argument is set to zero, the beep is stopped. The function returns `TRUE` if the pitch value is valid, that is, zero or greater than 18. Note that the symbol string specified in the `w2kCall08()` call includes the name of the target module, which is `hal.dll` in this case. In Listings 6-24 and 6-25, no module was specified, because the symbols referenced there are exported by the default module `ntoskrnl.exe`.

Although `HalMakeBeep()` is a silly function, I was extremely happy to see the `_HalMakeBeep()` thunk working. The PC speaker beeped on my request! And this was Windows 2000, not DOS with this proof that a Win32 application can call a HAL function that does direct hardware access. I ported my old beep sequencer from DOS to Windows 2000, resulting in the code shown in Listing 6-27. `w2kBeep()` issues a single tone of the specified pitch and duration. `w2kBeepEx()` takes an array of pitch/duration values and plays them in sequence until coming across a zero-duration value. Both functions are exported by `w2k_call.dll`. Maybe you can use them to add musical background with a classic DOS feeling to your Win32 applications.

```
BOOLEAN WINAPI
_HalMakeBeep (DWORD Pitch)
    {
    return w2kCall08 (FALSE, "hal.dll!HalMakeBeep", FALSE,
                      4, Pitch);
    }
```

LISTING 6-26. *Thunking Down to* `HalMakeBeep()`

```
BOOL WINAPI w2kBeep (DWORD dDuration,
                     DWORD dPitch)
    {
    BOOL fOk = TRUE;

    if (!_HalMakeBeep (dPitch)) fOk = FALSE;
    Sleep (dDuration);
    if (!_HalMakeBeep (0     )) fOk = FALSE;
    return fOk;
    }

// -----------------------------------------------------------------

BOOL WINAPI w2kBeepEx (DWORD dData,
                       ...)
    {
    PDWORD pdData;
    BOOL   fOk = TRUE;

    for (pdData = &dData; pdData [0]; pdData += 2)
        {
        if (!w2kBeep (pdData [0], pdData [1])) fOk = FALSE;
        }
    return fOk;
    }
```

LISTING 6-27. *A Simple Beep Sequencer*

My next step was to try a more useful function, such as `HalQueryRealTimeClock()`. I remember that accessing the on-board real-time clock in a DOS application was at one time considered difficult. This involves reading and writing a couple of hardware I/O ports. Listing 6-28 shows the thunks to `HalQueryRealTimeClock()` and its sibling `HalSetRealTimeClock()`, along with the `TIME_FIELDS` structure on which both functions operate. The `TIME_FIELDS` structure is defined in `ntddk.h`.

```
typedef struct _TIME_FIELDS
    {
    SHORT Year;
    SHORT Month;
    SHORT Day;
    SHORT Hour;
    SHORT Minute;
    SHORT Second;
    SHORT Milliseconds;
    SHORT Weekday; // 0 = sunday
    }
```

```
    TIME_FIELDS, *PTIME_FIELDS;

// -----------------------------------------------------------------

#define TIME_FIELDS_ \
        sizeof (TIME_FIELDS)

VOID WINAPI
_HalQueryRealTimeClock (PTIME_FIELDS TimeFields)
    {
    w2kCallV (NULL, "hal.dll!HalQueryRealTimeClock", FALSE,
              4, TimeFields);
    return;
    }

// -----------------------------------------------------------------

VOID WINAPI
_HalSetRealTimeClock (PTIME_FIELDS TimeFields)
    {
    w2kCallV (NULL, "hal.dll!HalSetRealTimeClock", FALSE,
              4, TimeFields);
    return;
    }
```

LISTING 6-28. *Thunks for* `HalQueryRealTimeClock()` *and* `HalSetRealTimeClock()`

Listing 6-29 provides a typical application case of `_HalQueryRealTimeClock()`, displaying the current date and time in a console window.

```
VOID WINAPI DisplayTime (void)
    {
    TIME_FIELDS tf;

    _HalQueryRealTimeClock (&tf);

    printf (L"\r\nDate/Time: %02hd-%02hd-%04hd %02hd:%02hd:%02hd\r\n",
            tf.Month, tf.Day,    tf.Year,
            tf.Hour,  tf.Minute, tf.Second);
    return;
    }
```

LISTING 6-29. *Displaying the Current Date and Time*

Although it is great news that the kernel call interface works, it is also somewhat alarming. After all, we have been taught for years that Windows NT/2000 is a secure operating system where an application can't do anything it likes. The average Win32 programmer was cut off from the hardware. A more experienced NT programmer at least knew how to call Native API functions via `ntdll.dll`. An NT wizard was able to write kernel-mode drivers to do things that were not allowed in user-mode. Now, with the DLL presented here, all Win32 programmers are able to call arbitrary kernel functions just like any other Win32 API function. Is this a big security hole in the Windows 2000 kernel? No—the only 100% secure system is one that grants applications no access at all, which would be a useless system. As soon as there is a way to interact with the system, the system becomes vulnerable. And as soon as an operating system vendor allows third-party developers to add components to the system, it is possible to smuggle a direct bridge into the kernel, such as the `w2k_spy.sys` / `w2k_call.dll` pair. There is no such thing as a 100% secure system as long as the system interacts with its environment.

DATA ACCESS SUPPORT FUNCTIONS

I have added several dozen kernel API thunks to `w2k_call.dll`. For example, the entire set of string management functions exposed by the Windows 2000 runtime library is made available by this DLL. However, as you experiment with these predefined thunks or thunks that you have added yourself, you will find that calling kernel API functions from user-mode is a bit different from calling ordinary Win32 functions. The simplicity of the kernel call interface introduced here tends to obscure the fact that the calling application is still a user-mode program with limited privileges. For example, an application might call a kernel function that returns a pointer to a `UNICODE_STRING` structure. Most likely, this will be a pointer into kernel-mode memory, which is invisible to the calling application. Any attempts to access the string data will terminate the application with an exception, stating that the instruction at an address tried to read from a forbidden address. To solve this problem I have added support functions to `w2k_call.dll` that provide easy access to the most common types of data involved in kernel API calls.

The `w2kSpyRead()` function in Listing 6-30 is a general-purpose function that copies arbitrary memory data blocks to a caller-supplied buffer. It is based on the IOCTL function `SPY_IO_MEMORY_BLOCK` offered by the `w2k_spy.sys` spy device, briefly described in Chapter 4. Use this function to read the contents or individual members of structures allocated in kernel memory. It is important to note that `w2kSpyRead()` fails if the address range spanned by the memory block contains invalid addresses. "Invalid" means that neither physical nor pagefile memory is associated with this address. `w2kSpyClone()` is an enhanced version of `w2kSpyRead()` that automatically allocates a properly sized buffer and copies the kernel data to this buffer.

```
BOOL WINAPI w2kSpyRead (PVOID pBuffer,
                        PVOID pAddress,
                        DWORD dBytes)
    {
    SPY_MEMORY_BLOCK smb;
    BOOL             fOk = FALSE;

    if ((pBuffer != NULL) && (pAddress != NULL) && dBytes)
        {
        ZeroMemory (pBuffer, dBytes);

        smb.pAddress = pAddress;
        smb.dBytes   = dBytes;

        fOk = w2kSpyControl (SPY_IO_MEMORY_BLOCK,
                             &smb,    SPY_MEMORY_BLOCK_,
                             pBuffer, dBytes);
        }
    return fOk;
    }

// -----------------------------------------------------------------

PVOID WINAPI w2kSpyClone (PVOID pAddress,
                          DWORD dBytes)
    {
    PVOID pBuffer = NULL;

    if ((pAddress != NULL) && dBytes &&
        ((pBuffer = w2kMemoryCreate (dBytes)) != NULL) &&
        (!w2kSpyRead (pBuffer, pAddress, dBytes)))
        {
        pBuffer = w2kMemoryDestroy (pBuffer);
        }
    return pBuffer;
    }
```

LISTING 6-30. *General-Purpose Data Access Functions*

Reading strings requires a bit more work. Please recall that the most common string type used by kernel-mode components is the `UNICODE_STRING` structure, comprising a string buffer pointer and information about the buffer size and the number of bytes currently occupied by the string. Reading a `UNICODE_STRING` is usually a two-part task. First, the `UNICODE_STRING` structure must be copied to find out the size and address of the string buffer. In a second step, the string data is read. To simplify this common task, `w2k_call.dll` provides the function set contained in Listing 6-31. `w2kStringAnsi()` and `w2kStringUnicode()` allocate and initialize empty `ANSI_STRING` and `UNICODE_STRING` structures, respectively, including a string buffer of the specified size. For reasons of simplicity, the string header and buffer are integrated into a single memory block. These structures can be used as targets for string copying, as demonstrated by `w2kStringClone()`. This function creates a faithful copy of a `UNICODE_STRING` in user-mode memory. The `MaximumLength` of the copy is usually equal to the original, except if the source string has inconsistent parameters. For example, if the indicated `MaximumLength` is less than or equal to the value of the `Length` member, it is invalid and therefore is set to `Length+2`. However, the `MaximumLength` of the copy will never be smaller than the original `MaximumLength`.

```
PANSI_STRING WINAPI w2kStringAnsi (DWORD dSize)
    {
    PANSI_STRING pasData = NULL;

    if ((pasData = w2kMemoryCreate (ANSI_STRING_ + dSize))
        != NULL)
        {
        pasData->Length        = 0;
        pasData->MaximumLength = (WORD) dSize;
        pasData->Buffer        = PTR_ADD (pasData, ANSI_STRING_);

        if (dSize) pasData->Buffer [0] = 0;
        }
    return pasData;
    }

// -----------------------------------------------------------------

PUNICODE_STRING WINAPI w2kStringUnicode (DWORD dSize)
    {
    DWORD           dSize1  = dSize * WORD_;
    PUNICODE_STRING pusData = NULL;

    if ((pusData = w2kMemoryCreate (UNICODE_STRING_ + dSize1))
        != NULL)
        {
        pusData->Length        = 0;
        pusData->MaximumLength = (WORD) dSize1;
        pusData->Buffer        = PTR_ADD (pusData, UNICODE_STRING_);

        if (dSize) pusData->Buffer [0] = 0;
        }
    return pusData;
    }

// -----------------------------------------------------------------
```

```
PUNICODE_STRING WINAPI w2kStringClone (PUNICODE_STRING pusSource)
    {
    DWORD           dSize;
    UNICODE_STRING  usCopy;
    PUNICODE_STRING pusData = NULL;

    if (w2kSpyRead (&usCopy, pusSource, UNICODE_STRING_))
        {
        dSize = max (usCopy.Length + WORD_,
                     usCopy.MaximumLength) / WORD_;

        if (((pusData = w2kStringUnicode (dSize)) != NULL) &&
            usCopy.Length && (usCopy.Buffer != NULL))
            {
            if (w2kSpyRead (pusData->Buffer, usCopy.Buffer,
                                             usCopy.Length))
                {
                pusData->Length = usCopy.Length;
                pusData->Buffer  [usCopy.Length / WORD_] = 0;
                }
            else
                {
                pusData = w2kMemoryDestroy (pusData);
                }
            }
        }
    return pusData;
    }
```

LISTING 6-31. *String Management Functions*

Another way of copying a kernel string down to the application memory space is to use one of the kernel runtime functions. For example, you can use a combination of the `_RtlInitUnicodeString()` and `_RtlCopyUnicodeString()` thunks provided by `w2k_call.dll` to achieve a similar effect. However, calling `w2kStringClone()` is usually easier, because this function automatically allocates the memory required for the string copy.

ACCESSING NONEXPORTED SYMBOLS

What we have achieved so far is to enable an application to execute operations that formerly were reserved to kernel-mode drivers. Can we enhance an application with capabilities that not even a kernel-mode driver has? Can we call internal functions that are neither documented nor exported? This sounds dangerous, but, as I will show in this section, it is not as bad as it might seem, if handled with care.

Looking Up Internal Symbols

The kernel call interface described in the previous sections delegated the task of looking up the addresses of exported symbols to the spy device, which has full access to the PE images of the kernel modules residing in the upper half of the linear address space. However, if the function to be called or the global variable to be accessed is not exported, the spy device has no chance to find out its address. While writing this chapter and examining some disassembly listing emitted by the Kernel Debugger, I frequently thought: "What a pity that they don't export this nifty function!" What made me especially angry was that the Kernel Debugger showed me the exact function name, but my application code was absolutely ignorant of it. Of course, I could have used my kernel call interface to jump through the plain binary entry point of the function, but that's not good programming style. The next service pack might shift this entry point to a completely different address.

I reasoned that if the Debugger can do it, my application also should be able to do it. A sample DLL described in Chapter 1 put me on the right track. The `w2k_img.dll` provides everything needed to look up the address of any symbol defined by the Windows 2000 kernel modules, provided that the operating system's symbol files are properly installed. So I extended the `w2k_call.dll` by an API function that first resolves an internal symbol to its linear address and then uses `w2kCall()` to execute it. Of course, an analogous function is provided for global variables.

Listing 6-32 shows the complete set of extended call interface functions. Again, a separate convenience function is provided for each major function type, corresponding to the functions in Listings 6-20 to 6-22. `w2kXCall()` is the main workhorse. It calls the `w2k_img.dll` API function `imgTableResolve()` to retrieve the address of the supplied symbol and, if successful, specifies it in a subsequent invocation of `w2kCall()`. Because `w2kCall()` is supposed to call an address instead of a symbol, a `NULL` pointer is passed in for its `pbSymbol` argument. The `pEntryPoint` argument is set to the symbol address `pie->pAddress` just retrieved from the symbol files. As explained in Chapter 1, `w2k_img.dll` is able to determine the calling conventions of most internal functions, so the `fFastCall` argument can be set up automatically by testing the value of `pie->dConvention` for `IMG_CONVENTION_FASTCALL`. The number of argument bytes and the pointer to the arguments are forwarded as received from the caller. It would have been possible to retrieve the number of arguments from the symbol information as well, but this works with `__stdcall` and `__fastcall` functions only. `__cdecl` symbols don't encode the argument stack size in their decoration.

```
BOOL WINAPI w2kXCall (PULARGE_INTEGER puliResult,
                      PBYTE           pbSymbol,
                      DWORD           dArgumentBytes,
                      PVOID           pArguments)
    {
    PIMG_TABLE pit;
    PIMG_ENTRY pie;
    BOOL       fOk = FALSE;

    if (((pit = w2kSymbolsGlobal (NULL))          != NULL) &&
        ((pie = imgTableResolve (pit, pbSymbol)) != NULL) &&
        (pie->pAddress != NULL))
        {
        fOk = w2kCall (puliResult, NULL, pie->pAddress,
                       pie->dConvention == IMG_CONVENTION_FASTCALL,
                       dArgumentBytes, pArguments);
        }
    else
        {
        if (puliResult != NULL) puliResult->QuadPart = 0;
        }
    return fOk;
    }

// -----------------------------------------------------------------

BOOL WINAPI w2kXCallV (PULARGE_INTEGER puliResult,
                       PBYTE           pbSymbol,
                       DWORD           dArgumentBytes,
                       ...)
    {
    return w2kXCall (puliResult, pbSymbol,
                     dArgumentBytes, &dArgumentBytes + 1);
    }

// -----------------------------------------------------------------

NTSTATUS WINAPI w2kXCallNT (PBYTE pbSymbol,
                            DWORD dArgumentBytes,
                            ...)
    {
    ULARGE_INTEGER uliResult;

    return (w2kXCall (&uliResult, pbSymbol,
                      dArgumentBytes, &dArgumentBytes + 1)

            ? uliResult.LowPart
            : STATUS_IO_DEVICE_ERROR);
    }
```

(continued)

```
// ----------------------------------------------------------------

BYTE WINAPI w2kXCall08 (BYTE  bDefault,
                        PBYTE pbSymbol,
                        DWORD dArgumentBytes,
                        ...)
    {
    ULARGE_INTEGER uliResult;

    return (w2kXCall (&uliResult, pbSymbol,
                      dArgumentBytes, &dArgumentBytes + 1)

            ? (BYTE) uliResult.LowPart
            : bDefault);
    }

// ----------------------------------------------------------------

WORD WINAPI w2kXCall16 (WORD  wDefault,
                        PBYTE pbSymbol,
                        DWORD dArgumentBytes,
                        ...)
    {
    ULARGE_INTEGER uliResult;

    return (w2kXCall (&uliResult, pbSymbol,
                      dArgumentBytes, &dArgumentBytes + 1)

            ? (WORD) uliResult.LowPart
            : wDefault);
    }

// ----------------------------------------------------------------

DWORD WINAPI w2kXCall32 (DWORD dDefault,
                         PBYTE pbSymbol,
                         DWORD dArgumentBytes,
                         ...)
    {
    ULARGE_INTEGER uliResult;

    return (w2kXCall (&uliResult, pbSymbol,
                      dArgumentBytes, &dArgumentBytes + 1)

            ? uliResult.LowPart
            : dDefault);
    }

// ----------------------------------------------------------------
```

```
QWORD WINAPI w2kXCall64 (QWORD qDefault,
                         PBYTE pbSymbol,
                         DWORD dArgumentBytes,
                         ...)
    {
    ULARGE_INTEGER uliResult;

    return (w2kXCall (&uliResult, pbSymbol,
                      dArgumentBytes, &dArgumentBytes + 1)

            ? uliResult.QuadPart
            : qDefault);
    }

// -----------------------------------------------------------------

PVOID WINAPI w2kXCallP (PVOID pDefault,
                        PBYTE pbSymbol,
                        DWORD dArgumentBytes,
                        ...)
    {
    ULARGE_INTEGER uliResult;

    return (w2kXCall (&uliResult, pbSymbol,
                      dArgumentBytes, &dArgumentBytes + 1)

            ? (PVOID) uliResult.LowPart
            : pDefault);
    }
```

LISTING 6-32. *The Extended Call Interface*

Note in Listing 6-32 that `w2kXCall()` invokes `w2kSymbolsGlobal()` before doing anything else. This function is included in Listing 6-33, along with some helpers, and its purpose is to load the `ntoskrnl.exe` symbol as soon as the first `w2kXCall()` is executed. The table is stored in the global `PIMG_TABLE` variable named `gpit`, so subsequent calls can reuse it. With support of some helper functions, `w2kSymbolsLoad()` returns one of the status codes listed in Table 6-2 via the optional `*pdStatus` argument. To avoid jumping to an invalid address because of unmatched symbol information, `w2kSymbolsLoad()` carefully checks the time stamp and check sum of the symbol files against the corresponding fields in the memory-resident image of the target module using the `w2kPeCheck()` API function (not reprinted) and discards the symbol table if they don't match exactly.

```
PIMG_TABLE WINAPI w2kSymbolsLoad (PBYTE  pbModule,
                                  PDWORD pdStatus)
    {
    PVOID      pBase;
    DWORD      dStatus = W2K_SYMBOLS_UNDEFINED;
    PIMG_TABLE pit     = NULL;

    if ((pBase = imgModuleBaseA (pbModule)) == NULL)
        {
        dStatus = W2K_SYMBOLS_MODULE_NOT_FOUND;
        }
    else
        {
        if ((pit = imgTableLoadA (pbModule, pBase)) == NULL)
            {
            dStatus = W2K_SYMBOLS_LOAD_ERROR;
            }
        else
            {
            if (!w2kPeCheck (pbModule, pit->dTimeStamp,
                                       pit->dCheckSum))
                {
                dStatus = W2K_SYMBOLS_CHECKSUM_ERROR;
                pit     = imgMemoryDestroy (pit);
                }
            else
                {
                dStatus = W2K_SYMBOLS_OK;
                }
            }
        }
    if (pdStatus != NULL) *pdStatus = dStatus;
    return pit;
    }

// -----------------------------------------------------------------

PIMG_TABLE WINAPI w2kSymbolsGlobal (PDWORD pdStatus)
    {
    DWORD      dStatus = W2K_SYMBOLS_UNDEFINED;
    PIMG_TABLE pit     = NULL;

    w2kSpyLock ();

    if ((gdStatus == W2K_SYMBOLS_OK) && (gpit == NULL))
        {
```

```
        gpit = w2kSymbolsLoad (NULL, &gdStatus);
        }
    dStatus = gdStatus;
    pit     = gpit;

    w2kSpyUnlock ();

    if (pdStatus != NULL) *pdStatus = dStatus;
    return pit;
    }

// -----------------------------------------------------------------

DWORD WINAPI w2kSymbolsStatus (VOID)
    {
    DWORD dStatus = W2K_SYMBOLS_UNDEFINED;

    w2kSymbolsGlobal (&dStatus);
    return dStatus;
    }

// -----------------------------------------------------------------

VOID WINAPI w2kSymbolsReset (VOID)
    {
    w2kSpyLock ();

    gpit     = imgMemoryDestroy (gpit);
    gdStatus = W2K_SYMBOLS_OK;

    w2kSpyUnlock ();
    return;
    }
```

LISTING 6-33. *The Symbol Table Manager Functions*

The `w2kSymbolsStatus()` and `w2kSymbolsReset()` functions at the bottom of Listing 6-33 are used to load and unload the symbol table on demand. `w2kSymbolsStatus()` attempts to load the symbol table if it isn't already present and returns its status. If `w2k_call.dll` already tried to load the table without success, the function simply returns the last error status (Table 6-2) unless the symbol table is reset by a `w2kSymbolsReset()` call. The latter function also destroys the memory block occupied by the symbol table, if any, forcing a complete symbol reload on the next request that involves the `ntoskrnl.exe` symbol table.

TABLE 6-2. *w2kSymbolsLoad() Status Codes*

STATUS CODE	DESCRIPTION
W2K_SYMBOLS_OK	The module's symbol table has been loaded
W2K_SYMBOLS_MODULE_ERROR	The module is not resident in memory
W2K_SYMBOLS_LOAD_ERROR	The module's symbol files couldn't be loaded
W2K_SYMBOLS_VERSION_ERROR	The symbol files don't match the resident module image
W2K_SYMBOLS_UNDEFINED	The symbol table status is undefined

The `w2kXCopy*()` function set making up the extended copy interface is shown in Listing 6-34, which corresponds to Listing 6-23 above. `w2kXCopy()` simply calls `w2kXCall()` with a negative value for `dArgumentBytes`, and the remaining copy functions are merely wrappers with simplified argument lists.

```
BOOL WINAPI w2kXCopy (PULARGE_INTEGER puliResult,
                      PBYTE           pbSymbol,
                      DWORD           dBytes)
    {
    return w2kXCall (puliResult, pbSymbol,
                     0xFFFFFFFF - dBytes, NULL);
    }

// -----------------------------------------------------------------

BYTE WINAPI w2kXCopy08 (BYTE  bDefault,
                        PBYTE pbSymbol)
    {
    ULARGE_INTEGER uliResult;

    return (w2kXCopy (&uliResult, pbSymbol, 1)
            ? (BYTE) uliResult.LowPart
            : bDefault);
    }

// -----------------------------------------------------------------

WORD WINAPI w2kXCopy16 (WORD  wDefault,
                        PBYTE pbSymbol)
    {
    ULARGE_INTEGER uliResult;

    return (w2kXCopy (&uliResult, pbSymbol, 2)
            ? (WORD) uliResult.LowPart
            : wDefault);
    }
```

```
// ----------------------------------------------------------------

DWORD WINAPI w2kXCopy32 (DWORD dDefault,
                         PBYTE pbSymbol)
    {
    ULARGE_INTEGER uliResult;

    return (w2kXCopy (&uliResult, pbSymbol, 4)
            ? uliResult.LowPart
            : dDefault);
    }

// ----------------------------------------------------------------

QWORD WINAPI w2kXCopy64 (QWORD qDefault,
                         PBYTE pbSymbol)
    {
    ULARGE_INTEGER uliResult;

    return (w2kXCopy (&uliResult, pbSymbol, 8)
            ? uliResult.QuadPart
            : qDefault);
    }

// ----------------------------------------------------------------

PVOID WINAPI w2kXCopyP (PVOID pDefault,
                        PBYTE pbSymbol)
    {
    ULARGE_INTEGER uliResult;

    return (w2kXCopy (&uliResult, pbSymbol, 4)
            ? (PVOID) uliResult.LowPart
            : pDefault);
    }

// ----------------------------------------------------------------

PVOID WINAPI w2kXCopyEP (PVOID pDefault,
                         PBYTE pbSymbol)
    {
    ULARGE_INTEGER uliResult;

    return (w2kXCopy (&uliResult, pbSymbol, 0)
            ? (PVOID) uliResult.LowPart
            : pDefault);
    }
```

LISTING 6-34. *The Extended Copy Interface*

IMPLEMENTING KERNEL FUNCTION THUNKS

The same guidelines apply to the implementation of thunks for internal kernel functions as for exported API functions, except that only functions inside `ntoskrnl.exe` can be called. This restriction is imposed by the symbol table manager inside `w2k_call.dll`, not by the call interface itself. To simplify matters, only the `ntoskrnl.exe` symbol table is loaded, because this is the module where the most interesting symbols are found (of course, `w2k_call.dll` could have been enhanced to load multiple tables on request). Listing 6-35 comprises two sample thunks for internal functions of the Windows 2000 object manager that return information about type objects (object types will be discussed in detail in Chapter 7).

Listing 6-36 shows three thunks for some very important internal data structures that will be used by the sample code in Chapter 7. Note that I have prefixed the names of all thunks that use the extended kernel call interface with two underscores. This is just a reminder that this function will work only with a proper set of symbol files. If you install a service pack without also updating the symbol files, `w2kSymbolsLoad()` will refuse to load any symbols and the thunks will fail and return default values. On the other hand, the thunks with a single leading underscore should continue to work with unmatched symbol files, because they resolve symbols on the basis of the memory-resident export tables of the new modules. However, they may fail as well after an update if the updated modules fail to export all referenced API functions or some argument lists have been changed.

```
NTSTATUS WINAPI
__ObQueryTypeInfo (POBJECT_TYPE      ObjectType,
                   POBJECT_TYPE_INFO TypeInfo,
   /* bytes     */ DWORD             TypeInfoLength,
   /* init to 0 */ PDWORD            ReturnLength)
    {
    return w2kXCallNT ("ObQueryTypeInfo",
                       16, ObjectType, TypeInfo, TypeInfoLength,
                           ReturnLength);
    }

// ----------------------------------------------------------------

NTSTATUS WINAPI
__ObQueryTypeName (POBJECT                  Object,
                   POBJECT_NAME_INFORMATION NameString,
       /* bytes */ DWORD                    NameStringLength,
```

```
                    PDWORD                    ReturnLength)
    {
    return w2kXCallNT ("ObQueryTypeName",
                       16, Object, NameString, NameStringLength,
                           ReturnLength);
    }
```

LISTING 6-35. *Sample Thunks for* `ObQueryTypeInfo()` *and* `ObQueryTypeName()`

```
PERESOURCE WINAPI
__ObpRootDirectoryMutex (VOID)
    {
    return w2kXCopyP (NULL, "ObpRootDirectoryMutex");
    }

// -------------------------------------------------------------------

POBJECT_DIRECTORY WINAPI
__ObpRootDirectoryObject (VOID)
    {
    return w2kXCopyP (NULL, "ObpRootDirectoryObject");
    }

// -------------------------------------------------------------------

POBJECT_DIRECTORY WINAPI
__ObpTypeDirectoryObject (VOID)
    {
    return w2kXCopyP (NULL, "ObpTypeDirectoryObject");
    }
```

LISTING 6-36. *Sample Thunks for Some Internal Variables*

This should suffice for now. You may be a bit disappointed that I am not adding sample code here to demonstrate the usage of the `w2k_call.dll` API functions. Don't worry—you *will* get your sample code in the next chapter.

CHAPTER 7

Windows 2000 Object Management

There is hardly anything more fascinating in the internals of Windows 2000 than the world of its objects. If the memory space of an operating system is viewed as the surface of a planet, the objects are the creatures living on it. Several types of objects exist—small and large ones, simple and complex ones—and they interact in various ways. Windows 2000 features a clever, well-structured object management mechanism that is almost completely undocumented. This chapter attempts to give you a small insight into this huge, complex universe. Unfortunately, this part of Windows 2000 is one of the best-kept secrets of Microsoft, and many questions must be left unanswered here. However, I hope that this chapter will serve as a starting point for others, helping them to go "where no man has gone before."

WINDOWS 2000 OBJECT STRUCTURES

The companion CD of this book contains a large header file named `w2k_def.h` in the `\src\common\include` directory that makes the heart of a Windows 2000 system programmer throb with joy. It is a large collection of constant and type definitions, resulting from years of Windows NT/2000 spelunking. The `w2k_def.h` file is designed to be included in Win32 applications as well as kernel-mode drivers, using conditional compilation to account for their different build environments. For example, Win32 applications can't make use of the `ntdef.h` and `ntddk.h` files that contain most of the kernel data type definitions. Therefore, `w2k_def.h` includes all `#define's` and `typedef's` found in the Device Documentation Kit (DDK) header files that are required in the definitions of the undocumented items. To avoid redefinition errors in a kernel-mode driver build, these definitions are put into an `#ifdef _USER_MODE_` clause, so they are ignored by the compiler if the `_USER_MODE_` symbol is not defined. This means that you must put a `#define _USER_MODE_` line into your source code before including `w2k_def.h` to enable the processing of the DDK definitions in a Win32 application or DLL build. The `#else` clause of the `#ifdef _USER_MODE_` construct contains a small number of definitions that are missing from the Windows 2000 DDK header files, such as the `SECURITY_DESCRIPTOR` and `SECURITY_DESCRIPTOR_CONTROL` types.

BASIC OBJECT CATEGORIES

Although objects are clearly the gist of the Windows 2000 operating system, you will find remarkably little information about their inner structure in the DDK. Out of the 21 `Ob*()` object manager API functions exported by `ntoskrnl.exe`, only 6 are listed in the DDK documentation. API functions that receive pointers to objects as arguments usually define these pointers as simple `PVOID` types. If you search the main DDK header files `ntdef.h` and `ntddk.h` for occurrences of type definitions that somehow are related to objects, you won't find much useful information. Some important object data types are defined as placeholders only. For example, the `OBJECT_TYPE` structure appears as `typedef struct _OBJECT_TYPE *POBJECT_TYPE;` just to keep the compiler happy, without revealing anything useful about its internals.

Whenever you come across an object pointer, you should view it as a linear address that divides a memory-resident structure into two parts: an `object header` and an `object body`. The object pointer doesn't point to the base address of the object itself, but to its body section that immediately follows the header. Therefore, the header parts of an object must be accessed by applying negative offsets to the object pointer. The internals of the object body are completely dependent on the type of object and may vary considerably. The most simple object is the event object with its 16-byte body. Among the most complex ones are thread and process objects, which are several hundred bytes. Basically, the object body types can be sorted into the following three main categories:

1. `Dispatcher objects` reside on the lowest system level and share a common data structure called `DISPATCHER_HEADER` (Listing 7-1) at the beginning of their object bodies. This header contains an object type ID and the length of the object body in 32-bit `DWORD` units. The names of all dispatcher object structures start with a `K` for "kernel." The presence of a `DISPATCHER_HEADER` makes an object "waitable." This means that the object can be passed to the synchronization functions `KeWaitForSingleObject()` and `KeWaitForMultipleObjects()`, which are the ones the Win32 API functions `WaitForSingleObject()` and `WaitForMultipleObjects()` are built upon.

```
typedef struct _DISPATCHER_HEADER
        {
/*000*/ BYTE       Type;         // DISP_TYPE_*
/*001*/ BYTE       Absolute;
/*002*/ BYTE       Size;         // number of DWORDs
/*003*/ BYTE       Inserted;
/*004*/ LONG       SignalState;
/*008*/ LIST_ENTRY WaitListHead;
/*010*/ }
        DISPATCHER_HEADER,
      * PDISPATCHER_HEADER,
     **PPDISPATCHER_HEADER;
```

LISTING 7-1. *Definition of the* `DISPATCHER_HEADER`

2. `I/O system data structures` are higher-level objects whose body starts with a `SHORT` member specifying an object type ID. Usually, this ID is followed by another `SHORT` or `WORD` member indicating the object body size in 8-bit `BYTE` units. However, not all objects of this category follow this guideline.
3. `Other objects`—some objects fit into neither of the above categories.

Note that the type IDs of dispatcher objects and I/O system data structures—named I/O objects from now on—are assigned independently and hence overlap. Table 7-1 lists the dispatcher object types of which I'm currently aware. Some of the structures in the "C Structure" column are defined in the DDK header file `ntddk.h`. Unfortunately, the most interesting ones, such as `KPROCESS` and `KTHREAD`, are missing. Don't worry, however—these special object types will be discussed in detail later in this chapter. All undocumented structures whose internals are at least partially known to me are included in the header file `w2k_def.h` on the companion CD, as well as in Appendix C of this book.

TABLE 7-1. *Summary of Dispatcher Objects*

ID	TYPE	C STRUCTURE	DEFINITION
0	DISP_TYPE_NOTIFICATION_EVENT	KEVENT	ntddk.h
1	DISP_TYPE_SYNCHRONIZATION_EVENT	KEVENT	ntddk.h
2	DISP_TYPE_MUTANT	KMUTANT, KMUTEX	ntddk.h
3	DISP_TYPE_PROCESS	KPROCESS	w2k_def.h
4	DISP_TYPE_QUEUE	KQUEUE	w2k_def.h

(continued)

TABLE 7-1. *(continued)*

ID	TYPE	C STRUCTURE	DEFINITION
5	DISP_TYPE_SEMAPHORE	KSEMAPHORE	ntddk.h
6	DISP_TYPE_THREAD	KTHREAD	w2k_def.h
8	DISP_TYPE_NOTIFICATION_TIMER	KTIMER	ntddk.h
9	DISP_TYPE_SYNCHRONIZATION_TIMER	KTIMER	ntddk.h

Table 7-2 summarizes the I/O objects I have identified so far. Only the first 13 IDs are defined in `ntddk.h`. Again, some of the structures in the "C Structure" column can be looked up in the DDK. Some of the remaining ones are included in `w2k_def.h` and in Appendix C of this book.

TABLE 7-2. *Summary of I/O Objects*

ID	TYPE	C STRUCTURE	DEFINITION
1	IO_TYPE_ADAPTER	ADAPTER_OBJECT	
2	IO_TYPE_CONTROLLER	CONTROLLER_OBJECT	ntddk.h
3	IO_TYPE_DEVICE	DEVICE_OBJECT	ntddk.h
4	IO_TYPE_DRIVER	DRIVER_OBJECT	ntddk.h
5	IO_TYPE_FILE	FILE_OBJECT	ntddk.h
6	IO_TYPE_IRP	IRP	ntddk.h
7	IO_TYPE_MASTER_ADAPTER		
8	IO_TYPE_OPEN_PACKET		
9	IO_TYPE_TIMER	IO_TIMER	w2k_def.h
10	IO_TYPE_VPB	VPB	ntddk.h
11	IO_TYPE_ERROR_LOG	IO_ERROR_LOG_ENTRY	w2k_def.h
12	IO_TYPE_ERROR_MESSAGE	IO_ERROR_LOG_MESSAGE	ntddk.h
13	IO_TYPE_DEVICE_OBJECT_ EXTENSION	DEVOBJ_EXTENSION	ntddk.h
18	IO_TYPE_APC	KAPC	ntddk.h
19	IO_TYPE_DPC	KDPC	ntddk.h
20	IO_TYPE_DEVICE_QUEUE	KDEVICE_QUEUE	ntddk.h
21	IO_TYPE_EVENT_PAIR	KEVENT_PAIR	w2k_def.h
22	IO_TYPE_INTERRUPT	KINTERRUPT	
23	IO_TYPE_PROFILE	KPROFILE	

The Object Header

The body of an object can assume any form suitable for the creator of the object. The Windows 2000 object manager doesn't impose any restrictions on the size and structure of the object body. Contrary to this, there is much less freedom with the header portion of an object. Figure 7-1 shows the memory layout of a full-featured object, with the maximum number of header fields. Every object features at least a basic `OBJECT_HEADER` structure, immediately preceding the object body, plus up to four optional structures that supply additional information about the object. As already noted, an object pointer always refers to the object body, not to the header, so the header fields are accessed via negative offsets relative to the object pointer. The basic header contains information about the availability and location of additional header fields, which are stacked up on the `OBJECT_HEADER` structure in the order shown in Figure 7-1, if present. However, this sequence isn't mandatory, and your programs should never rely on it. The information in the `OBJECT_HEADER` is sufficient to locate all header fields regardless of their order, as will be shown in a moment. The only exception is the `OBJECT_CREATOR_INFO` structure that always precedes the `OBJECT_HEADER` immediately if it is included.

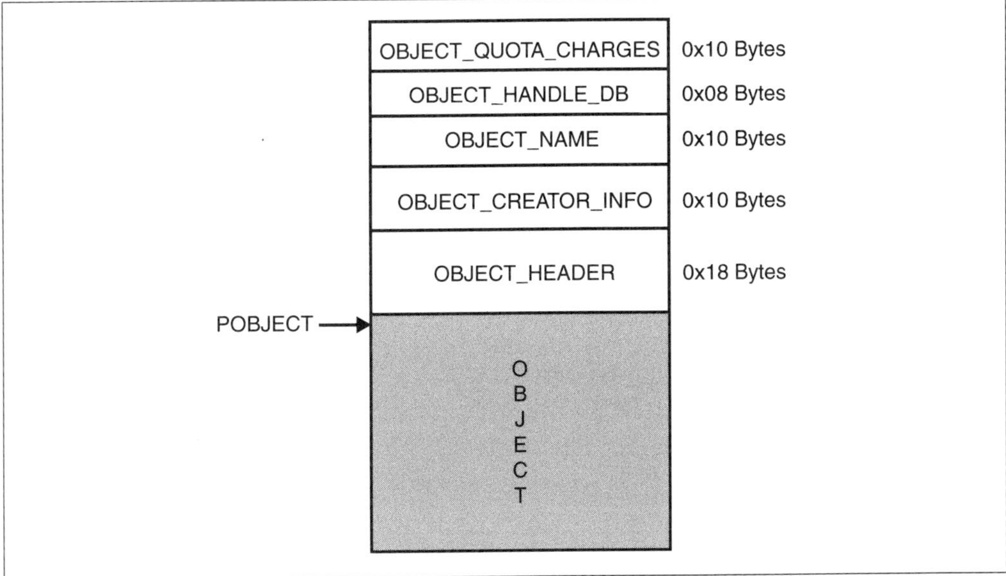

FIGURE 7-1. *Memory Layout of an Object*

Listing 7-2 shows the definition of the `OBJECT_HEADER` structure. Its members serve the following purposes:

- The `PointerCount` member indicates how many active pointer references to this object currently exist. This value is similar to the reference count maintained by Component Object Model (COM) objects. The `ntoskrnl.exe` API functions `ObfReferenceObject()`, `ObReferenceObjectByHandle()`, `ObReferenceObjectByName()`, and `ObReferenceObjectByPointer()` increment the `PointerCount`, and `ObfDereferenceObject()` and `ObDereferenceObject()` decrement it.
- The `HandleCount` member indicates how many open handles currently refer to this object.

```
#define OB_FLAG_CREATE_INFO    0x01 // has OBJECT_CREATE_INFO
#define OB_FLAG_KERNEL_MODE    0x02 // created by kernel
#define OB_FLAG_CREATOR_INFO   0x04 // has OBJECT_CREATOR_INFO
#define OB_FLAG_EXCLUSIVE      0x08 // OBJ_EXCLUSIVE
#define OB_FLAG_PERMANENT      0x10 // OBJ_PERMANENT
#define OB_FLAG_SECURITY       0x20 // has security descriptor
#define OB_FLAG_SINGLE_PROCESS 0x40 // no HandleDBList

typedef struct _OBJECT_HEADER
        {
/*000*/ DWORD        PointerCount;       // number of references
/*004*/ DWORD        HandleCount;        // number of open handles
/*008*/ POBJECT_TYPE ObjectType;
/*00C*/ BYTE         NameOffset;         // -> OBJECT_NAME
/*00D*/ BYTE         HandleDBOffset;     // -> OBJECT_HANDLE_DB
/*00E*/ BYTE         QuotaChargesOffset; // -> OBJECT_QUOTA_CHARGES
/*00F*/ BYTE         ObjectFlags;        // OB_FLAG_*
/*010*/ union
            { // OB_FLAG_CREATE_INFO ? ObjectCreateInfo : QuotaBlock
/*010*/     PQUOTA_BLOCK        QuotaBlock;
/*010*/     POBJECT_CREATE_INFO ObjectCreateInfo;
/*014*/     };
/*014*/ PSECURITY_DESCRIPTOR SecurityDescriptor;
/*018*/ }
        OBJECT_HEADER,
      * POBJECT_HEADER,
     **PPOBJECT_HEADER;
```

LISTING 7-2. *The* `OBJECT_HEADER` *Structure*

- The `ObjectType` member points to an `OBJECT_TYPE` structure (described later) representing the type object that has been used in the creation of this object.
- The `NameOffset` specifies the number of bytes to be subtracted from the `OBJECT_HEADER` address to locate the object header's `OBJECT_NAME` portion. If zero, this structure is not available.
- The `HandleDBOffset` specifies the number of bytes to be subtracted from the `OBJECT_HEADER` address to locate the object header's `OBJECT_HANDLE_DB` portion. If zero, this structure is not available.
- The `QuotaChargesOffset` specifies the number of bytes to be subtracted from the `OBJECT_HEADER` address to locate the object header's `OBJECT_QUOTA_CHARGES` portion. If zero, this structure is not available.
- The `ObjectFlags` specify various binary properties of an object, as listed in the top section of Listing 7-2. If the `OB_FLAG_CREATOR_INFO` bit is set, the object header includes an `OBJECT_CREATOR_INFO` structure that immediately precedes the `OBJECT_HEADER`. In `Windows NT/2000 Native API Reference,` Gary Nebbett mentions these flags with slightly different names in his description of the `SystemObjectInformation` class of the `ZwQuerySystemInformation()` function (Nebbett 2000, p. 24), as shown in Table 7-3.
- The `QuotaBlock` and `ObjectCreateInfo` members are mutually exclusive. If the `ObjectFlags` member has the `OB_FLAG_CREATE_INFO` flag set, this member contains a pointer to the `OBJECT_CREATE_INFO` structure (described later) used in the creation of this object. Otherwise, it points to a `QUOTA_BLOCK` that provides information about the usage of the paged and nonpaged memory pools. Many objects have their `QuotaBlock` pointer set to the internal `PspDefaultQuotaBlock` structure. The value of this `union` can be `NULL`.
- The `SecurityDescriptor` member points to a `SECURITY_DESCRIPTOR` structure if the `OB_FLAG_SECURITY` bit of the `ObjectFlags` is set. Otherwise, its value is `NULL`.

In the above list, several structures have been mentioned that weren't discussed in detail so far. Each of them will be introduced now, starting with the four optional header parts shown in Figure 7-1.

TABLE 7-3. *Comparison of* ObjectFlags *Interpretations*

SCHREIBER	VALUE	NEBBETT
OB_FLAG_CREATE_INFO	0x01	N/A
OB_FLAG_KERNEL_MODE	0x02	KERNEL_MODE
OB_FLAG_CREATOR_INFO	0x04	CREATOR_INFO
OB_FLAG_EXCLUSIVE	0x08	EXCLUSIVE
OB_FLAG_PERMANENT	0x10	PERMANENT
OB_FLAG_SECURITY	0x20	DEFAULT_SECURITY_QUOTA
OB_FLAG_SINGLE_PROCESS	0x40	SINGLE_HANDLE_ENTRY

THE OBJECT CREATOR INFORMATION

The `OBJECT_HEADER` of an object is immediately preceded by an `OBJECT_CREATOR_INFO` structure if the `OB_FLAG_CREATOR_INFO` bit of its `ObjectFlags` member is set. The definition of this optional header part is shown in Listing 7-3. The `ObjectList` member is a node within a doubly linked list (cf. Listing 2-7 in Chapter 2) that connects objects of the same type to each other. As usual, this list is circular. The list head where the object list originates and ends is located within the `OBJECT_TYPE` structure that represents the common type object of the list members. By default, only `Port` and `WaitablePort` objects include `OBJECT_CREATOR_INFO` data in their headers. The `SystemObjectInformation` class of the `ZwQuerySystemInformation()` API function uses the `ObjectList` to return complete lists of currently allocated objects, grouped by object type. Gary Nebbett points out in `Windows NT/2000 Native API Reference` that "[...] this information class is only available if `FLG_MAINTAIN_OBJECT_TYPELIST` was set in the `NtGlobalFlags` at boot time" (Nebbett 2000, p. 25).

```
typedef struct _OBJECT_CREATOR_INFO
        {
/*000*/ LIST_ENTRY ObjectList;      // OBJECT_CREATOR_INFO
/*008*/ HANDLE     UniqueProcessId;
/*00C*/ WORD       Reserved1;
/*00E*/ WORD       Reserved2;
/*010*/ }
        OBJECT_CREATOR_INFO,
      * POBJECT_CREATOR_INFO,
     **PPOBJECT_CREATOR_INFO;
```

LISTING 7-3. *The* `OBJECT_CREATOR_INFO` *Structure*

The `UniqueProcessId` is the zero-based numeric ID of the process that created the object. Although defined as a `HANDLE`, this member is not a handle in the usual sense. It might be described more accurately as an opaque 32-bit unsigned integer. Actually, the Win32 `GetCurrentProcessId()` API function returns these `HANDLE` values as `DWORD` types.

THE OBJECT NAME

If the `NameOffset` member of the `OBJECT_HEADER` is nonzero, it specifies the inverse offset of an `OBJECT_NAME` structure with respect to the base address of the `OBJECT_HEADER`. Typical values are `0x10` or `0x20`, depending on the presence of an `OBJECT_CREATOR_INFO` header part. Listing 7-4 shows the definition of the `OBJECT_NAME` structure. The `Name` member is a `UNICODE_STRING` whose `Buffer` member points to the name string, which is usually not part of the memory block containing the object. Not all named objects use an `OBJECT_NAME` structure in the header to store the name. For example, some objects rely on a `QueryNameProcedure()` provided by their associated `OBJECT_TYPE`.

If the `Directory` member is not `NULL`, it points to the directory object representing the layer in the system's object hierarchy where this object is located. Like files in a file system, Windows 2000 objects are kept in a hierarchically structured tree consisting of directory and leaf objects. More details about the `OBJECT_DIRECTORY` structure follow in a moment.

```
typedef struct _OBJECT_NAME
        {
/*000*/ POBJECT_DIRECTORY Directory;
/*004*/ UNICODE_STRING    Name;
/*00C*/ DWORD             Reserved;
/*010*/ }
        OBJECT_NAME,
      * POBJECT_NAME,
     **PPOBJECT_NAME;
```

LISTING 7-4. *The* `OBJECT_NAME` *Structure*

THE OBJECT HANDLE DATABASE

Some objects maintain process-specific handle counts stored in a so-called "handle database." If this is the case, the `HandleDBOffset` member of the `OBJECT_HEADER` contains a nonzero value. Just like the `NameOffset` described above, this is an offset to be subtracted from the base address of the `OBJECT_HEADER` to locate this header part. The OBJECT_HANDLE_DB structure is defined in Listing 7-5. If the OB_FLAG_SINGLE_PROCESS flag is set in the ObjectFlags, the Process member of the union at the beginning of this structure is valid and points to a process object. If more that one process holds handles to the object, the OB_FLAG_SINGLE_PROCESS flag is cleared, and the HandleDBList member becomes valid, pointing to an OBJECT_HANDLE_DB_LIST that constitutes an array of OBJECT_HANDLE_DB structures, preceded by a count value.

```
typedef struct _OBJECT_HANDLE_DB
        {
/*000*/ union
            {
/*000*/     struct _EPROCESS              *Process;
/*000*/     struct _OBJECT_HANDLE_DB_LIST *HandleDBList;
/*004*/     };
/*004*/ DWORD HandleCount;
/*008*/ }
        OBJECT_HANDLE_DB,
      * POBJECT_HANDLE_DB,
     **PPOBJECT_HANDLE_DB;

#define OBJECT_HANDLE_DB_ \
        sizeof (OBJECT_HANDLE_DB)

// -----------------------------------------------------------------

typedef struct _OBJECT_HANDLE_DB_LIST
        {
/*000*/ DWORD            Count;
/*004*/ OBJECT_HANDLE_DB Entries [];
/*???*/ }
        OBJECT_HANDLE_DB_LIST,
      * POBJECT_HANDLE_DB_LIST,
     **PPOBJECT_HANDLE_DB_LIST;

#define OBJECT_HANDLE_DB_LIST_ \
        sizeof (OBJECT_HANDLE_DB_LIST)
```

LISTING 7-5. *The* OBJECT_HANDLE_DB *Structure*

RESOURCE CHARGES AND QUOTAS

If a process opens a handle to an object, the process must "pay" for usage of system resources caused by this operation. The paid dues are referred to as charges, and the upper limit a process may spend for resources is termed the `quota`. In the glossary of the DDK documentation (Microsoft, 2000F), Microsoft defines the "quota" term in the following way:

QUOTA

> *A per-process limit on the use of system resources.*
> *For each process, Windows NT®/Windows® 2000 sets limits on certain system resources the process's threads can use, including quotas for paging-file, paged-pool, and nonpaged-pool usage, etc. For example, the Memory Manager "charges quota" against the process as its threads use page-file, paged-pool, or nonpaged-pool memory; it also updates these values when threads release memory.* (Windows 2000 DDK \ Kernel-Mode Drivers \ Design Guide \ Kernel-Mode Glossary \ Q \ quota)

By default, an object's `OBJECT_TYPE` determines the charges to be applied for paged/nonpaged pool usage and security. However, this default can be overridden by adding an `OBJECT_QUOTA_CHARGES` structure to the object header. The location of this data relative to the `OBJECT_HEADER` base address is specified by the `QuotaChargesOffset` member of the `OBJECT_HEADER` as an inverse offset, as usual. Listing 7-6 shows the structure definition. The usages of the paged and nonpaged pools are charged separately. If the object requires security, an additional `SecurityCharge` is added to the paged-pool usage. The default security charge is `0x800`.

If the `OB_FLAG_CREATE_INFO` bit of the `ObjectFlags` in the `OBJECT_HEADER` is zero, the `QuotaBlock` member points to a `QUOTA_BLOCK` structure (Listing 7-7) that contains statistical information about the current resource usage of the object.

```
#define OB_SECURITY_CHARGE 0x00000800

typedef struct _OBJECT_QUOTA_CHARGES
        {
/*000*/ DWORD PagedPoolCharge;
/*004*/ DWORD NonPagedPoolCharge;
/*008*/ DWORD SecurityCharge;
/*00C*/ DWORD Reserved;
/*010*/ }
        OBJECT_QUOTA_CHARGES,
      * POBJECT_QUOTA_CHARGES,
     **PPOBJECT_QUOTA_CHARGES;
```

LISTING 7-6. *The* `OBJECT_QUOTA_CHARGES` *Structure*

```
typedef struct _QUOTA_BLOCK
        {
/*000*/ DWORD Flags;
/*004*/ DWORD ChargeCount;
/*008*/ DWORD PeakPoolUsage [2]; // NonPagedPool, PagedPool
/*010*/ DWORD PoolUsage     [2]; // NonPagedPool, PagedPool
/*018*/ DWORD PoolQuota     [2]; // NonPagedPool, PagedPool
/*020*/ }
        QUOTA_BLOCK,
      * PQUOTA_BLOCK,
     **PPQUOTA_BLOCK;
```

LISTING 7-7. *The* QUOTA_BLOCK *Structure*

OBJECT DIRECTORIES

As already noted in the discussion of the OBJECT_NAME header part, the Windows 2000 object manager keeps individual objects in a tree of OBJECT_DIRECTORY structures, also known as "directory objects." An OBJECT_DIRECTORY is just another fancy type of object, with an ordinary OBJECT_HEADER and everything a real object needs. The Windows 2000 object directory management is quite tricky. As Listing 7-8 shows, the OBJECT_DIRECTORY is basically a hash table with 37 entries. This unusual size has probably been chosen because it is a prime number. Each table entry can hold a pointer to an OBJECT_DIRECTORY_ENTRY whose Object member refers to an object. When a new object is created, the object manager computes a hash value in the range 0 to 36 from the object name and creates an OBJECT_DIRECTORY_ENTRY. If the target slot of the hash table is empty, this slot is set up to point to the new directory entry. If the slot is already in use, the new entry is inserted into a singly-linked list of entries originating from the target slot, using the NextEntry members of the involved OBJECT_DIRECTORY_ENTRY structures. To represent hierarchical object relationships, object directories can be nested in a straightforward way by simply adding an OBJECT_DIRECTORY_ENTRY with an Object member that points to a subordinate directory object.

To optimize the access to frequently used objects, the object manager applies a simple most recently used (MRU) algorithm. Whenever an object has successfully been retrieved, it is put in front of the linked list of entries that are assigned to the same hash table slot. Moreover, a pointer to the updated list is kept in the CurrentEntry member of the OBJECT_DIRECTORY. The CurrentEntryValid flag indicates whether the CurrentEntry pointer is valid. Access to the system's global object directory is synchronized by means of an ERESOURCE lock called ObpRootDirectoryMutex. This lock is neither documented nor exported.

```
typedef struct _OBJECT_DIRECTORY_ENTRY
        {
/*000*/ struct _OBJECT_DIRECTORY_ENTRY *NextEntry;
/*004*/ POBJECT                         Object;
/*008*/ }
        OBJECT_DIRECTORY_ENTRY,
      * POBJECT_DIRECTORY_ENTRY,
     **PPOBJECT_DIRECTORY_ENTRY;

// -----------------------------------------------------------------

#define OBJECT_HASH_TABLE_SIZE 37

typedef struct _OBJECT_DIRECTORY
        {
/*000*/ POBJECT_DIRECTORY_ENTRY HashTable [OBJECT_HASH_TABLE_SIZE];
/*094*/ POBJECT_DIRECTORY_ENTRY CurrentEntry;
/*098*/ BOOLEAN                 CurrentEntryValid;
/*099*/ BYTE                    Reserved1;
/*09A*/ WORD                    Reserved2;
/*09C*/ DWORD                   Reserved3;
/*0A0*/ }
        OBJECT_DIRECTORY,
      * POBJECT_DIRECTORY,
     **PPOBJECT_DIRECTORY;
```

LISTING 7-8. *The* `OBJECT_DIRECTORY` *and* `OBJECT_DIRECTORY_ENTRY` *Structures*

OBJECT TYPES

The above object header part descriptions have frequently referred to "type objects" or `OBJECT_TYPE` structures, so it is now time to introduce these. Formally, a type object is nothing but a special kind of object, such as an event, device, or process, and as such has an `OBJECT_HEADER` and potentially some of the optional header substructures. The only difference is that type objects are related in a special way to other objects. A type object is sort of a "master object" that defines common properties of objects of the same kind, and optionally keeps all of its subordinate objects in a doubly-linked list, as explained earlier in the description of the `OBJECT_CREATOR_INFO` structure. Therefore, type objects are frequently referred to as "object types" to emphasize that they are more than just ordinary objects.

The body of a type object consists of an `OBJECT_TYPE` structure with an embedded `OBJECT_TYPE_INITIALIZER`, both of which are shown in Listing 7-9. The latter is used during object creation via `ObCreateObject()` to build a proper object header. For example, the `MaintainHandleCount` and `MaintainTypeList` members are used

```
typedef struct _OBJECT_TYPE_INITIALIZER
        {
/*000*/ WORD            Length;          //0x004C
/*002*/ BOOLEAN         UseDefaultObject;//OBJECT_TYPE.DefaultObject
/*003*/ BOOLEAN         Reserved1;
/*004*/ DWORD           InvalidAttributes;
/*008*/ GENERIC_MAPPING GenericMapping;
/*018*/ ACCESS_MASK     ValidAccessMask;
/*01C*/ BOOLEAN         SecurityRequired;
/*01D*/ BOOLEAN         MaintainHandleCount; // OBJECT_HANDLE_DB
/*01E*/ BOOLEAN         MaintainTypeList;    // OBJECT_CREATOR_INFO
/*01F*/ BYTE            Reserved2;
/*020*/ BOOL            PagedPool;
/*024*/ DWORD           DefaultPagedPoolCharge;
/*028*/ DWORD           DefaultNonPagedPoolCharge;
/*02C*/ NTPROC          DumpProcedure;
/*030*/ NTPROC          OpenProcedure;
/*034*/ NTPROC          CloseProcedure;
/*038*/ NTPROC          DeleteProcedure;
/*03C*/ NTPROC_VOID     ParseProcedure;
/*040*/ NTPROC_VOID     SecurityProcedure; // SeDefaultObjectMethod
/*044*/ NTPROC_VOID     QueryNameProcedure;
/*048*/ NTPROC_BOOLEAN  OkayToCloseProcedure;
/*04C*/ }
        OBJECT_TYPE_INITIALIZER,
     * POBJECT_TYPE_INITIALIZER,
    **PPOBJECT_TYPE_INITIALIZER;

// -----------------------------------------------------------------

typedef struct _OBJECT_TYPE
        {
/*000*/ ERESOURCE      Lock;
/*038*/ LIST_ENTRY     ObjectListHead; // OBJECT_CREATOR_INFO
/*040*/ UNICODE_STRING ObjectTypeName; // see above
/*048*/ union
            {
/*048*/     PVOID DefaultObject; // ObpDefaultObject
/*048*/     DWORD Code;          // File: 5C, WaitablePort: A0
            };
/*04C*/ DWORD                   ObjectTypeIndex; // OB_TYPE_INDEX_*
/*050*/ DWORD                   ObjectCount;
/*054*/ DWORD                   HandleCount;
/*058*/ DWORD                   PeakObjectCount;
/*05C*/ DWORD                   PeakHandleCount;
/*060*/ OBJECT_TYPE_INITIALIZER ObjectTypeInitializer;
/*0AC*/ DWORD                   ObjectTypeTag;   // OB_TYPE_TAG_*
/*0B0*/ }
```

```
        OBJECT_TYPE,
      * POBJECT_TYPE,
     **PPOBJECT_TYPE;
```

LISTING 7-9. *The* `OBJECT_TYPE` *and* `OBJECT_TYPE_INITIALIZER` *Structures*

by the internal `ntoskrnl.exe` function `ObpAllocateObject()` to decide whether all newly created objects will comprise `OBJECT_HANDLE_DB` and `OBJECT_CREATOR_INFO` header parts, respectively. Setting the `MaintainTypeList` flag has the nice side effect that the objects of this type will be tied to each other in a doubly linked list, originating from and ending at the `ObjectListHead` member of the `OBJECT_TYPE`. The `OBJECT_TYPE_INITIALIZER` also provides the default quota charges (mentioned earlier in the discussion of the `OBJECT_QUOTA_CHARGES` header component) via its `DefaultPagedPoolCharge` and `DefaultNonPagedPoolCharge` members.

Because type objects/object types are essential building blocks of the Windows 2000 object universe, `ntoskrnl.exe` stores them in named variables, making it easy to verify the type of an object by simply comparing the `ObjectType` member of its `OBJECT_HEADER` to the stored type object in question. Type objects are unique—the system never creates more than one type object for each kind of object. Table 7-4 summarizes the type objects maintained by Windows 2000. The information in the various columns has the following meaning:

TABLE 7-4. *Available Object Types*

INDEX	TAG	NAME	C STRUCTURE	PUBLIC	SYMBOL
1	"ObjT"	"Type"	OBJECT_TYPE	No	ObpTypeObjectType
2	"Dire"	"Directory"	OBJECT_DIRECTORY	No	ObpDirectoryObjectType
3	"Symb"	"SymbolicLink"		No	ObpSymbolicLinkObjectType
4	"Toke"	"Token"	TOKEN	No	SepTokenObjectType
5	"Proc"	"Process"	EPROCESS	Yes	PsProcessType
6	"Thre"	"Thread"	ETHREAD	Yes	PsThreadType
7	"Job "	"Job"		Yes	PsJobType
8	"Even"	"Event"	KEVENT	Yes	ExEventObjectType
9	"Even"	"EventPair"	KEVENT_PAIR	No	ExEventPairObjectType
10	"Muta"	"Mutant"	KMUTANT	No	ExMutantObjectType
11	"Call"	"Callback"	CALLBACK_OBJECT	No	ExCallbackObjectType

(continued)

TABLE 7-4. *(continued)*

INDEX	TAG	NAME	C STRUCTURE	PUBLIC	SYMBOL
12	"Sema"	"Semaphore"	KSEMAPHORE	Yes	ExSemaphoreObjectType
13	"Time"	"Timer"	ETIMER	No	ExTimerObjectType
14	"Prof"	"Profile"	KPROFILE	No	ExProfileObjectType
15	"Wind"	"WindowStation"		Yes	ExWindowStationObjectType
16	"Desk"	"Desktop"		Yes	ExDesktopObjectType
17	"Sect"	"Section"		Yes	MmSectionObjectType
18	"Key"	"Key"		No	CmpKeyObjectType
19	"Port"	"Port"		Yes	LpcPortObjectType
20	"Wait"	"WaitablePort"		No	LpcWaitablePortObjectType
21	"Adap"	"Adapter"	ADAPTER_OBJECT	Yes	IoAdapterObjectType
22	"Cont"	"Controller"	CONTROLLER_OBJECT	No	IoControllerObjectType
23	"Devi"	"Device"	DEVICE_OBJECT	Yes	IoDeviceObjectType
24	"Driv"	"Driver"	DRIVER_OBJECT	Yes	IoDriverObjectType
25	"IoCo"	"IoCompletion"	IO_COMPLETION	No	IoCompletionObjectType
26	"File"	"File"	FILE_OBJECT	Yes	IoFileObjectType
27	"WmiG"	"WmiGuid"	GUID	No	WmipGuidObjectType

- The "Index" column specifies the value of the `ObjectTypeIndex` member of the `OBJECT_TYPE` structure.
- The "Tag" is the 32-bit identifier stored in the `ObjectTypeTag` member of the `OBJECT_TYPE` structure. Windows 2000 tags are typically binary values generated by concatenation of four ANSI characters. During debugging, these characters can easily be identified in a hex dump listing. Testing the `ObjectTypeTag` value is the easiest way to verify that a given type object is of the expected kind. When allocating memory for an object, Windows 2000 also uses this value—logically OR'ed with `0x80000000`—to tag the new memory block.
- The "Name" column states the object name, as it is specified by the type object's `OBJECT_NAME` header component. It is obvious that the type tag is generated from the object name by truncating it to four characters, appending spaces if the name is shorter.
- "C Structure" is the name of the object body structure associated with the object type. Some of them are documented in the DDK and some in the

w2k_def.h header file on the CD provided with this book. If no name is present, the structure is currently unknown or unidentified.

- The "Symbol" column indicates the name of the pointer variable that refers to the type object. If the "Public" column contains "yes," the variable is exported and can be accessed by kernel-mode drivers or applications that link to the kernel via the w2k_call.dll library presented in Chapter 6.

The "Index" column requires further explanation. The value shown here is taken from the ObjectTypeIndex member of the corresponding OBJECT_TYPE structure. This value is not a predefined type ID as are the DISP_TYPE_* and IO_TYPE_* constants used by dispatcher and I/O objects (see Tables 7-1 and 7-2). It merely reflects the order in which the system created these type objects. Therefore, you should never use the ObjectTypeIndex to identify the type of an object. It is safer to use the ObjectTypeTag instead, which is certainly more stable across future operating system versions.

OBJECT HANDLES

Whereas a kernel-mode driver can directly contact an object by querying a pointer to its object body, a user-mode application cannot. When it calls one of the API functions that open an object, it receives back a handle that must be used in subsequent operations on the object. Although Windows 2000 applies the "handle" metaphor to a variety of things that are not necessarily related, there is a construct that can be called the handle in the strictest sense. This pure form of a handle is a process-specific 16-bit number that is usually a multiple of four and constitutes an index into a handle table maintained by the kernel for each process. The main HANDLE_TABLE structure is shown at the end Listing 7-10. This table points to a HANDLE_LAYER1 structure that consists of pointers to HANDLE_LAYER2 structures, which in turn are composed of HANDLE_LAYER3 pointers. Finally, the third indirection layer contains pointers to the actual handle table entries, represented by HANDLE_ENTRY structures.

```
// HANDLE BIT-FIELDS
// -----------------
//  1 1 1 1 1 1 1 1 1 1 1 1 1 1 1 1 0 0 0 0 0 0 0 0 0 0 0 0 0 0 0 0
//  F E D C B A 9 8 7 6 5 4 3 2 1 0 F E D C B A 9 8 7 6 5 4 3 2 1 0
//  _______________________________________________________________
//  |x|x|x|x|x|x|a|a|a|a|a|a|a|a|b|b|b|b|b|b|b|b|c|c|c|c|c|c|c|c|y|y|
```

(continued)

```
// | not used  | HANDLE_LAYER1 | HANDLE_LAYER2 | HANDLE_LAYER3 |tag|

#define HANDLE_LAYER_SIZE 0x00000100

// -----------------------------------------------------------------

#define HANDLE_ATTRIBUTE_INHERIT 0x00000002
#define HANDLE_ATTRIBUTE_MASK    0x00000007
#define HANDLE_OBJECT_MASK       0xFFFFFFF8

typedef struct _HANDLE_ENTRY // cf. OBJECT_HANDLE_INFORMATION
        {
/*000*/ union
            {
/*000*/     DWORD          HandleAttributes;// HANDLE_ATTRIBUTE_MASK
/*000*/     POBJECT_HEADER ObjectHeader;    // HANDLE_OBJECT_MASK
/*004*/     };
/*004*/ union
            {
/*004*/     ACCESS_MASK    GrantedAccess;   // if used entry
/*004*/     DWORD          NextEntry;       // if free entry
/*008*/     };
/*008*/ }
        HANDLE_ENTRY,
     * PHANDLE_ENTRY,
    **PPHANDLE_ENTRY;

// -----------------------------------------------------------------

typedef struct _HANDLE_LAYER3
        {
/*000*/ HANDLE_ENTRY Entries [HANDLE_LAYER_SIZE]; // bits 2 to 9
/*800*/ }
        HANDLE_LAYER3,
     * PHANDLE_LAYER3,
    **PPHANDLE_LAYER3;

// -----------------------------------------------------------------

typedef struct _HANDLE_LAYER2
        {
/*000*/ PHANDLE_LAYER3 Layer3 [HANDLE_LAYER_SIZE]; // bits 10 to 17
/*400*/ }
        HANDLE_LAYER2,
     * PHANDLE_LAYER2,
    **PPHANDLE_LAYER2;

// -----------------------------------------------------------------
```

```
typedef struct _HANDLE_LAYER1
        {
/*000*/ PHANDLE_LAYER2 Layer2 [HANDLE_LAYER_SIZE]; // bits 18 to 25
/*400*/ }
        HANDLE_LAYER1,
     * PHANDLE_LAYER1,
    **PPHANDLE_LAYER1;

// -----------------------------------------------------------------

typedef struct _HANDLE_TABLE
        {
/*000*/ DWORD             Reserved;
/*004*/ DWORD             HandleCount;
/*008*/ PHANDLE_LAYER1    Layer1;
/*00C*/ struct _EPROCESS *Process; // passed to PsChargePoolQuota ()
/*010*/ HANDLE            UniqueProcessId;
/*014*/ DWORD             NextEntry;
/*018*/ DWORD             TotalEntries;
/*01C*/ ERESOURCE         HandleTableLock;
/*054*/ LIST_ENTRY        HandleTableList;
/*05C*/ KEVENT            Event;
/*06C*/ }
        HANDLE_TABLE,
     * PHANDLE_TABLE,
    **PPHANDLE_TABLE;
```

LISTING 7-10. *Handle Tables, Layers, and Entries*

This three-layered addressing mechanism is a clever trick to be able to dynamically increase or decrease the storage needed for handle entries with minimum effort while also minimizing waste of memory. Because each handle table layer takes up to 256 pointers, a process can theoretically open `256 * 256 * 256, or 16,777,216` handles. With each handle entry consuming 8 bytes, the required maximum storage amounts to 128 MB. However, because a process rarely needs that many handles, it would be an immense waste of space to allocate the complete handle table from the start. The three-layered approach used by Windows 2000 starts out with the minimum set of a single subtable per layer. Not counting the `HANDLE_TABLE` itself, the required storage is `256 * 4 + 256 * 4 + 256 * 8, or 4,096` bytes. The initial handle table material fits exactly into a single physical memory page.

To look up the `HANDLE_ENTRY` of a `HANDLE,` the system divides the 32-bit value of the handle into three 8-bit fragments, discarding bits #0 and #1, as well as the topmost six bits. Given these three fragments, the handle resolution mechanism proceeds as follows:

1. Bits #18 to #25 of the HANDLE are used as an index into the Layer2 array of the HANDLE_LAYER1 block referred to by the Layer1 member of the HANDLE_TABLE.
2. Bits #10 to #17 of the HANDLE are used as an index into the Layer3 array of the HANDLE_LAYER2 block retrieved in the previous step.
3. Bits #2 to #9 of the HANDLE are used as an index into the Entries array of the HANDLE_LAYER3 block retrieved in the previous step.
4. The HANDLE_ENTRY retrieved in the previous step provides a pointer to the OBJECT_HEADER (see Listing 7-2) of the object associated to the HANDLE.

If this sounds confusing, Figure 7-2 may clarify what occurs in this situation. Actually, Figure 7-2 is remarkably similar in structure to Figure 4-3 in Chapter 4, where the i386 CPU's linear-to-physical address translation is depicted. Both algorithms break an input value into three fragments, with two of them used as offsets into two hierarchically arranged indirection layers and the third one selecting an entry from the target layer. Note that the layered handle table model is new to Windows 2000. Windows NT 4.0 provided a single-layered table that had to be expanded if the currently opened handles didn't fit into the memory block currently allocated for the handle table (cf. Custer 1993, Solomon 1998).

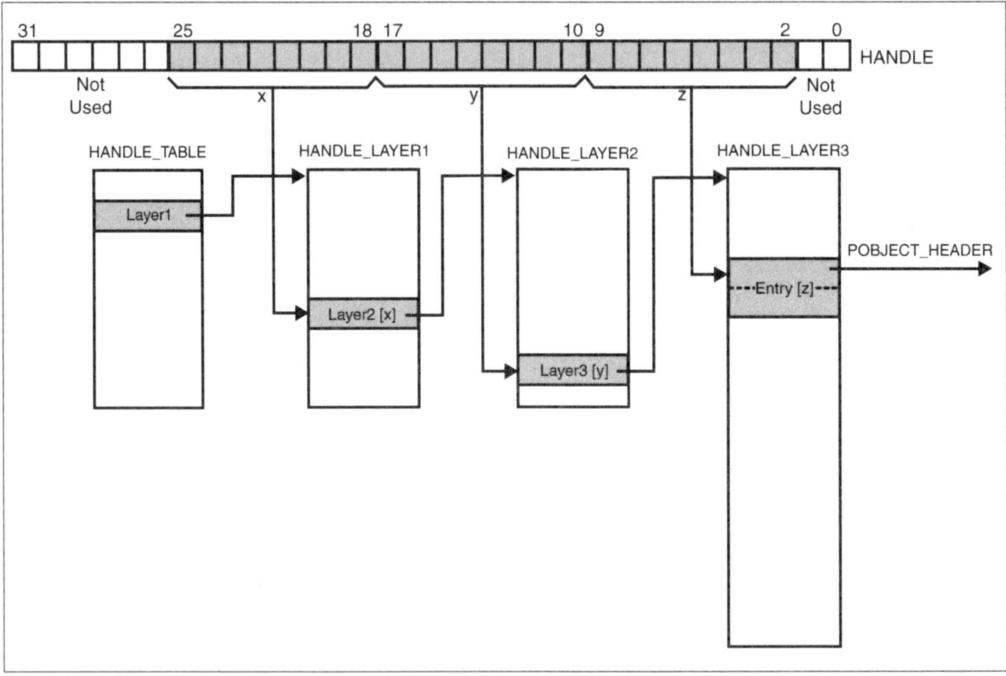

FIGURE 7-2. HANDLE *to* OBJECT_HEADER *Resolution*

Because each process has its own handle table, the kernel must somehow keep track of the currently allocated tables. Therefore, ntoskrnl.exe maintains a LIST_ENTRY variable named HandleTableListHead that is the root of a doubly linked list of HANDLE_TABLE structures, chained together by means of their HandleTableList members. When following their Flink or Blink pointers, you must always subtract the HandleTableList member offset 0x54 to get to the base address of the surrounding HANDLE_TABLE structure. The owning process of each table can easily be determined by consulting its UniqueProcessId member. The first HANDLE_TABLE in the list is usually owned by the System process (ID=8), followed by the table of the System Idle Process (ID=0). The latter HANDLE_TABLE is also reachable by an internal variable referred to as ObpKernelHandleTable.

When accessing handle tables, the system uses a couple of synchronization objects to preserve data integrity in multithreaded handle access scenarios. The entire handle table list is locked by means of the global HandleTableListLock inside ntoskrnl.exe, which is an ERESOURCE structure. This type of synchronization object allows exclusive or shared locks, acquired with the help of the ExAcquireResourceExclusiveLite() and ExAcquireResourceSharedLite() API functions, respectively. The lock is released by calling ExReleaseResourceLite(). After locking the handle table list for exclusive access, you are guaranteed that the system will not change any list entries until the lock is released. Each HANDLE_TABLE in the list entry has its own ERESOURCE lock, termed HandleTableLock in Listing 7-10. ntoskrnl.exe provides the internal functions ExLockHandleTableExclusive() and ExLockHandleTableShared() to acquire this ERESOURCE, and ExUnlockHandleTableShared() to release it (no matter whether the lock is exclusive or shared, even though the name suggests that it is good for shared locks only). These functions are simply wrappers around ExAcquireResourceExclusiveLite(), ExAcquireResourceSharedLite(), and ExReleaseResourceLite(), taking a pointer to a HANDLE_TABLE and passing over its HandleTableLock.

Unfortunately, all essential functions and global variables used by the kernel's handle manager are not only undocumented, but also inaccessible because they are not exported by the ntoskrnl.exe module. Although it is certainly possible to look up objects by their handles using the kernel call interface proposed in Chapter 6 and the scheme outlined in Figure 7-2, I don't recommend doing so. One reason is that this code would deliberately give up compatibility with Windows NT 4.0 because of the radical handle table design change. Another reason is that the kernel provides a luxurious function that returns the contents of all handle tables owned by the currently active processes. This function is NtQuerySystemInformation(), and the information class required to obtain the handle information is SystemHandleInformation (16). Please refer to Schreiber (1999) or Nebbett (2000) for extensive details on how to issue this API call. The SystemHandleInformation data are obtained from the internal function ExpGetHandleInformation() that relies on ObGetHandleInformation(). The latter in turn calls ExSnapShotHandleTables(), where the handle table list enumeration is ultimately performed. ExSnapShotHandleTables() expects a pointer to a callback function that is called for each HANDLE_ENTRY referring to an object. ObGetHandleInformation() uses the internal ObpCaptureHandleInformation() callback function to fill the caller's buffer with an array of structures containing information about each handle currently maintained by the system.

PROCESS AND THREAD OBJECTS

Probably the most interesting and complex inhabitants of the Windows 2000 object world are the process and thread objects. These are usually the top-level entities a software developer must deal with. A kernel-mode component always runs in the context of a thread, and this thread is often part of a user process. Therefore, it is quite natural that process and thread objects are object types that frequently are explored in debugging situations. The Windows 2000 Kernel Debugger accounts for this requirement by providing the "bang" commands !processfields and !threadfields, exported by the debugger extension kdextx86.dll. Both commands output a simple list of name/offset pairs describing the members of the EPROCESS and ETHREAD structures, respectively (cf. Examples 1-1 and 1-2 in Chapter 1). These object structures are undocumented, so these debugger commands are currently the only official source of information about them.

Unfortunately, the !processfields output (cf. Example 1-1) starts with a member named Pcb that refers to a substructure comprising 0x6C bytes, because the next member ExitStatus is located at this offset. Pcb is a KPROCESS structure that is completely undocumented. This arrangement is interesting: Obviously, a process is represented by a smaller kernel object embedded in a larger executive object. This nesting scheme reappears with the thread object. The debugger's !threadfields command (cf. Example 1-2) reveals a Tcb member of no less than 0x1B0 bytes at the beginning of the ETHREAD structure. This is a KTHREAD structure, representing another kernel object inside an executive object.

Although it is helpful that the Kernel Debugger provides symbolic information about the executive's process and thread objects, the plain member names do not necessarily provide enough cues to identify the members' data types. Moreover, the opacity of the Pcb and Tcb members makes it quite difficult to understand the nature of these objects. In a disassembly listing generated by the Kernel Debugger, you will frequently see instructions referencing data within the confines of these opaque members. The used offsets are completely useless without information about the name and type of the referenced data. Therefore, I have collected information from various sources plus results of my investigation, to figure out what these objects look like. Part one of the results is shown in Listings 7-11 and 7-12, defining the `KPROCESS` and `KTHREAD` structures, respectively. The `DISPATCHER_HEADER` at the beginning of both objects qualifies processes and threads as dispatcher objects, which in turn means they can be waited for using `KeWaitForSingleObject()` and `KeWaitForMultipleObjects()`. A thread object becomes signaled after execution of the thread has ceased, and a process object enters the signaled state after all of its threads have terminated. This is nothing new for Win32 programmers—it is quite common to wait for termination of a process spawned by another process by means of the Win32 API function `WaitForSingleObject()`. However, now you finally know why waiting for processes and threads is possible in the first place.

```
typedef struct _KPROCESS
        {
/*000*/ DISPATCHER_HEADER Header; // DO_TYPE_PROCESS (0x1B)
/*010*/ LIST_ENTRY        ProfileListHead;
/*018*/ DWORD             DirectoryTableBase;
/*01C*/ DWORD             PageTableBase;
/*020*/ KGDTENTRY         LdtDescriptor;
/*028*/ KIDTENTRY         Int21Descriptor;
/*030*/ WORD              IopmOffset;
/*032*/ BYTE              Iopl;
/*033*/ BOOLEAN           VdmFlag;
/*034*/ DWORD             ActiveProcessors;
/*038*/ DWORD             KernelTime; // ticks
/*03C*/ DWORD             UserTime;   // ticks
/*040*/ LIST_ENTRY        ReadyListHead;
/*048*/ LIST_ENTRY        SwapListEntry;
/*050*/ LIST_ENTRY        ThreadListHead; // KTHREAD.ThreadListEntry
/*058*/ PVOID             ProcessLock;
/*05C*/ KAFFINITY         Affinity;
/*060*/ WORD              StackCount;
/*062*/ BYTE              BasePriority;
/*063*/ BYTE              ThreadQuantum;
/*064*/ BOOLEAN           AutoAlignment;
/*065*/ BYTE              State;
/*066*/ BYTE              ThreadSeed;
/*067*/ BOOLEAN           DisableBoost;
/*068*/ DWORD             d68;
/*06C*/ }
        KPROCESS,
      * PKPROCESS,
     **PPKPROCESS;
```

LISTING 7-11. *The* `KPROCESS` *Object Structure*

```
typedef struct _KTHREAD
        {
/*000*/ DISPATCHER_HEADER         Header; // DO_TYPE_THREAD (0x6C)
/*010*/ LIST_ENTRY                MutantListHead;
/*018*/ PVOID                     InitialStack;
/*01C*/ PVOID                     StackLimit;
/*020*/ struct _TEB              *Teb;
/*024*/ PVOID                     TlsArray;
/*028*/ PVOID                     KernelStack;
/*02C*/ BOOLEAN                   DebugActive;
/*02D*/ BYTE                      State; // THREAD_STATE_*
/*02E*/ BOOLEAN                   Alerted;
/*02F*/ BYTE                      bReserved01;
/*030*/ BYTE                      Iopl;
/*031*/ BYTE                      NpxState;
/*032*/ BYTE                      Saturation;
/*033*/ BYTE                      Priority;
/*034*/ KAPC_STATE                ApcState;
/*04C*/ DWORD                     ContextSwitches;
/*050*/ DWORD                     WaitStatus;
/*054*/ BYTE                      WaitIrql;
/*055*/ BYTE                      WaitMode;
/*056*/ BYTE                      WaitNext;
/*057*/ BYTE                      WaitReason;
/*058*/ PLIST_ENTRY               WaitBlockList;
/*05C*/ LIST_ENTRY                WaitListEntry;
/*064*/ DWORD                     WaitTime;
/*068*/ BYTE                      BasePriority;
/*069*/ BYTE                      DecrementCount;
/*06A*/ BYTE                      PriorityDecrement;
/*06B*/ BYTE                      Quantum;
/*06C*/ KWAIT_BLOCK               WaitBlock [4];
/*0CC*/ DWORD                     LegoData;
/*0D0*/ DWORD                     KernelApcDisable;
/*0D4*/ KAFFINITY                 UserAffinity;
/*0D8*/ BOOLEAN                   SystemAffinityActive;
/*0D9*/ BYTE                      Pad [3];
/*0DC*/ PSERVICE_DESCRIPTOR_TABLE pServiceDescriptorTable;
/*0E0*/ PVOID                     Queue;
/*0E4*/ PVOID                     ApcQueueLock;
/*0E8*/ KTIMER                    Timer;
/*110*/ LIST_ENTRY                QueueListEntry;
/*118*/ KAFFINITY                 Affinity;
/*11C*/ BOOLEAN                   Preempted;
/*11D*/ BOOLEAN                   ProcessReadyQueue;
/*11E*/ BOOLEAN                   KernelStackResident;
/*11F*/ BYTE                      NextProcessor;
/*120*/ PVOID                     CallbackStack;
```

```
/*124*/ struct _WIN32_THREAD     *Win32Thread;
/*128*/ PVOID                     TrapFrame;
/*12C*/ PKAPC_STATE               ApcStatePointer;
/*130*/ PVOID                     p130;
/*134*/ BOOLEAN                   EnableStackSwap;
/*135*/ BOOLEAN                   LargeStack;
/*136*/ BYTE                      ResourceIndex;
/*137*/ KPROCESSOR_MODE           PreviousMode;
/*138*/ DWORD                     KernelTime; // ticks
/*13C*/ DWORD                     UserTime;   // ticks
/*140*/ KAPC_STATE                SavedApcState;
/*157*/ BYTE                      bReserved02;
/*158*/ BOOLEAN                   Alertable;
/*159*/ BYTE                      ApcStateIndex;
/*15A*/ BOOLEAN                   ApcQueueable;
/*15B*/ BOOLEAN                   AutoAlignment;
/*15C*/ PVOID                     StackBase;
/*160*/ KAPC                      SuspendApc;
/*190*/ KSEMAPHORE                SuspendSemaphore;
/*1A4*/ LIST_ENTRY                ThreadListEntry;  // see KPROCESS
/*1AC*/ BYTE                      FreezeCount;
/*1AD*/ BYTE                      SuspendCount;
/*1AE*/ BYTE                      IdealProcessor;
/*1AF*/ BOOLEAN                   DisableBoost;
/*1B0*/ }
        KTHREAD,
      * PKTHREAD,
     **PPKTHREAD;
```

LISTING 7-12. *The* KTHREAD *Object Structure*

A KPROCESS links to its threads via its ThreadListHead member, which is the starting and ending point of a doubly linked list of KTHREAD objects. The list nodes of the threads are represented by their ThreadListEntry members. As usual with LIST_ENTRY nodes, the base address of the surrounding object is computed by subtracting the offset of the LIST_ENTRY member from its address, because the Flink and Blink members always point to the next LIST_ENTRY inside the list, not to the owner of the list node. This makes it possible to interlink objects in multiple lists without any interference.

In Listings 7-11 and 7-12, as well as in the following listings, you see occasional members with names consisting of a lower-case letter and a three-digit hexadecimal number. These are members whose identity and purpose is currently unknown to me. The leading character reflects the supposed member type (e.g., d for DWORD or p for PVOID), and the numeric trailer specifies the member's offset from the beginning of the structure.

The EPROCESS and ETHREAD executive objects surrounding the KPROCESS and KTHREAD dispatcher objects are shown in Listings 7-13 and 7-14. These structures contain several unidentified members that hopefully will be analyzed soon by others, maybe encouraged by the material in this book. However, the most important and most frequently referenced members are included, and at least it is known what information is missing.

```
typedef struct _EPROCESS
        {
/*000*/ KPROCESS              Pcb;
/*06C*/ NTSTATUS              ExitStatus;
/*070*/ KEVENT                LockEvent;
/*080*/ DWORD                 LockCount;
/*084*/ DWORD                 d084;
/*088*/ LARGE_INTEGER         CreateTime;
/*090*/ LARGE_INTEGER         ExitTime;
/*098*/ PVOID                 LockOwner;
/*09C*/ DWORD                 UniqueProcessId;
/*0A0*/ LIST_ENTRY            ActiveProcessLinks;
/*0A8*/ DWORD                 QuotaPeakPoolUsage [2]; // NP, P
/*0B0*/ DWORD                 QuotaPoolUsage     [2]; // NP, P
/*0B8*/ DWORD                 PagefileUsage;
/*0BC*/ DWORD                 CommitCharge;
/*0C0*/ DWORD                 PeakPagefileUsage;
/*0C4*/ DWORD                 PeakVirtualSize;
/*0C8*/ LARGE_INTEGER         VirtualSize;
/*0D0*/ MMSUPPORT             Vm;
/*100*/ DWORD                 d100;
/*104*/ DWORD                 d104;
/*108*/ DWORD                 d108;
/*10C*/ DWORD                 d10C;
/*110*/ DWORD                 d110;
/*114*/ DWORD                 d114;
/*118*/ DWORD                 d118;
/*11C*/ DWORD                 d11C;
/*120*/ PVOID                 DebugPort;
/*124*/ PVOID                 ExceptionPort;
/*128*/ PHANDLE_TABLE         ObjectTable;
/*12C*/ PVOID                 Token;
/*130*/ FAST_MUTEX            WorkingSetLock;
/*150*/ DWORD                 WorkingSetPage;
/*154*/ BOOLEAN               ProcessOutswapEnabled;
/*155*/ BOOLEAN               ProcessOutswapped;
/*156*/ BOOLEAN               AddressSpaceInitialized;
/*157*/ BOOLEAN               AddressSpaceDeleted;
/*158*/ FAST_MUTEX            AddressCreationLock;
/*178*/ KSPIN_LOCK            HyperSpaceLock;
/*17C*/ DWORD                 ForkInProgress;
```

```
/*180*/ WORD                    VmOperation;
/*182*/ BOOLEAN                 ForkWasSuccessful;
/*183*/ BYTE                    MmAgressiveWsTrimMask;
/*184*/ DWORD                   VmOperationEvent;
/*188*/ HARDWARE_PTE            PageDirectoryPte;
/*18C*/ DWORD                   LastFaultCount;
/*190*/ DWORD                   ModifiedPageCount;
/*194*/ PVOID                   VadRoot;
/*198*/ PVOID                   VadHint;
/*19C*/ PVOID                   CloneRoot;
/*1A0*/ DWORD                   NumberOfPrivatePages;
/*1A4*/ DWORD                   NumberOfLockedPages;
/*1A8*/ WORD                    NextPageColor;
/*1AA*/ BOOLEAN                 ExitProcessCalled;
/*1AB*/ BOOLEAN                 CreateProcessReported;
/*1AC*/ HANDLE                  SectionHandle;
/*1B0*/ struct _PEB            *Peb;
/*1B4*/ PVOID                   SectionBaseAddress;
/*1B8*/ PQUOTA_BLOCK            QuotaBlock;
/*1BC*/ NTSTATUS                LastThreadExitStatus;
/*1C0*/ DWORD                   WorkingSetWatch;
/*1C4*/ HANDLE                  Win32WindowStation;
/*1C8*/ DWORD                   InheritedFromUniqueProcessId;
/*1CC*/ ACCESS_MASK             GrantedAccess;
/*1D0*/ DWORD                   DefaultHardErrorProcessing; // HEM_*
/*1D4*/ DWORD                   LdtInformation;
/*1D8*/ PVOID                   VadFreeHint;
/*1DC*/ DWORD                   VdmObjects;
/*1E0*/ PVOID                   DeviceMap; // 0x24 bytes
/*1E4*/ DWORD                   SessionId;
/*1E8*/ DWORD                   d1E8;
/*1EC*/ DWORD                   d1EC;
/*1F0*/ DWORD                   d1F0;
/*1F4*/ DWORD                   d1F4;
/*1F8*/ DWORD                   d1F8;
/*1FC*/ BYTE                    ImageFileName [16];
/*20C*/ DWORD                   VmTrimFaultValue;
/*210*/ BYTE                    SetTimerResolution;
/*211*/ BYTE                    PriorityClass;
/*212*/ union
            {
            struct
                {
/*212*/         BYTE                SubSystemMinorVersion;
/*213*/         BYTE                SubSystemMajorVersion;
                };
            struct
                {
/*212*/         WORD                SubSystemVersion;
                };
```

(continued)

```
            };
/*214*/ struct _WIN32_PROCESS *Win32Process;
/*218*/ DWORD                  d218;
/*21C*/ DWORD                  d21C;
/*220*/ DWORD                  d220;
/*224*/ DWORD                  d224;
/*228*/ DWORD                  d228;
/*22C*/ DWORD                  d22C;
/*230*/ PVOID                  Wow64;
/*234*/ DWORD                  d234;
/*238*/ IO_COUNTERS            IoCounters;
/*268*/ DWORD                  d268;
/*26C*/ DWORD                  d26C;
/*270*/ DWORD                  d270;
/*274*/ DWORD                  d274;
/*278*/ DWORD                  d278;
/*27C*/ DWORD                  d27C;
/*280*/ DWORD                  d280;
/*284*/ DWORD                  d284;
/*288*/ }
        EPROCESS,
      * PEPROCESS,
     **PPEPROCESS;
```

LISTING 7-13. *The* EPROCESS *Object Structure*

```
typedef struct _ETHREAD
        {
/*000*/ KTHREAD       Tcb;
/*1B0*/ LARGE_INTEGER CreateTime;
/*1B8*/ union
            {
/*1B8*/     LARGE_INTEGER ExitTime;
/*1B8*/     LIST_ENTRY    LpcReplyChain;
            };
/*1C0*/ union
            {
/*1C0*/     NTSTATUS      ExitStatus;
/*1C0*/     DWORD         OfsChain;
            };
```

```
/*1C4*/ LIST_ENTRY    PostBlockList;
/*1CC*/ LIST_ENTRY    TerminationPortList;
/*1D4*/ PVOID         ActiveTimerListLock;
/*1D8*/ LIST_ENTRY    ActiveTimerListHead;
/*1E0*/ CLIENT_ID     Cid;
/*1E8*/ KSEMAPHORE    LpcReplySemaphore;
/*1FC*/ DWORD         LpcReplyMessage;
/*200*/ DWORD         LpcReplyMessageId;
/*204*/ DWORD         PerformanceCountLow;
/*208*/ DWORD         ImpersonationInfo;
/*20C*/ LIST_ENTRY    IrpList;
/*214*/ PVOID         TopLevelIrp;
/*218*/ PVOID         DeviceToVerify;
/*21C*/ DWORD         ReadClusterSize;
/*220*/ BOOLEAN       ForwardClusterOnly;
/*221*/ BOOLEAN       DisablePageFaultClustering;
/*222*/ BOOLEAN       DeadThread;
/*223*/ BOOLEAN       Reserved;
/*224*/ BOOL          HasTerminated;
/*228*/ ACCESS_MASK   GrantedAccess;
/*22C*/ PEPROCESS     ThreadsProcess;
/*230*/ PVOID         StartAddress;
/*234*/ union
            {
/*234*/     PVOID         Win32StartAddress;
/*234*/     DWORD         LpcReceivedMessageId;
            };
/*238*/ BOOLEAN       LpcExitThreadCalled;
/*239*/ BOOLEAN       HardErrorsAreDisabled;
/*23A*/ BOOLEAN       LpcReceivedMsgIdValid;
/*23B*/ BOOLEAN       ActiveImpersonationInfo;
/*23C*/ DWORD         PerformanceCountHigh;
/*240*/ DWORD         d240;
/*244*/ DWORD         d244;
/*248*/ }
        ETHREAD,
      * PETHREAD,
     **PPETHREAD;
```

LISTING 7-14. *The* ETHREAD *Object Structure*

It is apparent that both the EPROCESS and ETHREAD object structures contain additional members after the ones listed by the !processfields and !threadfields debugger commands. You may wonder how I dare to claim that. Well, there are two principal ways to find out details about undocumented object structure members. One is to observe how system functions operating on objects access their members; the other one is to examine how objects are created and initialized. The latter approach yields the size of an object. The basic object creation function inside ntoskrnl.exe is ObCreateObject(). It allocates the memory for the object header and body and initializes common object parameters. However, ObCreateObject() is absolutely ignorant about the type of object it creates, so the caller must specify the number of bytes required for the object body. Hence, the problem of finding out the size of an object boils down to finding an ObCreateObject() call for this object type. Process objects are created by the Native API function NtCreateProcess(), which lets PspCreateProcess() do the dirty work. Inside this function, an ObCreateObject() call can be found that requests an object body size of 0x288 bytes. That's why Listing 7-13 contains a couple of unidentified trailing members until a final offset of 0x288 is reached. The situation is similar for the ETHREAD structure. The NtCreateThread() API function calls PspCreateThread(), which in turn calls ObCreateObject(), requesting 0x248 bytes.

The list of currently running processes is formed by interlinking the ActiveProcessLinks member of the EPROCESS structure. The head of this list is stored in the internal global variable PsActiveProcessHead, and the associated FAST_MUTEX synchronization object is named PspActiveProcessMutex. Unfortunately, the PsActiveProcessHead variable is not exported by ntoskrnl.exe, but PsInitialSystemProcess is, pointing to the EPROCESS structure of the System process with the process ID 8. Following the Blink of its ActiveProcessLinks list entry leads us directly to the PsActiveProcessHead. Basically, the linkage of processes and threads is structured as shown in Figure 7-3. Figure 7-3 is overly simplified because the illustrated process list contains only two items. In a real-world scenario, the list will be much longer. (While I am writing this paragraph, my task manager reports 36 processes!) To keep the picture as simple as possible, only the thread list of one process is shown, assuming that this process has two active threads.

Listings 7-12 and 7-13 suggest that there must be a third process and thread object layer above the kernel and executive layers, indicated by pointers to WIN32_PROCESS and WIN32_THREAD structures inside EPROCESS and KTHREAD. These undocumented structures constitute the process and thread representations of the Win32 subsystem. Although the purposes of some of their members are quite obvious, they still contain too many unidentified holes to be included here. This is another area of future research.

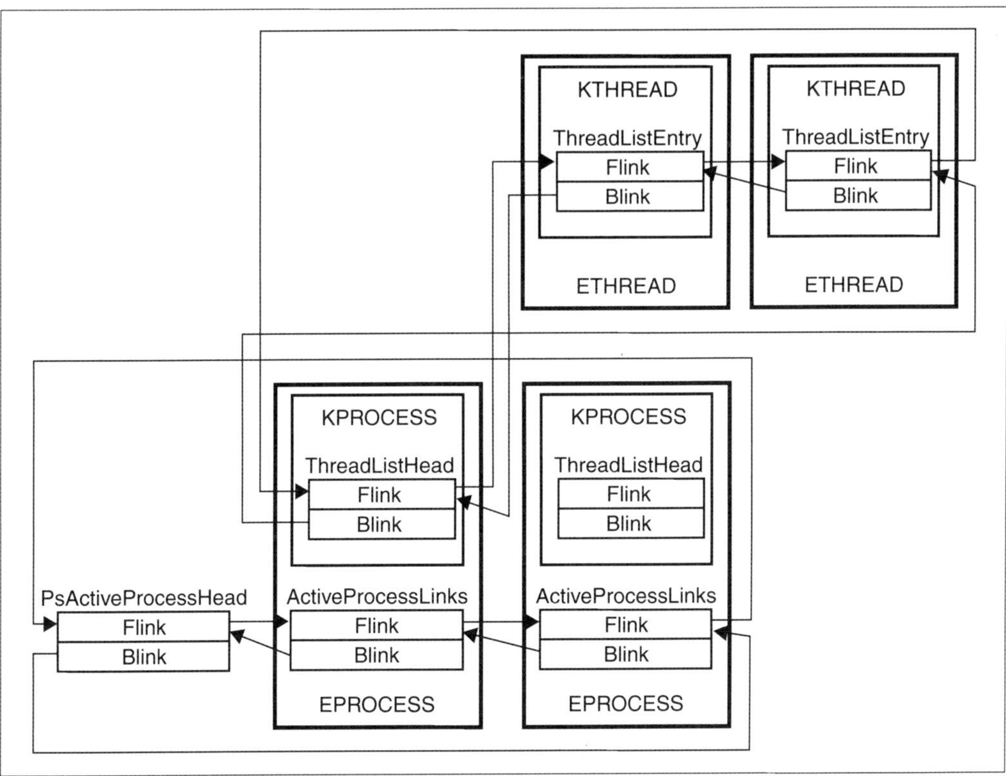

FIGURE 7-3. *Process and Thread Object Lists*

THREAD AND PROCESS CONTEXTS

While the system executes code, the execution always takes place in the context of a thread that is part of some process. In several situations, the system has to look up thread- or process-specific information from the current context. Therefore, the system always keeps a pointer to the current thread in the Kernel's Processor Control Block (`KPRCB`). This structure, defined in `ntddk.h,` is shown in Listing 7-15.

```
typedef struct _KPRCB // base address 0xFFDFF120
        {
/*000*/ WORD                MinorVersion;
/*002*/ WORD                MajorVersion;
/*004*/ struct _KTHREAD    *CurrentThread;
/*008*/ struct _KTHREAD    *NextThread;
/*00C*/ struct _KTHREAD    *IdleThread;
/*010*/ CHAR                Number;
/*011*/ CHAR                Reserved;
```

(continued)

```
/*012*/ WORD                    BuildType;/*014*/ KAFFINITY              SetMember;
/*018*/ struct _RESTART_BLOCK *RestartBlock;
/*01C*/ }
        KPRCB,
     * PKPRCB,
    **PPKPRCB;
```

LISTING 7-15. *The Kernel's Processor Control Block* (KPRCB)

The `KPRCB` structure is found at linear address `0xFFDFF120`, and a pointer to it is stored in the `Prcb` member of the Kernel's Processor Control Region (`KPCR`), also defined in `ntddk.h` (Listing 7-16) and located at address `0xFFDFF000`. As explained in Chapter 4, this essential data area is readily accessible in kernel-mode via the `FS` segment; that is, reading from address `FS:0` is equivalent to reading from linear address `DS:0xFFDFF000`. At address `0xFFDFF13C`, immediately following the `KPRCB`, the system keeps low-level CPU information in a `CONTEXT` structure (Listing 7-17).

```
typedef struct _KPCR // base address 0xFFDFF000
        {
/*000*/ NT_TIB             NtTib;
/*01C*/ struct _KPCR      *SelfPcr;
/*020*/ PKPRCB             Prcb;
/*024*/ KIRQL              Irql;
/*028*/ DWORD              IRR;
/*02C*/ DWORD              IrrActive;
/*030*/ DWORD              IDR;
/*034*/ DWORD              Reserved2;
/*038*/ struct _KIDTENTRY *IDT;
/*03C*/ struct _KGDTENTRY *GDT;
/*040*/ struct _KTSS      *TSS;
/*044*/ WORD               MajorVersion;
/*046*/ WORD               MinorVersion;
/*048*/ KAFFINITY          SetMember;
/*04C*/ DWORD              StallScaleFactor;
/*050*/ BYTE               DebugActive;
/*051*/ BYTE               Number;
/*054*/ }
        KPCR,
     * PKPCR,
    **PPKPCR;
```

LISTING 7-16. *The Kernel's Processor Control Region* (KPCR)

```
#define SIZE_OF_80387_REGISTERS 80

typedef struct _FLOATING_SAVE_AREA // base address 0xFFDFF158
        {
/*000*/ DWORD ControlWord;
/*004*/ DWORD StatusWord;
/*008*/ DWORD TagWord;
/*00C*/ DWORD ErrorOffset;
/*010*/ DWORD ErrorSelector;
/*014*/ DWORD DataOffset;
/*018*/ DWORD DataSelector;
/*01C*/ BYTE  RegisterArea [SIZE_OF_80387_REGISTERS];
/*06C*/ DWORD Cr0NpxState;
/*070*/ }
        FLOATING_SAVE_AREA,
      * PFLOATING_SAVE_AREA,
     **PPFLOATING_SAVE_AREA;

// -----------------------------------------------------------------

#define MAXIMUM_SUPPORTED_EXTENSION 512

typedef struct _CONTEXT // base address 0xFFDFF13C
        {
/*000*/ DWORD        ContextFlags;
/*004*/ DWORD        Dr0;
/*008*/ DWORD        Dr1;
/*00C*/ DWORD        Dr2;
/*010*/ DWORD        Dr3;
/*014*/ DWORD        Dr6;
/*018*/ DWORD        Dr7;
/*01C*/ FLOATING_SAVE_AREA FloatSave;
/*08C*/ DWORD        SegGs;
/*090*/ DWORD        SegFs;
/*094*/ DWORD        SegEs;
/*098*/ DWORD        SegDs;
/*09C*/ DWORD        Edi;
/*0A0*/ DWORD        Esi;
/*0A4*/ DWORD        Ebx;
/*0A8*/ DWORD        Edx;
/*0AC*/ DWORD        Ecx;
/*0B0*/ DWORD        Eax;
/*0B4*/ DWORD        Ebp;
/*0B8*/ DWORD        Eip;
/*0BC*/ DWORD        SegCs;
/*0C0*/ DWORD        EFlags;
/*0C4*/ DWORD        Esp;
/*0C8*/ DWORD        SegSs;
/*0CC*/ BYTE         ExtendedRegisters [MAXIMUM_SUPPORTED_EXTENSION];
/*2CC*/ }
        CONTEXT,
      * PCONTEXT,
     **PPCONTEXT;
```

LISTING 7-17. *The CPU's* CONTEXT *and* FLOATING_SAVE_AREA

According to Listing 7-15, the KPRCB contains three KTHREAD pointers at the offsets 0x004, 0x008, and 0x00C:

1. CurrentThread points to the KTHREAD object of the thread that is currently executing. This member is accessed very frequently by the kernel code.
2. NextThread points to the KTHREAD object of the thread scheduled to run after the next context switch.
3. IdleThread points to the KTHREAD object of an idle thread that performs background tasks while no other threads are ready to run. The system provides a dedicated idle thread for each installed CPU. On a single-processor machine, the idle thread object is named P0BootThread and is the only thread in the thread list of the PsIdleProcess object.

Because the first member of an ETHREAD is a KTHREAD, a KTHREAD pointer always points to an ETHREAD as well, and vice versa. This means that KTHREAD and ETHREAD can be typecast interchangeably. The same is true for KPROCESS and EPROCESS pointers.

Because the Windows 2000 kernel maps the linear address 0xFFDFF000 to address 0x00000000 of the CPU's FS segment in kernel-mode, the system always finds the current KPCR, KPRCB, and CONTEXT data at the addresses FS:0x0, FS:0x120, and FS:13C. When you are disassembling kernel code in a debugger, you will frequently see the system retrieve a pointer from FS:0x124, which is obviously the current thread object. Example 7-1 lists the output of the Kernel Debugger if the command u PsGetCurrentProcessId is issued, instructing the debugger to unassemble 10 lines of code, starting at the address of the symbol PsGetCurrentProcessId. The implementation of the PsGetCurrentProcessId() function simply retrieves the KTHREAD/ETHREAD of the current thread and returns the value of the member at offset 0x1E0, which happens to be the UniqueProcess ID of the CLIENT_ID Cid member of the ETHREAD, according to Listing 7-14. PsGetCurrentThreadId() is almost identical, except that it retrieves the UniqueThread ID at offset 0x1E4. By the way, the CLIENT_ID structure has been introduced in Chapter 2, Listing 2-8.

```
kd> u PsGetCurrentProcessId
u PsGetCurrentProcessId
ntoskrnl!PsGetCurrentProcessId:
8045252a 64a124010000     mov     eax,fs:[00000124]
80452530 8b80e0010000     mov     eax,[eax+0x1e0]
```

```
80452536 c3              ret
80452537 cc              int     3
ntoskrnl!PsGetCurrentThreadId:
80452538 64a124010000     mov     eax,fs:[00000124]
8045253e 8b80e4010000     mov     eax,[eax+0x1e4]
80452544 c3              ret
80452545 cc              int     3
```

EXAMPLE 7-1. *Retrieving Process and Thread IDs*

Sometimes, the system needs a pointer to the process object that owns the current thread. This address can be looked up quite easily by reading the `Process` member of the `ApcState` substructure inside the current `KTHREAD`.

THREAD AND PROCESS ENVIRONMENT BLOCKS

You may wonder about the purpose of the `Teb` and `Peb` members inside the `KTHREAD` and `EPROCESS` structures. The `Teb`, points to a `Thread Environment Block (TEB)`, outlined in Listing 7-18. The first part of the `TEB` the `Thread Information Block (NT_TIB)`, is defined in the Platform Software Development Kit (SDK) and DDK header files `winnt.h` and `ntddk.h`, respectively. The remaining members are undocumented. Windows 2000 maintains a `TEB` structure for each thread object in the system. In the address space of the current process, the `TEBs` of its threads are mapped to the linear addresses `0x7FFDE000`, `0x7FFDD000`, `0x7FFDC000`, and so on, always stepping down one 4-KB page per thread. As noted in Chapter 4, the `TEB` of the current thread is also accessible via the `FS` segment in user-mode. Many `ntdll.dll` functions access the current `TEB` by reading the value at address `FS:0x18`, which is the `Self` member of the embedded `NT_TIB`. This member always provides the linear address of the surrounding `TEB` within the 4-GB address space of the current process.

```
// typedef struct _NT_TIB // see winnt.h / ntddk.h
//         {
// /*000*/ struct _EXCEPTION_REGISTRATION_RECORD *ExceptionList;
// /*004*/ PVOID                                  StackBase;
// /*008*/ PVOID                                  StackLimit;
// /*00C*/ PVOID                                  SubSystemTib;
// /*010*/ union
```

(continued)

```
//              {
// /*010*/      PVOID FiberData;
// /*010*/      ULONG Version;
//              };
// /*014*/ PVOID            ArbitraryUserPointer;
// /*018*/ struct _NT_TIB *Self;
// /*01C*/ }
//         NT_TIB,
//       * PNT_TIB,
//      **PPNT_TIB;

// -----------------------------------------------------------------

typedef struct _TEB // base addresses 0x7FFDE000, 0x7FFDD000, ...
        {
/*000*/ NT_TIB    Tib;
/*01C*/ PVOID     EnvironmentPointer;
/*020*/ CLIENT_ID Cid;
/*028*/ HANDLE    RpcHandle;
/*02C*/ PPVOID    ThreadLocalStorage;
/*030*/ PPEB      Peb;
/*034*/ DWORD     LastErrorValue;
/*038*/ }
        TEB,
      * PTEB,
     **PPTEB;
```

LISTING 7-18. *The Thread Environment Block* (TEB)

Just as each thread has its own `TEB`, each process has an associated `PEB` or `Process Environment Block`. The `PEB` is much more complex than the `TEB`, as Listing 7-19 demonstrates. It contains various pointers to subordinate structures that refer to more subordinate structures, and most of them are undocumented. Listing 7-19 includes raw sketches of some of them, using tentative names and leaving much to be desired. The `PEB` is located at linear address `0x7FFDF000`, that is, in the first 4-KB page following the `TEB` stack of the process. The system can easily access the `PEB` by simply referencing the `Peb` member of the current thread's `TEB`.

```
typedef struct _MODULE_HEADER
        {
/*000*/ DWORD      d000;
/*004*/ DWORD      d004;
/*008*/ LIST_ENTRY List1;
/*010*/ LIST_ENTRY List2;
```

```
/*018*/ LIST_ENTRY List3;
/*020*/ }
        MODULE_HEADER,
     * PMODULE_HEADER,
    **PPMODULE_HEADER;

// -----------------------------------------------------------------

typedef struct _PROCESS_MODULE_INFO
        {
/*000*/ DWORD         Size; // 0x24
/*004*/ MODULE_HEADER ModuleHeader;
/*024*/ }
        PROCESS_MODULE_INFO,
     * PPROCESS_MODULE_INFO,
    **PPPROCESS_MODULE_INFO;

// -----------------------------------------------------------------

// see RtlCreateProcessParameters()

typedef struct _PROCESS_PARAMETERS
        {
/*000*/ DWORD          Allocated;
/*004*/ DWORD          Size;
/*008*/ DWORD          Flags; // bit 0: all pointers normalized
/*00C*/ DWORD          Reserved1;
/*010*/ LONG           Console;
/*014*/ DWORD          ProcessGroup;
/*018*/ HANDLE         StdInput;
/*01C*/ HANDLE         StdOutput;
/*020*/ HANDLE         StdError;
/*024*/ UNICODE_STRING WorkingDirectoryName;
/*02C*/ HANDLE         WorkingDirectoryHandle;
/*030*/ UNICODE_STRING SearchPath;
/*038*/ UNICODE_STRING ImagePath;
/*040*/ UNICODE_STRING CommandLine;
/*048*/ PWORD          Environment;
/*04C*/ DWORD          X;
/*050*/ DWORD          Y;
/*054*/ DWORD          XSize;
/*058*/ DWORD          YSize;
/*05C*/ DWORD          XCountChars;
/*060*/ DWORD          YCountChars;
/*064*/ DWORD          FillAttribute;
/*068*/ DWORD          Flags2;
/*06C*/ WORD           ShowWindow;
/*06E*/ WORD           Reserved2;
/*070*/ UNICODE_STRING Title;
/*078*/ UNICODE_STRING Desktop;
/*080*/ UNICODE_STRING Reserved3;
```

(continued)

```
/*088*/ UNICODE_STRING Reserved4;
/*090*/ }
        PROCESS_PARAMETERS,
     * PPROCESS_PARAMETERS,
    **PPPROCESS_PARAMETERS;

// ---------------------------------------------------------------

typedef struct _SYSTEM_STRINGS
        {
/*000*/ UNICODE_STRING SystemRoot;       // d:\WINNT
/*008*/ UNICODE_STRING System32Root;     // d:\WINNT\System32
/*010*/ UNICODE_STRING BaseNamedObjects; // \BaseNamedObjects
/*018*/ }
        SYSTEM_STRINGS,
     * PSYSTEM_STRINGS,
    **PPSYSTEM_STRINGS;

// ---------------------------------------------------------------

typedef struct _TEXT_INFO
        {
/*000*/ PVOID           Reserved;
/*004*/ PSYSTEM_STRINGS SystemStrings;
/*008*/ }
        TEXT_INFO,
     * PTEXT_INFO,
    **PPTEXT_INFO;

// ---------------------------------------------------------------

typedef struct _PEB // base address 0x7FFDF000
        {
/*000*/ BOOLEAN              InheritedAddressSpace;
/*001*/ BOOLEAN              ReadImageFileExecOptions;
/*002*/ BOOLEAN              BeingDebugged;
/*003*/ BYTE                 b003;
/*004*/ DWORD                d004;
/*008*/ PVOID                SectionBaseAddress;
/*00C*/ PPROCESS_MODULE_INFO ProcessModuleInfo;
/*010*/ PPROCESS_PARAMETERS  ProcessParameters;
/*014*/ DWORD                SubSystemData;
/*018*/ HANDLE               ProcessHeap;
/*01C*/ PCRITICAL_SECTION    FastPebLock;
/*020*/ PVOID                AcquireFastPebLock; // function
/*024*/ PVOID                ReleaseFastPebLock; // function
/*028*/ DWORD                d028;
/*02C*/ PPVOID               User32Dispatch;     // function
/*030*/ DWORD                d030;
```

```
/*034*/ DWORD                d034;
/*038*/ DWORD                d038;
/*03C*/ DWORD                TlsBitMapSize;      // number of bits
/*040*/ PRTL_BITMAP          TlsBitMap;          // ntdll!TlsBitMap
/*044*/ DWORD                TlsBitMapData [2];  // 64 bits
/*04C*/ PVOID                p04C;
/*050*/ PVOID                p050;
/*054*/ PTEXT_INFO           TextInfo;
/*058*/ PVOID                InitAnsiCodePageData;
/*05C*/ PVOID                InitOemCodePageData;
/*060*/ PVOID                InitUnicodeCaseTableData;
/*064*/ DWORD                KeNumberProcessors;
/*068*/ DWORD                NtGlobalFlag;
/*06C*/ DWORD                d6C;
/*070*/ LARGE_INTEGER        MmCriticalSectionTimeout;
/*078*/ DWORD                MmHeapSegmentReserve;
/*07C*/ DWORD                MmHeapSegmentCommit;
/*080*/ DWORD                MmHeapDeCommitTotalFreeThreshold;
/*084*/ DWORD                MmHeapDeCommitFreeBlockThreshold;
/*088*/ DWORD                NumberOfHeaps;
/*08C*/ DWORD                AvailableHeaps; // 16, *2 if exhausted
/*090*/ PHANDLE              ProcessHeapsListBuffer;
/*094*/ DWORD                d094;
/*098*/ DWORD                d098;
/*09C*/ DWORD                d09C;
/*0A0*/ PCRITICAL_SECTION    LoaderLock;
/*0A4*/ DWORD                NtMajorVersion;
/*0A8*/ DWORD                NtMinorVersion;
/*0AC*/ WORD                 NtBuildNumber;
/*0AE*/ WORD                 CmNtCSDVersion;
/*0B0*/ DWORD                PlatformId;
/*0B4*/ DWORD                Subsystem;
/*0B8*/ DWORD                MajorSubsystemVersion;
/*0BC*/ DWORD                MinorSubsystemVersion;
/*0C0*/ KAFFINITY            AffinityMask;
/*0C4*/ DWORD                ad0C4 [35];
/*150*/ PVOID                p150;
/*154*/ DWORD                ad154 [32];
/*1D4*/ HANDLE               Win32WindowStation;
/*1D8*/ DWORD                d1D8;
/*1DC*/ DWORD                d1DC;
/*1E0*/ PWORD                CSDVersion;
/*1E4*/ DWORD                d1E4;
/*1E8*/ }
        PEB,
      * PPEB,
     **PPPEB;
```

LISTING 7-19. *The Process Environment Block* (PEB)

ACCESSING LIVE SYSTEM OBJECTS

The preceding sections have provided a lot of theoretical information. As a practical example to illustrate object management in the most useful form, I thought of writing a kernel object browser. This would show how objects are arranged hierarchically and how some of their properties can be retrieved. Unfortunately, `ntoskrnl.exe` fails to export several key structures and functions required in an object browser application. This means that not even a kernel-mode driver has access to them—they are reserved for internal system use. On the other hand, Chapter 6 introduced a mechanism that allows access to nonexported data and code by evaluating the Windows 2000 symbol files, so the object browser seemed to be an ideal test case to check out the practical suitability of this approach. The symbolic call interface from Chapter 6 passed this test, so I have included the sample application `w2k_obj.exe` with full source code on the companion CD in the directory tree `\src\w2k_obj`. However, the most interesting parts of the code are not buried inside `w2k_obj.c`. The hard work is really done by the `w2k_call.dll` library introduced in Chapter 6. Hence, many of the subsequent code snippets are pulled from `w2k_call.c`.

ENUMERATING OBJECT DIRECTORY ENTRIES

You probably know the small `objdir.exe` utility in the Windows 2000 DDK, in the `\ntddk\bin` directory. `objdir.exe` retrieves object directory information via the undocumented Native API function `NtQueryDirectoryObject()` exported by `ntdll.dll`. Contrary to this, my object browser `w2k_obj.exe` bangs directly at the object directory and its leaf objects. This sounds rather scary, but actually it isn't. The best proof is that `w2k_obj.exe` works on both Windows 2000 and Windows NT 4.0 without a single line of version-dependent code. Admittedly, there are a couple of subtle differences in the object structures of both operating system versions, but the basic model has remained the same. Providing a sample application that works directly on the raw object structures rather than using higher-level API functions is an illustrative means to verify whether the structures shown in the preceding sections are accurate.

The most important thing to do before accessing global system data structures is to lock them. Otherwise it might happen that the system alters the data in the context of a concurrent thread, so the application unexpectedly reads invalid data or reaches into the void. Windows 2000 provides a large set of locks for the numerous internal data items it maintains. The problem with these locks is that they are usually not exported. Although a kernel-mode driver can do all sorts of things forbidden in user-mode, it can't safely access nonexported data structures. However, the extended kernel call interface discussed in Chapter 6 and implemented by the `w2k_call.dll` sample library `can` make the impossible possible by looking up the addresses of internal symbols from the operating system's symbol files. This DLL exports the following three object manager data thunks that allow access to the kernel's object directory:

1. `__ObpRootDirectoryMutex()` returns the address of the `ERESOURCE` lock that synchronizes access to the object directory as a whole.
2. `__ObpRootDirectoryObject()` returns a pointer to the `OBJECT_DIRECTORY` structure representing the root node of the object directory.
3. `__ObpTypeDirectoryObject()` returns a pointer to the `OBJECT_DIRECTORY` structure representing the `\ObjectTypes` subdirectory node of the object directory.

An application must be extremely cautious when it works with pointers to kernel objects, especially after acquiring a global lock. If the lock isn't properly released, the system might be left in a handcuffed state, unable to perform even the simplest tasks.

Although the root directory lock is named `ObpRootDirectoryMutex`, it isn't really a mutex in the strict sense of the word. It is an `ERESOURCE` rather than a `KMUTEX`, and as such must be acquired with the help of the `ExAcquireResourceExclusiveLite()` or `ExAcquireResourceSharedLite()` API functions. The "Lite" suffix is important—never use the siblings `ExAcquireResourceExclusive()` or `ExAcquireResourcShared()` on Windows 2000 or NT4 `ERESOURCE` locks. This structure has been revised quite a bit since Windows NT 3.x, and the latter pair of functions works only with the old-style `ERESOURCE` type, included in `w2k_def.h` as `ERESOURCE_OLD` (see also Appendix C). The counterpart of the `ExAcquireResource*Lite()` functions is named `ExReleaseResourceLite()` and should be carefully distinguished from its old-style sibling `ExReleaseResource()`.

The basic approach of my object browser is to lock the object directory, take a snapshot of all nodes found in its hierarchic structure, and display the snapshot data after releasing the directory lock. This procedure guarantees the least interference with the system, and the application can take as much time as it needs to display the data without overusing the system. Taking a faithful snapshot of the directory requires very intimate knowledge of the system's object structures, so this application is a great test case for the reliability of the object information I have supplied above. This job can be subdivided into the following two basic tasks:

1. Copying the `structure` of the object directory tree. This involves copying and interlinking several `OBJECT_DIRECTORY` structures, each one representing an individual nonleaf node.
2. Copying the `contents` of the object directory tree. This means copying the `OBJECT_HEADER` and its related structures of each leaf node in the tree.

The `w2kDirectoryOpen()` function shown in Listing 7-20 performs the first task. It locks the directory and enumerates all children of the supplied `OBJECT_DIRECTORY`. To capture the entire object tree, this function must be called recursively for each directory entry that is itself an `OBJECT_DIRECTORY`. Please recall that each object directory node consists of a hash table that can accommodate a maximum of 37 entries. Each hash table slot can in turn refer to an arbitrary number of entries by putting them into a linked list. Therefore, enumeration of directory entries requires two nested loops: The outer one scans all 37 hash table slots for non-`NULL` entries, and the inner one walks down the linked lists. This is about all the `w2kDirectoryOpen()` function does. The resulting data is structurally equivalent to the original model, except that all pointers refer to memory blocks reachable in user-mode. The basic copying including automatic memory allocation is performed by the powerful `w2kSpyClone()` function, also exported by `w2k_call.dll` (see Listing 6-30). The `w2kDirectoryClose()` function in Listing 7-20 undoes the work done by `w2kDirectoryOpen()`, simply deallocating all cloned memory blocks.

```
POBJECT_DIRECTORY WINAPI
w2kDirectoryOpen (POBJECT_DIRECTORY pDir)
    {
    DWORD                        i;
    PERESOURCE                   pLock;
    PPOBJECT_DIRECTORY_ENTRY ppEntry;
    POBJECT_DIRECTORY            pDir1 = NULL;

    if (((pLock = __ObpRootDirectoryMutex ()) != NULL) &&
        _ExAcquireResourceExclusiveLite (pLock, TRUE))
        {
        if ((pDir1 = w2kSpyClone (pDir, OBJECT_DIRECTORY_)) != NULL)
            {
            for (i = 0; i < OBJECT_HASH_TABLE_SIZE; i++)
                {
                ppEntry = pDir1->HashTable + i;

                while (*ppEntry != NULL)
                    {
                    if ((*ppEntry =
                            w2kSpyClone (*ppEntry,
                                         OBJECT_DIRECTORY_ENTRY_))
                        != NULL)
                        {
                        (*ppEntry)->Object =
                            w2kObjectOpen ((*ppEntry)->Object);

                        ppEntry = &(*ppEntry)->NextEntry;
                        }
                    }
                }
            }
```

```
            _ExReleaseResourceLite (pLock);
            }
        return pDir1;
        }

// ----------------------------------------------------------------

POBJECT_DIRECTORY WINAPI
w2kDirectoryClose (POBJECT_DIRECTORY pDir)
        {
        POBJECT_DIRECTORY_ENTRY pEntry, pEntry1;
        DWORD                   i;

        if (pDir != NULL)
            {
            for (i = 0; i < OBJECT_HASH_TABLE_SIZE; i++)
                {
                for (pEntry  = pDir->HashTable [i];
                     pEntry != NULL;
                     pEntry  = pEntry1)
                    {
                    pEntry1 = pEntry->NextEntry;

                    w2kObjectClose   (pEntry->Object);
                    w2kMemoryDestroy (pEntry);
                    }
                }
            w2kMemoryDestroy (pDir);
            }
        return NULL;
        }
```

LISTING 7-20. *The* `w2kDirectoryOpen()` *and* `w2kDirectoryClose()` *API Functions*

A closer look at Listing 7-20 reveals that `w2kDirectoryOpen()` and `w2kDirectoryClose()` call the functions `w2kObjectOpen()` and `w2kObjectClose()`, respectively. `w2kObjectOpen()` takes care of part two of the directory copying procedure: It clones leaf objects. It doesn't produce complete object copies, because this would require identifying each object type and copying the appropriate number of bytes from the object body. `w2kObjectOpen()` copies the entire header portion of an object, including most of its subordinate structures, and builds a fake object body that contains pointers to the real object body and to various parts of the object header copy. Listing 7-21 shows the data structures built and initialized by `w2kObjectOpen()`. `W2K_OBJECT_FRAME` is a monolithic data block that comprises the object header copy and the fake object body. The latter is represented by the `W2K_OBJECT` structure, which is just a collection of pointers to members of

W2K_OBJECT_FRAME. w2kObjectOpen() allocates memory for the W2K_OBJECT_FRAME structure, initializes it with data from the original object, and returns a pointer to the object frame's Object member. If you recall the foregoing description of object bodies and headers, it becomes apparent that the W2K_OBJECT_FRAME mimics the structure of a real object. That is, it has all header fields the original object has, and an application can access them in the same way that the system accesses its objects in kernel-mode memory, using the offsets and flags in the OBJECT_HEADER.

```
typedef struct _W2K_OBJECT
    {
    POBJECT                 pObject;
    POBJECT_HEADER          pHeader;
    POBJECT_CREATOR_INFO    pCreatorInfo;
    POBJECT_NAME            pName;
    POBJECT_HANDLE_DB       pHandleDB;
    POBJECT_QUOTA_CHARGES   pQuotaCharges;
    POBJECT_TYPE            pType;
    PQUOTA_BLOCK            pQuotaBlock;
    POBJECT_CREATE_INFO     pCreateInfo;
    PWORD                   pwName;
    PWORD                   pwType;
    }
    W2K_OBJECT, *PW2K_OBJECT, **PPW2K_OBJECT;

#define W2K_OBJECT_ sizeof (W2K_OBJECT)

// -----------------------------------------------------------------

typedef struct _W2K_OBJECT_FRAME
    {
    OBJECT_QUOTA_CHARGES QuotaCharges;
    OBJECT_HANDLE_DB     HandleDB;
    OBJECT_NAME          Name;
    OBJECT_CREATOR_INFO  CreatorInfo;
    OBJECT_HEADER        Header;
    W2K_OBJECT           Object;
    OBJECT_TYPE          Type;
    QUOTA_BLOCK          QuotaBlock;
    OBJECT_CREATE_INFO   CreateInfo;
    WORD                 Buffer [];
    }
    W2K_OBJECT_FRAME, *PW2K_OBJECT_FRAME, **PPW2K_OBJECT_FRAME;

#define W2K_OBJECT_FRAME_ sizeof (W2K_OBJECT_FRAME)
#define W2K_OBJECT_FRAME__(_n) (W2K_OBJECT_FRAME_ + ((_n) * WORD_))
```

LISTING 7-21. *Object Clone Structures*

I don't want to go into the details of w2kObjectOpen() and all of its subordinate functions. For illustrative purposes, the three-part set of functions shown in Listing 7-22 should suffice. w2kObjectHeader() creates a copy of an object's OBJECT_HEADER, and w2kObjectCreatorInfo() and w2kObjectName() copy the OBJECT_CREATOR_INFO and OBJECT_NAME header parts, if present. Again, w2kSpyClone() is the main workhorse. For more examples of this kind, please refer to the w2k_call.c source file on the accompanying CD.

```
#define BACK(_p,_d) ((PVOID) (((PBYTE) (_p)) - (_d)))

// -----------------------------------------------------------------

POBJECT_HEADER WINAPI
w2kObjectHeader (POBJECT pObject)
    {
    DWORD          dOffset = OBJECT_HEADER_;
    POBJECT_HEADER pHeader = NULL;

    if (pObject != NULL)
        {
        pHeader = w2kSpyClone (BACK (pObject, dOffset),
                               dOffset);
        }
    return pHeader;
    }

// -----------------------------------------------------------------

POBJECT_CREATOR_INFO WINAPI
w2kObjectCreatorInfo (POBJECT_HEADER pHeader,
                      POBJECT        pObject)
    {
    DWORD                dOffset;
    POBJECT_CREATOR_INFO pCreatorInfo = NULL;

    if ((pHeader != NULL) && (pObject != NULL) &&
        (pHeader->ObjectFlags & OB_FLAG_CREATOR_INFO))
        {
        dOffset = OBJECT_CREATOR_INFO_ + OBJECT_HEADER_;

        pCreatorInfo = w2kSpyClone (BACK (pObject, dOffset),
                                    OBJECT_CREATOR_INFO_);
        }
    return pCreatorInfo;
    }
```

(continued)

```
// ----------------------------------------------------------------

POBJECT_NAME WINAPI
w2kObjectName (POBJECT_HEADER pHeader,
               POBJECT        pObject)
    {
    DWORD        dOffset;
    POBJECT_NAME pName = NULL;

    if ((pHeader != NULL) && (pObject != NULL) &&
        (dOffset = pHeader->NameOffset))
        {
        dOffset += OBJECT_HEADER_;

        pName = w2kSpyClone (BACK (pObject, dOffset),
                             OBJECT_NAME_);
        }
    return pName;
    }
```

LISTING 7-22. *Object Cloning Helper Functions*

The bottom line of the story is that `w2kDirectoryOpen()` takes a pointer to a live `OBJECT_DIRECTORY` node and returns a copy that contains `W2K_OBJECT` pointers where the original directory stores its object body pointers. The object browser application calls this API function repeatedly, once for each directory layer it displays. Listing 7-23 is a heavily edited version of the browser code, stripped down to its bare essentials. The original code found in `w2k_obj.c` contains many distracting extras that would have obscured the basic functional layout. The top-level function is named `DisplayObjects()`. It requests the object root pointer from `w2k_call.dll` via `__ObpRootDirectoryObject()` and forwards it to `DisplayOject()`, which displays the type and name of the object and calls itself recursively if the object is an `OBJECT_DIRECTORY`. For each nesting level, `DisplayObject()` adds a line indentation of three spaces. I have added the functions in Listing 7-23 to `w2k_obj.c` on the companion CD under the section header "POOR MAN'S OBJECT BROWSER." However, this code is not called anywhere, although it does work.

```
VOID WINAPI _DisplayObject (PW2K_OBJECT pObject,
                            DWORD       dLevel)
    {
    POBJECT_DIRECTORY       pDir;
    POBJECT_DIRECTORY_ENTRY pEntry;
    DWORD                   i;
```

```
    for (i = 0; i < dLevel; i++) printf (L"    ");

    _printf (L"%+.-16s%s\r\n", pObject->pwType, pObject->pwName);

    if ((!lstrcmp (pObject->pwType, L"Directory")) &&
        ((pDir = w2kDirectoryOpen (pObject->pObject)) != NULL))
        {
        for (i = 0; i < OBJECT_HASH_TABLE_SIZE; i++)
            {
            for (pEntry  = pDir->HashTable [i];
                 pEntry != NULL;
                 pEntry  = pEntry->NextEntry)
                {
                _DisplayObject (pEntry->Object, dLevel+1);
                }
            }
        w2kDirectoryClose (pDir);
        }
    return;
    }

// -----------------------------------------------------------------

VOID WINAPI _DisplayObjects (VOID)
    {
    PW2K_OBJECT pObject;

    if ((pObject = w2kObjectOpen (__ObpRootDirectoryObject ()))
        != NULL)
        {
        _DisplayObject (pObject, 0);
        w2kObjectClose (pObject);
        }
    return;
    }
```

LISTING 7-23. *A Very Simple Object Browser*

In Example 7-2, I have compiled some characteristic parts of an object directory listing generated by the code in Listing 7-23. For example, the `\BaseNamedObjects` subdirectory comprises named objects that are typically shared between processes and can be opened by name. The `\ObjectTypes` subdirectory contains all 27 `OBJECT_TYPE` type objects (cf. Listing 7-9) supported by the system, as listed in Table 7-4.

```
Directory.......\
   Directory.......ArcName
      SymbolicLink....multi(0)disk(0)rdisk(0)
      SymbolicLink....multi(0)disk(0)rdisk(1)
      SymbolicLink....multi(0)disk(0)rdisk(1)partition(1)
      SymbolicLink....multi(0)disk(0)rdisk(0)partition(1)
      SymbolicLink....multi(0)disk(0)fdisk(0)
      SymbolicLink....multi(0)disk(0)rdisk(0)partition(2)
   Device..........Ntfs
   Port............SeLsaCommandPort
   Key.............REGISTRY
   Port............XactSrvLpcPort
   Port............DbgUiApiPort
   Directory.......NLS
      Section.........NlsSectionCP874
      Section.........NlsSectionCP950
      Section.........NlsSectionCP20290
      Section.........NlsSectionCP1255c_1255.nls
...
   Directory.......BaseNamedObjects
      Section.........DfSharedHeapE445BB
      Section.........DFMap0-14765686
      Mutant..........ZonesCacheCounterMutex
      Section.........DFMap0-14364447
      Event...........WINMGMT_COREDLL_UNLOADED
      Mutant..........MCICDA_DeviceCritSec_19
      Event...........AgentToWkssvcEvent
      Event...........userenv: Machine Group Policy has been applied
      SymbolicLink....Local
      Section.........DFMap0-15555297
      Section.........DfSharedHeapED2256
      Section.........DfSharedHeapE8F975
      Section.........DFMap0-15232696
      Section.........DFMap0-15170325
      Event...........Shell_NotificationCallbacksOutstanding
      Section.........DFMap0-14364985
      Event...........SETTermEvent
      Event...........winlogon:  User GPO Event 112121
...
   Directory.......ObjectTypes
      Type............Directory
      Type............Mutant
      Type............Thread
      Type............Controller
      Type............Profile
      Type............Event
      Type............Type
      Type............Section
```

```
      Type...........EventPair
      Type...........SymbolicLink
      Type...........Desktop
      Type...........Timer
      Type...........File
      Type...........WindowStation
      Type...........Driver
      Type...........WmiGuid
      Type...........Device
      Type...........Token
      Type...........IoCompletion
      Type...........Process
      Type...........Adapter
      Type...........Key
      Type...........Job
      Type...........WaitablePort
      Type...........Port
      Type...........Callback
      Type...........Semaphore
   Directory.......Security
      Event..........TRKWKS_EVENT
      WaitablePort....TRKWKS_PORT
      Event..........LSA_AUTHENTICATION_INITIALIZED
      Event..........NetworkProviderLoad
...
```

EXAMPLE 7-2. *Excerpts from an Object Directory*

The full-featured object browser code inside `w2k_obj.exe` not only displays the directory tree in a more pleasing visual form, but also allows display of additional object features and filtering of object types. Example 7-3 shows the various options offered by the `w2k_obj.exe` command line.

```
// w2k_obj.exe
// SBS Windows 2000 Object Browser V1.00
// 08-27-2000 Sven B. Schreiber
// sbs@orgon.com

Usage: w2k_obj [+-atf] [<type>] [<#>|-1] [/root] [/types]

       +a -a  : show/hide object addresses  (default: -a)
       +t -t  : show/hide object type names (default: -t)
       +f -f  : show/hide object flags      (default: -f)
```

(continued)

```
      <type> : show <type> objects only    (default:  *)
      <#>    : show <#> directory levels   (default: -1)
      -1     : show all directory levels
      /root  : show ObpRootDirectoryObject tree
      /types : show ObpTypeDirectoryObject tree

Example: w2k_obj +atf *port 2 /root

This command displays all Port and WaitablePort objects,
starting in the root and scanning two directory levels.
Each line includes address, type, and flag information.
```

EXAMPLE 7-3. *The Command Help of* `w2k_obj.exe`

In Example 7-4, I have issued the sample command `w2k_obj +atf *port 2 /root` mentioned in the help screen. It restricts the output to `Port` and `WaitablePort` objects by applying the type filter expression `*port` and includes object body addresses, type names, and flags for each entry. The display is limited to two subordinate directory layers.

```
Root directory contents: (2 levels shown)
------------

 8149CDD0 Directory_____ <32> \
> |_ E26A0540 Port__________ <24> SeLsaCommandPort
> |_ E130CC20 Port__________ <24> XactSrvLpcPort
> |_ E13E2380 Port__________ <24> DbgUiApiPort
> |_ E13E4BA0 Port__________ <26> SeRmCommandPort
> |_ E26A9D20 Port__________ <24> LsaAuthenticationPort
> |_ E13E4CA0 Port__________ <24> DbgSsApiPort
> |_ E13E3260 Port__________ <24> SmApiPort
> |_ E2707680 Port__________ <24> ErrorLogPort
  |_ 81499B70 Directory_____ <32> \ArcName
  |_ 812FDB60 Directory_____ <10> \NLS
  |_ 814940B0 Directory_____ <32> \Driver
  |_ 81490B30 Directory_____ <32> \WmiGuid
  |_ 81499A90 Directory_____ <32> \Device
  |    |_ 814AEA90 Directory_____ <32> \Device\DmControl
  |    |_ 814AE4F0 Directory_____ <32> \Device\HarddiskDmVolumes
  |    |_ 8148BE50 Directory_____ <32> \Device\Ide
  |    |_ 814AB3D0 Directory_____ <32> \Device\Harddisk0
  |    |_ 814852F0 Directory_____ <32> \Device\Harddisk1
  |    |_ 814A9F50 Directory_____ <22> \Device\WinDfs
```

```
  |   \_ 814AB030 Directory_____ <32> \Device\Scsi
  |_ 81319030 Directory_____ <30> \Windows
> |   |_ E2615520 Port__________ <24> SbApiPort
> |   |_ E260E1A0 Port__________ <24> ApiPort
  |   \_ 812FC810 Directory_____ <32> \Windows\WindowStations
  |_ 81319150 Directory_____ <30> \RPC Control
> |   |_ E26B6A20 Port__________ <24> tapsrvlpc
> |   |_ E3228440 Port__________ <24> OLE3c
> |   |_ E269F360 Port__________ <24> spoolss
> |   |_ E269B6E0 Port__________ <24> OLE2
> |   |_ E2C96C60 Port__________ <24> OLE3f
> |   |_ E1306BC0 Port__________ <24> OLE3
> |   |_ E269BD20 Port__________ <24> LRPC0000021c.00000001
> |   |_ E276D520 Port__________ <24> OLE5
> |   |_ E2699D40 Port__________ <24> OLE6
> |   |_ E2697C00 Port__________ <24> OLE7
> |   |_ E26F0AE0 Port__________ <24> ntsvcs
> |   |_ E26B6B20 Port__________ <24> policyagent
> |   |_ E2814CA0 Port__________ <24> OLEa
> |   |_ E29DC3C0 Port__________ <24> OLEb
> |   |_ E304C8A0 Port__________ <24> OLE40
> |   |_ E3165660 Port__________ <24> OLE41
> |   |_ E26979A0 Port__________ <24> epmapper
> |   |_ E13069A0 Port__________ <24> senssvc
> |   \_ E2C8D040 Port__________ <24> OLE42
  |_ 812FD030 Directory_____ <30> \BaseNamedObjects
  |   \_ 812FDF50 Directory_____ <30> \BaseNamedObjects\Restricted
  |_ 8149CBD0 Directory_____ <32> \??
  |_ 814B5030 Directory_____ <32> \FileSystem
  |_ 8149CCB0 Directory_____ <32> \ObjectTypes
  |_ 81499C50 Directory_____ <32> \Security
> |   \_ 8121EB20 WaitablePort__ <24> TRKWKS_PORT
  |_ 8149B2D0 Directory_____ <32> \Callback
  \_ 81446E90 Directory_____ <30> \KnownDlls

54 objects
```

EXAMPLE 7-4. *Output of the Command* `w2k_obj +atf *port 2 /root`

Note that `Directory` objects are always included in the list, even though the type name pattern doesn't match them. Otherwise, it would be unclear to which node in the directory hierarchy the matching objects are assigned. The > characters in the first display column act as visual cues that distinguish the objects with a matching object type from the additional `Directory` objects.

WHERE DO WE GO FROM HERE?

So much could still be said about Windows 2000 internals. But the number of words fitting into a reasonably sized book is limited, so it must end somewhere. The seven chapters of this book were tough reading, but maybe it was thrilling as well. If you are now seeing Windows 2000 with different eyes, I have reached my goal. If you are a programming or debugging tool developer, the programming and interfacing techniques in this book will help you add value to your products that none of the competitive tools can currently offer. If you are developing other kinds of software for Windows 2000, the understanding of the inner system dynamics imparted by this book will help you writing more efficient code that optimally exploits the features of your operating system. I also would like this book to spur the inquiring minds of developers everywhere, kicking off an avalanche of research that unveils the mysteries that still surround most parts of the Windows 2000 kernel. I never believed that treating the operating system as a black box was a good programming paradigm—and I still don't believe it.

APPENDIX A

Kernel Debugger Commands

The following tables provide a quick reference to the Windows 2000 Kernel Debugger's console command interface, described in Chapter 1.

TABLE A-1. *Built-in Kernel Debugger Commands*

<table>
<tr><th>COMMAND</th><th>DESCRIPTION</th></tr>
<tr><td>A [<address>]</td><td>Assemble</td></tr>
<tr><td>BA[#] <e|r|w|i><1|2|4> <address></td><td>Address breakpoint</td></tr>
<tr><td>BC[<bp>]</td><td>Clear breakpoint(s)</td></tr>
<tr><td>BD[<bp>]</td><td>Disable breakpoint(s)</td></tr>
<tr><td>BE[<bp>]</td><td>Enable breakpoint(s)</td></tr>
<tr><td>BL[<bp>]</td><td>List breakpoint(s)</td></tr>
<tr><td>BP[#] <address></td><td>Set breakpoint</td></tr>
<tr><td>C <range> <address></td><td>Compare memory</td></tr>
<tr><td>D[type][<range>]</td><td>Dump memory</td></tr>
<tr><td>E[type] <address> [<list>]</td><td>Enter</td></tr>
<tr><td>F <range> <list></td><td>Fill memory</td></tr>
<tr><td>G [=<address> [<address>...]]</td><td>Go to address</td></tr>
<tr><td>I<type> <port></td><td>Read from I/O port</td></tr>
<tr><td>J<expression> [']cmd1['];[']cmd2[']</td><td>Conditional execution</td></tr>
<tr><td>K[B] <count></td><td>Stack trace</td></tr>
<tr><td>KB = <base> <stack> <ip></td><td>Stack trace from specific state</td></tr>
</table>

(continued)

TABLE A-1. *(continued)*

<table>
<tr><th>COMMAND</th><th>DESCRIPTION</th></tr>
<tr><td>L{+|-}[lost*]</td><td>Control source options</td></tr>
<tr><td>LN <expression></td><td>List nearest symbols</td></tr>
<tr><td>LS[.] [<first>][,<count>]</td><td>List source file lines</td></tr>
<tr><td>LSA <address>[,<first>][,<count>]</td><td>List source file lines at address</td></tr>
<tr><td>LSC</td><td>Show current source file and line</td></tr>
<tr><td>LSF[-] <file></td><td>Load or unload a source file for browsing</td></tr>
<tr><td>M <range> <address></td><td>Move memory</td></tr>
<tr><td>N [<radix>]</td><td>Set / show number radix</td></tr>
<tr><td>P[R] [=<address>] [<value>]</td><td>Program step</td></tr>
<tr><td>Q</td><td>Quit debugger</td></tr>
<tr><td>#R</td><td>Multiprocessor register dump</td></tr>
<tr><td>R[F][L][M <expression>] [[<register> [= <expression>]]]</td><td>Get/set register/flag value</td></tr>
<tr><td>Rm[?] [<expression>]</td><td>Control prompt register output mask</td></tr>
<tr><td>S <range> <list></td><td>Search memory</td></tr>
<tr><td>SS <n | a | w></td><td>Set symbol suffix</td></tr>
<tr><td>SX [e|d [<event>|*|<expression>]]</td><td>Exception</td></tr>
<tr><td>T[R] [=<address>] [<expression>]</td><td>Trace</td></tr>
<tr><td>U [<range>]</td><td>Unassemble</td></tr>
<tr><td>O<type> <port> <expression></td><td>Write to I/O port</td></tr>
<tr><td>X [<*|module>!]<*|symbol></td><td>Examine symbols</td></tr>
<tr><td>.cache [size]</td><td>Set virtual memory cache size</td></tr>
<tr><td>.logopen [<file>]</td><td>Open new log file</td></tr>
<tr><td>.logappend [<file>]</td><td>Append to log file</td></tr>
<tr><td>.logclose</td><td>Close log file</td></tr>
<tr><td>.reboot</td><td>Reboot target machine</td></tr>
<tr><td>.reload</td><td>Reload symbols</td></tr>
<tr><td>~<processor></td><td>Change current processor</td></tr>
<tr><td>? <expression></td><td>Display expression</td></tr>
<tr><td>#<string> [address]</td><td>Search for a string in the disassembly</td></tr>
<tr><td>$< <filename></td><td>Take input from a command file</td></tr>
</table>

TABLE A-2. *Command Argument Types Used in Table 1-1*

ARGUMENT	DESCRIPTION
<address>	#<16-bit protect-mode [seg:]address>
	&<V86-mode [seg:]address>
<event>	ct, et, ld, av, cc
<expression>	operators: + - * / not by wo dw poi mod(%) and(&) xor(^) or(|) hi low
	operands: number in current radix, public symbol, <register>
<flag>	iopl, of, df, if, tf, sf, zf, af, pf, cf
<list>	<byte> [<byte> ...]
<pattern>	[(nt | <dll-name>)!]<var-name> (<var-name> can include ? and *)
<radix>	8, 10, 16
<range>	<address> <address>
	<address> L <count>
<register>	[e]ax, [e]bx, [e]cx, [e]dx, [e]si, [e]di, [e]bp, [e]sp, [e]ip, [e]fl
	al, ah, bl, bh, cl, ch, dl, dh, cs, ds, es, fs, gs, ss
	cr0, cr2, cr3, cr4, dr0, dr1, dr2, dr3, dr6, dr7
	gdtr, gdtl, idtr, idtl, tr, ldtr
<type>	b (BYTE)
	w (WORD)
	d[s] (DWORD [with symbols])
	q (QWORD)
	f (FLOAT)
	D (DOUBLE)
	a (ASCII)
	c (DWORD and CHAR)
	u (Unicode)
	s|S (ASCII/Unicode string)
	l (list)

TABLE A-3. *Bang Commands Exported by* `kdextx86.dll`

<table>
<tr><th>COMMAND</th><th colspan="3">DESCRIPTION</th></tr>
<tr><td>!acl <Address> [flags]</td><td colspan="3">Display the ACL</td></tr>
<tr><td>!apic [base]</td><td colspan="3">Dump local APIC</td></tr>
<tr><td>!arbiter [flags]</td><td colspan="3">Display all arbiters and arbitrated ranges</td></tr>
<tr><td></td><td>flags:</td><td>1</td><td>I/O arbiters</td></tr>
<tr><td></td><td></td><td>2</td><td>Memory arbiters</td></tr>
<tr><td></td><td></td><td>4</td><td>IRQ arbiters</td></tr>
<tr><td></td><td></td><td>8</td><td>DMA arbiters</td></tr>
<tr><td></td><td></td><td>10</td><td>Bus number arbiters</td></tr>
<tr><td>!arblist <address> [flags]</td><td colspan="3">Dump set of resources being arbitrated</td></tr>
<tr><td></td><td>flags:</td><td>1</td><td>Include Interface and Slot info per device</td></tr>
<tr><td>!bugdump</td><td colspan="3">Display bug check dump data</td></tr>
<tr><td>!bushnd</td><td colspan="3">Dump HAL "BUS HANDLER" list</td></tr>
<tr><td>!bushnd <address></td><td colspan="3">Dump HAL "BUS HANDLER" structure of handler <address></td></tr>
<tr><td>!ca <address> [flags]</td><td colspan="3">Dump control area of a section</td></tr>
<tr><td>!callback <address> [num]</td><td colspan="3">Dump callback frames for specified thread</td></tr>
<tr><td>!calldata <table name></td><td colspan="3">Dump call data hash table</td></tr>
<tr><td>!cbreg <BaseAddr> | %%<PhyAddr></td><td colspan="3">Dump CardBus registers</td></tr>
<tr><td>!cmreslist <CM Resource List></td><td colspan="3">Dump CM resource list</td></tr>
<tr><td>!cxr</td><td colspan="3">Dump context record at specified address</td></tr>
<tr><td>!db <physical address></td><td colspan="3">Display physical memory BYTEs</td></tr>
<tr><td>!dblink <address> [count] [bias]</td><td colspan="3">Dump a list via its blinks</td></tr>
<tr><td>!dcs <Bus>.<Dev>.<Fn></td><td colspan="3">Dump PCI ConfigSpace of device</td></tr>
<tr><td>!dd <physical address></td><td colspan="3">Display physical memory DWORDs</td></tr>
<tr><td>!defwrites</td><td colspan="3">Dump deferred write queue and triages cached write throttles</td></tr>
<tr><td>!devext <address> <type></td><td colspan="3">Dump device extension at <address> of type <type> <type> PCI, PCMCIA, USBD, OpenHCI, USBHUB, UHCD, HID</td></tr>
<tr><td>!devnode <node> [flags] [service]</td><td colspan="3">Dump device node</td></tr>
<tr><td></td><td>node:</td><td>0</td><td>List main tree</td></tr>
<tr><td></td><td></td><td>1</td><td>List pending removals</td></tr>
<tr><td></td><td></td><td>2</td><td>List pending ejects</td></tr>
<tr><td></td><td></td><td>addr</td><td>List specified node</td></tr>
<tr><td></td><td>flags:</td><td>1</td><td>Dump children</td></tr>
<tr><td></td><td></td><td>2</td><td>Dump CM Resource List</td></tr>
<tr><td></td><td></td><td>4</td><td>Dump I/O Resource List</td></tr>
<tr><td></td><td></td><td>8</td><td>Dump translated CM Resource List</td></tr>
<tr><td></td><td></td><td>10</td><td>Dump only nodes that aren't started</td></tr>
<tr><td></td><td></td><td>20</td><td>Dump only nodes that have problems</td></tr>
<tr><td></td><td>service:</td><td colspan="2">If present, only nodes driven by this service dumped</td></tr>
</table>

TABLE A-3. *Bang Commands Exported by* `kdextx86.dll`

COMMAND	DESCRIPTION
!devobj <device>	Dump device object and IRP queue
	<device> Device object address or name
!devstack <device>	Dump device stack associated with device object
!dflink <address> [count] [bias]	Dump a list via its flinks
bias	Mask of bits to ignore in each pointer
!drivers	Display information about all loaded system modules
!drvobj <driver> [flags]	Dump driver object and related information
	<driver> Driver object address or name
	flags: 1 Dump device object list
	2 Dump driver entry points
!eb <physical address> <BYTE list>	Enter BYTE values to physical memory
!ed <physical address>	Enter DWORD values to physical memory <DWORD list>
!errlog	Dump the error log contents
!exca <BasePort>.<SktNum>	Dump ExCA registers
!exqueue [flags]	Dump the ExWorkerQueues
	flags: 1/2/4 Same as !thread / !process
	10 Only critical work queue
	20 Only delayed work queue
	40 Only hypercritical work queue
!exr <address>	Dump exception record at specified address
!filecache	Dump information about the file system cache
!filelock <address>	Dump file lock structure
!filetime	Dump 64-bit FILETIME as a human-readable time
!fpsearch <address>	Find a freed special pool allocation
!frag [flags]	Display kernel mode pool fragmentation
	flags: 1 List all fragment information
	2 List allocation information
	3 Both
!gentable <address>	Dump the given rtl_generic_table
!handle <address> <flags> <process> <TypeName>	Dump handle for a process
	flags: 2 Dump nonpaged object
!heap <address> [flags]	Dump heap for a process
	address: Desired heap to dump or 0 for all
	flags: -v Verbose
	-f Free List entries
	-a All entries

(continued)

TABLE A-3. *Bang Commands Exported by* `kdextx86.dll`

COMMAND	DESCRIPTION	
	-s	Summary
	-x	Force a dump even if the data is bad
!help	Display command help	
!HidPpd <address> <flags>	Dump preparsed Data of HID device	
!ib <port>	Read a BYTE from an I/O port	
!id <port>	Read a DWORD from an I/O port	
!ioapic [base]	Dump I/O APIC	
!ioreslist <IO Resource List>	Dump I/O resource requirements list	
!irp <address> <dumplevel>	Dump IRP at specified address	
	address == 0	Dump active IRPs (checked only)
	dumplevel:0	Basic stack info
	1	Full field dump
	2	Include tracking information (checked only)
!irpfind [pooltype] [restart addr] [<irpsearch> <address>]	Search pool for active IRPs	
	pooltype: 0	Nonpaged pool (default)
	1	Paged pool
	2	Special pool
	restart addr If present, scan will be restarted from here in pool	
	<irpsearch> Specifies filter criteria to find a specific IRP:	
	userevent	Irp.UserEvent == <address>
	device	Stack location: DeviceObject == <address>
	fileobject	Irp.Tail.Overlay.OriginalFileObject == <address>
	mdlprocess	Irp.MdlAddress.Process ==<address>
	thread	Irp.Tail.Overlay.Thread == <address>
	arg	One of the arguments == <address>
!iw <port>	Read a WORD from an I/O port	
!job <address> [<flags>]	Dump JobObject at <address>, processes in job	
!locks [-v] <address>	Dump kernel-mode resource locks	
!lookaside <address> <options> <depth>	Dump lookaside lists	
	options: 1	Reset list counters
	2	Set list depth to <depth>
!lpc	Dump LPC ports and messages	
!memusage	Dump the page frame database table	
!mps	Dump MPS BIOS structures	
!mtrr	Dump MTTR	
!npx [base]	Dump NPX save area	
!ob <port>	Write a BYTE to an I/O port	

TABLE A-3. *Bang Commands Exported by* `kdextx86.dll`

COMMAND	DESCRIPTION		
!obja <TypeName>	Dump an object manager object's attributes		
!object <-r | Path | address | 0 TypeName>	Dump an object manager object		
	-r	Force reload of cached object pointers	
!od <port>	Write a DWORD to an I/O port		
!ow <port>	Write a WORD to an I/O port		
!patch	Enable and disable various driver flags		
!pci [flag] [bus] [device] [function]	Dump PCI type1 configuration [rawdump:minaddr] [maxaddr]		
	flag:	0x01	Verbose
		0x02	From bus 0 to 'bus'
		0x04	Dump raw BYTEs
		0x08	Dump raw DWORDs
		0x10	Do not skip invalid devices
		0x20	Do not skip invalid functions
		0x40	Dump capabilities if found
		0x80	Dump device specific on VendorID:8086
!pciir	Dump the PCI IRQ routing table		
!pcitree	Dump the PCI tree structure		
!pcr	Dump the Processor Control Region (PCR)		
!pfn	Dump the page frame database entry for the physical page		
!pic	Dump PIC (8259) information		
!pnpevent <address>	Dump specified PNP event, or all events if <address> == 0		
!pocaps	Dump system power capabilities		
!podev <devobj>	Dump power relevant data in device object		
!polist	Dump power IRP serial list		
!polist [<devobj>]	Dump power IRP serial list entries for specified devobj		
!ponode	Dump power device node stack (devnodes in power order)		
!popolicy	Dump system power policy		
!poproc <Address>	Dump processor power state.		
!pool <address> [detail]	Dump kernel mode heap		
	address:	0	Only the process heap (default)
		-1	All heaps in the process
		else	Pool entry
	detail:	0	Summary Information
		1	Summary + location/size of regions
		2	Display information only for address

(continued)

TABLE A-3. *Bang Commands Exported by* `kdextx86.dll`

COMMAND	DESCRIPTION		
		3	Summary + blocks in committed regions
		4	Summary + free lists
!poolfind <tag> [pooltype]	Find occurrences of the specified pool <tag>		
	<tag>	Four-character tag, * and ? are wild cards	
	pooltype:	0	Nonpaged pool (default)
		1	Paged pool
		2	Special pool
!poolused [flags [TAG]]	Dump usage by pool tag		
	flags:	1	Verbose
		2	Sort by NonPagedPool Usage
		4	Sort by PagedPool Usage
!poReqList [<devobj>]	Dump PoRequestedPowerIrp created Power IRPs		
!portcls <devobj> [flags]	Dump portcls data for portcls bound devobj		
	flags:	1	Port dump
		2	Filter dump
		4	Pin dump
		8	Device context
		10	Power info
		100	Verbose
		200	Really verbose
!potrigger <address>	Dump POP_ACTION_TRIGGER		
!process [flags] [image name]	Dump process at specified address		
	flags:	1	Don't stop after Cid/Image information
		2	Dump thread wait states
		4	Dump only thread states
		6	Dump thread states and stack
!processfields	Show offsets to all fields in the EPROCESS structure		
!pte	Dump the corresponding PDE and PTE for the entered address		
!ptov <PhysicalPageNumber>	Dump all valid physical/virtual mappings for a page directory		
!qlocks	Dump state of all queued spin locks		
!range <RtlRangeList>	Dump RTL_RANGE_LIST		
!ready	Dump state of all ready system threads		
!reghash	Dump registry hash table		
!regkcb <address>	Dump registry key-control-blocks		
!regpool [s|r]	Dump registry allocated paged pool		
	s	Save list of registry pages to temporary file	
	r	Restore list of registry pages from temporary file	

TABLE A-3. *Bang Commands Exported by* `kdextx86.dll`

COMMAND	DESCRIPTION
!rellist <relation list> [flags]	Dump PNP relation lists
	flags: 1 Not used
	2 Dump CM Resource List
	4 Dump I/O Resource List
	8 Dump translated CM Resource List
!remlock	Dump a remove lock structure
!sd <Address> [flags]	Display SECURITY_DESCRIPTOR
!sel [selector]	Examine selector values
!session <id> [flags] [image name]	Dump sessions
!sid <Address> [flags]	Display the SID structure at the specified address
!socket <address>	Dump PCMCIA socket structure
!srb <address>	Dump SCSI Request Block at specified address
!stacks <detail-level>	Dump summary of current kernel stacks
	detail-level: 0 Display stack summary
	1 Display stacks, no parameters
	2 Display stacks, full parameters
!sysptes	Dump the system PTEs
!thread <address> [flags]	Dump thread at specified address
	flags: 1 Not used
	2 Dump thread wait states
	4 Dump only thread states
	6 Dump thread states and stack
!threadfields	Show offsets to all fields in the ETHREAD structure
!time	Report PerformanceCounterRate and TimerDifference
!timer	Dump timer tree
!token <address> [flags]	Dump token at specified address
!tokenfields	Show offsets to all fields in a token structure
!trap [base]	Dump trap frame
!tss [register]	Dump TSS
!tunnel <address>	Dump a file property tunneling cache
!tz [<address> <flags>]	Dump thermal zones (No arguments: dump all zones)
!tzinfo <address>	Dump thermal zone information
!urb <address> <flags>	Dump an USB Request Block
!usblog <log> [addr] [flags]	Display an USB log
	<log> USBHUB, USBD, UHCD, OpenHCI

(continued)

TABLE A-3. *Bang Commands Exported by* `kdextx86.dll`

COMMAND	DESCRIPTION		
	addr:		Address to begin dumping from in <log>
	flags:	-r	Reset the log to dump from most recent entry
		-s L	Search for tags in comma-delimited list L
		-l N	Set number of lines to display at a time to N
!usbstruc <address> <type>	Display an USB HC descriptor of <type>		
	<type>	OHCIReg, HCCA, OHCIHcdED, OHCIHcdTD, OHCIEndpoint, DevData, UHCDReg	
!vad	Dump VADs		
!version	Version of extension DLL		
!vm	Dump virtual memory values		
!vpd <address>	Dump volume parameter block		
!vtop DirBase address	Dump physical page for virtual address		
!wdmaud <address> <flags>	Dump wdmaud data for structures		
	flags:	1	I/O control history dump given WdmaIoctlHistoryListHead
		2	Pending IRPs given WdmaPendingIrpListHead
		4	Allocated MDLs given WdmaAllocatedMdlListHead
		8	pContext dump given WdmaContextListHead
		100	Verbose
!zombies	Find all zombie processes		

TABLE A-4. *Bang Commands Exported by* `userkdx.dll`

COMMAND	DESCRIPTION
!atom	Dump atoms or atom tables
!dcls [pcls]	Dump window class
!dcss	Dump critical section stack traces
!dcur -aivp [pcur]	Dump cursors
!dde -vr [conv|window|xact]	Dump DDE tracking information
!ddesk -vh <pdesk>	Display objects allocated in desktop
!ddl [pdesk]	Dump desktop log
!ddk <pKbdTbl>	Dump deadkey table
!df [flags] | [-p pid]	Display or set debug flags
!dfa	Dump allocation fail stack trace
!dha address	Dump heap allocations and verify heap
!dhe [pointer|handle] | [-t[o[p]] type [pti/ppi]]	Dump handle entries
!dhk -ag [pti]	Dump hooks
!dhot	Dump registered hotkeys
!dhs -vpty [id|type]	Dump handle table statistics
!di	Display USER input processing globals
!dii <piiex>	Dump extended IME information
!dimc [-hrvus] -[wci] [imc|wnd,etc.]	Dump Input Context
!dimk [pImeHotKeyObj]	Dump IME Hotkeys
!dinp -v [pDeviceInfo]	Dump input diagnostics
!dkl -akv <pkl>	Dump keyboard layout structures
!dll [*]addr [l#] [b#] [o#] [c#] [t[addr]]	Dump linked list (can Ctrl-C)
!dlr <pointer|handle>	Display assignment locks for object
!dm -vris <menu|window>	Dump a menu
!dmon <pMonitor>	Dump MONITOR
!dmq [-ac] [pq]	List messages in queues
!dms <MenuState>	Dump a pMenuState
!dp -vcpt [id]	Display simple process information
!dpa -cvsfrp	Dump pool allocations
!dpi [ppi]	Display PROCESSINFO structure specified
!dpm <ppopupmenu>	Dump a popup menu
!dq -t [pq]	Display Q structure specified
!dsbt <pSBTrack>	Display Scroll Bar Track structure
!dsbwnd <psbwnd>	Dump extra fields of Scrollbar windows
!dsi [-bchmopvw]	Display SERVERINFO structure

(continued)

TABLE A-4. *(continued)*

<table>
<tr><th>COMMAND</th><th>DESCRIPTION</th></tr>
<tr><td>!dsms -vl [psms]</td><td>Display SMS (SendMessage structure) specified</td></tr>
<tr><td>!dso <Structure> [Field] [addr [*n]]</td><td>Dump structure field(s)'s offset(s) and value(s)</td></tr>
<tr><td>!dt -gvcp [id]</td><td>Display simple thread information</td></tr>
<tr><td>!dtdb [ptdb]</td><td>Dump Task Database</td></tr>
<tr><td>!dti [pti]</td><td>Display THREADINFO structure</td></tr>
<tr><td>!dtl [-t] [pointer|handle]</td><td>Display thread locks</td></tr>
<tr><td>!dtmr [ptmr]</td><td>Dump timer structure</td></tr>
<tr><td>!du [pointer|handle]</td><td>Generic object dumping routine</td></tr>
<tr><td>!dumphmgr [-s]</td><td>Dump object allocation counts (debug version only)</td></tr>
<tr><td>!dup</td><td>User preferences DWORDs</td></tr>
<tr><td>!dupm</td><td>User preference bit mask</td></tr>
<tr><td>!dvs -s</td><td>Dump sections and mapped views</td></tr>
<tr><td>!dw -aefhvsprwoz [hwnd/pwnd]</td><td>Display information on windows in system</td></tr>
<tr><td>!dwe [-n] [addr]</td><td>Display WinEvent hooks/notifies</td></tr>
<tr><td>!dwpi -p [pwpi | ppi]</td><td>Display WOWPROCESSINFO structure specified</td></tr>
<tr><td>!dws [pws]</td><td>Dump window stations</td></tr>
<tr><td>!dy [pdi]</td><td>Dump DISPLAYINFO</td></tr>
<tr><td>!find baseaddr addr [o#]</td><td>Find linked list element</td></tr>
<tr><td>!fno <address></td><td>Find nearest object</td></tr>
<tr><td>!frr <psrcLo> <psrcHi> <prefLo> [prefHi]</td><td>Find Range Reference</td></tr>
<tr><td>!help -v [cmd]</td><td>Display command help (-v verbose)</td></tr>
<tr><td>!hh</td><td>Dump gdwHydraHint</td></tr>
<tr><td>!kbd -au [pq]</td><td>Display key state for queue</td></tr>
<tr><td>!sas [-s] <addr> [length]</td><td>Stack Analysis Stuff</td></tr>
<tr><td>!test</td><td>Test basic debug functions</td></tr>
<tr><td>!uver</td><td>Show versions of USERTEXTS and WIN32K.SYS</td></tr>
</table>

APPENDIX B

Kernel API Functions

Appendix B contains a compilation of functions exported by the system modules `win32k.sys`, `ntdll.dll`, and `ntoskrnl.exe`, discussed in Chapter 2.

TABLE B-1. *The Windows 2000 Native API*

FUNCTION NAME	INT 2Eh	ntdll.Nt*	ntdll.Zw*	ntoskrnl.Nt*	ntoskrnl.Zw*
NtAcceptConnectPort	0x0000			N/A	N/A
NtAccessCheck	0x0001			N/A	N/A
NtAccessCheckAndAuditAlarm	0x0002			N/A	
NtAccessCheckByType	0x0003			N/A	N/A
NtAccessCheckByTypeAndAuditAlarm	0x0004			N/A	N/A
NtAccessCheckByTypeResultList	0x0005			N/A	N/A
NtAccessCheckByTypeResultListAndAuditAlarm	0x0006			N/A	N/A
NtAccessCheckByTypeResultListAndAuditAlarmByHandle	0x0007			N/A	N/A
NtAddAtom	0x0008				N/A
NtAdjustGroupsToken	0x0009			N/A	N/A
NtAdjustPrivilegesToken	0x000A				
NtAlertResumeThread	0x000B			N/A	N/A
NtAlertThread	0x000C			N/A	
NtAllocateLocallyUniqueId	0x000D				N/A
NtAllocateUserPhysicalPages	0x000E			N/A	N/A

N/A Not Available

(continued)

TABLE B-1. *(continued)*

FUNCTION NAME	INT 2Eh	ntdll.Nt*	ntdll.Zw*	ntoskrnl.Nt*	ntoskrnl.Zw*
NtAllocateUuids	0x000F				N/A
NtAllocateVirtualMemory	0x0010				
NtAreMappedFilesTheSame	0x0011			N/A	N/A
NtAssignProcessToJobObject	0x0012			N/A	N/A
NtBuildNumber	N/A	N/A	N/A		N/A
NtCallbackReturn	0x0013			N/A	N/A
NtCancelDeviceWakeupRequest	0x0016			N/A	N/A
NtCancelIoFile	0x0014			N/A	
NtCancelTimer	0x0015			N/A	
NtClearEvent	0x0017			N/A	
NtClose	0x0018				
NtCloseObjectAuditAlarm	0x0019			N/A	
NtCompleteConnectPort	0x001A			N/A	N/A
NtConnectPort	0x001B				
NtContinue	0x001C			N/A	N/A
NtCreateChannel	0x00F1			N/A	N/A
NtCreateDirectoryObject	0x001D			N/A	
NtCreateEvent	0x001E				
NtCreateEventPair	0x001F			N/A	N/A
NtCreateFile	0x0020				
NtCreateIoCompletion	0x0021			N/A	N/A
NtCreateJobObject	0x0022			N/A	N/A
NtCreateKey	0x0023			N/A	
NtCreateMailslotFile	0x0024			N/A	N/A
NtCreateMutant	0x0025			N/A	N/A
NtCreateNamedPipeFile	0x0026			N/A	N/A
NtCreatePagingFile	0x0027			N/A	N/A
NtCreatePort	0x0028			N/A	N/A
NtCreateProcess	0x0029			N/A	N/A
NtCreateProfile	0x002A			N/A	N/A
NtCreateSection	0x002B				
NtCreateSemaphore	0x002C			N/A	N/A
NtCreateSymbolicLinkObject	0x002D			N/A	

TABLE B-1. *(continued)*

FUNCTION NAME	INT 2Eh	ntdll.Nt*	ntdll.Zw*	ntoskrnl.Nt*	ntoskrnl.Zw*
NtCreateThread	0x002E			N/A	N/A
NtCreateTimer	0x002F			N/A	
NtCreateToken	0x0030			N/A	N/A
NtCreateWaitablePort	0x0031			N/A	N/A
NtCurrentTeb	N/A		N/A	N/A	N/A
NtDelayExecution	0x0032			N/A	N/A
NtDeleteAtom	0x0033				N/A
NtDeleteFile	0x0034				
NtDeleteKey	0x0035			N/A	
NtDeleteObjectAuditAlarm	0x0036			N/A	N/A
NtDeleteValueKey	0x0037			N/A	
NtDeviceIoControlFile	0x0038				
NtDisplayString	0x0039			N/A	
NtDuplicateObject	0x003A				
NtDuplicateToken	0x003B				
NtEnumerateKey	0x003C			N/A	
NtEnumerateValueKey	0x003D			N/A	
NtExtendSection	0x003E			N/A	N/A
NtFilterToken	0x003F			N/A	N/A
NtFindAtom	0x0040				N/A
NtFlushBuffersFile	0x0041			N/A	N/A
NtFlushInstructionCache	0x0042			N/A	
NtFlushKey	0x0043			N/A	
NtFlushVirtualMemory	0x0044			N/A	
NtFlushWriteBuffer	0x0045			N/A	N/A
NtFreeUserPhysicalPages	0x0046			N/A	N/A
NtFreeVirtualMemory	0x0047				
NtFsControlFile	0x0048				
NtGetContextThread	0x0049			N/A	N/A
NtGetDevicePowerState	0x004A			N/A	N/A
NtGetPlugPlayEvent	0x004B			N/A	N/A
NtGetTickCount	0x004C			N/A	N/A
NtGetWriteWatch	0x004D			N/A	N/A

(continued)

TABLE B-1. *(continued)*

FUNCTION NAME	INT 2Eh	ntdll.Nt*	ntdll.Zw*	ntoskrnl.Nt*	ntoskrnl.Zw*
NtGlobalFlag	N/A	N/A	N/A		N/A
NtImpersonateAnonymousToken	0x004E			N/A	N/A
NtImpersonateClientOfPort	0x004F			N/A	N/A
NtImpersonateThread	0x0050			N/A	N/A
NtInitializeRegistry	0x0051			N/A	N/A
NtInitiatePowerAction	0x0052			N/A	
NtIsSystemResumeAutomatic	0x0053			N/A	N/A
NtListenChannel	0x00F2			N/A	N/A
NtListenPort	0x0054			N/A	N/A
NtLoadDriver	0x0055			N/A	
NtLoadKey	0x0056			N/A	
NtLoadKey2	0x0057			N/A	N/A
NtLockFile	0x0058				N/A
NtLockVirtualMemory	0x0059			N/A	N/A
NtMakeTemporaryObject	0x005A			N/A	
NtMapUserPhysicalPages	0x005B			N/A	N/A
NtMapUserPhysicalPagesScatter	0x005C			N/A	N/A
NtMapViewOfSection	0x005D				
NtNotifyChangeDirectoryFile	0x005E				N/A
NtNotifyChangeKey	0x005F			N/A	
NtNotifyChangeMultipleKeys	0x0060			N/A	N/A
NtOpenChannel	0x00F3			N/A	N/A
NtOpenDirectoryObject	0x0061			N/A	
NtOpenEvent	0x0062			N/A	
NtOpenEventPair	0x0063			N/A	N/A
NtOpenFile	0x0064				
NtOpenIoCompletion	0x0065			N/A	N/A
NtOpenJobObject	0x0066			N/A	N/A
NtOpenKey	0x0067			N/A	
NtOpenMutant	0x0068			N/A	N/A
NtOpenObjectAuditAlarm	0x0069			N/A	N/A
NtOpenProcess	0x006A				
NtOpenProcessToken	0x006B				

TABLE B-1. *(continued)*

FUNCTION NAME	INT 2Eh	ntdll.Nt*	ntdll.Zw*	ntoskrnl.Nt*	ntoskrnl.Zw*
NtOpenSection	0x006C			N/A	
NtOpenSemaphore	0x006D			N/A	N/A
NtOpenSymbolicLinkObject	0x006E			N/A	
NtOpenThread	0x006F			N/A	
NtOpenThreadToken	0x0070			N/A	
NtOpenTimer	0x0071			N/A	
NtPlugPlayControl	0x0072			N/A	N/A
NtPowerInformation	0x0073			N/A	
NtPrivilegeCheck	0x0074			N/A	N/A
NtPrivilegedServiceAuditAlarm	0x0075			N/A	N/A
NtPrivilegeObjectAuditAlarm	0x0076			N/A	N/A
NtProtectVirtualMemory	0x0077			N/A	N/A
NtPulseEvent	0x0078			N/A	
NtQueryAttributesFile	0x007A			N/A	N/A
NtQueryDefaultLocale	0x007B			N/A	
NtQueryDefaultUILanguage	0x007C			N/A	
NtQueryDirectoryFile	0x007D				
NtQueryDirectoryObject	0x007E			N/A	
NtQueryEaFile	0x007F				
NtQueryEvent	0x0080			N/A	N/A
NtQueryFullAttributesFile	0x0081			N/A	N/A
NtQueryInformationAtom	0x0079				N/A
NtQueryInformationFile	0x0082				
NtQueryInformationJobObject	0x0083			N/A	N/A
NtQueryInformationPort	0x0085			N/A	N/A
NtQueryInformationProcess	0x0086				
NtQueryInformationThread	0x0087			N/A	N/A
NtQueryInformationToken	0x0088				
NtQueryInstallUILanguage	0x0089			N/A	
NtQueryIntervalProfile	0x008A			N/A	N/A
NtQueryIoCompletion	0x0084			N/A	N/A
NtQueryKey	0x008B			N/A	
NtQueryMultipleValueKey	0x008C			N/A	N/A

(continued)

TABLE B-1. *(continued)*

FUNCTION NAME	INT 2Eh	ntdll.Nt*	ntdll.Zw*	ntoskrnl.Nt*	ntoskrnl.Zw*
NtQueryMutant	0x008D			N/A	N/A
NtQueryObject	0x008E			N/A	
NtQueryOpenSubKeys	0x008F			N/A	N/A
NtQueryPerformanceCounter	0x0090			N/A	N/A
NtQueryQuotaInformationFile	0x0091				N/A
NtQuerySection	0x0092			N/A	
NtQuerySecurityObject	0x0093				
NtQuerySemaphore	0x0094			N/A	N/A
NtQuerySymbolicLinkObject	0x0095			N/A	
NtQuerySystemEnvironmentValue	0x0096			N/A	N/A
NtQuerySystemInformation	0x0097				
NtQuerySystemTime	0x0098			N/A	N/A
NtQueryTimer	0x0099			N/A	N/A
NtQueryTimerResolution	0x009A			N/A	N/A
NtQueryValueKey	0x009B			N/A	
NtQueryVirtualMemory	0x009C			N/A	N/A
NtQueryVolumeInformationFile	0x009D				
NtQueueApcThread	0x009E			N/A	N/A
NtRaiseException	0x009F			N/A	N/A
NtRaiseHardError	0x00A0			N/A	N/A
NtReadFile	0x00A1				
NtReadFileScatter	0x00A2			N/A	N/A
NtReadRequestData	0x00A3			N/A	N/A
NtReadVirtualMemory	0x00A4			N/A	N/A
NtRegisterThreadTerminatePort	0x00A5			N/A	N/A
NtReleaseMutant	0x00A6			N/A	N/A
NtReleaseSemaphore	0x00A7			N/A	N/A
NtRemoveIoCompletion	0x00A8			N/A	N/A
NtReplaceKey	0x00A9			N/A	
NtReplyPort	0x00AA			N/A	N/A
NtReplyWaitReceivePort	0x00AB			N/A	N/A
NtReplyWaitReceivePortEx	0x00AC			N/A	N/A
NtReplyWaitReplyPort	0x00AD			N/A	N/A

TABLE B-1. *(continued)*

FUNCTION NAME	INT 2Eh	ntdll.Nt*	ntdll.Zw*	ntoskrnl.Nt*	ntoskrnl.Zw*
NtReplyWaitSendChannel	0x00F4			N/A	N/A
NtRequestDeviceWakeup	0x00AE			N/A	N/A
NtRequestPort	0x00AF				N/A
NtRequestWaitReplyPort	0x00B0				
NtRequestWakeupLatency	0x00B1			N/A	N/A
NtResetEvent	0x00B2			N/A	
NtResetWriteWatch	0x00B3			N/A	N/A
NtRestoreKey	0x00B4			N/A	
NtResumeThread	0x00B5			N/A	N/A
NtSaveKey	0x00B6			N/A	
NtSaveMergedKeys	0x00B7			N/A	N/A
NtSecureConnectPort	0x00B8			N/A	N/A
NtSendWaitReplyChannel	0x00F5			N/A	N/A
NtSetContextChannel	0x00F6			N/A	N/A
NtSetContextThread	0x00BA			N/A	N/A
NtSetDefaultHardErrorPort	0x00BB			N/A	N/A
NtSetDefaultLocale	0x00BC			N/A	
NtSetDefaultUILanguage	0x00BD			N/A	
NtSetEaFile	0x00BE				
NtSetEvent	0x00BF				
NtSetHighEventPair	0x00C0			N/A	N/A
NtSetHighWaitLowEventPair	0x00C1			N/A	N/A
NtSetInformationFile	0x00C2				
NtSetInformationJobObject	0x00C3			N/A	N/A
NtSetInformationKey	0x00C4			N/A	N/A
NtSetInformationObject	0x00C5			N/A	
NtSetInformationProcess	0x00C6				
NtSetInformationThread	0x00C7				
NtSetInformationToken	0x00C8			N/A	N/A
NtSetIntervalProfile	0x00C9			N/A	N/A
NtSetIoCompletion	0x00B9			N/A	N/A
NtSetLdtEntries	0x00CA			N/A	N/A
NtSetLowEventPair	0x00CB			N/A	N/A

(continued)

TABLE B-1. *(continued)*

FUNCTION NAME	INT 2Eh	ntdll.Nt*	ntdll.Zw*	ntoskrnl.Nt*	ntoskrnl.Zw*
NtSetLowWaitHighEventPair	0x00CC			N/A	N/A
NtSetQuotaInformationFile	0x00CD				N/A
NtSetSecurityObject	0x00CE				
NtSetSystemEnvironmentValue	0x00CF			N/A	N/A
NtSetSystemInformation	0x00D0			N/A	
NtSetSystemPowerState	0x00D1			N/A	N/A
NtSetSystemTime	0x00D2			N/A	
NtSetThreadExecutionState	0x00D3			N/A	N/A
NtSetTimer	0x00D4			N/A	
NtSetTimerResolution	0x00D5			N/A	N/A
NtSetUuidSeed	0x00D6			N/A	N/A
NtSetValueKey	0x00D7			N/A	
NtSetVolumeInformationFile	0x00D8				
NtShutdownSystem	0x00D9			N/A	N/A
NtSignalAndWaitForSingleObject	0x00DA			N/A	N/A
NtStartProfile	0x00DB			N/A	N/A
NtStopProfile	0x00DC			N/A	N/A
NtSuspendThread	0x00DD			N/A	N/A
NtSystemDebugControl	0x00DE			N/A	N/A
NtTerminateJobObject	0x00DF			N/A	N/A
NtTerminateProcess	0x00E0			N/A	
NtTerminateThread	0x00E1			N/A	N/A
NtTestAlert	0x00E2			N/A	N/A
NtUnloadDriver	0x00E3			N/A	
NtUnloadKey	0x00E4			N/A	
NtUnlockFile	0x00E5				N/A
NtUnlockVirtualMemory	0x00E6			N/A	N/A
NtUnmapViewOfSection	0x00E7			N/A	
NtVdmControl	0x00E8				N/A
NtWaitForMultipleObjects	0x00E9			N/A	
NtWaitForSingleObject	0x00EA				
NtWaitHighEventPair	0x00EB			N/A	N/A
NtWaitLowEventPair	0x00EC			N/A	N/A

TABLE B-1. *(continued)*

FUNCTION NAME	INT 2Eh	ntdll.Nt*	ntdll.Zw*	ntoskrnl.Nt*	ntoskrnl.Zw*
NtWriteFile	0x00ED				
NtWriteFileGather	0x00EE			N/A	N/A
NtWriteRequestData	0x00EF			N/A	N/A
NtWriteVirtualMemory	0x00F0			N/A	N/A
NtYieldExecution	0x00F7			N/A	

TABLE B-2. *The GDI/Win32K Interface*

gdi32.dll	INT 2Eh	win32k.sys
N/A	0x1000	NtGdiAbortDoc
N/A	0x1001	NtGdiAbortPath
N/A	0x1002	NtGdiAddFontResourceW
N/A	0x1003	NtGdiAddRemoteFontToDC
N/A	0x1004	NtGdiAddFontMemResourceEx
N/A	0x1005	NtGdiRemoveMergeFont
N/A	0x1006	NtGdiAddRemoteMMInstanceToDC
N/A	0x1007	NtGdiAlphaBlend
N/A	0x1008	NtGdiAngleArc
AnyLinkedFonts	0x1009	NtGdiAnyLinkedFonts
FontIsLinked	0x100A	NtGdiFontIsLinked
N/A	0x100B	NtGdiArcInternal
N/A	0x100C	NtGdiBeginPath
N/A	0x100D	NtGdiBitBlt
N/A	0x100E	NtGdiCancelDC
N/A	0x100F	NtGdiCheckBitmapBits
N/A	0x1010	NtGdiCloseFigure
N/A	0x1011	NtGdiColorCorrectPalette
N/A	0x1012	NtGdiCombineRgn
N/A	0x1013	NtGdiCombineTransform
N/A	0x1014	NtGdiComputeXformCoefficients
GdiConsoleTextOut	0x1015	NtGdiConsoleTextOut
N/A	0x1016	NtGdiConvertMetafileRect
N/A	0x1017	NtGdiCreateBitmap

(continued)

TABLE B-2. *(continued)*

gdi32.dll	INT 2Eh	win32k.sys
N/A	0x1018	NtGdiCreateClientObj
N/A	0x1019	NtGdiCreateColorSpace
N/A	0x101A	NtGdiCreateColorTransform
N/A	0x101B	NtGdiCreateCompatibleBitmap
N/A	0x101C	NtGdiCreateCompatibleDC
N/A	0x101D	NtGdiCreateDIBBrush
N/A	0x101E	NtGdiCreateDIBitmapInternal
N/A	0x101F	NtGdiCreateDIBSection
N/A	0x1020	NtGdiCreateEllipticRgn
CreateHalftonePalette	0x1021	NtGdiCreateHalftonePalette
N/A	0x1022	NtGdiCreateHatchBrushInternal
N/A	0x1023	NtGdiCreateMetafileDC
N/A	0x1024	NtGdiCreatePaletteInternal
N/A	0x1025	NtGdiCreatePatternBrushInternal
N/A	0x1026	NtGdiCreatePen
N/A	0x1027	NtGdiCreateRectRgn
N/A	0x1028	NtGdiCreateRoundRectRgn
N/A	0x1029	NtGdiCreateServerMetaFile
N/A	0x102A	NtGdiCreateSolidBrush
N/A	0x102B	NtGdiD3dContextCreate
N/A	0x102C	NtGdiD3dContextDestroy
N/A	0x102D	NtGdiD3dContextDestroyAll
N/A	0x102E	NtGdiD3dValidateTextureStageState
N/A	0x102F	NtGdiD3dDrawPrimitives2
N/A	0x1030	NtGdiDdGetDriverState
N/A	0x1031	NtGdiDdAddAttachedSurface
N/A	0x1032	NtGdiDdAlphaBlt
N/A	0x1033	NtGdiDdAttachSurface
N/A	0x1034	NtGdiDdBeginMoCompFrame
N/A	0x1035	NtGdiDdBlt
N/A	0x1036	NtGdiDdCanCreateSurface
N/A	0x1037	NtGdiDdCanCreateD3DBuffer
N/A	0x1038	NtGdiDdColorControl

TABLE B-2. *(continued)*

gdi32.dll	INT 2Eh	win32k.sys
N/A	0x1039	NtGdiDdCreateDirectDrawObject
N/A	0x103A	NtGdiDdCreateSurface
N/A	0x103B	NtGdiDdCreateSurface
N/A	0x103C	NtGdiDdCreateMoComp
N/A	0x103D	NtGdiDdCreateSurfaceObject
N/A	0x103E	NtGdiDdDeleteDirectDrawObject
N/A	0x103F	NtGdiDdDeleteSurfaceObject
N/A	0x1040	NtGdiDdDestroyMoComp
N/A	0x1041	NtGdiDdDestroySurface
N/A	0x1042	NtGdiDdDestroyD3DBuffer
N/A	0x1043	NtGdiDdEndMoCompFrame
N/A	0x1044	NtGdiDdFlip
N/A	0x1045	NtGdiDdFlipToGDISurface
N/A	0x1046	NtGdiDdGetAvailDriverMemory
N/A	0x1047	NtGdiDdGetBltStatus
N/A	0x1048	NtGdiDdGetDC
N/A	0x1049	NtGdiDdGetDriverInfo
N/A	0x104A	NtGdiDdGetDxHandle
N/A	0x104B	NtGdiDdGetFlipStatus
N/A	0x104C	NtGdiDdGetInternalMoCompInfo
N/A	0x104D	NtGdiDdGetMoCompBuffInfo
N/A	0x104E	NtGdiDdGetMoCompGuids
N/A	0x104F	NtGdiDdGetMoCompFormats
N/A	0x1050	NtGdiDdGetScanLine
N/A	0x1051	NtGdiDdLock
N/A	0x1052	NtGdiDdLockD3D
N/A	0x1053	NtGdiDdQueryDirectDrawObject
N/A	0x1054	NtGdiDdQueryMoCompStatus
N/A	0x1055	NtGdiDdReenableDirectDrawObject
N/A	0x1056	NtGdiDdReleaseDC
N/A	0x1057	NtGdiDdRenderMoComp
N/A	0x1058	NtGdiDdResetVisrgn
N/A	0x1059	NtGdiDdSetColorKey

(continued)

TABLE B-2. *(continued)*

gdi32.dll	INT 2Eh	win32k.sys
N/A	0x105A	NtGdiDdSetExclusiveMode
N/A	0x105B	NtGdiDdSetGammaRamp
N/A	0x105C	NtGdiDdCreateSurfaceEx
N/A	0x105D	NtGdiDdSetOverlayPosition
N/A	0x105E	NtGdiDdUnattachSurface
N/A	0x105F	NtGdiDdUnlock
N/A	0x1060	NtGdiDdUnlockD3D
N/A	0x1061	NtGdiDdUpdateOverlay
N/A	0x1062	NtGdiDdWaitForVerticalBlank
N/A	0x1063	NtGdiDvpCanCreateVideoPort
N/A	0x1064	NtGdiDvpColorControl
N/A	0x1065	NtGdiDvpCreateVideoPort
N/A	0x1066	NtGdiDvpDestroyVideoPort
N/A	0x1067	NtGdiDvpFlipVideoPort
N/A	0x1068	NtGdiDvpGetVideoPortBandwidth
N/A	0x1069	NtGdiDvpGetVideoPortField
N/A	0x106A	NtGdiDvpGetVideoPortFlipStatus
N/A	0x106B	NtGdiDvpGetVideoPortInputFormats
N/A	0x106C	NtGdiDvpGetVideoPortLine
N/A	0x106D	NtGdiDvpGetVideoPortOutputFormats
N/A	0x106E	NtGdiDvpGetVideoPortConnectInfo
N/A	0x106F	NtGdiDvpGetVideoSignalStatus
N/A	0x1070	NtGdiDvpUpdateVideoPort
N/A	0x1071	NtGdiDvpWaitForVideoPortSync
N/A	0x1072	NtGdiDeleteClientObj
N/A	0x1073	NtGdiDeleteColorSpace
N/A	0x1074	NtGdiDeleteColorTransform
N/A	0x1075	NtGdiDeleteObjectApp
N/A	0x1076	NtGdiDescribePixelFormat
N/A	0x1077	NtGdiGetPerBandInfo
N/A	0x1078	NtGdiDoBanding
N/A	0x1079	NtGdiDoPalette
N/A	0x107A	NtGdiDrawEscape

TABLE B-2. *(continued)*

gdi32.dll	INT 2Eh	win32k.sys
N/A	0x107B	NtGdiEllipse
EnableEUDC	0x107C	NtGdiEnableEudc
N/A	0x107D	NtGdiEndDoc
N/A	0x107E	NtGdiEndPage
N/A	0x107F	NtGdiEndPath
N/A	0x1080	NtGdiEnumFontChunk
N/A	0x1081	NtGdiEnumFontClose
N/A	0x1082	NtGdiEnumFontOpen
N/A	0x1083	NtGdiEnumObjects
N/A	0x1084	NtGdiEqualRgn
N/A	0x1085	NtGdiEudcEnumFaceNameLinkW
N/A	0x1086	NtGdiEudcLoadUnloadLink
N/A	0x1087	NtGdiExcludeClipRect
N/A	0x1088	NtGdiExtCreatePen
N/A	0x1089	NtGdiExtCreateRegion
N/A	0x108A	NtGdiExtEscape
N/A	0x108B	NtGdiExtFloodFill
N/A	0x108C	NtGdiExtGetObjectW
N/A	0x108D	NtGdiExtSelectClipRgn
N/A	0x108E	NtGdiExtTextOutW
N/A	0x108F	NtGdiFillPath
N/A	0x1090	NtGdiFillRgn
N/A	0x1091	NtGdiFlattenPath
N/A	0x1092	NtGdiFlushUserBatch
N/A	0x1093	GreFlush
N/A	0x1094	NtGdiForceUFIMapping
N/A	0x1095	NtGdiFrameRgn
GdiFullscreenControl	0x1096	NtGdiFullscreenControl
N/A	0x1097	NtGdiGetAndSetDCDword
N/A	0x1098	NtGdiGetAppClipBox
N/A	0x1099	NtGdiGetBitmapBits
N/A	0x109A	NtGdiGetBitmapDimension
N/A	0x109B	NtGdiGetBoundsRect

(continued)

TABLE B-2. *(continued)*

gdi32.dll	INT 2Eh	win32k.sys
N/A	0x109C	NtGdiGetCharABCWidthsW
N/A	0x109D	NtGdiGetCharacterPlacementW
N/A	0x109E	NtGdiGetCharSet
N/A	0x109F	NtGdiGetCharWidthW
GetCharWidthInfo	0x10A0	NtGdiGetCharWidthInfo
N/A	0x10A1	NtGdiGetColorAdjustment
N/A	0x10A2	NtGdiGetColorSpaceforBitmap
N/A	0x10A3	NtGdiGetDCDword
N/A	0x10A4	NtGdiGetDCforBitmap
N/A	0x10A5	NtGdiGetDCObject
N/A	0x10A6	NtGdiGetDCPoint
N/A	0x10A7	NtGdiGetDeviceCaps
N/A	0x10A8	NtGdiGetDeviceGammaRamp
N/A	0x10A9	NtGdiGetDeviceCapsAll
N/A	0x10AA	NtGdiGetDIBitsInternal
N/A	0x10AB	NtGdiGetETM
N/A	0x10AC	NtGdiGetEudcTimeStampEx
N/A	0x10AD	NtGdiGetFontData
N/A	0x10AE	NtGdiGetFontResourceInfoInternalW
GetGlyphIndicesW	0x10AF	NtGdiGetGlyphIndicesW
N/A	0x10B0	NtGdiGetGlyphIndicesWInternal
N/A	0x10B1	NtGdiGetGlyphOutline
N/A	0x10B2	NtGdiGetKerningPairs
N/A	0x10B3	NtGdiGetLinkedUFIs
N/A	0x10B4	NtGdiGetMiterLimit
N/A	0x10B5	NtGdiGetMonitorID
N/A	0x10B6	NtGdiGetNearestColor
N/A	0x10B7	NtGdiGetNearestPaletteIndex
N/A	0x10B8	NtGdiGetObjectBitmapHandle
N/A	0x10B9	NtGdiGetOutlineTextMetricsInternalW
N/A	0x10BA	NtGdiGetPath
N/A	0x10BB	NtGdiGetPixel
N/A	0x10BC	NtGdiGetRandomRgn

TABLE B-2. *(continued)*

gdi32.dll	INT 2Eh	win32k.sys
N/A	0x10BD	NtGdiGetRasterizerCaps
N/A	0x10BE	NtGdiGetRealizationInfo
N/A	0x10BF	NtGdiGetRegionData
N/A	0x10C0	NtGdiGetRgnBox
N/A	0x10C1	NtGdiGetServerMetaFileBits
GdiGetSpoolMessage	0x10C2	NtGdiGetSpoolMessage
N/A	0x10C3	NtGdiGetStats
N/A	0x10C4	NtGdiGetStockObject
N/A	0x10C5	NtGdiGetStringBitmapW
N/A	0x10C6	NtGdiGetSystemPaletteUse
GetTextCharsetInfo	0x10C7	NtGdiGetTextCharsetInfo
N/A	0x10C8	NtGdiGetTextExtent
N/A	0x10C9	NtGdiGetTextExtentExW
N/A	0x10CA	NtGdiGetTextFaceW
N/A	0x10CB	NtGdiGetTextMetricsW
N/A	0x10CC	NtGdiGetTransform
N/A	0x10CD	NtGdiGetUFI
N/A	0x10CE	NtGdiGetUFIPathname
GetFontUnicodeRanges	0x10CF	NtGdiGetFontUnicodeRanges
N/A	0x10D0	NtGdiGetWidthTable
N/A	0x10D1	NtGdiGradientFill
N/A	0x10D2	NtGdiHfontCreate
N/A	0x10D3	NtGdiIcmBrushInfo
N/A	0x10D4	NtGdiInit
N/A	0x10D5	NtGdiInitSpool
GdiInitSpool	0x10D6	NtGdiIntersectClipRect
N/A	0x10D7	NtGdiInvertRgn
N/A	0x10D8	NtGdiLineTo
N/A	0x10D9	NtGdiMakeFontDir
N/A	0x10DA	NtGdiMakeInfoDC
N/A	0x10DB	NtGdiMaskBlt
N/A	0x10DC	NtGdiModifyWorldTransform
N/A	0x10DD	NtGdiMonoBitmap

(continued)

TABLE B-2. *(continued)*

gdi32.dll	INT 2Eh	win32k.sys
N/A	0x10DE	NtGdiMoveTo
N/A	0x10DF	NtGdiOffsetClipRgn
N/A	0x10E0	NtGdiOffsetRgn
N/A	0x10E1	NtGdiOpenDCW
N/A	0x10E2	NtGdiPatBlt
N/A	0x10E3	NtGdiPolyPatBlt
N/A	0x10E4	NtGdiPathToRegion
N/A	0x10E5	NtGdiPlgBlt
N/A	0x10E6	NtGdiPolyDraw
N/A	0x10E7	NtGdiPolyPolyDraw
N/A	0x10E8	NtGdiPolyTextOutW
N/A	0x10E9	NtGdiPtInRegion
N/A	0x10EA	NtGdiPtVisible
GdiQueryFonts	0x10EB	NtGdiQueryFonts
N/A	0x10EC	NtGdiQueryFontAssocInfo
N/A	0x10ED	NtGdiRectangle
N/A	0x10EE	NtGdiRectInRegion
N/A	0x10EF	NtGdiRectVisible
N/A	0x10F0	NtGdiRemoveFontResourceW
N/A	0x10F1	NtGdiRemoveFontMemResourceEx
N/A	0x10F2	NtGdiResetDC
N/A	0x10F3	NtGdiResizePalette
N/A	0x10F4	NtGdiRestoreDC
N/A	0x10F5	NtGdiRoundRect
N/A	0x10F6	NtGdiSaveDC
N/A	0x10F7	NtGdiScaleViewportExtEx
N/A	0x10F8	NtGdiScaleWindowExtEx
N/A	0x10F9	NtGdiSelectBitmap
N/A	0x10FA	NtGdiSelectBrush
N/A	0x10FB	NtGdiSelectClipPath
N/A	0x10FC	NtGdiSelectFont
N/A	0x10FD	NtGdiSelectPen
N/A	0x10FE	NtGdiSetBitmapBits

TABLE B-2. *(continued)*

gdi32.dll	INT 2Eh	win32k.sys
N/A	0x10FF	NtGdiSetBitmapDimension
N/A	0x1100	NtGdiSetBoundsRect
N/A	0x1101	NtGdiSetBrushOrg
N/A	0x1102	NtGdiSetColorAdjustment
N/A	0x1103	NtGdiSetColorSpace
N/A	0x1104	NtGdiSetDeviceGammaRamp
N/A	0x1105	NtGdiSetDIBitsToDeviceInternal
N/A	0x1106	NtGdiSetFontEnumeration
N/A	0x1107	NtGdiSetFontXform
N/A	0x1108	NtGdiSetIcmMode
N/A	0x1109	NtGdiSetLinkedUFIs
SetMagicColors	0x110A	NtGdiSetMagicColors
N/A	0x110B	NtGdiSetMetaRgn
N/A	0x110C	NtGdiSetMiterLimit
N/A	0x110D	NtGdiGetDeviceWidth
N/A	0x110E	NtGdiMirrorWindowOrg
N/A	0x110F	NtGdiSetLayout
N/A	0x1110	NtGdiSetPixel
N/A	0x1111	NtGdiSetPixelFormat
N/A	0x1112	NtGdiSetRectRgn
N/A	0x1113	NtGdiSetSystemPaletteUse
N/A	0x1114	NtGdiSetTextJustification
N/A	0x1115	NtGdiSetupPublicCFONT
N/A	0x1116	NtGdiSetVirtualResolution
N/A	0x1117	NtGdiSetSizeDevice
N/A	0x1118	NtGdiStartDoc
N/A	0x1119	NtGdiStartPage
N/A	0x111A	NtGdiStretchBlt
N/A	0x111B	NtGdiStretchDIBitsInternal
N/A	0x111C	NtGdiStrokeAndFillPath
N/A	0x111D	NtGdiStrokePath
N/A	0x111E	NtGdiSwapBuffers
N/A	0x111F	NtGdiTransformPoints

(continued)

TABLE B-2. *(continued)*

gdi32.dll	INT 2Eh	win32k.sys
N/A	0x1120	NtGdiTransparentBlt
N/A	0x1121	NtGdiUnloadPrinterDriver
N/A	0x1122	NtGdiUnmapMemFont
N/A	0x1123	NtGdiUnrealizeObject
N/A	0x1124	NtGdiUpdateColors
N/A	0x1125	NtGdiWidenPath
ActivateKeyboardLayout	0x1126	NtUserActivateKeyboardLayout
N/A	0x1127	NtUserAlterWindowStyle
N/A	0x1128	NtUserAssociateInputContext
AttachThreadInput	0x1129	NtUserAttachThreadInput
BeginPaint	0x112A	NtUserBeginPaint
N/A	0x112B	NtUserBitBltSysBmp
BlockInput	0x112C	NtUserBlockInput
N/A	0x112D	NtUserBuildHimcList
N/A	0x112E	NtUserBuildHwndList
N/A	0x112F	NtUserBuildNameList
N/A	0x1130	NtUserBuildPropList
N/A	0x1131	NtUserCallHwnd
N/A	0x1132	NtUserCallHwndLock
N/A	0x1133	NtUserCallHwndOpt
N/A	0x1134	NtUserCallHwndParam
N/A	0x1135	NtUserCallHwndParamLock
N/A	0x1136	NtUserCallMsgFilter
N/A	0x1137	NtUserCallNextHookEx
N/A	0x1138	NtUserCallNoParam
N/A	0x1139	NtUserCallOneParam
N/A	0x113A	NtUserCallTwoParam
ChangeClipboardChain	0x113B	NtUserChangeClipboardChain
N/A	0x113C	NtUserChangeDisplaySettings
N/A	0x113D	NtUserCheckImeHotKey
N/A	0x113E	NtUserCheckMenuItem
ChildWindowFromPointEx	0x113F	NtUserChildWindowFromPointEx
ClipCursor	0x1140	NtUserClipCursor

TABLE B-2. *(continued)*

gdi32.dll	INT 2Eh	win32k.sys
CloseClipboard	0x1141	NtUserCloseClipboard
CloseDesktop	0x1142	NtUserCloseDesktop
CloseWindowStation	0x1143	NtUserCloseWindowStation
N/A	0x1144	NtUserConsoleControl
N/A	0x1145	NtUserConvertMemHandle
CopyAcceleratorTableW	0x1146	NtUserCopyAcceleratorTable
CountClipboardFormats	0x1147	NtUserCountClipboardFormats
CreateAcceleratorTableW	0x1148	NtUserCreateAcceleratorTable
CreateCaret	0x1149	NtUserCreateCaret
N/A	0x114A	NtUserCreateDesktop
N/A	0x114B	NtUserCreateInputContext
N/A	0x114C	NtUserCreateLocalMemHandle
N/A	0x114D	NtUserCreateWindowEx
N/A	0x114E	NtUserCreateWindowStation
DdeGetQualityOfService	0x114F	NtUserDdeGetQualityOfService
N/A	0x1150	NtUserDdeInitialize
DdeSetQualityOfService	0x1151	NtUserDdeSetQualityOfService
DeferWindowPos	0x1152	NtUserDeferWindowPos
N/A	0x1153	NtUserDefSetText
DeleteMenu	0x1154	NtUserDeleteMenu
N/A	0x1155	NtUserDestroyAcceleratorTable
N/A	0x1156	NtUserDestroyCursor
N/A	0x1157	NtUserDestroyInputContext
DestroyMenu	0x1158	NtUserDestroyMenu
DestroyWindow	0x1159	NtUserDestroyWindow
N/A	0x115A	NtUserDisableThreadIme
N/A	0x115B	NtUserDispatchMessage
DragDetect	0x115C	NtUserDragDetect
DragObject	0x115D	NtUserDragObject
DrawAnimatedRects	0x115E	NtUserDrawAnimatedRects
N/A	0x115F	NtUserDrawCaption
N/A	0x1160	NtUserDrawCaptionTemp
N/A	0x1161	NtUserDrawIconEx

(continued)

TABLE B-2. *(continued)*

gdi32.dll	INT 2Eh	win32k.sys
N/A	0x1162	NtUserDrawMenuBarTemp
EmptyClipboard	0x1163	NtUserEmptyClipboard
N/A	0x1164	NtUserEnableMenuItem
EnableScrollBar	0x1165	NtUserEnableScrollBar
N/A	0x1166	NtUserEndDeferWindowPosEx
EndMenu	0x1167	NtUserEndMenu
EndPaint	0x1168	NtUserEndPaint
N/A	0x1169	NtUserEnumDisplayDevices
EnumDisplayMonitors	0x116A	NtUserEnumDisplayMonitors
N/A	0x116B	NtUserEnumDisplaySettings
N/A	0x116C	NtUserEvent
ExcludeUpdateRgn	0x116D	NtUserExcludeUpdateRgn
N/A	0x116E	NtUserFillWindow
N/A	0x116F	NtUserFindExistingCursorIcon
N/A	0x1170	NtUserFindWindowEx
FlashWindowEx	0x1171	NtUserFlashWindowEx
N/A	0x1172	NtUserGetAltTabInfo
GetAncestor	0x1173	NtUserGetAncestor
N/A	0x1174	NtUserGetAppImeLevel
N/A	0x1175	NtUserGetAsyncKeyState
GetCaretBlinkTime	0x1176	NtUserGetCaretBlinkTime
GetCaretPos	0x1177	NtUserGetCaretPos
N/A	0x1178	NtUserGetClassInfo
N/A	0x1179	NtUserGetClassName
N/A	0x117A	NtUserGetClipboardData
N/A	0x117B	NtUserGetClipboardFormatName
GetClipboardOwner	0x117C	NtUserGetClipboardOwner
GetClipboardSequenceNumber	0x117D	NtUserGetClipboardSequenceNumber
GetClipboardViewer	0x117E	NtUserGetClipboardViewer
GetClipCursor	0x117F	NtUserGetClipCursor
GetComboBoxInfo	0x1180	NtUserGetComboBoxInfo
N/A	0x1181	NtUserGetControlBrush
N/A	0x1182	NtUserGetControlColor

TABLE B-2. *(continued)*

gdi32.dll	INT 2Eh	win32k.sys
N/A	0x1183	NtUserGetCPD
N/A	0x1184	NtUserGetCursorFrameInfo
GetCursorInfo	0x1185	NtUserGetCursorInfo
GetDC	0x1186	NtUserGetDC
GetDCEx	0x1187	NtUserGetDCEx
GetDoubleClickTime	0x1188	NtUserGetDoubleClickTime
GetForegroundWindow	0x1189	NtUserGetForegroundWindow
GetGuiResources	0x118A	NtUserGetGuiResources
GetGUIThreadInfo	0x118B	NtUserGetGUIThreadInfo
N/A	0x118C	NtUserGetIconInfo
N/A	0x118D	NtUserGetIconSize
N/A	0x118E	NtUserGetImeHotKey
N/A	0x118F	NtUserGetImeInfoEx
GetInternalWindowPos	0x1190	NtUserGetInternalWindowPos
GetKeyboardLayoutList	0x1191	NtUserGetKeyboardLayoutList
N/A	0x1192	NtUserGetKeyboardLayoutName
GetKeyboardState	0x1193	NtUserGetKeyboardState
N/A	0x1194	NtUserGetKeyNameText
N/A	0x1195	NtUserGetKeyState
GetListBoxInfo	0x1196	NtUserGetListBoxInfo
GetMenuBarInfo	0x1197	NtUserGetMenuBarInfo
N/A	0x1198	NtUserGetMenuIndex
GetMenuItemRect	0x1199	NtUserGetMenuItemRect
N/A	0x119A	NtUserGetMessage
GetMouseMovePointsEx	0x119B	NtUserGetMouseMovePointsEx
GetUserObjectInformationW	0x119C	NtUserGetObjectInformation
GetOpenClipboardWindow	0x119D	NtUserGetOpenClipboardWindow
GetPriorityClipboardFormat	0x119E	NtUserGetPriorityClipboardFormat
GetProcessWindowStation	0x119F	NtUserGetProcessWindowStation
GetScrollBarInfo	0x11A0	NtUserGetScrollBarInfo
GetSystemMenu	0x11A1	NtUserGetSystemMenu
N/A	0x11A2	NtUserGetThreadDesktop
N/A	0x11A3	NtUserGetThreadState

(continued)

TABLE B-2. *(continued)*

gdi32.dll	INT 2Eh	win32k.sys
GetTitleBarInfo	0x11A4	NtUserGetTitleBarInfo
N/A	0x11A5	NtUserGetUpdateRect
N/A	0x11A6	NtUserGetUpdateRgn
GetWindowDC	0x11A7	NtUserGetWindowDC
GetWindowPlacement	0x11A8	NtUserGetWindowPlacement
N/A	0x11A9	NtUserGetWOWClass
N/A	0x11AA	NtUserHardErrorControl
HideCaret	0x11AB	NtUserHideCaret
HiliteMenuItem	0x11AC	NtUserHiliteMenuItem
ImpersonateDdeClientWindow	0x11AD	NtUserImpersonateDdeClientWindow
N/A	0x11AE	NtUserInitialize
N/A	0x11AF	NtUserInitializeClientPfnArrays
N/A	0x11B0	NtUserInitTask
N/A	0x11B1	NtUserInternalGetWindowText
InvalidateRect	0x11B2	NtUserInvalidateRect
InvalidateRgn	0x11B3	NtUserInvalidateRgn
IsClipboardFormatAvailable	0x11B4	NtUserIsClipboardFormatAvailable
KillTimer	0x11B5	NtUserKillTimer
N/A	0x11B6	NtUserLoadKeyboardLayoutEx
LockWindowStation	0x11B7	NtUserLockWindowStation
LockWindowUpdate	0x11B8	NtUserLockWindowUpdate
LockWorkStation	0x11B9	NtUserLockWorkStation
N/A	0x11BA	NtUserMapVirtualKeyEx
MenuItemFromPoint	0x11BB	NtUserMenuItemFromPoint
N/A	0x11BC	NtUserMessageCall
N/A	0x11BD	NtUserMinMaximize
N/A	0x11BE	NtUserMNDragLeave
N/A	0x11BF	NtUserMNDragOver
N/A	0x11C0	NtUserModifyUserStartupInfoFlags
MoveWindow	0x11C1	NtUserMoveWindow
N/A	0x11C2	NtUserNotifyIMEStatus
N/A	0x11C3	NtUserNotifyProcessCreate
N/A	0x11C4	NtUserNotifyWinEvent

TABLE B-2. *(continued)*

gdi32.dll	INT 2Eh	win32k.sys
N/A	0x11C5	NtUserOpenClipboard
N/A	0x11C6	NtUserOpenDesktop
OpenInputDesktop	0x11C7	NtUserOpenInputDesktop
N/A	0x11C8	NtUserOpenWindowStation
PaintDesktop	0x11C9	NtUserPaintDesktop
N/A	0x11CA	NtUserPeekMessage
N/A	0x11CB	NtUserPostMessage
N/A	0x11CC	NtUserPostThreadMessage
N/A	0x11CD	NtUserProcessConnect
N/A	0x11CE	NtUserQueryInformationThread
N/A	0x11CF	NtUserQueryInputContext
QuerySendMessage	0x11D0	NtUserQuerySendMessage
QueryUserCounters	0x11D1	NtUserQueryUserCounters
N/A	0x11D2	NtUserQueryWindow
RealChildWindowFromPoint	0x11D3	NtUserRealChildWindowFromPoint
RedrawWindow	0x11D4	NtUserRedrawWindow
N/A	0x11D5	NtUserRegisterClassExWOW
RegisterHotKey	0x11D6	NtUserRegisterHotKey
RegisterTasklist	0x11D7	NtUserRegisterTasklist
N/A	0x11D8	NtUserRegisterWindowMessage
RemoveMenu	0x11D9	NtUserRemoveMenu
N/A	0x11DA	NtUserRemoveProp
N/A	0x11DB	NtUserResolveDesktop
N/A	0x11DC	NtUserResolveDesktopForWOW
N/A	0x11DD	NtUserSBGetParms
N/A	0x11DE	NtUserScrollDC
N/A	0x11DF	NtUserScrollWindowEx
N/A	0x11E0	NtUserSelectPalette
SendInput	0x11E1	NtUserSendInput
N/A	0x11E2	NtUserSendMessageCallback
N/A	0x11E3	NtUserSendNotifyMessage
SetActiveWindow	0x11E4	NtUserSetActiveWindow
N/A	0x11E5	NtUserSetAppImeLevel

(continued)

TABLE B-2. *(continued)*

gdi32.dll	INT 2Eh	win32k.sys
SetCapture	0x11E6	NtUserSetCapture
N/A	0x11E7	NtUserSetClassLong
SetClassWord	0x11E8	NtUserSetClassWord
N/A	0x11E9	NtUserSetClipboardData
SetClipboardViewer	0x11EA	NtUserSetClipboardViewer
SetConsoleReserveKeys	0x11EB	NtUserSetConsoleReserveKeys
SetCursor	0x11EC	NtUserSetCursor
SetCursorContents	0x11ED	NtUserSetCursorContents
N/A	0x11EE	NtUserSetCursorIconData
PrivateSetDbgTag	0x11EF	NtUserSetDbgTag
SetFocus	0x11F0	NtUserSetFocus
N/A	0x11F1	NtUserSetImeHotKey
N/A	0x11F2	NtUserSetImeInfoEx
N/A	0x11F3	NtUserSetImeOwnerWindow
N/A	0x11F4	NtUserSetInformationProcess
N/A	0x11F5	NtUserSetInformationThread
SetInternalWindowPos	0x11F6	NtUserSetInternalWindowPos
SetKeyboardState	0x11F7	NtUserSetKeyboardState
SetLogonNotifyWindow	0x11F8	NtUserSetLogonNotifyWindow
N/A	0x11F9	NtUserSetMenu
SetMenuContextHelpId	0x11FA	NtUserSetMenuContextHelpId
SetMenuDefaultItem	0x11FB	NtUserSetMenuDefaultItem
N/A	0x11FC	NtUserSetMenuFlagRtoL
SetUserObjectInformationW	0x11FD	NtUserSetObjectInformation
SetParent	0x11FE	NtUserSetParent
SetProcessWindowStation	0x11FF	NtUserSetProcessWindowStation
N/A	0x1200	NtUserSetProp
PrivateSetRipFlags	0x1201	NtUserSetRipFlags
SetScrollInfo	0x1202	NtUserSetScrollInfo
SetShellWindowEx	0x1203	NtUserSetShellWindowEx
N/A	0x1204	NtUserSetSysColors
N/A	0x1205	NtUserSetSystemCursor
SetSystemMenu	0x1206	NtUserSetSystemMenu

TABLE B-2. *(continued)*

gdi32.dll	INT 2Eh	win32k.sys
SetSystemTimer	0x1207	NtUserSetSystemTimer
SetThreadDesktop	0x1208	NtUserSetThreadDesktop
N/A	0x1209	NtUserSetThreadLayoutHandles
N/A	0x120A	NtUserSetThreadState
SetTimer	0x120B	NtUserSetTimer
N/A	0x120C	NtUserSetWindowFNID
N/A	0x120D	NtUserSetWindowLong
SetWindowPlacement	0x120E	NtUserSetWindowPlacement
SetWindowPos	0x120F	NtUserSetWindowPos
N/A	0x1210	NtUserSetWindowRgn
N/A	0x1211	NtUserSetWindowsHookAW
N/A	0x1212	NtUserSetWindowsHookEx
N/A	0x1213	NtUserSetWindowStationUser
SetWindowWord	0x1214	NtUserSetWindowWord
N/A	0x1215	NtUserSetWinEventHook
ShowCaret	0x1216	NtUserShowCaret
ShowScrollBar	0x1217	NtUserShowScrollBar
ShowWindow	0x1218	NtUserShowWindow
ShowWindowAsync	0x1219	NtUserShowWindowAsync
N/A	0x121A	NtUserSoundSentry
SwitchDesktop	0x121B	NtUserSwitchDesktop
N/A	0x121C	NtUserSystemParametersInfo
N/A	0x121D	NtUserTestForInteractiveUser
N/A	0x121E	NtUserThunkedMenuInfo
N/A	0x121F	NtUserThunkedMenuItemInfo
N/A	0x1220	NtUserToUnicodeEx
TrackMouseEvent	0x1221	NtUserTrackMouseEvent
TrackPopupMenuEx	0x1222	NtUserTrackPopupMenuEx
N/A	0x1223	NtUserTranslateAccelerator
N/A	0x1224	NtUserTranslateMessage
UnhookWindowsHookEx	0x1225	NtUserUnhookWindowsHookEx
UnhookWinEvent	0x1226	NtUserUnhookWinEvent
N/A	0x1227	NtUserUnloadKeyboardLayout

(continued)

TABLE B-2. *(continued)*

gdi32.dll	INT 2Eh	win32k.sys
UnlockWindowStation	0x1228	NtUserUnlockWindowStation
N/A	0x1229	NtUserUnregisterClass
UnregisterHotKey	0x122A	NtUserUnregisterHotKey
N/A	0x122B	NtUserUpdateInputContext
N/A	0x122C	NtUserUpdateInstance
UpdateLayeredWindow	0x122D	NtUserUpdateLayeredWindow
SetLayeredWindowAttributes	0x122E	NtUserSetLayeredWindowAttributes
N/A	0x122F	NtUserUpdatePerUserSystemParameters
UserHandleGrantAccess	0x1230	NtUserUserHandleGrantAccess
N/A	0x1231	NtUserValidateHandleSecure
ValidateRect	0x1232	NtUserValidateRect
N/A	0x1233	NtUserVkKeyScanEx
N/A	0x1234	NtUserWaitForInputIdle
N/A	0x1235	NtUserWaitForMsgAndEvent
WaitMessage	0x1236	NtUserWaitMessage
Win32PoolAllocationStats	0x1237	NtUserWin32PoolAllocationStats
WindowFromPoint	0x1238	NtUserWindowFromPoint
N/A	0x1239	NtUserYieldTask
N/A	0x123A	NtUserRemoteConnect
N/A	0x123B	NtUserRemoteRedrawRectangle
N/A	0x123C	NtUserRemoteRedrawScreen
N/A	0x123D	NtUserRemoteStopScreenUpdates
N/A	0x123E	NtUserCtxDisplayIOCtl
EngAssociateSurface	0x123F	NtGdiEngAssociateSurface
EngCreateBitmap	0x1240	NtGdiEngCreateBitmap
EngCreateDeviceSurface	0x1241	NtGdiEngCreateDeviceSurface
EngCreateDeviceBitmap	0x1242	NtGdiEngCreateDeviceBitmap
EngCreatePalette	0x1243	NtGdiEngCreatePalette
N/A	0x1244	NtGdiEngComputeGlyphSet
EngCopyBits	0x1245	NtGdiEngCopyBits
N/A	0x1246	NtGdiEngDeletePalette
EngDeleteSurface	0x1247	NtGdiEngDeleteSurface
EngEraseSurface	0x1248	NtGdiEngEraseSurface

TABLE B-2. *(continued)*

gdi32.dll	INT 2Eh	win32k.sys
EngUnlockSurface	0x1249	NtGdiEngUnlockSurface
EngLockSurface	0x124A	NtGdiEngLockSurface
EngBitBlt	0x124B	NtGdiEngBitBlt
EngStretchBlt	0x124C	NtGdiEngStretchBlt
EngPlgBlt	0x124D	NtGdiEngPlgBlt
EngMarkBandingSurface	0x124E	NtGdiEngMarkBandingSurface
EngStrokePath	0x124F	NtGdiEngStrokePath
EngFillPath	0x1250	NtGdiEngFillPath
EngStrokeAndFillPath	0x1251	NtGdiEngStrokeAndFillPath
EngPaint	0x1252	NtGdiEngPaint
EngLineTo	0x1253	NtGdiEngLineTo
EngAlphaBlend	0x1254	NtGdiEngAlphaBlend
EngGradientFill	0x1255	NtGdiEngGradientFill
EngTransparentBlt	0x1256	NtGdiEngTransparentBlt
EngTextOut	0x1257	NtGdiEngTextOut
EngStretchBltROP	0x1258	NtGdiEngStretchBltROP
XLATEOBJ_cGetPalette	0x1259	NtGdiXLATEOBJ_cGetPalette
XLATEOBJ_iXlate	0x125A	NtGdiXLATEOBJ_iXlate
XLATEOBJ_hGetColorTransform	0x125B	NtGdiXLATEOBJ_hGetColorTransform
CLIPOBJ_bEnum	0x125C	NtGdiCLIPOBJ_bEnum
CLIPOBJ_cEnumStart	0x125D	NtGdiCLIPOBJ_cEnumStart
CLIPOBJ_ppoGetPath	0x125E	NtGdiCLIPOBJ_ppoGetPath
EngDeletePath	0x125F	NtGdiEngDeletePath
EngCreateClip	0x1260	NtGdiEngCreateClip
EngDeleteClip	0x1261	NtGdiEngDeleteClip
BRUSHOBJ_ulGetBrushColor	0x1262	NtGdiBRUSHOBJ_ulGetBrushColor
BRUSHOBJ_pvAllocRbrush	0x1263	NtGdiBRUSHOBJ_pvAllocRbrush
BRUSHOBJ_pvGetRbrush	0x1264	NtGdiBRUSHOBJ_pvGetRbrush
BRUSHOBJ_hGetColorTransform	0x1265	NtGdiBRUSHOBJ_hGetColorTransform
XFORMOBJ_bApplyXform	0x1266	NtGdiXFORMOBJ_bApplyXform
XFORMOBJ_iGetXform	0x1267	NtGdiXFORMOBJ_iGetXform
FONTOBJ_vGetInfo	0x1268	NtGdiFONTOBJ_vGetInfo
FONTOBJ_pxoGetXform	0x1269	NtGdiFONTOBJ_pxoGetXform

(continued)

TABLE B-2. *(continued)*

gdi32.dll	INT 2Eh	win32k.sys
FONTOBJ_cGetGlyphs	0x126A	NtGdiFONTOBJ_cGetGlyphs
FONTOBJ_pifi	0x126B	NtGdiFONTOBJ_pifi
FONTOBJ_pfdg	0x126C	NtGdiFONTOBJ_pfdg
FONTOBJ_pQueryGlyphAttrs	0x126D	NtGdiFONTOBJ_pQueryGlyphAttrs
FONTOBJ_pvTrueTypeFontFile	0x126E	NtGdiFONTOBJ_pvTrueTypeFontFile
FONTOBJ_cGetAllGlyphHandles	0x126F	NtGdiFONTOBJ_cGetAllGlyphHandles
STROBJ_bEnum	0x1270	NtGdiSTROBJ_bEnum
STROBJ_bEnumPositionsOnly	0x1271	NtGdiSTROBJ_bEnumPositionsOnly
STROBJ_bGetAdvanceWidths	0x1272	NtGdiSTROBJ_bGetAdvanceWidths
STROBJ_vEnumStart	0x1273	NtGdiSTROBJ_vEnumStart
STROBJ_dwGetCodePage	0x1274	NtGdiSTROBJ_dwGetCodePage
PATHOBJ_vGetBounds	0x1275	NtGdiPATHOBJ_vGetBounds
PATHOBJ_bEnum	0x1276	NtGdiPATHOBJ_bEnum
PATHOBJ_vEnumStart	0x1277	NtGdiPATHOBJ_vEnumStart
PATHOBJ_vEnumStartClipLines	0x1278	NtGdiPATHOBJ_vEnumStartClipLines
PATHOBJ_bEnumClipLines	0x1279	NtGdiPATHOBJ_bEnumClipLines
N/A	0x127A	NtGdiGetDhpdev
EngCheckAbort	0x127B	NtGdiEngCheckAbort
HT_Get8BPPFormatPalette	0x127C	NtGdiHT_Get8BPPFormatPalette
HT_Get8BPPMaskPalette	0x127D	NtGdiHT_Get8BPPMaskPalette
N/A	0x127E	NtGdiUpdateTransform

TABLE B-3. *The C Runtime Library*

FUNCTION NAME	ntdll.dll	ntoskrnl.exe
__isascii		N/A
__iscsym		N/A
__iscsymf		N/A
__toascii		N/A
_abnormal_termination	N/A	
_alldiv		
_allmul		
_alloca_probe		N/A

TABLE B-3. *(continued)*

FUNCTION NAME	ntdll.dll	ntoskrnl.exe
_allrem		
_allshl		
_allshr		
_atoi64		N/A
_aulldiv		
_aullrem		
_aullshr		
_chkstk		N/A
_CIpow		N/A
_except_handler2	N/A	
_except_handler3	N/A	
_fltused		N/A
_ftol		N/A
_global_unwind2	N/A	
_i64toa		N/A
_i64tow		N/A
_itoa		
_itow		
_local_unwind2	N/A	
_ltoa		N/A
_ltow		N/A
_memccpy		N/A
_memicmp		N/A
_purecall	N/A	
_snprintf		
_snwprintf		
_splitpath		N/A
_strcmpi		N/A
_stricmp		
_strlwr		
_strnicmp		
_strnset	N/A	
_strrev	N/A	

(continued)

TABLE B-3. *(continued)*

FUNCTION NAME	ntdll.dll	ntoskrnl.exe
_strset	N/A	
_strupr		
_tolower		N/A
_toupper		N/A
_ui64toa		N/A
_ultoa		N/A
_ultow		N/A
_vsnprintf		
_wcsicmp		
_wcslwr		
_wcsnicmp		
_wcsnset	N/A	
_wcsrev	N/A	
_wcsupr		
_wtoi		N/A
_wtoi64		N/A
_wtol		N/A
abs		N/A
atan		N/A
atoi		
atol		
ceil		N/A
cos		N/A
fabs		N/A
floor		N/A
isalnum		N/A
isalpha		N/A
iscntrl		N/A
isdigit		
isgraph		N/A
islower		
isprint		
ispunct		N/A

TABLE B-3. *(continued)*

FUNCTION NAME	ntdll.dll	ntoskrnl.exe
isspace		
isupper		
iswalpha		N/A
iswctype		N/A
iswdigit		N/A
iswlower		N/A
iswspace		N/A
iswxdigit		N/A
isxdigit		
labs		N/A
log		N/A
mbstowcs		
mbtowc	N/A	
memchr		
memcmp		N/A
memcpy		
memmove		
memset		
pow		N/A
qsort		
rand	N/A	
sin		N/A
sprintf		
sqrt		N/A
srand	N/A	
sscanf		N/A
strcat		
strchr		
strcmp		
strcpy		
strcspn		N/A
strlen		
strncat		

(continued)

TABLE B-3. *(continued)*

FUNCTION NAME	ntdll.dll	ntoskrnl.exe
strncmp		
strncpy		
strpbrk		N/A
strrchr		
strspn		
strstr		
strtol		N/A
strtoul		N/A
swprintf		
tan		N/A
tolower		
toupper		
towlower		
towupper		
vsprintf		
wcscat		
wcschr		
wcscmp		
wcscpy		
wcscspn		
wcslen		
wcsncat		
wcsncmp		
wcsncpy		
wcspbrk		N/A
wcsrchr		
wcsspn		
wcsstr		
wcstombs	N/A	
wctomb	N/A	
wcstol		N/A
wcstombs		N/A
wcstoul		N/A

TABLE B-4. *The Windows 2000 Runtime Library*

FUNCTION NAME	ntdll.dll	ntoskrnl.exe
RtlAbortRXact		N/A
RtlAbsoluteToSelfRelativeSD		
RtlAcquirePebLock		N/A
RtlAcquireResourceExclusive		N/A
RtlAcquireResourceShared		N/A
RtlAddAccessAllowedAce		
RtlAddAccessAllowedAceEx		N/A
RtlAddAccessAllowedObjectAce		N/A
RtlAddAccessDeniedAce		N/A
RtlAddAccessDeniedAceEx		N/A
RtlAddAccessDeniedObjectAce		N/A
RtlAddAce		
RtlAddActionToRXact		N/A
RtlAddAtomToAtomTable		
RtlAddAttributeActionToRXact		N/A
RtlAddAuditAccessAce		N/A
RtlAddAuditAccessAceEx		N/A
RtlAddAuditAccessObjectAce		N/A
RtlAddCompoundAce		N/A
RtlAddRange		
RtlAdjustPrivilege		N/A
RtlAllocateAndInitializeSid		N/A
RtlAllocateHandle		N/A
RtlAllocateHeap		
RtlAnsiCharToUnicodeChar		
RtlAnsiStringToUnicodeSize		
RtlAnsiStringToUnicodeString		
RtlAppendAsciizToString		
RtlAppendStringToString		
RtlAppendUnicodeStringToString		
RtlAppendUnicodeToString		
RtlApplyRXact		N/A
RtlApplyRXactNoFlush		N/A

(continued)

TABLE B-4. *(continued)*

FUNCTION NAME	ntdll.dll	ntoskrnl.exe
RtlAreAllAccessesGranted		
RtlAreAnyAccessesGranted		
RtlAreBitsClear		
RtlAreBitsSet		
RtlAssert		
RtlCallbackLpcClient		N/A
RtlCancelTimer		N/A
RtlCaptureContext	N/A	
RtlCaptureStackBackTrace		
RtlCharToInteger		
RtlCheckForOrphanedCriticalSections		N/A
RtlCheckRegistryKey		
RtlClearAllBits		
RtlClearBits		
RtlCompactHeap		N/A
RtlCompareMemory		
RtlCompareMemoryUlong		
RtlCompareString		
RtlCompareUnicodeString		
RtlCompressBuffer		
RtlCompressChunks	N/A	
RtlConsoleMultiByteToUnicodeN		N/A
RtlConvertExclusiveToShared		N/A
RtlConvertLongToLargeInteger		
RtlConvertPropertyToVariant		N/A
RtlConvertSharedToExclusive		N/A
RtlConvertSidToUnicodeString		
RtlConvertToAutoInheritSecurityObject		N/A
RtlConvertUiListToApiList		N/A
RtlConvertUlongToLargeInteger		
RtlConvertVariantToProperty		N/A
RtlCopyLuid		
RtlCopyLuidAndAttributesArray		N/A

TABLE B-4. *(continued)*

FUNCTION NAME	ntdll.dll	ntoskrnl.exe
RtlCopyRangeList		
RtlCopySecurityDescriptor		N/A
RtlCopySid		
RtlCopySidAndAttributesArray		N/A
RtlCopyString		
RtlCopyUnicodeString		
RtlCreateAcl		
RtlCreateAndSetSD		N/A
RtlCreateAtomTable		
RtlCreateEnvironment		N/A
RtlCreateHeap		
RtlCreateLpcServer		N/A
RtlCreateProcessParameters		N/A
RtlCreateQueryDebugBuffer		N/A
RtlCreateRegistryKey		
RtlCreateSecurityDescriptor		
RtlCreateTagHeap		N/A
RtlCreateTimer		N/A
RtlCreateTimerQueue		N/A
RtlCreateUnicodeString		
RtlCreateUnicodeStringFromAsciiz		N/A
RtlCreateUserProcess		N/A
RtlCreateUserSecurityObject		N/A
RtlCreateUserThread		N/A
RtlCustomCPToUnicodeN		
RtlCutoverTimeToSystemTime		N/A
RtlDebugPrintTimes		N/A
RtlDecompressBuffer		
RtlDecompressChunks	N/A	
RtlDecompressFragment		
RtlDefaultNpAcl		N/A
RtlDelete		
RtlDeleteAce		

(continued)

TABLE B-4. *(continued)*

FUNCTION NAME	ntdll.dll	ntoskrnl.exe
RtlDeleteAtomFromAtomTable		
RtlDeleteCriticalSection		N/A
RtlDeleteElementGenericTable		
RtlDeleteNoSplay		
RtlDeleteOwnersRanges		
RtlDeleteRange		
RtlDeleteRegistryValue		
RtlDeleteResource		N/A
RtlDeleteSecurityObject		N/A
RtlDeleteTimer		N/A
RtlDeleteTimerQueue		N/A
RtlDeleteTimerQueueEx		N/A
RtlDeNormalizeProcessParams		N/A
RtlDeregisterWait		N/A
RtlDeregisterWaitEx		N/A
RtlDescribeChunk	N/A	
RtlDestroyAtomTable		
RtlDestroyEnvironment		N/A
RtlDestroyHandleTable		N/A
RtlDestroyHeap		
RtlDestroyProcessParameters		N/A
RtlDestroyQueryDebugBuffer		N/A
RtlDetermineDosPathNameType_U		N/A
RtlDnsHostNameToComputerName		N/A
RtlDoesFileExists_U		N/A
RtlDosPathNameToNtPathName_U		N/A
RtlDosSearchPath_U		N/A
RtlDowncaseUnicodeString		
RtlDumpResource		N/A
RtlEmptyAtomTable		
RtlEnableEarlyCriticalSectionEventCreation	N/A	
RtlEnlargedIntegerMultiply		
RtlEnlargedUnsignedDivide		

TABLE B-4. *(continued)*

FUNCTION NAME	ntdll.dll	ntoskrnl.exe
RtlEnlargedUnsignedMultiply		
RtlEnterCriticalSection		N/A
RtlEnumerateGenericTable		
RtlEnumerateGenericTableWithoutSplaying		
RtlEnumProcessHeaps		N/A
RtlEqualComputerName		N/A
RtlEqualDomainName		N/A
RtlEqualLuid		
RtlEqualPrefixSid		N/A
RtlEqualSid		
RtlEqualString		
RtlEqualUnicodeString		
RtlEraseUnicodeString		N/A
RtlExpandEnvironmentStrings_U		N/A
RtlExtendedIntegerMultiply		
RtlExtendedLargeIntegerDivide		
RtlExtendedMagicDivide		
RtlExtendHeap		N/A
RtlFillMemory		
RtlFillMemoryUlong		
RtlFindClearBits		
RtlFindClearBitsAndSet		
RtlFindClearRuns	N/A	
RtlFindFirstRunClear	N/A	
RtlFindLastBackwardRunClear		
RtlFindLeastSignificantBit		
RtlFindLongestRunClear		
RtlFindMessage		
RtlFindMostSignificantBit		
RtlFindNextForwardRunClear		
RtlFindRange		
RtlFindSetBits		
RtlFindSetBitsAndClear		

(continued)

TABLE B-4. *(continued)*

FUNCTION NAME	ntdll.dll	ntoskrnl.exe
RtlFindUnicodePrefix	N/A	
RtlFirstFreeAce		N/A
RtlFormatCurrentUserKeyPath		
RtlFormatMessage		N/A
RtlFreeAnsiString		
RtlFreeHandle		N/A
RtlFreeHeap		
RtlFreeOemString		
RtlFreeRangeList		
RtlFreeSid		N/A
RtlFreeUnicodeString		
RtlFreeUserThreadStack		N/A
RtlGenerate8dot3Name		
RtlGetAce		
RtlGetCallersAddress		
RtlGetCompressionWorkSpaceSize		
RtlGetControlSecurityDescriptor		N/A
RtlGetCurrentDirectory_U		
RtlGetDaclSecurityDescriptor		N/A
RtlGetDefaultCodePage	N/A	
RtlGetElementGenericTable		
RtlGetFirstRange		
RtlGetFullPathName_U		N/A
RtlGetGroupSecurityDescriptor		
RtlGetLongestNtPathLength		N/A
RtlGetNextRange		
RtlGetNtGlobalFlags		
RtlGetNtProductType		N/A
RtlGetOwnerSecurityDescriptor		
RtlGetProcessHeaps		N/A
RtlGetSaclSecurityDescriptor		
RtlGetSecurityDescriptorRMControl		N/A
RtlGetUserInfoHeap		N/A

TABLE B-4. *(continued)*

FUNCTION NAME	ntdll.dll	ntoskrnl.exe
RtlGetVersion		N/A
RtlGUIDFromString		
RtlIdentifierAuthoritySid		N/A
RtlImageDirectoryEntryToData		
RtlImageNtHeader		
RtlImageRvaToSection		N/A
RtlImageRvaToVa		N/A
RtlImpersonateLpcClient		N/A
RtlImpersonateSelf		N/A
RtlInitAnsiString		
RtlInitCodePageTable		
RtlInitializeAtomPackage		N/A
RtlInitializeBitMap		
RtlInitializeContext		N/A
RtlInitializeCriticalSection		N/A
RtlInitializeCriticalSectionAndSpinCount		N/A
RtlInitializeGenericTable		
RtlInitializeHandleTable		N/A
RtlInitializeRangeList		
RtlInitializeResource		N/A
RtlInitializeRXact		N/A
RtlInitializeSid		
RtlInitializeUnicodePrefix	N/A	
RtlInitNlsTables		N/A
RtlInitString		
RtlInitUnicodeString		
RtlInsertElementGenericTable		
RtlInsertElementGenericTableFull	N/A	
RtlInsertUnicodePrefix	N/A	
RtlInt64ToUnicodeString		N/A
RtlIntegerToChar		
RtlIntegerToUnicodeString		
RtlInvertRangeList		

(continued)

TABLE B-4. *(continued)*

FUNCTION NAME	ntdll.dll	ntoskrnl.exe
RtlIsDosDeviceName_U		N/A
RtlIsGenericTableEmpty		
RtlIsNameLegalDOS8Dot3		
RtlIsRangeAvailable		
RtlIsTextUnicode		N/A
RtlIsValidHandle		N/A
RtlIsValidIndexHandle		N/A
RtlIsValidOemCharacter	N/A	
RtlLargeIntegerAdd		
RtlLargeIntegerArithmeticShift		
RtlLargeIntegerDivide		
RtlLargeIntegerNegate		
RtlLargeIntegerShiftLeft		
RtlLargeIntegerShiftRight		
RtlLargeIntegerSubtract		
RtlLargeIntegerToChar		N/A
RtlLeaveCriticalSection		N/A
RtlLengthRequiredSid		
RtlLengthSecurityDescriptor		
RtlLengthSid		
RtlLocalTimeToSystemTime		N/A
RtlLockHeap		N/A
RtlLookupAtomInAtomTable		
RtlLookupElementGenericTable		
RtlLookupElementGenericTableFull	N/A	
RtlMakeSelfRelativeSD		N/A
RtlMapGenericMask		
RtlMergeRangeLists		
RtlMoveMemory		
RtlMultiByteToUnicodeN		
RtlMultiByteToUnicodeSize		
RtlNewInstanceSecurityObject		N/A
RtlNewSecurityGrantedAccess		N/A

TABLE B-4. *(continued)*

FUNCTION NAME	ntdll.dll	ntoskrnl.exe
RtlNewSecurityObject		N/A
RtlNewSecurityObjectEx		N/A
RtlNextUnicodePrefix	N/A	
RtlNormalizeProcessParams		N/A
RtlNtStatusToDosError		
RtlNtStatusToDosErrorNoTeb	N/A	
RtlNumberGenericTableElements		
RtlNumberOfClearBits		
RtlNumberOfSetBits		
RtlOemStringToCountedUnicodeString	N/A	
RtlOemStringToUnicodeSize		
RtlOemStringToUnicodeString		
RtlOemToUnicodeN		
RtlOpenCurrentUser		N/A
RtlPcToFileHeader		N/A
RtlPinAtomInAtomTable		
RtlpNtCreateKey		N/A
RtlpNtEnumerateSubKey		N/A
RtlpNtMakeTemporaryKey		N/A
RtlpNtOpenKey		N/A
RtlpNtQueryValueKey		N/A
RtlpNtSetValueKey		N/A
RtlPrefixString		
RtlPrefixUnicodeString		
RtlProtectHeap		N/A
RtlpUnWaitCriticalSection		N/A
RtlpWaitForCriticalSection		N/A
RtlQueryAtomInAtomTable		
RtlQueryEnvironmentVariable_U		N/A
RtlQueryInformationAcl		N/A
RtlQueryProcessBackTraceInformation		N/A
RtlQueryProcessDebugInformation		N/A
RtlQueryProcessHeapInformation		N/A

(continued)

TABLE B-4. *(continued)*

FUNCTION NAME	ntdll.dll	ntoskrnl.exe
RtlQueryProcessLockInformation		N/A
RtlQueryRegistryValues		
RtlQuerySecurityObject		N/A
RtlQueryTagHeap		N/A
RtlQueryTimeZoneInformation		
RtlQueueWorkItem		N/A
RtlRaiseException		
RtlRaiseStatus		N/A
RtlRandom		
RtlReAllocateHeap		N/A
RtlRealPredecessor		
RtlRealSuccessor		
RtlRegisterWait		N/A
RtlReleasePebLock		N/A
RtlReleaseResource		N/A
RtlRemoteCall		N/A
RtlRemoveUnicodePrefix	N/A	
RtlReserveChunk	N/A	
RtlResetRtlTranslations		N/A
RtlRunDecodeUnicodeString		N/A
RtlRunEncodeUnicodeString		N/A
RtlSecondsSince1970ToTime		
RtlSecondsSince1980ToTime		
RtlSelfRelativeToAbsoluteSD		
RtlSelfRelativeToAbsoluteSD2		
RtlSetAllBits		
RtlSetAttributesSecurityDescriptor		N/A
RtlSetBits		
RtlSetControlSecurityDescriptor		N/A
RtlSetCriticalSectionSpinCount		N/A
RtlSetCurrentDirectory_U		N/A
RtlSetCurrentEnvironment		N/A
RtlSetDaclSecurityDescriptor		

TABLE B-4. *(continued)*

FUNCTION NAME	ntdll.dll	ntoskrnl.exe
RtlSetEnvironmentVariable		N/A
RtlSetGroupSecurityDescriptor		
RtlSetInformationAcl		N/A
RtlSetIoCompletionCallback		N/A
RtlSetOwnerSecurityDescriptor		
RtlSetSaclSecurityDescriptor		
RtlSetSecurityDescriptorRMControl		N/A
RtlSetSecurityObject		N/A
RtlSetSecurityObjectEx		N/A
RtlSetThreadPoolStartFunc		N/A
RtlSetTimer		N/A
RtlSetTimeZoneInformation		
RtlSetUnicodeCallouts		N/A
RtlSetUserFlagsHeap		N/A
RtlSetUserValueHeap		N/A
RtlShutdownLpcServer		N/A
RtlSizeHeap		
RtlSplay		
RtlStartRXact		N/A
RtlStringFromGUID		
RtlSubAuthorityCountSid		
RtlSubAuthoritySid		
RtlSubtreePredecessor		
RtlSubtreeSuccessor		
RtlSystemTimeToLocalTime		N/A
RtlTimeFieldsToTime		
RtlTimeToElapsedTimeFields		N/A
RtlTimeToSecondsSince1970		
RtlTimeToSecondsSince1980		
RtlTimeToTimeFields		
RtlTryEnterCriticalSection		N/A
RtlUlongByteSwap		
RtlUlonglongByteSwap		

(continued)

TABLE B-4. *(continued)*

FUNCTION NAME	ntdll.dll	ntoskrnl.exe
RtlUnicodeStringToAnsiSize		
RtlUnicodeStringToAnsiString		
RtlUnicodeStringToCountedOemString		
RtlUnicodeStringToInteger		
RtlUnicodeStringToOemSize		
RtlUnicodeStringToOemString		
RtlUnicodeToCustomCPN		
RtlUnicodeToMultiByteN		
RtlUnicodeToMultiByteSize		
RtlUnicodeToOemN		
RtlUniform		N/A
RtlUnlockHeap		N/A
RtlUnwind		
RtlUpcaseUnicodeChar		
RtlUpcaseUnicodeString		
RtlUpcaseUnicodeStringToAnsiString		
RtlUpcaseUnicodeStringToCountedOemString		
RtlUpcaseUnicodeStringToOemString		
RtlUpcaseUnicodeToCustomCPN		
RtlUpcaseUnicodeToMultiByteN		
RtlUpcaseUnicodeToOemN		
RtlUpdateTimer		N/A
RtlUpperChar		
RtlUpperString		
RtlUsageHeap		N/A
RtlUshortByteSwap		
RtlValidAcl		N/A
RtlValidateHeap		N/A
RtlValidateProcessHeaps		N/A
RtlValidRelativeSecurityDescriptor		
RtlValidSecurityDescriptor		
RtlValidSid		
RtlVerifyVersionInfo		N/A

TABLE B-4. *(continued)*

FUNCTION NAME	ntdll.dll	ntoskrnl.exe
RtlVolumeDeviceToDosName	N/A	
RtlWalkFrameChain		
RtlWalkHeap		N/A
RtlWriteRegistryValue		
RtlxAnsiStringToUnicodeSize		
RtlxOemStringToUnicodeSize		
RtlxUnicodeStringToAnsiSize		
RtlxUnicodeStringToOemSize		
RtlZeroHeap		
RTlZeroMemory		

APPENDIX C

Constants, Enumerations, and Structures

The code samples and descriptions in this book make frequent references to data definitions from the Windows 2000 Device Driver Kit (DDK), the Win32 Platform Software Development Kit (SDK), and header files found on the companion CD of this book. To allow easy lookup of these definitions, I have compiled the most important ones in Appendix C. Most of the definitions are drawn from the `w2k_def.h` header file found in the CD directory `\src\common\include`.

CONSTANTS

This section contains definitions of symbolic constants used throughout the book. They are also referred to in subsequent sections of this appendix.

DISPATCHER OBJECT TYPE CODES

```
#define DISP_TYPE_NOTIFICATION_EVENT        0
#define DISP_TYPE_SYNCHRONIZATION_EVENT     1
#define DISP_TYPE_MUTANT                    2
#define DISP_TYPE_PROCESS                   3
#define DISP_TYPE_QUEUE                     4
#define DISP_TYPE_SEMAPHORE                 5
#define DISP_TYPE_THREAD                    6
#define DISP_TYPE_NOTIFICATION_TIMER        8
#define DISP_TYPE_SYNCHRONIZATION_TIMER     9
```

File Object Flags

```
#define FO_FILE_OPEN                        0x00000001
#define FO_SYNCHRONOUS_IO                   0x00000002
#define FO_ALERTABLE_IO                     0x00000004
#define FO_NO_INTERMEDIATE_BUFFERING        0x00000008
#define FO_WRITE_THROUGH                    0x00000010
#define FO_SEQUENTIAL_ONLY                  0x00000020
#define FO_CACHE_SUPPORTED                  0x00000040
#define FO_NAMED_PIPE                       0x00000080
#define FO_STREAM_FILE                      0x00000100
#define FO_MAILSLOT                         0x00000200
#define FO_GENERATE_AUDIT_ON_CLOSE          0x00000400
#define FO_DIRECT_DEVICE_OPEN               0x00000800
#define FO_FILE_MODIFIED                    0x00001000
#define FO_FILE_SIZE_CHANGED                0x00002000
#define FO_CLEANUP_COMPLETE                 0x00004000
#define FO_TEMPORARY_FILE                   0x00008000
#define FO_DELETE_ON_CLOSE                  0x00010000
#define FO_OPENED_CASE_SENSITIVE            0x00020000
#define FO_HANDLE_CREATED                   0x00040000
#define FO_FILE_FAST_IO_READ                0x00080000
#define FO_RANDOM_ACCESS                    0x00100000
#define FO_FILE_OPEN_CANCELLED              0x00200000
#define FO_VOLUME_OPEN                      0x00400000
```

Portable Executable Section Directory IDs

```
#define IMAGE_DIRECTORY_ENTRY_EXPORT          0
#define IMAGE_DIRECTORY_ENTRY_IMPORT          1
#define IMAGE_DIRECTORY_ENTRY_RESOURCE        2
#define IMAGE_DIRECTORY_ENTRY_EXCEPTION       3
#define IMAGE_DIRECTORY_ENTRY_SECURITY        4
#define IMAGE_DIRECTORY_ENTRY_BASERELOC       5
#define IMAGE_DIRECTORY_ENTRY_DEBUG           6
#define IMAGE_DIRECTORY_ENTRY_COPYRIGHT       7
#define IMAGE_DIRECTORY_ENTRY_GLOBALPTR       8
#define IMAGE_DIRECTORY_ENTRY_TLS             9
#define IMAGE_DIRECTORY_ENTRY_LOAD_CONFIG    10
#define IMAGE_DIRECTORY_ENTRY_BOUND_IMPORT   11
#define IMAGE_DIRECTORY_ENTRY_IAT            12
#define IMAGE_DIRECTORY_ENTRY_DELAY_IMPORT   13
#define IMAGE_DIRECTORY_ENTRY_COM_DESCRIPTOR 14

#define IMAGE_NUMBEROF_DIRECTORY_ENTRIES     16
```

I/O System Data Structure Type Codes

```
#define IO_TYPE_ADAPTER                    1
#define IO_TYPE_CONTROLLER                 2
#define IO_TYPE_DEVICE                     3
#define IO_TYPE_DRIVER                     4
#define IO_TYPE_FILE                       5
#define IO_TYPE_IRP                        6
#define IO_TYPE_MASTER_ADAPTER             7
#define IO_TYPE_OPEN_PACKET                8
#define IO_TYPE_TIMER                      9
#define IO_TYPE_VPB                       10
#define IO_TYPE_ERROR_LOG                 11
#define IO_TYPE_ERROR_MESSAGE             12
#define IO_TYPE_DEVICE_OBJECT_EXTENSION   13

#define IO_TYPE_APC                       18
#define IO_TYPE_DPC                       19
#define IO_TYPE_DEVICE_QUEUE              20
#define IO_TYPE_EVENT_PAIR                21
#define IO_TYPE_INTERRUPT                 22
#define IO_TYPE_PROFILE                   23
```

I/O Request Packet Functions

```
#define IRP_MJ_CREATE                      0
#define IRP_MJ_CREATE_NAMED_PIPE           1
#define IRP_MJ_CLOSE                       2
#define IRP_MJ_READ                        3
#define IRP_MJ_WRITE                       4
#define IRP_MJ_QUERY_INFORMATION           5
#define IRP_MJ_SET_INFORMATION             6
#define IRP_MJ_QUERY_EA                    7
#define IRP_MJ_SET_EA                      8
#define IRP_MJ_FLUSH_BUFFERS               9
#define IRP_MJ_QUERY_VOLUME_INFORMATION   10
#define IRP_MJ_SET_VOLUME_INFORMATION     11
#define IRP_MJ_DIRECTORY_CONTROL          12
#define IRP_MJ_FILE_SYSTEM_CONTROL        13
#define IRP_MJ_DEVICE_CONTROL             14
#define IRP_MJ_INTERNAL_DEVICE_CONTROL    15
#define IRP_MJ_SHUTDOWN                   16
#define IRP_MJ_LOCK_CONTROL               17
#define IRP_MJ_CLEANUP                    18
#define IRP_MJ_CREATE_MAILSLOT            19
#define IRP_MJ_QUERY_SECURITY             20
```

```
#define IRP_MJ_SET_SECURITY                21
#define IRP_MJ_POWER                       22
#define IRP_MJ_SYSTEM_CONTROL              23
#define IRP_MJ_DEVICE_CHANGE               24
#define IRP_MJ_QUERY_QUOTA                 25
#define IRP_MJ_SET_QUOTA                   26
#define IRP_MJ_PNP                         27
#define IRP_MJ_MAXIMUM_FUNCTION            27

#define IRP_MJ_FUNCTIONS (IRP_MJ_MAXIMUM_FUNCTION + 1)
```

Object Header Flags

```
#define OB_FLAG_CREATE_INFO    0x01 // has OBJECT_CREATE_INFO
#define OB_FLAG_KERNEL_MODE    0x02 // created by kernel
#define OB_FLAG_CREATOR_INFO   0x04 // has OBJECT_CREATOR_INFO
#define OB_FLAG_EXCLUSIVE      0x08 // OBJ_EXCLUSIVE
#define OB_FLAG_PERMANENT      0x10 // OBJ_PERMANENT
#define OB_FLAG_SECURITY       0x20 // has security descriptor
#define OB_FLAG_SINGLE_PROCESS 0x40 // no HandleDBList
```

Object Type Array Indexes

```
#define OB_TYPE_INDEX_TYPE              1 // [ObjT] "Type"
#define OB_TYPE_INDEX_DIRECTORY         2 // [Dire] "Directory"
#define OB_TYPE_INDEX_SYMBOLIC_LINK     3 // [Symb] "SymbolicLink"
#define OB_TYPE_INDEX_TOKEN             4 // [Toke] "Token"
#define OB_TYPE_INDEX_PROCESS           5 // [Proc] "Process"
#define OB_TYPE_INDEX_THREAD            6 // [Thre] "Thread"
#define OB_TYPE_INDEX_JOB               7 // [Job ] "Job"
#define OB_TYPE_INDEX_EVENT             8 // [Even] "Event"
#define OB_TYPE_INDEX_EVENT_PAIR        9 // [Even] "EventPair"
#define OB_TYPE_INDEX_MUTANT           10 // [Muta] "Mutant"
#define OB_TYPE_INDEX_CALLBACK         11 // [Call] "Callback"
#define OB_TYPE_INDEX_SEMAPHORE        12 // [Sema] "Semaphore"
#define OB_TYPE_INDEX_TIMER            13 // [Time] "Timer"
#define OB_TYPE_INDEX_PROFILE          14 // [Prof] "Profile"
#define OB_TYPE_INDEX_WINDOW_STATION   15 // [Wind] "WindowStation"
#define OB_TYPE_INDEX_DESKTOP          16 // [Desk] "Desktop"
#define OB_TYPE_INDEX_SECTION          17 // [Sect] "Section"
#define OB_TYPE_INDEX_KEY              18 // [Key ] "Key"
#define OB_TYPE_INDEX_PORT             19 // [Port] "Port"
#define OB_TYPE_INDEX_WAITABLE_PORT    20 // [Wait] "WaitablePort"
#define OB_TYPE_INDEX_ADAPTER          21 // [Adap] "Adapter"
#define OB_TYPE_INDEX_CONTROLLER       22 // [Cont] "Controller"
#define OB_TYPE_INDEX_DEVICE           23 // [Devi] "Device"
```

```
#define OB_TYPE_INDEX_DRIVER          24 // [Driv] "Driver"
#define OB_TYPE_INDEX_IO_COMPLETION   25 // [IoCo] "IoCompletion"
#define OB_TYPE_INDEX_FILE            26 // [File] "File"
#define OB_TYPE_INDEX_WMI_GUID        27 // [WmiG] "WmiGuid"
```

Object Type Tags

```
#define OB_TYPE_TAG_TYPE             'TjbO' // [ObjT] "Type"
#define OB_TYPE_TAG_DIRECTORY        'eriD' // [Dire] "Directory"
#define OB_TYPE_TAG_SYMBOLIC_LINK    'bmyS' // [Symb] "SymbolicLink"
#define OB_TYPE_TAG_TOKEN            'ekoT' // [Toke] "Token"
#define OB_TYPE_TAG_PROCESS          'corP' // [Proc] "Process"
#define OB_TYPE_TAG_THREAD           'erhT' // [Thre] "Thread"
#define OB_TYPE_TAG_JOB              ' boJ' // [Job ] "Job"
#define OB_TYPE_TAG_EVENT            'nevE' // [Even] "Event"
#define OB_TYPE_TAG_EVENT_PAIR       'nevE' // [Even] "EventPair"
#define OB_TYPE_TAG_MUTANT           'atuM' // [Muta] "Mutant"
#define OB_TYPE_TAG_CALLBACK         'llaC' // [Call] "Callback"
#define OB_TYPE_TAG_SEMAPHORE        'ameS' // [Sema] "Semaphore"
#define OB_TYPE_TAG_TIMER            'emiT' // [Time] "Timer"
#define OB_TYPE_TAG_PROFILE          'forP' // [Prof] "Profile"
#define OB_TYPE_TAG_WINDOW_STATION   'dniW' // [Wind] "WindowStation"
#define OB_TYPE_TAG_DESKTOP          'kseD' // [Desk] "Desktop"
#define OB_TYPE_TAG_SECTION          'tceS' // [Sect] "Section"
#define OB_TYPE_TAG_KEY              ' yeK' // [Key ] "Key"
#define OB_TYPE_TAG_PORT             'troP' // [Port] "Port"
#define OB_TYPE_TAG_WAITABLE_PORT    'tiaW' // [Wait] "WaitablePort"
#define OB_TYPE_TAG_ADAPTER          'padA' // [Adap] "Adapter"
#define OB_TYPE_TAG_CONTROLLER       'tnoC' // [Cont] "Controller"
#define OB_TYPE_TAG_DEVICE           'iveD' // [Devi] "Device"
#define OB_TYPE_TAG_DRIVER           'virD' // [Driv] "Driver"
#define OB_TYPE_TAG_IO_COMPLETION    'oCoI' // [IoCo] "IoCompletion"
#define OB_TYPE_TAG_FILE             'eliF' // [File] "File"
#define OB_TYPE_TAG_WMI_GUID         'GimW' // [WmiG] "WmiGuid"
```

Object Attribute Flags

```
#define OBJ_INHERIT            0x00000002
#define OBJ_PERMANENT          0x00000010
#define OBJ_EXCLUSIVE          0x00000020
#define OBJ_CASE_INSENSITIVE   0x00000040
#define OBJ_OPENIF             0x00000080
#define OBJ_OPENLINK           0x00000100
#define OBJ_KERNEL_HANDLE      0x00000200
#define OBJ_VALID_ATTRIBUTES   0x000003F2
```

ENUMERATIONS

Some Windows 2000 constant definitions come in the form of enumerations. Following is an alphabetical collection of the most frequently used ones. The effective values of the enumeration members are shown in comments inserted before each definition line.

IO_ALLOCATION_ACTION

```
typedef enum _IO_ALLOCATION_ACTION
        {
/*001*/ KeepObject = 1,
/*002*/ DeallocateObject,
/*003*/ DeallocateObjectKeepRegisters
        }
        IO_ALLOCATION_ACTION;
```

LOOKASIDE_LIST_ID

```
typedef enum _LOOKASIDE_LIST_ID
        {
/*000*/ SmallIrpLookasideList,
/*001*/ LargeIrpLookasideList,
/*002*/ MdlLookasideList,
/*003*/ CreateInfoLookasideList,
/*004*/ NameBufferLookasideList,
/*005*/ TwilightLookasideList,
/*006*/ CompletionLookasideList
        }
        LOOKASIDE_LIST_ID;
```

MODE (SEE ALSO *KPROCESSOR_MODE)*

```
typedef enum _MODE
        {
/*000*/ KernelMode,
/*001*/ UserMode,
/*002*/ MaximumMode
        }
        MODE;
```

NT_PRODUCT_TYPE

```
typedef enum _NT_PRODUCT_TYPE
        {
/*000*/ NtProductInvalid,
/*001*/ NtProductWinNt,
```

```
/*002*/ NtProductLanManNt,
/*003*/ NtProductServer
        }
        NT_PRODUCT_TYPE;
```

POOL_TYPE

```
typedef enum _POOL_TYPE
        {
/*000*/ NonPagedPool,
/*001*/ PagedPool,
/*002*/ NonPagedPoolMustSucceed,
/*003*/ DontUseThisType,
/*004*/ NonPagedPoolCacheAligned,
/*005*/ PagedPoolCacheAligned,
/*006*/ NonPagedPoolCacheAlignedMustS,
/*007*/ MaxPoolType
        }
        POOL_TYPE;
```

STRUCTURES AND ALIASES

This section is an alphabetical collection of structure and alias type definitions used by kernel-mode drivers and low-level system programs. Parts of them are undocumented. Before the member names, I have inserted comments indicating the offsets of all structure members relative to the structure base address. This allows easy read-out of member values from a hex dump listing.

ANSI_STRING

```
typedef STRING ANSI_STRING;
```

CALLBACK_OBJECT

```
typedef struct _CALLBACK_OBJECT
        {
/*000*/ DWORD      Tag; // 0x6C6C6143 ("Call")
/*004*/ KSPIN_LOCK Lock;
/*008*/ LIST_ENTRY CallbackList;
/*010*/ BOOLEAN    AllowMultipleCallbacks;
/*014*/ }
        CALLBACK_OBJECT;
```

CLIENT_ID

```
typedef struct _CLIENT_ID
        {
/*000*/ HANDLE UniqueProcess;
/*004*/ HANDLE UniqueThread;
/*008*/ }
        CLIENT_ID;
```

CONTEXT

```
// base address 0xFFDFF13C

#define MAXIMUM_SUPPORTED_EXTENSION 512

typedef struct _CONTEXT
        {
/*000*/ DWORD        ContextFlags;
/*004*/ DWORD        Dr0;
/*008*/ DWORD        Dr1;
/*00C*/ DWORD        Dr2;
/*010*/ DWORD        Dr3;
/*014*/ DWORD        Dr6;
/*018*/ DWORD        Dr7;
/*01C*/ FLOATING_SAVE_AREA FloatSave;
/*08C*/ DWORD        SegGs;
/*090*/ DWORD        SegFs;
/*094*/ DWORD        SegEs;
/*098*/ DWORD        SegDs;
/*09C*/ DWORD        Edi;
/*0A0*/ DWORD        Esi;
/*0A4*/ DWORD        Ebx;
/*0A8*/ DWORD        Edx;
/*0AC*/ DWORD        Ecx;
/*0B0*/ DWORD        Eax;
/*0B4*/ DWORD        Ebp;
/*0B8*/ DWORD        Eip;
/*0BC*/ DWORD        SegCs;
/*0C0*/ DWORD        EFlags;
/*0C4*/ DWORD        Esp;
/*0C8*/ DWORD        SegSs;
/*0CC*/ BYTE         ExtendedRegisters [MAXIMUM_SUPPORTED_EXTENSION];
/*2CC*/ }
        CONTEXT;
```

CONTROLLER_OBJECT

```
typedef struct _CONTROLLER_OBJECT
        {
/*000*/ SHORT          Type; // IO_TYPE_CONTROLLER 0x02
/*002*/ SHORT          Size; // number of BYTEs
/*004*/ PVOID          ControllerExtension;
/*008*/ KDEVICE_QUEUE DeviceWaitQueue;
/*01C*/ DWORD          Spare1;
/*020*/ LARGE_INTEGER Spare2;
/*028*/ }
        CONTROLLER_OBJECT;
```

CRITICAL_SECTION

```
typedef struct _RTL_CRITICAL_SECTION
        {
/*000*/ PRTL_CRITICAL_SECTION_DEBUG DebugInfo;
/*004*/ LONG                        LockCount;
/*008*/ LONG                        RecursionCount;
/*00C*/ HANDLE                      OwningThread;
/*010*/ HANDLE                      LockSemaphore;
/*014*/ DWORD_PTR                   SpinCount;
/*018*/ }
        CRITICAL_SECTION;
```

DEVICE_OBJECT

```
typedef struct _DEVICE_OBJECT
        {
/*000*/ SHORT                    Type; // IO_TYPE_DEVICE 0x03
/*002*/ WORD                     Size; // number of BYTEs
/*004*/ LONG                     ReferenceCount;
/*008*/ struct _DRIVER_OBJECT   *DriverObject;
/*00C*/ struct _DEVICE_OBJECT   *NextDevice;
/*010*/ struct _DEVICE_OBJECT   *AttachedDevice;
/*014*/ struct _IRP             *CurrentIrp;
/*018*/ struct _PIO_TIMER       *Timer;
/*01C*/ DWORD                    Flags;           // DO_*
/*020*/ DWORD                    Characteristics; // FILE_*
/*024*/ PVPB                     Vpb;
/*028*/ PVOID                    DeviceExtension;
/*02C*/ DEVICE_TYPE              DeviceType;
/*030*/ CHAR                     StackSize;
/*034*/ union
            {
```

```
/*034*/     LIST_ENTRY         ListEntry;
/*034*/     WAIT_CONTEXT_BLOCK Wcb;
/*05C*/     } Queue;
/*05C*/ DWORD                      AlignmentRequirement;
/*060*/ KDEVICE_QUEUE              DeviceQueue;
/*074*/ KDPC                       Dpc;
/*094*/ DWORD                      ActiveThreadCount;
/*098*/ PSECURITY_DESCRIPTOR       SecurityDescriptor;
/*09C*/ KEVENT                     DeviceLock;
/*0AC*/ WORD                       SectorSize;
/*0AE*/ WORD                       Spare1;
/*0B0*/ struct _DEVOBJ_EXTENSION *DeviceObjectExtension;
/*0B4*/ PVOID                      Reserved;
/*0B8*/ }
        DEVICE_OBJECT;
```

DEVOBJ_EXTENSION

```
typedef struct _DEVOBJ_EXTENSION
        {
/*000*/ SHORT          Type; // IO_TYPE_DEVICE_OBJECT_EXTENSION 0x0D
/*002*/ WORD           Size; // number of BYTEs
/*004*/ PDEVICE_OBJECT DeviceObject;
/*008*/ }
        DEVOBJ_EXTENSION;
```

DISPATCHER_HEADER

```
typedef struct _DISPATCHER_HEADER
        {
/*000*/ BYTE       Type;          // DISP_TYPE_*
/*001*/ BYTE       Absolute;
/*002*/ BYTE       Size;          // number of DWORDs
/*003*/ BYTE       Inserted;
/*004*/ LONG       SignalState;
/*008*/ LIST_ENTRY WaitListHead;
/*010*/ }
        DISPATCHER_HEADER;
```

DRIVER_EXTENSION

```
typedef struct _DRIVER_EXTENSION
        {
/*000*/ struct _DRIVER_OBJECT *DriverObject;
/*004*/ PDRIVER_ADD_DEVICE     AddDevice;
/*008*/ DWORD                  Count;
/*00C*/ UNICODE_STRING         ServiceKeyName;
/*014*/ }
        DRIVER_EXTENSION;
```

DRIVER_OBJECT

```
typedef struct _DRIVER_OBJECT
        {
/*000*/ SHORT                 Type; // IO_TYPE_DRIVER 0x04
/*002*/ SHORT                 Size; // number of BYTEs
/*004*/ PDEVICE_OBJECT        DeviceObject;
/*008*/ DWORD                 Flags;
/*00C*/ PVOID                 DriverStart;
/*010*/ DWORD                 DriverSize;
/*014*/ PVOID                 DriverSection;
/*018*/ PDRIVER_EXTENSION     DriverExtension;
/*01C*/ UNICODE_STRING        DriverName;
/*024*/ PUNICODE_STRING       HardwareDatabase;
/*028*/ PFAST_IO_DISPATCH     FastIoDispatch;
/*02C*/ PDRIVER_INITIALIZE    DriverInit;
/*030*/ PDRIVER_STARTIO       DriverStartIo;
/*034*/ PDRIVER_UNLOAD        DriverUnload;
/*038*/ PDRIVER_DISPATCH      MajorFunction [IRP_MJ_FUNCTIONS];
/*0A8*/ }
        DRIVER_OBJECT;
```

EPROCESS

```
typedef struct _EPROCESS
        {
/*000*/ KPROCESS                  Pcb;
/*06C*/ NTSTATUS                  ExitStatus;
/*070*/ KEVENT                    LockEvent;
/*080*/ DWORD                     LockCount;
/*084*/ DWORD                     d084;
/*088*/ LARGE_INTEGER             CreateTime;
/*090*/ LARGE_INTEGER             ExitTime;
/*098*/ PVOID                     LockOwner;
/*09C*/ DWORD                     UniqueProcessId;
/*0A0*/ LIST_ENTRY                ActiveProcessLinks;
/*0A8*/ DWORD                     QuotaPeakPoolUsage [2]; // NP, P
/*0B0*/ DWORD                     QuotaPoolUsage     [2]; // NP, P
/*0B8*/ DWORD                     PagefileUsage;
/*0BC*/ DWORD                     CommitCharge;
/*0C0*/ DWORD                     PeakPagefileUsage;
/*0C4*/ DWORD                     PeakVirtualSize;
/*0C8*/ LARGE_INTEGER             VirtualSize;
/*0D0*/ MMSUPPORT                 Vm;
/*100*/ DWORD                     d100;
/*104*/ DWORD                     d104;
/*108*/ DWORD                     d108;
/*10C*/ DWORD                     d10C;
/*110*/ DWORD                     d110;
/*114*/ DWORD                     d114;
```

```
/*118*/ DWORD               d118;
/*11C*/ DWORD               d11C;
/*120*/ PVOID               DebugPort;
/*124*/ PVOID               ExceptionPort;
/*128*/ PHANDLE_TABLE       ObjectTable;
/*12C*/ PVOID               Token;
/*130*/ FAST_MUTEX          WorkingSetLock;
/*150*/ DWORD               WorkingSetPage;
/*154*/ BOOLEAN             ProcessOutswapEnabled;
/*155*/ BOOLEAN             ProcessOutswapped;
/*156*/ BOOLEAN             AddressSpaceInitialized;
/*157*/ BOOLEAN             AddressSpaceDeleted;
/*158*/ FAST_MUTEX          AddressCreationLock;
/*178*/ KSPIN_LOCK          HyperSpaceLock;
/*17C*/ DWORD               ForkInProgress;
/*180*/ WORD                VmOperation;
/*182*/ BOOLEAN             ForkWasSuccessful;
/*183*/ BYTE                MmAgressiveWsTrimMask;
/*184*/ DWORD               VmOperationEvent;
/*188*/ HARDWARE_PTE        PageDirectoryPte;
/*18C*/ DWORD               LastFaultCount;
/*190*/ DWORD               ModifiedPageCount;
/*194*/ PVOID               VadRoot;
/*198*/ PVOID               VadHint;
/*19C*/ PVOID               CloneRoot;
/*1A0*/ DWORD               NumberOfPrivatePages;
/*1A4*/ DWORD               NumberOfLockedPages;
/*1A8*/ WORD                NextPageColor;
/*1AA*/ BOOLEAN             ExitProcessCalled;
/*1AB*/ BOOLEAN             CreateProcessReported;
/*1AC*/ HANDLE              SectionHandle;
/*1B0*/ struct _PEB        *Peb;
/*1B4*/ PVOID               SectionBaseAddress;
/*1B8*/ PQUOTA_BLOCK        QuotaBlock;
/*1BC*/ NTSTATUS            LastThreadExitStatus;
/*1C0*/ DWORD               WorkingSetWatch;
/*1C4*/ HANDLE              Win32WindowStation;
/*1C8*/ DWORD               InheritedFromUniqueProcessId;
/*1CC*/ ACCESS_MASK         GrantedAccess;
/*1D0*/ DWORD               DefaultHardErrorProcessing; // HEM_*
/*1D4*/ DWORD               LdtInformation;
/*1D8*/ PVOID               VadFreeHint;
/*1DC*/ DWORD               VdmObjects;
/*1E0*/ PVOID               DeviceMap; // 0x24 bytes
/*1E4*/ DWORD               SessionId;
/*1E8*/ DWORD               d1E8;
/*1EC*/ DWORD               d1EC;
```

```
/*1F0*/ DWORD                  d1F0;
/*1F4*/ DWORD                  d1F4;
/*1F8*/ DWORD                  d1F8;
/*1FC*/ BYTE                   ImageFileName [16];
/*20C*/ DWORD                  VmTrimFaultValue;
/*210*/ BYTE                   SetTimerResolution;
/*211*/ BYTE                   PriorityClass;
/*212*/ union
            {
            struct
                {
/*212*/         BYTE                   SubSystemMinorVersion;
/*213*/         BYTE                   SubSystemMajorVersion;
                };
            struct
                {
/*212*/         WORD                   SubSystemVersion;
                };
            };
/*214*/ struct _WIN32_PROCESS *Win32Process;
/*218*/ DWORD                  d218;
/*21C*/ DWORD                  d21C;
/*220*/ DWORD                  d220;
/*224*/ DWORD                  d224;
/*228*/ DWORD                  d228;
/*22C*/ DWORD                  d22C;
/*230*/ PVOID                  Wow64;
/*234*/ DWORD                  d234;
/*238*/ IO_COUNTERS            IoCounters;
/*268*/ DWORD                  d268;
/*26C*/ DWORD                  d26C;
/*270*/ DWORD                  d270;
/*274*/ DWORD                  d274;
/*278*/ DWORD                  d278;
/*27C*/ DWORD                  d27C;
/*280*/ DWORD                  d280;
/*284*/ DWORD                  d284;
/*288*/ }
        EPROCESS;
```

ERESOURCE

```
typedef struct _ERESOURCE
        {
/*000*/ LIST_ENTRY   SystemResourcesList;
/*008*/ POWNER_ENTRY OwnerTable;
```

```
/*00C*/ SHORT        ActiveCount;
/*00E*/ WORD         Flag;
/*010*/ PKSEMAPHORE  SharedWaiters;
/*014*/ PKEVENT      ExclusiveWaiters;
/*018*/ OWNER_ENTRY  OwnerThreads [2];
/*028*/ DWORD        ContentionCount;
/*02C*/ WORD         NumberOfSharedWaiters;
/*02E*/ WORD         NumberOfExclusiveWaiters;
/*030*/ union
            {
/*030*/     PVOID      Address;
/*030*/     DWORD_PTR CreatorBackTraceIndex;
/*034*/     };
/*034*/ KSPIN_LOCK   SpinLock;
/*038*/ }
        ERESOURCE;
```

ERESOURCE_OLD

```
typedef struct _ERESOURCE_OLD
        {
/*000*/ LIST_ENTRY        SystemResourcesList;
/*008*/ PERESOURCE_THREAD OwnerThreads;
/*00C*/ PBYTE             OwnerCounts;
/*010*/ WORD              TableSize;
/*012*/ WORD              ActiveCount;
/*014*/ WORD              Flag;
/*016*/ WORD              TableRover;
/*018*/ BYTE              InitialOwnerCounts  [4];
/*01C*/ ERESOURCE_THREAD  InitialOwnerThreads [4];
/*02C*/ DWORD             Spare1;
/*030*/ DWORD             ContentionCount;
/*034*/ WORD              NumberOfExclusiveWaiters;
/*036*/ WORD              NumberOfSharedWaiters;
/*038*/ KSEMAPHORE        SharedWaiters;
/*04C*/ KEVENT            ExclusiveWaiters;
/*05C*/ KSPIN_LOCK        SpinLock;
/*060*/ DWORD             CreatorBackTraceIndex;
/*064*/ WORD              Depth;
/*066*/ WORD              Reserved;
/*068*/ PVOID             OwnerBackTrace [4];
/*078*/ }
        ERESOURCE_OLD;
```

ERESOURCE_THREAD

```
typedef DWORD_PTR ERESOURCE_THREAD;
```

ETHREAD

```
typedef struct _ETHREAD
        {
/*000*/ KTHREAD       Tcb;
/*1B0*/ LARGE_INTEGER CreateTime;
/*1B8*/ union
            {
/*1B8*/     LARGE_INTEGER ExitTime;
/*1B8*/     LIST_ENTRY    LpcReplyChain;
            };
/*1C0*/ union
            {
/*1C0*/     NTSTATUS      ExitStatus;
/*1C0*/     DWORD         OfsChain;
            };
/*1C4*/ LIST_ENTRY    PostBlockList;
/*1CC*/ LIST_ENTRY    TerminationPortList;
/*1D4*/ PVOID         ActiveTimerListLock;
/*1D8*/ LIST_ENTRY    ActiveTimerListHead;
/*1E0*/ CLIENT_ID     Cid;
/*1E8*/ KSEMAPHORE    LpcReplySemaphore;
/*1FC*/ DWORD         LpcReplyMessage;
/*200*/ DWORD         LpcReplyMessageId;
/*204*/ DWORD         PerformanceCountLow;
/*208*/ DWORD         ImpersonationInfo;
/*20C*/ LIST_ENTRY    IrpList;
/*214*/ PVOID         TopLevelIrp;
/*218*/ PVOID         DeviceToVerify;
/*21C*/ DWORD         ReadClusterSize;
/*220*/ BOOLEAN       ForwardClusterOnly;
/*221*/ BOOLEAN       DisablePageFaultClustering;
/*222*/ BOOLEAN       DeadThread;
/*223*/ BOOLEAN       Reserved;
/*224*/ BOOL          HasTerminated;
/*228*/ ACCESS_MASK   GrantedAccess;
/*22C*/ PEPROCESS     ThreadsProcess;
/*230*/ PVOID         StartAddress;
/*234*/ union
            {
/*234*/     PVOID         Win32StartAddress;
/*234*/     DWORD         LpcReceivedMessageId;
            };
/*238*/ BOOLEAN       LpcExitThreadCalled;
/*239*/ BOOLEAN       HardErrorsAreDisabled;
/*23A*/ BOOLEAN       LpcReceivedMsgIdValid;
/*23B*/ BOOLEAN       ActiveImpersonationInfo;
/*23C*/ DWORD         PerformanceCountHigh;
/*240*/ DWORD         d240;
/*244*/ DWORD         d244;
/*248*/ }
        ETHREAD;
```

ETIMER

```
typedef struct _ETIMER
        {
/*000*/ KTIMER     Tcb;
/*028*/ KAPC       Apc;
/*058*/ KDPC       Dpc;
/*078*/ LIST_ENTRY ActiveTimerList;
/*080*/ KSPIN_LOCK Lock;
/*084*/ LONG       Period;
/*088*/ BOOLEAN    Active;
/*089*/ BOOLEAN    Resume;
/*08C*/ LIST_ENTRY WakeTimerList;
/*098*/ }
        ETIMER;
```

FAST_MUTEX

```
typedef struct _FAST_MUTEX
        {
/*000*/ LONG             Count;
/*004*/ struct _KTHREAD *Owner;
/*008*/ DWORD            Contention;
/*00C*/ KEVENT           Event;
/*01C*/ DWORD            OldIrql;
/*020*/ }
        FAST_MUTEX;
```

FILE_OBJECT

```
typedef struct _FILE_OBJECT
        {
/*000*/ SHORT                     Type; // IO_TYPE_FILE 0x05
/*002*/ SHORT                     Size; // number of BYTEs
/*004*/ PDEVICE_OBJECT            DeviceObject;
/*008*/ PVPB                      Vpb;
/*00C*/ PVOID                     FsContext;
/*010*/ PVOID                     FsContext2;
/*014*/ PSECTION_OBJECT_POINTERS SectionObjectPointer;
/*018*/ PVOID                     PrivateCacheMap;
/*01C*/ NTSTATUS                  FinalStatus;
/*020*/ struct _FILE_OBJECT      *RelatedFileObject;
/*024*/ BOOLEAN                   LockOperation;
/*025*/ BOOLEAN                   DeletePending;
/*026*/ BOOLEAN                   ReadAccess;
/*027*/ BOOLEAN                   WriteAccess;
/*028*/ BOOLEAN                   DeleteAccess;
/*029*/ BOOLEAN                   SharedRead;
```

```
/*02A*/ BOOLEAN                     SharedWrite;
/*02B*/ BOOLEAN                     SharedDelete;
/*02C*/ DWORD                       Flags; // FO_*
/*030*/ UNICODE_STRING              FileName;
/*038*/ LARGE_INTEGER               CurrentByteOffset;
/*040*/ DWORD                       Waiters;
/*044*/ DWORD                       Busy;
/*048*/ PVOID                       LastLock;
/*04C*/ KEVENT                      Lock;
/*05C*/ KEVENT                      Event;
/*06C*/ PIO_COMPLETION_CONTEXT      CompletionContext;
/*070*/ }
        FILE_OBJECT;
```

FLOATING_SAVE_AREA

```
// base address 0xFFDFF158

#define SIZE_OF_80387_REGISTERS 80

typedef struct _FLOATING_SAVE_AREA
        {
/*000*/ DWORD ControlWord;
/*004*/ DWORD StatusWord;
/*008*/ DWORD TagWord;
/*00C*/ DWORD ErrorOffset;
/*010*/ DWORD ErrorSelector;
/*014*/ DWORD DataOffset;
/*018*/ DWORD DataSelector;
/*01C*/ BYTE  RegisterArea [SIZE_OF_80387_REGISTERS];
/*06C*/ DWORD Cr0NpxState;
/*070*/ }
        FLOATING_SAVE_AREA;
```

HANDLE_ENTRY

```
#define HANDLE_ATTRIBUTE_INHERIT 0x00000002
#define HANDLE_ATTRIBUTE_MASK    0x00000007
#define HANDLE_OBJECT_MASK       0xFFFFFFF8

typedef struct _HANDLE_ENTRY // cf. OBJECT_HANDLE_INFORMATION
        {
/*000*/ union
            {
/*000*/     DWORD          HandleAttributes;// HANDLE_ATTRIBUTE_MASK
/*000*/     POBJECT_HEADER ObjectHeader;    // HANDLE_OBJECT_MASK
/*004*/     };
```

```
/*004*/ union
            {
/*004*/     ACCESS_MASK    GrantedAccess;    // if used entry
/*004*/     DWORD          NextEntry;        // if free entry
/*008*/     };
/*008*/ }
        HANDLE_ENTRY;
```

HANDLE_LAYER1, HANDLE_LAYER2, HANDLE_LAYER3

```
#define HANDLE_LAYER_SIZE 0x00000100

typedef struct _HANDLE_LAYER1
        {
/*000*/ PHANDLE_LAYER2 Layer2 [HANDLE_LAYER_SIZE]; // bits 18 to 25
/*400*/ }
        HANDLE_LAYER1;

typedef struct _HANDLE_LAYER2
        {
/*000*/ PHANDLE_LAYER3 Layer3 [HANDLE_LAYER_SIZE]; // bits 10 to 17
/*400*/ }
        HANDLE_LAYER2;

typedef struct _HANDLE_LAYER3
        {
/*000*/ HANDLE_ENTRY Entries [HANDLE_LAYER_SIZE]; // bits 2 to 9
/*800*/ }
        HANDLE_LAYER3;
```

HANDLE_TABLE

```
typedef struct _HANDLE_TABLE
        {
/*000*/ DWORD             Reserved;
/*004*/ DWORD             HandleCount;
/*008*/ PHANDLE_LAYER1    Layer1;
/*00C*/ struct _EPROCESS *Process; // passed to PsChargePoolQuota ()
/*010*/ HANDLE            UniqueProcessId;
/*014*/ DWORD             NextEntry;
/*018*/ DWORD             TotalEntries;
/*01C*/ ERESOURCE         HandleTableLock;
/*054*/ LIST_ENTRY        HandleTableList;
/*05C*/ KEVENT            Event;
/*06C*/ }
        HANDLE_TABLE;
```

HARDWARE_PTE

```
typedef struct _HARDWARE_PTE
        {
/*000*/ unsigned Valid           :  1;
        unsigned Write           :  1;
        unsigned Owner           :  1;
        unsigned WriteThrough    :  1;
        unsigned CacheDisable    :  1;
        unsigned Accessed        :  1;
        unsigned Dirty           :  1;
        unsigned LargePage       :  1;
/*001*/ unsigned Global          :  1;
        unsigned CopyOnWrite     :  1;
        unsigned Prototype       :  1;
        unsigned reserved        :  1;
        unsigned PageFrameNumber : 20;
/*004*/ }
        HARDWARE_PTE;
```

IMAGE_DATA_DIRECTORY

```
typedef struct _IMAGE_DATA_DIRECTORY
        {
/*000*/ DWORD VirtualAddress;
/*004*/ DWORD Size;
/*008*/ }
        IMAGE_DATA_DIRECTORY;
```

IMAGE_EXPORT_DIRECTORY

```
typedef struct _IMAGE_EXPORT_DIRECTORY
        {
/*000*/ DWORD Characteristics;
/*004*/ DWORD TimeDateStamp;
/*008*/ WORD  MajorVersion;
/*00A*/ WORD  MinorVersion;
/*00C*/ DWORD Name;
/*010*/ DWORD Base;
/*014*/ DWORD NumberOfFunctions;
/*018*/ DWORD NumberOfNames;
/*01C*/ DWORD AddressOfFunctions;
/*020*/ DWORD AddressOfNames;
/*024*/ DWORD AddressOfNameOrdinals;
/*028*/ }
        IMAGE_EXPORT_DIRECTORY;
```

IMAGE_FILE_HEADER

```
typedef struct _IMAGE_FILE_HEADER
        {
/*000*/ WORD  Machine;
/*002*/ WORD  NumberOfSections;
/*004*/ DWORD TimeDateStamp;
/*008*/ DWORD PointerToSymbolTable;
/*00C*/ DWORD NumberOfSymbols;
/*010*/ WORD  SizeOfOptionalHeader;
/*012*/ WORD  Characteristics;
/*014*/ }
        IMAGE_FILE_HEADER;
```

IMAGE_NT_HEADERS

```
typedef struct _IMAGE_NT_HEADERS
        {
/*000*/ DWORD                 Signature;
/*004*/ IMAGE_FILE_HEADER     FileHeader;
/*018*/ IMAGE_OPTIONAL_HEADER OptionalHeader;
/*0F8*/ }
        IMAGE_NT_HEADERS;
```

IMAGE_OPTIONAL_HEADER

```
#define IMAGE_NUMBEROF_DIRECTORY_ENTRIES        16

typedef struct _IMAGE_OPTIONAL_HEADER
        {
/*000*/ WORD                 Magic;
/*002*/ BYTE                 MajorLinkerVersion;
/*003*/ BYTE                 MinorLinkerVersion;
/*004*/ DWORD                SizeOfCode;
/*008*/ DWORD                SizeOfInitializedData;
/*00C*/ DWORD                SizeOfUninitializedData;
/*010*/ DWORD                AddressOfEntryPoint;
/*014*/ DWORD                BaseOfCode;
/*018*/ DWORD                BaseOfData;
/*01C*/ DWORD                ImageBase;
/*020*/ DWORD                SectionAlignment;
/*024*/ DWORD                FileAlignment;
/*028*/ WORD                 MajorOperatingSystemVersion;
/*02A*/ WORD                 MinorOperatingSystemVersion;
/*02C*/ WORD                 MajorImageVersion;
/*02E*/ WORD                 MinorImageVersion;
/*030*/ WORD                 MajorSubsystemVersion;
/*032*/ WORD                 MinorSubsystemVersion;
/*034*/ DWORD                Win32VersionValue;
```

```
/*038*/ DWORD                SizeOfImage;
/*03C*/ DWORD                SizeOfHeaders;
/*040*/ DWORD                CheckSum;
/*044*/ WORD                 Subsystem;
/*046*/ WORD                 DllCharacteristics;
/*048*/ DWORD                SizeOfStackReserve;
/*04C*/ DWORD                SizeOfStackCommit;
/*050*/ DWORD                SizeOfHeapReserve;
/*054*/ DWORD                SizeOfHeapCommit;
/*058*/ DWORD                LoaderFlags;
/*05C*/ DWORD                NumberOfRvaAndSizes;
/*060*/ IMAGE_DATA_DIRECTORY DataDirectory
                             [IMAGE_NUMBEROF_DIRECTORY_ENTRIES];
/*0E0*/ }
        IMAGE_OPTIONAL_HEADER;
```

IO_COMPLETION

```
typedef struct _IO_COMPLETION
        {
/*000*/ KQUEUE Queue;
/*028*/ }
        IO_COMPLETION;
```

IO_COMPLETION_CONTEXT

```
typedef struct _IO_COMPLETION_CONTEXT
        {
/*000*/ PVOID Port;
/*004*/ PVOID Key;
/*008*/ }
        IO_COMPLETION_CONTEXT;
```

IO_ERROR_LOG_ENTRY

```
typedef struct _IO_ERROR_LOG_ENTRY
        {
/*000*/ SHORT               Type; // IO_TYPE_ERROR_LOG 0x0B
/*002*/ SHORT               Size; // number of BYTEs
/*004*/ LIST_ENTRY          ErrorLogList;
/*00C*/ PDEVICE_OBJECT      DeviceObject;
/*010*/ PDRIVER_OBJECT      DriverObject;
/*014*/ DWORD               Reserved;
/*018*/ LARGE_INTEGER       TimeStamp;
/*020*/ IO_ERROR_LOG_PACKET EntryData;
/*050*/ }
        IO_ERROR_LOG_ENTRY;
```

IO_ERROR_LOG_MESSAGE

```
typedef struct _IO_ERROR_LOG_MESSAGE
        {
/*000*/ WORD                Type; // IO_TYPE_ERROR_MESSAGE 0x0C
/*002*/ WORD                Size; // number of BYTEs
/*004*/ WORD                DriverNameLength;
/*008*/ LARGE_INTEGER       TimeStamp;
/*010*/ DWORD               DriverNameOffset;
/*018*/ IO_ERROR_LOG_PACKET EntryData;
/*048*/ }
        IO_ERROR_LOG_MESSAGE;
```

IO_ERROR_LOG_PACKET

```
typedef struct _IO_ERROR_LOG_PACKET
        {
/*000*/ BYTE          MajorFunctionCode;
/*001*/ BYTE          RetryCount;
/*002*/ WORD          DumpDataSize;
/*004*/ WORD          NumberOfStrings;
/*006*/ WORD          StringOffset;
/*008*/ WORD          EventCategory;
/*00C*/ NTSTATUS      ErrorCode;
/*010*/ DWORD         UniqueErrorValue;
/*014*/ NTSTATUS      FinalStatus;
/*018*/ DWORD         SequenceNumber;
/*01C*/ DWORD         IoControlCode;
/*020*/ LARGE_INTEGER DeviceOffset;
/*028*/ DWORD         DumpData [1];
/*030*/ }
        IO_ERROR_LOG_PACKET;
```

IO_STATUS_BLOCK

```
typedef struct _IO_STATUS_BLOCK
        {
/*000*/ NTSTATUS Status;
/*004*/ ULONG    Information;
/*008*/ }
        IO_STATUS_BLOCK;
```

IO_TIMER

```
typedef struct _IO_TIMER
        {
/*000*/ SHORT              Type;       // IO_TYPE_TIMER 0x09
/*002*/ WORD               TimerState; // 0 = stopped, 1 = started
/*004*/ LIST_ENTRY         TimerQueue;
/*00C*/ PIO_TIMER_ROUTINE TimerRoutine;
```

```
/*010*/ PVOID              Context;
/*014*/ PDEVICE_OBJECT     DeviceObject;
/*018*/ }
        IO_TIMER;
```

KAFFINITY

```
typedef DWORD KAFFINITY;
```

KAPC

```
typedef struct _KAPC
        {
/*000*/ SHORT               Type; // IO_TYPE_APC 0x12
/*002*/ SHORT               Size; // number of BYTEs
/*004*/ DWORD               Spare0;
/*008*/ struct _KTHREAD    *Thread;
/*00C*/ LIST_ENTRY          ApcListEntry;
/*014*/ PKKERNEL_ROUTINE    KernelRoutine;  // KiSuspendNop
/*018*/ PKRUNDOWN_ROUTINE   RundownRoutine;
/*01C*/ PKNORMAL_ROUTINE    NormalRoutine;  // KiSuspendThread
/*020*/ PVOID               NormalContext;
/*024*/ PVOID               SystemArgument1;
/*028*/ PVOID               SystemArgument2;
/*02C*/ CHAR                ApcStateIndex;
/*02D*/ KPROCESSOR_MODE     ApcMode;
/*02E*/ BOOLEAN             Inserted;
/*030*/ }
        KAPC;
```

KAPC_STATE

```
typedef struct _KAPC_STATE
        {
/*000*/ LIST_ENTRY          ApcListHead [2];
/*010*/ struct _KPROCESS   *Process;
/*014*/ BOOLEAN             KernelApcInProgress;
/*015*/ BOOLEAN             KernelApcPending;
/*016*/ BOOLEAN             UserApcPending;
/*018*/ }
        KAPC_STATE;
```

KDEVICE_QUEUE

```
typedef struct _KDEVICE_QUEUE
        {
/*000*/ SHORT       Type; // IO_TYPE_DEVICE_QUEUE 0x14
/*002*/ SHORT       Size; // number of BYTEs
```

```
/*004*/ LIST_ENTRY DeviceListHead;
/*00C*/ KSPIN_LOCK Lock;
/*010*/ BOOLEAN    Busy;
/*014*/ }
        KDEVICE_QUEUE;
```

KDEVICE_QUEUE_ENTRY

```
typedef struct _KDEVICE_QUEUE_ENTRY
        {
/*000*/ LIST_ENTRY DeviceListEntry;
/*008*/ DWORD      SortKey;
/*00C*/ BOOLEAN    Inserted;
/*010*/ }
        KDEVICE_QUEUE_ENTRY;
```

KDPC

```
typedef struct _KDPC
        {
/*000*/ SHORT              Type; // IO_TYPE_DPC 0x13
/*002*/ BYTE               Number;
/*003*/ BYTE               Importance;
/*004*/ LIST_ENTRY         DpcListEntry;
/*00C*/ PKDEFERRED_ROUTINE DeferredRoutine;
/*010*/ PVOID              DeferredContext;
/*014*/ PVOID              SystemArgument1;
/*018*/ PVOID              SystemArgument2;
/*01C*/ PDWORD_PTR         Lock;
/*020*/ }
        KDPC;
```

KEVENT

```
typedef struct _KEVENT
        {
/*000*/ DISPATCHER_HEADER Header; // DISP_TYPE_*_EVENT 0x00, 0x01
/*010*/ }
        KEVENT;
```

KEVENT_PAIR

```
typedef struct _KEVENT_PAIR
        {
/*000*/ SHORT  Type; // IO_TYPE_EVENT_PAIR 0x15
```

```
/*002*/ WORD   Size; // number of BYTEs
/*004*/ KEVENT Event1;
/*014*/ KEVENT Event2;
/*024*/ }
        KEVENT_PAIR;
```

KGDTENTRY

```
typedef struct _KGDTENTRY

        {
/*000*/ WORD  LimitLow;
/*002*/ WORD  BaseLow;
/*004*/ DWORD HighWord;
/*008*/ }
        KGDTENTRY;
```

KIDTENTRY

```
typedef struct _KIDTENTRY
        {
/*000*/ WORD Offset;
/*002*/ WORD Selector;
/*004*/ WORD Access;
/*006*/ WORD ExtendedOffset;
/*008*/ }
        KIDTENTRY;
```

KIRQL

```
typedef BYTE KIRQL;
```

KMUTANT, KMUTEX

```
typedef struct _KMUTANT
        {
/*000*/ DISPATCHER_HEADER Header; // DISP_TYPE_MUTANT 0x02
/*010*/ LIST_ENTRY        MutantListEntry;
/*018*/ struct _KTHREAD  *OwnerThread;
/*01C*/ BOOLEAN           Abandoned;
/*01D*/ BYTE              ApcDisable;
/*020*/ }
        KMUTANT, KMUTEX;
```

KPCR

```
// base address 0xFFDFF000


typedef struct _KPCR // processor control region
        {
/*000*/ NT_TIB             NtTib;
/*01C*/ struct _KPCR      *SelfPcr;
/*020*/ PKPRCB             Prcb;
/*024*/ KIRQL              Irql;
/*028*/ DWORD              IRR;
/*02C*/ DWORD              IrrActive;
/*030*/ DWORD              IDR;
/*034*/ DWORD              Reserved2;
/*038*/ struct _KIDTENTRY *IDT;
/*03C*/ struct _KGDTENTRY *GDT;
/*040*/ struct _KTSS      *TSS;
/*044*/ WORD               MajorVersion;
/*046*/ WORD               MinorVersion;
/*048*/ KAFFINITY          SetMember;
/*04C*/ DWORD              StallScaleFactor;
/*050*/ BYTE               DebugActive;
/*051*/ BYTE               Number;
/*054*/ }
        KPCR;
```

KPRCB

```
// base address 0xFFDFF120

typedef struct _KPRCB // processor control block
        {
/*000*/ WORD                  MinorVersion;
/*002*/ WORD                  MajorVersion;
/*004*/ struct _KTHREAD      *CurrentThread;
/*008*/ struct _KTHREAD      *NextThread;
/*00C*/ struct _KTHREAD      *IdleThread;
/*010*/ CHAR                  Number;
/*011*/ CHAR                  Reserved;
/*012*/ WORD                  BuildType;
/*014*/ KAFFINITY             SetMember;
/*018*/ struct _RESTART_BLOCK *RestartBlock;
/*01C*/ }
        KPRCB;
```

KPROCESS

```
typedef struct _KPROCESS
        {
/*000*/ DISPATCHER_HEADER Header; // DO_TYPE_PROCESS (0x1B)
/*010*/ LIST_ENTRY        ProfileListHead;
/*018*/ DWORD             DirectoryTableBase;
/*01C*/ DWORD             PageTableBase;
/*020*/ KGDTENTRY         LdtDescriptor;
/*028*/ KIDTENTRY         Int21Descriptor;
/*030*/ WORD              IopmOffset;
/*032*/ BYTE              Iopl;
/*033*/ BOOLEAN           VdmFlag;
/*034*/ DWORD             ActiveProcessors;
/*038*/ DWORD             KernelTime; // ticks
/*03C*/ DWORD             UserTime;   // ticks
/*040*/ LIST_ENTRY        ReadyListHead;
/*048*/ LIST_ENTRY        SwapListEntry;
/*050*/ LIST_ENTRY        ThreadListHead; // KTHREAD.ThreadListEntry
/*058*/ PVOID             ProcessLock;
/*05C*/ KAFFINITY         Affinity;
/*060*/ WORD              StackCount;
/*062*/ BYTE              BasePriority;
/*063*/ BYTE              ThreadQuantum;
/*064*/ BOOLEAN           AutoAlignment;
/*065*/ BYTE              State;
/*066*/ BYTE              ThreadSeed;
/*067*/ BOOLEAN           DisableBoost;
/*068*/ DWORD             d068;
/*06C*/ }
        KPROCESS;
```

KPROCESSOR_MODE

```
typedef CHAR KPROCESSOR_MODE;
```

KQUEUE

```
typedef struct _KQUEUE
        {
/*000*/ DISPATCHER_HEADER Header; // DISP_TYPE_QUEUE 0x04
/*010*/ LIST_ENTRY        EntryListHead;
/*018*/ DWORD             CurrentCount;
/*01C*/ DWORD             MaximumCount;
/*020*/ LIST_ENTRY        ThreadListHead;
/*028*/ }
        KQUEUE;
```

KSEMAPHORE

```
typedef struct _KSEMAPHORE
        {
/*000*/ DISPATCHER_HEADER Header; // DISP_TYPE_SEMAPHORE 0x05
/*010*/ LONG              Limit;
/*014*/ }
        KSEMAPHORE;
```

KTHREAD

```
typedef struct _KTHREAD
        {
/*000*/ DISPATCHER_HEADER          Header; // DO_TYPE_THREAD (0x6C)
/*010*/ LIST_ENTRY                 MutantListHead;
/*018*/ PVOID                      InitialStack;
/*01C*/ PVOID                      StackLimit;
/*020*/ struct _TEB               *Teb;
/*024*/ PVOID                      TlsArray;
/*028*/ PVOID                      KernelStack;
/*02C*/ BOOLEAN                    DebugActive;
/*02D*/ BYTE                       State; // THREAD_STATE_*
/*02E*/ BOOLEAN                    Alerted;
/*02F*/ BYTE                       bReserved01;
/*030*/ BYTE                       Iopl;
/*031*/ BYTE                       NpxState;
/*032*/ BYTE                       Saturation;
/*033*/ BYTE                       Priority;
/*034*/ KAPC_STATE                 ApcState;
/*04C*/ DWORD                      ContextSwitches;
/*050*/ DWORD                      WaitStatus;
/*054*/ BYTE                       WaitIrql;
/*055*/ BYTE                       WaitMode;
/*056*/ BYTE                       WaitNext;
/*057*/ BYTE                       WaitReason;
/*058*/ PLIST_ENTRY                WaitBlockList;
/*05C*/ LIST_ENTRY                 WaitListEntry;
/*064*/ DWORD                      WaitTime;
/*068*/ BYTE                       BasePriority;
/*069*/ BYTE                       DecrementCount;
/*06A*/ BYTE                       PriorityDecrement;
/*06B*/ BYTE                       Quantum;
/*06C*/ KWAIT_BLOCK                WaitBlock [4];
/*0CC*/ DWORD                      LegoData;
/*0D0*/ DWORD                      KernelApcDisable;
/*0D4*/ KAFFINITY                  UserAffinity;
/*0D8*/ BOOLEAN                    SystemAffinityActive;
/*0D9*/ BYTE                       Pad [3];
/*0DC*/ PSERVICE_DESCRIPTOR_TABLE pServiceDescriptorTable;
```

```
/*0E0*/ PVOID                       Queue;
/*0E4*/ PVOID                       ApcQueueLock;
/*0E8*/ KTIMER                      Timer;
/*110*/ LIST_ENTRY                  QueueListEntry;
/*118*/ KAFFINITY                   Affinity;
/*11C*/ BOOLEAN                     Preempted;
/*11D*/ BOOLEAN                     ProcessReadyQueue;
/*11E*/ BOOLEAN                     KernelStackResident;
/*11F*/ BYTE                        NextProcessor;
/*120*/ PVOID                       CallbackStack;
/*124*/ struct _WIN32_THREAD       *Win32Thread;
/*128*/ PVOID                       TrapFrame;
/*12C*/ PKAPC_STATE                 ApcStatePointer;
/*130*/ PVOID                       p130;
/*134*/ BOOLEAN                     EnableStackSwap;
/*135*/ BOOLEAN                     LargeStack;
/*136*/ BYTE                        ResourceIndex;
/*137*/ KPROCESSOR_MODE             PreviousMode;
/*138*/ DWORD                       KernelTime; // ticks
/*13C*/ DWORD                       UserTime;   // ticks
/*140*/ KAPC_STATE                  SavedApcState;
/*157*/ BYTE                        bReserved02;
/*158*/ BOOLEAN                     Alertable;
/*159*/ BYTE                        ApcStateIndex;
/*15A*/ BOOLEAN                     ApcQueueable;
/*15B*/ BOOLEAN                     AutoAlignment;
/*15C*/ PVOID                       StackBase;
/*160*/ KAPC                        SuspendApc;
/*190*/ KSEMAPHORE                  SuspendSemaphore;
/*1A4*/ LIST_ENTRY                  ThreadListEntry;  // see KPROCESS
/*1AC*/ BYTE                        FreezeCount;
/*1AD*/ BYTE                        SuspendCount;
/*1AE*/ BYTE                        IdealProcessor;
/*1AF*/ BOOLEAN                     DisableBoost;
/*1B0*/ }
        KTHREAD;
```

KTIMER

```
typedef struct _KTIMER
        {
/*000*/ DISPATCHER_HEADER Header; // DISP_TYPE_*_TIMER 0x08, 0x09
/*010*/ ULARGE_INTEGER    DueTime;
/*018*/ LIST_ENTRY        TimerListEntry;
/*020*/ struct _KDPC     *Dpc;
/*024*/ LONG              Period;
/*028*/ }
        KTIMER;
```

KWAIT_BLOCK

```
typedef struct _KWAIT_BLOCK
        {
/*000*/ LIST_ENTRY           WaitListEntry;
/*008*/ struct _KTHREAD     *Thread;
/*00C*/ PVOID                Object;
/*010*/ struct _KWAIT_BLOCK *NextWaitBlock;
/*004*/ WORD                 WaitKey;
/*006*/ WORD                 WaitType;
/*018*/ }
        KWAIT_BLOCK;
```

LARGE_INTEGER

```
typedef union _LARGE_INTEGER
        {
/*000*/ struct
            {
/*000*/     ULONG LowPart;
/*004*/     LONG  HighPart;
/*008*/     };
/*000*/ LONGLONG  QuadPart;
/*008*/ }
        LARGE_INTEGER;
```

LIST_ENTRY

```
typedef struct _LIST_ENTRY
        {
/*000*/ struct _LIST_ENTRY *Flink;
/*004*/ struct _LIST_ENTRY *Blink;
/*008*/ }
        LIST_ENTRY;
```

MMSUPPORT

```
typedef struct _MMSUPPORT
        {
/*000*/ LARGE_INTEGER LastTrimTime;
/*008*/ DWORD         LastTrimFaultCount;
/*00C*/ DWORD         PageFaultCount;
/*010*/ DWORD         PeakWorkingSetSize;
/*014*/ DWORD         WorkingSetSize;
/*018*/ DWORD         MinimumWorkingSetSize;
```

```
/*01C*/ DWORD         MaximumWorkingSetSize;
/*020*/ PVOID         VmWorkingSetList;
/*024*/ LIST_ENTRY    WorkingSetExpansionLinks;
/*02C*/ BOOLEAN       AllowWorkingSetAdjustment;
/*02D*/ BOOLEAN       AddressSpaceBeingDeleted;
/*02E*/ BYTE          ForegroundSwitchCount;
/*02F*/ BYTE          MemoryPriority;
/*030*/ }
        MMSUPPORT;
```

NT_TIB (Thread Information Block)

```
typedef struct _NT_TIB // see winnt.h / ntddk.h
        {
/*000*/ struct _EXCEPTION_REGISTRATION_RECORD *ExceptionList;
/*004*/ PVOID                                  StackBase;
/*008*/ PVOID                                  StackLimit;
/*00C*/ PVOID                                  SubSystemTib;
/*010*/ union
            {
/*010*/     PVOID FiberData;
/*010*/     ULONG Version;
            };
/*014*/ PVOID          ArbitraryUserPointer;
/*018*/ struct _NT_TIB *Self;
/*01C*/ }
        NT_TIB;
```

NTSTATUS

```
typedef LONG NTSTATUS;
```

OBJECT_ATTRIBUTES

```
typedef struct _OBJECT_ATTRIBUTES
        {
/*000*/ DWORD                       Length; // 0x18
/*004*/ HANDLE                      RootDirectory;
/*008*/ PUNICODE_STRING             ObjectName;
/*00C*/ DWORD                       Attributes;
/*010*/ PSECURITY_DESCRIPTOR        SecurityDescriptor;
/*014*/ PSECURITY_QUALITY_OF_SERVICE SecurityQualityOfService;
/*018*/ }
        OBJECT_ATTRIBUTES;
```

OBJECT_CREATE_INFO

```
typedef struct _OBJECT_CREATE_INFO
        {
/*000*/ DWORD                         Attributes; // OBJ_*
/*004*/ HANDLE                        RootDirectory;
/*008*/ DWORD                         Reserved;
/*00C*/ KPROCESSOR_MODE               AccessMode;
/*010*/ DWORD                         PagedPoolCharge;
/*014*/ DWORD                         NonPagedPoolCharge;
/*018*/ DWORD                         SecurityCharge;
/*01C*/ PSECURITY_DESCRIPTOR          SecurityDescriptor;
/*020*/ PSECURITY_QUALITY_OF_SERVICE SecurityQualityOfService;
/*024*/ SECURITY_QUALITY_OF_SERVICE  SecurityQualityOfServiceBuffer;
/*030*/ }
        OBJECT_CREATE_INFO;
```

OBJECT_CREATOR_INFO

```
typedef struct _OBJECT_CREATOR_INFO
        {
/*000*/ LIST_ENTRY ObjectList;      // OBJECT_CREATOR_INFO
/*008*/ HANDLE     UniqueProcessId;
/*00C*/ WORD       Reserved1;
/*00E*/ WORD       Reserved2;
/*010*/ }
        OBJECT_CREATOR_INFO;
```

OBJECT_DIRECTORY

```
#define OBJECT_HASH_TABLE_SIZE 37

typedef struct _OBJECT_DIRECTORY
        {
/*000*/ POBJECT_DIRECTORY_ENTRY HashTable [OBJECT_HASH_TABLE_SIZE];
/*094*/ POBJECT_DIRECTORY_ENTRY CurrentEntry;
/*098*/ BOOLEAN                 CurrentEntryValid;
/*099*/ BYTE                    Reserved1;
/*09A*/ WORD                    Reserved2;
/*09C*/ DWORD                   Reserved3;
/*0A0*/ }
        OBJECT_DIRECTORY;
```

OBJECT_DIRECTORY_ENTRY

```
typedef struct _OBJECT_DIRECTORY_ENTRY
        {
/*000*/ struct _OBJECT_DIRECTORY_ENTRY *NextEntry;
```

```
/*004*/ POBJECT                         Object;
/*008*/ }
        OBJECT_DIRECTORY_ENTRY;
```

OBJECT_HANDLE_DB

```
typedef struct _OBJECT_HANDLE_DB
        {
/*000*/ union
            {
/*000*/     struct _EPROCESS              *Process;
/*000*/     struct _OBJECT_HANDLE_DB_LIST *HandleDBList;
/*004*/     };
/*004*/ DWORD HandleCount;
/*008*/ }
        OBJECT_HANDLE_DB;
```

OBJECT_HANDLE_DB_LIST

```
typedef struct _OBJECT_HANDLE_DB_LIST
        {
/*000*/ DWORD            Count;
/*004*/ OBJECT_HANDLE_DB Entries [];
/*???*/ }
        OBJECT_HANDLE_DB_LIST;
```

OBJECT_HANDLE_INFORMATION

```
#define OBJ_HANDLE_TAGBITS 0x00000003

typedef struct _OBJECT_HANDLE_INFORMATION // cf. HANDLE_ENTRY
        {
/*000*/ DWORD       HandleAttributes; // cf. HANDLE_ATTRIBUTE_MASK
/*004*/ ACCESS_MASK GrantedAccess;
/*008*/ }
        OBJECT_HANDLE_INFORMATION;
```

OBJECT_HEADER

```
typedef struct _OBJECT_HEADER
        {
/*000*/ DWORD        PointerCount;       // number of references
/*004*/ DWORD        HandleCount;        // number of open handles
/*008*/ POBJECT_TYPE ObjectType;
/*00C*/ BYTE         NameOffset;         // -> OBJECT_NAME
/*00D*/ BYTE         HandleDBOffset;     // -> OBJECT_HANDLE_DB
/*00E*/ BYTE         QuotaChargesOffset; // -> OBJECT_QUOTA_CHARGES
```

```
/*00F*/ BYTE          ObjectFlags;         // OB_FLAG_*
/*010*/ union
            { // OB_FLAG_CREATE_INFO ? ObjectCreateInfo : QuotaBlock
/*010*/     PQUOTA_BLOCK         QuotaBlock;
/*010*/     POBJECT_CREATE_INFO ObjectCreateInfo;
/*014*/     };
/*014*/ PSECURITY_DESCRIPTOR SecurityDescriptor;
/*018*/ }
        OBJECT_HEADER;
```

OBJECT_NAME

```
typedef struct _OBJECT_NAME
        {
/*000*/ POBJECT_DIRECTORY Directory;
/*004*/ UNICODE_STRING    Name;
/*00C*/ DWORD             Reserved;
/*010*/ }
        OBJECT_NAME;
```

OBJECT_NAME_INFORMATION

```
typedef struct _OBJECT_NAME_INFORMATION
        {
/*000*/ UNICODE_STRING Name; // points to Buffer[]
/*008*/ WORD           Buffer [];
/*???*/ }
        OBJECT_NAME_INFORMATION;
```

OBJECT_QUOTA_CHARGES

```
#define OB_SECURITY_CHARGE 0x00000800

typedef struct _OBJECT_QUOTA_CHARGES
        {
/*000*/ DWORD PagedPoolCharge;
/*004*/ DWORD NonPagedPoolCharge;
/*008*/ DWORD SecurityCharge;
/*00C*/ DWORD Reserved;
/*010*/ }
        OBJECT_QUOTA_CHARGES;
```

OBJECT_TYPE

```
typedef struct _OBJECT_TYPE
        {
/*000*/ ERESOURCE      Lock;
/*038*/ LIST_ENTRY     ObjectListHead; // OBJECT_CREATOR_INFO
```

```
/*040*/ UNICODE_STRING ObjectTypeName; // see above
/*048*/ union
            {
/*048*/     PVOID DefaultObject; // ObpDefaultObject
/*048*/     DWORD Code;          // File: 5C, WaitablePort: A0
            };
/*04C*/ DWORD                   ObjectTypeIndex; // OB_TYPE_INDEX_*
/*050*/ DWORD                   ObjectCount;
/*054*/ DWORD                   HandleCount;
/*058*/ DWORD                   PeakObjectCount;
/*05C*/ DWORD                   PeakHandleCount;
/*060*/ OBJECT_TYPE_INITIALIZER ObjectTypeInitializer;
/*0AC*/ DWORD                   ObjectTypeTag;   // OB_TYPE_TAG_*
/*0B0*/ }
        OBJECT_TYPE;
```

OBJECT_TYPE_ARRAY

```
typedef struct _OBJECT_TYPE_ARRAY
        {
/*000*/ DWORD               ObjectCount;
/*004*/ POBJECT_CREATOR_INFO ObjectList [];
/*???*/ }
        OBJECT_TYPE_ARRAY;
```

OBJECT_TYPE_INFO

```
typedef struct _OBJECT_TYPE_INFO
        {
/*000*/ UNICODE_STRING  ObjectTypeName; // points to Buffer[]
/*008*/ DWORD           ObjectCount;
/*00C*/ DWORD           HandleCount;
/*010*/ DWORD           Reserved1 [4];
/*020*/ DWORD           PeakObjectCount;
/*024*/ DWORD           PeakHandleCount;
/*028*/ DWORD           Reserved2 [4];
/*038*/ DWORD           InvalidAttributes;
/*03C*/ GENERIC_MAPPING GenericMapping;
/*04C*/ ACCESS_MASK     ValidAccessMask;
/*050*/ BOOLEAN         SecurityRequired;
/*051*/ BOOLEAN         MaintainHandleCount;
/*052*/ WORD            Reserved3;
/*054*/ BOOL            PagedPool;
/*058*/ DWORD           DefaultPagedPoolCharge;
/*05C*/ DWORD           DefaultNonPagedPoolCharge;
/*060*/ WORD            Buffer [];
/*???*/ }
        OBJECT_TYPE_INFO;
```

OBJECT_TYPE_INITIALIZER

```
typedef struct _OBJECT_TYPE_INITIALIZER
        {
/*000*/ WORD            Length;           //0x004C
/*002*/ BOOLEAN         UseDefaultObject;//OBJECT_TYPE.DefaultObject
/*003*/ BOOLEAN         Reserved1;
/*004*/ DWORD           InvalidAttributes;
/*008*/ GENERIC_MAPPING GenericMapping;
/*018*/ ACCESS_MASK     ValidAccessMask;
/*01C*/ BOOLEAN         SecurityRequired;
/*01D*/ BOOLEAN         MaintainHandleCount; // OBJECT_HANDLE_DB
/*01E*/ BOOLEAN         MaintainTypeList;    // OBJECT_CREATOR_INFO
/*01F*/ BYTE            Reserved2;
/*020*/ BOOL            PagedPool;
/*024*/ DWORD           DefaultPagedPoolCharge;
/*028*/ DWORD           DefaultNonPagedPoolCharge;
/*02C*/ NTPROC          DumpProcedure;
/*030*/ NTPROC          OpenProcedure;
/*034*/ NTPROC          CloseProcedure;
/*038*/ NTPROC          DeleteProcedure;
/*03C*/ NTPROC_VOID     ParseProcedure;
/*040*/ NTPROC_VOID     SecurityProcedure; // SeDefaultObjectMethod
/*044*/ NTPROC_VOID     QueryNameProcedure;
/*048*/ NTPROC_BOOLEAN  OkayToCloseProcedure;
/*04C*/ }
        OBJECT_TYPE_INITIALIZER;
```

OEM_STRING

```
typedef STRING OEM_STRING;
```

OWNER_ENTRY

```
typedef struct _OWNER_ENTRY
        {
/*000*/ ERESOURCE_THREAD OwnerThread;
/*004*/ union
            {
/*004*/     LONG  OwnerCount;
/*004*/     DWORD TableSize;
/*008*/     };
/*008*/ }
        OWNER_ENTRY;
```

PEB (PROCESS ENVIRONMENT BLOCK)

```
// located at 0x7FFDF000

typedef struct _PEB
        {
/*000*/ BOOLEAN                InheritedAddressSpace;
/*001*/ BOOLEAN                ReadImageFileExecOptions;
/*002*/ BOOLEAN                BeingDebugged;
/*003*/ BYTE                   b003;
/*004*/ DWORD                  d004;
/*008*/ PVOID                  SectionBaseAddress;
/*00C*/ PPROCESS_MODULE_INFO ProcessModuleInfo;
/*010*/ PPROCESS_PARAMETERS  ProcessParameters;
/*014*/ DWORD                  SubSystemData;
/*018*/ HANDLE                 ProcessHeap;
/*01C*/ PCRITICAL_SECTION      FastPebLock;
/*020*/ PVOID                  AcquireFastPebLock; // function
/*024*/ PVOID                  ReleaseFastPebLock; // function
/*028*/ DWORD                  d028;
/*02C*/ PPVOID                 User32Dispatch;     // function
/*030*/ DWORD                  d030;
/*034*/ DWORD                  d034;
/*038*/ DWORD                  d038;
/*03C*/ DWORD                  TlsBitMapSize;      // number of bits
/*040*/ PRTL_BITMAP            TlsBitMap;          // ntdll!TlsBitMap
/*044*/ DWORD                  TlsBitMapData [2];  // 64 bits
/*04C*/ PVOID                  p04C;
/*050*/ PVOID                  p050;
/*054*/ PTEXT_INFO             TextInfo;
/*058*/ PVOID                  InitAnsiCodePageData;
/*05C*/ PVOID                  InitOemCodePageData;
/*060*/ PVOID                  InitUnicodeCaseTableData;
/*064*/ DWORD                  KeNumberProcessors;
/*068*/ DWORD                  NtGlobalFlag;
/*06C*/ DWORD                  d6C;
/*070*/ LARGE_INTEGER          MmCriticalSectionTimeout;
/*078*/ DWORD                  MmHeapSegmentReserve;
/*07C*/ DWORD                  MmHeapSegmentCommit;
/*080*/ DWORD                  MmHeapDeCommitTotalFreeThreshold;
/*084*/ DWORD                  MmHeapDeCommitFreeBlockThreshold;
/*088*/ DWORD                  NumberOfHeaps;
/*08C*/ DWORD                  AvailableHeaps; // 16, *2 if exhausted
/*090*/ PHANDLE                ProcessHeapsListBuffer;
/*094*/ DWORD                  d094;
/*098*/ DWORD                  d098;
/*09C*/ DWORD                  d09C;
```

```
/*0A0*/ PCRITICAL_SECTION    LoaderLock;
/*0A4*/ DWORD                NtMajorVersion;
/*0A8*/ DWORD                NtMinorVersion;
/*0AC*/ WORD                 NtBuildNumber;
/*0AE*/ WORD                 CmNtCSDVersion;
/*0B0*/ DWORD                PlatformId;
/*0B4*/ DWORD                Subsystem;
/*0B8*/ DWORD                MajorSubsystemVersion;
/*0BC*/ DWORD                MinorSubsystemVersion;
/*0C0*/ KAFFINITY            AffinityMask;
/*0C4*/ DWORD                ad0C4 [35];
/*150*/ PVOID                p150;
/*154*/ DWORD                ad154 [32];
/*1D4*/ HANDLE               Win32WindowStation;
/*1D8*/ DWORD                d1D8;
/*1DC*/ DWORD                d1DC;
/*1E0*/ PWORD                CSDVersion;
/*1E4*/ DWORD                d1E4;
/*1E8*/ }
        PEB;
```

PHYSICAL_ADDRESS

```
typedef LARGE_INTEGER PHYSICAL_ADDRESS;
```

PROCESS_PARAMETERS

```
typedef struct _PROCESS_PARAMETERS
        {
/*000*/ DWORD          Allocated;
/*004*/ DWORD          Size;
/*008*/ DWORD          Flags; // bit 0: all pointers normalized
/*00C*/ DWORD          Reserved1;
/*010*/ LONG           Console;
/*014*/ DWORD          ProcessGroup;
/*018*/ HANDLE         StdInput;
/*01C*/ HANDLE         StdOutput;
/*020*/ HANDLE         StdError;
/*024*/ UNICODE_STRING WorkingDirectoryName;
/*02C*/ HANDLE         WorkingDirectoryHandle;
/*030*/ UNICODE_STRING SearchPath;
/*038*/ UNICODE_STRING ImagePath;
/*040*/ UNICODE_STRING CommandLine;
/*048*/ PWORD          Environment;
/*04C*/ DWORD          X;
/*050*/ DWORD          Y;
/*054*/ DWORD          XSize;
/*058*/ DWORD          YSize;
/*05C*/ DWORD          XCountChars;
```

```
/*060*/ DWORD          YCountChars;
/*064*/ DWORD          FillAttribute;
/*068*/ DWORD          Flags2;
/*06C*/ WORD           ShowWindow;
/*06E*/ WORD           Reserved2;
/*070*/ UNICODE_STRING Title;
/*078*/ UNICODE_STRING Desktop;
/*080*/ UNICODE_STRING Reserved3;
/*088*/ UNICODE_STRING Reserved4;
/*090*/ }
        PROCESS_PARAMETERS;
```

QUOTA_BLOCK

```
typedef struct _QUOTA_BLOCK
        {
/*000*/ DWORD Flags;
/*004*/ DWORD ChargeCount;
/*008*/ DWORD PeakPoolUsage [2]; // NonPagedPool, PagedPool
/*010*/ DWORD PoolUsage     [2]; // NonPagedPool, PagedPool
/*018*/ DWORD PoolQuota     [2]; // NonPagedPool, PagedPool
/*020*/ }
        QUOTA_BLOCK;
```

RTL_BITMAP

```
typedef struct _RTL_BITMAP
        {
/*000*/ DWORD  SizeOfBitMap;
/*004*/ PDWORD Buffer;
/*008*/ }
        RTL_BITMAP;
```

RTL_CRITICAL_SECTION_DEBUG

```
#define RTL_CRITSECT_TYPE 0
#define RTL_RESOURCE_TYPE 1

typedef struct _RTL_CRITICAL_SECTION_DEBUG
        {
/*000*/ WORD                          Type;
/*002*/ WORD                          CreatorBackTraceIndex;
/*004*/ struct _RTL_CRITICAL_SECTION *CriticalSection;
/*008*/ LIST_ENTRY                    ProcessLocksList;
/*010*/ DWORD                         EntryCount;
/*014*/ DWORD                         ContentionCount;
/*018*/ DWORD                         Spare [2];
/*020*/ }
        RTL_CRITICAL_SECTION_DEBUG;
```

SECTION_OBJECT_POINTERS

```
typedef struct _SECTION_OBJECT_POINTERS
        {
/*000*/ PVOID DataSectionObject;
/*004*/ PVOID SharedCacheMap;
/*008*/ PVOID ImageSectionObject;
/*00C*/ }
        SECTION_OBJECT_POINTERS;
```

SECURITY_DESCRIPTOR

```
typedef struct _SECURITY_DESCRIPTOR
        {
/*000*/ BYTE                        Revision;
/*001*/ BYTE                        Sbz1;
/*002*/ SECURITY_DESCRIPTOR_CONTROL Control;
/*004*/ PSID                        Owner;
/*008*/ PSID                        Group;
/*00C*/ PACL                        Sacl;
/*010*/ PACL                        Dacl;
/*014*/ }
         SECURITY_DESCRIPTOR;
```

SECURITY_DESCRIPTOR_CONTROL

```
typedef WORD SECURITY_DESCRIPTOR_CONTROL;
```

SERVICE_DESCRIPTOR_TABLE

```
typedef struct _SERVICE_DESCRIPTOR_TABLE
        {
/*000*/ SYSTEM_SERVICE_TABLE ntoskrnl;  // ntoskrnl.exe (native api)
/*010*/ SYSTEM_SERVICE_TABLE win32k;    // win32k.sys   (gdi/user)
/*020*/ SYSTEM_SERVICE_TABLE Table3;    // not used
/*030*/ SYSTEM_SERVICE_TABLE Table4;    // not used
/*040*/ }
        SERVICE_DESCRIPTOR_TABLE;
```

STRING

```
typedef struct _STRING
        {
/*000*/ WORD  Length;
/*002*/ WORD  MaximumLength;
```

```
/*004*/ PBYTE Buffer;
/*008*/ }
        STRING;
```

SYSTEM_SERVICE_TABLE

```
typedef NTSTATUS (NTAPI *NTPROC) ();
typedef NTPROC *PNTPROC;

typedef struct _SYSTEM_SERVICE_TABLE
        {
/*000*/ PNTPROC ServiceTable;           // array of entry points
/*004*/ PDWORD  CounterTable;           // array of usage counters
/*008*/ DWORD   ServiceLimit;           // number of table entries
/*00C*/ PBYTE   ArgumentTable;          // array of byte counts
/*010*/ }
        SYSTEM_SERVICE_TABLE;
```

TEB (Thread Environment Block)

```
// located at 0x7FFDE000, 0x7FFDD000, ...

typedef struct _TEB
        {
/*000*/ NT_TIB    Tib;
/*01C*/ PVOID     EnvironmentPointer;
/*020*/ CLIENT_ID Cid;
/*028*/ HANDLE    RpcHandle;
/*02C*/ PPVOID    ThreadLocalStorage;
/*030*/ PPEB      Peb;
/*034*/ DWORD     LastErrorValue;
/*038*/ }
        TEB;
```

TIME_FIELDS

```
typedef struct _TIME_FIELDS
        {
/*000*/ SHORT Year;
/*002*/ SHORT Month;
/*004*/ SHORT Day;
/*006*/ SHORT Hour;
/*008*/ SHORT Minute;
/*00A*/ SHORT Second;
/*00C*/ SHORT Milliseconds;
/*00E*/ SHORT Weekday; // 0 = sunday
/*010*/ }
        TIME_FIELDS;
```

ULARGE_INTEGER

```
typedef union _ULARGE_INTEGER
        {
/*000*/ struct
            {
/*000*/     ULONG LowPart;
/*004*/     ULONG HighPart;
/*008*/     };
/*000*/ ULONGLONG QuadPart;
/*008*/ }
        ULARGE_INTEGER;
```

UNICODE_STRING

```
typedef struct _UNICODE_STRING
        {
/*000*/ WORD  Length;
/*002*/ WORD  MaximumLength;
/*004*/ PWORD Buffer;
/*008*/ }
        UNICODE_STRING;
```

VPB (VOLUME PARAMETER BLOCK)

```
#define MAXIMUM_VOLUME_LABEL        32
#define MAXIMUM_VOLUME_LABEL_LENGTH (MAXIMUM_VOLUME_LABEL * WORD_)

typedef struct _VPB // volume parameter block
        {
/*000*/ SHORT                   Type; // IO_TYPE_VPB 0x0A
/*002*/ SHORT                   Size; // number of BYTEs
/*004*/ WORD                    Flags;
/*006*/ WORD                    VolumeLabelLength; // bytes (no term.)
/*008*/ struct _DEVICE_OBJECT *DeviceObject;
/*00C*/ struct _DEVICE_OBJECT *RealDevice;
/*010*/ DWORD                   SerialNumber;
/*014*/ DWORD                   ReferenceCount;
/*018*/ WORD                    VolumeLabel [MAXIMUM_VOLUME_LABEL];
/*058*/ }
        VPB;
```

WAIT_CONTEXT_BLOCK

```
typedef struct _WAIT_CONTEXT_BLOCK
        {
/*000*/ KDEVICE_QUEUE_ENTRY WaitQueueEntry;
/*010*/ PDRIVER_CONTROL     DeviceRoutine;
/*014*/ PVOID               DeviceContext;
/*018*/ DWORD               NumberOfMapRegisters;
/*01C*/ PVOID               DeviceObject;
/*020*/ PVOID               CurrentIrp;
/*024*/ PKDPC               BufferChainingDpc;
/*028*/ }
        WAIT_CONTEXT_BLOCK;
```

Bibliography

Asche, R. *Using the Windows NT Custom Driver Wizard.* Redmond, WA: Microsoft Corporation, 1995a.

Asche, R. *Wizards Simplify Windows NT Kernel-Mode Driver Design.* Redmond, WA: Microsoft Corporation, 1995b.

Baker, A. *The Windows NT Device Driver Book: A Guide for Programmers.* Upper Saddle River, NJ: Prentice Hall PTR, 1997.

Booth, R. Inner Loops. *A Sourcebook for Fast 32-bit Software Development.* Reading, MA: Addison-Wesley, 1997.

Brown, R., and Kyle, J. *PC Interrupts: A Programmer's Reference to BIOS, DOS, and Third-Party Calls.* Reading, MA: Addison-Wesley, 1991.

Brown, R., and Kyle, J. *PC Interrupts, Second Edition: A Programmer's Reference to BIOS, DOS, and Third-Party Calls,* 2nd ed. Reading, MA: Addison-Wesley, 1994.

Brown, R., and Kyle, J. *Network Interrupts: A Programmer's Reference to Network APIs.* Reading, MA: Addison-Wesley, 1994.

Chappell, G. *DOS Internals.* Reading, MA: Addison-Wesley, 1994.

Custer, H. *Inside Windows NT.* Redmond, WA: Microsoft Press, 1993.

Custer, H. *Inside the Windows NT File System.* Redmond, WA: Microsoft Press, 1994.

Dabak, P., Phadke, S., and Borate, M. *Undocumented Windows NT.* Foster City, CA: IDG Books Worldwide, 1999.

Dekker, E. N., and Newcomer, J. M. *Developing Windows NT Device Drivers: A Programmer's Handbook.* Reading, MA: Addison-Wesley, 1999.

Gircys, G. R. *Understanding and Using COFF.* Sebastopol, CA: O'Reilly & Associates, 1988.

Hummel, R. L. *PC Magazine Programmer's Reference: The Processor and Coprocessor.* Emeryville, CA: Ziff-Davis Press, 1992.

Intel Corporation. *Intel Architecture Software Developer's Manual. Volume 1: Basic Architecture.* Santa Clara, CA: Intel Corporation, 1999a. Available online: *ftp://download.intel.com/design/PentiumII/manuals/24319002.pdf.*

Intel Corporation. *Intel Architecture Software Developer's Manual. Volume 2: Instruction Set Reference.* Santa Clara, CA: Intel Corporation, 1999b. Available online: *ftp://download.intel.com/design/PentiumII/manuals/24319102.pdf.*

Intel Corporation. *Intel Architecture Software Developer's Manual. Volume 3: System Programming.* Santa Clara, CA: Intel Corporation, 1999c. Available online: *ftp://download.intel.com/design/PentiumII/manuals/24319202.pdf.*

Johnson, M. *PC Programmer's Guide to Low-Level Functions and Interrupts.* Indianapolis, IN: SAMS Publishing, 1994.

Microsoft Corporation. *MSDN Library–April 2000.* Redmond, WA: Microsoft Corporation, 2000a.

Microsoft Corporation. *HOWTO: Enumerate Applications in Win32.* Microsoft Knowledge Base, Q175030. Redmond, WA: Microsoft Corporation, 2000b. Available online: *http://support.microsoft.com/support/kb/articles/q175/0/30.asp.*

Microsoft Corporation. *Information on Application Use of 4GT RAM Tuning.* Microsoft Knowledge Base, Q171793. Redmond, WA: Microsoft Corporation, 2000c. Available online: *http://support.microsoft.com/support/kb/articles/q171/7/93.asp.*

Microsoft Corporation. *INFO: PDB File Format Information Not Documented.* Microsoft Knowledge Base, Q182043. Redmond, WA: Microsoft Corporation, 2000d. Available online: *http://support.microsoft.com/support/kb/articles/q182/0/43.asp.*

Microsoft Corporation. *INFO: PDB and DBG Files-What They Are and How They Work.* Microsoft Knowledge Base, Q121366. Redmond, WA: Microsoft Corporation, 2000e. Available online: *http://support.microsoft.com/support/kb/articles/q121/3/66.asp.*

Microsoft Corporation. *Microsoft Windows 2000 Driver Development Kit.* Redmond, WA: Microsoft Corporation, 2000f.

Nagar, R. *Windows NT File System Internals.* Cambridge, MA: O'Reilly & Associates, 1997.

Nebbett, G. *Windows NT/2000 Native API Reference.* Indianapolis, IN: Macmillan Technical Publishing (MTP), 2000.

Open Systems Resources. *Make WinDbg Your Friend: Creating Debugger Extensions. The NT Insider* 6, no. 5, September/October (1999a). Amherst, NH: OSR Open Systems Resources.

Open Systems Resources. *More On Kernel Debugging: KMODE_EXCEPTION_NOT_HANDLED. The NT Insider* 6, no. 6, November/December (1999b). Amherst, NH: OSR Open Systems Resources.

Open Systems Resources. *Throw the book at 'Em: Books on Writing NT and WDM Device Drivers. The NT Insider* 6, no. 6, November/December (1999c). Amherst, NH: OSR Open Systems Resources.

Open Systems Resources. 2000: *There's a New WinDBG in Town, and It Doesn't Suck Anymore. The NT Insider* 7, no. 3, May/June (2000). Amherst, NH: OSR Open Systems Resources.

Pietrek, M. *Windows Internals: The Implementation of the Windows Operating Environment.* Reading MA: Addison-Wesley, 1993.

Pietrek, M. *Windows 95 Secrets.* Foster City, CA: IDG Books Worldwide, 1995.

Pietrek, M. Under the Hood. *Microsoft Systems Journal* 11, no. 4, April (1996a). San Francisco, CA: Miller Freeman.

Pietrek, M. Under the Hood. *Microsoft Systems Journal* 11, no. 5, May (1996b). San Francisco, CA: Miller Freeman.

Pietrek, M. Under the Hood. *Microsoft Systems Journal* 11, no. 6, June (1996c). San Francisco, CA: Miller Freeman.

Pietrek, M. Under the Hood. *Microsoft Systems Journal* 11, no. 8, August (1996d). San Francisco, CA: Miller Freeman.

Pietrek, M. Under the Hood. *Microsoft Systems Journal* 12, no. 12, December (1996e). San Francisco, CA: Miller Freeman.

Pietrek, M. Under the Hood. *Microsoft Systems Journal* 12, no. 5, May (1997a). San Francisco, CA: Miller Freeman.

Pietrek, M. Under the Hood. *Microsoft Systems Journal* 12, no. 8, August (1997b). San Francisco, CA: Miller Freeman.

Pietrek, M. Under the Hood. *Microsoft Systems Journal* 14, no. 3, March (1999). San Francisco, CA: Miller Freeman.

Podanoffsky, M. *Dissecting DOS: A Code-Level Look at the DOS Operating System.* Reading, MA: Addison-Wesley, 1995.

Richter, J. *Advanced Windows.* 3rd ed. Redmond, WA: Microsoft Press, 1997.

Robbins, J. Bugslayer. *Microsoft Systems Journal* 14, no. 10, October (1999). San Francisco, CA: Miller Freeman.

Russinovich, M., and Cogswell, B. Windows NT System-Call Hooking. *Dr. Dobb's Journal,* no. 261, January (1997). San Francisco, CA: CMP Media. Source code available online: *http://www.ddj.com/ftp/1997/1997_01/ntregmon.zip*, *http://www.ddj.com/ftp/1997/1997_01/ntfilmon.zip*.

Russinovich, M. *Inside the Native API.* (1998). Web Site "Systems Internals," *http://www.sysinternals.com/ntw2k/info/ntdll.shtml.*

Sargent III, M., and Shoemaker, R. L. *The Personal Computer from the Inside Out.* 3rd ed. *The Programmer's Guide to Low-level PC Hardware and Software.* Reading, MA: Addison-Wesley, 1994.

Schreiber, S. B. A Spy Filter Driver for Windows NT. *Windows Developer's Journal* 8, no. 2, February (1997). San Francisco, CA: CMP Media. Source code available online: *http://www.wdj.com/archive/0802/.*

Schreiber, S. B. Inside Windows NT System Data. *Dr. Dobb's Journal,* no. 305, November (1999). San Francisco, CA: CMP Media. Source code available online: *http://www.ddj.com/ftp/1999/1999_11/ntinfo.zip.*

Schreiber, S. B. *Developing LDAP and ADSI Clients for Microsoft Exchange.* Boston, MA: Addison-Wesley, 2000.

Schulman, A., Michels, R. J., Kyle, J., Paterson, T., Maxey, D., and Brown, R. *Undocumented DOS: A Programmer's Guide to Reserved MS-DOS Functions and Data Structures.* Reading, MA: Addison-Wesley, 1990.

Schulman, A., Brown, R., Maxey, D., Michels, R. J., and Kyle, J. *Undocumented DOS:* 2nd ed. *A Programmer's Guide to Reserved MS-DOS Functions and Data Structures.* Reading, MA: Addison-Wesley, 1992.

Schulman, A., Maxey, D., and Pietrek, M. *Undocumented Windows: A Programmer's Guide to Reserved Microsoft Windows API Functions.* Reading, MA: Addison-Wesley, 1992.

Schulman, A. *Unauthorized Windows 95: Developer's Resource Kit.* Foster City, CA: IDG Books Worldwide, 1994.

Solomon, D. A. *Inside Windows NT.* 2nd ed. Redmond, WA: Microsoft Press, 1998.

Solomon, D. A., and Russinovich, M. *Inside Windows 2000.* 3rd ed. Redmond, WA: Microsoft Press, 2000.

Tomlinson, P. How to Write an NT Service. *Windows Developer's Journal* 7, no. 2, February (1996a). San Francisco, CA: CMP Media.

Tomlinson, P. Understanding NT: Interactive Services. *Windows Developer's Journal* 7, no. 6, June (1996b). San Francisco, CA: CMP Media.

van Gilluwe, F. *The Undocumented PC: A Programmer's Guide to I/O, CPUs, and Fixed Memory Areas.* Reading, MA: Addison-Wesley, 1993.

Viscarola, P. G., and Mason, W. A. *Windows NT Device Driver Development.* Indianapolis, IN: Macmillan Technical Publishing (MTP), 1999.

Index

C

D

E

F

K

Q

R

S

X

Z

CD-ROM Warranty

Addison-Wesley warrants the enclosed disc to be free of defects in materials and faulty workmanship under normal use for a period of ninety days after purchase. If a defect is discovered in the disc during this warranty period, a replacement disc can be obtained at no charge by sending the defective disc, postage prepaid, with proof of purchase to:

Editorial Department
Addison-Wesley Professional
Pearson Technology Group
75 Arlington Street, Suite 300
Boston, MA 02116
Email: AWPro@awl.com

Addison-Wesley makes no warranty or representation, either expressed or implied, with respect to this software, its quality, performance, merchantability, or fitness for a particular purpose. In no event will Addison Wesley, its distributors, or dealers be liable for direct, indirect, special, incidental, or consequential damages arising out of the use or inability to use the software. The exclusion of implied warranties is not permitted in some states. Therefore, the above exclusion may not apply to you. This warranty provides you with specific legal rights. There may be other rights that you may have that vary from state to state. The contents of this CD-ROM are intended for personal use only.

More information and updates are available at:
http://www.awl.com/cseng/titles/ 0-201-72187-2

Operating systems: Windows 2000, restricted compatibility to Windows NT 4.0, Windows 9x not supported.
CPU: x86 Pentium 90 and up.
RAM: 64 MB and up.
Compiler/Linker: MS Visual C/C++ 6.0.
Developer packages: MS Platform SDK, MS Device Driver Kit (DDK).
Document viewer: MS Internet Explorer 5.0 and up.